*Track-Two Diplomacy toward an
Israeli-Palestinian Solution,
1978–2014*

Track-Two Diplomacy toward an Israeli-Palestinian Solution, 1978–2014

Yair Hirschfeld

Woodrow Wilson Center Press
Washington, D.C.

Johns Hopkins University Press
Baltimore

EDITORIAL OFFICES

Woodrow Wilson Center Press
Woodrow Wilson International Center for Scholars
One Woodrow Wilson Plaza
1300 Pennsylvania Avenue, NW
Washington, DC 20004-3027
www.wilsoncenter.org

ORDER FROM

Johns Hopkins University Press
Hopkins Fulfillment Services
P.O. Box 50370
Baltimore, MD 21211-4370
Telephone: 1-800-537-5487
www.press.jhu.edu/books/

Printed in the United States of America
2 4 6 8 9 7 5 3 1

Library of Congress Cataloging-in-Publication Data

Hirschfeld, Yair P., 1944–
Track-two diplomacy toward an Israeli-Palestinian solution, 1978–2014 /
Yair Hirschfeld.
        pages cm
Includes bibliographical references and index.
ISBN-13: 978-1-4214-1414-0
1. Arab-Israeli conflict—1973–1993—Peace. 2. Arab-Israeli conflict—1993– —Peace.
3. Israel—Politics and government—1967–1993. 4. Israel—Politics and government—1993–
5. West Bank—International status. 6. Gaza Strip—International status. I. Title.
 DS119.7.H5397 2014
 956.9405'4—dc23
                        2014009613

Wilson Center

The Wilson Center, chartered by Congress as the official memorial to President Woodrow Wilson, is the nation's key nonpartisan policy forum for tackling global issues through independent research and open dialogue to inform actionable ideas for Congress, the Administration, and the broader policy community.

Conclusions or opinions expressed in Center publications and programs are those of the authors and speakers and do not necessarily reflect the views of the Center staff, fellows, trustees, advisory groups, or any individuals or organizations that provide financial support to the Center

Please visit us online at www.wilsoncenter.org.

Jane Harman, Director, President, and CEO

To Boaz Karni and everyone at the Economic Cooperation Foundation, without whom neither the events that took place nor the writing of this book could have happened, and to Ambassador Edward Djerejian, whose friendship and professional advice have guided me throughout the last two decades and who has always helped to translate conceptual track-two work into practical diplomacy.

Contents

Tables and Figures

Preface

Two years ago, Steve McDonald invited me to participate in a workshop on multitrack diplomacy at the Woodrow Wilson International Center for Scholars. Following the workshop, he suggested that I write a study on the experience gained in the work that led to the September 1993 Oslo Accords, and he offered me a resident scholarship at the Wilson Center.

It was a tempting proposal. I knew that if I were to undertake the challenge, the book would need to be an analytical review of the peace work in which my colleagues and I have been involved throughout the past thirty years. To carry out the research, I knew I could rely on my personal archive of policy papers, briefings, correspondence, and other materials that I had gathered between 1980 and today. Back home, I began to carefully review the vast amount of private material at my disposal. I soon found out that my memory is tricky and was, at times, misleading; the documentation written at the time of action told a more precise story. In studying the written material, I made four "discoveries."

First, my own role was less decisive than I liked to remember. In fact, Yossi Beilin and Nimrod Novik played leading roles far more than I did during the first twenty years of our work, between 1980 and 2000. This is not to say, however, that my own task was not important. I did shape the vision and the execution of the track-two and multitrack diplomacy work of the Economic Cooperation Foundation (ECF). However, it was Nimrod and Yossi who translated these conceptual understandings into political reality. In fact, during the past decade of the ECF's work, senior experts worked with us and, as at times they went in and out of government, they made it possible to translate even more of the strategic ideas that we had developed into reality.

Second, the documents at hand showed that the impact of our small group had been far more important than I remembered. In fact, I dare say that any study dealing with the development of strategic and political thinking in Israel with regard to the Arab-Israeli peace process cannot be carried out seriously if it ignores the ideas and concepts that we, the ECF, created. Furthermore, any serious study must acknowledge the impact that we had on the actual development of a two-state solution.

Third, it was necessary to check how political thought and action within the Israeli government structure evolved in response to the track-two and multitrack diplomacy work of the ECF. To do so, I interviewed many of the senior actors involved several times and compared their oral descriptions, seeking further information from secondary sources, memory, and public documentation. I then repeated the interviews to clarify contradictions and gain additional information on still-remaining loopholes of knowledge.

Finally, the research clearly exposed the ECF's successes and failures, and it often clarified where and how some ECF ideas got stuck and other ECF ideas could be implemented. More important, it enabled me to compare the lessons learned at the time with lessons and conclusions drawn in hindsight. On a personal level, this was an important and painful exercise, for it exposed shortcomings and mistakes that I had made, along with those made by the entire ECF.

Because the ECF worked with the Israeli government structure on one hand, and with the most senior Palestinian, Jordanian, Egyptian, American, and European interlocutors on the other hand, its story as told in this book constitutes a classic case study of multitrack diplomacy that exposes not only the strengths but also the weaknesses and shortcomings of this approach.

Acknowledgments

It was Amatzia Baram who got me in touch with the wonderful people at the Woodrow Wilson International Center for Scholars in Washington, D.C., who set off the process for this book, and I want to thank him for that.

At the Wilson Center, Steve McDonald asked me to participate on a panel on track-two and multitrack diplomacy in the service of conflict resolution, and afterward suggested that I engage in a research project covering the track-two and multitrack diplomacy work I had been engaged in. He also proposed that I critically evaluate the results, successes, failures, lessons learned, and theoretical findings in regard to this work. This suggestion challenged me to research and review three different but interrelated perspectives: the historical ups and downs of the Israeli-Palestinian negotiating process from 1978 onward, my personal perspective emerging from track-two and multitrack diplomacy activities that I had the privilege to be involved in, and the perspective (as much as I can glean) of the official decisionmakers and actors. I thus owe Steve McDonald for both the proposal of the research project and the definition of the necessary focus, without which this study never would have been possible.

Also at the Wilson Center, Michael van Dusen has been a great friend and made this work possible by offering a grant to organize two workshops: the first on track-two and multitrack diplomacy and the second on the historical development of the Israeli-Palestinian negotiating process and the lessons learned. Steve McDonald and Alyson Lyons did a wonderful job in helping me prepare the first workshop, and Haleh Esfandiari and Aaron David Miller were essential in helping me develop the second. Kendra Heideman and Mona Youssef also provided vital support for the organization of the second workshop.

Xiomara Hurni-Cranston, whose wonderful work I owe to the Economic Cooperation Foundation (ECF) for providing additional funds necessary, has accompanied me in this entire project from its inception until its final moment, doing research in both the ECF's and my own expansive personal archives and guiding me in identifying and carrying out additional research. Later, when the process of writing started, she was an extremely effective editor and a rigorous assistant who held me tightly to my deadlines and cooperated with me throughout the entire process of moving from a first draft to a final manuscript.

At the Woodrow Wilson Center Press, Joe Brinley made a major contribution in turning the first draft into a readable book. He suggested expanding the historical narrative to make it more accessible to nonprofessionals, and carefully guided me through the necessary procedure to obtain the final go-ahead for publication. I am very grateful for his friendship and support. Shannon Granville also did a superb job in editing the text. She was always available to answer any question I might have and patiently offered the most useful advice. Shannon showed me how best to focus my arguments, made me aware of unnecessary repetitions, and, most important, insisted that I change general statements to specific and down-to-earth descriptions. I have no doubt that she substantially upgraded the readability of the book.

This book could not have been written without the continuous commitment of the ECF team:

- Boaz Karni had already played a quiet and important role in promoting a better understanding between Israelis and Palestinians ten years before the ECF was founded and has continued in this vein since. His commitment and his analytical and critical mind have guided the entire team through various ups and downs.
- Nimrod Novik did much of the work of our small group before the ECF was founded. He then served many years as chairman of the ECF board of directors and more recently has joined the team as a colleague. His work is much referred to in this study, attention that is deserving considering the great contribution he has made to the promotion of a peaceful two-state solution.

- Baruch Spiegel has worked untiringly behind the scenes, playing an exceptionally important role in improving Israel's relations with Jordan, developing working relations with Palestinian counterparts, and improving coordination and cooperation with Egyptian interlocutors.
- Dov (Fufi) Sedaqa's work has been similarly important. His personal network and his ability to develop cooperation and coordination structures between former enemies and against all odds has helped to diminish hardships, minimize misunderstandings, and provide a sense of dignity and friendship to the Israeli-Palestinian relationship.
- Ron Shatzberg's resourceful mind and his ability to build bridges between track-one and track-two actors have played a central part in the improvement of Palestinian access and movement and the expansion of Palestinian activities beyond areas A and B, thus also providing a supporting role to Palestinian statebuilding. Ron has also played a leading role in promoting humanitarian security.
- Celine Touboul has led the ECF team in defining a policy concept regarding Gaza. Her ideas have been translated into track-one action, particularly under Ehud Barak's term as minister of defense. Similarly, her work on how to deter and minimize Jewish hate crimes has been largely adopted by the Israeli ministries of Defense, Justice, and Internal Security.
- Anat Kaufmann has worked tirelessly to build economic networks with Palestinian counterparts and has taken upon herself much of the tedious work that had to be done.
- Alissa Rabinowitz and Rahel Oren have been exceptionally loyal and professional secretaries to the ECF team.

I owe all of them—Boaz, Nimrod, Baruch, Fufi, Ron, Celine, Anat, Alissa, and Rahel—many thanks for their continuing friendship and for the important work they are committed to.

Miriam Hirschfeld, my sister, patiently read all the different versions of the emerging manuscript and improved my English. Miriam has also given me important ongoing advice, since my birth, but particularly in pursuing the unfolding story of my engagement in seeking a peaceful and good neighborly Israeli-Palestinian relationship. Her understanding of and compassion for people undoubtedly has had an important influence upon me and possibly helped to develop necessary negotiation skills.

Finally, I owe a tremendous debt to my wife, Ruthie, and my four children, Michal, Naomi, David, and Yehonathan. Ruthie has not only accompanied me through the many ups and downs of my work, but in one specific moment she played a decisive role in contributing to the success of the Oslo negotiations. In 1993, after the Palestinians had renewed direct negotiations in Washington and Abu Ala' had gone to Norway for the next round of discussions, I was given the order to stay home. Ruthie understood that leaving Abu Ala' alone in Norway, out in the cold, would destroy his reputation with Yasser Arafat and most likely would cause the negotiations to fail. It was Ruthie's insistence that made me ask Shimon Peres for permission to go to Norway immediately and explain the Israeli position to Abu Ala'. Abu Ala' later told me how decisive for the success of our negotiations this gesture had been. My deepest thanks go to Ruthie and my children for their love, their companionship, and their support.

Yair Hirschfeld
March 2014

Track-Two Diplomacy toward an Israeli-Palestinian Solution, 1978–2014

Chapter 1

The Camp David Accords
Lay the Foundations for a
Two-State Solution, 1978–79

The Unique Opportunity of the Camp David Accords

On September 17, 1978, Egyptian president Anwar Sadat and Israeli prime minister Menachem Begin signed the Camp David Accords, a guide for a comprehensive peace settlement of the long-standing territorial and other disputes between Israel and the Arab states since the establishment of Israel in 1948. The accords comprised three parts: (1) *A Framework for Peace in the Middle East*, a detailed description on how to proceed in solving the Palestinian problem; (2) *A Framework for the Conclusion of a Peace Treaty between Egypt and Israel*, provisions to guide negotiations for an Israeli-Egyptian peace agreement; and (3) "Associated Principles" to be applied in negotiating peace treaties between Israel and its other Arab neighbors, Jordan, Syria, and Lebanon.[1]

In many ways, the conclusion of the Camp David Accords seemed to be a dream coming true. After eighty years of conflict and multiple wars (in 1948, 1956, 1967, 1969–70, and 1973), Egypt, the most powerful Arab state, under the leadership of President Sadat, offered Israel a blueprint to achieve a comprehensive peace with the entire Arab world. Even if most Arab states would at first oppose the proposed blueprint, the argument in favor of it was compelling. From the start of the negotiations in November 1977, Sadat had argued that without Egypt the other Arab states had no chance of succeeding in a war against Israel, and sooner or later they would have to follow the Egyptian leadership and come to the negotiating table.[2] However, for Israel there was a clear price attached to the accords: Agree on the withdrawal from all territories occupied during the Six-Day War of June 1967 (including the Sinai Peninsula, the Gaza Strip, the West Bank, and the Golan Heights) and recognize "the fundamental rights of the Palestinian People and their right to self-determination, including their right to establish their own state."[3]

When the Camp David Accords were signed ten months later, Sadat laid the foundations for a negotiating process that aimed to establish the State of Palestine through a peaceful Israeli-Palestinian two-state solution. The process involved a two-stage solution broken down into three time periods: first, an open-ended period to negotiate the modalities for establishing an elected Palestinian self-governing authority in the West Bank and Gaza Strip; second, a five-year transitional period to begin "when the self-governing authority (administrative council) in the West Bank and Gaza is established and inaugurated";[4] and third, negotiations that would take place "as soon as possible, but not later than the third year after the beginning of the transitional period . . . [to determine] the final status of the West Bank and Gaza and its relationship with its neighbors."[5]

At the end of August 1978, shortly before presidents Carter and Sadat and Prime Minister Begin met at Camp David to conclude an agreement, 400,000 Israelis demonstrated in support of peace in Tel Aviv's central square. My wife Ruthie, my daughters Michal and Naomi, and my son David (just one year old) were among the demonstrators. My future partners in working for peace—Yossi Beilin, Boaz Karni, and Nimrod Novik—were also present at the demonstration. When I studied the complete text of the Camp David Accords later that year, I found that the agreement presented a unique opportunity for a comprehensive peace settlement. Moreover, four provisions of the agreed-on text led me to conclude that successful negotiations would lead to a peaceful Israeli-Palestinian two-state solution, possibly linked to the Hashemite Kingdom of Jordan:

1. Negotiations on the "final status of the West Bank and Gaza . . . shall be based on all the provisions and principles of UN Security Council Resolution 242," which provided for Israeli withdrawal from territories occupied in June 1967;

2. "The negotiations will resolve, among other matters, the location of the boundaries and the nature of security arrangements";

3. "The solution from the negotiations must also recognize the legitimate right of the Palestinian peoples and their just requirements"; and
4. The agreement will have to be submitted to a vote "by the elected representatives of the inhabitants of the West Bank and Gaza."[6]

One needed little fantasy or foresight to understand that these four conditions made it evident that the most likely outcome of negotiations would be the establishment of a separate Palestinian state. Theoretically, negotiations on the location of boundaries based on United Nations Security Council Resolution 242 (adopted in November 1967, in the aftermath of the Six-Day War) might simply return the West Bank territories to Jordan. However, the specific references to the *legitimate right of the Palestinian peoples and their just requirements* and to the proposed vote *by the elected representatives of the inhabitants of the West Bank and Gaza* made it highly probable that the Palestinian (and possibly other Arab) negotiators would insist the Palestinian people had a legitimate right to self-determination, and accordingly would demand that the State of Palestine be established alongside Israel.

It turned out that both of my conclusions—the Camp David Accords' unique opportunity for a comprehensive Arab-Israeli peace settlement, and the expected outcome of a peaceful Israeli-Palestinian two-state solution—were shared by other Israelis. Most important among them was Yossi Beilin, who at the time was working closely with Israeli Labor Party (ILP) chairman, Shimon Peres. Beilin was joined by Boaz Karni, who would help him organize an ideologically oriented ILP activist group to seek a solution to the conflict with the Palestinians and Israel's Arab neighbors; and by Nimrod Novik, who in 1984 would become Peres's political adviser. Over the following decades, the four of us would work together with many others, all determined not to let the emerging opportunity for peace to slip away.

Israeli Opposition and Fears of a Two-State Solution

Israel's main leaders and decisionmakers did not necessarily share our conviction that the hoped-for outcome of negotiations would be an Israeli-Palestinian two-state solution. Rather, the opposite was the case: The opposition within Israel toward a two-state solution was overwhelming.

On the Israeli extreme right, opposition to any understanding with the Palestinians derived from the national-religious camp, which viewed the

1967 Six-Day War and the "liberation" of Judea (the southern part of the West Bank), Samaria (the northern part of the West Bank), and Gaza as a God-ordained development. It was believed that "the main purpose of the Jewish people is to attain physical and spiritual redemption by living in and building up an integral "Eretz Yisrael" (i.e., the Land of Israel, including Judea and Samaria). The territory of Eretz Yisrael is assigned a sanctity that obligates its retention once liberated from foreign rule, as well as its settlement, even in defiance of (Israeli) government authority."[7] As a result, the National Religious Party (Miflaga Datit Leumit, MAFDAL), which between 1948 and 1967 had placed itself on the dovish spectrum of Israeli politics, became a proactive agitator for a "Great Israel" policy that sought to keep the captured areas and encourage Jewish settlement there. Out of their ranks emerged the radical leadership of the settler movement, gradually pushing out the more moderate leadership headed by Joseph Burg.[8] More than a decade after the signing of the Camp David Accords, Rabbi Shlomo Goren, former chief rabbi of Israel, demanded that the Israeli government assert Israel's sovereignty over Judea and Samaria. To achieve this aim, he said, it would be necessary "to exert force against the Arabs living there." And he added: "The Government is permitted to take the nation into an elective war and is not punished, even if a sixth of the population falls. And in an obligatory war there is no limitation on the percentage of casualties."[9] The reason for this belligerent approach was based on the belief that God had promised the Land of Israel to the Jewish people, and not to the Palestinians. Moreover, many religious directives given in the Bible to the Jewish people are related to Eretz Yisrael, particularly to Jerusalem, Hebron, and the other holy places situated in the occupied West Bank. Following this belief, it would be a fatal mistake to grant sovereignty over these areas to the Palestinian people, who then would have the power to prevent the Jewish people from exercising their religious duties.

Prime Minister Begin had to face opposition against his peace policy toward Egypt from political groups to the right of his movement, and also from within his party. In 1967, Begin had strongly supported the "Greater Israel" movement, and in 1970 he and his party left a national-unity government in protest against Israel's acceptance of UN Security Council Resolution 242, which provided for the "territory for peace" principle: an Israeli withdrawal from the occupied territories in exchange for a peace agreement. Now, in 1978, Begin was signing an agreement that was based on the self-same territory-for-peace formula. Thus, other leaders within his party, such as Yitzhak Shamir (who would succeed Begin as Israel's prime minister), and some of the rank and file opposed the concessions to which Begin had agreed in the Camp David Accords.[10] Dan Meridor, who as government secretary had the task of coordinating the work of Prime Minister Begin with all the ministers in his government, told me that Begin would have been willing to withdraw from the Golan Heights in order to conclude peace with Syria, but under no circumstances was he willing to give up Israeli control over Judea and Samaria. Begin believed that peace with Syria provided for manageable security risks but would offer important political benefits. In the West Bank, however, Begin was convinced that the security risks of ceding Israeli control would be too high and the political costs would be immense.[11]

Peres, who at the time was the ILP's chairman, envisaged what he called "a functional" solution: a concept that would enable Israel and the Hashemite Kingdom of Jordan to divide their powers and control mechanisms over the Palestinian people, instead of creating a truly separate Palestinian state. Peres had held this idea of a functional solution since the end of the Six-Day War, and he would oppose the move for a full two-state solution for many years to come.[12] In his memoirs, *Battling for Peace*, he wrote:

> In our view, a Palestinian state, though demilitarized at first, would over time inevitably strive to build up a military strength of its own, and the international community, depending upon massive Second and Third World support at the United Nations, would do nothing to stop it. That army, eventually, would be deployed at the very gates of Jerusalem and down the entire, narrow length of Israel. It would pose a constant threat to our security and to the peace and stability of the region.[13]

Many senior members of Israel's security establishment shared Peres's views. Among them was Israeli army commander Ariel Sharon. For the May 1977 Knesset elections, Sharon had established a party of his own; but after gaining only two seats, he rejoined his former party, Likud. In his view at that time, Jordan should become the state of the Palestinian people, but he did not oppose the idea of offering self-government to the Palestinian inhabitants of the West Bank and Gaza as long as Israel maintained a full and undivided security presence in the occupied territories.

Yitzhak Rabin, an ILP politician and Begin's predecessor as Israeli prime minister, was ideologically closest to supporting a "territorial solution." Rabin was by all means committed to going all the way to reach peace with the Palestinians, but he was hesitant to openly declare his support for a two-state solution. In a speech to the Knesset in October 1995, he would point out his objections to the formation of the State of Palestine. He envisaged the creation of a Jordanian-Palestinian confederation rather than a fully independent State of Palestine. He insisted that the Jordan River should remain Israel's security border and that settlements within settlement blocs should be annexed to Israel, while others could stay where they were situated. Accordingly, he also rejected a return to the June 4, 1967, cease-fire lines. Last but not least, he insisted on maintaining the unity of the city of Jerusalem.[14]

Different Interpretations of the Camp David Accords

Begin and his advisers were aware that the text of the Camp David Accords largely took care of Sadat's political intentions, which sought to establish a State of Palestine alongside Israel. To create the necessary counterarguments, and to ensure the outcome that he envisioned and hoped for, Begin insisted that the following six elements be included either in the Camp David Accords or in legally obliging side letters:

1. The representatives of the Palestinian people would not participate in the negotiations through a delegation of their own, but within the Egyptian or Jordanian delegations.
2. The Palestinian members of this delegation would have to be mutually agreed upon (i.e., Israel would have to approve their participation in the negotiations).
3. Israel would be allowed to "construe or understand" the expressions "Palestinians" and "the Palestinian People" as "Arawej Eretz Yisrael" (Arabs of the Land of Israel), in accordance with President Jimmy Carter's acceptance of the use of this term.
4. Israel would be permitted to refer to the West Bank as "Judea and Samaria," and no limitation of Israeli settlement activities was to be enforced.[15]
5. There would be no links between negotiations on the solution of the Palestinian problem, Israeli-Egyptian peace settlements, or peace negotiations with other Arab neighbors of Israel.
6. The provisions regarding the solution of the Palestinian problem were not yet applicable as long as no full agreement on the self-government regime had been achieved.

In spite of these restrictions on the negotiations, Begin did want to grant the Palestinians of the West Bank and Gaza autonomous rights. In a speech addressing more than two thousand Jewish leaders in New York on September 20, 1978, he said:

> Concerning Judea, Samaria and the Gaza District: We have also signed a very serious agreement. Yes, it is based on our peace proposal. . . . Now, on the basis of our peace plan, the agreement says that the Palestinian Arabs residing in Judea, Samaria and the Gaza District will have autonomy. Full autonomy. They will themselves select their administrative council. And eleven departments. And deal themselves with the daily affairs of their lives.[16]

Begin added that the Israeli Defense Forces would remain in the West Bank and Gaza beyond the five-year transitional period established in the Camp David Accords. He also stated, in response to Sadat's interpretation of the 1967 UN Security Council Resolution 242, which indicated the "inadmissibility of the acquisition of territory by war," that this language would not provide the Palestinians with an important negotiating card in order to demand Israel's withdrawal to the pre–June 1967 lines:

> We explained to them [the Egyptians] that these words are taken from the preamble to Resolution 242 of the United Nations Security Council of November 1967. Under international law a preamble is not an integral part of the resolution itself. It does not have binding force. Therefore it stands separately as a doctrine. If it is a doctrine, it must mean a war of aggression. The aggressor must never get away with the spoils. But, if it is a war of legitimate national self-defense, this is the Golden Rule, under international law, then territorial changes are not only permissible, but necessary.[17]

Evidently, Begin intentionally ignored the fact that the United States understood and interpreted UN Security Council Resolution 242 very differently: Washington clearly advocated a "territory for peace" agreement, in which the pre-1967 cease-fire lines would be a guiding principle for border and security negotiations.[18] This would seem to indicate American approval for a two-state solution. Yet when the Camp David Accords were signed, the United States—similar to Israel's leadership—opposed the creation of a Palestinian state. Later on, early in September 1982, President Reagan would state this opposition very clearly and advocate the "Jordanian

Option": the return of the West Bank and Gaza to Jordan, and the establishment of Palestinian self-government under Jordanian sovereignty.[19]
The US administration feared that a Palestinian state would undermine the
stability of the Hashemite Kingdom of Jordan. Inadvertently, the Palestine
Liberation Organization (PLO) also helped to reinforce American opposition to the creation of a Palestinian state. The PLO did not accept either
the Camp David Accords or UN Security Council Resolution 242, and
according to its Covenant, the PLO opposed the very existence of the State
of Israel.

Since 1978, the differing interpretations of the substance of the Camp
David Accords on the question of the two-state solution have largely
influenced and even dominated the entire effort of the Israeli-Palestinian
and wider Israeli-Arab peacemaking effort. Although this constructive
ambiguity has enabled the accords to serve as a negotiating tool for conflict resolution in the Middle East, the contradictions and disagreements
between the participants' positions have often frustrated the peacemaking process. This book relates the efforts undertaken since 1978 to bridge
the gap between these positions, and it aims to describe in some detail
the related process of trial and error in the search for a workable two-
state solution.

Track-Two Diplomacy and My Involvement in the
Two-State Solution

In a 1981 *Foreign Policy* article, US State Department employee Joseph
Montville defined *track-two diplomacy* as "a specific kind of informal
diplomacy, in which non-officials (academic scholars, retired civil and
military officials, public figures, and social activists) engage in dialogue,
with the aim of conflict resolution and confidence building."[20] The major
task of track-two diplomacy is to assist the official negotiating tracks,
known as track-one diplomacy, to succeed. The historical and political
process of drafting a peaceful Israeli-Palestinian two-state solution, both
on track one and track two, is the major theme of this book. The story is
told from the vantage point of a small group of Israeli activists to whom
I belong, who at times successfully and at times unsuccessfully contributed to the historic development of the two-state negotiations. In the pages
that follow, I describe and analyze the track-two and conflict resolution
techniques that we employed, with the hope that some general lessons, as
pointed out in each chapter, may be learned from our experiences.

My involvement unfolded more by coincidence than by design. When Ayatollah Ruhollah Khomeini returned to Iran on February 1, 1979, and the Islamic Revolution changed Iran's government and history, I was invited by Austrian TV to participate in a discussion on the events in Iran. Austrian chancellor Bruno Kreisky saw the program and asked to see me.

Kreisky was Jewish and ideologically rooted in the pre–World War II Austrian Social Democratic movement. He personally subscribed to an anti-Zionist ideology, but he cared deeply for the Jewish people and was dedicated to promoting peace between Israel and all its neighbors. After President Sadat's historic visit to Jerusalem in November 1977, Kreisky played a significant role in helping to overcome Israeli-Egyptian differences.[21] He organized meetings in Austria between Sadat and Peres, then the leader of the opposition ILP, in February and July 1978. Sadat impressed upon Peres his determination to conclude peace in the Middle East, and thus led Peres to support the emerging peace effort. The meetings between Sadat and Peres helped to create a supportive public atmosphere in Israel for a peaceful solution to the Arab-Israeli conflict, a factor that influenced the Israeli government's decision to conclude the September 1978 Camp David Accords. (The demonstration I had attended in Tel Aviv in the summer of 1978 was one such display of Israeli popular support for peace.)

In 1976, Kreisky had organized track-two negotiations between an Israeli leftist group (headed by Uri Avnery, the publisher of a left-wing weekly and later a member of the Knesset), and Arieh Eliav, a former ILP secretary-general, and PLO representatives. These negotiations ended with a letter to Kreisky from PLO representative Izzam Sartawi. To prevent the letter from appearing to be an official PLO policy statement, it was written on the letterhead of the Hotel Imperial, Vienna, rather than the PLO letterhead. In the letter, Sartawi warned that any US or Israeli attempt to circumvent the PLO and pursue peace first with Egypt would cause a further conflagration in the Middle East. The PLO demanded full Israeli withdrawal from all occupied territories, as well as from two further enclaves of Himma (on the Israel-Syria border) and Auja (on the Israel-Egypt border), and it offered in return a "nonbelligerency" commitment rather than peace. According to the letter, peace would only be possible if Israel "accepted and implemented" the right of Arab refugees to return to their original homes if they wished to do so, or to be compensated if they freely elected not to return.[22] The hardly hidden threatening tone of Sartawi's letter, the excessive demands, and the unwillingness to offer peace but instead only a rather dubious concept of nonbelligerency caused these track-two negotiations to end in failure. Nonetheless, Kreisky remained committed to playing an important role in promoting peace in the Middle East.[23]

When Kreisky asked to see me, he hoped to receive professionally valuable input with regard to the political thinking of the Israeli leadership. Our first meeting in February 1979 was a success. Kreisky shared a great cultural affinity with my parents; they spoke the same language and cracked the same jokes, their intonations of speech were almost identical, and most important, they shared the ideology of the Austrian Social Democratic movement. When Kreisky called me at my parents' house, my mother would answer and say to him, "Your phone call brings sunshine and light to my heart." This was not flattery; she really meant it. This shared Austro-Jewish background provided a sociocultural atmosphere that eased and supported our dialogue.

However, in spite of our shared cultural background, my dialogue with Kreisky was, in substance, confrontational. I told him that it would make no sense to follow up on the 1976 track-two dialogue between the Israeli left and the PLO. In a meeting held in May 1980, I suggested that action be taken to identify common ground among Israelis, Jordanians, and the Palestinian leadership of the West Bank and Gaza. My proposal seemed simple: Kreisky, as chancellor of Austria, would allow me to send an invitation to a Palestinian delegation to visit Vienna. Kreisky would discuss the possibility of offering economic aid to the Palestinians. Because he was scheduled to visit Jordan from October 2 through 4, 1980, he could discuss the same concept with King Hussein of Jordan, and follow that discussion with similar words with PLO chairman Yasser Arafat and, finally, with the Israeli government. In return, I would try to obtain the support of ILP chairman Peres. Kreisky gave me the go-ahead, and it was up to me to decide to whom to turn in order to organize the Palestinian delegation. Given that I had suggested to Kreisky that he discuss the concept with both King Hussein and Chairman Arafat, the optimal choice would be to identify a Palestinian delegation that represented both Jordanian and PLO interests.

Paradoxically enough, the organized opposition to the Camp David Accords made it possible to identify exactly such a group. At the Arab Summit Conference, held in Baghdad in November 1978, the leaders of the Arab states (without Egypt) condemned the Camp David Accords and formed the so-called steadfastness front. The main purpose of this front was to isolate Egypt and prevent, if possible, the implementation of the Camp David Accords. The Arab leadership sensed that the accords would empower the Palestinian leadership of the West Bank and Gaza, and feared this would offer a sufficient incentive for the Palestinians to participate independently in negotiations with Israel and Egypt. To prevent this outcome, and despite the differences that lay between them, Jordan and the PLO decided to form a joint committee to support the Palestinian inhabitants financially and thus oblige them to refrain from entering negotiations on the suggested Palestinian self-government arrangements.[24]

In response to the November 1978 Baghdad Conference negotiations, the Palestinian "inside" (referring to the West Bank and Gaza) leadership formed a coalition between PLO and Jordanian supporters. The coalition was led by Fahd Qawassme, the mayor of Hebron in the West Bank. To stress the economic nature of this effort, Qawassme and his supporters formed the Arab Industrial Committee and the Arab Cement Company, the latter being an effort to raise money from the Palestinian public to finance the construction of publicly owned Palestinian industrial compounds.[25] Because the aim of the committee and its affiliated company would be to create a policy of economic empowerment, it was not difficult for me to contact the group and convince it to send a delegation to meet with Kreisky. However, in May 1980, in response to a PLO terror attack in Hebron that killed a Jewish worshipper, the Israeli military authorities in Hebron forced Qawassme into exile, which meant that he would not be able to participate in the delegation's visit to Vienna.

Early in September 1980, the Palestinian delegation of pro-Jordanian and pro-PLO activists went to Vienna. In Qawassme's absence, the delegation's leading personalities were Khalid Iseily, who many years later would succeed Qawassme as mayor of Hebron; a leading West Bank industrialist, Kamal Hassouneh, from Hebron; and a Greek Orthodox industrialist, Rajah Salti, from Ramallah. To avoid further irritating the Israeli authorities, the members of the delegation were all known businessmen who had refrained from taking political positions. Some of them had even enjoyed Israeli subsidies. The meeting between the Palestinian delegation and Kreisky was friendly, but in hindsight not well prepared. Kreisky's initial overtures of promised economic aid resulted in unrealistic Palestinian expectations that frightened Kreisky and his aides into feeling that Austria was making commitments it could not and did not want to deliver. Although no practical results were achieved at the time, the visit was an important beginning of an unfolding process in search of Palestinian self-government.

Kreisky wanted to discuss the concept that I had proposed with the Jordanian leadership. In preparation for Kreisky's visit to Jordan, Crown Prince Hassan, the brother of King Hussein, submitted a comprehensive paper to the Austrian government titled "Some Suggestions for Aiding the

West Bank Economy." This paper, which was dated September 30, 1980, and was handed to Kreisky by King Hussein, pointed out that

> ... *any aid* given to the *West Bank* should be *linked to Jordan*. In this way, aid would be *credible* to the people of the West Bank itself as suspicion to direct foreign assistance would be minimized. Moreover, *coordination* with other investment and aid policies is maintained so as to assure the greatest benefit. This holds whether aid is coming from private organizations, governments or international institutions. Jordan, of course, is the legal authority in the West Bank, recognized by the international community [emphasis in original].[26]

The paper defined the strategic aim of "strengthening the attachment of the people of the West Bank to their land" and of "job creation" and requested the creation of indigenous credit facilities and the establishment of an economic planning agency.[27] It also pointed to "the importance of the industrial sector" and suggested support for local industries, with special attention to be paid to modernizing handicrafts and establishing maintenance workshops. It requested support for agriculture and housing cooperatives, and investments in health and education. Kreisky was shocked by the volume of economic aid that was being requested, and he told me that it was necessary to make an effort to get other governments involved in the suggested political concept.

The Emergence of Mashov:
Pursuing Ben Gurion's Political Heritage

The policy paper written by Crown Prince Hassan of Jordan provided me with a most effective introduction to Peres and Beilin. At the time, Peres was chairman of the ILP, and Beilin was his spokesman and closest adviser. Beilin had recently founded a small group of young ILP activists called Mashov (Hebrew for "feedback"). The aim of Mashov was to create a kind of an ideological hub for rethinking all the components of accepted ILP policies, with regard to envisaged Israeli peace policies as well as various social and economic matters. I was asked to join Mashov, and soon I would lead its committee dealing with the Palestinian question and Israel's policies in the occupied territories. Apart from Beilin and myself, the core of our small group included Novik and Karni. Novik had completed a doctorate in the United States on US policy in the Middle East, and he would soon become Peres's political adviser. Karni lived on a kibbutz, and he would come to manage Beilin's political interests both inside and outside the ILP.

The four of us had all been politically educated and influenced by the teachings of the ILP movement, particularly by the political thought of David Ben Gurion, Israel's first prime minister.[28] Five elements of Ben Gurion's political thinking deeply influenced us:

1. The belief that the partition of the former British Mandate territory of Palestine between Israel and its Arab neighbor was essential to maintain Israel's Jewish identity and functioning democracy. As a result, we understood that Israel had a strategic interest in ending the occupation of the West Bank and Gaza and in negotiating the optimal conditions for a stable, secure, and peaceful withdrawal from these territories.

2. A deep identification and commitment to the Land of Israel (Eretz Yisrael), the Jewish people, and their religion and traditions. However, Ben Gurion believed that these traditional values could only be maintained if they were adapted to changing realities, and thus he encouraged intellectual discussions of different interpretations of biblical texts in the context of the current political realities in Israel. Beilin's mother had headed several of these discussions within Ben Gurion's own Tanakh-Bible circle, so we had a first-hand example of his interest in promoting such intellectual discussions.

3. An understanding of both the importance and the limitations of military power. Following Ben Gurion's reflections on the works of the Prussian military theorist Carl von Clausewitz, we understood "the need to maintain the unity of the government, the army and the people" perfectly.[29] Clausewitz had explained the difficulties of maintaining public support and military effectiveness during a long-term occupation of enemy territory.[30] Because we knew that military power in itself could not create long-term stability, we fully subscribed to the cooperative security principles of the Camp David Accords, and we believed that a solution to the Palestinian problem and a withdrawal from the territories would make it possible to achieve a more stable security structure in the Middle East.

4. An awareness that political means were required to transform military success into long-term success; otherwise, these military achievements could be all too easily reversed.[31] Like Clausewitz, Ben Gurion understood military victories as tactical achievements and insisted that definite success could only be achieved by political

and diplomatic means.[32] We had a prime example of this ethos in Ben Gurion's conduct over the control of Jerusalem during the 1948 War of Independence. Even though he identified with Jerusalem's central role in the Jewish and Israeli national ethos, he calculated that Israel alone would be unable to withstand international pressure to internationalize Jerusalem. By permitting King Abdullah of Jordan to maintain a stake in controlling the holy places of Jerusalem, Ben Gurion effectively created a joint Arab-Israeli interest in preventing the internationalization of Jerusalem, thus making it possible for Israel to establish and maintain its capital in the western part of the city.[33] The lesson learned was mainly to seek possible cooperative coalitions between Israel and potential Arab partners where and whenever possible.

5. An understanding that conflict resolution efforts cannot always address all the outstanding issues, and second-best solutions need to be tested and should be achieved.[34] When Israeli-Palestinian final status negotiations failed in 2000–2001 and again in 2008, the spirit of this strategic approach strongly affected our thinking and the search for the optimal path to a peaceful Israeli-Palestinian two-state solution, even if all the outstanding core issues of conflict could not be solved. (For more context, see chapters 8, 9, and 10.)

In addition to sharing a connection to Ben Gurion's way of thought and the teachings of the ILP movement, Beilin, Karni, Novik, and I had all been through a second formative experience: the October 1973 Yom Kippur War. Our generation had been badly shaken by the loss of the close to three thousand Israelis who were killed during the October 1973 war. We had sufficient knowledge to understand that the war could have been prevented. In February 1971, President Sadat had suggested an interim agreement to Prime Minister Golda Meir that would have permitted Egypt to reopen the Suez Canal and would have created a 35-kilometer-wide buffer zone between the Egyptian and Israeli armies. This arrangement would have permitted Israel to maintain control over the eastern, central, and southern parts of the Sinai Peninsula, and the buffer zone between the armies undoubtedly would have made an Egyptian surprise attack impossible. At the time, Meir had rejected Sadat's proposal, but on September 1, 1975—less than two years after the October War—Israel and Egypt signed an interim agreement that by and large was identical to what Sadat had offered in February 1971.[35] The lesson we drew from the experience was that Israel had to be careful not to miss the opportunities for a peaceful settlement. To paraphrase former Israeli foreign minister Abba Eban, the

Palestinians were not the only ones who would miss an opportunity to miss every opportunity. In the context of the late 1970s and the 1980s, Israel could not be permitted to miss the opportunity for peace offered by the Camp David Accords.

We had also learned a second lesson from the Yom Kippur War: the need for political activism. We simply could not rely solely on the official decisionmaking process and the wisdom of Israel's leadership; we had to find ways and means to make an impact on the decisionmaking process ourselves. This propelled us into action.

Thus, by and large, the ideological and political thinking of our small group was based on three major political guidelines and one action concept. First was the need to maintain Israel's Jewish and democratic identity. For this reason, it was necessary to renew the partition of Israel and Palestine under controlled and secure conditions. Second, Israel's security could not always depend on the use of weapons; it was essential to create a political process that, under controlled conditions, could enable stability and movement toward peace. Third, peace negotiations enabled Israel to open up to the world, reinforce its alliance with the United States, and build crucial regional and international relationships. This approach would provide Israel with important political and diplomatic safety networks, but it also would open up important avenues for Israel's economic and social development.

Toward Our First Multitrack Diplomacy Efforts of the 1980s

With these basic principles in mind, our small group set out on a multitrack diplomacy effort that would be marked by both failure and success. Our first effort would last nearly a decade, from 1979 until 1988. Its main strategic aim would be to involve Jordan in the peace process by obtaining substantial support for such a move from the Palestinian inhabitants of the West Bank and Gaza. Although this effort, known as the "Jordanian Option," brought together people from multiple countries as participants in and facilitators of the peace negotiations, it ended in absolute failure in July 1988, with King Hussein's announcement that neither he nor the Kingdom of Jordan would negotiate with Israel to solve the Palestinian question. Yet both the techniques of multitrack diplomacy that we used and their total failure in this context had an impact on subsequent negotiations.

Chapter 2

The First Multitrack Diplomacy Efforts and the Unsuccessful "Jordanian Option," 1979–88

Between 1978 and 1988, the United States and Israel attempted to involve Jordan in the negotiating process to implement the Camp David Accords. Under the leadership of King Hussein, Jordan had long been an important US ally in the Middle East. Ever since the mid-1950s, the United States had attempted to diffuse possible tension between Israel and Jordan, and from 1963 onward King Hussein pursued a secret dialogue with the Israeli leadership.[1] King Hussein's relationship with the Palestinian citizens of his kingdom along with the power equation between various forces in the Arab world, as much as the content of the Camp David Accords, all separately and together necessitated Palestinian support for the inclusion of Jordan in negotiating with Israel for a solution to the Palestinian problem.

During these years, our small group was involved in a multitrack diplomacy effort, pursued by official track-one negotiators in coordination with our track-two efforts. The strategy chosen was known as the "Jordanian Option." At the time, the most senior policymakers and decisionmakers in Washington, Jerusalem, and Amman supported this approach, which would enable Jordan in coordination with the Palestinians to negotiate peace with Israel. However, it turned out to be a classic case in which each side, in spite of the best intentions, refrained from taking the decisive action that would be needed to make the hoped-for strategy work.

Thus, this multitrack diplomacy effort ended in failure on July 31, 1988, with King Hussein's announcement that the Kingdom of Jordan under his leadership would exclude itself from negotiations with Israel to solve the Palestinian question. This chapter tells the story of the combined efforts of track-one and track-two diplomacy, and it analyzes the techniques of action and the causes for failure, referring to lessons learned and their impact on subsequent negotiations.

Israel, Egypt, and the Initial Attempt to Negotiate Palestinian Self-Government in the West Bank and Gaza

On March 26, 1979, six months and twelve days after the conclusion of the Camp David Accords in September 1978, the Egypt-Israeli Peace Treaty was signed. In line with the obligations laid out in the treaty, Israel withdrew from the Sinai Peninsula in April 1982 and the settlements there were evacuated and destroyed. During the same period, the first serious effort was undertaken to negotiate a self-government agreement for the Palestinian inhabitants of the West Bank and Gaza.

This was not an easy feat, given that almost all doors for such negotiations were closed to both nations. Immediately after signing the Camp David Accords in September 1978, the United States and Israel tried to convince King Hussein to join the negotiations. After some reflection, having posed questions about the US position in the envisioned negotiations and their outcome, King Hussein refused to get involved and joined the Arab states in opposing the Camp David Accords.[2] In the aftermath of the November 1977 Arab Summit Conference in Baghdad, the Palestine Liberation Organization (PLO), Jordan, and the other Arab states would apply severe pressure on the Palestinian inhabitants of the West Bank and Gaza to oblige them to oppose the Camp David Accords and to refrain from engaging in negotiations that would have offered them self-government arrangements.

The only option that remained was to start negotiations between Israel and Egypt in order to develop an agreed-on concept for Palestinian self-government. These negotiations started in May 1979 and finally ended in failure at the end of 1981. The gap between the Egyptian and Israeli concepts of self-government was tremendous. Israel, under Prime Minister Menachem Begin's leadership, insisted on maintaining Israeli control of the West Bank and Gaza territories, and offered only limited powers to the Palestinians.[3] Egypt, in contrast, viewed the self-government arrangement as a kind of corridor to Palestinian independence. With regard to the proposed self-government council, Israel preferred an administrative body that would assert only those powers transferred to it by Israel, with all residual powers remaining under Israeli control, making it evident that Israel remained the "source of authority." The Egyptian-proposed model vested the self-governing authority with full autonomy: "It is a self-governing authority, which means that it governs itself by itself. . . . No outside source vests it with its authority."[34] Furthermore, questions of security, water rights, land usage (including settlements), and the voting rights of Palestinians residing in East Jerusalem remained unresolved. The gap between the Egyptian and Israeli positions was clearly too wide to make an acceptable US bridging proposal possible.

The Logic in Favor of Palestinian Economic Empowerment

In the face of early difficulties in Israeli-Egyptian negotiations on Palestinian self-government, the idea of Palestinian economic empowerment began to make sense. If their economic empowerment was successful, sooner or later the Palestinian elites of the West Bank and Gaza would need to attempt to translate the economic power they had gained into political power. Thus, the concept that I had suggested to Austrian chancellor Bruno Kreisky in Vienna in the spring of 1980 intended to build Palestinian self-government from the bottom up. Kreisky's capability to speak with both King Hussein of Jordan and Chairman Arafat of the PLO added to the political logic. Kreisky spoke to me often about what he called "the vehicle theory." Because the 1974 Arab Summit had decided to recognize the PLO as "the sole legitimate representative of the Palestinian people," Kreisky argued, King Hussein could not negotiate without a prior consensus from the PLO. However, because the United States and Israel would not recognize the PLO even though they were willing to engage in negotiations with King Hussein, Arafat could not get involved in the negotiating process without King Hussein's assistance. Thus, the question was whether King Hussein would become "the vehicle" for Arafat to get involved in the negotiations or whether Arafat would become a similar vehicle for King Hussein's participation. Our hope was that the Palestinian delegation from the West Bank and Gaza, which represented both Jordanian and PLO interests, could help to create the necessary political support structure that would permit King Hussein to participate with Chairman Arafat's consent.

Viewing the developments from a historical and society-oriented perspective, I hoped that the economic empowerment obtained through an optimally all-inclusive internal Palestinian coalition could help to overcome the prevailing internal divisions within the Palestinian society of the West Bank and Gaza. Theoretically, the Palestinians residing in the West Bank and Gaza constituted the group that had the most to gain from the self-government negotiations. However, the Palestinians were a society torn by history.[5] The 1947–49 Palestine War had displaced the majority of the Palestinian people and made them refugees.[6] Even before the June 1967 Israeli occupation,[7] neighboring Arab states had dominated formerly Palestinian territory, following Jordan's annexation of the West Bank in April 1950 and Egypt's military control of Gaza between 1949 and 1967.[8] The continuous interference of outside powers[9] had eroded Palestinian national identity and contributed to tremendous internal rifts in Palestinian society.[10] The intended aim of economic empowerment was to assist in overcoming these rifts.

Translating the Idea into a Track-Two Diplomacy Effort

Getting Other European Actors Involved

When Kreisky returned from his visit to Jordan early in October 1980, he understood that Austria alone could not offer enough economic assistance to the Palestinians of the West Bank and Gaza to make any meaningful difference. He wanted to engage other European actors to participate in this endeavor without taking too much responsibility or commitment upon himself. To do so, he invited me to come to a Socialist International meeting in Madrid in November 1980.

In Madrid, I met Bernt Carlsson, the Swedish secretary-general of the Socialist International, who later died in the 1988 explosion of Pan Am Flight 103 over Lockerbie, Scotland. Carlsson listened carefully to what I suggested, and his response was supportive but not without sarcasm: "Yair, can't you choose another conflict for your conflict resolution attempts; the Israeli-Palestinian one is too difficult." I also met with Hans-Eberhard Dingels, the international secretary of the German Social Democratic Party; Leopoldo J. Niilus, president of the World Council of Churches; and Gro Harlem Brundtland, then chairman of the Norwegian Parliament. (When we came to Oslo in 1993, Brundtland had become Norway's prime minister; she did not, of course, remember our conversation in November 1980.)

I attempted to report all that occurred in Madrid to Shimon Peres, who was chairman of the Israeli Labor Party (ILP). At the time, these reports were channeled through two people: ILP member of the Knesset Yossi Sarid, who was publicly perceived as one of the most articulate leaders of the Israeli peace camp, and ILP international secretary Israel Gat. Kreisky was very fond of Sarid, and told me that ideologically he had "two sons: Izzam Sartawi from the PLO and Yossi Sarid from the Labor Party." I made the mistake of reporting this remark to Sarid, who was upset by it because he feared that it would cause him substantial political damage in Israel if it became public. He thus broke off all contact with me, and I do not know whether he maintained contact with Kreisky. Gat, in contrast, tended to monopolize his intense relations with the leaders of Europe's socialist parties and was not too happy about the fact that Kreisky had chosen to speak with me and to develop new political initiatives with my assistance. Gat promised to arrange a meeting with Shimon Peres and me, but did not deliver.

After the Socialist International meeting in Madrid, Kreisky suggested that a second visit of the Palestinian delegation to Europe be organized. The delegation would again visit Vienna, and Kreisky himself would ask the German Social Democratic Party to receive the Palestinian delegation after their visit. I was asked to arrange a series of meetings in Denmark, which I did with the help of Herbert Pundik,[11] the father of one of my students and, more important, the chief editor of the popular Danish daily newspaper *Politiken*.

The Palestinian delegation for the second trip was more political than the first one and was closer to the PLO. In hindsight, the PLO did not want to alienate Kreisky, although it did want to participate in a "hands-on" approach to prevent any turn of events in which it might not be interested. At this second round, in April 1981, some practical results were achieved. The Austrian government committed itself to giving its first economic aid to the Palestinians. In Bonn, the Bundestag's Economic Aid Committee chairman, Wolfgang Roth, proposed that the requested economic aid to the West Bank be channeled through German government loans to the Kingdom of Jordan. In Copenhagen, Lasse Budtz, chairman of the Danish Parliament's Foreign Political and Security Committee, together with the members of the hosting Danish Federation of Industries, looked into the possibilities of soft loans and export credit facilities. The Austrian, German, and Danish governments also promised political support, but the success of the planned initiative would largely depend on a hoped-for victory for Peres and the ILP in the upcoming June 1981 Israeli elections.

The ILP in Opposition: Making Track-Two Diplomacy Possible

In the 1981 Knesset elections, the ILP gained an additional fifteen seats, but still received one seat less than Likud. Under Begin, Likud was able to form a governing coalition and keep the ILP in opposition. During the first four years of the Likud government, Prime Minister Begin followed the ILP's policy intentions in pursuing peace with Egypt. In this context, Peres and the ILP as a whole supported Prime Minister Begin in his peace negotiations and voted in the Knesset in favor of the Camp David Accords. However, from that point on, the ideological positions and the resulting policies of Likud and the ILP diverged. Under Peres's leadership, the ILP wanted to strengthen Jordanian influence in the West Bank and possibly also in Gaza, whereas Likud was mainly interested in driving Israeli settlement expansion in the occupied territories. Being in opposition, and thus without any government power, an optimal way for the ILP to pursue an independent foreign policy agenda was to adopt the technique of track-two diplomacy.

In this context, for Peres, being in opposition led him to change his initial position on the settlement issue. In a 1975 interview with Yossi Beilin (who at the time was a young reporter for the ILP newspaper *Davar*), Peres had said that the settlements "represented Israel's eyes and roots." However, according to Beilin, by 1982 Peres's position in opposition had made him far more aware of the dangers inherent in the Likud-backed settlement expansion. The growing opposition against the policies pursued by the Likud government created the necessary space for our small group, under the leadership of Beilin, to seek a well-defined alternative strategic concept.[12]

Shimon Peres and Yossi Beilin:
A Strategic Concept for a Track-Two Effort Emerges

Beilin and Peres were particularly intrigued by the policy paper presented by Crown Prince Hassan of Jordan. For a long time, Peres had advocated the "Jordanian Option": negotiating the future of the West Bank and Gaza with King Hussein of Jordan. Peres was willing and interested in employing economic statecraft to engage the Palestinian elites of the West Bank and Gaza in support of a negotiating formula that would allow King Hussein to lead the negotiations with Israel on the basis of the 1978 Camp David Accords. To achieve this goal, five steps had to be taken:

- Support a coalition of pro-PLO and pro-Jordanian Palestinian inhabitants of the West Bank and Gaza to gain economic power.
- Obtain Jordanian support and increase Jordanian influence in the occupied territories.
- Obtain US support and proactive diplomatic encouragement for the suggested approach.
- Allow Jordan to develop agreed-on terms of reference with the PLO that would empower King Hussein to negotiate with Israel on how to implement the Camp David Accords.
- Create an Israeli-Jordanian understanding on how to follow a successful negotiating path.

Early in 1982, Beilin and I started to work on the described five-component strategic concept. At that time, Israel was preparing to fully withdraw from the Sinai Peninsula and dismantle all Israeli settlements there. At the same time, there were activities behind the scenes to prepare for the intensification of Israeli-Egyptian economic and cultural relations.[13] It was only sensible to take this opportunity to ask for international support to develop an economic power base for the Palestinians in the West Bank and Gaza. Fully aware that such an initiative could not be launched from Israel, Beilin and I developed a sophisticated proposal largely in line with Kreisky's demand that other European governments become involved. I therefore submitted the following five-point proposal to Shimon Peres:[14]

1. Establish an international committee in charge of financing and overseeing the equivalent of a Marshall Plan for economic aid to the West Bank and Gaza, as well as for Israeli activities in Africa (and particularly in Egypt).
2. Establish a professional committee from the West Bank and Gaza to lead and oversee development in agriculture, regional planning, education, health, social services, and other spheres.
3. Establish a parallel Israeli committee.
4. Permit the established international committee to negotiate an economic development plan for the West Bank and Gaza with the Palestinian and the Israeli committees.
5. Permit the international committee to negotiate Israeli involvement in Asia and Africa, including Egypt, with the Israeli team.[15]

Luck was on my side. On February 14, 1982, two weeks after I had submitted the proposal to Peres, Elias Freij, the Palestinian mayor of

Bethlehem, published his proposal for a Palestinian Peace Initiative in the *Washington Post*. He suggested that Palestinians "recognize the right of Israel to exist as a sovereign and independent state within defined and internationally recognized borders on a reciprocal, mutual and simultaneous basis," and he indicated that an Israeli proposal "to give us our right to self-determination, and to reach it in stages, might be considered."[16] The idea of recognizing the Palestinians' right to self-determination in stages clicked with me. In teaching my students about the content of self-determination, I had fancifully compared the right to self-determination to a large cupboard with many drawers and compartments. I had argued that in the modern world, some of the drawers in the "cupboard of self-determination" could be given up voluntarily—as in the case of the European Union, which enacted provisions that clearly impeded some of the sovereign rights of its member states. Other compartments of self-determination and national sovereignty might be limited by agreements—as was the case in the deployment of Egyptian armed forces in Sinai, which by agreement were confined to specific areas of Sinai and were prohibited from being stationed closer to the Israeli border, even though Egypt had unquestioned sovereignty over the entire Sinai Peninsula. In line with this way of thinking, I argued, it should be possible to offer the Palestinian inhabitants of the West Bank the right of self-determination with regard to economic development.

I wanted to be able to respond to Mayor Freij's proposal with two trump cards in my hand: backing from Peres (and the ILP), and an international support structure.[17] I received cautious approval from Peres and Beilin to prepare the suggested initiative in cooperation with Kreisky, Dingels, Budtz, and Carlsson.

The War in Lebanon Changes the Equation

On June 5, 1982, Israel invaded Lebanon. The announced purpose of the Israeli military campaign was to destroy the military and terrorist infrastructure of the PLO, which politically and militarily controlled southern Lebanon and had launched terrorist acts against Israel from there.[18] However, Prime Minister Begin had two other political aims in mind: First, he and his government hoped to strengthen the position of the Maronite president of Lebanon, Bashir Gemayel, as well as his minority community; and second, he hoped to conclude a peace agreement between Israel and Lebanon under Gemayel's leadership.[19] The Israeli government also hoped that weakening and possibly evicting the PLO from Lebanon would make it easier to deal with the Palestinian inhabitants of the West Bank and Gaza.[20]

Within the first week of the war, I was mobilized to go to Lebanon to lecture Israeli troops about Lebanon and the Middle East. I was sure that the war could not be won, given that the Israeli government was relying on the support of the Maronites, a minority group within the complicated political structure of Lebanon. The Maronites were a Christian denomination, one of whose members had traditionally always occupied the powerful post of president of Lebanon, but they represented only about 25 percent of the Lebanese population. Furthermore, they were fiercely opposed by all the country's other minority groups—the Shi'a Muslims, the Sunni Muslims, the Druze, and the Greek Orthodox Christian communities. Given this fragmentation, it was not difficult to foresee that the Lebanese political, social, and governmental structure offered only two options: Either Israel would need to become more heavily invested in Lebanon over a long period, which would be unsustainable; or, with Israel failing to do so, the Maronites would turn against Israel and seek a coalition with Syria and Israel's other enemies.[21]

After weeks of serving in Lebanon and feeling extremely depressed, I visited my parents in Vienna—hoping, at the same time, to convince Chancellor Kreisky to convene the suggested study group of the Socialist International. Instead of receiving his support, I learned that he had decided to suggest to the Socialist International that it expel the ILP because of its (conditional) support for the war effort. It turned out that on this issue, Kreisky remained isolated, and other European leaders did not by any means follow his advice. However, I permitted myself to get carried away emotionally and argued that expelling the ILP from the Socialist International could be compared to the Roman Catholic Church's policy during the Middle Ages of trying to solve the "Jewish problem" without consulting the Jewish community, thus harming the latter. I compared Kreisky's proposal that the Socialist International cooperate instead with Mapam, a small and marginalized left-wing Israeli political party, to the policies of Karl Lueger, the anti-Semitic mayor of Vienna at the end of the nineteenth century. Lueger had encouraged anti-Semitism in order to obtain mass support for his party, even as he independently maintained personal relations with several Jewish families, saying: "I decide who is a Jew."[22] Comparing Kreisky to Lueger was the worst possible thing I could have done. And then I exacerbated this insult by going to the press and asking for a public discussion of the issues with Kreisky. This was the end of our relationship; Kreisky never forgave me. (Later—I do not fully remember when—I phoned Kreisky on his direct line, which was open to everyone every Monday morning, and suggested that we "smoke the peace pipe." He told me that he was not ready to do so, and we were unable to make amends before he died at the end of July 1990.)

On the Israeli front, however, I received important support. In mid-August 1982, Peres asked me to organize meetings with Mayor Freij of Bethlehem and with Rashad Shawwa, the deposed mayor of Gaza. Peres wanted to communicate with the pro-Jordanian Palestinian leaders in the West Bank and Gaza in order to convince them to pursue a coordinated Jordanian-Palestinian approach.

Because it seemed valuable to obtain American support, I informed Samuel Lewis, the US ambassador to Tel Aviv, of the unfolding dialogue between Peres and the Palestinian mayors. Lewis asked his political officer, Daniel Kurtzer, to get in touch with me, beginning a friendship that has lasted ever since and will hopefully prevail for many more years.

The Reagan Plan and the First (Failed) Attempt of the King Hussein–Arafat Dialogue

The US administration, as a cosigner of the 1978 Camp David Accords, was committed to finding a solution to the Palestinian question. In July 1982, newly appointed Secretary of State George Shultz stated at his confirmation hearing before the Senate Foreign Relations Committee that "the crisis in Lebanon makes painfully and totally clear a central reality in the Middle East: the legitimate needs and problems of the Palestinian people must be addressed and resolved—urgently and in all their dimensions."[23] Accordingly, Shultz initiated a policy review, which concluded that the PLO was at a point of maximum weakness, offering a unique opportunity for an initiative on the Palestinian question.[24] Thus, on September 1, 1982, President Ronald Reagan delivered a surprise speech on the Middle East, presenting American ideas on the final shape of a Palestinian settlement.

Reagan rejected both an independent Palestinian state and Israeli sovereignty over the West Bank and Gaza. Instead, he argued, "self-government by the Palestinians of the West Bank and Gaza in association with Jordan offers the best chance for a durable, just and lasting peace." This time, the United States announced more specific ideas for its proposed settlement: The Palestinians should have real authority over land and resources, and

Palestinians living in East Jerusalem should be allowed to vote in elections for a self-governing authority. Reagan called upon Israel to freeze all settlement activity on the West Bank, and added that although he believed that Israel could not be expected to return to the narrow and indefensible frontiers it had endured before 1967, the withdrawal provision of UN Security Council Resolution 242 had to be applied.[25]

In reaction to the Reagan Plan, King Hussein started a dialogue with Chairman Arafat in order to develop a possible modus operandi that would permit the king to enter negotiations with Israel. The hope of encouraging King Hussein to join the negotiations on the basis of this plan and its attached talking points was very much in line with Peres's thinking and ambitions.[26] Because Peres opposed and feared the possibility of creating an independent Palestinian state and had no confidence in Chairman Arafat, he preferred to come to a political solution with King Hussein, whom he highly respected.[27]

In this context, the confidential discussions between Peres, Freij, and Shawwa that we had begun two weeks before the Reagan Plan was announced had taken on greater importance. The discussions aimed to achieve three goals:

1. Permit Peres to get a better understanding of what was going on within the Jordanian-PLO dialogue;
2. Obtain the necessary Palestinian support to enable King Hussein to engage in negotiations with Israel on the basis of the Reagan Plan; and
3. Send messages to Amman, via Bethlehem and Gaza, about what would be needed on the Israeli side to be able to start negotiations on the basis of the Reagan Plan.

On November 21, 1982, I was invited to Peres's home in Ramat Aviv for the first time, to be present at a meeting with Shawwa. The meeting would focus on the substance of the Israeli-Jordanian peace agreement. Shawwa was accompanied by his son, Mansur, and all sorts of nuts, fruit, and desserts were laid out for us to eat. (Peres and Shawwa were both fully immersed in their conversation and did not partake of any of the temptations on the table, and I was too shy to touch anything.) Peres pointed out that he aspired to a peace agreement with Jordan but saw negotiations on Palestinian self-government as a possible and constructive step toward an Israeli-Jordanian peace solution, rather than as his first choice. He argued that negotiations over the powers of a self-government body were not the essential matter at hand; more important was the creation of a new reality and momentum toward a final peace agreement. He added that in order to obtain Palestinian control over land and water rights and to contain settlement expansion, "the best you could achieve would be a joint Israeli-Palestinian administration based on a 50:50 approach."[28] When Shawwa asked how this arrangement would help the Palestinian cause, Peres responded, "In a situation of 50:50, you would have the right to vote." (Originally, in my notes from the meeting I had written Peres's statement as "you would have the right to veto," but Peres himself reviewed my notes and provided handwritten corrections to this statement.) Peres continued to explain, "You could adopt procrastinating tactics; make all kinds of inquiries. The decision would have to be taken together. True, you would be dependent upon the Israeli side, but the Israeli side would also be dependent upon you."[29]

In April 1983, King Hussein prepared and signed a draft agreement and Arafat promised to sign it, but these negotiations failed. Arafat asked to consult with his people and went to Kuwait before signing the draft agreement; however, he never returned to Amman to attend the planned signing ceremony.[30] According to the *Wall Street Journal*, King Hussein had written a five-page letter that explained the failure of negotiations as follows:

1. The Reagan Plan had, by pointedly excluding the possibility of a Palestinian state, given Arafat and his associates too little incentive to support it.
2. The Soviets had directly opposed the plan and worked against it through their Syrian surrogates.
3. The United States, through its failure to induce the withdrawal of Israeli forces from Lebanon, had severely undermined its credibility in Arab capitals.
4. Arafat had proved incapable of standing up to radicals within the bitterly divided PLO.
5. Hussein's supposed supporters among Arab moderates had proved to be more meddlesome than helpful.[31]

A few weeks after the failure of the Hussein-Arafat dialogue, Peres and Shawwa discussed the lessons to be learned from the experience. Peres argued that the Americans would continue to pursue progress in negotiations in line with the Reagan Plan by aiming to convince Israel to withdraw from Lebanon, encouraging the Palestinians to offer more substantial support to King Hussein, and asking King Fahd of Saudi Arabia to offer his undivided support. Shawwa did not oppose such steps, but he added two further suggestions: to find ways to include the Soviet Union in the negotiating process, and to offer further incentives to the PLO.[32]

Unfortunately, the dialogue between Peres and the pro-Jordanian Palestinian mayors could not prevent the failure of the Hussein-Arafat dialogue. Nor could it offer any public Palestinian support for King Hussein to proceed without the PLO and Arafat's endorsement. Nevertheless, these discussions set off an important exchange of ideas that would have an impact upon the policy planning of the future Peres government.

Beilin and I made an effort to follow up on Shawwa's suggestions. When, a year after the failure of the Hussein-Arafat negotiations, Kurtzer from the American Embassy paid a visit to Jordan and Saudi Arabia, we were informed that King Fahd of Saudi Arabia would support King Hussein's role in the negotiations only if King Hussein reached an agreement with Chairman Arafat beforehand.

Incorporating the Americans' "Quality of Life" Policy

Our small group was still committed to advocating the concept of granting economic empowerment to the Palestinian leadership of the West Bank and Gaza. As discussed above, the aim was to improve the power base of the Palestinian leadership; to unite, as much as possible, the conflicting Palestinian groups; to improve the living conditions of the Palestinian people as a whole; and to mobilize international support and assistance. We also understood that the policy of economic empowerment could not stand alone but would need to become an integral part of a more complex political strategy that would permit King Hussein to obtain sufficient local, regional, and international support to engage in peace negotiations with Israel.

Early in 1983, I contacted Naftali Blumenthal, then chairman of Koor Industries (a powerful industrial conglomerate owned by the Histadruth, Israel's trade union), to ask him to help me prepare concrete proposals for a viable economic policy concept. For several months, Blumenthal and I traveled around the West Bank, where we engaged in meetings with the Palestinian business community to discuss a variety of economic plans and specific projects of interest. To minimize the Palestinians' economic dependence upon Israel, we suggested economic and business plans that would interest the US business community. Finally, to get the necessary political backing from the United States, Blumenthal and I reported our efforts to the US Embassy in Tel Aviv. Our reports about planned economic activities in the West Bank and Gaza impressed our American interlocutors.

In a meeting on November 17, 1983, Kurtzer explained to me that the following points were emerging in US policy:

- Secretary of State George Shultz believed in a twofold approach. First, he aimed to promote political moves regarding the peace process; and second, Shultz was convinced of the necessity of improving the living conditions of the Palestinians residing in the territories, irrespective of progress in the peace process.
- The US Agency for International Development had been given the necessary funding to carry out an economic development plan for the West Bank and Gaza.
- Political caution was necessary so as not to set off any counterproductive reactions. It was thus essential that the Israeli government's support and cooperation be obtained and that the plan's economic aspects be stressed over its political intentions. It was also crucial to cooperate exclusively with the "traditional moderates."
- It was assumed that it would be realistic to expect obtaining the support of the Jordanian government.[33]

This approach contradicted my original intention of working together with a wide coalition of pro-Jordanian as well as pro-PLO Palestinian supporters. The American approach tended to exclude PLO supporters, who were not seen to be "traditional moderates." Although this approach was at odds with my own policy understanding, as a track-two actor it appeared nearly impossible for me alone to change the mind of the American policymakers.

Kurtzer and I also discussed possible ways to achieve the Israeli government's support for these goals. I insisted that it was important to stress that this was not a "Peres Plan," in order to avoid unnecessary objections from the incumbent minister of defense, Moshe Arens. Arens had taken over from Ariel Sharon, who had resigned over the Israeli military's failure to stop the September 1982 massacre of Palestinians by a Lebanese Christian militia at the Sabra and Shatilia refugee camps in Beirut. Arens was a hard-liner on political and security affairs, but he tended to be a liberal and had a positive view on improving economic conditions for the Palestinians. The difference in style between Sharon's and Arens's performances was striking. When our Palestinian negotiators at the time asked for support on a particular issue, Sharon would give a positive answer that was never translated into reality. He wanted to make the point that it did not make sense for the Palestinians to make demands to the head of the opposition. With Arens, however, any request was first checked according to its merits, and then we would receive either a positive answer that would be implemented or a well-founded explanation for rejecting the request. Arens's approach simultaneously encouraged the Americans to pursue the emerging concept of "quality of life."

Throughout the summer and early autumn of 1983, the Americans worked on the details of this new policy concept. On November, 1983, in an address to the Council of Jewish Federations and Welfare Funds in Atlanta, Secretary of State George Shultz announced the Quality of Life policy for the Palestinians in the West Bank and Gaza. Shultz said:

> I am thinking in particular of the 1.3 million Palestinians living in the West Bank and Gaza. Their well-being, their desire for a greater voice in determining their own destiny, must be another issue of moral concern, even while we continue to pursue an agreed solution to the final status of the occupied territories. If their acceptance of a peaceful future with Israel is to be nurtured, they must be given some stake in that future by greater opportunities for economic development, by fairer administrative practices, and by greater concern for the quality of their lives.[34]

The United States viewed the planned economic empowerment of the Palestinians of the West Bank and Gaza as an important bottom-up approach and as a possible tactic for achieving Palestinian support for King Hussein to pursue negotiations with Israel on the basis of the Reagan Plan.[35] This seemed to be the first sign of success of our multitrack diplomacy effort.

However, both Jordan and Israel voiced concerns about this approach. The Jordanian authorities insisted that all economic aid be directed to the West Bank via Amman, a demand that the Americans rejected. Although the American decision made sense, because it kept a free hand for American action in support of the Palestinians, it did not help create Jordanian support for the policy and thus diminished the political support needed. The Israeli authorities were concerned that they would lose control, and they feared that sooner rather than later they would be overruled in their policy action by US intervention.

To move matters ahead on the ground, Shultz pursued an intense dialogue with Arens that led to an agreement to focus on specific projects.

On the basis of this understanding, Brigadier General Benjamin Ben-Eliezer (known as Fuad), the head of the Israeli Office of the Coordinator of Government Activities in the Territories (COGAT), was invited to Washington in December 1983. He came with a number of specific suggestions. For Gaza, he proposed tackling the problem of water drainage; construction plans for a school, a slaughterhouse, and roads; and the provisioning of medical equipment for hospitals. For the West Bank, he proposed the construction of a modern telephone network, roads, hospitals, and schools.

The American officials viewed these proposals with great suspicion. Instead of enabling the Palestinians to create an economic power base, these projects would at best increase the Israeli government's control over the Palestinians. Or at worst, the projects might be directed so as to provide the infrastructure for increased Israeli settlement activities. The US counterproposals followed the strategic concept of economically empowering the Palestinian inhabitants of the West Bank and Gaza. They suggested permitting the Arab Cement Company to establish a cement factory near Hebron, establishing an Arab- and United States–owned bank, and creating an Arab Development Association to be an economic planning agency on both the macro and micro levels. Furthermore, the Americans suggested establishing an Export Institute for local Palestinian industries and development centers for each of the major regions of the West Bank: Jenin, Nablus, Ramallah, Bethlehem, and Hebron.[36]

Though the Jordanian and Israeli governments made efforts to manipulate the direction of the US Quality of Life policy to increase their political control, the kiss of death came from the PLO. The PLO, or groups within the PLO, were afraid of losing control mechanisms over most of the Palestinian leadership in the occupied territories, and thus asserted political pressure and threats to prevent meaningful Palestinian support for the effort. Later on, this led to the assassinations of Fahd Qawassme and Zafer al-Masri by PLO splinter groups that wanted to assert their power and control over events.[37]

In essence, the US Quality of Life policy failed shortly after it had been announced. Washington had supported the idea of Palestinian economic empowerment, but in the face of Jordanian and Israeli administrative opposition and PLO death threats, no major effort was undertaken to enforce this policy concept in the territories. As an afterthought, rather than as the implementation of the policy concept, the Jewish-Arab American Business Group was encouraged to take action and the US Agency for International Development financed a related health project.

Mashov's Comprehensive Policy Planning Efforts

In August 1983, under Beilin's leadership, Mashov had established a Committee on Policies in the West Bank and Gaza. I chaired and led this effort, whose intention was to prepare policy ideas for Peres and to test potential support from within the ILP and the relevant government authorities.

Our approach was, first and foremost, to listen to a wide range of Palestinian positions to identify common interests and possible policy approaches. We then tested those ideas by speaking with Israeli experts and government officials and evaluating ongoing tendencies on the ground that could become barriers to the pursuance of a suggested strategic approach.

Seeking Common Interests in a Dialogue with the Palestinians

The Mashov committee members held discussions with leading Palestinian administrators, journalists, business people, and intellectuals. We spoke with Palestinian mayors and prominent local leaders such as Shawwa of Gaza, Freij of Bethlehem, Mustafa Nabi Natche of Hebron, and Karim Khalaf of Ramallah; with the journalists Raymonda Tawwil (the mother of Suha Arafat, wife of Yasser Arafat) and Ibrahim Kar'im; with business people such as Kamal Hassouneh from Hebron and Ibrahim Abdul Hadi from Nablus; and with academic and legal intellectuals such as Sari Nusseibeh and Hatem Abu Ghazaleh. Our planning effort was based on three rounds of discussions with the Palestinians, which were followed by input from our American interlocutors and discussions with Israeli experts and officials.

At the beginning of the first round of meetings, our interlocutors repeatedly gave us the official PLO position, which went along the following lines:

The PLO was the sole legitimate representative of the Palestinian people and Arafat was its leader. The aim of peace talks would be to realize the right of self-determination for the Palestinian people and move toward the establishment of a Jordanian-Palestinian Confederation, with two separate capitals; one would be Amman, the other Arab Jerusalem. The Palestinian State, forming part of the confederation, would control all the areas occupied in June 1967. The Palestinian refugees would have to obtain the right to choose between the option of going back to their former houses in Jaffa and Haifa, or to where they had originally come from. Or, alternatively, the Palestinian refugees could choose to receive reparation payments. Probably, most of them could be convinced to take the money and give up their right to return to their former homes. The Camp David Accords and the Israeli autonomy proposals were totally unacceptable, as they did not refer specifically to the PLO.[38]

The first round had, in effect, only a ceremonial character. I assume that after these first meetings, our Palestinian interlocutors checked us out, and only when they understood that our small group was politically relevant were they prepared to discuss emerging policy options more openly and freely. As a result, the second round was devoted to the question of the necessary conditions for bringing about peace negotiations. The Palestinians were by no means united on this issue. Mayors Freij and Shawwa accepted the Reagan Plan and UN Security Council Resolution 242 as a basis for negotiations. Shawwa even went so far as to give a telephone interview to Radio Monte Carlo, calling upon Chairman Arafat to accept the Reagan Plan and Resolution 242 as a basis for negotiations and to join the negotiating process with King Hussein.[39] In contrast, Mayor Khalaf of Ramallah opposed the Reagan Plan, stressing that it expressly excluded the establishment of a Palestinian state in the West Bank and Gaza. Both PLO and Jordanian supporters repeatedly gave us the following statement:

> All Palestinians unanimously agree that Hussein and Arafat had to reach an understanding before negotiations could start, and that the Palestinian leadership of the West Bank and Gaza could not act alone, but only in complete coordination with Hussein and Arafat.[40]

When we asked what should be done if Arafat decided to block negotiations, responses differed. Shawwa made the far-reaching suggestion that if this were the case, we should return to step one and start negotiations between Israel and Egypt and between Israel and Jordan in order to return the Gaza Strip to Egypt and the West Bank to Jordan. Nobody else made the same proposal. Although Israeli policymakers might have liked the idea, it was completely detached from the political and diplomatic reality determining US and Arab policies.

In this round, we also tested the ground for other possible negotiating options. The idea of having President Mubarak of Egypt, King Hussein of Jordan, King Fahd of Saudi Arabia, and King Hassan II of Morocco jointly nominate a Palestinian delegation (with the quiet understanding of Israel) was rejected, because it ignored the role of the PLO. At the same time, the discussions revealed strong opposition to the idea of a unilateral Israeli withdrawal from the West Bank and Gaza. Khalaf in particular vehemently opposed this suggestion. He said that such a move would produce a civil war–like state of affairs in the territories, with one Palestinian political group fighting the others and increasing the likelihood of intensified terror. Khalid Iseily, a businessman from (and later mayor of) Hebron, simply shook his head in total rejection. Similarly, the idea of unilaterally transferring political control or government authority to the Palestinians was rejected, because it threatened to upset the existing balance of power in the territories and would invite additional interference from both Jordan and Syria and also the PLO, thus causing added internal strife.

Our Palestinian interlocutors made several suggestions and demands. First, they insisted that a settlement freeze in the territories be announced. Israel would need to recognize the PLO as "*a* legitimate representative of the Palestinian people" (though not necessarily as *the* legitimate representative of the Palestinian people), and the ILP government should permit Palestinians from the territories to attend meetings of the Palestinian National Council either in Tunis or elsewhere in the Arab world, because their voting power could tip the balance in favor of the moderates.

All in all, the second round of talks gave us an in-depth understanding of two basic facts that had to be accounted for in any policy planning exercise: the enormous gap that prevailed between the moderate Palestinian and Israeli positions, and the internal divisions within the Palestinian camp. The Israeli government, led by Begin and (after 1983) by Yitzhak Shamir, was mainly engaged in expanding Israeli settlements in the West Bank and Gaza and opposed the provisions of the Reagan Plan. The Israeli opposition, led by Peres, wanted to avoid any PLO role in negotiations and was not in a position to bring about a settlement freeze. At the same time, internal Palestinian divisions could all too easily negate or foil possible progress. Ironically, however, any hopeful step in negotiations made it easy for outside actors—such as Egypt, Iraq, Jordan, the Soviet Union, Syria, and the PLO—to manipulate Palestinian positions.

Identifying First Recommendations

Listening carefully to the Palestinians' demands during the first and second rounds of discussion, we identified seven initial policy recommendations for expanding the economic and administrative power base of the Palestinian leadership of the West Bank and Gaza.

- Palestinian cooperative movements should be supported to carry out programs of land reclamation. The physical enlargement of areas under Palestinian agricultural production would symbolize and substantiate the diminishing threat of Israeli land expropriations.
- Palestinian farmers and industrialists should be encouraged and enabled to compete more effectively on the Jordanian market and to create an economic basis for Arab investments in the territories.
- Arab banks in the territories should be established and enabled to trade not only in Israeli but also in American and Jordanian currencies.
- Capital import restrictions should be lifted.
- Plots of "state land" should be returned to Arab private and public ownership.
- Fahd Qawassme, the mayor of Hebron, who had been exiled to Jordan in May 1979, should be permitted to return in order to lead and strengthen the formation of a pro-Jordanian, pro-PLO coalition. (Although Qawassme was categorized as a PLO supporter, he was from a family of entrepreneurs residing in Jordan and had strong contacts with the Jordanian-PLO delegations to Austria, Germany, and Denmark in 1980.)
- Harsh prison sentences for political prisoners should be reduced.[41]

The strategic purpose of these recommendations was fourfold: (1) provide for economic empowerment of the Palestinian elites residing in the West Bank; (2) enhance economic growth and prosperity; (3) create conditions for increasing social and economic Palestinian-Jordanian cooperation; and (4) create a public atmosphere supportive of a Jordanian-Palestinian involvement in peace negotiations with Israel.

Evaluating Ideas with Israeli Experts and Government Officials

To obtain acceptance for our proposals, we knew that we had to obtain optimal support from the professional echelon of Israel experts who had been or still were determining Israel's policy in the occupied territories. We discussed our proposals with three former heads of COGAT (generals Shlomo Gazit, Rehevam Vardi, and Benjamin Ben-Eliezer), as well as with the former governor of Nablus, Zvie el-Peleg, and former Israeli chief of staff Lieutenant General Motta Gur. We also spoke with generals Shlomo Ilya and Shmuel Goren, the officials who were in charge of West Bank affairs at the time.

Regarding the overall strategy, we received unanimous support for a policy that would enable King Hussein (with Palestinian support) to negotiate with Israel on the basis of the Reagan Plan. The idea of founding an Arab Bank in coordination with Jordan was generally supported as well, though we were told that the Central Bank of Jordan would put up too many demands and that ultimately it would not work out. However, positions were divided on the lifting of restrictions on importing capital. Motta Gur in particular argued that even if capital were to be imported for the purposes of investment, in the end it would help finance terrorist activities.[42] Finally, the idea of permitting Qawassme to return to the West Bank was viewed as counterproductive, because it would strengthen PLO interests and limit Jordanian influence in the territories. Qawassme's interest in building a strong Jordanian-PLO coalition was regarded as irrelevant, as was the fact that his family had substantial business interests in Jordan.[43]

We were also concerned about how to best limit settlement expansion. The first Likud government (1977–81) had taken care to identify uncultivated land that was referred to in the land register as "state land," a legal category that was based on Ottoman law.[44] Pliah Albek, the custodian of government and abandoned territory in the Israeli Ministry of Justice, was engaged in identifying these lands in order to prepare them for settlement construction. Aerial surveys were carried out, and areas available for seizing land were delineated on low-scale maps. In 1980, the areas defined and seized as state land amounted to 700,000 dunams (1 dunam is 1,000 square meters). By September 1984, when Peres formed his government, 1.4 million dunams had been defined as state land, 800,000 dunams of which had actually been seized by law.[45] We understood that even if a Peres government decided to stop settlement construction, the land seizures were controlled by the judiciary, which would make Israeli government intervention a complex undertaking. Moreover, we feared that the planned confidence-building measures toward the West Bank Palestinians would be perceived as a cover-up, aimed at quieting Palestinian opposition to the ongoing seizure of land.

In our meetings with former and current officials, we received some insight regarding the bureaucratic barriers that might impede our negotiations strategy. The Civil Administration, which was subordinate to the Ministry of Defense, viewed the control of all the civil affairs of the

Palestinian inhabitants of the West Bank and Gaza as an essential policy instrument that could not be abolished or even limited. This thinking was largely dominated by a zero-sum game approach that viewed pro-PLO supporters as the enemy. This went so far that General Shmuel Goren, head of COGAT during the mid-1980s, offered support to the Islamic fundamentalists who would later create the Hamas movement in order to contain and limit the influence of the PLO.[46] We suggested to Daniel Kurtzer that he propose to his superiors at the US embassy an official US protest against this policy of strengthening the Islamic fundamentalists. Kurtzer did so, but with little result.[47]

Policy Proposals for the First Hundred Days of the Peres Government

In early 1984, anticipating victory in the July 1984 elections, Peres established a One Hundred Day Team. The idea was based on the tremendous changes that American president Franklin Delano Roosevelt had brought about soon after his inauguration in March 1933. Led by Beilin, this team prepared two different policy proposals for the Palestinian issue. One related to the question of how to open negotiations with Jordan on the Reagan Plan; the other related to changing the realities on the ground. The basic idea for the first proposal was to assist King Hussein in building the necessary international, regional, and local support to negotiate with Israel. We understood the need for more flexible language than that used in the Reagan Plan, particularly with regard to the PLO. For the second proposal, we explored the need to limit the Likud-backed settlement drive and prepare the necessary preconditions for Palestinian self-government. In our proposals, we made the following suggestions:

- The Civil Administration should be abolished, and control over daily affairs in the West Bank and Gaza should be given to the Central Command of the Israeli Defense Forces (IDF), while an interdepartmental committee under the authority of the prime minister would oversee activities in the territories, particularly those involving land expropriation and settlements.
- Control of the municipalities should be returned to the Palestinian leadership, possibly by establishing public committees to be chaired by Shawwa in Gaza, by supporters of Hassouneh in Hebron, and by al-Masri in Nablus.
- Restrictions on capital import should be eased, but not fully lifted.[48]

We were told that Peres had endorsed all these proposals. At the time, however, we did not fully understand that Peres's endorsement was almost immaterial, because the prime minister would not, as a rule, deal with West Bank and Gaza policies. Theoretically, this was the task of the minister of defense; however, not even he would deal with these issues. The professional echelons of the Israeli security authorities were the ones who determined and managed Israeli policy in the West Bank and Gaza.[49] Thus, the effectiveness of the work of the Economic Cooperation Foundation (ECF), the nongovernmental organization we founded at the end of 1990, became largely based on our cooperation with these professional echelons. Later on, between 2001 and the present, many ECF successes stemmed from our understanding that substantial changes on the ground could be achieved by cooperating with the relevant senior military or civil servants rather than with senior decisionmakers in the government.

When Peres formed his government at the end of the summer of 1984, Beilin was nominated for secretary of government and Nimrod Novik became political adviser to the prime minister. Boaz Karni and I continued to work from the outside. However, track-two diplomacy was largely marginalized, while multitrack diplomacy gained clout.

Peres Forms a National Unity Government

The July 1984 Elections and Their Repercussions

Although the July 23, 1984, election results were disappointing for us, the ILP, under Peres's leadership, became the biggest party in the Knesset.[50] However, this partial victory occurred against the trend of political polarization that was a reaction to the war in Lebanon. One segment of Israel's population wanted to end the war, while the other drifted more toward radical positions in support of intensified violence. On the day of the elections, while I was in Sidon, Lebanon, carrying out my reserve duties in the IDF, one of the higher-ranking officers, in a clear breach of military ethics, was loudly asserting his support for radical right-wing rabbi Meir Kahane.[51] It appeared that the military conditions in Lebanon were teaching two lessons to the Israelis serving there: First, there is no reason to differentiate between allies and enemies, as long as both are Arabs; and second, the sooner and stronger force is applied, the more secure your position will be.

Despite economic difficulties, inflation, and rising poverty under the Likud government, Likud remained strong enough after the elections to block the establishment of a center-left government under Peres. To form a coalition with Likud, Peres had to agree to a principle of rotation whereby he would be prime minister for the first half of the four-year term and Shamir would be minister of foreign affairs. After two years, they would rotate, and Shamir would become prime minister while Peres would take over the Foreign Ministry. All the other positions would remain the same, including Rabin's position as the minister of defense.

Ideologically, Likud was committed to pursuing its settlement policy to prevent territorial compromises, such as Israeli withdrawal from parts of the West Bank and Gaza. The West Bank Data Project, a research project led by Meron Benvenisti, a researcher and former vice mayor of Jerusalem, was documenting the ongoing de facto annexation of the West Bank in great detail and publicly arguing that the situation was no longer reversible.[52] Although this work was carried out with the best of intentions of stopping the trend, its public effect was to enhance the drive for further land expropriation and settlement construction.[53]

At the same time, Likud maintained control over a number of ministries with executive powers of great relevance to the implementation of policies in the territories. Most important among these was the Ministry of Justice, through which the custodian of government and abandoned property, Pliah Albek, continued to seize land for further settlement activities. Another important portfolio under Likud control was the Ministry of Finance, which could hide budgetary support to the settlements under various innocent titles. We worried that the Bank of Israel, headed by National Religious Party supporter Moshe Mandelbaum, would obstruct the plan of founding an Arab Bank in the territories.[54]

Similarly, the Trade and Industry, Labor and Social Welfare, and Housing ministries fell under Likud control. We expected that Sharon, as minister of trade and industry, would create difficulties for our proposals to promote Palestinian industrial projects. Moreover, if capital investment for such projects were to actually be obtained, Sharon could be counted on to make a public case for encouraging similar industrialization projects for Jewish settlers in the West Bank and Gaza. The Ministry of Housing was headed by David Levy, who, along with Mattityahu Drobless at the Jewish Agency's Department for Settlement, was a strong supporter of the hard-core settlement movement. Levy was thus in charge of offering practical assistance to Jewish settlement activities in the territories. Both Levy and Drobless argued that settlement activities had to be connected more effectively to Israel proper in order to enable Israelis to live in the settlements and commute to their workplaces in Tel Aviv or other cities on the Mediterranean coast. As a result, these Likud-led ministries were able to provide cheap housing facilities in the beautiful West Bank, not far from employment opportunities in Israel, which attracted young couples that otherwise had no special ideological commitment to the settlement enterprise. However, the presence of even these ideologically uncommitted Israelis in the territories gave the settlement enterprise an immediate and future boost. Likud's control of the Ministry of Transport also enabled the relevant executive branches to plan the construction of road networks that would ease commuting from the West Bank and Gaza settlements to the Gush Dan area, the economic center of Israel.[55]

The need to build a functioning and stable coalition government with Likud made it necessary to drop our most important proposal: to control affairs in the West Bank through an interdepartmental committee chaired by the prime minister. Under Peres's chairmanship, our small group might have been able to work together with a wider, pro-Jordanian, and pro-PLO Palestinian coalition for a breakthrough in peace negotiations. However, the more conservative leadership of the IDF and the Ministry of Defense would oppose such a policy, and no effective bureaucratic structure was created to prevent substantial settlement expansion. The ILP itself contributed to settlement expansion in line with the provisions of the Alon Plan, a concept developed in 1967 by leading ILP member Yigal Alon. His plan demanded Israeli military and civilian control of the Jordan Valley as an essential security buffer against any possible Arab attack from the east. Several ILP members of the Knesset were also sympathetic to Othniel Schneller, the secretary-general of the settler movement, who successfully mobilized support in the Knesset to allocate further funds for settlement activities.[56]

The Tactics of "Reaching Out"

Three and a half weeks after Peres formed his national unity government in September 1984, he was scheduled for his first official visit to Washington as Israeli prime minister. His main concern was the disastrous economic and fiscal situation that the Likud government had left behind.[57] Thus, he dedicated his visit to achieving only one aim: obtaining the necessary US support and guarantees that would enable him to overcome the economic crisis.[58] In hindsight, it was a major mistake not to conclude a possible US-Israeli strategic understanding for the implementation of the Reagan Plan. When Peres and King Hussein of Jordan eventually signed the London Agreement in April 1987, a prior American commitment to support such an achievement probably would have prevented the failure of the obtained understanding. However, immediately after taking office, Peres also pursued a policy of reaching out to King Hussein, largely along the lines of the work that Mashov had prepared in the two preceding years. His policy and its related activities consisted of the following points:

1. Peres would not exclude from his official statements the possibility of forming a Palestinian state based on the results of future negotiations. It was hoped that this would contribute to greater maneuverability for King Hussein to obtain active or passive support from the Egyptian and Palestinian leadership.
2. Regarding the control of the municipalities in the territories, Peres intended to make an effort to consult with the Jordanian authorities as to how to turn the municipalities over to Palestinian control.
3. Peres met with Najaf Halaby, King Hussein's father-in-law, in New York in the autumn of 1984 to boost the activities of the Jewish-Arab American Business Group.[59]
4. In January 1985, the Israeli government decided to withdraw its troops from most Lebanese territory and remained only in a small security zone in the south. Both Mashov and the Hundred Day Team had suggested that the troops be moved back to the Israel-Lebanon border, but were overruled by the security establishment.
5. Peres supported and actively pursued the idea of establishing an Arab Bank in the territories. After complex secret negotiations with the chairman of the Jordanian Central Bank, in 1986 an agreement was concluded that would make it possible to open the doors of the Cairo Amman Bank in Ramallah.[60]
6. To widen the scope of Israel's diplomatic activities, Peres led an intense dialogue with and visited both Italy and Romania. Both states were viewed as close to the PLO.[61] Their support was requested in order to make it easier for King Hussein to come to terms with Chairman Arafat while simultaneously making it more difficult for Arafat to avoid concluding an agreement with the king.

All these activities required a confidential dialogue between Peres and King Hussein. The king made it clear that he needed an umbrella in the form of an international conference to establish negotiations. Thus, it was

necessary to start a dialogue with the Soviet Union. Novik, as Peres's political adviser, was given the go-ahead to engage with Ambassador Gennady
Tarasov, a senior Soviet diplomat. The good news was that early contact
with both King Hussein and the Soviets showed that neither expected nor
intended to demand an international conference that would have the power
to impose a settlement.[62]

To understand in greater detail the necessary conditions that would
have to be agreed upon when convening the requested international conference, Beilin formed a small committee headed by Shimshon Zellniker.
Karni, David Twersky, and I were members. We were to meet with experts
and submit a report on reactions to the idea of an international conference.
Most of the people we met with opposed the idea, and our task was to
anticipate internal and external opposition, as well as practical, political,
and possible procedural pitfalls.

Abba Eban, who at the time was a member of the Knesset, remarked
that if we wanted the United States and the Soviet Union to jointly chair the
conference—hoping that they would effectively mediate between the parties—we would first require a mediator between the United States and the
Soviet Union. In our report, we enumerated all the dangers outlined by the
experts: the fear that the conference would lead to an imposed settlement, the
danger that various Arab participants would radicalize each other, the possibility that the Soviet Union would try to outbid the Americans during the
negotiations and thus lead to a destructive polarization of Soviet-Arab versus
US-Israeli positions, and the need to maintain bilateral negotiations between
Israel and a Jordanian-Palestinian delegation separate from other possible
(but unlikely) negotiating channels. We submitted the report to Peres and
made practical suggestions regarding issues that had to be agreed upon.[63]

Novik was tasked with speaking to the Soviets and adopted a strategic
rather than technical approach. First of all, two bilateral issues on the agenda
were to be pursued simultaneously: the renewal of diplomatic relations
between the Soviet Union and Israel, and the lifting of travel restrictions
on Soviet Jews, permitting them to leave the country and come to Israel
or go elsewhere. Moreover, in order to enable King Hussein to negotiate
with Israel, Soviet influence on both Syria and the PLO was essential.
What helped Novik in his deliberations was the fact that the Soviet leadership was interested in improving relations with the United States, partly
because of Soviet entanglement in Afghanistan but also because of Mikhail
Gorbachev's emerging policy of glasnost, which necessitated an economic
opening to the West. Jerusalem was seen not as a detour on the way from
Moscow to Washington, but rather as a useful interim station.[64]

These efforts were welcome in Amman and created a constructive impetus for change, allowing King Hussein to conclude the envisaged agreement with Chairman Arafat on February 11, 1985. The agreement provided for a commitment to establishing "the framework of an Arab confederation that is intended to be established between the two states of Jordan and Palestine." The operational paragraph indicated that

> . . . peace negotiations should be held within the framework of an international conference to be attended by the five UN Security Council permanent member states and all parties to the conflict, including the PLO, which is the Palestinian people's sole legitimate representative, within a joint delegation—a joint Jordanian-Palestinian delegation.[65]

Paradoxically, the Hussein-Arafat agreement of February 1985 eased Jordanian-Israeli relations while intensifying, rather than diminishing, the rift between Jordan and the PLO. King Hussein and Arafat differed substantially over the context and substance of the jointly proposed Jordan-Palestine confederation. For Arafat, this meant two states, with a nominal leadership that would rotate between King Hussein and himself.[66] In contrast, King Hussein told Peres and Beilin that he would not permit—not "even only for ten minutes"—the establishment of an independent State of Palestine as a preliminary step to the formation of the confederation.[67]

Although Arafat and King Hussein differed on issues of substance, the procedure for setting up the negotiations was relatively simple. In the context of the provisions of the Camp David Accords, this meant that the membship of the Jordanian-Palestinian delegation had to be agreed upon with Israel. Chairman Arafat therefore provided King Hussein with a list of seven PLO-nominated candidates to participate in the Jordanian-Palestinian delegation. The list was given to the Americans, who handed it on to Israel. This process worked, and Peres accepted two of Arafat's candidates: Hana Siniora, a Christian journalist from Jerusalem, and Faiz Abu Rahme, a lawyer from Gaza (who happened to be related to the militant Palestinian politician Khalil al-Wazir, also known as Abu Jihad).[68]

To promote the process, Peres twice met with King Hussein in secret. In July 1985, they agreed to follow three stages. In the first stage, a joint Jordanian-Palestinian delegation would meet with Richard Murphy, the US assistant secretary of state for Near East and East Asia affairs. In the second stage, the PLO would meet the American conditions for a dialogue. In the final stage, peace negotiations would begin. More details were discussed on October 5, 1985, when Beilin accompanied Peres and Jordanian prime minister Zaid al-Rifai accompanied King Hussein to meet and discuss the proposed international conference.[69]

To achieve the desired support from the West Bank Palestinians for King Hussein's negotiations with Israel, we introduced the economic development measures we had proposed as part of Peres's One Hundred Days Team. In consultation with the Jordanian Court, al-Masri was appointed mayor of Nablus. An agreement was concluded to establish a Jordanian bank in the West Bank, the Jordanians launched an economic development plan for the West Bank and Gaza, and Israel eased the restrictions on importing capital.[70]

I was given the task of establishing close contact with Siniora, who was personally very committed to the peace process. He was, however, an outsider in the complicated social and political fabric of the Palestinian leadership network of the West Bank and Jerusalem. Undoubtedly, this was why Arafat chose him to communicate with us; in order to be effective and to obtain the support of the inside leadership, Siniora would need to rely upon Arafat's daily support and intervention. My tasks were to listen carefully to Siniora to gain an in-depth understanding of the ups and downs of Palestinian policies, provide him with input regarding the Israeli political scene, and start testing emerging Palestinian positions regarding envisaged negotiations on Palestinian self-government. Though little headway was achieved at that time, I remained in contact with Siniora; and several years later, after the negotiations at the Madrid Conference in October 1991, he gave me a detailed table describing the common ground and discrepancies between the Israeli and Palestinian positions regarding Palestinian self-government. This table was essential in enabling me to plan effectively for the Oslo negotiations in 1993.[71]

Assassinations, Terrorism, and the Cancellation of the King Hussein–Arafat Agreement

At the end of December 1984, the exiled former Hebron mayor Fahd Qawassme was assassinated in Amman, apparently by a radical splinter group of the PLO.[72] On January 15, 1985, the PLO-controlled newspaper *al-Mithaq* published a threatening piece against "collaborators" with the Jewish-Arab American Business Group. The piece quoted Arafat as condemning Khalid Iseily, Hisham Awartani, and others for having met with the business group, and compared them to the members of the

Israeli-controlled "village leagues." The village league was an Israeli attempt to create a new power structure in the occupied territories between 1981 and 1983, during Sharon's tenure as minister of defense. Israeli officials tried to create a Palestinian political leadership, known as the village leagues, to replace PLO and Jordanian influence in the West Bank and Gaza.[73] The warning in *al-Mithaq* produced its intended response; in a public statement in April 1985, eleven Palestinians—including Freij, Shawwa, and Iseily—stressed that the PLO was the sole legitimate representative of the Palestinian people and demanded that United States recognize the PLO and direct negotiations.[74]

Early in October 1985, another PLO splinter group hijacked the Italian cruise ship *Achille Lauro* and murdered a retired Jewish American businessman named Leon Klinghofer, throwing him overboard in his wheelchair.[75] The international community and King Hussein requested that Arafat distance himself from this act. But Arafat, afraid of estranging hard-liners within the PLO, refused to do so.[76]

After several failed attempts by King Hussein to sustain the understanding with the PLO, and after having obtained the necessary reassurances from Washington, Damascus, Moscow, and Jerusalem, King Hussein canceled the agreement with Arafat in a three-hour speech on February 19, 1986.[77] Shortly afterward, in early March, the PLO instigated the assassination of al-Masri, the new mayor of Nablus.[78] According to Avi Shlaim, al-Masri's assassination showed that the PLO intended to fight for its position as the sole representative of the Palestinian people, and further undermined the Jordanian-PLO joint attempt to improve the economic well-being of the West Bank's population.[79] It appeared that the only way forward would be to initiate an Israeli-Jordanian attempt to get the peace negotiations back on track. Without doubt, the internal divisions within the Palestinian political system and the use of terrorism, death threats, and assassinations would make it extremely difficult to create an ongoing sustainable process.

The Failure of the London Agreement

Throughout 1986, Jordanian involvement in the West Bank and Gaza accelerated with the full support of the Israeli government. The Jordanian Central Bank and the Bank of Israel concluded an agreement to establish the Cairo Amman Bank in the West Bank. Jordanian prime minister Zaid al-Rifai announced that emergency funds would be allocated for social, educational, and health institutions in the West Bank until money for a five-year plan would become available, a project for which the Jordanians hoped to receive substantial American aid.[80] However, instead of the requested $1.5 billion, the United States merely granted $90 million.[81] Avi Shlaim, in his biography of King Hussein, also argues that replacing Taher el-Qanaan, who had the confidence of the Palestinians of the West Bank, with Marwan Dudin as minister of the occupied territories had a detrimental effect.[82]

Middle Eastern policy structures are dominated by the characteristics of neopatrimonial societies.[83] Political loyalties depend largely upon the social and economic support offered by political stakeholders and the related control mechanisms. A generous supply of funds most likely would have enabled the pro-Jordanian coalition of Palestinian notables to strengthen their own support structure in the territories, preparing ground for wider support for a Jordanian-led political initiative. Because sufficient US support was not forthcoming before the negotiations started, our small group hoped that if Israel and Jordan would agree to start negotiations, US political and financial support would then be made available. Although the promotion of Israeli-Jordanian negotiations was fully in line with the concept of the Reagan Plan, the hope that sufficient US support would be forthcoming turned out to be unrealistic.

Peres appealed to King Hussein that it would be best to finalize an agreement before November 1986, when Shamir would become prime minister. However, Peres's argument was to no avail, and the king procrastinated for unclear reasons.[84] Eventually, most of the pieces of the puzzle appeared to be falling into place, and on April 11, 1987, after the political rotation, Peres and Beilin met once again with King Hussein and al-Rifai in London. Because Peres had not officially asked the new prime minister for permission to go to London for this meeting, Peres and Beilin had to travel in disguise—complete with wigs and sunglasses.[85] On this occasion, however, the agreement was finalized and included the following points:

1. The international conference would not impose any solutions or veto any agreements arrived at between the parties.
2. The negotiations would be conducted directly in bilateral committees.
3. The Palestinian issue would be dealt with by the committee of the Jordanian-Palestinian and Israeli delegations.
4. The representatives of the Palestinians would be included in the Jordanian-Palestinian delegation.

5. Participation in the conference would be based on the parties' acceptance of United Nations Security Council Resolution 242 and Resolution 338 and the renunciation of violence and terrorism.
6. Each committee would negotiate independently.
7. Other issues would be decided by mutual agreement between Jordan and Israel.[86]

However, it was too early to celebrate. Peres and Beilin anticipated Shamir's opposition and had prepared two fallback options. First, they hoped that Peres and Defense Minister Rabin could convince a Likud member of the cabinet, the final government decisionmaking body, to vote in favor of the agreement. Such success had previously been achieved for the decision to withdraw from Lebanon, which Housing Minister David Levy had supported, and in support of the economic reform program, when Yitzhak Moda'i, the Likud finance minister, voted with the ILP. This time, however, the effort failed. The second fallback plan was to ask Secretary of State Shultz to put his weight behind the agreement. Because the Americans had made no prior commitment, Shultz retracted and permitted the London Agreement to falter. Shultz initiated a dialogue with Shamir, who demanded that King Hussein engage in direct negotiations with Israel without the cover of an international conference. Not unexpectedly, King Hussein rejected the offer.[87]

Peres neither forgave nor forgot Shultz's lack of support. During my negotiations in Oslo in 1993, he remained suspicious of American interference, and in May 1993—before negotiations even moved toward a secret official track—I was ordered to refrain from briefing Dan Kurtzer.

The Intifada Puts an End to Jordanian Involvement in Peace Negotiations

On December 9, 1987, the first intifada—meaning "uprising" or "the revolution of the stone," as the Palestinians called it—began in Gaza. It was a sporadic outbreak of violence caused initially by the growing rivalry between the PLO and several emerging Islamic extremist groups, who would soon after form Hamas. The emergence of a younger militant generation challenged the rule of the older, traditional Palestinian leadership. Israeli settlement expansion and emerging verbal and physical expressions of violence also radicalized the Palestinian youth; for instance, former

IDF chief of staff General Eitan Rafael referred to the Palestinians as "cockroaches in a bottle," and a Jewish underground group carried out terrorist attacks against several Palestinian mayors.[88] In historical context, the intifada became a game changer. But even before others realized its implications, the intifada strongly affected the thinking and action of our small group.

In June 1988, Karni and I went to Gaza for a meeting with Shawwa, who sent a closed transit van to take us from the Israel-Gaza border to his house in the center of Gaza City. The vehicle created the impression that goods, rather than Israelis, were being transported, but even as we drove along dirt roads to avoid the main streets, heavy bricks were thrown at us by youth who evidently recognized the van as belonging to Shawwa. We arrived safely, though shocked and scared, at Shawwa's villa—where he told us, upon our arrival, that he had lost all his former political influence and that his ability to pursue peace had come to a final and irreversible end. It was the last time we saw him. Several months later, in September 1988, Shawwa died, apparently a broken man.

It was difficult not to read the writing on the wall, yet King Hussein was the first to do so and take action. Toward the end of July, the Jordanian Development Plan for the West Bank and Gaza was canceled. Political quarters in Amman stressed that these steps would leave Israel and the United States with no choice but to negotiate directly with the PLO.[89] King Hussein also changed the decades-old direction of Jordanian policy aspirations. Since Trans-Jordan's establishment in 1921, the Hashemite Dynasty had tried to expand its influence over the Palestinian territory. Jordan annexed the West Bank in 1950 in line with this policy and, after the West Bank was lost to Israel in 1967, King Hussein aimed at negotiations that would return those Palestinian territories to Jordan. In his speech on July 31, 1988, however, King Hussein announced Jordan's disengagement from both peace negotiations and the West Bank and Gaza:

> Jordan is not Palestine and the independent Palestinian state will be established on the occupied Palestinian territory after its liberation. God willing. On this territory the Palestinian identity will be embodied and the Palestinian struggle will blossom as confirmed by the blessed uprising of the Palestinian people under occupation.[90]

From the Jordanian point of view, the issue was not merely about Palestinian identity but also about Jordanian identity. As much as our group and the

Israeli center and left-wing parties wanted to maintain the Jewish and democratic identity of Israel by repartitioning the former British Mandatory
Palestine to create the State of Palestine alongside Israel within agreed-on
boundaries, the Jordanians wanted to maintain the Jordanian identity of
the Hashemite Kingdom.[91] Ever since Jordan withdrew from negotiations
with Israel over the Palestinian question, the Jordanian leadership has
defended this Jordanian identity by supporting the PLO's efforts to establish the State of Palestine.[92] After almost a decade of negotiation attempts,
the Jordanian Option had died.

Successes, Failures, and Lessons Learned, 1979–88

Successes

At the time of action, the successes our small group achieved appeared
impressive. I personally had come out of nowhere and succeeded in kick-
ing off a serious track-two effort, and Beilin translated our track-two work
into a multitrack diplomacy exercise. Finally, under Peres's leadership, the
work we had started was affecting Israeli government policy. The strategic
idea of building a Palestinian economic power basis contributed to the formulation of Secretary of State Shultz's Quality of Life policy; the dialogue
that Peres and our group had led with the pro-Jordanian and pro-PLO
Palestinian leadership in the West Bank and Gaza contributed to Peres's
tactics in his dialogue with King Hussein in the autumn of 1984. This
made it easier for King Hussein to conclude the February 1985 agreement
with Chairman Arafat. Furthermore, many (although not all) of our policy
proposals on the West Bank and Gaza were being implemented, which
in 1986 enabled the Israeli government to obtain full Jordanian support
and thus increased Amman's involvement and influence in the Palestinian
territories. Finally, the policy planning work we had carried out assisted
Peres and Beilin in negotiating and formulating what became the London
Agreement of April 1987.

The Failure and Its Causes

As successful as these achievements may sound, the major strategic
aim of bringing about Israeli-Jordanian negotiations with support
from the Palestinian leadership of the West Bank and Gaza did not

simply fail; it produced the exact opposite of what had been hoped for. Jordan excluded itself from dealing with the Palestinian issue, and the Jordanian Option died. A combination of four factors caused this monumental failure.

First, in order to obtain the political support of the West Bank and Gaza's Palestinian leadership, our small group envisaged empowering them by offering far-reaching control over their own economic power base. This strategic idea, which I believe might have changed the equation, was opposed by the Israeli, Jordanian, and PLO bureaucracies. Each of these power brokers feared losing influence and control. The relatively little economic support that was being given was manipulated to increase Israeli and Jordanian control mechanisms over the Palestinian population and leadership, instead of giving them sufficient space to build a power base of their own. This manipulation made it easier for the PLO to strengthen its opposition to a development that threatened to weaken PLO influence and control.

Second, although we understood that King Hussein had to embrace the PLO in order to continue negotiations, the renunciation of the Jordanian-PLO agreement of February 1985, which obliged King Hussein to consult with and include PLO supporters in the envisaged negotiations, enhanced PLO opposition. Shlaim's biography of King Hussein argues that this was the decisive cause of the failure.[93] From that moment on, when the PLO had been excluded, we underestimated its capability to undermine the coordinated US-Israeli-Jordanian negotiation attempts through coercion, bribes, and assassinations.

Third, the coalition agreement concluded in the summer of 1984 provided Shamir and his Likud ministers with a veto power over all major Israeli government political decisions. This power allowed Likud to substantially enlarge Israel's settlement activities in the West Bank and Gaza and to create an atmosphere that eventually led to the Palestinian intifada, instead of establishing a relationship of trust that would have created a supportive atmosphere for negotiations.

Fourth and finally, US support for the envisaged strategy remained lukewarm. Even though Peres was pursuing the Reagan Plan's policies on Israeli-Jordanian negotiations, Secretary of State Shultz refrained from offering the necessary support for the London Agreement—a move that Peres perceived as nothing less than betrayal. Similarly, US support for Jordan fell short of what King Hussein had hoped for, as the United States refrained from providing the economic assistance required to rebuild Palestinian support in the West Bank and Gaza.

Lessons Learned

LESSON ONE: COALITION BUILDING AROUND A SIMPLE CONCEPT IS THE KEY TO THE SUCCESS OF TRACK-TWO WORK

Looking at the hoped-for transition from track-two work to multitrack diplomacy, and from there to government policy toward the conclusion of an agreement (i.e., the Hussein-Arafat Agreement of February 1985, and the London Agreement of April 1987), the question arises: What was the key to our success in getting as far as we did? I would reply that the idea of Palestinian economic empowerment enabled us to build a wide, supportive coalition among Peres, several Palestinian leaders, Jordan, and the United States.

LESSON TWO: SUCCESS CAN BE MISLEADING: ALWAYS BE AWARE OF THE BARRIERS AND THE SPOILERS

It turned out that all the achievements—the US Quality of Life policy, Peres's opening-up tactics, the 1985 Hussein-Arafat Agreement, the nomination of the Palestinian mayors in West Bank cities, the Jordanian economic development plan for the West Bank and Gaza, and the 1987 London Agreement—were important but not sufficient. The basic strategy of permitting King Hussein to lead negotiations with Israel on the Palestinian issue failed bitterly. Far greater awareness of the barriers to success and the probable action of spoilers would have been necessary.

LESSON THREE: THE FALLACY OF A POLITICAL EXCLUSIVE STRATEGY

Our Palestinian interlocutors suggested accepting the PLO as *a* legitimate, and not *the only* legitimate, representative of the Palestinian people. This formula would have indicated that Jordan, as well as the Palestinian leadership of the West Bank and Gaza, were similarly legitimate representatives of the Palestinian people. In a way, the 1985 Hussein-Arafat Agreement did provide for such an understanding. Our small group learned that a way would have to be found to permit the Palestinian leadership in the West Bank and Gaza to play a more dominant role in the negotiations by offering the PLO some as-yet-undefined role.

At the same time, we understood that it had been counterproductive to ignore the concerns of Israel's right-wing parties. Before developing a new strategic approach (which is described in chapter 3), we decided to listen carefully to the political thinking and concerns of Likud supporters.

LESSON FOUR: THE LONG-TERM DANGER OF NEGLECTING THE EXPANSION OF SETTLEMENTS

From the outset, we were aware of the need to change the reality on the ground and limit the expansion of Israeli settlement activities. It was a concern that was not only expressed by our small group but also discussed between Peres and Shawwa. However, when the moment of truth came and the ruling coalition of a Peres-led government was formed, Likud received most of the control functions for the support of settlement activities. In hindsight, this allocation had more devastating effects on the long-term strategy for seeking a two-state solution than the failure of the London Agreement.

In preparing for the next phase, we took the first three lessons into account. We would intensify our dialogue with the Palestinian inside leadership and plan to obtain the PLO's support and involvement. Fearing that we would have to overcome barriers and spoiler tendencies from the PLO, we would also intensify our dialogue with Egypt in order to ensure Egyptian influence over Arafat. We learned to be far more alert about Likud's sensitivities and political thinking. Afraid of Likud opposition, we thought of developing a fallback strategy by intensifying contacts with the religious parties. Finally, assuming that we had no means available to influence the reality on the ground, we would direct all our attention to initiating Israeli-Palestinian negotiations.

Chapter 3

A Multitrack Approach to Israeli-Palestinian Negotiations, 1989–91

A far more successful multitrack diplomacy effort was built largely on the lessons learned from the first period. This effort helped pave the way for the Arab-Israeli negotiations at the Madrid Conference in October 1991. From the outset, the strategic aim of this effort was to build confidential relations with the Palestinian inside leadership from the West Bank and Gaza and thereby build a bridge toward the leadership of the Palestine Liberation Organization (PLO) in Tunis. In many ways, the work of this period laid the foundations for the Oslo negotiations in 1993. This chapter considers the performance of this multitrack diplomacy effort as an important model, both in substance and in applied techniques, and provides important tools for comparison with other multitrack diplomacy efforts elsewhere in other conflict situations.

Historical Background: Political Thinking and New Developments

By the end of the 1980s, the Israeli-Palestinian peace process was suffering from low expectations and deteriorating local conditions. The early excitement and enthusiasm of the late 1970s and the early 1980s had given way to disillusionment and pessimism. Early in 1982, it had become evident that Israeli-Egyptian negotiations on the Palestinian issue had failed. The Israeli-Jordanian negotiations of the mid-1980s had similarly failed. Instead of a stronger peace camp, Israeli and Palestinian public radicalization appeared to dominate the political scene and undermine the legitimacy of the leadership on both sides, leaving regional leaders unable to bridge prevailing gaps to start negotiations. Furthermore, the Israeli settlement community in the West Bank and Gaza had grown from a mere 6,000 in 1979 to about 80,000 in the years 1988–89, and its presence continued to pose problems for the future of the negotiations.[1]

Despite such setbacks, there was evident need and opportunity to renew the peace efforts in the late 1980s. Mikhail Gorbachev's ascent to power in the Soviet Union in 1985 and his unfolding dialogue with US president Ronald Reagan became a prelude to the changes that would lead to the end of the Cold War. The United States and the Soviet Union had a common interest in preventing a military buildup of regional powers in the Middle East, and after the 1986 Reykjavik Summit the Soviets agreed to begin a serious reduction of troops in Central and Eastern Europe, which promoted wider US-Soviet understandings across the board. These understandings eventually would also pertain to Middle Eastern affairs.[2] In 1987, the American and Russian Middle East teams met for the first time in Washington to coordinate policies that would support further peace negotiations between Israel and its neighbors.[3]

Regional and local considerations also affected the push for further negotiations. Iraqi president Saddam Hussein's aggressive policies toward Iran and other Arab countries in the late 1980s were cause for concern in Saudi Arabia and other Persian Gulf countries, leading them to rely on American military capabilities for their own defense. As a result, Washington was able to strengthen its power and influence in the Middle East. On the local Israeli-Palestinian level, the unfolding of the intifada in December 1987 created a mutual understanding among the Israeli and Palestinian leadership that a military solution to the conflict was not possible. Violent action by the Palestinians would not bring about an end to the Israeli occupation of the West Bank and Gaza, whereas Israeli military force, if not applied proportionately, would only cause stronger opposition locally, regionally, and internationally against Israel.[4] Accordingly, peace negotiations were the only feasible path. The political thinking and action at the level of senior Palestinian, American, and Israeli decisionmakers clearly reflected the emerging conceptual change and created momentum for our track-two and multitrack diplomacy effort.

Developments on the Palestinian Front

The December 1987 intifada and subsequent events caused five important changes in the Palestinian camp. First, the internal leadership and population of the West Bank and Gaza gained both prestige and political influence, as they were seen as the new heroes of the struggle for Palestinian independence. Second, the official founding of Hamas in 1987 presented a challenge to the PLO, not least because of the former's tendency to commit acts of terrorism to assert their political role and challenge the latter's leadership. The PLO, however, had stronger political representation in the Arab world and internationally. Along with PLO leader Yasser Arafat's capacity to finance (at least in part) the costs of the uprising, the PLO's reemergent role in the Palestinian camp was the third change caused by the intifada.

The fourth repercussion was probably the most significant: The intifada boosted the Palestinian leadership's need to negotiate. It became clear to the Palestinian leadership after only a few months of the intifada that no political breakthrough could be achieved through anger, violence, and boycotts. However, ending the intifada without achieving clear political gains made no sense. The only way out of the situation was for the Palestinian leadership to seek negotiations with Israel. This idea first became evident when, against all odds, the maverick PLO adviser Bassam Abu Sharif published an article in June 1988 titled "PLO View: Prospects of a Palestinian Israeli Settlement."[5] In it, Sharif wrote:

> If the support of the Palestinians for the PLO is regarded as an unreliable expression of the Palestinian free will, then give the Palestinians the chance to express their free will in a manner that will convince all doubters: arrange for an internationally supervised referendum in the West Bank and the Gaza Strip and allow the population to choose between the PLO and any other group of Palestinians that Israel or the United States or the international community wishes to nominate. The PLO is ready to abide by the outcome and step aside for any alternative leadership, should the Palestinian people choose one.

The idea of a referendum in the West Bank and Gaza—or better, simply elections—particularly appealed to Yitzhak Rabin, then the Israeli minister of defense. Rabin would include this idea in developing the "Rabin

Plan," which would later inform the official Israeli government policy.[6] Finally, Jordan's departure from the Palestinian political scene in July 1988 would become a crucial diplomatic and political factor, because it forced both the US and Israeli governments to deal directly with the Palestinian leadership.

Developments on the US Front

In early November 1987, after the London Agreement fell apart, Yossi Beilin—who at the time was a political director-general (equivalent to undersecretary) at the Israeli Foreign Office—flew to the United States to try to convince the American leadership to launch a policy initiative to get negotiations under way. His visit was to no avail.[7] Instead, it would take the showing of pictures of wounded Palestinian children on American television screens after the outbreak of the intifada to change the US government's stance and, in March 1988, Secretary of State George Shultz published the "Shultz Initiative."[8] The US peace team had drawn important lessons from the failure of earlier negotiations on self-government and created a new approach. The main idea was to enable the parties to move to Permanent Status negotiations with or without a comprehensive Interim Agreement on the exact details of Palestinian self-government. It was thus suggested that negotiations on Palestinian self-government begin May 1, 1989, and that the negotiations would move toward discussions on Permanent Status after seven months, even without an agreement. The Shultz Initiative proposed to convene an international conference two weeks before the start of negotiations in order to create the necessary framework and terms of reference for the negotiating partners. All the provisions laid out in the 1987 London Agreement were applied, obliging the participants to accept UN Security Council Resolution 242 and Resolution 338, and to renounce violence and terrorism. The Palestinian representatives would be included within the proposed Jordanian-Palestinian delegation.[9]

The idea of starting negotiations on borders, security issues, refugee concerns, and the status of Jerusalem—even without an agreement on the structure of Palestinian self-government—appealed to our small group. In our view, Israel's central interest was to negotiate a secure and recognized border with its Arab neighbors. However, the Shultz Initiative appealed to our small group for the same reasons that it was opposed by Prime

Minister Yitzhak Shamir, who wanted to prevent any foreign government from exercising sovereign control over any part of the West Bank and Gaza, at any cost. Accordingly, Shamir immediately rejected the initiative. Secretary Shultz, angered, sent his close confidant Charles Hill to Jerusalem in May 1988 with one specific task: to sit down with Shamir and find out whether a US peace initiative could be defined or whether every proposal would be rejected. Hill returned to the United States and reported that Shamir would say "no" to every suggestion.[10]

After the Hill-Shamir encounter, American thinking and action changed. Until that point, the PLO had made sporadic efforts to begin a dialogue with the United States, and President Jimmy Carter had made an unsuccessful effort to test whether it would be possible to include the PLO in peace negotiations. However, the PLO's demands had remained unacceptable.[11] In September 1975, the United States, in a Memorandum of Agreement with the Government of Israel, had committed not to engage in dialogue with the PLO for as long as the PLO refused to recognize Israel's right to exist, irreversibly renounce terrorism, and accept UN Security Council Resolution 242.[12] It was made clear that the PLO's stance on all three positions would need to change for a US-PLO dialogue to begin. However, in the face of Shamir's rejection of any possible United States–led peace initiative, Shultz needed to find out it if it would be possible to convince Chairman Arafat to accept American conditions independent of Israeli concerns.

Developments on the US-PLO Front

Shortly after Hill's return from Israel, in the summer of 1988 the United States began indirect dialogue with the PLO with the help of Swedish foreign minister Sten Andersson, the Jewish Republican politician Rita Hauser, and Peace Now's New York representative, Dvora Kesse. With Jordan out of the picture, UN Security Council Resolution 242 was now acceptable to the Palestinians, given that it advocated the formula of "territory for peace," which meant that if a Palestinian delegation were to negotiate with Israel, sooner or later Israel would have to withdraw from the West Bank and Gaza in return for peace, thus making it feasible to establish a Palestinian state. Although the indirect US dialogue with the PLO via Sweden remained secret, Secretary of State Shultz publicly addressed a largely Jewish audience and made it clear that he expected the

PLO to accept UN Security Council Resolution 242, and that in return he would acknowledge the "political rights" of the Palestinians.[13]

Between November 12 and 14, 1988, the Palestine National Council—the highest Palestinian representative decisionmaking body—met in Algiers and adopted eight major decisions on the peace process with Israel. Ever since, these decisions have guided Palestinian policies and negotiations with Israel. The decisions made demanded the following points:

> . . . an effective international conference . . . under the auspices of the United Nations; Israeli withdrawal from all the Palestinian and Arab territories that it has occupied since 1967, including Arab Jerusalem; removal of the settlements Israel has established since 1967; a demand to place the Palestinian territories included Arab Jerusalem under the supervision of the United Nations for a limited period; settlement of the Palestinian refugees issue in accordance with the resolutions of the United Nations; the right of worship at the holy places in Palestine for the followers of all religions; and Security Council guarantee and arrangements for security and peace "among all affected states in the region." Finally, the Palestine National Council confirmed that "the future relationship between the two states of Jordan and Palestine will be established on a confederal basis."[14]

The council subsequently announced the Palestinian Declaration of Independence on November 15, 1988. The eight decisions and the declaration of independence became the PLO's conceptual, ideological, and political framework for negotiations with Israel during the forthcoming decades. If the PLO wanted to keep unity among an internally divided nation, it had to respect the constraints that had been outlined by these decisions.

On the basis of these decisions, Chairman Arafat committed the PLO to a prenegotiated statement on December 13, 1988, accepting all three conditions in the September 1975 US-Israel Memorandum of Agreement. The following day, the United States announced that a dialogue with the PLO would begin, led by the American ambassador to Tunis, Robert Pelletreau. The subtext of the American message to Israel was clear: Though the United States viewed Israel, not the PLO, as its ally, Washington was not receiving any constructive policy proposals to begin peace negotiations from Jerusalem and therefore was turning to a US-PLO dialogue in the hope that some other ideas might emerge.[15]

Developments on the Israeli Front

At the beginning of November 1988, elections were held in Israel. In the face of a stronger Likud and a weakened Israeli Labor Party (ILP), which had lost eight seats in the Knesset, Yitzhak Shamir was able to form a second National Unity Government. Because Shamir had no need to offer Peres the rotation of the premiership, Peres received the finance portfolio and Beilin became his deputy minister. Rabin became defense minister.

As defense minister, Rabin became the prime mover in support of an Israeli peace plan. After the end of the Iran-Iraq war in 1988, he feared that Iran, and also Pakistan, would engage in a major effort to acquire military nuclear capabilities, and he understood that such a development would undermine Israel's deterrence capacity. To face such a challenge, his strategy was to promote peace with Syria and the Palestinians.[16] As minister of defense, he was also responsible for finding ways and means to put an end to the intifada.

According to Rabin's close adviser, Eitan Haber, three different experiences affected Rabin's thinking on the intifada. After visiting the Israeli troops in Gaza, he asked the military censors to submit to him the content of letters that soldiers stationed there would write home. Although the troops he had met seemed to be enthusiastic, he sensed that behind their expressed commitment many questions remained unasked and hence unanswered; for this reason, he asked for an overview of their personal thoughts in the letters they wrote to their families. Many of the letters questioned the rationale of seeking to subdue the intifada by the use of force and violent action against "kids" and the civilian Palestinian population.[17] Rabin's second formative experience happened when he visited the Kezioth prison camp, where the intifada's leaders were incarcerated. A discussion with two Palestinian leaders in particular struck him; they said that Israel could imprison ten, twenty, thirty, or even forty thousand Palestinians, but the intifada would not stop. Sooner or later, Israel would have to negotiate with the PLO leadership in Tunis.[18] The third formative experience came when Rabin realized that every Palestinian leader he met with reported, in detail, to the PLO. Over a period of two months after his visit to the prisoner camp, he met with Palestinian leaders in groups once a week to identify local leaders, with the hope that they would help negotiate the Palestinian self-government agreement provided for in the Camp David Accords. Israeli military intelligence informed Rabin that every one of the leaders with whom he had met sent detailed messages to Tunis and asked for instructions from the PLO.[19]

Still, Rabin was reluctant to deal directly with the PLO, because he viewed them as a terrorist organization and he understood that their main aim was to demand and fight for the unlimited Palestinian right of return to Israel and also to the West Bank and Gaza. Instead, he believed, the Palestinian residents of the West Bank and Gaza had to come to terms with Israel if they wanted to pursue their national rights and a decent living alongside Israel. Understanding the dominant political power of the PLO, Rabin decided to adopt PLO adviser Bassam Abu Sharif's idea of organizing elections in the West Bank and Gaza. The Rabin Plan proposed that a Palestinian negotiating team be determined by elections in the West Bank and Gaza and that negotiations with Israel on the conditions and steps necessary to reach Palestinian self-government in the territories subsequently begin. With some changes, the Rabin Plan became the Shamir Plan that was officially adopted by the Israeli government in May 1989.[20]

The Multitrack Diplomacy Challenge and the Emerging Strategy

The conditions for our multitrack diplomacy work had both worsened and improved. The fact that Likud had been strengthened in the 1988 elections clearly strengthened Prime Minister Shamir's hand, and his tendency was to maintain the status quo, expand settlements in the West Bank and the Gaza Strip, and if possible avoid meaningful negotiations that would necessitate Israel's withdrawal from occupied territories. Under Shamir's plan, Israeli government policy toward peace negotiations included three major "no's": no to the establishment of an additional Palestinian state, no to negotiations with the PLO, and no change of status of the West Bank and Gaza (which Israel referred to as "Judea, Samaria, and Gaza"). However, Rabin's commitment to peace negotiations was supported by Israel's security establishment. No less important was the determination of the Americans, Egyptians, and Palestinians to get the Israeli-Palestinian negotiating process going.

In practical terms, the challenge was multifaceted and required a complicated chain of understandings. For the Palestinian leadership residing in the West Bank and Gaza to be able to agree to a negotiating concept, they needed the consent and endorsement of the PLO leadership residing in Tunis. Furthermore, whatever ideas our small group might come up with, we needed Rabin's and Peres's consent and endorsement. For their part, they needed the consent of Prime Minister Shamir. The challenge was to bridge the gap between the PLO's hard-line positions on one hand and the parallel uncompromising approach of Shamir on the other.

The aim of our multitrack diplomacy effort was to seek common ground among the more moderate actors and to mobilize the United States and Egypt to provide assurance and support and, if necessary, pressure the harder-line actors to reach an agreement. Traditional diplomacy had almost no chance to succeed in such conditions. Despite the fact that the United States had started to speak directly to the PLO, it was inconceivable that the United States would be able to submit a concept that both the PLO and Shamir would accept. However, if we on track two could develop a concept that the internal Palestinian leadership would accept and then build a wide coalition including the leadership of the ILP, the United States, and Egypt around it, then it would be more feasible for the US peace team to clinch a deal. US secretary of state James Baker expressed this thinking when he said, "Let me know that there is a rabbit to hunt." Our challenge was not only to show that there was a rabbit but also to detail where, when, and how it could be hunted.

Our small group saw eye to eye with Rabin with regard to the need to start negotiations with a Palestinian team. We also understood that the formula for starting negotiations had to be in line with the provisions of the Rabin-turned-Shamir Plan. The multitrack diplomacy strategy that we developed was based on a four-phase approach:

- First, attempt to identify, in a track-two negotiating effort, agreed-upon principles to start Israeli-Palestinian negotiations.
- Second, obtain endorsement from Peres and the ILP's governing institutions.
- Third, gain the support and diplomatic intervention of the United States and Egypt (which would enable the fourth point).
- Fourth, convince Prime Minister Shamir to accept and begin negotiations.

In case our four-phase strategy were to fail and Prime Minister Shamir and the Likud party were to reject the suggested policy, we had two fall-back plans. The first was an attempt by the ILP to form an alternative government. If this were to fail, we would turn to our second fallback plan, whereby the ILP would leave the government altogether and move to the opposition.

The Unfolding Track-Two Negotiations

Getting Started

Toward the end of December 1988 and the start of January 1989, track-two discussions took place with our Palestinian partners in Jerusalem, Hebron, and Ramallah. I invited Immanuel Halperin, a nonpolitical insider (he was Menachem Begin's nephew) and a well-known television journalist with access to the most intimate circles of Likud's leadership, to participate in some of these meetings. In these discussions, the substantial gaps between Likud's and the Palestinian policy positions became very evident.

Halperin loyally presented Likud's thinking. He adopted a very soft tactical position and stated that the prohibition of meetings with the PLO was a mistake.[21] He insisted that Likud was "the first [party] to recognize the legitimate rights of the Palestinians," and he encouraged negotiations.[22] He also argued that Shamir would want a breakthrough "in the last term of his office. He will want to be remembered by history as a man of peace."[23] Regarding the substance of autonomy, Halperin said, "Autonomy is nowhere granted to an area of land, but always to a people; otherwise autonomy would bring about foreign sovereignty."[24] Finally, on strategy, Halperin's statements were not very encouraging. He stated that Israel would never be able to agree to a statement that said that Eretz Yisrael between the Jordan and the Mediterranean is the land to be divided between Israelis and Palestinians. In his opinion, it would be more historically accurate and politically acceptable to say that the Israeli and the Palestinian peoples inhabit the area between the Mediterranean and the desert, and that if at any time a new division or solution to the problem of the West Bank and Gaza should come about, it would be of essential importance for the Palestinians to know that they would receive the greater portion of the divided land, and not merely a piece of land that amounts to less than 20 percent of the area lying between the Mediterranean and the Jordan.[25]

The message was clear. Likud, which had historically claimed that "both sides of the River Jordan" had to be part of the Jewish state in the original area of British-occupied Palestine, wanted a deal that would recognize Jordan as "Palestine" and an agreement that would give personal autonomy to the Palestinians in the West Bank. It also wanted to prevent any "foreign sovereignty" over the territories of the West Bank and Gaza.

Our Palestinian interlocutors were similarly soft on tactics and hard on strategy. On tactics, the most forthcoming were Hana Siniora, a journalist who formerly had been nominated by Arafat to become a member of a joint Jordanian-Palestinian peace delegation, and Hebron mayor Mustafa Abdel Nabi Natche. They said that the PLO would endeavor to bring about the beginning of negotiations with Israel at an international conference, that elections in the West Bank and Gaza could become a possible step in the evolving process, and that an Interim Agreement was possible. Any negotiations would need to be coordinated with the PLO, whether through the Palestinian leadership in the territories, the US-PLO dialogue, the Egyptian government, the Israeli left, or the American Jewish community.[26] On strategy, however, it was abundantly clear that only full Israeli recognition of the Palestinian right to self-determination, leading to the creation of a Palestinian state, was acceptable.

Comparing the positions presented by Halperin and those by our Palestinian interlocutors, we clearly understood that the zone of possible agreement was very narrow. There was too little common ground to achieve a full agreement on self-government, and there was no room to work on a concept that would substantially diffuse the causes of conflict. What remained was to seek an agreement that would get Israeli-Palestinian negotiations going.

Our Palestinian interlocutors also told us that we would need to work with Faisal Husseini.[27] Husseini was the son of Abd el-Qadar el-Husseini, who had led the Palestinian armed forces in the 1948 war until his death in the Battle of the Qastal near Jerusalem, and a descendant of the most important branch of the Husseini clan, which had played a dominant political role in the Jerusalem region for several centuries. Immediately after Husseini was released from prison at the end of January 1989, I met him in his home in East Jerusalem. This was the beginning of a long working relationship that lasted until his untimely death in Kuwait in 2001. In this first meeting, I suggested to Husseini that we organize a meeting at Jerusalem's Notre Dame Hotel that would be attended by an Israeli team under the leadership of Beilin. There would be seven members on the Israeli side, and Husseini should come with whoever he decided should be there—the wider and more all-embracing the Palestinian team, the better. The location of the hotel on the former border between Jewish and Arab Jerusalem was of both political and symbolic significance, and indicated that we perceived that the area east of that line was Palestinian territory and that the Palestinians would simultaneously perceive that the area west of the line was Israeli territory.

In preparation for the Notre Dame meeting, I wrote a short position paper pointing out that the PLO was permitting "a certain degree of flexibility" (or soft tactics) as a means of achieving international recognition. I also made it clear that although the internal PLO leaders in the West Bank and Gaza were not an alternative to the PLO leaders in Tunis, they would be able to act as intermediaries. I anticipated that the PLO would permit negotiations on elections, as long as the following conditions w ere maintained:

1. The amorphous power structure in the territories and PLO control over them would be maintained.
2. The PLO would receive additional international recognition.
3. Elections would open the way for UN involvement in the peace process.
4. Elections would lead the way to PLO involvement (and domination) of the peace process.[28]

To be effective and to convince the Israeli government to move toward negotiations, we had to tread very carefully.

From Notre Dame to The Hague

On February 15, 1989, at 8 p.m., the Palestinian and Israeli delegations gathered at the Notre Dame Hotel on the "border" between East and West Jerusalem. The Palestinian team, chaired by Husseini, was composed of many future delegates to the coming negotiations in Washington. Hanan Ashrawi, an articulate Palestinian woman from a Protestant family, was a close friend of Husseini. As both a female and a non-Muslim (and as someone who was not even from one of the major Christian communities), Ashrawi was cast as a political outsider, but she had studied in Beirut and was personally close to Shafiq al-Khut, Abu Sharif, and several other PLO leaders.[29] Two years after the Notre Dame meeting, Ashrawi would become the Palestinian spokeswoman at the 1991 Madrid Conference. Husseini was also accompanied by Sari Nusseibeh (who later would become president of Al-Quds University in Jerusalem), who had led many discussions, particularly with members of Likud, and had been beaten up by Palestinian thugs for his attempts to build bridges;[30] by Mamdouh el-Akr, a physician; by Ziyyad Abu Zayyad, a lawyer who spoke perfect Hebrew and often appeared in the Israeli media; by Ghassan al-Khatib, who would later become a minister in the Palestinian Authority and represented the Communist Party; and by Saaman Khuri of the Popular Front for the Liberation of Palestine, a PLO member group led by George Habash.

The Israeli team was led by Beilin and consisted of Avrum Burg, who would later become chairman of the Knesset; Efraim Sneh, who would later serve as minister of health, minister of transport, and deputy minister of defense; Nimrod Novik, who at the time was a political adviser to Shimon Peres; Arie Ofri, a member of Peres's 100-day team; my friend Boaz Karni, who was Beilin's closest friend and adviser; and myself.

At the beginning of the meeting, Beilin laid out the basic working assumptions and guidelines for the intended track-two dialogue. He opened the meeting by saying:

> All of us Israelis belong to the ILP. Here lies our influence and our effectiveness. We are not the party and not the government. Yet, we represent a large segment within the party. . . . The general situation has changed after Arafat's speech in Geneva of 15 [*sic*] December 1988. . . . The PLO itself and PLO supporters in the territories get more legitimization in Israel. Even Rabin and his people have met with you. . . . The question is, how to use our power and influence? There is Rabin's Plan. Perhaps we can move from there. . . . Let us take the skeleton of the Rabin Plan and make something out of it.[31]

However, Beilin added a warning:

> If the PLO is using violence and will employ terrorism it is the end of the story. It will undermine and kill any political effort aimed at achieving understanding and will totally undermine our own positions and influence.[32]

Husseini and the other Palestinians present took a harder-line approach than had been presented to us in the preparatory meetings. As a precondition for going to elections, Husseini asked whether the Israeli side was willing to accept the Palestinian demand "for the end of occupation and the right to self-determination."[33]

The Palestinians leaked the events of the Notre Dame meeting to the press.[34] Ehud Yaari, a prominent television journalist, stated that the meeting had been an absolute failure. On the surface, his statement was accurate; the Israeli team had come to discuss how to move toward elections in the territories, and the Palestinians had preconditions that, from the Israeli point of view, were totally unrealistic. However, the meeting was more complex than what the media had sensed. The Israeli side had stated that we viewed dialogue with the inside leadership as a stepping-stone toward dialogue with the PLO in Tunis, and we suggested elections in the territories that would provide the internal leadership with both indigenous and international legitimacy at a time when Israel was questioning the PLO's legitimacy. The Palestinian team was telling us, more indirectly than directly, that the space in which the internal PLO could maneuver depended on its ability to offer Chairman Arafat and the PLO in Tunis a greater degree of international recognition and control of the evolving negotiating process. As long as it was not evident that this would be the case, little or no headway could be made.

The significance of the Notre Dame meeting was not in its immediate results but in the fact that it was an opening move that made it clear to both sides that their representative groups were interested in a dialogue to begin Israeli-Palestinian negotiations. The message we received from those meetings was twofold: The Palestinians were willing to develop a political concept that would make negotiations and elections in the territories possible, but in order to do so another gesture was needed to indicate goodwill toward the PLO from the Israeli side. At the same time, Ashrawi sent us various international observers who offered their services in arranging direct or indirect dialogue with the PLO.

Evidently, more in-depth discussions had to be pursued in a more intimate setting. Novik and I understood that the decisive thinking and decisionmaking rested with Husseini and Ashrawi. From then on, I would visit Ashrawi—sometimes alone, sometimes with different members of Mashov, and often accompanied by Karni—and later, when progress had been made, Husseini participated in the meetings.[35] These meetings were important for Husseini and Ashrawi, because they allowed them to better understand internal Israeli politics. Similarly, we gained a better understanding of internal Palestinian affairs.

Although our meetings with Husseini and Ashrawi were part of a track-two effort, we were also kept informed of parallel efforts on the track-one level, the most relevant being the unfolding dialogue between the United States and the PLO. My American Embassy contact, Daniel Kurtzer, had made the following points to me in mid-May 1989:[36]

1. The dialogue with the PLO was being taken seriously on the American side, and Ambassador Robert Pelletreau in Tunis was receiving handwritten instructions from Secretary of State Schulz. On the Palestinian

side, the PLO ambassador to Tunis, Hakam Balawi, was leading the dialogue, but it did not seem that Chairman Arafat was taking the discussions seriously. The Americans hoped that the Palestinians would upgrade the dialogue on their side and involve leading PLO figures Mahmoud Abbas (also known as Abu Mazen) and Saleh Khalaf (also known as Abu Iyad), but Washington would not ask for their involvement.[37] Washington also understood that the PLO in Tunis would only go along with the proposal for elections if the PLO's gains were made clear. The PLO wanted an international conference that would lead to the establishment of a Palestinian state, and it hoped that the Americans would identify some common ground between this idea and the Israeli plan. The Americans, however, were still opposed to the idea of an independent Palestinian state. Because they could not, and would not, promise to recognize one, they wanted only to achieve an agreement on fair and honest elections that would lead to negotiations for a final settlement.

2. Outside the Palestinian territories, the Democratic Front for the Liberation of Palestine, a left-wing member of the PLO, led by Naif Hawatme, stressed that more influence should be given to the Palestinian community in the territories and emphasized the fact that it supported elections. The position of Habash's group, the Popular Front for the Liberation of Palestine, was not clear; nor was it clear whether it possessed a spoiler capacity (as in its role in the assassination of Zafer al-Masri in February 1986).[38]

3. Estimates indicated that Hamas might get up to 40 percent of the vote of elections held in Gaza. However, the PLO wanted to see that Hamas remained as weak as possible.

4. The Soviets were supporting the idea of elections, and they promised the Americans that they would assert their influence upon the leftist groups within the PLO.[39]

The information we received from Kurtzer and other sources indicated that the international community at large, not just the Americans, supported the idea of elections, and that a gesture made on our side to the PLO through track-two channels might make a difference. In a meeting with Peres, Max van der Stoel, the former Dutch minister of foreign affairs, offered to forge a link with the PLO. Without Peres's knowledge, his political adviser, Novik, suggested that van der Stoel get in touch with me and simultaneously asked that I get in touch with him. I was later told that Ashrawi had also insisted that van der Stoel meet with me. Novik wanted to create a fully deniable channel to the PLO. At that point, our relationship with Ashrawi was close enough for her to make the same proposal. This led to a request from van der Stoel that, after receiving the "green light" from Beilin, I should go to Paris to meet him and prepare the envisaged meeting.

In our short discussion with van der Stoel in Paris, I made it clear that according to Israeli law, Beilin and I were not allowed to meet with the PLO delegation. What we had in mind were proximity talks; van der Stoel and Robert Serry, the head of the Middle Eastern desk at the Dutch Ministry of Foreign Affairs (who later would become the UN peace envoy to the Middle East), would need to meet the Palestinian delegation in one location, then come and see us in another. We, the Israeli side, would not be willing to meet face-to-face with the Palestinians because it would delegitimize our own position and the entire initiative by breaking the law prohibiting direct meetings between Israelis and PLO officials. However, our message was clear: We understood that the PLO had a dominant role in the negotiating process, and we would lead the way to such negotiations with Israel.

There was no need for a joint statement by the Israeli and Palestinian delegations about the proximity talks. Rather, we hoped that our discussions would make it possible for the Dutch Labor Party to publish policy principles that could aid in reaching a final understanding on how to start negotiations. A statement by the Dutch Labor Party, rather than a bilateral Israeli-Palestinian statement, would also make it possible to ensure that Beilin's and my own visits to The Hague would not be leaked to the press. As a cover story for the visit to the Netherlands, Beilin would arrange for talks with his counterpart in the Dutch Ministry of Finance, Deputy Minister J. N. van Cuntereen.[40]

Meeting in The Hague

On June 26, 1989, Beilin and I arrived at the Amsterdam Schiphol Airport. We were welcomed by heavily armed security officials, who immediately formed a secure ring around Beilin, leaving me outside the ring to face a possible terrorist attack on my own. An armed tank also drove beside us, creeping along the lengthy corridors of Schiphol to protect us against a possible attack from the airfield.

Our meeting with the Ministry of Finance was as awkward and amusing as our dramatic welcome. The subject of discussion was the complicated Dutch arrangements for control of customs and the linked Foreign Trade

Computer System. In essence, the discussion was aimed at enlightening Israel about the Dutch way of handling and controlling customs affairs without interfering in the movement of goods and carriers, an effective system that substantially eased the flow of goods in ports and other border areas. It was, however, surreal to be taught about a system that necessitated open borders and friendly relations with all neighbors, one that was neither relevant nor adaptable to the Israeli situation. Furthermore, it was obvious during the meeting that the relationship between the Israeli deputy minister of finance (Beilin) and his aide (me) was unusual: The deputy minister had clearly mastered all the relevant and professional information and bureaucratic issues, whereas his aide had neither the slightest idea of nor interest in the discussion.

We were set up in a hotel close to the sea and Scheveningen, in the southern part of The Hague not too far from the International Court of Justice. The Palestinian delegation was staying in a hotel situated in the center of The Hague. We, of course, neither met with nor saw the Palestinian delegation, and it took van der Stoel and Serry almost half an hour to move from one site to the other. We were told that the Palestinian delegation was composed of four people: delegation chair Abdallah Hourani, who was in charge of cultural affairs in the PLO; Hisham Mustafa, who was Abbas's chief of staff and was responsible for contacts and possible negotiations with Israel; Hassan Asfour, an agricultural engineer from Rafah in the Gaza Strip;[41] and Afif Safiyeh, the PLO representative (ambassador) in the Netherlands.[42]

At The Hague, Beilin's messages to the PLO delegation, delivered by van der Stoel and Serry, were as follows:[43]

1. Eventually, Israel and the PLO would negotiate directly with one another. There was strong support for this within the Israeli political camp, because Ezer Weitzmann of Likud and Moshe Shahal and Beilin of the ILP were advocating such an approach.
2. The ILP and the Israeli peace camp had been weakened by the intifada, which had brought about the loss of eight ILP seats in the Knesset in the last elections.
3. Israel would have to accept the idea of Palestinian self-determination, though its practical implementation could not be on Israel's account. Israel would also need to eventually withdraw from most of the territories, which would permit Palestinian sovereignty.
4. Negotiations on the relationship between the Palestinian territories and Jordan (whether in the form of a federation or a confederation) would be necessary.[44]

5. There would be a need for interim solutions while the permanent solution was being negotiated.
6. To allow the Israeli political system to adopt the necessary positions, the next steps would need to be planned very carefully, and eventually elections in Israel would be necessary to obtain the legitimacy needed to continue.

In my handwritten notes on the discussion, I did not record any messages from the PLO delegation to us. The approach taken by van der Stoel and Serry was to listen carefully to each side and, based on what they had heard, to prepare a Dutch text and show this text to both sides. In substance, what we were pursuing was not a dialogue with intermediaries but rather two parallel, interrelated dialogues in which the Dutch side could not, of course, conclude a paper without receiving the full consent of both sides.

We did not reach an agreement on the paper while in The Hague. Instead, we left with the impression (right or wrong) that the PLO delegation had been dogmatic and had not reciprocated or appreciated the goodwill and the willingness to take political risk that Beilin had shown in coming to the proximity talks.

As it turned out, Beilin had taken a very serious personal risk, and Prime Minister Shamir demanded his resignation upon our return. Peres backed Beilin and refused to dismiss him. This caused a Likud member of the Knesset, Zachi Hanegbi, to demand legislation that would permit the prime minister to dismiss deputy ministers.[45] Despite the internal political anger, our visit to The Hague had been a success. Once in Israel, we realized that our proximity talks had not failed to have a constructive impact on our dialogue with Husseini and Ashrawi. We also continued to work with the Dutch Labor Party on a proposed statement from the talks, and on July 19, 1989, van der Stoel sent us the following draft statement:[46]

> In my capacity as chairman of the Middle East committee of the Netherlands Labour Party . . . during the last few months, I have conducted a number of separate conversations with prominent members of the Israeli Labor Party and of the Palestinian Liberation Organization. On the basis of these contacts I have reason to believe that there exists an understanding on the following basic principles as the basis for a comprehensive and lasting settlement of the Arab-Israeli conflict:
>
> 1. Implementation of [UN Security Council] Resolution 242 and Resolution 338.

2. Respect for and implementation of the security (P) [of all states in the region including Israel], (I) [needs of Israel].
3. Respect for and implementation of the (P) [right to self-determination of the Palestinian people], (I) [full political rights of the Palestinian people which the Palestinians consider to include the right to self-determination].
4. Acceptance of the need to move towards a settlement in stages and of the principle of linkage amongst them: interim agreements have to be part of an ongoing process of negotiations leading to a comprehensive permanent settlement. Agreement that all options will be considered.
5. Agreement that a permanent settlement must include an equitable solution of the Palestinian refugee problem.
6. Rejection of terrorism in all its forms.

The peace process to be agreed upon will be based on the above-mentioned principles. Elections amongst the Palestinian people in the (P) [territories occupied since 1967]. (I) [West Bank and Gaza, including East Jerusalem] are considered as an important step in this process.

In order to agree on the modalities of the elections, negotiations between Israel and representatives of the Palestinian people will start immediately. The PLO will appoint the Palestinian delegation to these negotiations which will comprise (I) [eight] representatives from the West Bank, East Jerusalem and the Gaza Strip, as well as two representatives from elsewhere as mutually agreed upon.

The agreement, to be concluded within the framework of an international conference, will be final and permanent and supported by international guarantees.[47]

After The Hague: A Formula for Negotiations, and Mubarak's Ten Points

After the proximity talks in Netherlands, we were more aware of the gap between the PLO's demands and what we could achieve on the Israeli side. At the same time, we were aware that no Palestinian delegation could come to negotiations on the basis of the May 1989 Israeli Peace Plan, which expressly negated much of the five main Palestinian demands: (1) a Palestinian state, (2) the right to self-determination, (3) Israeli withdrawal to the 1967 lines, (4) the "right of return," and (5) recognition of the PLO as the sole representative of the Palestinian people. In order to advance, we needed to get these five seemingly imperative PLO demands out of the way without negating the possibility of their raising these demands again at a later stage. It was thus essential that the Israeli and Palestinian delegations be able to attend negotiations on different platforms that would not be allowed to negate each other outright.

Egypt was ideally situated to assist in bridging the gap between us and the Palestinians. Egypt was committed to the conditions of the 1978 Camp David Accords with Israel; but during negotiations on Palestinian self-government, Egypt had submitted a proposal fully in line with the PLO demand for self-determination leading to the establishment of the State of Palestine.[48] Furthermore, the Palestinian perspective—and Arafat's own—was that Egypt could play a central role in legitimizing the PLO and allowing Arafat to play a dominant role, even if for the time being it was "behind the curtains."

Novik, as Peres's political adviser, had built a close and effective working relationship with the Egyptian ambassador to Israel, Mohammed Bassiouni—a relationship similar to the ones that I had developed with our Palestinian interlocutors. In early July 1989, Novik and Bassiouni discussed Egypt's potential role in bridging the Israeli-Palestinian gap. On a paper napkin, Novik jotted down nine points that outlined how it would be possible for the Palestinians to attend negotiations at which Israel would also be present. These points described the minimal demands of the Palestinians necessary to guarantee free and undisturbed elections, and repeated the "territory for peace formula" as a basis for negotiations. Novik and Bassiouni concluded that both sides would check with their superiors as to whether such an approach might work.[49] Avi Gil, another member of Peres's support team and future director-general of the Ministry of Foreign Affairs, added a tenth point to Novik's nine: the need to refrain from building new settlements during negotiations. Ambassador Bassiouni quickly received a positive response from Cairo: President Hosni Mubarak (who had succeeded Anwar Sadat following Sadat's assassination in 1981) was interested in adopting the ten points as a basis for convincing Arafat and the PLO to permit a Palestinian delegation to engage in negotiations with Israel. To do so, Mubarak needed to receive positive indications from Jerusalem and Washington that such an approach had a serious chance of success.[50] Peres and Rabin demonstrated their seriousness by deciding to leave the government if Likud opposed the unfolding peace initiative.[51]

Finalizing the Formula

Beilin, Novik, and I thought that we had achieved a breakthrough in our deliberations in the Netherlands and in the ongoing dialogue with van der Stoel and Serry. The eighth point of van der Stoel's July 19, 1989, draft statement was operationally significant because it suggested that the Palestinian delegation be composed of eight representatives from the West Bank, Jerusalem, and Gaza, along with two representatives from outside. Furthermore, it said that the PLO would appoint the Palestinian delegation, although the Israeli government would have the right to veto nominations. Such a system ensured that each representative was mutually agreed upon.

However, two important points still needed to be clarified. Israel had a reason for insisting on negotiating with an inside Palestinian delegation as opposed to an outside one. Discussions with an inside delegation would focus on ending the June 1967 occupation and creating good and viable neighborly relations, while negotiations with an outside delegation would sooner or later turn to the 1948 conflict and the "right of return" of the members of the Palestinian Diaspora to their homes within Israel. This latter demand would undermine Israel's very existence. Therefore, we needed a formula of constructive ambiguity that would allow each delegation to interpret the same reality differently. It was also necessary to get the Palestinians to agree to the proviso that the "two representatives from elsewhere" in the Palestinian delegation be former inhabitants of the West Bank and/or Gaza who had been expelled by Israel. In this case, the ILP (and later the Government of Israel) could claim that negotiations had been with the inside leadership, and the PLO could simultaneously claim that the Palestinian delegation had genuinely represented the outside leadership. Husseini, with consent from Tunis, accepted this formula.

Thus, Beilin, Novik, Karni, and I decided to go public and ask Husseini to submit a first formula for the beginning of negotiations to an Israeli audience. We had to make it evident that the negotiating formula was being presented to Israel by Husseini and had not been agreed upon by our small group, as we had no authority to do so. Thus, on July 30, 1989, all Mashov members were invited to a gathering at the ILP headquarters in Tel Aviv. The meeting room was so full that people stood outside to hear what Husseini had to say. He opened with these words: "Under occupation there are no leaders, only fighters." Furthermore, he explained, both sides had to "give up our dreams, and get rid of our nightmares." The Palestinians had to give up on their dream of a Palestinian state from the

Mediterranean Sea to the Jordan, and Israel would have to give up on its dream of "Greater Israel."[52]

I had agreed before the meeting that we would ask Husseini three questions and that his answers would make it possible to define the proposed formula as how to start negotiations. Our first question was, "What would enable the Palestinians to start negotiations with Israel?" Husseini's response was, "Israel to sit opposite a Palestinian delegation, representing all parts of the Palestinian people." We followed this with, "What does this mean in practice?" His answer was, "A delegation comprising of eight members from the West Bank, East Jerusalem, and the Gaza Strip, as well as two representatives from the 'outside.'" Our final question was, "Is it possible that the two other representatives of the delegation will be former inhabitants from the West Bank or Gaza who have been expelled by Israel, permitting us to view the entire delegation as a delegation from 'inside'?" His answer was a simple "Yes."[53]

Ultimately, our track-two efforts resulted in a formula that still had to be fine-tuned by official government negotiators. Nevertheless, the proposed formula made it clear that (referring to the picture drawn by James Baker) the rabbit had been located in the forest but the hunting grounds had not yet been narrowed down. In other words, the task ahead was to translate track-two understandings into an official agreement that would be accepted by all the concerned parties. In order to do so, we needed to help create a supportive diplomatic structure that would permit the Israeli government under Prime Minister Shamir and the PLO under Chairman Arafat to go along with the agreement. Further deliberations of the exact formula would be still necessary.

Support from Israel, Egypt, and the United States

On August 8, 1989, several days after our meeting with Husseini, the ILP's Central Committee welcomed and supported an ongoing dialogue with the internal Palestinian leadership. The party developed and accepted a twelve-point program that provided for negotiations with a Palestinian delegation on how to arrange elections, to be followed by negotiations on an Interim Agreement and then a Permanent Status Agreement on the basis of UN Security Council Resolution 242 and the principle of territory for peace. It was agreed that during the interim period, the Palestinians should obtain political rights, particularly the right to free elections and the establishment of a representative body. This recognition of Palestinian political rights negated the Palestinian demand for Israel to recognize Palestinian self-determination during the interim period, but it did not negate the possibility of such a demand in final status negotiations. The ILP also committed to refrain from new settlements until an interim Palestinian self-government had been established, when the settlement issue would then be negotiated between Israel and the self-governing Palestinian Authority.[54]

On the very same day, at its Fifth General Congress, Fatah adopted a very radical political program "to continue, intensify and escalate armed action and all forms of struggle to eliminate the Zionist Israeli occupation of our occupied Palestinian soil" and rejected Prime Minister Shamir's proposed elections in the West Bank and Gaza.[55] In light of Fatah's response, Husseini and Ashrawi informed us that for Arafat to overcome opposition from within, he needed further concessions from Israel. They also informed us that the US-PLO talks had created a deadlock, and we were being asked to find a way out by going a second time to the Netherlands. Our Palestinian interlocutors said that during the discussions in Tunis, the Americans had adopted a policy line identical to the Shamir position, and explicitly negated the possibility of establishing a Palestinian state. That made it impossible to achieve any progress.[56] However, the US Embassy in Tel Aviv gave us a different account of the US-PLO dialogue. The United States had not categorically opposed discussing the issue of self-determination with the PLO, but insisted that it was necessary to agree on a common understanding of "all the components of the concept" of self-determination as well as its limitations. The PLO also rejected speaking of elections in the West Bank and Gaza, which the Americans wanted to discuss.[57]

While the US-PLO dialogue was under way, US secretary of state James Baker was pursuing an intense US-Israeli dialogue, with particular attention to the various components of the emerging peace proposal that went beyond the idea of elections. Prime Minister Shamir had repeatedly expressed to the Americans his determination to move ahead with the peace process, and he successfully convinced both President George H. W. Bush and Baker of the sincerity of his intentions.[58] In mid-August, Baker wrote a note to his Egyptian counterpart, Ahmed Asmat Abdel-Meguid, stressing three specific points:[59]

1. That it was too early for the United States to intervene, as the concerned parties had not made a sufficient effort to bridge the remaining gaps;
2. That Egypt had an important competitive advantage, as it possessed close relations with both sides and was committed to promoting peace

in the Middle East. Therefore, Egypt should take action to encourage the parties involved to move one step closer to an agreement; and

3. That Egypt should convince the PLO to authorize a Palestinian delegation to negotiate with Israel regarding elections in the West Bank and Gaza.[60]

Kurtzer made it clear to us that the Americans viewed a second round of talks in The Hague as potentially damaging to both the ongoing US-Israeli and US-PLO dialogues. Such talks might give the PLO hope for what would likely be unrealistic demands that neither the United States nor Israel could satisfy, which would then allow them to adopt hard-line tactics and block, rather than enhance, the ongoing talks. Kurtzer suggested that a more feasible option would be to intensify the dialogue with Egypt, to enable Cairo to play a bridging role. It quickly turned out that Rabin was willing to promote the dialogue with Egypt in order to help to make this new strategy work.

At the very beginning of September, Faisal and Ashrawi appealed again to Beilin and me to go for a second round of talks in the Netherlands. Several days later, I discussed this request on the phone with van der Stoel.[61] Immediately after speaking with van der Stoel, Novik phoned and informed me that Mubarak and Arafat had reached an understanding in Belgrade, and Arafat would accept the Ten Points.

On the Israeli side, Rabin did not at first believe that the PLO would permit the diplomatic process to unfold. But once the PLO agreed with the concept, Rabin adopted a proactive and supportive position.[62] He wanted Jordan to take part in negotiations if possible, though Israel would not demand this. At the same time, he did not believe that Likud would make peace, but he was determined to see to it that the ILP "go all the way." In practice, this meant that Rabin supported the basic strategy of trying to convince Prime Minister Shamir to move toward negotiations. If this should fail, Rabin would support the fallback plan of trying to form an alternative government under the leadership of Peres. If that too should fail, then he would support the ILP's leaving the government altogether. In support of Rabin's initiative, Rabbi Arieh Der'i, a member of the Sephardic orthodox religious Shas party and minister of interior affairs, and Transportation Minister Moshe Katzav wanted to convince the Egyptians to invite Prime Minister Shamir to Cairo.[63] They argued that Shamir would accept both outside participation in the Palestinian delegation and the participation of delegates from East Jerusalem if President Mubarak would agree to receive him in Cairo.[64]

Attempting to Close the Gap

Getting Shamir on Board: Mubarak's Ten Points and Baker's Five-Point Proposal

Early in September 1989, Rabin visited the United States, where the Americans officially informed him of Mubarak's achievement in convincing Arafat to engage in dialogue. They asked for an official Israeli government response "before we start to chase the rabbit," though it was clear that the Americans intended to "chase the rabbit" regardless, because they arranged for Rabin to visit Cairo.[65]

In preparation for his visit to Cairo, Rabin asked Prime Minister Shamir for clear instructions. Despite three rounds of discussions, Shamir, Peres, and Rabin could not come to a full agreement. However, Shamir was willing to support three points: (1) Israel was prepared to engage in dialogue with the Palestinians on the components of the Israeli peace initiative, (2) this dialogue should take place in Cairo, and (3) Israel would be willing to accept Egypt's central role during this dialogue.[66] At the same time, Peres visited Washington. Before his departure (and before Rabin's visit to Cairo), Peres gave an interview to Menachem Shalev and Jeff Black of the *Jerusalem Post*, in which he said, "To my mind, the residents of the territories can seek and get advice from whomever they wish."[67] His statement clearly provided a behind-the-scenes role for the PLO in the forthcoming initiative.

Encouraged by Peres's statements and by discussions with Rabin, President Mubarak announced his Ten-Point Initiative on September 11:

1. An Israeli commitment to accept any and all results of the poll.
2. The placing of international observers for the elections.
3. The granting of total immunity to elected representatives.
4. A withdrawal of the Israeli Defense Forces from the balloting area.
5. An Israeli commitment to start talks on the final status on a "date certain" (a specific, predetermined date).
6. An end to all settlement activities.
7. Complete freedom of election propaganda.
8. A ban on the entry of all Israelis to the territories on election day.
9. The participation of East Jerusalem residents in the elections.
10. Israeli acceptance, in advance, of the four principles of US Middle East policy as stated in recent months by the State Department:
    a. A solution based on UN Security Council Resolution 242 and Resolution 338,

    b. The principle of peace for territories,
    c. Security for all states in the region, and
    d. Political rights for the Palestinians.[68]

In response to Mubarak's points, Arafat called for a meeting with the ambassadors of France, Greece, Italy, Spain, and the United Kingdom on September 21. He gave them a detailed report of the meeting between Mubarak and Rabin and said that the positions taken by Rabin were "nearly positive." He asked that the ambassadors encourage their governments to offer their full support for Mubarak's endeavor.[69] On the same day, immediately after his return from Cairo, Rabin addressed the ILP's Central Committee, demanding that the Israeli government pursue the evolving peace initiative. On that occasion, Rabin suggested that a trilateral meeting with the United States, Israel, and Egypt be held in New York to prepare for the Israeli-Palestinian meeting in Cairo and to keep the PLO behind the scenes.[70]

Within Likud, however, opposition to the emerging Mubarak initiative became stronger, and criticism was mainly directed at two points. First, Arafat should not be permitted to nominate and control the Palestinian delegation to the envisaged talks in Cairo. Second, the "land-for-peace" formula could not be accepted because negotiations should focus merely on the issue of elections in the West Bank and Gaza. Although Prime Minister Shamir had had no reason to prevent Rabin from going to Cairo, after the announcement of Mubarak's Ten Points and the growing internal opposition within Likud, Shamir needed to show that he was in control of events and could not be manipulated into action by the ILP's leadership. He threatened to break up the government by dismissing all ILP ministers if Rabin and Peres supported the Mubarak initiative.[71] While threatening to break up the coalition, Shamir and Moshe Arens (then minister of foreign affairs) simultaneously proposed continuing the effort to engage in dialogue with the Palestinians if the agenda for the meeting in Cairo could be limited. Ultimately, Shamir and Arens were trying to overcome Likud's internal opposition to starting negotiations.[72]

Early in October, the American, Egyptian, and Israeli foreign ministers (James Baker, Ahmed Asmet Abdel-Meguid, and Moshe Arens) met in Washington. According to American sources, Arens proposed a trilateral US-Egyptian-Israeli committee to define the composition of the Palestinian delegation. The Egyptians refused this idea, indicating that they could not speak for the Palestinians. Arens, on behalf of the Israeli government, suggested that the meeting with the Palestinians remain ceremonial and that negotiations on the conditions for elections in the West Bank and Gaza be held with Egypt, leaving negotiations with the elected Palestinian representatives on substantial issues to begin after the elections.[73]

To bridge the prevailing gaps while simultaneously summing up the positions made by Arens and Meguid, Secretary of State Baker announced his Five-Point Proposal in November 1989:

1. The United States understands that because Egypt and Israel have been working hard on the peace process, there is an agreement that an Israeli delegation will conduct a dialogue with a Palestinian delegation in Cairo.
2. The United States understands that Egypt cannot substitute itself for the Palestinians and that Egypt will consult with the Palestinians on all aspects of that dialogue. Egypt will also consult with Israel and the United States.
3. The United States understands that Israel will attend the dialogue only after a satisfactory list of Palestinians has been worked out. Israel will also consult with Egypt and the United States.
4. The United States understands that the Government of Israel will come to the dialogue on the basis of the Israeli government's May 14th initiative. Furthermore, the United States understands that the Palestinians will come to the dialogue prepared to discuss elections and negotiations in accordance with the Israeli initiative. The United States understands, therefore, that the Palestinians will be free to raise issues that related to their opinion on how to make elections and negotiations succeed.
5. In order to facilitate the process, the United States proposes that the foreign ministers of Israel, Egypt, and the United States meet in Washington within two weeks.[74]

Another Round of Multitrack Diplomacy Efforts

Both the Israeli government and the PLO agreed to James Baker's five points, but with reservations, necessitating another concerted multitrack diplomacy effort to close the remaining gaps:

- At the center would be the most senior track-one actors, such as US secretary of state Baker and his staff; Egyptian president Mubarak, with Egyptian foreign minister Meguid; and Israeli vice prime minister and finance minister Peres, with Israeli defense minister Rabin and their staffs. These groups would work together closely, maintaining an ongoing flow of information between one another to maintain the process of reaching a final agreement on the beginning of negotiations.

- On the flanks of this structure, and making substantial demands for change, would be Israeli prime minister Shamir and Israeli foreign minister Arens, both of whom wanted to move forward but were limited in their maneuvering capacity by opposition from Likud hard-liners (mainly Ariel Sharon, David Levy, and Yitzhak Moda'i),[75] and by the basic content of Likud's ideology of advocating a Greater Israel approach.[76] Chairman Arafat, who was strongly encouraged to move forward by the Egyptians and the inside PLO leadership, while simultaneously facing strong opposition from within the PLO, particularly from Faruq Kaddumi and Abu Iyad, would also be on the flanks.[77]
- In the background was the track-two effort led by Karni and me. Its task was no longer to develop a breakthrough formula, but rather to check with Palestinians such as Husseini and Ashrawi about possible flexibilities and to brief the track-one actors, who would then put the final touches on the formula for negotiations.

The main issues of contention and discussion between Prime Minister Shamir and Chairman Arafat were the following:

- Each side wanted to obtain guarantees that its concerns were fully taken care of by the Americans.
- The Israeli side wanted to be seen as having had a hand in determining the composition of the Palestinian delegation while opposing any visible role of the PLO. In direct contradiction, the PLO wanted to be seen as the "sole legitimate representative of the Palestinian people" and the only authority to announce the composition of the Palestinian delegation.
- Regarding the composition of the Palestinian delegation, the Israeli side was not willing to accept an unambiguous representative of Jerusalem nor of the outside.
- Regarding the agenda of the meeting, the Israeli side wanted the negotiations to start after the elections, whereas the Palestinians wanted to deal immediately with the substantive issues that had to be negotiated.

In track two, we discussed these issues again and again. We sensed that there was room for flexibility on the Palestinian side over the composition of its delegation. I argued with Husseini, Ashrawi, and Radwan Abu Ayyash that on the issue of Jerusalem, constructive ambiguity would be easy to achieve, given that most of the Palestinian candidates from Jerusalem who were to participate in the delegation had two places of residence. Husseini lived in Jerusalem, but his official place of residence was actually in Eyn Siniya in the West Bank. Ashrawi had a Jerusalem identity card and her family owned a small flat there, but in reality she lived with her family in Ramallah. Thus, Palestinian delegates who resided in both the West Bank and Jerusalem could be perceived by the Palestinians as Jerusalemites and by Israel as West Bank residents. Another matter we discussed in depth was the possibility of agreeing that the two members from the outside be permitted to return to the territories before negotiations, thus being seen by Israel as representing the inside rather than the outside.[78]

Although we had made some headway on the composition of the Palestinian delegation, we were unable to come to a conclusion on who would announce the delegation through a track-two dialogue. We suggested Husseini, but he flatly rejected the offer and proposed that the United Leadership of the Intifada make the announcement instead. This suggestion was unacceptable to both Likud and the ILP, because one of Israel's original demands was that the Palestinians announce the end of the intifada before coming to negotiations. Also, on the issue of the agenda, we argued that the meeting in Cairo would create a momentum of its own that could hardly be stopped. The track-one dialogue substantiated this line of thought and said that each side could present any subject it wanted, including a concept for a final agreement.[79]

Toward the end of February 1990, the United States brought about a final understanding on all outstanding issues, along the following lines:

- No further moves would be made on the issue of US guarantees.
- The Palestinian delegates from the outside would return to the territories before the beginning of the dialogue.
- The Palestinian delegation would include two members from the West Bank who had a second address in Jerusalem.
- Egypt would announce the Palestinian delegation.
- The relationship between the Palestinian delegation and the PLO would be in line with the Peres-Rabin suggestion that "the members of the Palestinian delegation may consult with whomever they want from the Arab world."

- Neither Egypt nor the PLO would insist on the participation of the five permanent members of the Security Council.
- Each side could present any subject for the agenda, including an envisioned concept of the final agreement.
- The opening speeches and the discussions would focus on the conditions for the elections and the interlock between the elections and the negotiating process.[80]

Both the Palestinian side and Prime Minister Shamir and Minister of Foreign Affairs Arens accepted the proposed concepts. However, at the session in which the proposal was submitted to Likud's Central Committee, Ariel Sharon pulled the microphone out of Shamir's hand, threatening to resign and arguing very loudly that Likud would never support terrorism.[81] David Levy and Yitzhak Moda'i, Sharon's backers, had had time to organize Likud's internal opposition since October 1989, and consequently Shamir and Arens lost the vote. They had to inform Baker that they would be rejecting the proposed terms for the negotiations, even though they had constructively participated in creating the compromises that the United States had submitted to all parties.[82]

The ILP Moves into Opposition

With Likud's decision to reject the proposed negotiations in Cairo, the ILP's initial plan had failed. Although the ILP had remained in the government after Shamir and Arens rejected the 1987 London Agreement that Peres and Rabin had negotiated with King Hussein of Jordan, this time would be different. In accordance with our fallback plan, the ILP left the government and Peres made an effort to form an alternative government with Shas, the Sephardic orthodox religious party. The Shas leader, Rabbi Arieh Der'i, who had taken a proactive position in support of the peace initiative, suggested to Peres and Rabin that they form an alternative government and replace Shamir as prime minister.

Within the ILP, however, Rabin was skeptical and Peres was hesitant, while Haim Ramon, who was one of the young party leaders, was advocating that they follow Der'i's suggestion.[83] It also seemed at the time that Ashkenazi rabbi Eliezer Menahem Schach and Sephardic rabbi Ovadia Yosef would support such a development, given that both had made supportive approaches on issues of peace.[84] However, at the decisive moment,

Schach accused the ILP of having "severed the past from the Jewish people" and of raising "rabbits and pigs" in the kibbutz, which made it impossible for Yossef (and Der'i, who was under his direction) to participate in the center-left coalition led by Peres.[85] Ultimately, the entire exercise to form an alternative government failed, placing the ILP in the opposition until the June 1992 elections.

Keeping Track-Two Relations Going during Tough Times

Although our track-two activities had been marginalized in the preceding months, they became the ILP's safety net under the new and increasingly difficult conditions. From February 1990 to February 1991, Beilin and I remained in close contact with Husseini and Ashrawi. To show that we intended to lead the way toward the eventual involvement of the PLO in peace negotiations, I attended a Conference on Palestinian Economic Affairs in Nijmegen, the Netherlands, in mid-April 1990. Israeli law permitted attendance at such academic meetings, and thus some of Israel's most outstanding economists (including Assaf Razin, Efraim Kleimann, and Michael Shalev) participated. The Palestinian participants, however, were all PLO officials: Nabil Shaath, Kamal Mansur, Afif Safiyeh, Hisham Mustafa, and Laila Shaheen.[86]

At Nijmegen, I was shocked by statements made by Mustafa, Abbas's chief of staff. He began with statements that at first sounded constructive. However, as he went on, the nature of his remarks became more threatening:

> I want to focus on the question, whether peace is obtained by choice, by interest, or by need. We need peace to develop our national personality and our people. . . . We will not present peace on a platter. . . . There is an interest in the region for peace. We must find a formula. . . . It is true the Iraqis became a power. Their missiles can arrive in Tel Aviv. I know that Israel could not sustain psychologically the effect of a missile attack on Israel with all its victims. I read the reactions of some Israeli generals. They say Saddam will not use the missiles. Chemical and biological weapons cannot be used, if human rights are to be honored. We do accept this, but you do not accept us. Historically, we are a part of an area that reaches from Iran to Morocco. We will not offer peace very cheaply.[87]

Several months later, on January 16, 1991, the first Gulf War broke out. Even though Israel was not involved in the war, throughout the following weeks Saddam Hussein launched thirty-eight missiles against Israel, while Chairman Arafat and the PLO ostentatiously supported the Iraqi dictator. Ever since, I have kept Mustafa's threat in mind and understood how volatile the Palestinian commitment to peace might be. Israel experienced the fast-moving pendulum of Palestinian politics in January and February 1991—as it later would in the autumn of 1996 and again in the autumn of 2000—from peace-seeking approaches toward aggression and then back again.[88]

In spite of our setbacks, Beilin, Novik, Karni, and I all kept in touch and maintained a dialogue with our inside Palestinian interlocutors. Ashrawi would later say that while other Israelis from the peace camp broke off relations with them during the 1991 Iraq crisis, the fact that we maintained contact and an ongoing dialogue strengthened their confidence in working with us. Our continuation of such dialogue was driven by an understanding of Israel's strategic needs, not by a desire to satisfy justifiable or unjustifiable Palestinian expectations.

Lessons Learned

In many ways, the 1989–91 experience can be seen as a model for multitrack diplomacy efforts. As seldom happens, we were lucky to have most of the components necessary for success intact, and were able to react accordingly to mitigate failures as much as possible.

Lesson One: Establish a Well-Defined Strategy Concept at the Beginning

At the very beginning of the effort, we were fully aware of an apparent contradiction: The Palestinian intifada of the years 1987–89 had made it evident to both sides that negotiations were the only way forward, but the gap between the basic positions of the main stakeholders—Likud's leadership and the PLO—was still tremendous. To bridge that gap, we had to develop a process wherein the basic demands of either side would neither be granted nor negated on the way to starting negotiations. Our strategy concept was based on a four-phase approach. First, we would engage in fact-finding to identify existing common ground. Then we would obtain authorization for the emerging ideas from the ILP's leadership. As a third step, we attempted to create the regional and international legitimacy necessary for the conditions to be met. And fourth, in the end, however, it would be the task of the official decisionmakers to conclude the deal.

Lesson Two: Understand the "Focal Points" of the Negotiations

Leigh Thompson defines the "focal points" of intended negotiations as the central issues that can either make or break the outcome.[89] In our situation, we identified the following focal points:

1. Our ability to convince the Palestinian inside and outside leadership under the control of the PLO to engage in dialogue;
2. The need to maneuver Prime Minister Shamir and his party into a funnel situation toward accepting a negotiating concept. Eventually, the Rabin Plan—which would become the Peace Plan of the Government of Israel—would be key in this approach;
3. The awareness that the American government, particularly the US peace team under Secretary of State James Baker's able leadership, would have a decisive impact in putting the various pieces of the puzzle together; and
4. The key role that Egypt could play in bridging gaps between the PLO and the Israeli government.

Lesson Three: Possess Full Access to Decisionmakers

Multitrack diplomacy depends substantially on full, free, and ongoing access among track-two actors, track-one officials, and final decisionmakers. Between 1989 and 1991, the ideal conditions for this level of access were almost completely available. Within the Israeli political system, we had full access to the ILP's leadership; to Beilin and Novik, who were acting out of government (track-one) positions; to Likud's leadership; and to other political stakeholders. Novik also had access to the Egyptian leadership via Ambassador Bassiouni. In the meantime, I had full access to the American diplomats who dealt with the peace process, while Beilin and Novik had access to the most senior American decisionmakers. Finally, our access to the Palestinian inside leadership was available at all times because we had already developed a relationship of mutual confidence.

Lesson Four: Maintain the Flow of Information

Free access to different stakeholders also provides the preconditions for ongoing flows of information in all directions. By definition, a multitrack diplomacy exercise must proceed simultaneously through several different channels. To pursue our strategy, we had to be aware of the emerging positions within the Israeli government and between the ILP and Likud leaderships; we also needed to understand developments in the Israeli-US and the Israeli-Egyptian dialogues, as well as in the PLO inside/outside dialogue and the developments of US-PLO and US-Egyptian dialogues.

We were fortunate to enjoy and be educated by an ongoing full flow of information. We were also able to evaluate and verify the information we received through one channel by comparing it with reports received through other channels. This is not possible in most multitrack diplomacy efforts, because the instinctive behavioral pattern of track-one actors, diplomats, senior officials, and decisionmakers is to control the flow of information in order to feel (and have others perceive) that they are maintaining full control of events and nobody else can interfere. Preventing the flow of information can be justified when track-two actors do not impose upon themselves the necessary discipline and believe that they can impose their opinion upon the legitimate decisionmakers, instead of adapting ideas and concepts to the needs of the track-one actors. In a track-two effort, one has to understand that any attempt to manipulate information, such as by leaking it to the press, will cut off the flows of information. As we were fully aware of the fears of the track-one actors, we were able to maintain optimal discipline in controlling the flow of information from us to the decisionmaking echelons, and thereby secured the continued flow of information from them to us.

Another difficulty faced by track-two actors is that they are often dependent on information from the one and only channel which with they deal. This not only raises the problem of potential misinformation but also results in the track-two actors being dependent on their interlocutors. We were fortunate enough to be able to check our various sources of information against each other, and thus we did not suffer from this particular concern.

Lesson Five: Understand the Complexity of a Multitrack Diplomacy Exercise

Any multitrack diplomacy effort is, by definition, a complicated undertaking that combines and requires interaction among different political and diplomatic structures and levels. In our case, we had to manage, oversee, and passively observe a variety of different channels: the dialogue with the inside Palestinian leadership; the dialogue with the Dutch (and, through them, with the PLO); the US-PLO dialogue; the ongoing US-Egyptian dialogue; and, most important, the internal Israeli dialogues (within the ILP between Peres and Rabin, and between the ILP and Likud leaderships). We had to keep the following rules in mind:

- *Keep the general effort in mind, not merely your "own" channel:* The most common fallacy in managing multiple dialogue channels is to defend your own channel at all costs, even if it impedes parallel channels. According to Karni's and my vantage point, the dialogue channel with Husseini, Ashrawi, and other inside Palestinian leaders was our domain. In engaging in proximity talks in the Netherlands with the outside PLO leadership, we understood that dialogue with the outside, pursued with the assistance of our Dutch interlocutors, upgraded and strengthened our efforts. However, even though developments along the Israeli-Egyptian, Egyptian-PLO, and US-PLO channels might easily impede our channel and even render it obsolete, we understood the complexity of the general effort and the necessity of downgrading our effort when track-one activities on the Israeli, Egyptian, and US sides were taking the lead. This assertion of discipline and understanding was vital.

- *Create a well-sequenced "butterfly effect" among the different channels:* In our case, the epicenter of our activity was the small group led by Beilin, Novik, Avrum Burg, Karni, and me, which was supported by Yossi's political allies within the ILP, particularly Haim Ramon and Uzi Baram. From within that epicenter, we had to create an impact on what might be called the inner Labor circle. Being fully aware of the personal rivalry between Peres and Rabin, we understood the essential importance of coordinated action between those two leaders. When, at the end of 1988, Rabin prepared his plan, Beilin and Novik convinced Peres to offer his full support, which made it easier to obtain the undivided support of the party. From here, the butterfly effect had to make waves among the Palestinians, our European interlocutors, the Egyptians, and the Americans most of all. The logic and sequence of the effect were clear: We gained the trust, support, and motivation of the internal Palestinian leadership by maintaining ongoing contact with them and agreeing, with Dutch support, to engage in proximity talks with the outside PLO. The goodwill created in Tunis offered the Egyptians the sense that if President Mubarak decided to "chase the rabbit," his chances of success would be relatively high. With the Egyptians fully on board, the entire supportive structure would make it worthwhile for the Americans to "chase the rabbit" as well.

- *Maintain a sense of humility:* In Israel, as in any democratic system, the legitimacy of decisionmaking is given to the duly elected leadership, and thus not to track-two actors. This has several practical ramifications. First, it creates the need to adapt to policy decisions that are outside one's control. Second, it makes the low-key standing of the track-two effort essential. Third, it ensures that track-two actors can function effectively only if the duly elected decisionmakers—Peres and Rabin, in our case—understand that the track-two and other multitrack efforts provide them with an important policy tool but do not challenge, diminish, or manipulate their decisionmaking power. Finally, it is essential that one enable the leadership to take credit instead of claiming it for oneself.

Lesson Six: Identify the Zone of Possible Agreement and a Plan to Get There

To be able to identify a potential zone of possible agreement, it was necessary to have a solid understanding of the negotiation and ideological positions of each of the adversaries. This was the purpose for arranging meetings between Likud insider Immanuel Halperin and various Palestinian interlocutors. These meetings made it clear that the feasible path at the time was to seek agreement on the terms necessary to start negotiations.

Our second challenge was to devise a methodology on how to move from nonagreement to the envisaged zone of possible agreement. We understood that both the US-PLO dialogue that had begun in December 1988 and the Israeli Peace Plan of May 1989 had maneuvered both Prime Minister Shamir and Chairman Arafat toward a "funnel situation" in which it would be difficult, though not impossible, for them to turn back. Arafat had to deal with pressure from the inside leadership, supported by PLO activists in Tunis, which was determined to move toward negotiations with Israel. Abu Sharif's article in June 1988 did not oblige Arafat to support the idea of elections in the West Bank and Gaza, but it made it difficult for him to oppose the idea outright. Likewise, Shamir had to deal with Rabin's and Peres's activist political approach to achieve a nonmilitary solution to the intifada. As Israeli army circles had understood in 1988 that there was no military solution to the intifada and that Rabin and Peres had developed a policy plan out of the quagmire, Shamir had to respond to the challenge—which he did in May 1989 by committing himself and his government to the Israeli Peace Plan for Palestinian elections in the West Bank and Gaza, as proposed by Rabin.

From our point of view, this put both Shamir and Arafat close to the opening of the funnel. The difficulty was how to get both of them to the point where negotiations could start. Mubarak's Ten Points were important, as they kept Arafat in support of the unfolding approach; Baker's Five Points aimed at doing the same thing with Shamir while simultaneously taking care of Egyptian needs. Thus, Egyptian and US bridging concepts asserted effective political and diplomatic pressure from Washington onto Jerusalem and from Cairo onto Tunis. Our task was to devise a policy with which both Shamir and Arafat could go along in order to move them through the funnel until we could begin the negotiations.

Lesson Seven: Deal with Dilemmas

There were two methods of overcoming the prevailing gap between the two adversary positions. The first was constructive ambiguity, or the fact that the formulas we suggested could be interpreted by each side differently. The second was the necessity of permitting the policy demands to be postponed to a later date, as long as they were not negated in the beginning. However, as a result of these methods we had to deal with three major dilemmas: (1) the problematic effect of constructive ambiguity and the postponement of policy demands to a later point in time, (2) the question of how to deal with blockages introduced by either side in the unfolding negotiations, and (3) the question of when to move from our primary plan to our fallback plans.

CONSTRUCTIVE AMBIGUITY AND POSTPONING POLICY DEMANDS: HANDLING A TWO-EDGED SWORD

The advantages gained from constructive ambiguity and postponing policy demands were self-evident. However, constructive ambiguity can all too easily lead to misunderstandings—or worse, to intended manipulations of one side by the other. We therefore made a major effort to minimize the possible dangers involved in this approach. We made sure that the practical implications of the constructively ambiguous negotiating formulas were clearly defined and understood by all parties. Similarly, we established a clear public interpretation to ensure that what was agreed upon was in no way damaging to the other side.

It was more difficult to deal with the negative effects of postponing policy demands. In any negotiating process, it is essential that one define the red lines of one's own position at a very early stage and never move them. To reach an agreement on starting to negotiate, we gave up on drawing any red lines and actually suggested the opposite: legitimizing the postponement of further demands to a later phase of the negotiations.

BLOCKAGES OR DECIDING TO CREATE A CRISIS: AVOIDING THE "DEAD CAT ON THE DOORSTEP"

Both the Israeli and the Palestinian negotiating tactics included the creation or threat of crises or blockages along the way. Shamir did this intentionally at the end of September 1988, when he threatened to dismiss the ILP ministers from his government and to dissolve the coalition. Arafat likewise created blockages in August 1989 at the Fifth General Congress of Fatah, and later on in November, when the PLO Council met in Baghdad and Palestinian demands hardened. The dilemma of a multitrack diplomacy effort is whether to go along with the demands and try to satisfy them, thus potentially encouraging further blockages down the road, or to go for a confrontation instead and put what US secretary of state James Baker called the "dead cat on the doorstep"—the blame for the deadlock—in front of the side creating the crisis.[90]

Our tendency was to deal with the policy demands that had caused the blockages and to try to find solutions. Baker and Mubarak would permit some space to adapt the proposed working concept to the political needs of both sides; but at a certain point, in February 1990, they simply submitted the final proposal on a take-it-or-leave-it basis. Although track-two actors may be able to test possibilities for widening common ground, the track-one actors clearly have to draw a line and put an end to the otherwise unending demands of each side.

INITIAL PLANS AND FALLBACK PLANS: FINDING THE RESERVATION POINT

Negotiation theory is very clear about when one moves from an initial plan to a secondary or fallback plan. At the beginning of negotiations, one must identify the "reservation point"—the point in negotiations at which one moves from the initial plan to the fallback plan—for oneself.[91]

Theoretically, the answer to this question was to go all the way with Prime Minister Shamir until he, or Likud, turned down the suggested agreement. Then we would go for our fallback plan. In practice, however, our response was more complicated. An interesting difference of opinion emerged between us and our Palestinian interlocutors. Husseini, Ashrawi, and others repeatedly expressed to us—and particularly to Beilin and Novik—that they were afraid that the ILP would not be able to deliver on the negotiation proposals without Likud's support.[92] The difference of opinion lay not only in our different evaluations of the political situation in Israel but also in our different cultures; we dealt with reality differently and related to different psychologies of negotiation. Our group, led by Beilin, was immersed in the internal Israeli political power struggle and the ideological conflict between the peace camp's goal of a two-state solution in order to strengthen Israel's identity as a Jewish and democratic state, and the desire of Israel's right wing to maintain a strong presence in "Judea and Samaria"—that is, the West Bank. We were impatient by nature, and we perceived that time was working against Israel's interests. Our Palestinian interlocutors, conversely, were more patient and were uninvolved in the internal Israeli power game.

In hindsight, I would argue that we failed to play one important card of which we had been aware before moving from our initial plan to our fallback plans. In coordination with our Palestinian interlocutors, we should have launched an effective public campaign directed at Israeli political stakeholders, the moderate wing of Likud, the orthodox religious parties, and the public.[93] Planning for and implementing such a public relations effort would have served two parallel aims: It would have created, among the public, an atmosphere in which Likud could have supported the unfolding initiative to start Israeli-Palestinian negotiations (as was the case before Menachem Begin went to Camp David in September 1978 when public pressure created an important incentive to conclude an agreement), and/or it could have prepared the ground for the public support necessary to implement our ILP fallback plans to attempt to form a new coalition or finally leave the government.

Lesson Eight: Be Able to Sustain Failures

Likud's rejection of the Five Baker Points and their amendments was undoubtedly a failure. Although the writing had been on the wall from the beginning of October 1989, we had underestimated Likud's internal opposition. We had also overestimated the willingness and determination of Rabbi Ovadia Yosef and Rabbi Arieh Der'i to support our fallback plan of a center-left government under the leadership of Peres. However, despite our failures, we maintained our close relationships with our Palestinian, Egyptian, American, and European interlocutors. This network of relations later made it possible for us to assist our Palestinian interlocutors Husseini and Ashrawi to get in touch with the Americans, which eventually led, at the end of October 1991, to the Madrid Conference (which is discussed in chapter 4).

On the Palestinian side, and in full accordance with Chairman Arafat, Husseini and Ashrawi played the leading role in negotiating the conditions for getting to the Madrid conference and starting negotiations. On the American side, Molly Williamson—to whom I had introduced Ashrawi in the autumn of 1989—had become the US consul-general in Jerusalem.[94] It was her task, on behalf of Secretary of State Baker, to negotiate the conditions for Palestinian participation.

Our small group—Beilin, Novik, Karni, and I—knew what was necessary from the Israeli point of view to get to the negotiating table, and they provided encouragement and advice. We suggested to our American interlocutors that they incorporate into the Madrid approach the various components for negotiations agreed upon in the April 1988 London Agreement with King Hussein and those developed during the 1989–90 effort, such as those limiting the negotiations to the immediately concerned parties and preventing outside interference. In addition, Prime Minister Shamir insisted that the Palestinian delegation be joined by the Jordanian delegation, while the key formula permitting the Palestinian delegation "to consult with whomever they want to in the Arab world" was maintained, thereby opening a door for the PLO to dominate the negotiating process.

The political strategy that we had developed in January and February 1989, seeking the beginning of Israeli-Palestinian negotiations supported by the PLO, was becoming a reality. Our track-two efforts had laid the ground for a political dialogue with the Palestinian leadership that over the next two years would lead the way to the 1993 Oslo negotiations.

Chapter 4

Back-Channel Negotiations in Norway: The Challenges, the Planning, and the Track-Two Efforts of the Oslo Accords, 1991–93

This chapter describes the conceptual preparations for the 1993 Oslo negotiations, the various policy and negotiating options tested during this period, and the conclusions drawn from this exercise. This is followed by the story of the Oslo negotiations, with special emphasis on the back-channel negotiating efforts that began in London in December 1992 and ended in the successful transition toward secret official negotiations on May 20, 1993. It analyzes the original strategic concept that was pursued in the context of back-channel negotiations, the successes and shortcomings of the back-channel effort, and the subsequent failure of this concept and its replacement by a more conservative approach.

Historical Background: The 1991 Gulf War and the Madrid Conference

Several historical processes culminated in 1991: the demise of the Soviet Union (following the fall of the Berlin Wall two years earlier); the defeat of Saddam Hussein's army and the restoration of Kuwait as an independent state, thereby eliminating the threat of an Iraqi attack against Saudi Arabia; and a growing Israeli and Palestinian interest in ending the intifada by reaching a political understanding along the guidelines laid out in the Camp David Accords.

The aftermath of the 1991 Gulf War strengthened the United States' influence in the Middle East and affected the positions of many other regional players. Successful US military intervention had restored Kuwait's independence and territorial integrity, and reestablished the security of Saudi Arabia and the other Arab Gulf states. Syria was opening up to American diplomacy because the Soviet Union under Mikhail Gorbachev refused to back President Hafez el-Assad's ambition of reaching strategic (military) parity with Israel. Jordan, which had been seen to support Saddam Hussein, had emerged from the war internally united but politically isolated and economically devastated. Under these conditions, King Hussein's first order of business was to overcome the crisis in US-Jordanian relations resulting from Jordan's support for Iraq, which would involve an effort to assist Washington in pursuing a peace policy.[1] Palestine Liberation Organization (PLO) chairman Yasser Arafat's decision to also side with Saddam Hussein against the United States–led coalition markedly weakened the PLO, and provided important diplomatic maneuvering space to the Palestinian inside leadership headed by Faisal Husseini and Hanan Ashrawi, who were determined to get negotiations with Israel under way. Arafat understood that in order to reestablish his own legitimacy, he had to permit the Palestinian inside leadership to move forward with negotiations. Finally, Israeli prime minister Yitzhak Shamir understood that it would be wise for Israel to go along with an American diplomatic initiative rather than oppose it. He needed US support to help Israel absorb the flow of Jewish immigrants from the former Soviet Union. Shamir understood that Israel could obtain an important upgrade in US-Israeli security relationships and was determined to convince Washington to rebuild a strong alliance relationship with Amman.[2]

The American leadership understood these regional concerns very well. At the end of the Gulf War, US president George H. W. Bush, in his address to the nation, said, "We must now begin to look beyond victory and war. We must meet the challenge of security and peace."[3] What followed was a US diplomatic offensive by Secretary of State James Baker between March and October 1991, leading the way to the Madrid Conference.[4]

The concept behind the Madrid Conference was to negotiate issues of past Israeli-Arab conflicts and to try to solve them bilaterally between Israel and a Jordanian-Palestinian delegation, between Israel and a Syrian delegation, and between Israel and a Lebanese delegation. Negotiations in a multilateral structure were intended to address various current and potential problems: arms control and regional security, economic development, water rights and usage, the environment, and refugees. The success of the conference would depend on the ability of the participating delegations to move from the opening ceremony and speeches to the bilateral negotiations, which were scheduled to start on November 3, 1991, and were to be followed by the beginning of multilateral negotiations.[5]

The Madrid Conference began on October 31. In many ways, it was a triumph of American diplomacy and determination. Only eighteen days prior to the opening of the conference, Daniel Kurtzer, who at the time was deputy assistant secretary of state for Near Eastern affairs, and in this position was a member of Secretary of State Baker's policy planning staff, had been ordered to work with the Spanish government to prepare the meeting facilities. The room where the official negotiations were to take place was decorated with a tapestry illustrating the violent expulsion of the Muslims from Spain in the seventeenth century. Kurtzer insisted that the tapestry be taken down and that a friendlier welcome be provided, going so far as to threaten the Spanish government that the Americans would cancel the event otherwise.[6] In spite of that difficult start, on the first day of the conference the opening speeches made by the Americans and the Soviets created a sense of hope by committing to work together for peace.[7] However, on the second day the Syrian delegation attacked Israeli prime minister Shamir, resulting in a rather hostile Israeli response. By the end of that day, it seemed as if the conference would end in failure. The Syrian team threatened to go home, and it was unclear whether the Jordanian-Palestinian team would dare come to the planned negotiations without them.

At the behest of Israeli Labor Party (ILP) leader Shimon Peres, I had traveled to Madrid to observe the Palestinian and the American negotiating teams and to maintain contact with the European observers. Although I was watching events from the sidelines, I had several meetings with Daniel Kurtzer and with Palestinian leader Faisal Husseini, and I watched the way the Palestinian delegation at the conference was directed by the PLO. I met the American peace team on November 2 and learned that, with the help of Saudi Arabia, the Jordanian-Palestinian team would turn up for negotiations the following morning as planned. That same evening, in a meeting with Husseini, I was assured before others that the members of the Palestinian delegation and their Jordanian colleagues would indeed start the bilateral negotiation effort with Israel on the following day. I also knew that they would attend independently, whether or not the Syrian delegation would attend parallel bilateral negotiations. Finally, on November 3, 1991, the Israeli-Palestinian peace negotiations were able to begin.

The clear aim ahead was to seek ways and means to bring about the success of the unfolding Israeli-Palestinian negotiations. We had some time for planning, as not much would happen before the Knesset elections scheduled for June 1992. We had to understand the difficulties that needed to be overcome, plan for an optimal negotiating strategy and test possible options, and find a way to best feed our thinking and action into the official track, hopefully under a government that would be led by the ILP.

The First Challenge: Understanding the Difficulties

The Composition of the Palestinian Delegation

When Husseini met the US delegation for the first time in Madrid, he seemed to walk hunched over and appeared almost as if he had two broken arms and a shoulder torn out. Out of concern for his health, US ambassador Edward Djerejian, who had become assistant secretary of state for Near Eastern affairs, asked him what had happened. Husseini answered that the "suit that the American peace team tailored for the negotiations does not fit my body."[8] He was referring to the facts that the Palestinian delegation had no standing of its own but was only a part of the larger Jordanian-Palestinian delegation; that the outside leadership (i.e., the PLO) was not permitted to participate in the negotiations; and that, officially, Palestinian residents of Jerusalem were not to be part of the delegation.

In Madrid, from the outset both the Palestinians and the Jordanians insisted on negotiating separately with Israel. After the first meeting between the Israelis and the united Jordanian-Palestinian negotiating team, I received the handwritten protocol of the meeting with its corrections from the Palestinian side. The Jordanian-Palestinian team insisted on referring to separate Israeli-Palestinian and Israeli-Jordanian negotiating tracks. When the negotiating teams moved to Washington shortly after the Madrid Conference, this became a major issue. Both the Jordanian and the Palestinian team members refused to enter the negotiating room together, and instead remained outside in the corridor until the Israelis, still under Prime Minister Yitzhak Shamir, gave in and agreed to negotiate separately with the Palestinians and the Jordanians.[9] Israel's entire prenegotiation effort, during which it had insisted on meeting a joint Jordanian-Palestinian team, turned out to have been nothing but a nuisance. However, one of the most difficult problems to solve was the fact that the PLO leadership from Tunis was officially excluded from the negotiating effort.

The Mistrust and Tension between Arafat and the Palestinian Negotiators

In Madrid, I witnessed the detrimental impact of Arafat's mistrust of his own negotiators. On November 3, shortly after midnight in the early hours of the morning, I met Husseini at the Hotel Victoria, where the Palestinian delegation was staying. Never before had I seen Husseini under such stress. To make it clear to everyone that orders for the Palestinian negotiating team were being given by Chairman Arafat, the entire delegation had been flown to Tunis, where, undoubtedly as the result of advance planning, a member of the Palestinian delegation accused Husseini of being a traitor and of working with the Israelis and the Americans behind Arafat's back. I knew that this was nonsense and that in fact the opposite was true. After the Gulf War, the Saudis, resentful of Arafat's support for Saddam Hussein, had offered Husseini an open check, suggesting that he fill it in with any sum of billions of dollars to finance a Palestinian national movement to replace the PLO. But Husseini refused, explaining to me that he did not want to repeat the tragedy of the period 1936–39, when the Palestinian national movement split into different groups that then fought one another.[10]

Arafat probably knew that Husseini was exceedingly loyal to him; nevertheless, he remained suspicious and did almost everything he could to undermine Husseini's authority. And the related yet bigger problem was that Arafat mistrusted the entire Palestinian delegation, which he viewed as a competitor that derogated his authority. His demand for self-legitimization took precedence over the need to formulate the official Palestinian position for the talks in Washington. As Daniel Kurtzer and his colleagues would later state, "Arafat wanted to demonstrate to both the United States and Israel that no agreement could be reached unless it were to be negotiated directly with him.[11]

The Gap in the Negotiating Positions

As the bilateral negotiations got under way in Washington, the gap between the Israeli and Palestinian positions on substance became more and more evident. In May 1992, Hana Siniora handed me a table detailing the gap between the Israeli-Palestinian negotiating positions, which is reproduced here as table 4.1. With all these differences laid out, it would be no small challenge to bridge the gap.

The Second Challenge: Planning for Negotiations

The Economic Cooperation Foundation's Study on the Israeli-Palestinian Peace Process

Late in December 1990, Yossi Beilin, Boaz Karni, and I founded the Economic Cooperation Foundation (ECF). We arranged for a bipartisan board of directors, which included two Likud members (Tel Aviv mayor Shlomo Lahat and Herzliya mayor Eli Landau); Labor politician Ya'akov Zur, a former minister for agriculture who was identified with the Rabin camp; Knesset members Avrum Burg and Yossi Beilin; and three members of the Mashov group, Ehud Kaufman, Boaz Karni, and me. At first, the ECF had no money, and my home address was given as its office address. By the summer of 1991, however, we had received our first EU grant to prepare a study on "Israel, the Palestinians, and the Middle East: From Dependency to Interdependence." I completed this study in September 1992, just in time for it to be used as the first strategic blueprint for what later became the Oslo negotiations.

The aim of the ECF study was to prepare a strategy with three very ambitious aims: reach progress in negotiations for the establishment of a Palestinian self-government, change the reality on the ground by moving toward a two-state solution, and seek a way to move from there toward comprehensive peace agreements in line with the provisions of the 1978 Camp David Accords. The study's opening assumption stated:

> The inherent causes of instability in the Middle East are too strong, as to enable a sudden and complete change from the old political order to a new one. Rather, a long and protracted struggle for a new and more stable order may be anticipated. As banal as it may sound, the success of the forces of pragmatism will depend on finding and implementing pragmatic solutions to existing conflicts, as well as assuring failure of political, terrorist or military tactics of the radical camp.[12]

Testing Three Different Models for Negotiations

To prepare for the Israeli-Palestinian negotiations, I interviewed more than thirty Palestinians as well as experts from the ILP and officials in the prime minister's office. I tested three different strategic approaches to a possible agreement: a minimalist one, a maximalist one, and a compromise. All three negotiating options had two issues in common: first, the goal of pursuing an Israeli-Palestinian Declaration of Principles, which would define the issues on which both sides agreed while avoiding the main points of contention; and second, the question of how to define a strategy that would change realities on the ground in order to make a two-state solution possible:

- *The minimalist approach*, which was largely in line with the Shamir Peace Plan of May 1989, suggested detailed arrangements for elections and agreed-on action in support of economic development in the territories before negotiating the final powers of the self-government agreement. Through the elections, this approach would provide the internal Palestinian leadership in the West Bank and Gaza with popular and constitutional legitimacy independent of the PLO. The support for economic development was intended to create an economic power base for the elected leaders that would enable them to negotiate the proposed self-government agreement without outside interference.
- *The maximalist approach* tackled the main issues of contention head on by first negotiating a settlement-freeze agreement and then establishing three working committees: one on economic development to negotiate an envisaged Palestinian Development Program, one on security affairs to negotiate the conditions for establishing a Palestinian police force and for improving Israeli-Palestinian anti-terrorism cooperation, and one on the conditions for electing the Palestinian self-government body. The strategic concept behind this approach was simple: An agreed-on settlement freeze would prepare the ground for negotiating recognized and secure boundaries, economic development and security for both sides would create the necessary supportive environment for negotiating Permanent Status, and Palestinian elections would provide for a legitimate Palestinian negotiating partner for Permanent Status.
- *The compromise approach* proposed the establishment of a Palestinian Preparatory Authority and the institutional framework for

Table 4.1. The Gap between the Israeli and Palestinian Negotiating Positions, May 1992

Issue	Palestinian Position
The substance of the agreement	Recognize right to self-determination
Connection between Interim Agreement and Permanent Agreement	Interim Agreement to be linked to Permanent Agreement
Terms of reference	UN Security Council Resolution 242 and Resolution 338 to apply to all territories
Source of authority	Palestinian self-government
Powers of self-government	Unlimited, with any exceptions to its powers qualified and agreed upon
Territorial extension	Jurisdiction over all territories of the West Bank, East Jerusalem, and the Gaza Strip
Legislative powers	Complete legislative and judicial powers
Jurisdiction	Full jurisdiction over land, natural resources and water, subsoil, territorial sea and air space, and jurisdiction over all Palestinian inhabitants
Executive power	Full executive power without foreign intervention
Foreign policy	Foreign policy powers demanded for the self-government regime
Judiciary	Fully independent Palestinian judiciary
Police force and security	Strong Palestinian police force responsible for public order and security
Peacekeeping forces	UN peacekeeping
Standing committee	A five-member standing committee demanded
Date of elections	An election date must be set
Purpose of elections	To establish a 180-member legislative assembly
Functions of elected body	Exercise the full national and political rights of the Palestinians
Laws defining campaigning for elections	Demand to rescind all existing orders, regulations which prohibit assembly, movement, participation and campaigning
Administrative detention and return of deportees	Demand an end to administrative detention and the return of deportees
Participation of Palestinian inhabitants of Jerusalem in elections	Palestinian inhabitants of Jerusalem can vote and be nominated as candidates

Israeli Position
Agree on autonomy arrangements
Interim stage to be open-ended
No reference to the Security Council resolutions or to the Camp David Accords
Will be military government; Israel will transfer some authority
Powers of self-government to be based on full coordination with Israeli and Jordanian governments; residual powers stay with Israel
No territorial dimension
Functional administrative arrangements
Jurisdiction limited to people, not to land and not to natural resources
Limited executive powers only as stated in agreement; Israel maintains residual powers with military government
Foreign policy powers opposed for the self-government regime
Palestinians will have the right to participate in the administration of justice
Responsibility for security stays with Israel, with Palestinians to cooperate on granting public order
No room for the UN
Rejection of the standing committee
Israel will not set a date
To establish a twelve-person administrative council
Exercise limited administrative functions
Prepared to negotiate these issues
Israel does not relate to this point (under the prime minister, this issue will be negotiated in a different channel)
Palestinian inhabitants of Jerusalem should not participate; later might vote by proxy

a Palestinian self-government authority that would nominate working groups to form joint Israeli-Palestinian committees, enabling a gradual and orderly transfer of authority. The joint committees would discuss security issues, the concepts and structure of elections, and the mechanisms for transferring authority. This last committee would also create subcommittees on more specific topics such as finance and investment, regional planning and zoning issues,[13] water and agricultural management, transportation, and communication.

The Palestinian side unanimously rejected the minimalist approach, while the maximalist approach faced strong opposition from Israel's right-wing parties. Israel's center and left-wing parties did not have the ability to obtain the necessary majority to ensure the success of the maximalist approach without the support of the right. The compromise strategy, which offered many advantages, was supported by both sides. The concept of gradualism allowed Prime Minister Rabin to maintain the military government and the Civil Administration and to postpone all military withdrawals that had been provided for in the 1978 Camp David Accords. It also made it possible to achieve progress in one joint committee while moving at a slower pace in another, which made it unnecessary to reach a comprehensive agreement on Palestinian self-government all at once. Finally, it provided a mechanism to allow delays in dealing with the difficult issues that would arise in negotiating Palestinian self-government, such as the source of authority and the control of the residual authorities.

The proposed compromise approach gave us a clear path toward Permanent Status negotiations. In this context, my thinking was influenced by the March 4, 1988, Shultz Initiative, in which then–US secretary of state George Shultz suggested that final status negotiations should start even before negotiations over the transitional period were completed.[14] The gradual and ongoing transfer of authorities would create a Palestinian interest in stability and could serve as an important safety net in case Permanent Status negotiations failed. Nonetheless, it seemed dangerous to leave the core issues of conflict unsolved, because struggles over Jerusalem, refugees, territories, settlements, and security could all too easily jeopardize any future understanding. For Yossi Beilin and me, the most important strategic issue on which to agree was the border, but we were convinced that on all outstanding core issues of conflict, a policy of diminishing existing frictions could be developed and implemented.

Moving Toward a Comprehensive Israeli-Arab Peace Settlement

I carried out the EU-funded study for the ECF between June 1991 and June 1992. This was a time of optimism, when bilateral and multilateral negotiations were under way and Israeli and Arab delegations from thirteen Arab states were meeting each other for the first time to discuss the future as well as the past. Opposing these developments were the Islamic fundamentalist State of Iran and Saddam Hussein's radical militant leadership in Iraq, both of which threatened to build a strong coalition of forces in the Middle East that would be against the peace process. Under these circumstances, I argued that the "present regional diplomatic constellation provides a key position to three forces: Syria, the PLO, and Saudi Arabia":

> Islamic militant forces derived their strength from four basic complementary functions: the defense of traditional Islamic society, providing social functions of welfare, an alternative political leadership, and a messianic Islamic message to society. These four factors made it possible for them to build powerful bases in most Middle Eastern countries, often in opposition to the ruling elites. In addition to the political power and influence acquired, Iran and her non-state proxies such as Hezbollah and various jihadist movements sustained their power with military means, which included the development of terror capacities as well as the acquisition of non-conventional weapons, including the effort to develop military nuclear power.[15]

Saudi Arabia, Syria, and the PLO had the power to join either the radical or the peacemaking coalitions. The decisive strategic task of the Madrid process was to draw these three actors away from the radical coalition and into the pragmatic, pro-Western, and pro-peace camp.[16] The way to do this was to pursue both the Palestinian and Syrian tracks and to gain Egypt's and Saudi Arabia's political and diplomatic support for these peace negotiations.

We hoped that by the end of this process, broad regional organizations would be in place to focus on security issues and on water, energy, and tourism concerns. At the same time, I was fully aware of the threat posed by militant Islamic fundamentalist forces and argued that the struggle had to be led by the local participants. The various countries and regions involved had different local actors. In the West Bank and Gaza, only the Fatah organization seemed able to face the challenge of Hamas. Jordan would need a united coalition of the Hashemite establishment, the PLO, and the Palestinian national leadership of the West Bank and Gaza to defeat the forces of militant Islam. In Egypt, by contrast, a coalition of state, party, and Islamic clergy could cope with the powerful but divided forces of militant Islam.[17]

We also understood that a broader regional community organization on water, energy, and tourism necessitated the reduction of the Palestinians' economic dependence on Israel and the political and social dependence of the Palestinian inhabitants of the West Bank and Gaza on the PLO in Tunis. In this context, we stressed the need to prevent further expansion of Israeli settlements through negotiated agreements and to create a viable physical and institutional infrastructure for a Palestinian state.

Opening a Back Channel in Norway

Yitzhak Rabin's 1992 Labor Government and Negotiations with the Palestinian "Outside"

Many of our ideas were reflected in the ILP's 1992 political platform. The platform expressed willingness to negotiate an agreement on self-government with a separate Palestinian delegation (i.e., not insisting on a joint Jordanian-Palestinian delegation) and to include any Palestinian in the delegation who recognized the State of Israel's right to exist, opposed terrorism, and accepted UN Security Council Resolution 242. Because the PLO had agreed to these terms in December 1988, it created a certain amount of flexibility without specifically referring to negotiations with the PLO. The ILP also committed to changing the law prohibiting meetings with members of the PLO. However, its platform opposed the establishment of a separate Palestinian state and requested an accepted joint Jordanian-Palestinian "framework."[18]

In the June 1992 Knesset elections, the ILP received 44 seats, the left-wing (peace-oriented) Meretz party won 12 seats, and the Arab parties received 5 seats, providing the Israeli center-left with a majority of 61 out of a total 120 mandates. Rabin formed a government together with the religious Shas party, and Peres was nominated as foreign minister. Rabin and Peres also signed an agreement defining their individual roles and their relationship; Rabin took full responsibility for bilateral negotiations, and Peres for multilateral negotiations. To create an effective working relationship, they agreed to meet at short intervals. These meetings, dubbed the "Meeting of the Two," became the most important decisionmaking forum at the time.

With regard to the Palestinian track, the overriding idea was to negotiate an agreement on autonomy with the Palestinian inside leadership:
those who were living in the West Bank, Arab Jerusalem, and Gaza. To
strengthen the Palestinian inside leadership, Peres agreed to accept outside
Palestinian participation in multilateral negotiations, with an agreed-upon
role for the PLO. I was asked to work with Hanan Ashrawi to prepare a
concept that would define the multilateral negotiation participation rules
for the Palestinian outside leadership. After having discussed what did
and did not seem possible, Ashrawi scribbled the formula that she was
suggesting on a yellow piece of paper. In essence, no official members of
the PLO could participate in the multilateral negotiations, but Palestinians
who resided outside the West Bank and Gaza (and who were supported
by the PLO) could participate. I subsequently showed this piece of paper
to Peres, who accepted it. Ashrawi, however, asked us to wait until she
received the necessary green light from Tunis, which never came. Instead,
Osama al-Baz, President Mubarak's powerful senior foreign policy
adviser—who was obviously sent by Arafat—flew in from Cairo about
a week later offering a formula that was less favorable to the Palestinian
side. Arafat's message was clear: He would block negotiations again and
again until Israel agreed to talk directly to the PLO. It was also clear that
if he were allowed to control the negotiations, the positions he would offer
would be more forthcoming.

Rabin and Peres both understood the message, and at the end of
November 1992, Rabin compared Arafat to Nahum Goldmann, who had
served as the leader of the World Zionist Organization for decades. This
comparison was an obvious attempt to de-demonize Arafat, and in early
January 1993 Peres suggested that Rabin "propose to Arafat and his staff
that they move to Gaza. Once there, they would have the right to vote and
to stand in elections; and if elected, they would represent the Palestinians
directly in negotiations with Israel."[19] This proposal became the deal-making
issue for Arafat and was a move that evidently needed to be worked on in
direct negotiations with the PLO.

The Need to Adopt the Back-Channel Technique

Rabin's original plan was to negotiate with the Palestinian delegation in
Washington and to permit them "to consult with whomever they wanted
to," offering the PLO a place outside the negotiating table. However,
no headway was made in Washington. Worse, after Hamas kidnapped

and killed an Israeli policeman, Nissim Toledano, in mid-December 1992, Rabin decided to expel more than four hundred Hamas activists to Lebanon.[20] The Palestinians subsequently broke off the negotiations in Washington.

In a way, this was a very awkward situation. Rabin and Peres understood, and they were committed to finding a way to convince Arafat and the PLO to fully support the negotiations. But for good reasons, they were reluctant to start an official dialogue. Israel's official recognition of the PLO would pave the way for the PLO's international acceptance and would provide its leadership with substantial international legitimacy. Israel had every interest in playing this card carefully, making its quid pro quo for recognizing the PLO the conclusion of a peace agreement. Thus the back-channel technique would be needed to test the ground while maintaining full deniability.

Under these circumstances, Ashrawi repeatedly asked me to start a track-two dialogue with the PLO's senior members. Early in December 1992, the five multilateral negotiating groups that had been designed in Madrid were meeting in London. We knew that PLO leader Abu Ala' was directing the Palestinian delegation. Husseini and Ashrawi arranged for me to meet with Abu Ala', and I got the political backing of Beilin. By participating in this first meeting in London, I actually did break Israeli law. The outcome of this meeting remained inconclusive, but our discussions were important enough for us to agree to meet again in Norway the following month.[21]

The Way to the Sarpsborg Document: "The Principles of an Israeli-Palestinian Understanding" of March 21, 1993

The first three meetings in Norway all took place in Sarpsborg, a small industrial town in the southern part of the country. We were accommodated at Borregard, a beautiful mansion belonging to a former Norwegian industrialist. During the first meeting, held on January 21 and 22, Abu Ala' offered what Israel had demanded earlier: a Gaza-first agreement. He wanted it to be based on three understandings:

• Israel would agree to withdraw from Gaza "in two to three years,"
• An economic development "Marshall Plan" would be immediately introduced for the Gaza Strip, and
• A structure for Israeli-Palestinian economic cooperation would be immediately created.[22]

The Palestinians expressed their understanding that a parallel withdrawal from the West Bank could not be expected, and thus they proposed that the "keys to Gaza" should be given, at first, to a third party in order to permit negotiations to proceed on all the outstanding issues.

The Palestinian team presented several ideas for economic cooperation, which would build on existing resources and help to develop new ones, knowing (or at least assuming correctly) that these ideas would suit Peres. The ideas included the construction of an Israeli-Palestinian-Egyptian water desalination plant and power station on the Gaza-Sinai border, a free trade zone between Ashdod and Gaza to connect the two harbors, cooperation to develop the Dead Sea's natural resources, the creation of a joint Israeli-Palestinian automobile factory that would make cars for the Arab world, and the construction of gas and oil pipelines and refineries, incorporating the existing Tap Line.[23]

However, Abu Ala' also made several demands:

- UN Security Council Resolutions 242 and 338 should be accepted as guidelines not only for permanent status but also for the Interim Agreement.
- The Palestinian Authority's jurisdiction should extend over all the Palestinian territories occupied in 1967, though administrative exceptions could be agreed upon.
- The Transitional Council "should be allowed to exercise all legislative powers."
- All existing laws should be subject to review.
- An international body, whose composition would be agreed upon, should supervise the elections.[24]
- Israel should allow those who had been deported since 1967 to return home.
- The PLO's role in the peace process should be reinstated.
- The Government of Israel should take immediate steps to halt all settlement activities.[25]

It was clear to us that many of these demands had no chance of being accepted by the Israeli government. However, we also understood that the willingness of Abu Ala' to pursue a Gaza-first approach and his suggestions for economic development provided ground for further exploration. Furthermore, he had the appealing idea of working on an agreement that would be submitted to the parties as an American proposal.[26]

After discussing our report of the first meeting in Norway, Beilin asked me to prepare a paper that we could talk over to test common positions and gaps between our two teams. This was the only way in which we could complete the fact-finding experiment and test, in detail, whether we could define enough common ground to move toward an agreement. I sat at home in Ramat Yishai for several days in February 1993 and prepared a document titled "The Principles of an Israeli-Palestinian Negotiating Plan," which included three draft components: (1) a Declaration of Principles, (2) an Israeli-Palestinian Cooperation and Working Program, and (3) "Preparing a Marshall Plan for the West Bank, Gaza Strip, and the Region."[27] The basic guidelines in this document would later become the Israel-PLO Declaration of Principles that would be signed on the White House lawn seven months later, on September 13. Yet even at this draft stage, the written concept for a proposed agreement made it possible to identify common ground and prevailing gaps.

Several major differences became evident. The most important gap in the positions was in the jurisdiction over territory. The Israeli position that we suggested read "the jurisdiction of the Palestinian Interim Council will cover control over land, as mutually agreed upon"; the Palestinian version read "the jurisdiction of the Palestinian Interim Council will cover the Palestinian territories occupied in 1967. Any administrative exception hereto should be discussed during negotiations, stipulated these exceptions should not prejudice UN Security Council Resolutions 242 and 338 and the principles of international law." The other major difference related to the issue of arbitration. The proposed Israeli version stated that both sides "may decide by agreement to seek arbitration. The conditions for arbitration will then have to be fully and mutually agreed upon." The Palestinian suggestion read "An arbitration committee will be created to whom all issues of disputes will be submitted, in case no Israeli-Palestinian agreement will have been achieved, otherwise. The committee will include representatives of the cosponsors of the Madrid Conference, of Egypt, Jordan and the UN Secretariat, and furthermore a representative from Israel and from the Palestinian Interim Council."[28]

Although considerable gaps in substance remained during the February 1993 Sarpsborg meeting, an agreement on procedure was achieved, and its understanding was incorporated into the joint paper. It read: "It is suggested that the US Secretary of State will go to Jerusalem and will submit to the Government of Israel on the one hand, and to the Palestinian leadership [Faisal Husseini and Hanan Ashrawi] on the other hand, an American draft for a DoP [Declaration of Principles]; an outline of a proposed Israeli-Palestinian CWP [Cooperation and Working Program], and an outline of a proposed 'Marshall Plan' for the West Bank, the Gaza Strip and the

Region."[29] To close the prevailing gaps, a US shuttle diplomacy effort was proposed. Abu Ala' told us that Arafat would ask Faisal Husseini to go to Tunis, where Arafat and Abu Ala' would fully brief Husseini and then decide how to move from there.[30]

After returning from Sarpsborg, Beilin organized two meetings between Peres and Husseini, on February 21 and 27, 1993. At the first meeting, Faisal read a message from Arafat to Peres that carried the tone and language of the meetings in Sarpsborg:

> We are concerned about the peace process, our commitment is so strong. It is important for us, for the region; it is not only the shape of the new world that can help us, we also can help the new world order. So far we are enemies, but in this peace process there is a partnership, so do not make more problems for both of us. . . . Both of us are not completely free to do steps exclusively without consideration of the other side.[31]

Peres referred to US secretary of state Warren Christopher's forthcoming visit, and I expressed hope that the idea of a US shuttle diplomacy effort on both tracks would be discussed.[32] However, this did not happen. What was apparently discussed instead was the preparation for a joint US-Russian invitation to the parties to restart bilateral Israeli-Palestinian negotiations in Washington.

The Palestinians conditioned their return to negotiations on an agreement to solve the issue of the Palestinian deportees. But Rabin was not willing to accept this condition. Instead, on March 10, in the follow-up to Christopher's visit to Israel and without having achieved an agreement on how to solve the deportee question,[33] a US-Russian announcement was made that the parties were invited to attend a ninth round of negotiations, which was to start in late April and continue, without interruption, until early May.[34]

Following this US-Russian announcement, ECF member Ron Pundak and I were given the green light to return to Norway. This time, Peres verbally instructed me to ask Abu Ala' when Arafat wanted to return to Gaza. At the same time, Beilin instructed me to bridge the gaps between the two sides and to return with an agreed-upon paper. Beilin hoped that the existence of this paper would provide sufficient enticement to Arafat to overrule possible internal opposition to the renewal of negotiations in Washington.[35]

The third meeting was held again in Sarpsborg from March 20 through 22, 1993. We managed to close all the outstanding gaps and to produce a paper titled "The Principles of an Israeli-Palestinian Understanding."

We explained at the beginning of the paper that "an agreement has been achieved in Sarpsborg regarding the concept of a mutually *envisaged* Israeli-Palestinian understanding" (emphasis added).[36] This ensured that the commitments made were not binding and were still deniable by the official track. Table 4.2 shows the results achieved and compares the original Palestinian demands with the agreements reached in Sarpsborg.

I was convinced that our results were impressive. The Sarpsborg Document maintained all the necessary control mechanisms for Israel; the source of authority and all residual power remained with Israel; and there was no need for any immediate withdrawal of the military government and/or the Civil Administration or for a redeployment of the Israeli Defense Forces. The concessions that the Sarpsborg paper granted to the Palestinians were also in line with the strategic approach that our group had pursued throughout the past decade: A series of Palestinian institutions would be established to provide the Palestinians with the capability to prepare a bottom-up approach for Palestinian state building and to limit the expansion of Israeli settlements in the West Bank and Gaza. The Sarpsborg Document made clear provisions for Palestinian empowerment, but it intentionally did not provide for the conclusion of a comprehensive Interim Agreement on Palestinian self-government. The understandings were substantive enough to conclude a Declaration of Principles and to enable the parties to move on to negotiate the outstanding core issues of conflict in order to reach a Permanent Status Agreement.

In the context of Permanent Status negotiations, the term of reference was UN Security Council Resolution 242, which agreed upon the concept of territory for peace. The acceptance in paragraph four, which stated that the "jurisdiction of the Palestinian Interim Council will cover West Bank and Gaza Strip land," was connected to paragraph six, which provided for immediate powers to the Palestinian Land Committee and the Water Administration Committee and the need to negotiate a coordinated land and water resources development plan.[37] These conditions would create, for the duration of negotiations, a mutual veto power on control over land and water resources, and were thus meant to limit the expansion of Israeli settlements. This concept was fully in line with what Peres had suggested to Rashad Shawwa in November 1982 and to Husseini and Ashrawi early in January 1993.[38] It was also in keeping with the logic suggested in my policy planning paper, which was subtitled "From Dependence to Interdependence."[39]

The proposal permitting Palestinians living in Jerusalem to participate in elections for a Palestinian Council and to cast their votes in the al-Aqsa Mosque and the Church of the Holy Sepulchre was also part of my win-win thinking. We offered the Palestinians what was essentially a symbolic gesture that would enable their leadership to gather both Palestinian and wider Arab support for the agreement by permitting the Palestinians living in Jerusalem to vote every four years in the city, while Israel continued to maintain full administrative and security control over Jerusalem.[40]

Committing to the establishment of a strong Palestinian police force responsible for internal security and public order—in liaison with Israel, Jordan, and Egypt—was fully in line with the provisions laid down in the 1978 Camp David Accords. We hoped that liaison functions with Egypt and Jordan could lay the foundations for wider Israeli-Palestinian-Jordanian security cooperation toward the east, as well as wider Israeli-Palestinian-Egyptian security cooperation toward the south and the west of Israel.

The Gaza-first approach was based on wide political support in Israel. Furthermore, the introduction of an international trusteeship to take over the administration of Gaza after an Israeli withdrawal—two years after the conclusion of the 1993 Declaration of Principles—would serve three different purposes. First, it would free Chairman Arafat from the need to run his own administration and permit him to concentrate on Permanent Status negotiations with Israel. Second, the emerging Palestinian state would be managed and overseen by Western standards, preventing abuses while institutionalizing public accountability of the executive and the judiciary and thus helping to establish a commitment to constitutional practices from the very beginning. And third, the trusteeship could institutionalize proper coordination between the Israeli, Palestinian, and Egyptian security forces.

However, from Peres's perspective, matters looked different. He opposed the idea of establishing a Palestinian trusteeship and would later explain his opposition, writing that "international trusteeships in recent history were almost always . . . designed to lead eventually to full independence. Israel's declared position was that it opposed the creation of an independent Palestinian state following the interim period of self-government."[41] Peres was also very critical of the paragraphs dealing with elections in Jerusalem and arbitration.[42] And what may have irritated Peres even more than those points was the fact that we had bridged the existing gaps in Sarpsborg and concluded a jointly supported document. Because Prime Minister Rabin had not clarified or preauthorized the conclusion of a joint "mutually envisaged understanding," Peres feared that this approach might be interpreted as if he was working against Rabin behind his back, and he thus gave Pundak and me a serious verbal beating.[43] Nothing specific was said, but it seemed to me that the Norwegian back-channel negotiations had come to an end.

Table 4.2. The Pre-Oslo Palestinian Demands and the
Sarpsborg Principles, March 1993

Subject	The Palestinian Position before Oslo	The Sarpsborg Principles
The substance of the agreement	For Israel to recognize the Palestinian right for self-determination	The clock toward negotiating Permanent Status began ticking during a period of ongoing transfer of authority and comprehensive bilateral and regional cooperation procedures
The connection between the Interim Agreement and Permanent Agreement	The Interim Agreement was to be linked to the Permanent Agreement	The Interim Agreement was to be linked to permanent status negotiations
Terms of reference	UN Security Council Resolution 242 and Resolution 338 had to apply to all territories	Interim arrangements for a transitional period leading to a permanent settlement based on Resolution 242 and Resolution 338
Source of authority	Palestinian self-government	A temporary and partial transfer of authorities that would permit Israel's military authority to remain the source of authority
Elections	Demand to rescind all existing orders and regulations which prohibit assembling, movement and participation in elections	Direct, free and general elections to be agreed on and held under international supervision
Participation of Palestinians of Jerusalem in elections	The right to participate in the elections as voters and as candidates	The right to participate in the elections as voters and as candidates. Jerusalem voters will vote in the al-Aqsa Mosque and in the Church of the Holy Sepulchre
Powers of self-government	Unlimited; exceptions to be qualified and agreed upon	The transfer of authorities would be of a temporary nature and would include control over taxation, tourism, education, health and social welfare and other areas, as agreed upon
Territorial extension	Jurisdiction over all territories of the West Bank, East Jerusalem, and the Gaza Strip	The Palestinian Interim Council's jurisdiction would cover "West Bank land" and Gaza (para. 4). The Palestinian Land Committee and the Palestinian Water Administration would be given immediate mutually agreed upon powers. A coordinated land and water resource development plan would be negotiated between the Palestinian committees and the Government of Israel
Legislative powers	Complete legislative and judicial powers	The Palestinian Interim Council would be empowered to legislate all mutually agreed upon authorities. Both parties would jointly reassess all laws and military orders in force at the time

Subject	The Palestinian Position before Oslo	The Sarpsborg Principles
Executive powers	Full executive powers without foreign intervention	The establishment of a Palestinian Land Authority, Palestinian Water Authority, Palestinian Electricity Authority, Palestinian Development Bank, Palestinian Export Promotion Board, Environment Authority and a strong police force. The necessary relevant agreements defining the executive powers of these bodies would be negotiated with Israel
Foreign policy	Demand foreign policy powers	The Palestinian self-government would not obtain official authority to pursue an independent foreign policy. However, Israel's recognition would as a matter of fact offer international legitimacy to the PLO's diplomatic missions
Judiciary	The Palestinian judiciary should be fully independent	The transfer of authority to a Palestinian judiciary would be negotiated at a later point in time
Police force and security	A strong Palestinian police force responsible for public order and security	The Palestinian Interim Council would establish a strong police force responsible for internal security and public order. External security would be under exclusive Israeli control
Peacekeeping force	UN peacekeeping force	After an Israeli withdrawal from Gaza, a trusteeship for Gaza would be established
Date of the elections	The Palestinians would decide the date	Elections would be held three months after the signing of the Declaration of Principles
Purpose of elections	A legislative assembly of 180 members would be established	The Palestinian Interim Council would be elected and the number of its members was to be negotiated
Functions of elections	To permit the elected assembly to assert full control of Palestinians political rights	A significant preparatory step toward the realization of the legitimate rights of the Palestinian people and their just requirements
Participation of Palestinian inhabitants of Jerusalem	The right to participate in the elections as voters and as candidates	The right to participate in elections as voters and as candidates
Defining the right to participate in elections	All displaced Palestinians who were registered on the 4th of June 1967 would have the right to participate	All displaced Palestinians who were registered on June 4, 1967, would have the right to participate. Even if they lived abroad and were not allowed to return and hence would be unable to participate in the elections, their right to do so will not be prejudiced.[a]
International supervision	International supervision of elections	The mode of international supervision was to be negotiated

a The addition indicated that the principle of the right to participate in elections did not provide the right of displaced persons to return.

From Sarpsborg to Oslo: Legitimizing the Norwegian Channel and Breaking through the Deadlock

The Americans Start to Bridge the Gap

Almost unexpectedly, the opposite happened. In fact, it took about two weeks for us to get back to business. On April 13, Kurtzer spoke to Pundak and me about the Washington talks between President Bill Clinton, Secretary of State Warren Christopher, Prime Minister Rabin, the American peace team, and Israeli delegation head Elyakim Rubinstein.

The Americans were very critical of Israeli negotiating tactics. Clinton told Rabin that progress was too slow. The American peace team told Rubinstein that the proposals he had submitted to the Palestinians had been counterproductive; instead of creating hope for the Palestinians, the official Israeli proposals and demands had caused the Palestinian delegation to conclude that success in the ongoing effort was not possible. Worse, the legitimacy of the Palestinian delegation to the Washington talks was undermined by the fact that it had not been able to achieve any visible results.

It was in this context that Kurtzer referred to the meetings in Sarpsborg. Evidently, the Americans were ambivalent about the dialogue that was going on in Norway. On one hand, they understood and said that the continuation of meetings with the senior PLO leaders represented a very important confidence-building measure.[44] They also stressed that they thought it was useful to continue the dialogue in Norway. On the other hand, they did not want to permit the creation of an alternative to the negotiations in Washington. Accordingly, they remained cautious about offering any support for maintaining direct contact with the PLO.[45]

Kurtzer stressed to us that the paper that had been concluded in Norway showed substantial headway on several accounts. So that we would not lose our momentum, Kurtzer made four proposals:

- Continue the dialogue in Sarpsborg to help renew the Washington negotiations.
- Ask the Palestinians to agree to change some of the Sarpsborg Document's provisions on Jerusalem and arbitration that were not acceptable to the Israeli government.
- Introduce agreed-on points from Sarpsborg into the Washington talks.
- Permit the Americans to submit the Sarpsborg concept as an alternative proposal to the Washington negotiations, if the gap between

the parties could not be bridged directly. This would require an early understanding between Israel and the PLO.[46]

At about the same time, Terje Larsen, the head of the Norwegian Trade Union Research Institute (who was very close to the Norwegian labor leadership), came to see us in Tel Aviv. Larsen had been hosting our meetings in Norway and managing the liaison work between the meetings. He told Beilin that Abu Ala' had been calling almost daily, clearly indicating how eager Abu Ala' was to continue or renew the dialogue in Norway. Larsen had also been informed of a meeting between Chairman Arafat and Egyptian president Hosni Mubarak, as well as of Mubarak's intentions to discuss with President Clinton possible progress along the lines of the understandings that had been reached in Sarpsborg. Beilin hinted to Larsen that Prime Minister Rabin was now personally directing future moves, and that the reason why the Israelis did not intend to renew the meetings in Sarpsborg until the Palestinians renewed bilateral negotiations in Washington was to be able to incorporate the understandings reached in Norway into the official negotiating channel in Washington.[47]

The achievements of the Sarpsborg document—which gave advance notice to the Palestinian team of the need to agree to certain future changes; showed the PLO's willingness to make further concessions in order to upgrade the Norwegian back-channel to an official level; and permitted the United States, Norway, and Egypt to play a supportive role in a multitrack diplomacy effort—turned out to be good enough to renew negotiations in Washington, even before the issue of the Hamas deportees in Lebanon had been resolved. This development not only ensured the continuation of the Norwegian channel but also opened the way for Rabin to take full control of both the official negotiations in Washington and the secret negotiations in Oslo.

Renewing the Official Negotiations in Washington

On April 27, 1993, the Israeli-Palestinian negotiations in Washington were renewed. Notably, Arafat imposed this renewal on his negotiators even against almost unanimous opposition from the entire Palestinian delegation. The Palestinians had reacted badly to both the unproductive negotiations and ongoing events in the occupied territories, which included Palestinian houses being destroyed and Palestinians being prevented from traveling and working in both Israel and in the territories.

As Abu Ala' explained, summarizing the delegation's general mood at the time:

> The entire delegation was against the chairman's decision. Ghassan al-Khatib and Samir Abdallah boycotted the decision. Haidar Abd al-Shafi was strongly against it. Another strong group against it came from Gaza: the people around Dr. [Zakaria] al-Agha. This is due to the particularly difficult situation in the Gaza Strip and lack of confidence in any progress. Hanan Ashrawi was against the resumption of negotiations. Saeb Erekat wanted to write his memoirs, rather than to go to Washington.[48]

On the Israeli side, by contrast, the renewal of negotiations in Washington gave strong impetus to our work. Peres had fully informed his most intimate advisers—the director-general of the Israeli Ministry of Foreign Affairs, Uri Savir, and the head of his office, Avi Gil—of what had been achieved in Sarpsborg. From then on, Savir and Gil participated in joint planning sessions with Peres, Beilin, Pundak, and me.

In the meantime, and without our knowledge, Peres was leading an intense dialogue with Egypt about the content that was being discussed in Oslo. Responding to a request by President Mubarak, Peres willingly added an understanding that included Jericho in the Gaza-first approach. This addition would enable the Palestinians to obtain a visible foothold in the West Bank. In response to the proposal of turning the Gaza-first approach into a Gaza- and Jericho-first approach, Abu Ala' demanded that the Jericho area should include control of the King Hussein Bridge (Allenby Bridge)—that is, the bridge connecting the West Bank with Jordan. This demand clearly contradicted the understanding that the Palestinians would only have control over internal security. The entire concept of self-government as an interim move meant not only that Israel would maintain all powers over the external security of the self-government authority but also that Israel would exercise complete control over external borders. The Jericho request would later become a point of contention, even after we received initial concessions from the Palestinians on this proposal (see chapter 5).[49] In Oslo, however, no mention of this request had ever been made, and its introduction came as a complete surprise to Pundak and me.[50] Apparently, Peres had discussed the Jericho idea with Mubarak without a specific agreement from Rabin. It was then convenient for Peres to tell Rabin that the idea had come up in Oslo instead of telling him that the concept had emerged in his own dialogue with Mubarak. Thus, we were accused of having brought up the Jericho idea without having been told to do so and without reporting it.[51]

At the first joint planning session with Savir and Gil, Peres explained his criticism of the Sarpsborg document. He stated that regarding Jerusalem, Palestinians residing in the city could be permitted to vote but could not be elected because their election would indicate Palestinian sovereignty rights over the areas where they lived, which was unacceptable to Israel. Furthermore, the arbitration clause was unacceptable because it would encourage the Palestinians to refrain from engaging seriously in negotiations, as they would prefer to bring every little issue to arbitration by a third party instead. Peres also asked for clarification regarding the implications of the electoral register, which would include Palestinians residing in the West Bank and Gaza who had registered before June 4, 1967. He feared that the proposed understanding on the electoral registry would offer all Palestinians who had been deported and/or exiled since 1967 the right to participate in elections and would open the door to their request to return. In order to work on the Sarpsborg Understanding, Peres suggested inviting a lawyer to a meeting, in which we would all review the document and decide what changes had to be made. I, somewhat defensively, argued that the Palestinians knew that they had to adapt the paper to further changes and that their demands with regard to Jericho offered a perfect lever to bring about the necessary changes.[52]

Peres also discussed, in detail, the emerging Israeli approach to the Washington negotiations. There, the Israeli delegation was instructed to suggest important improvements regarding humanitarian affairs, land, and elections. Regarding the control of land, Rubinstein proposed that privately owned land, which constituted about 60 percent of the land in the West Bank and Gaza, be controlled by the Palestinian self-government authority.[53]

To create a complementary approach to the simultaneous pursuit of negotiations in Washington and in Oslo, Peres asked us to concentrate on the economic issues in Oslo. He also suggested that many of these issues be dealt with in the multilateral channels, where Israel had a greater capacity to be flexible (and where Rabin would not question concessions to which Peres might agree). Peres added that he was interested in negotiating Permanent Status, especially if the Palestinians agreed to form a confederation with Jordan and create a trilateral economic confederation for Israel, Jordan, and Palestine based on the Benelux (Belgium, Netherlands, and Luxembourg) structure.[54]

We raised all these issues at our next meeting in Oslo, on April 30 and May 1, 1993. Referring to the policy suggestions submitted by the Israeli delegation in Washington, Abu Ala' made the following comments:

The renewal of negotiations has created an additional problem. All the issues we discussed are thrown in Washington at our Palestinian delegation: Often proposals made by Rubinstein are identical to the letter with concepts formulated in the Sarpsborg Document. Our delegation does not understand it and our situation is becoming more and more precarious, for two reasons: First, the entirety of the approach and the balance of the give and take is not being preserved. Second, the credibility of the internal nucleus of the leadership, Arafat, Abu Mazen [Mahmoud Abbas] and Abu Ala', is being challenged. Presently, Nabil Qassis and Saeb Erekat are in Tunis. On the basis of the information they have, the bits and pieces presented to them in Washington, it is impossible to take a decision.[55]

Abu Ala' had no interest in reviewing the issues of economic development and cooperation to which Peres had referred as isolated matters. Rather, he wanted to continue the discussion on political moves, matters of public opinion, security, and economic development and cooperation. He made a number of constructive proposals, with immediate steps as well as medium- and long-term arrangements. Immediate general steps included discussing a timetable for the return of the PLO's leaders (possibly including Arafat) to the West Bank and Gaza, agreeing on a security plan to dismantle Palestinian terrorist forces and develop Palestinian and multinational police forces for the region, obtaining financial support from Saudi Arabia for economic development projects, and working to create "responsive public opinion" for the peace proposals among Israelis and Palestinians. For the Gaza Strip specifically, he proposed an immediate economic recovery program to develop housing and local infrastructure, as well as immediate steps for a long-term stabilizing and demilitarization program and for the establishment of a United States–Jordan–Egypt trusteeship for Gaza to be overseen by the United Nations. Medium- and long-term arrangements would involve detailed proposals with practical arrangements for Israeli-Palestinian cooperation (especially in the Israeli settlements in Gaza), along with political and economic confederation plans between Jordan and Palestine and the Benelux-style trilateral economic system under consideration.[56]

The renewal of negotiations in Washington, the willingness of the PLO delegation in Oslo to accept changes to the Sarpsborg Document, and the constructive proposals made by Abu Ala' at the beginning of May were all in line with what I had called the legitimizing phase. These steps documented the PLO's prevailing interest in concluding an agreement along the terms that had been discussed. Thus, Rabin and Peres received confirmation that the Oslo channel had enabled important headway to be achieved in the negotiations.

Moving to Secret Official Negotiations in Oslo

Pundak and I returned to Oslo on May 9, 1993, and, following clear instructions, I demanded that Abu Ala'—with the help of the newly appointed Norwegian minister of foreign affairs, Johan Jørgen Holst—convince Arafat to permit Husseini to join and lead the delegation in Washington. Abu Ala' woke me early on the morning of May 10 and informed me that Husseini was on his way to Washington. Abu Ala' was, of course, interested in strengthening his own role in Norway, and accordingly he did not like the fact that we wanted the Washington channel to have a leading function. Nevertheless, he accepted it and described some emerging difficulties to us. He explained that Arafat's insistence on returning to negotiations had created the political need to achieve visible progress, whether in Oslo or Washington. He also asked that money from the World Bank's Trust Fund help finance activities in the West Bank and Gaza and asked for a variety of confidence-building measures, such as the return of deportees, family reunions, and the release of prisoners.[57]

It was clear to us that an upgrade of the Oslo talks to the official level would offer substantial encouragement, not only to Abu Ala' but also to Arafat, so we proposed that Peres come to Oslo. He suggested the idea to Rabin, who vetoed it.[58] Instead, Rabin agreed that Savir, the director-general of the Ministry of Foreign Affairs and a close confidant of Peres, would join the talks in Oslo and head the Israeli delegation. Thus, on May 20, 1993, we returned to Oslo, this time accompanied by Savir. Official secret negotiations had started, and Abu Ala' was justifiably jubilant; I had kept my promise, and we had reached the breakthrough stage.

Early in June, it was decided that we would ask Yoel Singer to join the Oslo channel. Singer was a lawyer and former head of the International Legal Department of the Israeli Defense Forces who had worked closely with Rabin while he was minister of defense and prime minister. Early in May 1993, Rabin had decided that he wanted the Oslo channel to define a strategic concept that would lead the way to an Israeli-Palestinian agreement on Palestinian self-government, instead of the looser understandings for Palestinian empowerment that would pave the way directly to Permanent Status negotiations.[59] Under Singer's quiet yet impressive leadership, the concept of the Sarpsborg Understanding was replaced by the draft and, finally, by the conclusion of the Declaration of Principles that was signed on the White House lawn on September 13, 1993.

The official Israeli delegation to Oslo included Pundak and me in addition to Savir and Singer. My role was mainly to help explain and support the transition from the Sarpsborg concept to the newly emerging approach and to see to it that Abu Ala' did not renew the demands that we had rejected earlier. Peres also asked me to convince Abu Ala' to give up on the concept of a trusteeship over Gaza. Fully aware that I did not have the means to oppose Peres or to try to convince him otherwise, I told him that it would take me five minutes to do so. In practice, it took one minute. I simply asked Abu Ala' if it would be better if the PLO obtained direct control over Gaza instead of handing it over to a trusteeship managed by foreign actors. He asked me if this was what Israel wanted, and after I answered in the affirmative, he consented—and the concept of trusteeship that Peres so fervently opposed was eliminated from the equation.[60]

From mid-June to early July, a revised concept of the Sarpsborg Understanding was prepared and negotiated. The basic structure of the document, the order of the paragraphs and the language, remained by and large the same. Singer was acting upon instructions not to change too much. Adapting to the emerging changes, Abu Ala' went through three phases. At first, he was thrilled that a representative of Peres and Rabin had joined the negotiations, but when Singer presented the suggested changes in the form of questions, Abu Ala' was taken aback because he feared that many of the issues that had been discussed would have to be renegotiated. However, after he had adapted to the change in approach, he went along with it.

On July 6, 1993, we sensed that an almost-complete agreement had been reached on practically all matters. I reported to Norwegian minister of foreign affairs Holst that all outstanding issues had been solved but that we did not want to conclude the agreement without obtaining a final approval from both Rabin and Arafat. I also stated that we hoped that at the next round of negotiations everything could be concluded. I was wrong.

During the next round, and throughout all of July, the negotiations went through a major crisis. The Palestinians clearly wanted to test the room for potential further Israeli concessions, but the red lines that I had laid down at the beginning of the back-channel exercise played an important role in containing this effort. At the meeting in Halvorsbole, Norway, on July 11–12, 1993, the Palestinians demanded full Israeli withdrawal from Gaza and the "Jericho district," which according to Palestinian interpretation included most of the Jordan Valley. The Palestinians also demanded that immediate authority for the West Bank be given to the Palestinians, along with the return of 10,000 Palestinian "police-men" to the territories. The explanation given was that Arafat could not return to these territories while Israel still maintained its presence there. Not being able to accept the sudden Palestinian demands, the Israeli team broke off negotiations. And I made it clear to the Palestinian delegation that none of the recently tabled Palestinian demands had been accepted at an earlier stage and that those demands contradicted the understandings that we had concluded in Sarpsborg.[61]

The negotiations, however, did not come to an end. Savir and Abu Ala' developed not only the ability to manage the unfolding crisis but also an impressive personal relationship. Early in August, the Palestinians informed us that they had reviewed their demands and wanted to adjust them according to Israel's needs. Thus, I was sent to Paris alone on August 7 to receive from Abu Ala' the final Palestinian "make or break" proposal. I worked with Abu Ala' throughout the entire night, making it evident to him what would be acceptable to Peres and Rabin. Because the Palestinians clearly wanted to finalize an agreement, on the morning of August 8, 1993, Abu Ala' handed me a paper that was "still to be finalized." However, I knew that the way to the conclusion of the Oslo agreements had been paved.[62]

Anticipating the conclusion of an agreement with the PLO, Singer had already in June 1993 tried to convince Rabin that letters of mutual recognition between Israel and the PLO were essential. He argued that only mutual recognition would create the necessary legal responsibility for the PLO to implement all components of the agreement. Singer further argued that the Norway negotiations between official Israeli and PLO teams constituted a de facto recognition of the PLO. It would make sense, Singer contemplated, to negotiate the necessary quid pro quo, when the PLO was still highly interested in obtaining Israel's recognition. This concept contradicted the approach we had pursued, which was to bring the whole agreement to Washington and to permit the Israeli and Palestinian delegations there to sign it. Rabin told Singer that he could suggest the idea of negotiating mutual recognition as a private proposal of his. By that point, however, the concept of a private proposal had lost its credibility with the Palestinians. Too often, we in the back channel had argued that everything we were saying was only in "our private capacity," so Abu Ala' and his team had nothing but a smile for the private nature of the idea.

Ultimately, the decision was made to first conclude the Declaration of Principles and to later negotiate the conditions for mutual recognition. Accordingly, when the official document was initialed in a ceremony in Oslo shortly after midnight on August 20, the text of the Declaration of Principles still named the Palestinian delegation to the Washington talks as the Palestinian signatory.[63] On September 9, the official mutual letters of recognition were concluded and exchanged—and finally, on September 13, the Declaration of Principles between the Government of Israel and the PLO was concluded.[64]

Reflections on the Back-Channel Approach

The advantage of the back-channel technique over a more orthodox negotiating approach is that it maintains ample space for creative innovation. In official negotiations, the decisionmakers offer clear instructions to the negotiators on what subjects to touch and what outcomes to obtain, and the negotiators tend to ask for permission to test even the smallest diversion from existing instructions. Back-channel negotiations turn this approach upside down: The negotiators have a conceptual understanding of the direction in which the decisionmakers want to go, but a variety of ideas can be freely checked and brought back to the leadership only after obtaining a comprehensive response from the other side. The back-channel technique thus allows for far greater maneuverability for the negotiators. However, because of the principle of deniability, the leadership can cut off the back-channel negotiator from the chain of information and action at any given time. Accordingly, the back-channel technique requires a great deal of circumspection and very clear rules that have been agreed upon with the negotiating partner at the beginning of the exercise.

With these realities in mind, I consistently pursued five different components essential for the success of any back-channel exercise: maintaining complete deniability, demonstrating our relevance to the official decisionmaking process, refraining from exploiting the other side's internal political rivalries, creating a great degree of reliability, and being aware of what can and cannot be done in these types of negotiations.

Maintaining Complete Deniability

The entire logic of back-channel negotiations is to provide the leadership on your side with enough knowledge to informally test policy options. In 1957 and 1958, David Ben Gurion had authorized back-channel talks in London to allow his left-wing Zionist Mapam party to test whether it would be possible to establish a constructive relationship with the emerging radical opposition Ba'ath parties in Jordan, Lebanon, and Syria. Ben Gurion's official policy at the time was to strengthen US-Israeli relations and Israeli relations with the Jordanian and Lebanese regimes supported by Washington. Mapam's idea was to check whether it made sense for Israel to work instead with the upcoming "progressive" forces of the Ba'ath parties. With the assistance of the British Labour Party politician Anthony Wedgwood Benn, the London Mapam representative engaged in a back-channel dialogue for several months, leading to the conclusion that the Mapam-suggested approach of cooperation with the Ba'ath parties had no realistic chance of success.[65] In 1976, Yitzhak Rabin had authorized back-channel negotiations between Israeli and PLO representatives with assistance from Austrian chancellor Bruno Kreisky, aiming to lead the way to direct negotiations between Israel and the PLO. This effort was concluded in January 1977 with a letter from PLO representative Izzam Sartawi to Kreisky, which made it absolutely clear that there was no sufficient common ground to start negotiations.[66]

In both these earlier cases, the back-channel effort was successful from the point of view of Ben Gurion and Rabin. They tested an alternative strategy and were given sufficient information to learn that it would not work.[67] Accordingly, the failure of a policy pursued in back-channel negotiations may be seen by the leadership as a successful test of what not to do. Because the main purpose of the exercise is to test a policy option so far not taken, complete deniability is of its essence.

Therefore, I knew that in engaging in a dialogue with the PLO, I had to maintain absolute deniability for Rabin. At the first meeting in London, on December 4, 1993, I made this very clear, as Mahmoud Abbas recounted:

> Hirschfeld tried to give the impression that the meeting was unofficial, and that he was speaking as an academic who was not committed to anything and could not commit anyone else to anything either, and that, although he was close to Israeli officials, he had no authority to speak for them, and his words were not binding.[68]

Abu Ala', referring to the fourth round of negotiations in Norway (the second-to-last back-channel meeting), stated that Pundak and I "continued to maintain an apparently deliberate air of vagueness to the point of being rather irritating."[69] Although he knew that we had no official status, we also seemed to be in touch with the decisionmakers in the Israeli government, which made us worthwhile negotiating partners.

Beyond allowing Rabin to pursue or reject the findings of the Oslo channel, the denial of the ongoing dialogue with the PLO was based on the rationale of avoiding negotiations with the Palestinian Diaspora. In a meeting on January 9, 1993, Peres explained this rationale to Husseini:

> We know the situation: you speak to Tunisia. We do not prevent you from doing this. However, we cannot negotiate with Arafat, as there are a few problems: First, he wants to negotiate for the Palestinian Diaspora. We have also our Diaspora, but we never negotiated on behalf of our Diaspora. . . . We are now speaking on issues related to the West Bank and Gaza. Only 1/5 of the Jewish people are living in Israel. We have never negotiated in Israel negotiations of the Diaspora.[70]

One aspect of the logic of this approach was to permit PLO officials to go to Gaza and/or to the West Bank and to stand for election there. Another aspect of this logic was to maintain complete deniability about the ongoing dialogue with the PLO officials.

Demonstrating Relevance to the Official Decisionmaking Process

The relevance of the back-channel exercise depended on the support of the senior leadership, and on our capacity to officially deny this support while hinting at its presence. We knew, of course, that our reports of the meetings in Norway were discussed between Rabin and Peres from the very beginning.[71] Rabin also let the Americans know that he was interested in advancing the Palestinian track, and he knew that Arafat was the only Palestinian leader capable of making and enforcing a decision.[72]

In December 1992, after Rabin had ordered more than four hundred Hamas activists in the West Bank and Gaza to be deported to southern Lebanon, the Palestinian negotiation team, expressing solidarity with Hamas, demanded an agreed-on solution of the issue of the deportees as a precondition for restarting negotiations in Washington. But Rabin wanted Arafat to renew the negotiations without solving the deportee issue in advance. This would be a clear indication as to whether Arafat was willing to act in clear opposition to and contradiction of Hamas's demands. Accordingly, Rabin gave Peres the green light needed for pursuing the Norwegian back channel, although he would only become actively involved in the Norway negotiating efforts after Arafat had renewed negotiations in Washington.[73]

Peres had a far more hands-on approach. The Palestinians needed to be shown that the back-channel exercise was relevant and that it was supported by Israel's senior decisionmakers. The need for relevance was a two-way street and had to be based upon constructive input from both the Tunis- and Jerusalem-based Palestinians. To create a sense of relevance, Beilin and I arranged regular meetings between Peres, Husseini, and Ashrawi. We saw to it that the meeting protocols mentioned our presence—knowing, of course, that these protocols were sent to Tunis and read very carefully. We believed that Abu Ala' and Arafat would notice that Peres included Beilin and me, and sometimes Pundak, in these meetings with Husseini. Our presence at these meetings clearly indicated the intimate relationship that we had with Peres and demonstrated the relevance of our work. As it turned out, Abu Ala' not only read Peres's statements to Husseini and Ashrawi but, in order to please Peres, he also proposed ideas that had been discussed in the Peres-Husseini meetings, knowing in advance what Peres's reaction would be.

Similarly, many of the issues that we discussed in Norway had been discussed often before, and sometimes afterward, in the Peres-Husseini meetings. Several instances illustrate the connections between Peres's meetings with Husseini and Ashrawi and the Norway discussions. In a January 9, 1993, meeting with Husseini, discussing the relevance of UN Security Council Resolution 242 and Resolution 338, Peres explained that although the permanent solution could and should be based on these resolutions, this could not be the case for the interim phase of Palestinian self-government.[74] The same idea was reflected in the first draft that we submitted to Abu Ala' and his team on February 11 in Sarpsborg, whose first paragraph read: "The aim of Israeli-Palestinian negotiations is to obtain agreement regarding arrangements for establishing a Palestinian Interim Self-Governing Authority (Body), the elected Palestinian Interim Council, for a period leading to a permanent settlement based on Resolutions 242 and 338."[75] The January 9 meeting also discussed more specific issues, such as land and water rights, regarding which Peres said:

Land, where there is Palestinian life, will be under Palestinian control; land where there is Israeli life, will be under Israeli control; and other areas will be jointly controlled. . . . We refer in the issue of land to three categories: sovereignty, ownership and management. We say sovereignty is open: We are not annexing any territory: ownership will remain as it is; management can be largely under your control, or joint, or certain areas under direct Israeli control.[76]

Our draft proposal in Sarpsborg included provisions for a Palestinian Land Committee and a Palestinian Water Administration Committee, as well as a coordinated land and water resources development plan to be negotiated between these committees and the Israeli government.[77]

In another meeting of Peres, Husseini, and Ashrawi on January 23, Peres asked, "Why do you not take over part of the authority now: treasure, home tax, education, tourism. Why do you have to have it all at once? Begin gradually. In our nation we have always cherished the gradual approach."[78] Paragraph four of the Sarpsborg draft seemed to confirm his advice:

4. Immediately after the signing of this DOP, a transfer of authority from the Israeli military government and the Israeli Civil Administration to the Palestinians and such committees that will be appointed by the Palestinian delegation, will start. . . . The transfer of authority to the Palestinian committees will be of temporary and preparatory nature and will include Palestinian control over taxation, tourism, education, health and social welfare, as well as other agreed upon spheres.[79]

In at least one instance, our back-channel meetings showed how information was being shared among the negotiating parties. At our first meeting in Sarpsborg, on January 21, Abu Ala' referred to the suggestion that feasibility studies begin immediately[80]—a suggestion that Peres had made at the January 9 meeting with Husseini.[81] Abu Ala' also welcomed the idea of speaking of a Gaza-first approach, and he added that

Gaza needs a Mini-Marshall Plan. There can be a free-zone area and it can be extended to Ashdod. There can be joint operations, serving the entire area with two seaports [Ashdod and Gaza]; this will enable us to enhance trade, tourism and other areas of development. . . . We can start by commissioning studies very discreetly.[82]

It was evident that this suggestion was a direct response to the suggestion that Peres had made to Husseini less than two weeks earlier.

Refraining from Exploiting the Other Side's Internal Political Rivalries

The policy of Arafat and Abu Ala' was to make it evident that only they could bring about an agreement. Therefore, they would read and rely on reports they received from Husseini and Ashrawi, and at the same time Abu Ala' would insist on keeping Husseini and Ashrawi out of the loop. Abu Ala' told me in no uncertain terms never to report anything from our meetings in Norway back to Husseini, because the dialogue in Norway would come to an immediate end the moment I did. This prohibition from Abu Ala' contradicted advice that Sari Nusseibeh had given me early in December 1992, before the secret negotiations in Norway had started. Nusseibeh argued that it was necessary to work together with the three major pillars of power within the PLO: with Arafat, because of the political and psychological importance of his leadership; with Mahmoud Abbas, because he represented the PLO's organizational structure; and with Husseini, because he represented the inside leadership of the West Bank and Gaza.

Although the logic of this advice was very convincing, I understood that within the back-channel approach, it was essential to make it evident to Abu Ala' that the Israeli side was not attempting to manipulate one Palestinian political actor against the other. Accordingly, Pundak and I would painstakingly follow the demand by Abu Ala' not to speak to Husseini and Ashrawi about what we were discussing in Norway. The result of this prohibition was that the entire inside leadership remained uninformed throughout the whole process.[83]

Creating a Sense of Reliability

Negotiating with a PLO delegation without specifically recognizing the PLO made it necessary for us to adapt expectations to reality. I described the phases of the exercise ahead of us to Abu Ala' on a small piece paper with four aims: "fact-finding; partial authorization; legitimization and breakthrough." I explained that fact-finding meant that both sides would have to find out whether enough common ground for an understanding could be identified. For partial authorization, indications that the leadership on both sides supported the exercise was needed. In the third phase, that of legitimization, we had to prepare the ground for the officials to come in. Finally, breakthrough was our way of saying that negotiations would be moved from the back-channel approach toward a track-one continuation and conclusion.

We moved relatively quickly along this path. Our first two meetings in Sarpsborg, in late January and mid-February 1993, focused on the fact-finding effort. By our third meeting in March, as well as in the ensuing visit by Terje Larsen to Israel in April, it was made clear to the Palestinians that the Israeli team—Pundak and I—had partial authorization from the official Israeli leadership to negotiate. We then demanded that the PLO team legitimize the back-channel negotiating effort by asking Arafat to refrain from using inciting language (in any form), to renew negotiations in Washington, and to encourage multilateral negotiations on water, economic development, and refugees.

After having laid out the anticipated phases of our exercise, Abu Ala' and I defined and agreed upon seven rules. The first rule was absolute secrecy. Both Abu Ala' and his team and Pundak and I painstakingly kept to this commitment, as did the political leadership in Israel and Tunis. The second rule was to maintain full deniability. Given that Pundak and I were unknown to the press, it was very easy for us to maintain complete deniability during the back-channel phase of the negotiations. When the officials came in, and questions were being asked, deniability was maintained by offering evasive and largely misleading answers. The third rule was to look for a solution-oriented approach and to refrain from disputing the historical development of the Israeli-Palestinian conflict, because we understood that neither side could accept the other's historical narrative. The fourth rule was to refrain from writing a joint protocol; each side would write its own notes, which was useful for maintaining the second rule of deniability.[84] The fifth rule was to refrain from defining an agenda ahead of time while keeping the discussions in Norway open, in order to deal with all possible upcoming subjects and to be able to effectively and carefully listen to the other side. The sixth rule related to an understanding that common ground might, at times, necessitate adopting a language of constructive ambiguity and/or postponing contentious issues for later negotiations. This had a clear impact on the wording of the final Declaration of Principles, and it meant that the phrase "to be agreed upon" was used repeatedly. The seventh and final rule was "the wastepaper basket principle." The rationale of back-channel negotiations was to test different ideas and possibly pursue them for a while, while maintaining the option to throw them out later on.[85]

Understanding What Can and Cannot Be Done in Back-Channel Negotiations

Back-channel negotiations, if pursued professionally, are advantageous for the official negotiators, as they solve the inherent contradictions in any official negotiating process. At the beginning of any negotiations, two contradictory aims must be achieved. It is essential to demonstrate the seriousness of intentions and the willingness to go all the way to reach an agreement, but it is also essential to lay down red lines that can never be crossed in order to create realistic expectations for the possible outcome of the negotiations. If red lines are not defined at the beginning of negotiations, each side (hoping to achieve an optimal outcome) will tend to make demands that cannot be accepted, and thus might all too easily cause the negotiations to break down. Thus, it is essential to be clear with the other side about the limits of concessions, right from the beginning of the negotiations, to prevent crises later on.

Back-channel negotiations make what may be called backward negotiations possible. In a track-one negotiating setup, the first proposals tend to be of a minimalist nature and necessitate substantial further concessions down the line. This results in a serious problem, because the rejection of a minimalist proposal makes it necessary to reward the rejection with a better offer. Thus, in track-one negotiations, the tendency to start with minimal offers may well encourage the negotiating parties to reject proposals made later on. In such a situation, the negotiator is put in a difficult position: If further concessions are rejected, the negotiating process may come to an end; however, if those concessions are made, another rejection may necessitate further concessions.[86]

In backward negotiations, beyond the fact that those negotiations are deniable, the basic aim is to turn the other side into the *demandeur* (i.e., the side that is most interested in reaching an agreement before the official negotiations start). Thus, in any back-channel setup, four parallel tasks can and should be pursued simultaneously:

1. Develop an agreed-on framework for a proposed agreement. For us, this framework came in the first paper submitted to Abu Ala' in Norway.

2. Identify the deal-making concession that the other side is keen to obtain, as in the offer for Arafat to come to Gaza and the proposed empowerment of the Palestinians.
3. Define the red lines that will need to be respected later on when the negotiations move to the official track-one setup. We made it evident that the source of authority would stay with Israel, which meant that Israeli control with regard to security, settlements, and Jerusalem would be maintained.
4. Leave sufficient space to allow for additional demands or even a change of concept later on. For us, this occurred when Singer joined the negotiating effort.

All these tasks were achieved in Norway. However, the back-channel technique also had a threefold downside. First, the back-channel negotiator must be extremely careful not to preempt the decisions of the leadership and create unrealistic expectations. Second, in back-channel negotiations, the official senior echelons of state institutions dealing with all the issues related to the negotiations are excluded, and time and effort are needed to bring them on board. And third, the secrecy of the negotiations does not permit the necessary creation of public legitimacy, and time and patience must be invested to achieve this legitimacy later on.

Pundak and I were extremely careful and thus prevented the creation of false expectations among our Palestinian negotiating partners. But we did not succeed in overcoming the mistrust and anger of the official senior echelons of Israel's state institutions. It was easier for them to direct their anger at having been excluded against us than against Rabin or Peres. However, this was the smaller problem; the more serious problem was their initial mistrust toward the agreement that was concluded. During the follow-up phase, however, after the Declaration of Principles was signed in September 1993, senior officials of the Israeli Defense Forces and other officials in leading positions participated in the negotiations, and this approach eventually overcame the mistrust and the opposition that had been created.

One of the reasons for the many setbacks that were experienced in the Oslo Process was the fact that sufficient work had not been done to create the necessary public legitimacy. On the contrary, the Oslo Agreement was oversold as a peace agreement, which it was not, and this created unrealistic expectations that helped its opponents undermine it.[87]

Successes, Failures, and Lessons Learned, 1991–93

Successes

The Israeli-PLO Declaration of Principles signed on September 13, 1993, followed, in its basic concepts, the provisions laid out in the 1978 Camp David Accords, which supported a two-stage solution to the Palestinian problem. Earlier negotiations between Israel and Egypt and between Israel and Jordan, and also an attempt to reach an agreement between Israel and the inside Palestinian leadership, had all failed. Having learned from the mistakes and pitfalls of the past, it finally became possible to bridge the existing gaps and reach an understanding. The planning exercise carried out in the period 1991–92 laid the foundations for the success of the Oslo back channel in 1993, and the concepts of Palestinian empowerment and the language of a win-win approach helped to overcome the gaps in positions and aims.

When the back-channel exercise started on January 21, 1993, the official Israeli-Palestinian negotiations in Washington had been broken off and the agenda of the Israeli-Palestinian dialogue was dominated by the question of how to solve the issue of the Palestinian deportees who had been sent to Lebanon in December 1992. For Rabin, it was essential that negotiations in Washington be renewed before solving the deportee issue. The work carried out in Norway and the understandings reached in the Sarpsborg document clearly made this possible. Equally important was the fact that the Norwegian back-channel negotiations had created a substantial commitment to engage on the Palestinian side. This turned out to be a commitment strong enough to overcome the substantial changes that Israel demanded from the Palestinian side when negotiations moved from the back channel to track one.

From its inception, the back-channel exercise was embedded in a wider multitrack diplomacy effort supported by the United States, Norway, and Egypt. For the United States, Daniel Kurtzer's support and advice gave us backing from the American peace team during a time of great difficulty, through the end of March and early April 1993. Equally important was the Norwegian contribution. Although the Norwegian team was not permitted to be present during the actual negotiations, because both Abu Ala' and I viewed it as essential that we work out and solve prevailing Israeli-Palestinian problems bilaterally and without outside interference, the Norwegians splendidly facilitated the negotiating effort, both during the back-channel talks and later on, when the negotiations had become official. They played a central and essential supporting role in overcoming the asymmetry between the official Palestinian and unofficial Israeli teams by helping the Israeli team maintain full deniability while simultaneously providing the Palestinian team with assurance of the exercise's relevance. Between meetings, the Norwegians also maintained an important liaison role between the two teams and served as the bearers of messages between both parties.

The importance of the Norwegian contribution increased after the back-channel exercise ended and the secret negotiating effort began at the end of May 1993. Norwegian foreign minister Johan Jørgen Holst leveraged his personal prestige with both sides to achieve mutual confidence-building gains and overcome a serious crisis in July 1993. Norway also offered important logistical support and provided necessary funds. In many ways, Norwegian support for the back-channel exercise also upgraded Norway's diplomatic standing in international affairs, as expressed in the Norwegian chairmanship of the Ad Hoc Liaison Committee, the international forum that oversees and coordinates international support for the Palestinian Authority.

Egypt's supportive role was also of great importance, particularly to the Palestinian team and to the Egyptians themselves. President Clinton, Prime Minister Rabin, and Chairman Arafat all recognized Egypt's leadership position in the Middle East and consulted with Cairo on how best to proceed. For Rabin and Minister of Foreign Affairs Peres, this was a welcome development. It permitted Israel to improve its existing dialogue with Egypt and to develop an additional channel for exchanging information and testing ideas. Part of this dialogue between Rabin, Peres, and Mubarak went on secretly, without our knowledge. It helped the Israeli leadership to check the accuracy of our reports and obtain additional information.

The back-channel effort brought about a historic change. Most parts of the language and the structure of the original Sarpsborg Understanding were introduced into the final official Declaration of Principles that was signed on September 13, 1993. On the Palestinian side, the Oslo Accords resulted in the establishment of the Palestinian Authority in the West Bank and Gaza and permitted the outside leadership to return to the West Bank and Gaza. Furthermore, the concept of gradualism that had been introduced at the planning stage resulted in the signing of six follow-up agreements, which were all concluded within the framework of the Oslo Process:

- The Paris Agreement (April 1994), which would regulate the economic relationship between the emerging Palestinian Authority and Israel;
- The Cairo Agreement, or the Gaza-Jericho Agreement (May 1994),

which provided for the detailed implementation of the Declaration of Principles and the return of Yasser Arafat to Gaza;

- The Oslo II Agreement (September 1995), which established the Palestinian Authority;
- The Hebron Protocol (January 1997), which provided for Israel's withdrawal from parts of Hebron and defined further steps in the negotiating process;
- The Wye River Agreement (October 1998), which provided for an agreed-on Israeli redeployment of forces and for an agreed-on prisoner release; and
- The Sharm el-Sheikh Protocol (September 1999), which summed up the achievements and agreements made until then, and defined the agreed-on next steps.[88]

The strategic impact achieved by the signing of the Oslo Accords was meaningful for Israel's position in both the world and its region. And this achievement paved the way for much more intense US-Israeli security cooperation and the upgrading of Israel's technological capacities. It also contributed largely to the opening of worldwide markets, enabling a substantial increase in the Israeli gross national product per capita in only a few years. The signing of the Declaration of Principles also opened the way to peace negotiations with Jordan and the conclusion of the October 1994 Israeli-Jordanian Treaty of Peace. Moreover, it opened diplomatic relations with several Arab states, as well as security and trade relations for those Arab states that preferred to maintain an informal relationship with Israel.

The Oslo Process also strengthened the commitment to reaching a two-state solution within Israel. The influence of our small group within the ILP was strong enough to commit the party in its May 1997 political platform "to recognize the Palestinian right to self-determination and not to rule out in this connection the establishment of a Palestinian state with limited sovereignty."[89] Eventually, the United States and the entire international community would accept and support the concept of a peaceful, two-state solution between Israel and Palestine.

Failures

In spite of these successes, the strategic concept expressed in the Sarpsborg Document did not survive the change from the back-channel setup to the official negotiations. The decisive change in the concept was the addition of Article VI of the Declaration of Principles, the Interim Agreement. It made the conclusion of a comprehensive Interim Agreement obligatory and necessitated the resolving of all outstanding interim issues instead of providing for a more flexible transition to Permanent Status negotiations.

Another failure, in my opinion, was the deletion of the article that provided for the establishment of an international trusteeship over Gaza. This trusteeship would have made it possible to start security reform from the very beginning, creating a united security structure and a monopoly over the use of force, thus making it far more difficult for the Palestinian leadership to return to violence. Furthermore, the Israeli right wing and settlers' movements would not have been able to accuse Rabin's government of "having given arms to Arafat." No less important, an international trusteeship would have eased the Palestinian state-building effort and would have probably minimized the abuses of corruption and waste. Finally, a trusteeship would have freed Arafat from dealing with state-building tasks and would have enabled him to focus most of his time on the promotion of Permanent Status negotiations. Peres's argument that a trusteeship "was designed to lead eventually to full independence" was accurate.[90] However, we did not succeed in convincing the ILP's leadership at this early stage that a two-state solution was the necessary outcome of the entire process—even though we did succeed in doing so five years later.

Both the Gaza trusteeship and the transition of authorities to Palestinian state-building institutions, without concluding a full Interim Agreement on Palestinian self-government, were intended to support a move toward Permanent Status negotiations as quickly as possible. At the time, we did not expect that the Interim Agreement would become permanent, and we were more afraid of not solving the outstanding core issues of conflict: the nature of the Palestinian national entity, borders, security, settlements, Jerusalem, and refugees.

In hindsight, the most dramatic failure was that massive settlement expansion was not prevented. Although the ILP government of 1992–96 had made the political decision to freeze settlement construction, this did not include construction that was already under way. When Rabin formed his government in July 1992, 40,000 housing units were under construction in the West Bank and Gaza, and the completion of 10,000 of these units was legalized. With the exception of the Jerusalem area, no more construction was permitted. In 1992, the settler population was 106,000; in 1996, when Likud's Benjamin Netanyahu was elected prime minister, it was 145,000—a

37 percent increase.[91] We clearly failed to create the institutional mechanism necessary to limit settlement expansion, as the Palestinian right to veto the expansion of new settlement activities was not granted.

Other Palestinian institutions should have been established. Negotiations defining the powers of Palestinian electrical, trade, environment, and banking authorities should have started immediately, as preliminary understandings for most of these agreements would not have been too difficult to reach and would have increased the prestige of the Palestinian leadership and laid the foundations for a solid process of Palestinian state building. Furthermore, though language of empowerment was maintained in the official Declaration of Principles, the substance was severely curtailed by the fact that negotiations to establish these institutions were subordinated to negotiations on the entire Interim Agreement, which made it necessary to deal with more general issues of jurisdiction, powers and responsibilities, and broad legislative powers.[92]

I wrote the final text of annexes 3 and 4 of the Declaration of Principles—based on the ideas expressed in, respectively, the Israeli-Palestinian Cooperation and Working Program, and the Draft for Preparing a Marshall Plan for the West Bank. The aim of these annexes was to use economic development and cooperation to rebuild grassroots support and legitimacy for the peacemaking and Palestinian state-building effort and to overcome the hate and resentment that had erupted as a reaction to the 1987–93 intifada. I was very proud of the fact that Rabin did not change a single word of my text. At the time, however, I did not understand the fact that Rabin's lack of corrections did not indicate strong support, as I had thought, but a lack of supportive focus. Rabin was concerned and preoccupied with leading peace negotiations with both Syria and Jordan and with overseeing the negotiations for an Interim Agreement with the Palestinians. The cooperation plans described in annex 3 had to be dealt with by Israel's Trade and Industry, Energy, and Environment ministries and the like, and Rabin had neither the time nor the energy to interfere with them or guide them. Rabin also felt that annex 4, the economic initiative, would be Peres's domain. However, Peres was engaged in developing economic and other relations with the Arab world and was reticent to give the Palestinians a monopolizing role in this endeavor.

On a more personal level, I overestimated the rationale to seek common ground between the Israeli and the Palestinian national interests and underestimated the power of internal politics and the drive to oppose change. I also failed to understand, at the time, what a dangerous uphill battle awaited us.

Analytical Reflections and Lessons Learned

THE MISSING STRATEGIC FOCUS

The 1978 Camp David Accords laid down negotiating guidelines that, sooner or later, would lead the way to an agreement on a two-state solution, preferably on the basis of a Jordanian-Palestinian confederation formed by the State of Palestine and the Hashemite Kingdom of Jordan. The Oslo Accords of 1993 created the political and institutional framework for such a strategic outcome of negotiations. However, the political and historical constraints accompanying this process were tremendous, and they were manifest in the lack of strategic focus displayed not only by the Israeli and Palestinian sides but also by the other parties that attempted to contribute to the peace process.

In his study *Imagined Peace, Discourse of War: The Failure of Leadership, Politics, and Democracy in Israel, 1992–2006*, Lev Grinberg argues that the political space created by the Israeli political system dramatically limited the decisionmaking capacities of the Israeli leadership.[93] The Israeli electoral system tended to create a highly divisive political landscape that did not permit the formation of governments with workable majorities. Small splinter parties that were able to obtain one or two Knesset seats often could control the balance in favor of or against the government and thus had to be bought off, which as a rule caused public outrage and opposition to whatever the government would then decide to do. The political division of the Israeli public into a roughly 20:60:20 structure—with 20 percent of the population opposing any concessions to the Palestinians, 20 percent willing to offer far-reaching concessions to the Palestinians in order to achieve peace, and the remaining 60 percent undecided—created an extremely volatile political environment. In this explosive environment, the Israeli leadership promoting the peace process, Labor's Rabin and Peres, lacked a clear strategic focus. Peres at the time opposed a two-state solution and hoped to create a kind of Israeli-Palestinian-Jordanian condominium over the West Bank and Gaza, dividing various authorities among those three stakeholders. Rabin wanted to stabilize the interim phase of Palestinian self-government, and he had not yet made up his mind where to take it from there. Together, the prevailing personal and strategic differences between the two leaders also contributed to their inability to form a single strategic approach.

On the Palestinian side, the situation was not much better. The PLO's ideological ethos was based on fighting for "the right of return" (i.e., the return of all refugees to their former homes in what had become Israel) and "the right of resistance" (the need to adopt the armed struggle against Israel), and as a result it clearly lacked the ethos of state building. Likewise, PLO chairman Arafat thought and acted like the leader of a revolutionary movement. Over a twenty-five-year period, he had developed survival strategies, tactics, and techniques that all clearly contradicted ways to meet the basic needs of creating functioning institutions of state. Most political decisions, for example, were made by manipulating the different echelons of Palestinian leadership, outside the existing institutions. And as long as he would live, Arafat would play one armed Palestinian group against the other and would refrain from creating a monopoly on the use of force and a clear chain of command, both of which were basic preconditions for Palestinian state building.

The United States tended to support the peace process, but it similarly lacked a clear strategic focus. The common assumption in Washington was that "the United States could not want peace more than the parties themselves."[94] Kurtzer and his colleagues were even more critical: "In general, we are astounded by America's poor performance; some advances have been made along the way. . . . But these steps have not been translated into an overall success owing to alternating bouts of peace process frenzy and freeze, too much or too little involvement, the persistent lack of preparations even for summit meetings, the absence of strategy at key moments and the degree to which inside warfare in Washington undercut opportunities for making progress."[95] And the role of the United States in providing the parties with necessary political, security, and financial assurances and support, creating supportive regional and international coalitions assisting in the implementation of agreements made, or putting the blame on one or the other side, in order to create a new momentum for peacemaking, was not replaceable by any other power.

This situation made it evident at the time of signing the Oslo Accords, and even more today, that the direction toward a two-state solution had been taken. However, the following lessons learned from the Oslo Process would not prevent further ups and down in subsequent negotiations.

THE DANGER OF OVERSELLING ACHIEVEMENTS AND THE NEED TO PROVIDE THE PUBLIC WITH A CREDIBLE OUTLOOK OF ANTICIPATED UNFOLDING DEVELOPMENTS

Moving from conflict situations toward peace building creates no small challenges. The first issue with which we had to deal was how to present the Oslo Accords to the public. Rabin and Peres were tempted to present the September 1993 Declaration of Principles as a complete and final peace agreement, and this was the general implication they gave of it. But it would have been more accurate for them to describe it as the beginning of a peace process that might face further difficulties down the road. It was undoubtedly a great mistake to create unrealistic public expectations for the Oslo Accords. Any public wants to be reassured, but it also wants and needs to be prepared for potential difficulties. A more in-depth socio-psychological understanding of how to manage public expectations for a major diplomatic process is still needed.[96]

THE NECESSITY (AND THE DANGER) OF EXCLUDING THE SENIOR ECHELONS OF GOVERNMENT FROM THE BACK-CHANNEL EFFORT

Because deniability was necessary for the success of the back-channel negotiating effort, Prime Minister Rabin excluded the senior echelons of Israel's professional leadership—including the military and intelligence chiefs and the official diplomatic corps—from the entire exercise. However, when it came to implementing the agreement, the professional leadership was required to take on this responsibility, even though it had not participated in its development. Rabin solved the problem by defining a difference between the Declaration of Principles—the political principles of the agreement—and its implementation. He empowered the professional leadership of Israel's government authorities to lead the follow-up negotiations and to translate the principles that had been agreed upon into practice. The discussions on implementation led to the conclusion of the May 4, 1994, Cairo Agreement (for more on this agreement and its conclusion, see chapter 5).

In hindsight, this approach was not good enough. Senior government officials resented the fact that they had been excluded from the Norwegian negotiating experience, which caused them to oppose the agreement with the PLO. Various techniques could have been adopted to avoid such a reaction. For example, in most cases the opposition was based on personal rather than substantial strategic or technical factors. If the prime minister had dedicated more time to speaking with the heads of the Israeli Defense Forces, the security services, and other important agencies, he might have been able to better overcome their opposition. Planning seminars or other direct types of involvement might also have helped to mitigate the opposition of those who had been excluded from the back-channel negotiation exercises.

The Need to Define the Tasks of Third-Party Support and Gradual Development

In the original Sarpsborg Document, I had gone far in proposing an international trusteeship for Gaza as well as a third-party arbitration clause for negotiations on all outstanding issues. Neither of these suggestions was acceptable to Peres and Rabin. Instead, Peres made a great effort to mobilize substantial economic aid for the Palestinians. Seen from hindsight, it would have been necessary to add four other functions for international oversight and support in addition to this economic aid effort: (1) helping the Palestinian Authority to create a unified chain of command, (2) holding the Palestinians responsible for taking actions against acts of terrorism and violence committed by Hamas or other Palestinian actors, (3) overseeing and controlling the expansion of Israeli settlements, and (4) providing greater oversight for the implementation (or nonimplementation) of the economic aid agreements. However, none of these functions received support, either from the Israelis and Palestinians or from a third party.

Observers of the Oslo Process have tended to argue that the principle of gradualism—taking incremental steps—was a mistake. In this context, Kurtzer and his coauthors wrote: "The Oslo Process, built on the foundations of the 1978 Camp David Accords, was predicated on the assumption that the prospects of a comprehensive settlement would be enhanced if the parties passed through interim phases during which implementation of agreements and changes in behavior would instill confidence and trust. The theory failed, however, when confronted with reality."[97] To sustain this argument, Kurtzer and his coauthors refer to continued Palestinian acts of terrorism, continuing Israeli settlement activities, the lack of Palestinian institution building, and Israeli security checks preventing Palestinian economic growth.[98]

This argument criticizes the option taken and suggests a different approach that was not tested; that is, one that did not move incrementally but rather was a single step toward a comprehensive Permanent Status Agreement. The historical truth is that in 1993, neither the Israelis nor the Palestinians had matured enough in their political thinking to make a two-state solution possible. In essence, the argument against the incremental approach that was taken seeks a quick fix and fails to understand that protracted existential conflicts, as in the Israeli-Palestinian context, can only be resolved in a time frame of many decades.[99] To assume that a full Permanent Status Agreement dealing with Jerusalem, territory, borders, refugees, and settlements would not be tested most forcefully by massive violent opposition similarly appears to be unrealistic and under-estimates the ideological and emotional commitment of the many Israeli and Palestinian groups opposing a two-state solution. The same criticism fails to understand that the process of Palestinian state building—the cre-ation of the essential state institutions, the establishment of a functioning state apparatus, and the transition from revolutionary fighting units to an enforced monopoly on the use of force—all need time. Finally, the process of reconciliation between the Israeli and Palestinian societies will need even more time.[100]

The problem was not the incremental approach. More justified criti-cism would be to argue that a hands-on approach was needed from the beginning to contain the expansion of Israeli settlements, to assist in Palestinian state building, and to offer Israel and the Palestinians sufficient support in fighting terrorism and violence. What could be achieved, and was achieved, by concluding the Israel-PLO Declaration of Principles of September 13, 1993, was to show the best direction forward—albeit along a painful and difficult path.

Chapter 5

Preparing for Permanent Status:
The First Attempt, 1993–96

From September 1993 to May 1996, our group worked to conclude principles and guidelines for a Permanent Status Agreement with our Palestinian partners. These efforts brought about the conclusion of the "Beilin–Abu Mazen Understanding." From a theoretical point of view, this was a pure track-two exercise that did not obtain its political goal; however, this chapter discusses the lessons learned from our work.

Historical Background

From September 13, 1993, when the Oslo Agreements were signed, to May 29, 1996, when Benjamin Netanyahu and those who opposed the Oslo Agreements won the Knesset elections in Israel, two parallel processes were working against each other. On the government level, the negotiating process was continuing successfully. On May 4, 1994, Israel and the Palestine Liberation Organization (PLO) signed the Gaza-Jericho Agreement (also called the Cairo Agreement). This document specified Israel's military withdrawal from most of the Gaza Strip, excluding Jewish settlements and the land around them, and from Jericho in the West Bank. Even after the negotiations, Jericho remained a point of contention. After agreeing on a map that limited a Palestinian self-government to the Jericho area and clearly excluded access to the King Hussein Bridge that connected the West Bank with Jordan, Arafat refused, during the signing ceremony in Cairo, to sign the map, causing a major incident and an extremely angry remark from Mubarak.[1] Following the agreement, Arafat left Tunis and took up residence in Gaza early in July 1994 to assume his position as the head of the Palestinian Authority (PA), the representative body under the Oslo Agreements.

On September 28, 1995, the Interim Agreement on the West Bank and the Gaza Strip (commonly referred to as the Oslo II Agreement) was signed in Washington. This agreement divided the West Bank into three regions: Area A, comprising 12 percent of the territory and including the main Palestinian towns (except Hebron and East Jerusalem) under full Palestinian control; Area B, comprising 27 percent of the territory (including most of the Palestinian villages in the West Bank) under Palestinian administrative and Israeli security control; and Area C, the remaining 61 percent of the West Bank that included settlements, army facilities, public land and roads, and the entire Jordan Valley and Dead Sea area, which would remain under Israeli security and administrative control.[2]

In October 1994, the Israel-Jordan Peace Treaty was signed. Multilateral negotiations on arms control, economic development, water usage, environmental concerns, and refugees continued until 1996, enabling Israeli negotiators to touch base with partners from thirteen Arab states. Simultaneous efforts were made, unsuccessfully, to try to achieve peace between Israel and Syria.[3]

These agreements, however, were overshadowed by bad developments. Opposition to the Oslo Accords turned violent on both the Israeli and Palestinian sides. On the Israeli side, the Oslo Accords and the establishment of the PA destroyed the dream of "Greater Israel," aimed at incorporating Judea and Samaria (the West Bank) and the Gaza Strip into Israel's sovereign territory.[4] The Palestinian side claimed that the Oslo Accords contradicted the original PLO Covenant and the Covenant of the Islamic Resistance Movement, Hamas. Both covenants spoke of the Palestinian ambition to rule over the entire area of Palestine, and advocated an ongoing armed struggle against Israel.[5] On February 25, 1994, Baruch Goldstein, a settler from Hebron, murdered twenty-nine Palestinians during prayer at the Ibrahimi Mosque at the Tomb of the Patriarchs in Hebron, bringing about a vicious circle of retaliatory Palestinian suicide bombings against Israeli targets.[6] These actions led to a steadily growing Israeli right-wing incitement against Prime Minister Yitzhak Rabin and the so-called Oslo Criminals—Shimon Peres, Yossi Beilin, Ron Pundak, and me. Jewish militants led by several extremist rabbis, such as Rabbi Dov Lior in Hebron, were (and still are) convinced that God had ordained the Jewish people to return to all of Judea and Samaria and prevent any foreign sovereignty there.[7] In the eyes of these religious extremists, the ongoing terrorist acts against Israeli targets were a direct outcome of Rabin's willingness to "give up" parts of "Eretz Yisrael," and several rabbis issued statements denouncing Rabin as a traitor.[8] This radical right-wing sentiment culminated on November 4, 1995, when a Jewish extremist named Yigal Amir assassinated Rabin. The political implications of Rabin's assassination, according to one analysis, "may have had more impact on the failure of the peace process to move rapidly than almost anything else," leading many of those involved in the process to conclude that Rabin's death was "the single most significant setback for reaching a final status settlement between Israel and the Palestinians."[9]

No less destructive than the vicious circle of violence and incitement was the lack of trust created by Arafat's behavior toward the Israeli side, from the very day that the Oslo Accords were signed in Washington. The Declaration of Principles that had been initialed in Oslo by both sides on August 20, 1993, referred to "the Government of the State of Israel and the Palestinian team (in the Jordanian-Palestinian delegation to the Middle East Peace Conference) (the "Palestinian Delegation").[10] This wording maintained the Israeli claim that Israel was negotiating not with the PLO but with a Palestinian delegation from the West Bank and the Gaza Strip. Only three weeks later did both delegations exchange formal letters of mutual recognition, which offered Israeli recognition of the PLO and committed the PLO to recognize the right of existence of the State of Israel, to refrain from violence, and to act to prevent any acts of terrorism against Israel.[11] The Israeli side anticipated that the text signed in Washington would be identical to the text that had been signed in Oslo, but at the very last moment on the day of the Washington ceremony, Arafat demanded that the Washington text be changed to refer to the PLO as the official negotiating partner. The Israeli side fully understood the reasoning and substance of his demand, because it offered important additional legitimacy to the agreement and gave the PLO an important internationally recognized legal standing. However, the way in which the request was put forward—at the last moment, creating for Rabin the dilemma of whether to cancel the ceremony or to give in to blackmail—caused much anger on the Israeli side. This was the real reason for Rabin's hesitation to shake Arafat's hand during the signing ceremony on September 13: a scene that was seen by the entire world and created a bad start, reflecting a lack of trust.

Exacerbating the mutual mistrust, Arafat smuggled arms and a Palestinian militant (who had been refused entry by Israel) into Gaza when he entered it at the beginning of July 1994.[12] More detrimental, Arafat refused to fully cooperate to prevent Palestinian acts of terrorism and to change the text of the Palestinian Covenant, which contradicted his obligations in the agreement. Late in 1994, Rabin had asked Arafat to arrest Muhammad Deiff, one of the masterminds of Hamas's terror activities. Although Israeli intelligence knew that Arafat had met with Deiff the day before, Arafat lied to Rabin's face, denying any knowledge of Deiff. Arafat's reply was seen not merely as a lie but also as an indication that he had given at least a "yellow light" to Deiff's planned terrorist acts.[13] The Israeli interlocutors, among them the military intelligence chief and future defense minister Moshe Yahalon, felt betrayed. This did not create the trust necessary for negotiations and the conclusion of any agreement.

I would argue that as long as Rabin was leading the Israeli government, the Palestinians had few reasons for grievance. The Israeli side was by no means perfect, and the vicious circle of terrorism and enforced Israeli security action caused hardship on the Palestinian side. Nevertheless, Rabin made a major effort to create a fair and decent partnership with Arafat—a fact that the Palestinians and Arafat personally acknowledged.[14] In this situation, the strategic question for Israel was whether Rabin's five-phase approach of disengagement, diffusion, trust, negotiations, and then peace should be pursued[15]—indicating a prolonged process of disengaging and diffusing tension with the Palestinians that only then would be followed by building trust and negotiating a peace agreement—or whether our group's approach to move faster toward Permanent Status negotiations and peace should be undertaken as soon as possible.

The Track-Two Effort to Prepare a Permanent Status Draft Concept

Initial Considerations

The official Israeli and Palestinian track-one negotiating teams were concerned with reaching headway toward an interim solution and had no time to think ahead about how to prepare for Permanent Status. In the Sarpsborg Document, we had suggested moving as fast as possible to permanent status negotiations. Thus, from a practical as well as an analytical point of view, we thought it was essential to prepare a draft concept for Permanent Status in a track-two dialogue with the relevant Palestinian partners. In an April 1994 policy paper that I prepared for Beilin (at the time deputy foreign minister), influenced by Goldstein's murderous attacks and unfolding Palestinian terrorist acts, I referred to the dangers ahead of us:

> First, elections being set at the latest for the autumn of 1996, will create tremendous time pressure and the need to obtain visible achievements very quickly and thus may encourage the Palestinians to adopt either dilatory and/or brinkmanship tactics. Second, during the coming months, whether negotiations on final status will start or not, continued acts of terror—both Jewish and Arab—have to be anticipated. Third, management problems of the newly estab- lished Palestinian Self-Government Authority (PNA) and internal difficulties within the Palestinian body politic may be anticipated and will tend to create radicalizing and/or demoralizing overspill effects upon Israel. Fourth, ongoing negotiations between the GoI [Government of Israel] and the PLO will tend to encourage the Palestinian leadership to stress the existing gap and raise demands regarding Jerusalem, return to the 1967 borders, implementing the "right of return" etc. . . . Thus, moving towards final status negoti- ations, tactics will have to be formulated that will minimize those dangers and will provide the Israeli public with the awareness that security threats are being diminished and substantial political gains are being achieved.[16]

To continue negotiations, we needed to find Palestinian partners for a track-two exercise. We had to analyze the difficulties ahead of us, test various negotiating approaches, and explore the best ways and means to feed our ideas and the emerging concepts to the Israeli political, military, and economic leadership.

Identifying the Track-Two Negotiating Partners

In October 1993, shortly after the signing ceremony in Washington, Beilin, Pundak, and I traveled to Tunis for multilateral negotiations, hoping to find a way to continue our efforts. We wanted to suggest to Chairman Arafat that preparing preliminary understandings for Permanent Status on a track-two basis be done with his chosen interlocutors.

Pundak and I met Arafat without Beilin. After our meeting with Arafat in Tunis in October 1993, we waited until May 1994 before Arafat suggested that Pundak and I work with the "Londoners": Ahmed Khalidi[17] and Hussein Agha.[18] Khalidi was from a leading Palestinian family in Jerusalem, and Agha was a Lebanese Shi'ite. They had attended grammar school together in Beirut in the 1950s and had joined the Fatah movement in the early 1960s. They then moved to London to continue their studies and had remained there, working as experts on the Middle East and developing close personal relationships with PLO leaders such as Arafat and Mahmoud Abbas.

The Swedish government, which was interested in competing with the Norwegians in sponsoring headway in the Israeli-Palestinian peace process, decided to take Khalidi, Agha, Pundak, and me under its wing. It provided us with all the necessary facilities to meet in Sweden on a regular basis. To prepare the dialogue with Khalidi and Agha, we revisited the June 1992 Israeli Labor Party (ILP) platform as our basic guidelines for negotiations. (Knowing that we might have to go beyond the constraints of this platform, Beilin repeatedly discussed with me the rather narrow maneuvering space that had to be respected.)

In Norway, I had tested the negotiating approach and the various political arguments that I would present to the Palestinian negotiators in cooperation with Pundak, whose role was to anticipate the expected Palestinian response. We tried to forsee what concepts and arguments would be useful and where a different line of thinking and arguing needed to be adopted. In the back-channel negotiations in Norway, we had obtained well-defined guidelines and knew what our maneuvering space was. In the track-two set up in Sweden, the maneuvering space appeared to be substantially larger. It was my task to pursue concepts that would be acceptable to the Israeli leadership; Pundak's task was to seek concepts that would obtain an agreement from the Palestinian side. (In my opinion, Pundak identified too well with the Palestinian position at times, and seemed to cross the line to the other side. This remained, of course, a matter of interpretation, though I found it to be rather worrisome.)

Analyzing the Difficulties Ahead

The First Difficulty: Contradicting Narratives

Pundak and I understood that the biggest obstacle to an agreement was the diametrically opposing narrative on both sides of most of the core issues:

the nature and existence of both Israel and Palestine, the question of territory and boundaries, the existence of Israeli settlements, the status of Jerusalem, and the position of Palestinian refugees. It was clear that the conflicting narratives would make it extremely difficult to seek public support for a compromise formula in either Israel or Palestine. In many ways, the narratives dictated the negotiating demands of each side, and on certain issues they simply diverged too much.

THE NATURE AND EXISTENCE OF ISRAEL AND PALESTINE

In the 1978 Camp David Accords, the Government of Israel recognized "the legitimate rights of the Palestinian people and their just requirements."[19] Nevertheless, for decades many Israelis had denied the existence of the Palestinian people and accordingly opposed the establishment of a Palestinian state. Moreover, the West Bank was (and still is) referred to in Israel's official language as Judea and Samaria, the biblical names that imply the denial of the legitimacy of a Palestinian state in that territory.

On the Palestinian side, the recognition of the State of Israel's right to exist was nominally achieved on December 14, 1988. Responding to the US demand, PLO chairman Arafat had formally declared this right in a speech in Geneva.[20] However, the State of Israel's existence from May 1948 continued to be perceived as the *Naqba*, or "catastrophe," that had resulted from an ongoing imperialist and colonialist process of exploitation, impoverishment, and expropriation of the Palestinian people. A sector of the Palestinian people that supported the Hamas movement rejected the recognition of Israel altogether and remained committed to the struggle against Israel's very existence.[21]

TERRITORIAL AND BOUNDARY QUESTIONS

The moderate Palestinian approach was to say that the outcome of the 1948 war and the cease-fire lines in force until June 4, 1967, had divided British Mandatory Palestine in such a way as to permit Israel to gain 78 percent of the territory, leaving only 22 percent for the Palestinians. Thus, the Palestinian moderate and minimalist views were that there was no way that the Palestinians could make any further concessions on territory.[22]

The Palestinian position left no common ground for a compromise formula that would seem acceptable to a wide coalition within Israel. Both the Israeli right wing and the Israeli peace camp believed that the

Jewish people had a legitimate claim to its historical homeland, Judea and Samaria. The Israeli national-religious camp did not want to give up control over Judea and Samaria (i.e., the West Bank) for ideological reasons, while others took the same position due to security considerations. The Israeli peace camp argued against these positions, stating that, ideologically, the maintenance of the Jewish and democratic character of the State of Israel necessitated giving up the territories of the West Bank and Gaza. It also argued that conditions had to be negotiated that would augment Israel's security not only with security provisions but also with provisions for peace and cooperation.

To bridge the diverging internal Israeli positions and interests, the ILP advocated a territorial compromise, arguing that the return to the June 4, 1967, lines was neither acceptable for security reasons nor legally necessary, given that the June 4, 1967, borders of the West Bank and Gaza had never been internationally recognized, and it was therefore up to the parties to negotiate such a line.[23]

ISRAELI SETTLEMENTS

The Palestinian position was that, according to international law, the occupying power was not permitted to establish settlements; such an act could be persecuted as a war crime.[24] The Israeli legal position was that settlements on state land, rather than on private Palestinian land, were in line with international law.[25] (See chapter 2 for a discussion of the state land/ private land definitions and discrepancies.) The narrative gap seemed unbridgeable as long as the Palestinians demanded categorically that Israeli withdraw and evacuate all settlements to the pre–June 1967 cease-fire lines, and the Israeli narrative necessitated a territorial compromise beyond those lines.

THE STATUS OF JERUSALEM

Historically, the association of the Jewish people with Jerusalem dates back to the Patriarch Abraham, the founding father of Judaism, because it is where he fought the kings of Sodom and Gomorra and where he established an altar for the sacrifice of Isaac at God's behest. King David made Jerusalem the cornerstone of the religious and political unification of Israel when he transferred the Ark of the Covenant to Jerusalem and laid the foundations for the Holy Temple. The concept of Jerusalem as "the Holy City" dates from this time and is the reason for Jewish laws that accorded legal status to the holiness of the city. The destruction of the First Temple in 586 BCE and the Second Temple in 70 CE added substantial historical, emotional, and religious weight to the connection of the Jewish people to Jerusalem.[26] This connection is further strengthened by the Jewish religious belief that the Day of Judgment will occur in Jerusalem on the Temple Mount.[27]

The emotional strength and impact of the Jewish connection to Jerusalem became very apparent to one of our Palestinian interlocutors, Hikmat Ajouri, when he and I attended the wedding of an employee of the Economic Cooperation Foundation (ECF). I translated what was being said in the wedding ceremony, including the passage "If I forget thee, Jerusalem, my tongue shall get stuck on my cheek and my right hand should get paralyzed," and explained the tradition of stepping on and breaking a glass during the ceremony in order to remember the destruction of the Temple. Ajouri said to me, "This is terrible." I asked him what was terrible about the marriage of a lovely young couple, and he responded that that was not his point. "The point," he said, "is that you will never give up Jerusalem."

Another part of the Jewish narrative on Jerusalem was to argue that in Islam the importance of Jerusalem is far less central than in Judaism. Jerusalem's religious importance is second to the cities of Mecca and Medina for Muslims, and Jerusalem never became a capital of any Muslim empire. Furthermore, under Mamluk and Ottoman rule, from the thirteenth until the twentieth centuries CE, Jerusalem remained a small provincial town of little importance.[28] In Judaism, however, Jerusalem is the holiest place, and no place in the world can compare to its importance and holiness. I discussed the essence of this approach with Faisal Husseini, whose response was simple, but convincing. "True," he said, "but because Jerusalem is of such importance to you, it has gained tremendous political importance with the Palestinians, the Arabs, and the Islamic world."[29]

The Palestinian narrative denied any Jewish connection to Jerusalem. Even as late as the Camp David Conference in July 2000, Arafat sat with the Israeli team and argued that there had never been a Jewish presence in Jerusalem. Perhaps, he insisted, what Israel referred to as Jerusalem had been in Yemen or in Nablus.[30] In the Muslim narrative, the basic argument is that Jerusalem was originally a Palestinian city and was only later conquered by the Jews. The city is "most holy to Christianity and Islam," and its sanctity must be defended against any transgression.[31] On Jerusalem, it seemed almost impossible to recognize any rights of the other side, and it was most likely that any agreement would be seen as a zero-sum game, causing each side to protest any concession offered to the other side.

THE POSITION OF PALESTINIAN REFUGEES

The narratives related mainly to the question of guilt. The Israeli position was simple: On November 29, 1947, Israel had accepted UN General Assembly Resolution 181, partitioning British Mandatory Palestine into Jewish and Arab states. The following day, the Palestinians started the war in order to prevent the implementation of the UN resolution, which would have provided for the establishment of a Jewish state in substantial parts of the territory of British Mandatory Palestine. But because the Palestinian forces were not strong enough to defeat the Israelis alone, the neighboring Arab states invaded Israel on May 15, 1948, with the intention of destroying it. And because the Palestinian military struggle against Israel was in defiance of the UN decision of November 1947, and the Arab invasion of Israel in May 1948 was a war of aggression in denial of the international legitimacy of Israel gained by the UN General Assembly resolution, from the Israeli point of view Israel's 1947–49 War of Independence was a defensive war and the Palestinian refugee problem was the direct outcome of Palestinian and wider Arab aggression against Israel.[32]

The Palestinians' narrative was quite different. For them, Israel's presence in the Middle East was a by-product of European colonialism, and Israel had driven the Palestinian people out of their homes in the 1948 war. Arab leaders throughout the region had promised the Palestinians that they would be able to return to their former homes, and UN General Assembly Resolution 194 of December 1948, along with the Progress Report of the UN mediator on Palestine, suggested (among other proposals) that Palestinian refugees had the right to return to their homes or ask for compensation. To stress the desire and determination to return to their former homes in Palestine, most refugee families kept the keys to the homes that they (or their grandparents) had left behind in order to be able to return. Keeping a "key" in the homes in every refugee camp had both symbolic and political importance, given that no Palestinian leader could agree to give up the "right of return."[33]

Because no Palestinian leader would have the legitimacy to give up the Palestinian right of return, and the Israelis perceived the Palestinian right of return as an attempt to outnumber the Jewish population in Israel and eventually eliminate Israel's existence as a state where the Jewish people exercise their right to self-determination, it appeared that only strong leadership on both sides would make it possible to reach an agreement on any compromise formula that the negotiators (whether track one or track two) might devise.

The Second Difficulty: The Gap between the November 1988 Resolutions of the Palestinian National Council and the ILP's 1992 Platform

The very essence of our work was to bridge the gap between the Palestinian National Council's November 15, 1988, peace process decisions, which demanded that Israel withdraw from all territories occupied in June 1967, including Arab Jerusalem, and the right of return for all Palestinian refugees,[34] and the ILP's 1992 electoral policy platform, which spoke of the need to reach a territorial compromise, requested maintaining the municipal borders of Jerusalem as demarcated after the June 1967 war, and rejected the Palestinian right of return.[35]

In spite of the obvious gap between the positions of each side, these policy guidelines provided both good and bad news. The good news was that the Palestinian side was very flexible on tactical issues. It was not only willing to adapt Palestinian short-term demands to Israeli political needs but was also interested in meeting Israeli demands in order to pave the way for a comprehensive agreement. The bad news was that on strategic issues of Permanent Status and the finality of claims, there was little or no room for Palestinian flexibility.[36] All the Palestinians could do was to postpone demands to a later stage.

On the Israeli side, we quickly realized that the provisions of the ILP's 1992 platform did not permit reaching comprehensive common ground. Our political understanding was that with regard to the territorial solution, we could go beyond the ILP's provisions demanding a compromise over West Bank territory. In return, we would need a forthcoming Palestinian position on Jerusalem and refugees and, more important, a Palestinian agreement that if a compromise solution was reached, they would commit to forgo any further demands at a later date. Applying the language of negotiations, we demanded that the Palestinians commit to the "finality of claims" and not necessarily to the "end of conflict," as the ILP's 1992 platform demanded. Paradoxically, room for compromise was relatively large where it was not needed, and it was very narrow in areas where it was needed to achieve the necessary historical breakthrough.

The Third Difficulty: How to Bridge the Gaps between the Leadership on Both Sides

The decisive breakthrough needed to move toward an agreement had to be made by the leadership on both sides. Both Rabin and Peres were afraid of dealing with the Permanent Status issues, although they understood that it had to be done.[37] Rabin was thinking of a territorial solution and clearly understood that this would lead to the establishment of a Palestinian state, which he publicly opposed for a number of tactical reasons. He had not fully made up his mind on how to deal with the issues of borders and Jerusalem, and he wanted an Interim Agreement on the West Bank and the Gaza Strip to create a temporary stabilizing effect with favorable starting conditions for dealing with the Permanent Status issues. His attitude toward the settlements was ambivalent; although he respected or even admired the drive for pioneer work shown by the settlers, he understood that it was necessary to evacuate the settlements to reach a peaceful understanding with the Palestinians.[38] The track-two negotiating team understood that if we could convince the Palestinians to provide effective answers to Rabin's concerns, Rabin would agree to the envisaged two-state solution and the renewed partition of the land, exactly as Ben Gurion had done in 1948.[39]

Peres's views were different. He argued that the world was moving toward a postsovereignty stage, where different components of sovereignty might be divided or shared by different actors. He supported the establishment of a Jordanian-Palestinian confederation and the parallel establishment of a Benelux-style economic arrangement for Jordan, Israel, and Palestine. In such a complex configuration, Peres wanted to negotiate functional arrangements for the West Bank, permitting a division of authority among Israel, Jordan, and the Palestinians that would offer the Palestinians sovereign rights while maintaining Israel's sovereign powers over security arrangements and settlements.[40] On Jerusalem, Peres wrote in his memoirs: "Jerusalem in Israel's view—all of Jerusalem—is sovereign Israeli territory and the capital of our state."[41] His position was to oppose any substantial concession with regard to Jerusalem during the negotiations for an Interim Agreement, while accepting that the issue of Jerusalem would have to be negotiated later on.[42] And Peres viewed the Palestinian refugees' peaceful integration in a new and modern Middle East through economic and social development as the necessary solution.[43]

For Arafat, the essential concern was, first and foremost, that he be able to strengthen his own dominant position and his ability to build a strong internal Palestinian coalition for whatever decisions he made. In addition, he needed support from most of the Arab leadership, particularly from President Hosni Mubarak of Egypt and the kings of Saudi Arabia and Jordan. The Arab states had for decades interfered in Palestinian affairs, and their support for any Permanent Status Agreement was important in order to obtain support from the Palestinians living in the occupied territories, residing in other Arab countries, and living elsewhere. Saudi Arabia, Jordan, and Morocco all had conflicting aspirations with regard to Jerusalem, and it was also for this reason essential to obtain their support. Arafat personally relied particularly on the support of Egypt. He had grown up there and his adored older sister lived there, and Egypt's political role within the Arab world was especially important.

We had to find out whether it was possible to identify common ground between these diverging positions. Beilin's approach was to move one big step forward in order to enable Rabin and Peres to receive substantial political rewards for the necessary concessions that would have to go substantially beyond the limits outlined in the ILP's 1992 platform.[44]

The Fourth Difficulty: Palestinian Terrorism and Israeli Right-Wing Incitement

Responding to Palestinian terrorism, Rabin stated, "We shall fight terror as if there was no negotiating process, and we shall negotiate as if there was no terror." The logic was that it did not make sense to give the terrorists veto power over the negotiating process.[45] However, terrorism created fertile ground for resentment and incitement, and thus unleashed a vicious circle of violence. This eroded the legitimacy of peacemaking and offered ample opportunity for Israel's radical right wing to escalate vicious incitement against Rabin.[46]

In the April 1994 policy paper that I submitted to Beilin, I also discussed "the practical implementation approach" as a possible alternative or fallback. The idea was to combine the struggle against terrorism with a policy of separation between Israel and the Palestinian areas, creating a two-state reality on the ground by reinforcing mutual travel restrictions for Palestinians and Israeli settlers; constructing roads to both separate the Palestinians and the Israeli settlers and enable them to move in and around Jerusalem, the West Bank, and the Gaza Strip; developing low-cost housing programs for Palestinians; improving trade conditions in the area and with Jordan; and reducing the Israeli military presence in Palestinian areas.[47]

The idea of a de facto separation between Israel and the Palestinian territories also circulated within government institutions. The concept had two parts: to construct a security fence to impede movement, and to prepare a detailed plan for the separation of the road, electricity, and water networks. By 1994, a security fence had been constructed around the Gaza Strip and impeded the launching of terror acts from there.[48] However, when Rabin was given the budgetary costs, he decided to postpone most components of the emerging plan for separation and only continue work on the security fence.[49] The political guideline was to conceptually keep to the Green Line (i.e., the June 4, 1967, cease-fire lines) and to build the fence east of the Green Line in order to include settlements west of the line elsewhere in order to compensate. A first pilot version of the fence was put in place in 1996.[50]

Planning Our Work, Step by Step

In pursuing our track-two negotiation strategy, we had six steps in mind:

- First, we would work with our Palestinian interlocutors in Stockholm, Ahmed Khalidi and Hussein Agha, to identify optimal common ground and prevailing gaps in understanding.
- Second, we would test some of the emerging ideas or alternative concepts.
- Third, we would work to bridge prevailing gaps or replace an emerging concept with alternative ideas. This included exploring the range of actors on both sides and the feasibility of possible support from third parties.
- Fourth, we would move toward concluding an understanding that would remain confidential but would form the basis for a more definite policy concept of a fully coordinated Israeli-Palestinian position before May 1996, when Permanent Status negotiations were to start.
- Fifth, we would sell the concept to the senior decisionmakers and adapt it to their ideas.
- Sixth and finally, on the basis of a common Israeli-Palestinian understanding, we would launch a public diplomacy effort to obtain substantial majority support on both sides and to take forceful, coordinated action against terrorism and incitement.

Step One: Identifying Common Ground and Gaps in Understanding

Yossi Beilin's Guidelines

To get Peres and Rabin on board with a Permanent Status Agreement as quickly as possible, Beilin instructed us on the following positions that had to be achieved.

On the nature of the Palestinian state, the ILP's 1992 platform advocated support for a Jordanian-Palestinian confederation. We knew that Peres, however, wanted to create a double structure that permitted the establishment of a Jordanian-Palestinian confederation, which was to be supported by a parallel Israeli-Jordanian-Palestinian economic structure. We also knew that the Palestinians wanted to establish a state of their own. Strategically, we fully supported the idea of a two-state solution that permitted the establishment of a Palestinian state alongside Israel as long as Israel's vital demands were met.

On territory and borders, the ILP's platform advocated a territorial compromise and rejected any return to the June 4, 1967, cease-fire lines. Beilin believed that the two real issues at stake were settlements and security; as long as a maximum number of settlements could be integrated into Israel and become recognized Israeli sovereign territory, and as long as Israel's security needs could be fully addressed, we might be able to accommodate Palestinian territorial demands. As a result, *on settlements*, it was extremely important for Beilin that the settlers who wanted to stay in their residences under Palestinian sovereignty be permitted to do so.

On refugees, much exploratory work on all the components of the question was necessary. However, the basic deal was simple: Palestinian refugees would have the right of return to Palestine, parallel to the right of return of the Jewish people to the State of Israel.[51] Issues of compensation and rehabilitation had to be discussed and agreed upon.

On Jerusalem, Beilin was determined that sovereignty over the disputed areas of East Jerusalem be postponed for twenty-five years. Until then, the capital of Palestine should be outside the city borders of Jerusalem, in Abu Dis and/or al-Eizariya (both of which are former villages that have been integrated in the larger Jerusalem municipal area). Beilin hoped that this arrangement would let the Palestinians assert that they had gained a foothold within Jerusalem, while their claim for sovereignty over the rest of the Arab city of Jerusalem still would be dealt within an agreed-upon time frame.

On security, it was essential that the Palestinian state remain demilitarized, permitting residual Israeli forces to control the Jordan River and maintain early warning stations and other military installations along the Alon axis, which ran east of the mountain ridge crossing the West Bank from north to south, and west of the Jordan Valley, overseeing the eastern littoral of the Jordan River. Israeli security presence in these areas was seen to be essential by Israel's security experts and by general public opinion, in order to deter any Palestinian or other Arab conventional or terrorist attack from the east that would threaten Israel's population centers between Haifa in the north and Ashkelon in the south.[52] The members of our group fully recognized these security concerns, but at the same time we tended to view the security challenges to Israel in the wider context of Israeli-Palestinian-Jordanian relations. We assumed that both the Palestinians and Israel had a common vested interest in preventing any external military or terrorist attacks against Jordan, and we believed that peaceful relations and well-defined security arrangements would make it possible to turn Palestine and Jordan into a bridge between Israel and the Arab world at large.

In Stockholm, Identifying Common Ground and Gaps

The first meeting in Stockholm at the end of the summer of 1994 was friendly and explorative. Our Palestinian interlocutors, Pundak, and I produced four understandings aimed at laying down the rules of our exercise and the issues to be dealt with.[53] At the second meeting in Stockholm, in October 1994, we presented a first written concept as to how to reach a Permanent Status Agreement. During the third meeting in Stockholm, in mid-November 1994, the contours of agreement and disagreement became apparent.

On the nature of the Palestinian entity, our guidelines were to commit our interlocutors to the creation of a Jordanian-Palestinian confederation. Ahmed Khalidi and Hussein Agha did not offer any strong opposition to this, but remarked rather drily that they believed this was not a realistic proposition. *On territory and boundaries,* Khalidi and Agha showed great flexibility under one simple but tough condition: the Israeli annexation of territories beyond the June 4, 1967, cease-fire lines could be acceptable if there was a one-for-one exchange of territory with the Palestinians. *On security,* the Israeli demand to keep residual forces and security installations in the West Bank seemed acceptable to the Palestinians. In fact, movement toward a regional security system on the basis of bilateral arrangements (e.g., Israeli-Jordanian and Israeli-Syrian arrangements) appeared to even be desirable for the Palestinians.

On Jerusalem and refugees, however, it seemed less evident that common ground was achievable. We discussed an approach whereby Arab Jerusalem (i.e., the Arab neighborhoods of the city of Jerusalem) would become the capital of a future Palestinian entity, over which the Palestinians would obtain sovereign rights.[54] The Jewish settlement areas close to (but outside) Jerusalem, as well as Arab areas outside the city border, would be incorporated within the new city limits of Jerusalem. The Municipality of Jerusalem would be formed by its boroughs on the basis of a 2:1 Israeli-Palestinian ratio, and the boroughs would elect the mayor and the municipal council. The Israeli-dominated municipality would establish a municipal police force responsible for the entire Jerusalem area. The mayor and council would direct zoning and planning issues for the entire city, while the limitations of jurisdiction of both governments remained to be defined. This meant that Israel would have complete sovereignty over West Jerusalem and shared sovereignty over East Jerusalem. As a result, Jewish religious rulings with regard to Jerusalem could be fully maintained; Jerusalem could develop further as the cultural center of the Jewish people, wherever they might live; the Jewish population of Jerusalem could live there undisturbed and under secure conditions; security conditions for the wider Jerusalem area could to be controlled and overseen by the Israeli security authorities; and on issues of zoning and planning and municipal management, Israel would maintain a decisive but not exclusive say. In short, all these provisions would ensure that the Jewish character of the city would be maintained within this multicultural setup. At the same time, because the 2:1 ratio would remain intact irrespective of demographic changes, the incentive for Palestinians to move to Jerusalem for political reasons would be diminished. Finally, because zoning and planning would remain under Israeli control, Israel would be able to employ procedural and political means to maintain the city's tolerant and liberal character, which had been created under Jerusalem mayor Teddy Kollek's leadership.[55] It was evident from the discussions in Stockholm that all this could only be achieved in return for Israel's recognition of Al-Quds (the Arab name for Jerusalem) as the capital of Palestine. At the time, I wrote in my diary, "Evidently, selling the idea of Jerusalem as a capital of the Palestinian state at home will not be an easy job—although I am convinced that any agreement without that would only incite Palestinian irredentism."[56]

On refugees, common ground was even less evident than on Jerusalem. Although Khalidi and Agha addressed the issue in very soft tones, their message was clear: A plethora of practical arrangements could be discussed to limit the Palestinians' demand to return to their former homes in Israel, but using the term "right of return" was politically and symbolically essential to make the agreement acceptable.[57] From an Israeli point of view, the Palestinian demand for this right of return clearly contradicted the very essence of the idea of a two-state solution. Partitioning former British Mandatory Palestine into two states meant that the Palestinians had the right of return to their state and the Jewish people had the right of return to Israel; the Palestinians could not ask for a state of their own and simultaneously claim the right of return to Israel, with the intent of turning Israel into a second Palestinian state through demographic change.

Our deliberations in Stockholm with Khalidi and Agha resulted in a dilemma. On one hand, it appeared that substantial concessions from the Palestinian side could be reached. These would delineate the minimum concessions that the Palestinians required from Israel to reach a Permanent Status Agreement and would demonstrate that the Palestinians were undertaking a remarkable effort to achieve peace. On the other hand, the guidelines for compromise that Beilin had laid out could not be maintained. The common ground that we were identifying in Stockholm needed to go beyond these guidelines by further delineating Israeli concessions to the Palestinians. The challenge ahead was tremendous. We needed to check the viability of a Jordanian-Palestinian confederation, overcome prevailing substantial gaps with regard to Jerusalem and refugees, and work on security issues in much more detail.

Step Two: Testing Emerging Ideas or Alternative Concepts

GETTING ORGANIZED AND ASKING A FIRST QUESTION

To advance to the second step, we made several procedural moves. We enlarged the number of Palestinian interlocutors substantially and pursued, in addition to our work with Khalidi and Agha, dialogues with our other Palestinian contacts, including Nabil Shaath, Faisal Husseini, and Sari Nusseibeh. In cooperation with the Jordanian leadership, we tested the issue of moving toward a Jordanian-Palestinian confederation. Finally, we asked for support from international actors—namely, the governments of France and the Netherlands—to establish multilateral working groups to deal with most of the outstanding issues, while conferring with other international actors (e.g., the Americans, the Austrians, and senior European Union officials) to seek possible supportive solutions.

The first question we posed was whether it made sense to deal with all outstanding core issues at once or whether it was preferable to take a sequential approach. Three different approaches were discussed. General Yehia Abdel-Razzeq, an elderly Palestinian who joined Shaath in a meeting with us in Stockholm in mid-February 1995, suggested negotiating one Permanent Status issue after the other, starting with security and moving on (in order) to dealing with border issues, agreeing on solving the settlement question, seeking a solution over Jerusalem, and finally dealing with the refugee issue.[58] Back at home, Nimrod Novik took the same approach, saying that only a "security and border first approach" could succeed.[59] In contrast, Khalidi and Agha argued that all the core issues were interrelated and thus had to be dealt with as a package deal. In my own opinion, the deal-making Israeli concession was to accept a one-for-one swap deal on territory. I believed that in return we could, and had to, achieve substantial concessions with regard to Jerusalem and refugees. Dealing with security and territory up front would make it more difficult for us to obtain the necessary quid pro quo on other issues later on.

Nusseibeh, interestingly enough, offered us a third approach. At a seminar in Paris on the Jerusalem question in May 1995, he argued that seeking to solve the outstanding core issues would cause further fragmentation of Palestinian society and thus result in terrorist acts against Israel. A slowed-down process pursued by a Likud government in Israel might, however, permit the Palestinian leadership to consolidate in opposition to Likud and to develop closer cooperation between the Palestinian and the Israel peace camps.[60] We did not agree with Nusseibeh, because we doubted the willingness of a Likud government to move ahead, even slowly. However, looking back at the unfolding Israeli-Palestinian dynamics during Netanyahu's first government between May 1996 and May 1999, Nusseibeh's reasoning was not far off. During those years, intense coordination of policies among Beilin, Novik, Haim Ramon (who had been Israeli health minister, trade union secretary-general, and interior minister before May 1996, and thereafter remained a member of the Knesset), Mahmoud Abbas, and Palestinian chief negotiator Saeb Erekat, did occur and kept the Oslo Process on track.[61]

The conclusion that we drew from these discussions was that it was important to tackle all the core issues of the conflict together in order to create a fair give-and-take dynamic between agreements on territory, settlements, Jerusalem, and refugees. Understanding the great distance that both sides had to travel in order to reach acceptable compromise solutions, we anticipated the need for a two-phase approach on Permanent Status.[62]

MAKING HEADWAY ON THE SYRIAN TRACK

The second question was whether we should deal with the Israeli-Palestinian track first or give priority to the Israeli-Syrian track. Interestingly enough, the Palestinians repeatedly gave us the same answer at the time: Conclude an agreement with Syria first. Khalidi and Agha argued that movement toward peace with Syria was essential because it would change the terrorism scene and open up relations with the Arab Gulf states. Headway with the Palestinians was also important, but Arafat and the system needed time to develop a two-stage approach and only later would they be able to move to the final step.[63]

Shaath repeated the same idea to Beilin at a meeting in New York. More important, Mahmoud Abbas took the same position. He wanted Hamas to participate in elections and argued that this could happen only if Israel finalized negotiations with Syria. He added that Assad "keeps his word" and concluded with, "If you finish with him, you will help us."[64]

As a result, we pursued the Syrian track first. With regard to Syria, I developed a track-two channel with Abe Suleiman, an elderly Syrian man who had lived in the United States for decades and was a professor of mathematics at an American university. He was also an Alawite, and his brother had been then–Syrian president Hafez al-Assad's commander in the Syrian army decades earlier. The Syrian Alawite elite, including the Assad family, regularly asked Suleiman to assist them in facilitating their visits to the United States, and sometimes to Europe.[65] For more than a year, I went back and forth from Tel Aviv to Washington or New York and, at times, to Europe, to meet with Suleiman and work on a peace treaty that would not demand that Israel give up the entire eastern littoral of the Sea of Galilee, north of Ein Gev, which was the central sticking point in the Israeli-Syrian negotiations. (In the end, it was a difference of a few hundred meters; see the more detailed discussion in chapter 7.)[66] Whereas I was positively impressed by Suleiman's assurances in support of the Israeli position, I wanted proof that such an approach was acceptable to President Assad, so I asked Suleiman to go to Damascus with Steve Cohen, a Jewish American whom we trusted, as he had cooperated with our small group for an entire decade. Suleiman never did. It became clear that the discussions with Suleiman were a classic example of a track-two exercise "running on neutral"—disconnected from the process of decisionmaking, and hence ineffective and redundant.

After the episode with Suleiman ended, we made another effort with regard to Syria. From May to September 1994, we talked with the

Austrian government and to Eberhard Rhein, the head of the European Commission's Middle East Department. I also established close contact with French businessman Loik Le-Floc Prigent, who had worked closely with French president Jacques Chirac in the early autumn of 1995. The concept was to prepare, in cooperation with the European Union, a substantial economic development package for Syria that would come into play after reaching a basic understanding with President Assad. We knew that to conclude peace with Syria, we needed an agreement on a territorial solution and a decision as to whether Israel would have to withdraw to the 1923 international border established by the British and French colonial governments of the Palestinian and Syrian mandates, or withdraw from all territories occupied in June 1967, which were based on the cease-fire lines that had been determined by the Israeli and Syrian military movements during the war.[67] On June 19, 1967, the Israeli government decided that, in return for peace, agreed-on security arrangements, and full normalization of relations with Syria, it would withdraw to the international border between the two countries. However, President Assad demanded the return of all territory occupied in the June 1967 War, which differed from the international line.[68] Beilin suggested that both Israel and Syria agree on international arbitration in order to solve the border issue. Altogether, we suggested a three-component deal: (1) obtain Assad's prior commitment to finalize peace negotiations with Israel at a given date, and if this was not achievable, to renew negotiations after Israeli elections; (2) define in negotiations the conditions for an international arbitration on the final demarcation of the Israeli-Syrian border; and (3) suggest, together with Germany, Russia, France, and the United States, a coordinated strategy that would permit Assad to discuss regional affairs with these powers and adopt a leading Syrian role in the region.[69]

At the time, we were unaware of the fact that Rabin had given the famous "deposit" regarding his willingness to withdraw fully from Syrian territory, specifically from the Golan Heights, if certain conditions were met.[70] Rabin had stated that he would agree to withdraw if the peace treaty could "stand on its own feet" independent of any other Arab-Israeli agreement, lead to normalized relations, be implemented in multiple phases that would not require immediate evacuation of Israeli settlements on the Golan Heights, and provide for sufficient security arrangements. Regardless, we received the same message from all sides—the Austrians, Rhein, and our French interlocutor Le-Floc Prigent—that only a complete withdrawal to the June 4, 1967, cease-fire lines would make peace with Syria possible.

At the beginning of October 1995, Novik discussed the matter with Martin Indyk, who had become the US ambassador to Israel. Indyk reported that President Clinton had sensed that Rabin was hesitant about the proposed withdrawal and wanted to postpone the decision to withdraw until after the scheduled autumn 1996 Knesset elections. Assad was aware of this hesitation and was not interested in dealing with Peres on the issue, arguing that it was Rabin who had to decide.[71] Rabin's unwillingness to take the plunge in order to conclude peace with Syria made it evident that the Syria-first approach was no longer achievable under Rabin's premiership.

TESTING THE IDEA OF A JORDANIAN-PALESTINIAN CONFEDERATION

The third question related to a possible Jordanian-Palestinian confederation. Most of our Palestinian interlocutors supported this idea, mainly in order to please Rabin and Peres. However, Khalidi and Agha argued that neither the Jordanians nor the Palestinians wanted a confederation. This was confirmed when Beilin visited Amman in March and met with Abdel Karim Kabariti, Jordan's minister of foreign affairs, who opposed the idea in strong terms.[72] However, because we were unwilling to take no for an answer, I asked the Dutch government to arrange for a trilateral seminar on the issue. The Jordanians rejected the idea once again.

Coincidentally, Queen Beatrix of the Netherlands was visiting Israel at the time, and we asked her to intercede.[73] The queen spoke with Crown Prince Hassan, who graciously invited us to Jordan. When, at the end of April, we arrived at the border, two royal cars were waiting for us. We spent four very informative days in Amman, though the agenda arranged for us made the delicate Jordanian-Palestinian relationship in Jordan most evident. Ultimately, we did not meet Prince Hassan. Instead, we met with Jawad Anani, who would later become foreign minister. On the political concept of a confederation, we received a resounding "no." However, regarding trilateral economic cooperation aimed at stabilizing the West Bank, we received a supportive answer. Upon my return home, I concluded, "For the first time, I understand their determination to keep out of Palestinian politics and leave the West Bank and Gaza to the Palestinians. Why, for heaven's sake, do they need this additional headache?"[74]

The peace treaty that Israel had signed in October 1994 with Jordan permitted the Jordanians to observe Israeli-Palestinian peace negotiations without being directly involved. They were also able to observe every move by maintaining a close dialogue with both the Israeli and the

Palestinian sides. In 1988, the Jordanians had disengaged from the West Bank in order to maintain their Jordanian national identity and a balance between the Jordanians and Palestinians living in Jordan. In order to do so, the Hashemite Kingdom wanted good relations with Israel and good relations with the Palestinian leadership, but it had no interest in forming a Jordanian-Palestinian confederation. We finally understood that we had to accept this reality, at least for the time being.

EVALUATING ALTERNATIVE CONCEPTS: PERES'S SEVENTEEN-POINT AND SEGAL'S TWENTY-POINT PROPOSAL

Peres was seeking, one way or another, what he called a "functional" agreement. The strategic aim was to permit Israel to maintain a foothold in the West Bank while coordinating various functional powers with Jordan and the Palestinian Authority. In contrast, we believed that only a "territorial" agreement with the necessary security arrangements was desirable and achievable. This difference of opinion reflected a discussion within the ILP that had begun as early as 1968, when Israeli finance minister Pinhas Sapir, believing in the need to preserve Israel's Jewish identity, had argued that the incorporation of the Palestinian population of the West Bank and Gaza, along with the Palestinian Arab minority in Israel, would permit the Arabs to become the majority sooner or later. Sapir warned that if Israel held on to the territories, the territories would take hold of Israel.[75] Accordingly, Sapir advocated a territorial solution and was willing to negotiate borders that were not very different from the June 4, 1967, cease-fire lines.[76]

In contrast, Moshe Dayan (at the time defense minister) and Peres (at the time transport minister) advocated a functional solution that would permit Israel to maintain control functions in the West Bank, with the Palestinians as citizens of and voters in Jordan.[77] In line with Dayan's thinking, Peres produced an updated seventeen-point plan that would establish a Palestinian state in Gaza but would not include the West Bank; the Palestinians residing in the West Bank were to choose whether they would have Israeli, Palestinian, or Jordanian citizenship.[78]

Our small group was convinced that Peres's proposed functional solution would hurt Israel's future. I wrote in my diary:

> . . . if we get that ["Peres's "Gaza-first concept"], we probably shall never have a solution over the West Bank. A Likud government would do everything to eternalize the situation and even Peres and

Rabin might fall in love with the idea. It could delegitimize Arafat in the West Bank, probably cause further terror and thus delegitimize the peace process even further.[79]

However, it was not difficult to understand that confronting Peres's leadership would seriously undermine the chances of success for our exercise. I summarized what was to come:

For us, his [Peres's] position will have major repercussions. Until yesterday, I hoped to sell Peres the Stockholm concept—yet we are light years apart. I am not sure, whether Peres's positions represents his strategic thinking, or whether they are tactics. . . . If Peres thinks in these terms, the consequences are many: First, the chance of moving quickly and effectively ahead in Stockholm are, so I understand, close to zero. . . . Second, this would mean that the Stockholm concept may only become politically relevant after a long perpetuated political struggle and public campaign.[80]

Beilin was more optimistic than I was. He was convinced that Peres could eventually be convinced to support the concept that was emerging in Stockholm and support a two-state solution.[81]

In hindsight, we could have pursued the compromise approach proposed by Jerome Segal, an American professor at the University of Maryland's Center for International and Security Studies and president of the Jewish Peace Lobby. Segal had been working on his concept throughout the first half of 1995, and we knew of it then. His final twenty-point concept was submitted in May 1995 to Peres and Arafat. In hindsight, his ideas would have taken care of most of our concerns.

The essence of the Segal's Twenty-Point Proposal was to establish the State of Palestine in Gaza and to maintain Palestinian claims for sovereignty over Arab Jerusalem and the West Bank. The Palestinian state would replace the PLO, "taking the Covenant with it" (point 20). Segal continued, stating that "Palestinian nationalism crosses into the ethos of the world of states. The state asserts its monopoly over the use or threat of violence and the establishment of foreign policy."[82] The assumption behind this point was far reaching. It meant that the Palestinian revolutionary movement—which was embodied in the PLO and had come into existence with the definite aim of destroying the State of Israel—would fulfill its national struggle by establishing the State of Palestine, which had to act responsibly as a neighbor of the State of Israel.

Segal's sixth point added another important component:

Israel recognizes a Palestinian right to self-determination, but states that like all rights, it is not absolute and needs to be adjudicated in reference to Israel's right to peace and security. It defines the negotiations as an attempt to satisfy these two rights.

A great number of points benefiting the Palestinians were made: full membership in the United Nations, control of the borders, defined sovereign rights over Gaza and Jericho, administrative powers in the West Bank, and the right to grant citizenship to all Palestinian inhabitants of the West Bank and Gaza and, if they so decided, to the Palestinians of the Diaspora. Furthermore, points 13, 14, and 17 related to the settlement issue, providing for an agreement on a freeze or controlled growth of settlements, negative subsidies of the Government of Israel to encourage relocation to Israel's sovereign territory, and the possibility of leasing the land of the settlements in Gaza for a given period.

Beilin and I discussed Segal's concepts at an early stage, and we both feared that an agreement on Gaza would entrench the Israeli presence in the West Bank and would ultimately undermine the possibility of reaching a fair, two-state solution. We also discussed the concept with Shaath in Stockholm in February 1995, and we learned that if this concept been offered officially to the Palestinians he, Shaath, would have bought the idea.[83]

When Segal submitted his concepts to Peres and Arafat in May 1995, we ignored him. Embarrassingly, we had arrogantly considered his work "not serious" and thus did not follow up. In hindsight, I am convinced that we made a big mistake in not following his approach and trying to convince Peres and Rabin to pursue it.

Step Three: Working to Bridge Gaps

During the spring of 1995, we held three workshops in Caesarea over a period of several months. These workshops dealt extensively with the issues of security, settlements, refugees, and Jerusalem. The participants included political, military, and academic representatives: Brigadier General Gadi Zohar, who had been head of the Office of the Coordinator of Government Activities in the Territories (COGAT); Brigadier General Fredy Zach, Zohar's second in command at COGAT; Major General Janosh Ben Gal, a former chief of the Northern Command; Colonel Yonathan

Lerner, a member of the Strategic Planning Department;[84] General Shlomo Gazit, who had been one of the first commanders in charge of West Bank affairs;[85] Professor Gad Gilbar of the University of Haifa, and Professor Asher Susser of Tel Aviv University; Ambassador Harry Knej Tal, head of the Planning Department in the Ministry of Foreign Affairs; advocate Meir Linzen; and Beilin, Boaz Karni, Pundak, and me.

On security, we discussed Israel's perceptions of threats and its need to maintain a military presence along the Jordan River. Most participants made it evident that Israel's security border could not be only the Jordan River. The defense against a possible assault from the east had to be based on the nonvulnerability of the territory of Jordan. General Ben Gal was most outspoken on this point, and he argued that an isolated Israeli military presence along the Jordan River was both a political and military liability in pursuing negotiations with the Palestinians. The Israeli presence along the Jordan River would make it necessary to negotiate conditions in which the Israeli army could move through the West Bank to the east beyond the river. Other trilateral Israeli-Palestinian-Jordanian security arrangements should be sought—ones that would not make it necessary to define such conditions. Furthermore, Israel would need to maintain its right to enter the West Bank under any threat scenario. It would be essential to reach an understanding with Jordan on regional security issues—turning Jordan's external border into a common security border for Jordan, Palestine, and Israel, possibly in coordination with the Palestinians.[86]

We tested this concept with Major General Amram Mitzna, former chief of Israel's Central Command (responsible for the West Bank) and with other Israelis. They took a less radical position and argued that Israeli military withdrawal from the Jordan Valley was possible, as long as access routes to it could be used in times of "emergency."[87] We reached a simple conclusion: The security of Israel, of the future Palestinian State, and of the Hashemite Kingdom of Jordan all depended on both preventing hostile forces from entering Jordan and taking effective coordinated action against terrorism. In the short term, due to continuing threats of violence, which the simple signing of an agreement could not eliminate, Israeli forces had to remain at strategic points in the West Bank, including the Jordan River. These arrangements would eventually be replaced by a trilateral Israeli-Palestinian-Jordanian security agreement, to be endorsed by the international community, to guarantee the security of Jordan. The peace treaty that Israel had signed with Jordan in October 1994 deterred any threat against Israel from the east. Thus, as long as Israel was not threatened from the east and the Palestinians did not threaten Israel through acts of terrorism, there was no need for Israel to physically control Palestinian territory, and an effective Palestinian security plan could be established in coordination with Israel and Jordan.

On the basis of these conclusions, and with help from the Belgian government, we created a trilateral Israeli-Palestinian-Jordanian security working group, which presented its recommendations to the three governments in 1999 and again in 2000 (see chapter 7 for more on this working group). A trilateral Israeli-Palestinian-Jordanian security agreement served all three parties. If Israel could be sure that no Arab army would move into Jordan and joint action against acts of terrorism was effectively pursued, it would be easier to withdraw Israeli forces from the West Bank.[88]

On settlements, opinions remained largely divided. Gadi Zohar, Fredy Zach, and Pundak strongly insisted on the complete evacuation of settlements located in areas that would become part of the sovereign Palestinian State, because this would be the only way to ensure the security of the settlers, and any other solution would not be acceptable to the Palestinian side. Beilin and I, aware of the political difficulty of evacuating the settler population, thought of a threefold strategy. First, knowing that the Palestinians had indicated that they would agree to a one-for-one swap deal for territorial concessions, we would make the effort to include an optimal number of settlements and settlers within the agreed-on recognized sovereign territory of the State of Israel. In effect, most settlers lived in settlement blocs in the Jerusalem area, in the Gush Etzion bloc, and in the Ariel–Karnej Shomrom bloc. It was evident to us that these areas had to be incorporated into Israel by agreement. Second, we spoke of a ten-year period during which the Israeli Defense Forces would withdraw from areas in a several-phase approach and the Israeli government would offer the settler community substantial financial incentives to move out. Third, for those settlers who wanted to remain under Palestinian sovereignty and without military protection, basic understandings with the Palestinian government would be negotiated to guarantee their safety under a Palestinian state.[89] I personally understood that we had to start an intense dialogue with the settler community, and I have endeavored to do this ever since.

On refugees, we had to deal with numerous questions. Should we acknowledge Israeli responsibility for the Palestinian refugee problem? How could we deal with the demand for the "right of return"? Would it be possible to acknowledge the theoretical "right" while committing the Palestinians to practical measures necessary to prevent the return and the demand to return to Israel proper? Should it be made clear, instead, that a two-state solution meant that Jews living in the Diaspora had the right to return to Israel, whereas the Palestinians living in the Diaspora had the right to return to Palestine? What should be the substance of compensation proposals for property taken by the State of Israel? If we acknowledged partial responsibility, in order to satisfy a seemingly unbendable Palestinian demand, would there have to be compensation "for suffering"? Should compensation for properties taken be given to individuals, or should we negotiate a lump sum with the PLO? How could compensation for Palestinian refugees be linked to the demand for compensation for properties left behind by the Jewish populations of Iraq, Syria, Egypt, Morocco, Algeria, Tunisia, and Libya? Should compensation be offered in money or in kind, and what conditions would have to be met to receive payments? Would the compensation process be carried out directly between Israel and the Palestinians, or would it be better to establish an international commission to carry out this work? What steps could be taken to help refugees integrate in the countries where they were living, or to create programs to permit them to resettle in third countries? What would be the best way to finance and organize the refugee rehabilitation process and the renouncing of refugee status? What rehabilitation and integration choices should be given to the individual refugee families? What could be done in the meantime to prepare to solve the refugee question? It was clear that a lot more work needed to be done on solving the refugee issue. Beilin discussed the principles with Abbas, and hoped to obtain an understanding that Israel would not be able to accept Palestinian refugees. However, no final understandings were reached on this point.[90]

On Jerusalem, we understood that the future of the city and its holy places would be the deal maker or deal breaker on both sides, and we thus dedicated much time and effort to finding a possible solution. The challenge was to postpone the question of sovereignty for twenty-five years while providing sufficient support for the Palestinians' aspiration to establish their capital in Al-Quds.

On the basis of the discussions in Stockholm with Ahmed and Hussein, as well as in consultations with Zohar and Zach, I developed a stage-to-stage approach to the question of Jerusalem. In the first stage, the physical and institutional infrastructure of Jerusalem would be created to permit both the unity and the division of the city; for instance, the necessary municipal institutions for the Palestinians would be created while still maintaining the current structure of the city. During the second stage, a borough system would be established, leading to the establishment of two capitals by the third stage. Beilin rejected this idea because he was convinced that Rabin would oppose it. The way out, Beilin believed, would be to permit the Palestinians to establish a temporary capital in Abu Dis, on the outskirts of Jerusalem, while keeping the difficult issues with regard to Jerusalem unsolved for a period of twenty-five years.[91] To check the ways and means of achieving an agreement on the Jerusalem issue, we worked on several fronts.[92]

In the early 1980s, I had learned an interesting discussion technique from Chancellor Kreisky of Austria. He would raise a roughly planned idea and absorb criticism from various positions, listening to alternative suggestions, and then would put the idea to rest for a time while taking the criticism and suggestions into consideration. In May 1995, at a seminar on Jerusalem in Paris organized by the Institut Français des Relations Internationales, I exercised Kreisky's technique by suggesting that Abu Dis become the Palestinian capital for twenty-five years.[93]

The seminar participants rejected this temporary-capital idea, but it led them to put forward other ideas. Dan Seidemann, an Israeli lawyer specializing on issues of Jerusalem, made three suggestions: (1) Take measures against expropriations (on a case-by-case basis) and against the illegal measures by the settlers, (2) prevent the breaking of the last links remaining between East Jerusalem and the West Bank, and (3) promote the economic development of East Jerusalem.[94] Izchak Reiter, a senior lecturer at Beit Berl College on the outskirts of Kfar Saba in central Israel, spoke at that same meeting of an autonomy plan for Palestinian Jerusalem on four levels, ranging from Level A (full Palestinian autonomy for educational, cultural, and religious affairs) through Level D (security powers that remained under Israeli control, albeit with a Palestinian police force).[95]

The result of the Paris seminar was that Husseini and I agreed to ask the Dutch government to support a trilateral Dutch-Israeli-Palestinian working group to plan for Jerusalem. In his request to Dutch foreign minister Hans van Mierlo, Husseini wrote:

> Any Palestinian-Israeli settlement of Jerusalem will require a clear functional division between the Palestinian and Israeli side of the city. In light of this realization and understanding, we have assembled a team of Palestinian and Israeli architects and city planners to investigate the creation of a "Draft Master Plan for Jerusalem" that provides for the joint design of the proposed divisions. . . . The political and economic stability of the city of Jerusalem depends on the achievement of such a functional division.[96]

To tentatively plan the structure of a borough system in particular, we asked Amir Heshin, who had been Jerusalem mayor Teddy Kollek's adviser on Arab affairs, to provide us with a detailed policy paper.[97] Heshin described how to achieve the functional division in the city, enabling Palestinian control over the city's Palestinian areas in great detail, and presented a conflict transformation concept, rather than aiming to achieve a full resolution of the Jerusalem issue. As we were seeking to obtain a two-stage agreement on Permanent Status, Heshin's concept made a lot of sense and could help us discuss what would have to be achieved during the first stage.

Between August 18 and 20, 1995, work on coordinated planning for Jerusalem started at The Hague. We obtained input that could help us conclude a comprehensive and coherent policy concept as to how to proceed on the way to a Permanent Status Agreement. It seemed as if we were making important progress in our effort to bridge the prevailing gaps with regard to Jerusalem.

Step Four: Agreeing on Policy Concepts and Adapting Them for Israeli Decisionmakers

BEILIN'S POLICY MOTIVATIONS

In July 1995, two important events changed the rules of the game. The first event was Beilin's appointment as minister for economic planning. At a meeting with the European Commission's Eberhard Rhein, Beilin explained that he answered directly to Prime Minister Rabin and that he was expected to prepare policy plans for the present government, as well as plans for the first hundred days of an expected future Rabin government. Such policy plans related to a proposed reform of social security policy concepts to influence cultural and perceptional attitudes of the population and to practical proposals with regard to the peace process and other outstanding issues.[98] Belin explained that he was trying to "find ways and means to replace God and War," in order to create educational attitudes that would help Israel become a twenty-first-century success story instead of the focus of messianic beliefs. After accepting the nomination as economic planning minister, Beilin stressed in his inaugural speech his determination to prepare for final status negotiations and aimed to conclude an agreement with the Palestinians before the next elections. Having worked closely with Peres for more than a decade, he argued that Peres would not tolerate anyone who did not have a mind of his own, and that now that the ILP was in the government, it was the task of "our generation" to take responsibility for Israel's future.[99]

The second important development was the news that PLO leader Mahmoud Abbas had taken full control of and responsibility for negotiations on the Palestinian side. These two nominations turned our purely track-two exercise into something more formal. Although our deliberations were unofficial on both sides, Abbas' official responsibility for overseeing negotiations with Israel and Beilin's position as the official policy planner for the Israeli government gave our exercise "real" relevance.

To begin, Beilin tried to convince Prime Minister Rabin to conclude agreed guidelines for Permanent Status with Arafat instead of finalizing interim status arrangements for the West Bank and Gaza (which would become the Oslo II Agreement). The arguments in favor of this approach were overwhelming. Going to elections in the autumn of 1996 without having moved ahead on the Israeli-Palestinian front would be a disaster. If no prior understandings were reached, Palestinian opening positions in the negotiations would enhance the fears of the Israeli public, who were being told that negotiations with the Palestinians would be a bottomless enterprise resulting in one Israeli concession after another without reaching an end to the conflict. Even worse, Likud would present itself as a more efficient negotiator. However, if we could finalize an agreement on guidelines for Permanent Status in the spring or summer of 1996—or some basic understandings that would appeal to the Israeli electorate and would be in line with Palestinian thinking—the elections would become a vote for or against peace.[100]

We had two problems convincing Rabin to adopt the policy concept on which we had worked. One problem, of which I was not aware at the time, was personal. Years earlier, Beilin had told the press that whenever difficulties occurred between Peres and Rabin, Peres would send Rabin a box of whiskey. Rabin had resented this statement, never forgave Beilin for making it, and thus tended to reject any advice from Beilin automatically.[101] The second problem had to do with the substance of the proposed strategy. Rabin was facing two major threats: Palestinian terrorism and radical right-wing incitement against him. Under these conditions, the question was whether it would be more effective to "go fast," as Beilin proposed, or to "go slow," as our Palestinian contact Nusseibeh had argued. Rabin's choice was not to decide for the time being but to build a working relationship with Arafat.[102]

Major General Danny Rothschild, who at the time was the head of COGAT and was in charge of ongoing relations with Arafat, told me that whenever Rabin met with Arafat, Rothschild was asked to prepare talking and action points. However, not once was there a discussion on what strategy to adopt. As Rabin had apparently not yet made up his mind as to how to proceed, he avoided policy discussions, even on tactical matters. For the time being, Rabin was interested in simply managing the relationship with the Palestinians. In one instance, before a meeting with Arafat at Erez (on the border between Israel and the Gaza Strip), Rabin asked Rothschild to prepare Israeli confidence-building measures. Rabin and Rothschild discussed twenty such measures in the car, and Rothschild suggested that Rabin offer five or six such steps to Arafat; then, depending on the tone and substance of Arafat's reaction, he should decide when to offer the other measures. When the meeting took place, Rabin met with Arafat alone. After about six minutes, Rothschild was asked to join them, and Rabin, in his deep voice, whispered, "I gave him all twenty points, can you give me some more?"[103]

This anecdote provides insight into Rabin's way of thinking. His main concern was building confidence and legitimacy for Arafat in order to make the Interim Agreement work and prepare for Permanent Status negotiations, keeping all options of possible fallback positions open. His thinking and action were fully in line with the five phases of his "peace doctrine," as Martin Gilbert has described it: disengagement—diffusion—trust—negotiations—peace.[104] For Rabin, the 1993 Declaration of Principles with the PLO represented the "disengagement" phase; the May 1994 Cairo Agreement and the September 1995 Oslo II Agreement apparently represented the "diffusion" phase by removing the major causes of friction. To prepare for negotiations, his main aim was to gain time by a policy of trust building. However, Rabin knew that negotiations were imminent, as he had committed to start Permanent Status negotiations no later than May 4, 1996. Thus, on October 5, 1995, in a speech to the Knesset, Rabin laid out his terms for those negotiations:

- He viewed the Jordan River as Israel's security border to the east, and therefore the West Bank had to be demilitarized.
- He opposed the dismantlement of settlements.
- He opposed a return to the June 4, 1967, cease-fire lines.
- He believed that the unity of the city of Jerusalem had to be maintained within the borders of the present municipality.

- He believed that a solution to the Palestinian refugee problem—permitting the refugees' rehabilitation, integration, and absorption outside Israel—was necessary.
- He believed that the political framework had to be a Jordanian-Palestinian confederation.[105]

Despite Rabin's public opposition, however, in confidential private conversations he understood that negotiations would lead to the establishment of the State of Palestine, obviously along conditions that took Israeli interests fully into account.[106] We were addressing most of these issues and were adopting solutions that could be presented to Rabin and the public, fully in line with his six conditions. Beilin, Novik, Pundak, and I believed that Rabin's demands could be addressed in our effort to conclude guidelines for a Permanent Status Agreement. However, the difficult issue that did not fit Rabin's demands was Jerusalem. This issue was Beilin's main motive for seeking an approach in line with Rabin's thinking: a two-phase Permanent Status Understanding that would allow Abu Dis to be established as the capital of the State of Palestine, while reaching a final resolution of the Jerusalem issue at a later date.

EMERGING DILEMMAS

The ongoing dialogue in Stockholm did not make matters easier. Ahmed Khalidi and Hussein Agha categorically rejected the suspension of sovereignty over East Jerusalem for twenty-five years. This, in my opinion, put the entire exercise in jeopardy, and I wrote in my diary (and argued in Stockholm),

> There is no way the Israeli leadership, nor the Israeli public, could accept all Palestinian demands: Agree to the establishment of a Palestinian State, agree to the exchange of territories based on the lines of June 4, 1967, agree to a solution of the refugee problem, and also make major concessions in Jerusalem.[107]

In response, Agha suggested that an agreement on preparing a more ambiguous Memorandum of Understanding be reached instead.[108] In hindsight, this statement would have been exactly what Rabin needed in order to win the next elections, if he had not been assassinated. It is difficult to speculate what would have happened "if," but it makes sense that such a general Israeli-PLO Memorandum of Understanding would have been agreed upon, with or without the involvement of our small group.

In the meantime, Beilin told us that Peres would tease him about the unrealistic approach of wanting to get to a Permanent Status deal immediately and argued that, due to Jerusalem, an agreement would be impossible.[109] Peres spoke with Arafat, who was willing to accept a state in Gaza temporarily instead.[110] Our small group, however, feared that a Gaza-first approach would enable further settlement expansion on the West Bank and would eventually create further obstacles on the way to a two-state solution. Nevertheless, I did see the possibility of building a bridge between the Beilin and the Peres concepts agreeing, in final status negotiations, to adopt "a slow step-to-step approach," which would discuss the dismantlement of settlements in the Gaza Strip and the widening of Palestinian sovereignty rights in the area.[111] I also commented that this approach could form the basis for a National Unity Government, which might be necessary after the next Knesset elections. At the same time, in my diary I admitted the downside of such an approach and assumed that this policy line of limiting settlement activity would increase friction between the settler community and the Palestinians. In fact, I even assumed that a prolonged struggle over the West Bank would blur the lines between Israeli Arab citizens and the Palestinians of the West Bank.[112]

Beilin tried to bridge that gap. In a meeting with Hassan Asfour, Khalidi, Agha, Pundak, and me, he reported that Chairman Arafat had told him, "Go ahead with the Permanent Status solution but do not tear relations with Rabin and Peres. What should be done is to refer to the link between Interim and Permanent Status."[113] In order to do so, the idea was to conclude the parameters of an understanding on all outstanding core issues of conflict. Thus, Beilin hoped to establish two institutions: a Permanent Israeli-Palestinian Secretariat to lead the way from Interim to Permanent Status, and a trilateral Israeli-Jordanian-Palestinian committee on economic issues. Agha wanted the Egyptians to join the second committee, but Beilin argued that though this would be politically acceptable from an economic point of view, Egypt's different economic agenda would make this a burdensome undertaking.

CONCLUDING THE BEILIN–ABU MAZEN UNDERSTANDING

Rabin's October 5, 1995, speech to the Knesset created a challenge for both us and the Palestinians. Rabin's commitment to reaching an agreement on Permanent Status within a year made our exercise more important and challenged us to deal with Rabin's conditions. In response to his speech, we made two decisions: Novik joined Pundak and me in our discussions in Stockholm, and Asfour joined the discussions on the Palestinian team.

Our intention was to conclude a joint concept paper on Permanent Status that would address Rabin's reservations. We assumed that if we took Rabin's concerns into account, Rabin would support the two-state solution. Developing a jointly accepted concept paper on Permanent Status and laying out the substance of a possible agreement would be the first step; the second step would be preparing the coordinated management of the political process needed to get there.

Beilin decided that the effort with Abbas needed to be concluded by the end of October 1995. The meeting took place on October 31, 1995, at the ECF's office in Tel Aviv. Present were Beilin and Abbas, along with the original small team—Khalidi, Agha, Pundak, and me. Beilin stressed that what we had prepared was not a final agreement; nor was it a shot in the blue that was detached from what could be concluded in the official negotiations. Rather, it was a basis from which negotiations would start, and it would help us to make progress.

Beilin envisaged two possibilities toward the conclusion of an agreement on track one. Either make minor changes to the document and sign it, or reopen negotiations. In any case, the document, which became known as the Beilin–Abu Mazen Understanding (using Abbas's Palestinian nom de guerre) would remain a term of reference at hand. What was essential, however, was adding a map. Yossi could give Rabin and Peres a map without an agreement, but he could not hand them an agreement without a map. Abbas's response was that "the paper was a good start." This was not good enough for us. Our Palestinian interlocutors, Agha and Khalidi, had told us before the meeting that Abbas fully supported the document that we had prepared. To obtain the necessary commitment, Agha had turned to Abbas and said, "We will ask Arafat to say 'yes.' You can say you know, and go with us to the next step." Abbas's response was a short "okay." Thus, the Beilin–Abu Mazen Understanding was concluded. It was, however, still unfinished business—and steps five and six of our planned track-two negotiation strategy would not be forthcoming, due to the murder of the Israeli prime minister.

Rabin's Assassination in November 1995 and Netanyahu's Electoral Victory in May 1996

On November 4, five days after the conclusion of the Beilin–Abu Mazen Understanding and toward the end of a peace gathering at which hundreds of thousands of Israelis were present, Rabin was assassinated by an Israeli

Jew who had been influenced by an atmosphere of right-wing and radical religious orthodox incitement. Peres was sworn in as prime minister.

Several days later, on November 11, Beilin presented the Beilin–Abu Mazen Understanding and its map to Peres and received a very polite but firm rejection. Peres wanted to negotiate peace with Syria and to stabilize Israeli-Palestinian relations on the basis of the Interim Agreement that had been signed on September 26, 1995. We should have expected Peres's rejection and prepared the next steps ahead of time. However, Rabin's assassination, a tremendous shock to us all, overturned all former plans and calculations.

Now that Beilin, Novik, Boaz Karni, Pundak, and I were in close vicinity to Peres, we were asked to deal with other emerging issues that had to be dealt with in the aftershock of Rabin's assassination. Because of Rabin's assassination, we wanted to build bridges between the Israeli peace camp and Israel's right-wing movements, particularly the settlers, and so I engaged in a dialogue with settler movement leader Israel Harel. However, instead of being apologetic for having permitted the creation of an atmosphere of hate and incitement among the ideological radical groups supporting the settler community, Harel denied any responsibility and submitted a paper to me that contained clear demands for maintaining and expanding settlement activities.[114]

At the time, Arafat was preparing for elections for the presidency and the Palestinian Legislative Council, scheduled for January 20, 1996. Although his original intention to convince Hamas to participate in the elections had not been achieved, he hoped to reach an understanding with Hamas in order to prevent disturbances during the election campaign and on the day of the elections. Thus, in December 1995, the Palestinian Authority and Hamas concluded an agreement in Cairo, in which the PA would release Hamas inmates and would cease to strike at its infrastructure in exchange for Hamas' refraining from terrorist attacks against Israel and a commitment from Hamas not to oppose the PA and not to disturb the Legislative Council elections.[115] However, Hamas claimed that its commitment to refrain from terrorist acts obliged it not to launch any terrorist acts from territory controlled by the PA, and did not refer to terrorist acts that were launched from areas still under Israeli control.[116] The Israeli security authorities obtained information that, despite the agreement between Arafat and Hamas, Hamas's militant wing under Yehyia Ayyash was planning to carry out terrorist acts against Israel. Peres asked Arafat to arrest Ayyash, but Arafat refused, leaving Peres with little choice but to order direct action to have Ayyash assassinated.[117]

Early in February 1996, the Beilin–Abu Mazen Understanding was leaked to the main Israeli newspaper, *Haaretz*.[118] Its publication came at the worst possible moment. Throughout February and March, a wave of terrorist acts hit Israel, killing fifty-six Israelis.[119] These acts of terrorism by Hamas, Peres stated, had occurred even though the Israeli army had been redeployed from numerous villages and cities in the West Bank. Peres added, "Instead of thanks, we got bombs."[120] The message to the Israeli public was one of terrorism, fear, and destruction, not of peace-making. Under these circumstances, contemplating far-reaching Israeli concessions to the Palestinians and establishing a Palestinian state that could turn into a refuge for terrorists did not make sense, either to the Israeli public or to Israel's professional elites, who largely determined Israeli policy obligations.

In those times of despair, when any reference to peace appeared to be unrealistic or, at best, naïve, the Israeli public was unwilling to accept any concessions to the Palestinians. Likud thus exploited the Beilin–Abu Mazen Understanding to attack Beilin, Pundak, and myself—and, by extension the entire ILP—for intending to "divide Jerusalem." Likud leader Benjamin Netanyahu ran his election campaign on the basis that, unlike Peres, he would not "divide Jerusalem." Moreover, Beilin's response to Netanyahu's accusation was that we had suggested establishing the Palestinian capital of Al-Quds in Abu Dis. This delegitimized Abbas in the eyes of the Palestinian public and led him to deny his previously given commitment to the agreed-on document, causing further harm. Nusseibeh drily described what happened: "By the time Israeli elections rolled around in May 1996, Hamas had murdered enough Israeli civilians to bring Bibi Netanyahu to power."[121]

Failures, Lessons Learned, and One Important Success, 1993–96

By concluding the Beilin–Abu Mazen Understanding, we created an important blueprint for a Permanent Status Agreement. When US president Bill Clinton saw the document, he reportedly said: "Let us change some words and sign the Agreement."[122] The document and its concept were fully in line with the paradigm proposed by the 1978 Camp David Accords: Negotiations for a Palestinian self-government agreement were to be followed by an agreement on all outstanding core issues of conflict, such as borders, security, Jerusalem, and refugees. On all these issues, the formulas on which we agreed with our Palestinian partners became important terms of reference for all the negotiations that followed. We made it evident that the outcome of negotiations had to be a two-state solution, with Israel and Palestine living side by side.

On the issue of territory, we recognized the Palestinian demand that the June 4, 1967, cease-fire lines be the reference point for any agreed exchange of territories on the basis of a 1:1 ratio. On Jerusalem, we achieved the recognition of West Jerusalem and the Jewish neighborhoods in East Jerusalem as the capital of Israel in return for recognizing the Palestinian neighborhoods of Jerusalem as Al-Quds, the capital of Palestine. We also defined understandings for the management of the city and the holy places. On refugees, we reached the Palestinian recognition that "Palestine was the homeland of all Palestinians," clearly implying that in practical terms, the Palestinian right of return was to Palestine and not to Israel. We also conceded that "the right of the Palestinian refugees to return to their homes is enshrined in international law and natural justice," and we acknowledged the "moral and material suffering of the Palestinian people." However, we were careful to maintain that we "recognized the Palestinian refugees' right of return to the Palestinian state and the right to compensation and rehabilitation for moral and material losses."[123] Most important, we obtained a commitment that "no additional claims or demands will be made upon the implementation of this Framework Agreement" from the Palestinian side.[124] These concepts and formulas would be repeatedly revisited in the coming years, at each (so far) unsuccessful attempt to negotiate or renegotiate a Permanent Status Agreement.

In hindsight, despite the impressive track record, it is doubtful whether this was the best way to pursue. In fact, we had built a house on floating sand. We failed to achieve the main aim of our exercise: reaching an Israeli-Palestinian understanding before the planned Israeli elections of 1996 that would turn the elections into a vote for or against peace. Our hope had been to thus enable Rabin to reach a Permanent Status Agreement with Arafat on the basis of wide Israeli electoral support. The failure to do so was one of historic dimensions. We reinforced a paradigm that would fail again and again.

In South Africa, a 1991–92 scenario planning exercise (known as the Mont Fleur Scenario Exercise) referred to four scenarios for the future of a nation: the "ostrich" scenario, where the leaders put their heads in the sand and ignore reality, which sooner or later leads to a major disaster; the "Icarus" scenario, named after the myth of the young man who flew too close to the sun, suggesting a government that creates unachievable hopes that lead to failure and disappointment; the "lame duck" scenario, where one agreement after another is reached without actually bringing about the hoped-for change; and the final positive scenario, the "flight of the flamingos," where the government enables a successful flight of "the choir of the flamingos" to a better future. For us, the final positive scenario would have meant that we had gained support from a majority of political leaders who enjoyed the backing of sufficient public support in favor of proposed conditions for a peace agreement with the PLO. By contrast, the Beilin–Abu Mazen Understanding turned out to be a "soft" Icarus scenario. We remained "lonely birds" and failed to gain even the support of the second echelon of the ILP's leadership. This failure stemmed from a variety of factors.

No appropriate answer was developed to counteract the damaging effect of the vicious circle of violence and incitement perpetrated by Hamas and other Palestinian opposition groups, and also by Israel's radical right wing and its supporters within Likud. The concept of "we will negotiate with the Palestinians as if there was no terrorism, and we will fight terrorism as if there were no negotiations" failed bitterly. The outcome of this approach was detrimental on two accounts. First, the continuing and escalating acts of terrorism brought about a dwindling of popular support for Prime Minister Rabin, contributing to the public atmosphere that led to his assassination. Second, the commitment to negotiate in spite of Palestinian terrorist acts created neither a stick nor carrot incentive for Arafat to take effective action against Palestinian terrorism. The lesson to be learned was simple: *Effective Israeli-Palestinian security cooperation would be a necessary precondition for a successful negotiating exercise.*

We did understand that it was necessary to create wide popular support on both sides for peace and reconciliation. Accordingly, we had suggested and agreed to a plethora of "people-to-people" activities, which were detailed in the third and fourth annexes of the September 1993 Declaration of Principles and in the sixth annex of the Oslo II Agreement.[125] However, we failed to implement these commitments. On the Israeli side, Rabin was occupied with leading the negotiations with Jordan, Syria, and the Palestinians, while Peres looked outward to the Arab world, rather than inward toward promoting reconciliatory relations between Israelis and Palestinians. Without their leadership, the various Israeli government departments pursued business as usual, rather than building bridges to the Palestinian side.

On the Palestinian side, the situation was even worse. In cooperation with Fathi Arafat (Yasser Arafat's brother) and with financial support from the Norwegian and Dutch governments, the ECF developed a broad program for people-to-people activities. It was agreed that joint Israeli-Palestinian teams would go to the United Nations in New York for a public kick-off, which aimed to achieve wide attention as well as political and further financial support. However, the UN visit was called off at the last minute when Nasr al-Qidwa, the PLO's representative to the United Nations, vetoed the entire program. Confidentially, I was told that al-Qidwa wanted to maintain an anti-Israeli stance at the UN by opposing any Israeli-Palestinian cooperation in support of peace.[126] The lesson to be learned was that *we had to engage in a serious and comprehensive effort to create vested interests for peace among the wide Israeli and Palestinian public.*

We did understand that the diverging Israeli and Palestinian narratives with regard to the core issues of conflict made it extremely difficult to bridge prevailing gaps in "one go." Agha offered to conclude a relatively vague Memorandum of Understanding that would serve the ILP before elections as a document illustrating the Palestinian commitment to peace. Beilin, similarly aware of the dramatic gap with regard to the Palestinian and Israeli positions on Jerusalem, agreed with Husseini on pursuing Permanent Status on the basis of a two-step approach. Beilin even suggested creating the necessary joint institutions in order to connect, or to "handcuff," the first move toward Permanent Status with the second move—even, and particularly, if a ten-year period in between was being envisaged. The lesson to be learned was to *keep the final aim in mind and devise agreed-on steps that would stand the test of political and public acceptability and sustainability.* (Later, we would act and plan our work accordingly after Netanyahu had become prime minister.)

We did oppose the conclusion of the Oslo II Agreement in September 1995. It was too long (314 pages), and thus too complicated for implementation. Worse, the agreement did not deal effectively with the two major issues on the way to a Permanent Status Agreement: preventing terrorism, and limiting Israeli settlement activity. In fact, the Oslo II Agreement generated the opposite; it was followed by violent acts of terrorism and a substantial Israeli expansion of settlement activities that was eased by the fact that about 60 percent of the West Bank territory remained under full Israeli control. However, the agreement did serve some of Arafat's political interests, because it laid the ground for his election as president of the PA. The lesson to be learned was to understand that *any Interim Agreement should not be defined according to the immediate political needs of the leadership of one side or the other, but interim steps or agreements had to serve the purpose of conflict transformation: to decrease the causes of friction and to prepare steps toward conflict resolution.*

We fully understood that our Palestinian interlocutors were interested in and committed to seeking common ground with the Israeli side on a tactical level, even while they showed close to zero flexibility on strategic issues. The guidelines for an agreement with Israel had been largely laid out at the November 1988 meeting of the *Palestinian National Council*, and the Palestinian leadership had little maneuvering room and no intention of disregarding its own guidelines and principles. We also understood that this situation was by and large symmetric. Peres strongly opposed the strategic breakthrough we had in mind. Rabin wanted the territorial separation that we supported, but he was not ready to agree to the Israeli concessions we thought necessary in order to achieve a strategic breakthrough. I would argue that *track-two actors must be fully aware of the political constraints of their own leadership and adopt their working concepts accordingly.* It should be added that Beilin did not view himself as a track-two actor, but rather as a politician who was fighting to achieve what he believed were the strategic necessities that his country faced.

In hindsight, I am convinced that Segal's Twenty-Point Proposal was far more in tune with the political realities and constraints of the time than the Beilin–Abu Mazen Understanding. The lesson to be learned in this context is bitter: *Do not ever disrespect the strategic work of potential competitors, and make every effort to prevent "tunnel thinking."*[127]

Politically and historically, the Beilin–Abu Mazen Understanding created the belief among many diplomats and observers that the paradigm of going immediately to Permanent Status was preferable to the gradual and incremental approach laid out by the Oslo Process. The belief in the need to go directly to a Permanent Status Agreement has been maintained in spite of the repeated failures of this approach. Taking the direct approach to Permanent Status failed three times: in 1995–96, in 1999–2001, and again in 2008 (see chapters 7, 8, and 9). Although our small group hoped that the Beilin–Abu Mazen Understanding would serve as an important blueprint for a final agreement, at the decisive moment of negotiations, in August 2000, Abbas withdrew his support for the understanding (see chapter 7). He did not act out of malice or because he was not committed to peace. Rather, he withdrew his support because he could not mobilize the necessary political legitimacy from the Palestinian top leadership, middle-range leadership, or grassroots. These problems were not restricted to the Palestinians; at about the same time, Ehud Barak lost his majority in the Knesset for the equivalent reasons.

As will be seen in later chapters, in 2008 an optimal Permanent Status proposal made by Prime Minister Ehud Olmert was effectively rejected by the Palestinian leadership. The cause for these failures cannot be seen to be merely coincidental. Paul Lederach explains in his theoretical study *Building Peace: Sustainable Reconciliation in Divided Societies* that peace must be built simultaneously along all dimensions of the societal pyramid: by the top-level leadership, in a top-down approach; by the middle-range leadership (e.g., religious leaders, academics, and intellectuals), in a middle-out approach; and by the grassroots actors, on the basis of bottom-up work.[128] In all the attempts made to reach a Permanent Status Agreement—the preliminary effort of 1995–96, and the 1999–2001 and 2006–8 peace negotiations—the entire effort rested purely upon the top leadership. No serious effort was undertaken to create the conditions that would make middle-out and bottom-up peace efforts possible. To develop the enabling conditions for the entire societal pyramid to move on top-down, middle-out, and bottom-up dimensions toward peace, six conditions in support for a peaceful, two-state solution had to be put in place: (1) a guided process of Palestinian institution and state building, (2) the creation of functioning Israeli-Palestinian security cooperation, (3) people-to-people and government-to-government activities that would create the necessary institutional cooperation for achieving a sustainable good neighborly relationship; (4) agreed-on measures to stop settlement activities and prepare for a territorial agreement; (5) regional involvement of the neighboring Arab states in support of Palestinian state building and security and regional legitimacy for Israeli; and (6) effective links to create a resilient chain connecting each interim step toward a peaceful Israeli-Palestinian two-state solution.

In spite of all the difficulties and setbacks that were experienced during our track-two work between 1993 and 1996, we did achieve one important success: Our small group attained the confidence of Abbas and most of the Palestinian leadership. This was no small achievement. It laid the foundations that enabled us to pursue an intense and constructive dialogue with the Palestinian leadership as to how to maintain the Oslo Process under Prime Minister Netanyahu's government and how to translate the lessons learned into flexible and achievable policy concepts. This was our challenge in the three years to come.

Chapter 6

Keeping the Oslo Process on Track: Multitrack Diplomacy during the First Netanyahu Government, May 1996–May 1999

This chapter covers the period of the first Netanyahu government from the end of May 1996 until May 1999. It includes our group's multitrack diplomacy work, which influenced Netanyahu and the Palestinians to accept the American leadership's proposals to conclude the Hebron Protocol with its attached "Note for the Record" (January 1997), providing for the partial withdrawal of Israel from Hebron, and the Wye River Agreement (October 1998), providing for Israeli Further Redeployment from 13 percent of its West Bank territory. It describes the tools we used to keep the Oslo Process on track, in spite of the initial strong opposition of Netanyahu and the Likud party to the Oslo Process, as well as the development of people-to-people activities and joint track-two policy planning, which provided for a gradual move toward a two-state solution. This period provides an interesting example of how effective multitrack diplomacy can partially overcome the opposition of a reluctant government.

Historical Background

Likud's electoral victory in May 1996 put the continuation of the Oslo Process into question. Benjamin Netanyahu, who would form Israel's new government, had played a leading role in opposing the Oslo Process and had participated in radical right-wing demonstrations that had portrayed Yitzhak

Rabin as a Nazi SS officer. Legally, the incoming government was obliged to honor agreements signed by the preceding government. Diplomatically, there was no doubt that the United States and the entire international community would demand the continuation of the Oslo Process. On the regional level, Israel's relations with Egypt and Jordan were at stake.

In this situation, in order to keep the Oslo Process on track, the challenge ahead was to pursue track-two and multitrack diplomacy. On a personal level, there were reasons for my concern. Several days before the elections, Likud demonstrators in Tel Aviv had recognized me and "promised" that they would put me on trial and hang me in a public execution after they won the elections. Although I knew that these were empty threats, I feared that the internal situation would get rough. At the same time, I remembered Sari Nusseibeh's May 1995 argument that in dealing with a Likud government, the Palestinian leadership would need to seek assistance from Israeli partners, enabling slow movement toward an agreed-on solution. In fact, Nusseibeh had stated that rapid progress pursued under an Israeli Labor Party (ILP) government would increase internal Palestinian friction and thus cause terrorism and other setbacks.[1] The three years pursuant would clearly test the accuracy of Nusseibeh's thesis. If he were right, I knew that the task of building a partnership between the Palestinian leadership and the Israeli peace camp depended largely upon our Economic Cooperation Foundation (ECF). The challenge of achieving small progress toward a solution of the Israeli-Palestinian conflict under a Likud government would thus depend on the effective use of track-two and multitrack diplomacy, as a kind of pacemaker, to provide the necessary impetus in times of stagnation or retreat, for track-one officials to pursue the Oslo Process.

The First Two Weeks: May and June 1996

In contrast to the threat I had received of being put on trial and hanged, the entire ECF team received support and encouragement from all sides immediately after Netanyahu's electoral victory. On May 30, 1996, the day after the Israeli elections, I drove to Jerusalem for a number of meetings. My first meeting that day was with Hikmat Ajouri of the Palestinian Council of Health. He made three very surprising statements: first, that the Palestinians had to come to terms with the new administration; second, that people-to-people efforts were more important than ever before; and third, that it was essential to widen the circle of dialogue to include the

Israeli settler population. Two hours later, I got the same message from Rami Nasrallah, who worked closely with Faisal Husseini.

That afternoon, I met with Eberhard Rhein, the head of the European Commission's Middle East Department, and Jean Paul Jesse, the European Union's ambassador to Israel. At the meeting, the ECF received a promise for a grant of 600,000 European currency units (ECUs) for people-to-people projects, such as creating an Israeli-Palestinian hub for youth activities and coordinated work for environmental and nature protection, which had to be carried out in full cooperation because of the geographical proximity of Israel and Palestine.[2] Later that same evening, I had a meeting with Mark Eijlenberg, a Dutch businessman and banker who was seeking ways to finance joint Israeli-Palestinian economic development projects.[3]

On May 31, Ron Pundak and I met with our Palestinian contact, Husseini, and received three requests and a warning. First, he wanted to establish contact with Likud as soon as possible and asked us to help; second, he wanted to intensify work on a Jerusalem solution and continue the work that we had started in the Netherlands a year earlier (see chapter 5); and third, he wanted to work out the "new rules" of "give and take" with us and with Likud. Finally, he warned that if the Likud government were to close down the Orient House—which was the seat of Husseini's office and, more important, the symbol of Palestinian political presence in Jerusalem—and block the connection between Jerusalem and the West Bank, an intifada would break out in Jerusalem.

After meeting with Husseini, we met with Ed Abbington, the US consul-general to Jerusalem and the man responsible for leading US relations with the Palestinian Authority (PA). He told us that Yasser Arafat was in shock following the Likud electoral victory and was telling his close entourage that his dream of establishing the State of Palestine during the coming three years "had floated away." Abbington, by contrast, was less pessimistic. He was convinced that the American commitment to the peace process would result in Washington defining red lines that Netanyahu would not be permitted to cross. Regarding Jerusalem, Abbington was less worried. He pointed out that Arafat had agreed to play down the Jerusalem issue time and again, and had repeatedly refrained from backing some of Husseini's "unrealistic" demands on the city, which he did not specify. Abbington was more concerned with the position of the city of Hebron. Most of the Hamas and Islamic Jihad terrorists lived in Hebron and used the area as the base for their actions. It would therefore be of paramount importance to permit the PA's security forces to get into Hebron as soon as possible in order to contain Hamas and other radical Arab influences there.

Among our small group, Nimrod Novik, who had left government and had become a businessman, was the one to establish contact with incoming Prime Minister Netanyahu on behalf of Shimon Peres in order to provide general background information.[4] Apparently, Netanyahu was surprised when briefed on the depth and effectiveness of the Israeli-Palestinian security cooperation that had developed in the last few months following the Palestinian terrorist acts of February and March 1996.[5]

On June 1, Pundak and I took Mahmoud Abbas, who still was Arafat's second in command and in charge of negotiations with Israel, and Hassan Asfour of the Gaza leadership of the Palestine Liberation Organization (PLO), from Egyptian ambassador Bassiouni's Herzliya residence to our office for a meeting with Yossi Beilin. (At the time, Beilin was spending his last days as minister of planning in Peres's government before having to hand over his file to his successor.) As Peres would remain the incumbent prime minister until Netanyahu presented his government to the Knesset, Abbas raised the question of what could be done in the coming days, before Netanyahu moved into the Prime Minister's Office.

Beilin, Pundak, and I strongly opposed the idea of a hasty Israeli withdrawal from Hebron. We believed that such a move would be difficult without a specific public request (not merely approval) from Netanyahu. The Israeli public would view such a move as illegitimate: contradicting the will of the people, who had elected Netanyahu as prime minister. If Netanyahu was unwilling to ask specifically for the agreed-on withdrawal from Hebron, then it would be best to leave it to Netanyahu to deal with the issue. This approach made also sense to the Palestinians. Their main concern was how to quickly establish a working relationship with the incoming Israeli government.

We were told that Dore Gold, Netanyahu's political adviser and a participant in several previous Israeli-Palestinian track-two meetings, had phoned Abbas and had started a dialogue with him on Netanyahu's behalf. Gold had been given the Palestinian portfolio and had become the main channel of communication between Netanyahu and Abbas. Beilin promised Abbas that the ILP would be "a watchdog in the Knesset and demand steadfastly the fulfillment of the agreement,"[6] accurately assuming that we would be able to work with leading Likud figures such as Gold, Finance Minister Dan Meridor, and Foreign Minister David Levy to build bridges, and that we could mobilize support from the international community to keep the peace process going.[7]

Later that same day, I brought Abbas and Asfour back to Ambassador Bassiouni's residence. In the car, we discussed various issues. Abbas wanted to create both formal and informal dialogues with Netanyahu, his advisers, and his coalition partners. To arrange an informal channel, Abbas wanted Hussein Agha to come to Israel and renew his dialogue with Gold, which had started at one of the earlier track-two meetings in Europe. Abbas also aimed at creating a working relationship with the Orthodox religious Shas Party. He wanted to speak with President Hosni Mubarak of Egypt and King Hassan II of Morocco about inviting the Shas leadership to Morocco in order to engage in a dialogue with them and to get them to support a policy of moving toward a peaceful resolution of the Israeli-Palestinian conflict. Abbas's third remark related to the "Beilin–Abu Mazen Understanding." He asserted that this concept was the "real basis for an understanding and we will get there," adding a waving movement with his hands that apparently meant that we would get there, one way or another.[8]

The following day, June 2, I flew to Vienna to see my mother. That evening, my sister and I met with Austrian chancellor Bruno Kreisky's former chief secretary, Margit Schmid; Patricia Kahane, who had worked with us in 1995 to develop the Syrian channel; the widow of well-known Austrian Jewish writer Friedrich Torberg; and Doron Grossman, who was serving as number two at the Israeli Embassy in Vienna. Kahane and Schmid promised on the spot to donate $40,000 for people-to-people activities.[9]

On June 4, I met Pundak in Brussels for another meeting with Rhein, who suggested that the ILP join the Likud government. The Friedrich Ebert Foundation, a German political entity associated with the German Social Democratic Party, also offered further financial support to the continuing work of the ECF.[10] On June 5, Pundak and I flew to Stockholm. Our main assigned task was to diminish, as realistically as possible, Palestinian fears. We advised Agha and Khalidi that Netanyahu would not be interested in rocking the boat and that crisis situations could emerge from misunderstandings rather than from intent.

To prevent misunderstandings between the Palestinians and Netanyahu's incoming government, I asked Ambassador Anne Dismorr from Sweden to finance a stay for Agha in Israel in order for him to be able to meet with Gold and create a working channel of communications. Ideally, this channel could be used to help relate both Netanyahu's and Arafat's acts and intentions. Ambassador Dismorr immediately agreed, enabling Agha to come to Israel on June 13. The subsequent dialogue between Agha and Gold opened the possibility for Agha to meet with Netanyahu. Though this dialogue channel did not eliminate the basic political and ideological gaps that divided the Likud government and the Palestinians, it did create the opportunity to verify mutual perceptions and diffuse irrational fears.[11]

Around this time, Novik met with Osama al-Baz, President Mubarak's foreign affairs adviser. We learned that Netanyahu had sent very constructive messages to President Mubarak, informing him that the incoming Likud government knew that Arafat was the only one who could deliver an effective solution, that it would look for solutions to the Hebron problem, and that it would not close the Orient House unless it was provoked to do so.[12] Novik was told that Mubarak sent two messages to Netanyahu in response: "1. Don't try to drive a wedge between Palestinians and Jordanians. 2. Do not get too close to King Hussein, in order not to drive Arafat into the hands of [Syrian president] Assad."[13]

These initial postelection meetings with a great variety of Israelis, Palestinians, and international representatives enabled us to define a coherent ECF strategy:

- Maintain and reinforce a mutually supportive relationship with the Palestinian leaders, while keeping their commitment to the "Beilin-Abu Mazen Understanding."
- Offer support to Netanyahu's government in order to sustain the Oslo Process and move toward Permanent Status.
- Enlarge the supportive coalition within Israel for a negotiated Israeli-Palestinian peace agreement and define agreed-on principles for the envisaged Permanent Status negotiations.
- Promote Israeli-Palestinian people-to-people programs to create the broadest legitimacy for concluding a Permanent Status Agreement.
- Work with various groups of experts to prepare detailed working concepts on most of the core issues of conflict: Jerusalem, refugees, security, and the economy.
- Work to prepare incoming ILP chairman Ehud Barak for negotiations to come.[14]

To pursue these strategy aims, we needed to employ and maintain the existing network of relations with other regional and international players, particularly with Egypt, the United States, and various European governments.

The First Seven Months: Initial Track-Two Failures

Soon after the formation of Netanyahu's government, the ECF established close contact with several government ministers: the finance minister, Meridor; the internal security minister, Avigdor Kahalani; and the foreign minister, Levy. Following our suggestion, at the end of July Meridor had met with Arafat's economic advisers, Maher el-Kurd and Muhammad Rashid, to develop a working relationship and better understand Palestinian economic difficulties. Kahalani consulted with Beilin in order to determine who would lead the dialogue with Husseini in order to create quiet in Jerusalem. We also had full access to the Foreign Ministry through a former assistant of Novik, Yuval Frankl-Rotem, who had been appointed Levy's chief of staff.[15] Although Gold controlled the Palestinian file, Levy had served as foreign minister in the early 1990s, and we knew that the Europeans liked him. During his time as foreign minister, Levy had told the Europeans, "These are my red lines; as long as you accept them, we can speak about all other options, and I am willing to listen and accept your suggestions and advice."[16] We thus hoped Levy would be willing to listen to policy suggestions that came either directly from us or (through Frankl-Rotem) could be presented to him as the ideas of others. We also understood that Yitzhak Mordechai, the newly appointed minister of defense, was politically closer to Rabin than to Likud, possibly opening another avenue of influence.

Those on the Palestinian side impressed us with their apparent need and desire to consult with us on a regular basis and to seek political understandings with Netanyahu's government. Novik's relationship with Ambassador Bassiouni and the most senior Egyptian leadership also offered us reason for optimism. The first tactical question we discussed with Abbas and other Palestinians was whether they should speak only with the prime minister and his office, or whether they should engage in dialogue with the second echelon of Israeli decisionmakers. We argued that the wider their contacts and their dialogue, the better. Possibly, following our advice, Chairman Arafat decided to forgo the demand to speak only to Prime Minister Netanyahu, and he agreed to meet with Foreign Minister David Levy, despite the original Palestinian opposition to such a move. The Palestinians had assumed that contacting Levy would undermine efforts to establish an effective dialogue with the prime minister, and in retrospect the Palestinian assumption turned out to be more accurate than the advice we had given. Immediately after the Arafat-Levy meeting on July 23, Abbas gave us a detailed account. He did not like Levy's rhetoric but was impressed by the substance of what he heard and by Levy's outgoing personality. Several days later, however, we were informed that Prime Minister Netanyahu had brushed away all the understandings on which Levy had agreed.[17]

At the end of August 1996, the "helicopter incident" occurred. Arafat had planned to fly from Gaza to Ramallah to meet with Peres. However, at the last minute, just as Arafat was marching on the red carpet toward the helicopter, permission to fly was withdrawn. According to the rules of the Israeli Defense Forces (IDF), the decision to do so could only have been made by the prime minister (Netanyahu) or by the minister of defense (Mordechai).[18] Several minutes later, Maher el-Kurd phoned me, literally in tears, saying, "These bastards, they could have woken me up at 2 a.m. and told us ahead of time instead of humiliating the chairman in front of his soldiers."[19] A first meeting between Arafat and Netanyahu was offered for early September, in exchange for which Arafat would agree to close three Palestinian institutions in Jerusalem.[20] The Palestinian side agreed to do so. One day later, the municipality of Jerusalem carried out an earlier legal decision to demolish an illegally built Palestinian house in the Old City, which led the Palestinians to believe that the demand to close Palestinian institutions in Jerusalem and the subsequent building demolition were intentional acts aimed at humiliating them.[21] Although the new government definitely wanted to limit and minimize Palestinian institutional presence in Jerusalem, the demolition of the house was an administrative municipal decision, independent of central government action.

Soon, a more serious crisis unfolded over a Jerusalemite municipal decision. The Jerusalem municipality, intending to create a tourist attraction, had reconstructed an old Hasmonean Tunnel that dated back to 19 BC. The tunnel led underground to the Wailing Wall and was close to two Muslim holy sites, the Dome of the Rock and the al-Aqsa mosque, which are both situated on the Haram ash-Sharif / Temple Mount. Pundak and I knew about the tunnel and had spoken with Husseini about it several times.[22] We tried to convince him that the reconstruction of the tunnel offered important advantages; of particular importance, it would help separate the movement of Jews and Palestinians by enabling Jewish worshippers to reach the Wailing Wall without crossing the Muslim areas adjacent to the Haram ash-Sharif, and thus might decrease friction. Husseini, however, argued fervently against the tunnel, saying that its proximity to the Muslim holy places and its underground location would incite trouble, encouraging extremists to spread rumors that Israel was taking control of the sacred Muslim sites. Accordingly, Rabin and Peres had prohibited the opening of the tunnel.[23]

The internal security minister, Kahalani, who had been made aware of the sensitivity of the issue and the related dangers, wanted to meet Husseini in order to be able to diffuse rising tension. However, Netanyahu feared that official meetings with Husseini would symbolize Israeli recognition of Palestinian authority over parts of Jerusalem and hence refused to permit the meetings. Moreover, Jerusalem mayor Olmert was determined to open the tunnel, and he gave the order to open it on September 25. Coordination between the Israeli police and the Orient House might have prevented the subsequent disaster; immediately after the tunnel opened, Palestinian demonstrators hiding behind the Palestinian police opened fire on Israeli targets, both soldiers and civilians. Sixteen Israelis and fifty Palestinians were killed in the ensuing violence.[24]

Our Palestinian contacts hinted that the outbreak of violence had been planned in order to create a reset and dictate, as far as possible, the emerging terms of engagement between the PA and the Israeli government. Just as I had been shocked in the spring of 1990 by the Palestinian verbal threat to unleash Iraqi rockets against Israel,[25] I was stunned once again by the ease with which negotiations disintegrated into violence.[26] I did not yet realize that the shootings in response to the tunnel opening would have far-reaching implications for thinking of and planning violent action on both sides of the Israeli/Palestinian divide.

The eruption of violence at the end of September 1996 led both Israelis and Palestinians to plan for even more violence. The IDF, reacting to the fact that the Palestinian police forces had been the main leaders of the violent action at the Hasmonean Tunnel, planned for "Operation Field of Thistles"—suggesting the employment of overwhelming firepower, "one million bullets," to deter any further acts of violence.[27] From this scenario, the Palestinians learned that the violence of September 1996 was a valid political response. Muhammad Dahlan, the Palestinian security forces head in Gaza (who had a close personal and professional relationship with American and Israeli intelligence officials), as well as Hassan Asfour, who had been a member of the Palestinian negotiating team in Norway and in January 1996 had been elected member of the Palestinian Legislative Council for the Khan Yunis district, did not keep this a secret. In February 1998, more than a year after the attacks, they told Novik that the lesson they had learned from the September 1996 violence was that violence was the only realistic response against an "unfolding US-Israeli conspiracy against the Palestinians."[28]

The events of September 1996 also mobilized the international community. On September 28, the UN Security Council announced Resolution 1073, calling for the immediate cessation of violence. Over the next few days, American, Russian, and European Union statements followed this call for peace, as did Pope John Paul II, with an "Appeal for Peace in the Middle East."[29] Following up on his call to action, US president Bill Clinton asked King Hussein of Jordan, Prime Minister Netanyahu, and Chairman Arafat to come to Washington for a Middle East summit. The

Americans believed that the opening of the Hasmonean Tunnel had been an Israeli provocation, and when the Israeli delegation arrived in Washington, the American peace team demanded the immediate closure of the tunnel.[30] The frosty treatment that the Americans gave to Netanyahu and his delegation indicated that the tunnel incident and the ensuing summit were intended to pressure the Israeli prime minister to make concessions. Dennis Ross, the special Middle East envoy named by President Clinton to work with both sides of the conflict, later observed that Netanyahu was under substantial pressure to put down the riots with overwhelming military force (at the risk of an increase in suicide bombings), but that outside his right-wing political and religious base he was also being criticized for his irresponsible action in opening the tunnel. "Though loath to cave in to our pressure," Ross continued, "he would want to show the mainstream of Israel that he had not destroyed Oslo."[31] It was now necessary to negotiate the conditions to allow the PA to take control over Hebron, and agree on how to implement the "Further Israeli Redeployment" that had been agreed to under the Oslo II Agreement.

The ECF's efforts to create a stable working relationship between the PA and the Israeli government were undermined by the substantial US backing for the Palestinians. One such story illustrates the failure of a track-two negotiation effort. After his meeting with Israeli finance minister Meridor, Maher el-Kurd asked me to help prepare a conference in the United States that would commit the United States, Israel, and the Palestinians to promoting economic development and international investment in the Palestinian territories. I convinced Timothy J. Sullivan, the president of the College of William and Mary in Williamsburg, Virginia, to take on such a task. We gained Meridor's support for this venture and prepared "the William and Mary Declaration," requesting economic initiatives such as support for joint Israeli-Palestinian business ventures and cooperation between nongovernmental and private-sector organizations; encouragement for private investors in major infrastructure projects; and greater freedom of movement of Palestinian workers, capital, and goods in the West Bank, Gaza, and Israel.[32]

The conference was scheduled for the end of December 1996, when negotiations for the Hebron Protocol were reaching a decisive moment. Meridor, who had committed to coming to the conference, asked to be excused to support the passage of his budget in the Knesset. He ordered that Ohad Maharani, the Israeli economic attaché to Washington, represent him personally at the conference. However, Maher el-Kurd and all the other Palestinian participants canceled their participation at the very last moment. Apparently, the Palestinians feared that Israeli goodwill and commitment to support Palestinian economic development would diminish US pressure on Israel over issues such as transferring authority over Hebron to the PA. The conference and the William and Mary Declaration were called off, resulting in a substantial financial loss to the college as well as the loss of a trilateral US-Palestinian-Israeli commitment to promote vital Palestinian economic projects. For me, it was a déjà vu experience; in 1995, the Palestinians had called off a people-to-people workshop at the United Nations on which the ECF had been working for months with Fathi Arafat, a younger brother of Yasser Arafat.

Novik experienced a similar situation. Toward the end of December 1996, at the height of the negotiations for the Hebron Protocol, he and a number of other Israeli participants were invited to a meeting with Egyptian president Mubarak. To ease the right-wing political pressure on Prime Minister Netanyahu, the Israeli delegation asked for the release of Azam Azam, a Druze who had been arrested in November 1996, having been accused by Egyptian intelligence first of industrial espionage and later of having worked for the Mossad as an Israeli spy.[33] Mubarak responded that the publicity created by Israel would make it difficult to release Azam. Novik remarked that Azam was not Jewish, which complicated the matter for Israel as its success or failure would affect relations with the Arab minority. Mubarak's first reaction was that Jews and Arabs were equal for him, and as a result it did not matter. Novik explained that because Azam was Arab, Israel was afraid that keeping quiet would result in an accusation of racism, which they would not have faced if the prisoner was Jewish. This argument convinced Mubarak, who said, "Tell Prime Minister Netanyahu, if he will sign the Hebron Protocol, I will release Azam Azam."[34] Two weeks later, Netanyahu signed the Hebron Protocol, but Azam was not released. (He remained in Egyptian prison until December 2004, when he was released and returned to his village in Israel.)

Preparing a Joint National Platform, January 22, 1997

The ECF's strategic aim was to turn the Beilin-Abu Mazen Understanding into a basic document that would lead to a Permanent Status Agreement with the Palestinians. According to the Cairo (or Gaza-Jericho) Agreement that had been signed on May 4, 1994, Permanent Status negotiations should be concluded by May 1999—five years later.[35] To meet this target date, we knew that support from Likud and other right-wing organizations and individuals were essential. Thus, in the autumn of 1996, Beilin started a dialogue with Likud member of the Knesset Michael Eitan, who was joined by other members of Likud and from the related political parties Gesher (Foreign Minister David Levy's party) and Tzomet (former IDF chief of staff Rafael Eitan's party). After several months of discussions, the Beilin-Eitan dialogue successfully concluded the "National Agreement Regarding the Negotiations on the Permanent Settlement with the Palestinians."[36] The leading term of reference for a common platform was to recognize the reality created by "the Camp David Agreements, the Oslo Accords, the Mutual Recognition between Israel and the PLO and the settlements in the territories under Israeli control since 1967."[37]

The commitment to establishing an independent State of Palestine was replaced by the need "to permit the establishment of a Palestinian entity whose status will be determined in negotiations." In essence, Israeli right-wing politicians committed themselves to the partition of Eretz Yisrael, giving up the dream of a "Greater Israel," and endorsing the PLO as a partner for negotiations on Permanent Status along the provisions of the 1978 Camp David Accords and the 1993 and 1995 Oslo Accords. In return, Beilin was willing to accommodate their concerns. Israeli settlements would not be evacuated; a return to the June 4, 1967, cease-fire lines was negated; and Israeli armed forces would be deployed along the Jordan River, which would be recognized as a special security zone. Jerusalem, the capital of Israel in its existing municipal borders, would be "a single unified city within sovereign Israel."[38] And on the issue of refugees, "the right of the State of Israel to prevent the entry of Palestinian refugees into its sovereign territory will be recognized."[39] Nevertheless, the language of the document was chosen carefully enough to enable its adjustment to reach understandings with the Palestinian side that would lead the way to the Beilin-Abu Mazen Understanding. It was obvious that adjustments had to be two-sided and be accepted by the Palestinians, as well as by a wide Israeli political coalition of left- and right-wing parties.

Even before the document was signed, the leaking of early drafts resulted in strong protests, particularly from the Jordan Valley Settlements Committee, whose members feared that an Israeli united national front would agree during negotiations with the Palestinians to evacuate all the settlements in the Jordan Valley.[40] As a result, Netanyahu was quick to deny any support or commitment to the Beilin-Eitan paper, diminishing the practical political implications of this effort.[41]

The Hebron Protocol and the Note for the Record

In mid-January 1997, Prime Minister Netanyahu signed the Hebron Protocol and the Note for the Record.[42] The Hebron Protocol demarcated the areas in Hebron from which Israel would withdraw, and organized similarly coordinated and separated arrangements for Jewish and Muslim worshippers at the Tomb of the Patriarch Abraham. The Note for the Record defined Israeli and Palestinian obligations for implementation and for negotiation, particularly regarding the release of prisoners and the territorial extension of Further Redeployment. Part of the agreement stated that Israel was obliged to transfer areas under full Israeli administrative and security control (areas "C") to the PA "not later than mid-1998." The idea was to enlarge territory in the West Bank under Palestinian administrative control in time to prepare for the May 4, 1999, target date, when Permanent Status negotiations were supposed to be finalized. These "Further Redeployments," as the transfers were known, had been referred to in the September 1995 Oslo II Agreement, but the agreement had not specified the percentages of territory that had to be transferred. Moreover, the Note for the Record stated that the Further Redeployments from defined West Bank territories were "Issues for Implementation" rather than "Issues for Negotiation."[43] Netanyahu and Gold quietly celebrated a victory, because this wording implied that the Israeli government could unilaterally determine the extent of the Israeli withdrawal, and therefore the withdrawal could be negligible.[44]

At first, Netanyahu's signing of the Hebron Protocol and the conclusion of the Beilin-Eitan concept seemed to indicate the accuracy of Nusseibeh's thesis, which stated that slow progress with a Likud government and parallel improved cooperation between the Palestinian leadership and the Israeli peace camp would be the best path. Netanyahu was now committed to the Oslo Process by his own signature. Beilin, in the dialogue with Eitan and the members of various right-wing groups, had defined a possible common approach toward Permanent Status. This appeared to have created favorable conditions for preparing, in a multitrack diplomacy effort, the way toward a two-state solution.

However, the Hebron Protocol and the Note for the Record widened the gap of expectations rather than narrowing it.[45] Arafat's strategic approach was to reach an understanding on the three Further Redeployments that would permit him to gain control over 90 percent of the West Bank territory and would create the necessary conditions to obtain a full 100 percent in negotiations, whereas the Israeli government intended to offer far less.[46]

In order to understand where Netanyahu was heading, President Clinton asked him to present his strategic approach. Thus, in February 1997, Netanyahu and Gold presented the Israeli "map of interests" to President Clinton and his adviser Mark Paris (who previously had served as deputy chief of mission in the US Embassy in Tel Aviv) at the White House. The IDF had prepared the map in 1994 as a guide for negotiations on the Interim Agreement; it described, in great detail, Israel's security threats and interests, concerns for the care of the settlements, environmental protection and water resource interests, and more. By adopting the 1994 "map of interests" as his strategic concept, Netanyahu implied his government's interest in protecting and preserving existing assets in the West Bank and Gaza.[47] Netanyahu and Gold made the first part of the strategic presentation to President Clinton. Following their presentation, General Amos Gilead was asked to present threats emerging against Israel from Syria, while General Shlomo Brom was asked to present security threats facing Israel from the east, mainly from Iraq and Jordan.[48]

The strategic and technical gaps between the ECF and Likud agendas were substantial. Likud's strategy was to ensure security, settlement, and water interests, mainly by continuing business as usual while expanding the settlements. The ECF's strategy was to find a way to end the occupation under secure and stable conditions and to agree on a secure and recognized border between Israel and an emerging State of Palestine. Moreover, the ECF aimed at seeking common ground and creating mutual confidence-building measures as a safeguard against violence, while Netanyahu believed in the need to demonstrate Israel's strength and ability to withstand pressure.

Netanyahu also had a vested interest in improving relations with Egypt, building bridges to Saudi Arabia and the other Arab Gulf states, isolating threats from Saddam Hussein's Iraq, and creating the necessary understandings with Cairo and Amman to support the peace process with both the Palestinians and Syria. Accordingly, Novik spoke with Netanyahu immediately after the signing of the Hebron Protocol and proposed that Netanyahu engage in an intimate dialogue with President Hosni Mubarak on all regional matters, an offer that received the green light from Egypt. Osama al-Baz, who was President Mubarak's all-powerful adviser on foreign affairs and reflected Egyptian thinking, even suggested expanding an initial Israeli-Egyptian dialogue and pursuing multilateral discussions with the World Bank and senior Palestinian, Jordanian, and US professional experts to encourage regional economic cooperation. The intended outcome of such a dialogue was to strengthen Israel's ties and standing in the Arab world.[49]

However, Netanyahu's main concern was to keep the right wing of his party content. After the signing of the Hebron Protocol, Netanyahu unilaterally decided on a Further Deployment of only 2 percent, making it clear that he would not even try to meet Arafat's expectations half, or even one third, of the way. Worse, the foundations to build Har Homa, a settlement in the south of Jerusalem, were laid. The strategic task of Har Homa was to block the connecting roads between the southern West Bank and Bethlehem (to the south) and between Jerusalem and the northern West Bank (to the north). The United States, Egypt, and the Palestinians perceived these two moves as provocative, and caused them to drop the idea of promoting a dialogue and coordinated action with Israel on regional issues.[50]

Planning for Multitrack Diplomacy: A Four-Pronged ECF Strategy

Analyzing events unfolding, we developed a new four-point ECF strategy:

1. *Identify the zone of possible agreement and attempt to get there.* The only zone of possible agreement for which we could now hope was to reach a negotiated understanding on Further Redeployment. The American negotiating team set the tone, making it clear to Netanyahu that any Israeli unilateral decision on Further Redeployment was "not an option.[51] The Americans demanded a credible figure for the redeployments, and they coined a formula for a "two-digit" redeployment, clearly indicating that Israel would need to deploy from more than 10 percent. This formula guided the negotiations and would lead to the October 1998 Wye River Agreement. The ECF's input was twofold. Beilin, Novik, and ILP member of the Knesset Haim Ramon would meet regularly with Abbas and Saeb Erekat, and occasionally joined by others, at the Herzliya residence of Egyptian ambassador Mohammed Bassiouni. At these meetings, they attempted to lower Palestinian expectations to realistic terms and convince them to go for an agreement on Further Redeployment, even if it would be far lower than what Arafat had expected. Complementing our effort, Novik maintained ongoing contact with Ambassador Bassiouni in Herzliya and with Osama al-Baz in Cairo. The Egyptians could communicate with both Arafat and Netanyahu and could try to bridge the gap, helping the official effort to succeed.

2. *Create principles for Permanent Status negotiations.* Knowing that Permanent Status negotiations had to be concluded by May 1999,

Pundak and I worked with Agha and Khalidi on a document that we called "The Logic of Peace." In essence, it was a code of conduct, defining guidelines and principles for Permanent Status negotiations and guaranteeing a secure and stable environment for negotiations, independent of the speed of progress that could be achieved.

3. *Create popular legitimacy for peacemaking.* The ECF would engage in an intensive effort to promote Israeli-Palestinian people-to-people activities in order to create the necessary public legitimacy for peacemaking.

4. *Prepare, in bilateral or trilateral working groups, detailed work concepts for dealing with the core issues.* The core issues addressed were security, economic relations, Jerusalem, and refugees.

Identifying a Zone of Possible Agreement: Moving Toward Further Redeployment

In March 1997, the gaps in positions were apparent. The Palestinians were upset about the Har Homa settlement and what they perceived as a ridiculous Israeli suggestion of a 2 percent redeployment. In response to American and Palestinian anger, Netanyahu decided to refrain from implementing the 2 percent redeployment. This was a constructive decision, as it left space to negotiate an agreed-on Further Redeployment. Because both sides were willing to discuss a possible solution, Levy and Abbas met again, but their discussions produced little results.[52]

To overcome the crisis, the ECF suggested an eight-point package to the Egyptians that would serve the interests of all parties and could be marketed as the Mubarak Initiative.[53] One of the aims was to also strengthen Beilin's political position and enable him to work closely with the newly elected ILP chairman, Barak. The idea was to invite Beilin and Abbas to Cairo, where they would pursue informal consultations with the United States' and the European Union's representatives, enable Foreign Minister Levy to visit Cairo and present him informally with the Mubarak Initiative, announce the eight-point initiative, and then proceed with informal consultations with all parties. This program would be followed by a Mubarak speech to the region, inviting the parties to a summit meeting in Egypt. The basic idea was to renew the momentum created by the Madrid process earlier in the decade, pursue negotiations between Israel and the PLO on both Further Redeployments and Permanent Status, renew Israeli-Syrian and Israeli-Lebanese negotiations to achieve bilateral peace agreements, intensify the common struggle against terrorism, and pursue a normalization of relations with Israel, mainly in the sphere of economic activity.[54] Although neither President Mubarak nor Prime Minister Netanyahu accepted the eight-point concept, its ideas were seriously discussed in both Cairo and Washington, thus contributing to a US-Egyptian dialogue on how best to negotiate.

During the first half of 1997, an internal discussion evolved within the American peace team. Newly appointed Secretary of State Madeleine Albright and National Security Adviser Sandy Berger were convinced that Netanyahu had wanted to derail the Oslo Process.[55] They both wanted to adopt the tactic employed by former secretary of state James Baker: putting Netanyahu to the test of furthering the peace process, and putting the "dead cat on his doorstep" if he failed. Dennis Ross, however, was more lenient with Netanyahu and wanted to pursue a policy in line with Netanyahu's needs to preserve his coalition.[56]

Our position was somewhere in between the two American camps. We believed that it was important to create, within Netanyahu's government, a supportive coalition in favor of reaching an agreement and providing supportive input where necessary. At the same time, we did not oppose the idea of testing Netanyahu and putting the blame of failure on him.

To create a supportive coalition within Netanyahu's government, we once again suggested the creation of multiple dialogue channels, as we knew that different government actors were interested in pursuing such an approach. The Americans and the Israelis were in favor of procedural arrangements, and they did not need to be convinced to agree to a well-structured multichannel dialogue. We did, however, convince Arafat and Abbas of the usefulness of this approach at this time. Thus, four dialogue channels were established: (1) the Mahmoud Abbas–David Levy channel, which coordinated four committees on security cooperation, Further Redeployment preparations, settlement restrictions (known at the time as a "time out"), and Permanent Status arrangements; (2) the Erekat–Danny Naveh channel,[57] which was responsible for general coordination of the Israeli-Palestinian relationship, mainly between the various government ministries on both sides; (3) the Abu Ala'–Yizhak Molcho channel, which considered the core issues of the conflict (including Jerusalem and refugees); and (4) the Yasser Arafat–Benjamin Netanyahu channel, which supervised all activities and all other issues. The Americans were kept informed about the content discussed in all channels, which provided their peace team with important information needed for a US mediation effort. While these discussions were unfolding, Novik and Beilin maintained contact with both the Israeli and Palestinian sides.[58]

Because we were in a position where we could make policy suggestions to all sides, we felt that the multichannel dialogue process could lead to one of four potential scenarios. The first (and from our point of view, the best) scenario was that Netanyahu would accept and conclude the next agreement and his government coalition would fall apart, making it necessary to form a new national unity government with the ILP that could lead the way to Permanent Status. The second good scenario was that Netanyahu would sign the agreement and keep his government intact. The third, less desirable, scenario would be for Netanyahu to reject the agreement and for the US government to lay "the dead cat" of failure on Netanyahu's doorstep, creating the necessary conditions to allow for an ILP electoral victory. The final negative scenario allowed Netanyahu to reject the agreement and maintain his government one way or the other.

As Palestinian confidence in Netanyahu vanished, our main task was to rebuild confidence and lower expectations through multitrack diplomacy. Between the autumn of 1997 and 1998, US secretary of state Madeleine Albright fought to achieve the hoped-for agreement on a meaningful Further Redeployment. From her point of view, it was a three-front battle—on the first side with Arafat, on the second side with Netanyahu, and on the third side with the US political system—because she was afraid that putting the blame on Netanyahu would create congressional opposition. Her steadfastness led the way to the Wye River Agreement, while Beilin, Novik, and Ramon did the "footwork" in convincing the Palestinian leadership to stay on board and sign an agreement that provided for the transfer of 13 percent rather than 40 percent of the West Bank territory. In the meetings in Herzliya with Abbas and Erekat, weekly updates on Israeli and Palestinian internal developments helped to convince the Palestinians of the need to conclude the envisaged agreement. The Beilin-Ramon-Novik trio also mobilized support from Egypt to offer additional encouragement to the Palestinians.

At first, the meetings at the Herzliya residence of Egyptian ambassador Bassiouni were limited to trying to convince Abbas and Erekat of the need to get Netanyahu to sign another agreement with them. Later, Abbas widened the circle, inviting Asfour and Dahlan from Gaza to attend. The Beilin-Ramon-Novik trio again had to reason with this forum to gain wider support for the future Wye Agreement. Multiple internal ECF reports provide witness to the ECF's investment in this effort, and all these reports were sent to Barak to keep him fully informed and to try to educate him about the ECF's strategic approach.[59]

Albright was a tough and successful negotiator opposed to taking any shortcuts.[60] She finally had her way, and both Netanyahu and Arafat went along with her original proposed strategy. In October 1998, the Wye River Agreement was signed, providing for a 13 percent transfer of territory in the West Bank, a well-defined obligation for Arafat to fight terrorism, and an Israeli commitment for prisoner release.[61]

Creating the Principles for Permanent Status Negotiations: "The Logic of Peace"

The idea of developing principles and a code of conduct for Permanent Status negotiations was simple: In case an agreement on the three Further Redeployments was achieved, the agreed-upon principles would have to guide Netanyahu (or any other Israeli government), as well as the PLO, in pursuing Permanent Status negotiations. We knew that the gaps between the Palestinian and current Israeli government positions on outstanding core issues were too wide to be bridged. However, we believed that it made sense to define, in very general and nonobliging terms, the zone of possible agreement in order to permit headway either to a conflict resolution approach (an avenue an ILP government would choose) or to a conflict transformation approach (an avenue we believed a Likud government might choose, or might be influenced to choose).

Khalidi, Agha, Pundak, and I worked on the envisaged principles in the zone of possible agreement. After the conclusion of the Wye River Agreement, we made an effort to translate those ideas into a detailed concept. Khalidi and Agha translated the concepts into text for a speech, which Arafat delivered in Stockholm on December 5, 1998.[62]

The first principle in Arafat's speech referred to a mutual commitment to nonviolence:

> . . . we see that our first task is to undertake a qualitative change in our political discourse. This means the transition from the logic of war and confrontation to the logic of peace in our mutual dealings. For actions and words that may be appropriate to the era of war and confrontation can no longer be useful or appropriate in the era of peace and co-operation. . . . There can be no alternative to

resolving the disputed issues between the two sides except through negotiations.[63]

The second principle was a commitment to a two-state solution: "the state of Palestine alongside the state of Israel, co-existing by mutual agreement and acceptance, and in a manner that does not infringe on the vital interests of either side."[64] On the related issues of Jerusalem and refugees, Arafat acknowledged the vital interests of both sides and agreed that any resolution to the status of Jerusalem and the final position of refugees would have to consider these interests. On security, he said:

> ... the Palestinian side is ready to consider any security arrangements that do not conflict with the principle of Palestinian sovereignty over Palestinian soil. . . . In return for a final agreement that ends the Israeli occupation of Palestinian land, we believe it will be possible to deal with Israeli security concerns via the following mechanisms:
> • agreed arrangements on the ground,
> • bilateral and multilateral agreements,
> • international guarantees and agreements,
> • and finally, last but not least, true reliance on the logic of peace.[65]

We distributed Arafat's speech to all 120 members of the Knesset and received a very positive response from right-wing politicians, particularly Nathan Sharansky, who was an important ally of Netanyahu.[66] On the basis of those principles, we later prepared an "Israeli-Palestinian Understanding Regarding Guidelines for Permanent Status Negotiations," and prepared more detailed guidelines for Permanent Status negotiations.[67]

In preparing for the eventuality that an ILP government should be elected in the May 1999 elections, the ECF suggested a three-step strategy: (1) Conclude a framework and timetable for negotiations along the principles of "the logic of peace," (2) conclude a third Further Redeployment and establish a "transition to state" plan, and (3) move from there to conclude a Permanent Status Agreement.[68] The concept we had prepared made much sense. However, over the next one and a half years, we would learn that Arafat's speech had been nothing but a theatrical gesture aimed at pleasing his Swedish hosts. He by no means felt committed to speak or act accordingly. Arafat's repeated zig-zagging caused more harm than good, as the Israeli decisionmakers and public began to perceive him as being completely unreliable.

Creating Legitimacy for Peace: Promoting People-to-People Cooperation

Peacemaking evidently requires the support of the people on both sides of the divide. However, conflict situations tend to foster hate and resentment among people instead of creating a drive for reconciliation. We understood that the years of the intifada, 1987 to 1993, had created an understanding among various echelons of the Israeli and Palestinian leadership that movement toward negotiations and an agreement was necessary, whereas the grassroots reaction to violence was one of enhanced hate, resentment, and hostility. This state of affairs created a dangerous discrepancy that could all too easily minimize the legitimacy of the leadership to make concessions for peace. It seemed essential to convince wider segments of both societies to get on board the peace-finding wagon and establish the necessary bottom-up support for the envisaged Permanent Status negotiations.

With this in mind, the ECF had, from its inception, endeavored to promote people-to-people understandings, with little success. We failed at implementing the economic cooperation and regional development annexes of the Oslo I Accords, and our earlier attempts from 1994 to 1996 had similarly ended in failure (see chapter 5). Paradoxically, Netanyahu's electoral victory provided our people-to-people efforts with a substantial boost. With Israel under a Likud government, the European Union and various European governments became far more willing to listen to our advice and to provide more substantial funding. The EU's experience in dealing with the conflict resolution process in Northern Ireland demonstrated how important and effective a comprehensive people-to-people program could become.[69] Thus, between the summer of 1996 and the end of September 2000, we made substantial conceptual and practical headway in understanding and promoting people-to-people activities. In doing so, we analytically passed through four different phases.

First, we pursued people-to-people activities on the basis of a Norwegian-sponsored program. Forty-four projects were financed in the first cycle (1996–97), for a total of $850,000.[70] However, I was critical of this approach, as the programs were donor-driven and therefore were dominated by a cultural bias alien to the region. Another counterproductive factor was that the Palestinian side preferred working with Israeli groups that fully submitted to Palestinian political demands and tended to be most critical of Israeli government policies, and also of the general mood of the Israeli public. However, this approach—preaching to the converted—targeted the wrong group of people in Israel. The strategic aim of the people-to-people activities was to expand legitimacy for peace in Israeli and Palestinian society, especially among those who most resented and opposed concessions. An additional problem was the fact that project funding was, as a rule, given only once to the same group, so Palestinian and Israeli recipients that did not obtain follow-up funding might easily become disillusioned. Another downside was the inability of small groups to deal effectively with the administrative and logistical problems that had to be overcome in dealing with closures, obtaining travel permits, and handling other logistic issues.

Before the May 1996 elections, we developed a second approach, the P2P [People-to-People] Hub Concept, in a meeting with Muna Yuul from Norway and Ed Abbington from the United States. With the help of the European Union and the Dutch, Swedish, and Belgian governments, we created four hubs: (1) health and social welfare, (2) the environment, (3) research, and (4) education and reconciliation. The hubs permitted joint professional Israeli and Palestinian teams to coordinate a strategy for a sustained effort that could be maintained despite crises in the peace process, and made it possible to establish organizational facilities to overcome political, psychological, and logistical obstacles.

The health and social welfare hub focused on issues such as primary health care, substance abuse, occupational health and safety, rehabilitation, and trauma. Organizations such as the Palestinian Council of Health, the Red Crescent Society, the American Jewish Joint Distribution Committee, and the Brookdale Institute participated and pursued similar activities. Palestinian doctors from Gaza and the West Bank trained in Israeli hospitals, and Israeli Arab physicians, mainly from the north of Israel, trained in family medicine at Palestinian primary health stations. The Palestinian side was mainly interested in obtaining professional input from Israeli health professionals, while the Israeli side was interested in building bonds for peace. This partial asymmetry of interests helped us reach and affect a wider Palestinian public than would have otherwise been possible, as Palestinian hate and resentment against Israel was overcome by addressing practical and immediate needs. An important factor in enabling this work was Fathi Arafat's and Hikmat Ajouri's interest in building these activities as a bridge for peace.[71]

In 1997, the environment hub launched its main project. The ECF and the Society for the Protection of Nature in Israel, with the support of the Palestinian Environment Authority and the Israeli Ministry of Environment, established the Palestinian-Israeli Environmental Secretariat. The secretariat's mission was to educate Israelis and Palestinians about their common environment and to create a widespread awareness of the need for environmental protection. These activities were generously funded by the Dutch government, and several other Israeli-Palestinian nongovernmental organizations engaged in parallel activities.[72]

Early in 1996, we formed the research hub. The concept emerged from a dialogue that I had with Marc Otte, then the Belgian ambassador to Israel. Otte raised an initial annual contribution from his government, and the Israeli side raised a further contribution from the Charles Bronfman Foundation in Jerusalem. With a $1 million budget, the Israeli foundation gave research grants for Israeli-Palestinian projects in agriculture, water exploitation, sociology, health, and even Middle Eastern studies. Additional monies were provided for human resources development and necessary equipment for laboratories on the Palestinian side.[73] In establishing this research hub, we achieved an important political breakthrough. To circumvent the boycott that Palestinian universities had implemented against Israel, Nusseibeh, who had become the president of Al-Quds University, created the Palestinian Consultancy Group and received the necessary blessing from the Palestinian political and security echelons to work with Israeli researchers and their academic institutions.[74]

The Rothschild Foundation managed the education and reconciliation hub. The aim was to develop, as far as possible, a common understanding of history and to convey a message of reconciliation to schoolchildren. This approach was based on research that had been carried out in Germany, which showed that the perspectives and attitudes in pre–World War I German history books had contributed to the political and social mindset that made both World War I and World War II possible. An institute in Braunschweig, Germany, specialized in rewriting French, German, and Polish history textbooks to mitigate these negative influences. Based on this experience, we participated in jump-starting a similar rewriting work with the Rothschild Institute on Israeli-Jordanian and Israeli-Palestinian textbooks.

I respected the importance of these activities, but I understood their limitations. These activities tended to mobilize peace camp supporters on both sides, but did not reach the population groups that needed to be won over the most. When Pundak went to see Abu Humus, the director-general of the Palestinian Ministry of Education, to ask to extend education and reconciliation activities to schools, he got a negative answer. Humus explained, "We cannot do this. We have 1 million pupils in our schools and all of them hate you." The implication was that the Palestinian leadership did not have the social authority to build the legitimacy for peace.

We needed to create an ongoing impact on the existential interests of the people on both sides of the divide. Thus, two complementary concepts formed our next approach: cross-border cooperation, and a strategic alliance between the police forces of both sides.

The area best suited for cross-border cooperation was in the north of the West Bank and Israel, between the Jenin Governorate and the neighboring Israeli municipalities of Gilboa, Bet Shean, and Haifa. Preliminary contacts between the mayor of Gilboa, Dani Atar, and the governor of Jenin, Zuheir el-Menasreh, began in the mid-1990s. Our task was to conceptualize and systemize the relationship between them and raise international support. The Friedrich Ebert Foundation helped make headway possible, just as it had many times before, by organizing a workshop with us on "Israeli-Palestinian Cooperation at the Municipal Level" in Brussels in mid-December 1997.[75]

At the workshop, el-Menasreh and I formed a lasting bond. Although he had played a major role in pursuing the strategy of violence against Israel, at the Brussels meeting he turned toward peacemaking as he and I developed our first principles for cross-border cooperation. We were helped by the fact that the border between Israeli and the Jenin Governorate was along the Green Line (the June 4, 1967, cease-fire lines) and that there was no dispute over territory. It was therefore possible for Governor el-Menasreh to exploit the practical advantages that could be obtained in cross-border cooperation. For all practical purposes, the market for goods from the Jenin Governorate was Israel, especially given that exports to Europe and other Western destinations would need to pass through the port at Haifa, and exports to Jordan and further east also had to pass through Israel. In addition, a new industrial park on the border would create thousands of direct and indirect employment opportunities for the inhabitants of the Jenin Governorate. Finally, from Palestinians' political point of view, it made sense to demonstrate that they wanted to pursue good neighborly relations with Israel in an area where no border dispute overshadowed the relationship.

El-Menasreh and I thus worked toward a cross-border cooperation agreement. All the participants, both Israeli and Palestinian, were interested in concluding it. One particular problem to overcome was competition and jealousy on the Israeli side between the relatively poor local council of the Gilboa district and the more well-to-do council of Emek Hamaayanot. It would be no small feat to create an effective model, bringing different actors with different and rivaling interests together to commit to an agreement. To do so, we established a steering committee of four Israelis and four Palestinians. The Israeli members represented the ECF and each of the Israeli municipalities, while the Palestinian members were Governor el-Menasreh and three representatives of PA government offices. All steering committee decisions had to be made by an Israeli-Palestinian agreement, while no Israeli participant would have the right to veto another cooperation project of a rivaling Israeli municipal council. We agreed to engage in five areas:

- *Economic cooperation*, mainly to establish an industrial park near the border in Jalameh and to encourage cross-border trade and Palestinian agricultural exports to Israel, all of which required intense cooperation to manage quality checks, health provisions, and other bureaucratic measures that necessitated joint business operations and a close dialogue with the relevant Israeli authorities;
- *Regional infrastructure*, to guarantee sufficient water, sewage, and drainage systems for the Jenin Governorate, and to coordinate the road network and plan a joint railway connection that would help to market goods from the industrial park and the entire Jenin region;
- *Civil security*, whereby Israeli and Palestinian forces would struggle together against theft (mainly of agricultural machinery from Israel) and the smuggling of illegal goods into Jenin;
- *Human resources development*, to enable municipal employees, planners, and administrative staff to develop parallel professional capacities that would help coordinate work among the municipalities on both sides; and
- *Cooperation in education*, particularly to protect the environment but also in the other spheres of culture and sports.

In several workshops, the participating parties in the cross-border cooperation effort identified spheres for common action. After detailed discussions, and in order to prevent never-ending negotiations, I asked Tom Sheahy, who had worked for the European Union, to table a final draft and made it clear to all sides that it was a take-it-or-leave-it matter. Thus, on February 15, 1999, the signing ceremony took place in the municipality of Haifa. The document, which presented a model for Israeli-Palestinian cross-border cooperation, carried the signatures of Mayor Amram Mitzna of Haifa, Mayor Yael Shaltieli of Emek Hamaayanot, Mayor Danni Atar of the Gilboa region, and Governor Zuheir el-Menasreh of Jenin.[76]

It took more than another year to obtain the necessary funding for our work from the European Union, while the ECF continued to work with all parties involved without the necessary financial support.

Regardless, the impact of the cross-border cooperation concept was substantial. Palestinian exports from the Jenin area to Israel reached the yearly amount of about $150 million. With the help of Deputy Minister for Defense Efraim Sneh, we also convinced the Israeli government to change the designation of the area allocated for the industrial park from Area C to Area B. This change in status would enable the Governorate of Jenin to have full administrative control over the planning for the industrial park. A variety of joint business projects were planned, some of which were executed.[77]

The regional infrastructure working group drafted water and sewage plans that would provide environmental protection to the Kishon River, which flows into Israel and enters the Mediterranean at Haifa Bay, and would recycle treated water for agricultural purposes in Israel.[78] At the same time, the Israeli Railway planned a new railway line to Jordan, with a stop at the area of the planned Palestinian industrial park, which would carry Palestinian-produced goods to the region and beyond. Similar plans for connecting the Palestinian road network on a north-south line with Israel were pursued.[79]

Probably the most important success in winning over opponents of peace was in the field of civil security. Cooperation against crime, particularly against the theft of agricultural equipment, had a major confidence-building effect.[80] In the other two areas of human resources development, and of education, culture, and sports, activities were planned, but not much was achieved before the outbreak of the second intifada at the end of September 2000.[81] Our cross-border cooperation activities helped to prevent the outbreak of violence in the Jenin area until May 2001, but Jenin eventually became a hotbed of Palestinian violence and terror against Israel until 2005. Despite the violence, the practical benefits that had been achieved for the inhabitants of both sides of the border area through extended cross border-trade, civil security, increased industrial development, and more made it possible to renew cooperation from 2005 onward. At the time of writing (from the spring of 2012 to the autumn of 2013), the ECF was engaged in promoting cooperation in regional tourism, trade, and infrastructure development. Two important lessons came out of these efforts: to enable cooperation at the grassroots level with as little government interference as possible, and to anchor the cross-border cooperation concept into a wider bilateral agreement between the governments.

Inspired by the impact of our cross-border civil security cooperation, we understood how important it was to prepare for more comprehensive cooperation in police-to-police work. Accordingly, we pursued a strategic dialogue between the national headquarters of the Israeli and Palestinian police forces to coordinate cooperation against crime and the protection of civil interests on both sides.[82] Before we could achieve substantial results, however, the September 2000 intifada put an end to this endeavor.

In other people-to-people activities, we led a dialogue between the ILP and the Fatah movement. We met with the Fatah leadership—including Marwan Barghouti, Qadura Fares, Jamil Shabahe, and members of the Palestinian Legislative Council and the Fatah Supreme Council—with one central aim: to convince them that the Israeli peace camp could not mobilize the public to demonstrate in support of peace when there was ongoing Palestinian violence.[83] We failed in this endeavor; eventually, Barghouti would lead Fatah activists and the military wing of the movement to renew the violence against Israeli targets (see chapter 7).

We also engaged in preparing the Israeli and Palestinian public to deal with the Palestinian refugee problem by organizing bus tours for interested Israelis to visit refugee camps in Gaza. The results were astounding. The Israelis' initial attitude toward the refugee problem was that this was not an Israeli concern, but the visits created an awareness of the need to solve the problem, as well as empathy for the Palestinian refugees.[84] We also took Palestinian refugees to Jaffa, making it clear that Israel was no longer the country that they or their parents had left, and that it would not be possible to turn back time and return them to the Jaffa they had known.[85]

The second intifada put an end to almost all people-to-people activities.[86] Those that continued were almost exclusively pursued on the Israeli side by radical left-wing groups, and included demonstrations against the security fence and other similar activities. As important as these activities might have been, they did not serve the purpose of widening the public legitimacy for peacemaking and did not embrace wider circles within Israeli and Palestinian society. The general tendency was for the opposing camps within Israel to turn away from each other.

Preparing Detailed Work Concepts for Permanent Status

In preparation for Permanent Status negotiations, the ECF teams worked with Palestinian and other partners to prepare detailed work concepts on security, economic relations, Jerusalem, and refugees.

PLANNING FOR AN ISRAELI-PALESTINIAN FRAMEWORK AGREEMENT ON
SECURITY, PERMANENT STATUS, AND A TRILATERAL JORDANIAN-ISRAELI-
PALESTINIAN SECURITY EFFORT

On the Israeli-Palestinian front, the official track had been negotiating understandings to coordinate the struggle against terrorism.[87] The ECF directed its attention to the envisaged security conditions for a Permanent Status Agreement, and Gilead Sher, who personally was very close to Barak and enjoyed his full confidence, led the ECF's work on this concept. To assist track-one negotiations without preempting the official decisionmaking process, the security working group finished an intentionally incomplete but comprehensive draft for an Israeli-Palestinian security agreement with sixteen articles. The articles included a framework for security relations and coordination, Israel-Palestine and Palestinian external borders, arrangements for "safe passage" roads between the West Bank and Gaza, rules of conduct in the case of external threat, airspace and port security concerns, security plans for holy sites, and confidence- and security-building measures.[88]

It was understood that a complementary trilateral understanding between Israel, Jordan, and the Palestinians was necessary because the major external threats against Israel, Palestine, and Jordan would potentially come from the east—from Saddam Hussein's Iraq in particular, and possibly also from Iran and Syria. In 1991, during the first Gulf War, thirty-eight Iraqi missiles attacked Israel across Jordanian territory, even though Israel did not participate in the war. This experience influenced the October 1994 Israeli-Jordanian peace treaty, which contained provisions to deal with external threats against Jordan and Israel alike, and a commitment to turn Israeli-Jordanian security understandings into an effective lever for wider regional security cooperation.[89] It made sense to extend these understandings to the Palestinians. The idea was to incorporate Israeli-Palestinian, Israeli-Jordanian, and Jordanian-Palestinian security arrangements into a trilateral Israeli-Palestinian-Jordanian security regime. This concept had to include the functions of an envisaged peacekeeping force, early warning arrangements, intelligence cooperation and sharing, mutual trilateral security guarantees, and international guarantees. In line with obligations laid out in the peace treaty, the proposed text included provisions on how to create a regional security structure. The joint paper was developed in an intense dialogue with the Amman Center for Peace and Development, where the Jordanian experts were led by General Mansur Abu Rashed and the Palestinians were led by Ahmed Khalidi and Hussein Aqa, at times joined by General Abdel Razzeq Yehia.[90]

PLANNING FOR ECONOMIC PERMANENT STATUS

Parallel to the effort of preparing a concept for Permanent Status security arrangements, we worked on an Economic Permanent Status (EPS) concept to define the envisaged economic relationship between Israel and the future State of Palestine. David Brodet, who had negotiated the Paris Agreement that had governed economic relations between Israel and the PA since May 1994, led the Israeli team. The Palestinian team was led by Maher el-Kurd, who had been with us in Norway in 1993, and who was an economic adviser to Chairman Arafat. Gidi Grinstein, who at first was my assistant at the ECF and then became project director, coordinated the work of the Israeli team, while I dealt with some of the negotiating issues. In early 1999, we concluded the work and signed, on a track-two basis, the Economic Permanent Status Agreement. The agreement discussed the trade regimen, the status of the Palestinian labor market, currency and monetary policy considerations, and other long-term policy coordination plans.[91]

After the agreement was concluded and signed on track two, we submitted the concept to the Israeli Ministry of Finance. The reception of the draft agreement was conditionally positive, with one critical remark. We were told that the proposed arrangements left too many loopholes for coordinated Palestinian-Israeli corruption which would cause major damage to the Israel tax and customs authorities. On the basis of these inputs, we prepared a preliminary strategy that drew on the European Union's experience in defining accession criteria for entry, stressing a focus on actual practices, the stability of institutions, free and fair elections, the judiciary, and anticorruption measures.[92] The Israeli and Palestinian track-two teams then went together to the United States twice, first in early March 1999 and second in October 1999. In early March 1999, we presented the Economic Permanent Status concept to the World Bank, the International Monetary Fund, the US Department of State, and President Clinton's Council of Economic Advisers.[93] We had a follow-up workshop in October 1999.

PLANNING FOR AGREEMENTS ON JERUSALEM AND REFUGEES

We worked in much detail on the Jerusalem and refugee questions but, unlike on security and on economic issues, we did not achieve a final track-two agreement on these important issues.[94]

Successes, Failures, and Lessons Learned, May 1996–May 1999

Successes (with Built-In Failures)

Nusseibeh's thesis that slow progress under a Likud government would enable close cooperation among the Palestinian leadership, the ILP, and the peace camp—and would keep the Oslo Process on track—proved to be accurate. Under Netanyahu's government, the Hebron Protocol and Note for the Record (January 1997) and the Wye River Agreement (October 1998) were concluded. Israeli-Palestinian security cooperation was rebuilt after the violence following the Hasmonean Tunnel's opening in late September 1996, resulting in a decrease in terrorism-related deaths and permitting the economic recovery of the Palestinians.[95]

People-to-people activities affected large sections of both societies and created the beginning of important grassroots contacts that would help build the necessary social capital to support peacemaking. In preparing for Permanent Status negotiations, joint Israeli and Palestinian track-two teams, as well as a trilateral Israeli-Palestinian-Jordanian team, succeeded in signing security and economic agreements. Husseini and his team helped carry out intense work on the status of Jerusalem, providing a basic understanding of principles that had to be respected by both sides. Important headway had been made on the refugee issue as well, as we pursued ongoing dialogues with Assad Abdel Rahman, who had been nominated by Arafat as the "minister of the expatriates," and Daud Barakat, who was responsible for the PLO's refugee portfolio. No less important, we prepared guidelines for Permanent Status negotiations that committed to a two-state solution but otherwise took care to create a stable and secure environment and left substantial maneuvering space for negotiations on the difficult outstanding core issues. Finally, we prepared a three-step strategy toward a Permanent Status Agreement: (1) define obligatory guidelines or a code of conduct, (2) agree to a third Further Redeployment and "transition to state," and (3) move toward Permanent Status based on the creation of a stable fallback state of affairs.

The credit for the January 1997 Hebron Protocol and the Note for the Record and the October 1998 Wye River Agreement had to go, first and foremost, to the American peace delegation. Albright's leadership kept the Oslo track alive and made the Wye River Agreement possible. The ECF-led multitrack diplomacy effort played an important auxiliary role, in which Novik marketed ideas to the American, Egyptian, and Israeli leadership, enriching the policy discussions in Washington, Cairo, and Jerusalem. Beilin, Novik, and Ramon successfully kept the Palestinian negotiators on board and helped reduce their expectations on land transfer to a more realistic level. Finally, Agha, Khalidi, Pundak, and I provided important and regular inputs for emerging policy ideas, as well as information on the political constellations in the Israeli and Palestinian political communities.

Failures

Although the successes achieved were impressive, they provided only a partial picture of reality. Fundamentally, the political, security, and economic situation was still extremely volatile. The combined effort of the US peace team with Egyptian and Jordanian support, and the parallel track-two dialogues between Beilin, Novik, and Ramon and the Palestinian leadership, created the dangerous illusion of having developed a diplomatic formula for achieving one agreement after another.[96] It was not understood that successful diplomacy was not and could not be the main instrument for achieving a Permanent Status Agreement. What was needed was to identify all the components necessary to prepare for the "flight of the flamingos"—to create a coalition that was as wide as possible on both sides of the divide to make a Permanent Status Agreement possible.

The ECF's initial activities had, in fact, been aimed at the conclusion of the Joint National Platform that Beilin had been negotiating with members of the right-wing Likud, Gesher, and Tzomet parties, which presented a wide political coalition for the envisaged peace negotiations. The "Logic of Peace" concept, developed in coordination with Arafat and our Palestinian contacts, created an important code of conduct for negotiations. Promoting people-to-people activities and reaching wide sectors of the Israeli and Palestinian populations offered to provide public legitimacy and support for the negotiations. The track-two agreements that we concluded with Palestinian partners on Economic Permanent Status and with Palestinian and Jordanian partners on Security Permanent Status provided important, detailed concepts for agreement. These preparations were strengthened by the senior IDF echelons' strong commitment to the peace process,[97] based on effective security cooperation with the Palestinian security forces that had decreased Palestinian acts of terrorism substantially between 1998 and 2000.[98] Last but not least, our small group developed a close relationship with Barak, the newly elected ILP chairman. Novik would submit ECF policy papers to Ehud Barak on an ongoing basis, and we created a working relationship with Barak's closest confidant, Gilead Sher.

For each of these "flight of the flamingos" components, success remained partial at best. The logic of creating the Joint National Platform necessitated continued cooperation and the development of a joint negotiating plan. This approach would have made it essential to give up some important parts of the earlier Beilin–Abu Mazen Understanding and to speak mainly of a "Palestinian entity" rather than the Palestinian state, which would have necessitated a commitment on behalf of our group and the ILP to seek an agreement that would be less than Permanent Status. What would have been achievable was the opportunity for Israel's right-wing political parties to fully recognize the PLO, to negotiate a severe restriction on settlement activities, and, most important, to offer substantial concessions in support of Palestinian state building.[99] However, Beilin was unwilling to compromise on the earlier understanding he had achieved, thereby discontinuing the dialogue with members of Likud, Gesher, and Tzomet—which undoubtedly was a mistake.

The Logic of Peace concept experienced a similar fate. Neither Arafat nor Barak, who was elected Israeli prime minister in May 1999, felt bound by it. Arafat resorted to violent speech and, worse, to violent action—as happened first at the end of May 2000 and again, with far greater consequences, at the end of September 2000. Barak pursued an "everything or nothing" approach, and thus he was not seriously interested in concluding and committing to a code of conduct for an unlimited time of negotiations (see chapter 7).

The headway we had made in promoting people-to-people activities did create substantial Israeli-Palestinian coordination and also boosted Palestinian exports to Israel. However, it soon turned out that this was only a partial, temporary, and volatile achievement. Great segments of the Palestinian public were alienated by the corruption and oppression of the PA, and expanding settlements caused a loss of confidence in the peace process.

In spite of the "partial success" with regard to security cooperation, the September 1996 violence in reaction to the opening of the Hasmonean Tunnel had a devastating effect. The Palestinians saw the Israeli response to the violence as proof that violence could get negotiations back on track on their terms.[100] On the other side, the IDF's reaction was to prevent a repetition of Palestinian violence by contemplating the use of overwhelming firepower, of "one million bullets." By the start of the second intifada in September 2000, the contradictory but complementary lessons learned by both sides from the September 1996 fighting would cause the breakdown of peace negotiations and a return to a prolonged cycle of accelerating violence.

It also would turn out that the close relationship we established with Barak would be a one-way street. He would carefully read the papers that the ECF prepared, but in direct contrast to our experience gained, he would consistently support an "everything or nothing" approach. It would soon become clear that this was a recipe for disaster.[101]

Lessons Learned

LESSON ONE: IDENTIFY THE NECESSARY STARTING POINT FOR A MULTITRACK DIPLOMACY EFFORT

This study is concerned with identifying the moment at which a track-two activity can successfully turn into a multitrack diplomacy effort. Three times—in October 1991, in January 1997, and again in October 1998—the United States succeeded in encouraging an Israeli right-wing government to pursue negotiations and conclude agreements. In all three cases, substantial US interest and commitment was there, but this was not enough. A clear conceptual framework about where to start and where to go was needed. The Rabin-turned-Shamir Plan of May 1989 was, in many ways, the starting point that permitted the United States and Egypt to move on from there. The ten-point Mubarak Initiative, the Five Baker Points, and the letter of invitation to the Madrid Conference helped to overcome various setbacks and reach the desired endpoint: the beginning of Israeli-Palestinian negotiations. Five years later, under Prime Minister Benjamin Netanyahu, the starting points were the Cairo Agreement of May 1994 and the Oslo II Agreement of September 1995, both of which had been officially endorsed by the United States and which had as their endpoint an agreement on Israeli withdrawal from Hebron (in January 1997) and an agreed-on Further Redeployment in October 1998.

In each of these three diplomatic efforts, track-two and multitrack diplomacy was successfully employed to help narrow the prevailing gap. Evidently, track-two diplomacy can start and end at any given point. Unfortunately, without translating its attempt to track-one diplomacy, track-two efforts will remain ineffective. However, for a combined official and unofficial diplomatic effort to take off, well-defined beginning points and end points are essential. Thus, track-two diplomacy has the potential to develop a starting point for more official diplomatic action.

LESSON TWO: UNDERSTAND THE FOUR COMPLEMENTARY CONDITIONS FOR ACHIEVING SUCCESS

For success, it was essential to identify a realistic zone of possible agreement that, in principle, would be acceptable to all concerned parties. This could be done by satisfying four necessary conditions.

The first condition was that there had to be a preliminary agreement of the "what" that would be done. Under Shamir in the late 1980s, the "what" was the beginning of direct negotiations; under Netanyahu in the mid-1990s, the "what" was an agreed-on Further Redeployment. Only then could negotiations be confined to the "how"—the concessions and agreements needed from each side in order to obtain the "what."

The second condition for success was the US leadership's decision to put its political weight behind the envisaged effort. To overcome the reluctance of Prime Minister Shamir, Secretary of State James Baker had had to assert his political determination to bring about the beginning of the negotiations. Secretary of State Madeline Albright needed to demonstrate the same determination toward Netanyahu to bring about an agreed-on Further Redeployment. Both Baker and Albright needed the full backing of their respective presidents, George H. W. Bush and Bill Clinton.

The third condition was a track-two effort working behind the scenes to establish realistic expectations on all sides. Between 1989 and 1991, we worked with Husseini and Hanan Ashrawi and also undertook proximity talks with the PLO in the Netherlands. Between 1996 and 1998, the ECF and Ramon coordinated an intensive dialogue with Israeli government actors and with the Palestinian leadership in order to adapt expectations to what was realistically achievable for both sides.

The final condition necessary for success was that all the actors involved—the US peace team, the Israeli government, Beilin, and Novik—invested great efforts into obtaining the necessary regional support from Egypt and Jordan to help the Palestinian side conclude the envisaged agreement. The combined effort of these four factors was strong enough to convince Shamir and Netanyahu on one side and Arafat on the other to overcome their own doubts and the internal political opposition to the deal.

LESSON THREE: UNDERSTAND THE NECESSITY OF AN INTERNATIONAL
MONITORING AND FOLLOW-UP CONCEPT

After the conclusion of an agreement, threefold follow-up action is necessary: first, to establish an informal (or, if possible, a formal) monitoring mechanism to hold both sides accountable for implementation; second, to identify the next realistic zone of possible agreement; and third, to stabilize the achievement by providing the necessary support for security cooperation, economic development, and a process of ongoing reconciliation. In other words, the United States' determination to conclude the Hebron Protocol and the Wye River Agreement was important, but that success remained unstable without an achievable zone of possible agreement for the next step and the necessary political investment.

LESSON FOUR: PLAN FOR A SUSTAINED PROCESS OF CONFLICT TRANSFORMATION

The basic underlying assumption of the US peace team was to proceed along the classical path of conflict resolution—negotiations, agreement, ratification, implementation—and to offer support to both parties at each stage. Observing the difficulties and setbacks that occurred during the Oslo Process, US diplomats concluded that it was dangerous to move along a step-by-step approach, and they thus advocated an "everything or nothing" strategy. As Daniel Kurtzer and his colleagues explain:

> For one thing, a lengthy and precarious process was inevitably going to be particularly vulnerable to extremists on both sides. But even for leaders who aimed for a peace agreement to end the conflict, there was a built in Catch 22: The more concessions they made in the interim, the weaker their position would be in negotiating the more important final status issues. . . . Does one want to jeopardize the whole process by making an incremental step a central issue of contention and undermine what leverage may be needed in mediating the more important final status issues?[102]

Alas, these arguments ignore four crucial realities. First, it is argued that extremists can cause difficulties during a lengthy process. But does this mean that one can assume that extremists will cause fewer difficulties by reaching compromise agreements on final status issues? Would Palestinian and other Arab extremists accept the concessions that the PLO has to make on giving up the "right of return"? Would Jewish extremists accept the concessions that Israel must make on Jerusalem? Would extremists on both sides not oppose any possible agreement on borders and territory?

Second, in order to marginalize the opposition of extremists to any final status agreement, the foundations of stability have to be created ahead of the final status negotiations. In our case, this required effective Israeli-Palestinian security cooperation, regional support, a limitation of Israeli settlement activities, the creation of substantial economic opportunities for both societies, and a process of reconciliation.

Third, a stable environment for conflict resolution requires optimal political inclusiveness. Opposition groups must be included, and attitudinal changes must be encouraged to accept the reality that in spite of resentment and hate, both societies need to live alongside each other. This perspective necessitates a process of conflict transformation.

Fourth, the argument that Nusseibeh presented to me in May 1995 was in many ways accurate on all accounts: Slow and gradual movement toward a two-state solution under an Israeli right-wing government enhanced the partnership between the Palestinian leadership and the Israeli peace camp and provided the United States with sufficient opportunities to keep the Oslo Process on track. Its downside was the steady expansion of Israeli settlement activities. Fast movement pursued under an ILP government tended to create too much tension within the Palestinian political system, and eventually it led to violence and confrontation during Barak's premiership of 1999–2001, and to the breakdown of the peace process and the de facto elimination of the Israeli peace camp. Seen from hindsight, the United States should have taken serious action to limit Israeli settlement activities in a dialogue with a right-wing Israeli government, rather than pursue a Permanent Status Agreement that was not yet achievable.

The conflict transformation approach that ECF started to develop— defining a national unity platform aimed at developing a wide supportive coalition in Israel for a two-state solution; developing a code of conduct, along the "Logic of Peace" concept, aimed at creating regulatory guidelines to diffuse tension; expanding people-to-people activities in order to create the necessary social capital for peace; and planning for the necessary economic and security state-building agreements—were seen both then and now as essential peace-building measures. The repeated attempts to adopt a shortcut to Permanent Status have all failed. Today, as much as in 1999, it is essential to adopt the path of a comprehensive conflict transformation strategy.

Chapter 7

The March of Folly: Ehud Barak's Attempt to Conclude a Permanent Status Agreement, May 1999–February 2001

This chapter covers the period from May 1999 to February 2001, during Ehud Barak's premiership. Because our small group worked very closely with both Prime Minister Barak and the Palestinian and American peace teams, this chapter adds important new information to the unfolding of events and provides empirical and analytical observations on the causes for the breakdown of negotiations. The description also provides insights into both the power and the impotence of multitrack diplomacy techniques.

Historical Background

The May 1999 elections in Israel brought about a landslide victory for Israeli Labor Party (ILP) leader Ehud Barak. In direct personal elections for the position of prime minister, Barak beat Benjamin Netanyahu with a majority of more than 10 percent.[1] Similarly important was the fact that Barak could count on potential support for a peace policy with a majority of eighty-two members of the Knesset (MKs), against only thirty-eight who were still committed to a Great Israel policy (see table 7.1).

The potential peace camp, however, was anything but unified. On its left wing were the Arab parties and Meretz, which together controlled twenty MKs; on its right wing were the religious parties Shas, United Torah, and Meimad (the last being part of the ILP's One Israel Alliance),

Table 7.1. Peace Policy Support, by Knesset Party, May 1999 (members of Knesset)

The Potential Peace Camp		The Opposition	
One Israel Alliance (Labor, Meimad, and Gesher)	26	Likud	19
Shas	17	Yisrael B'Aliyah	6
Meretz	10	National Religious Party	5
Shinui	6	Heruth	4
Center Party	6	Israel Beiteinu	4
United Torah	5		
United Arab List	5		
Hadash (Arab)	3		
Balad (Arab)	2		
Am Ehad (former Labor)	2		
Total	**82**	**Total**	**38**

which controlled twenty-four MKs; in the center were the ILP, Shinui, and Am Ehad, which controlled thirty-eight MKs.

In a less favorable situation in 1992, Yitzhak Rabin created a political space in his government coalition by including the orthodox religious parties on his right and Meretz and the Arab parties on his left, leaving the national religious party outside. With a potential majority of eighty-two MKs, it would have made sense for Barak to follow Rabin's example. The twenty MKs to Barak's left offered an important counterbalance to the twenty-two MKs of the religious camp (Shas and United Torah). If either of these two blocs left the coalition, Barak would still maintain his government. Even if the religious bloc moved to the right, the near-equal division in the Knesset would not allow the opposition to cause the government to fall.

Shas and the United Torah parties would be wary of any possible agreement on Jerusalem and would oppose granting the Palestinians sovereignty rights over the Temple Mount / Haram ash Sharif.[2] Shas had left Rabin's government in September 1993, when the Israel–Palestine Liberation Organization (PLO) Declaration of Principles was signed. However, Shas and United Torah were willing to agree to a substantial limitation of Israeli settlement activities in the West Bank and the Gaza Strip, and politically they chose Barak's ILP as their ally.[3] Thus, it was feasible to uphold a policy of implementing Israeli's obligations under the 1998 Wye River Agreement and moving toward a "transition to state" while keeping Shas on board. However, in light of their previous hesitations on Jerusalem and related issues, completing a Permanent Status Agreement might be problematic in this political constellation.

It was of similar importance to keep the Israeli Arab parties on board and to offer the Arab community in Israel a sense of partnership. The Israeli Arab parties strongly supported the establishment of the State of Palestine alongside Israel, yet simultaneously were concerned about the rights and duties of Arab Israelis. Israel's Arab citizens tended to identify in many ways with Yasser Arafat. Rabin's approach of sustaining Arafat's legitimacy by offering confidence-building measures (see chapter 5) while moving ahead slowly was acceptable to the Israeli Arab community.[4] However, Barak feared that by including the Israeli Arabs in his coalitions, he would be stigmatized as a left-wing politician and thus might lose the support of Israel's right-wing parties and their rank and file.

Barak wanted to move very fast on the peace process: Withdraw from Lebanon, conclude peace with Syria, and conclude a Permanent Status Agreement with the PLO—all before the end of President Bill Clinton's term of office in January 2001. This rapid timetable was motivated by considerations relevant to US politics, by Palestinian inputs, and by internal Israeli political considerations. Gidi Grinstein and I had gone to see Daniel Kurtzer in Egypt in mid-April 1999. In that meeting, Kurtzer outlined a timeline that was largely based on the American electoral calendar in anticipation of the November 2000 US presidential elections. Kurtzer suggested that Barak should work with the Palestinians through January 2000 to enable Clinton to lead the negotiations and close the gap. He argued that by April or May, Clinton would have to turn most of his attention to internal affairs, and he suggested that June 2000 was the last date for a planned Israeli withdrawal from Lebanon.[5] Internal Palestinian discussions were contemplating a unilateral announcement of the State of Palestine, and it was essential to continue the negotiations and preempt such an option, which all too easily could lead to a dangerous Israeli-Palestinian confrontation.[6] From an internal Israeli perspective, it would be easier to keep Barak's coalition together during the first one and a half years of his premiership, as most parties would prefer to avoid early elections that might cause each of them substantial losses.

In forming the government coalition, Barak argued internally that he had three potential choices in forming his government: (1) a center-left government that would be dependent on the Arab MKs to maintain its majority; (2) a grand coalition with Likud that would tend to paralyze any movement ahead; or (3) a government supported by (and dependent on) small right-wing parties, particularly Shas and the National Religious Party (NRP). Barak formed his coalition from the third option, and he decided to exclude the Arab parties and instead invited the NRP and Yisrael B'Aliyah to join his government.[7]

Policy Struggles with Ehud Barak

Hoping for a Barak victory, the Economic Cooperation Foundation (ECF) had developed a close relationship with him. Since Barak's election as the ILP chairman in 1997, Nimrod Novik had kept him informed of ongoing negotiations between Prime Minister Netanyahu and Chairman Arafat and of the emerging thinking on the Palestinian side. Barak had even developed some reliance upon Novik's steady reports and would, at times, phone him and ask for further input.[8] In preparing for Barak's premiership, we submitted two documents to him: a condensed concept of an ECF-proposed strategy titled "Israeli-Palestinian Six Point Plan of Action for the Promotion of the Process of Peace,"[9] and a list of all the papers on which we had worked.[10]

We believed that much mutual confidence between Israel and the Palestinian leadership had been eroded under Netanyahu, and that the first task of a Barak government was thus to rebuild confidence. The Six Point Plan aimed at creating the necessary supportive structure for negotiations and securing a fallback position in case Permanent Status negotiations led to a deadlock. Thus, point one suggested the reciprocal implementation of the 1998 Wye River Agreement, further confidence-building measures, and a commitment to honoring interim arrangements "until the conclusion of the Permanent Status Agreement." Point two requested the establishment of a joint working group for Permanent Status that would agree on an agenda, principles, and a timeline. Point three related to security cooperation to prevent terrorism and fight criminal activities. Point four obliged economic cooperation and the enhancement of Palestinian economic development and growth in the service of Palestinian state-building activities. Point five committed both parties to intensifying people-to-people activities and civil society cooperation. Finally, point six requested

coordination with the donor community to establish the necessary political, diplomatic, and economic support. In case of a possible breakdown
in the negotiations, we suggested an international damage control mechanism backed by European governments and the European Union. This idea
was based on the argument that Europe had a vested interest in regional
stability, while the Palestinians had confidence in the Europeans and
needed their support.[11]

Thus, we hoped to be able to influence the policy planning process along
the way. There were some positive indications. Immediately after forming
his government, Barak established a peace administration responsible for
planning for both the Israeli-Palestinian and Israeli-Syrian negotiations.
Gilead Sher, who had led the ECF's working group on Security Permanent
Status, became Barak's closest adviser and his candidate for leading
the negotiations with the PLO. Gidi Grinstein, who had been my assistant for several years, was brought into the negotiating team and became
Sher's closest assistant. Throughout the negotiations, Grinstein had all
the ECF's policy planning papers at hand. Other members of this "Peace
Administration" were close to the ECF and would regularly consult with
us. Shaul Arieli was the coordinating secretary-general; Motti Kristal,
who worked on the Palestinian file, had cooperated with us before. We
also had functioning working relations with leading members of Barak's
government, including the tourism minister, Amnon Lipkin-Shachak, who
was the leading force in the Center Party, and the deputy defense minister,
Dalya Rabin. The minister of interior security, Shlomo Ben Ami, and the
minister without portfolio, Haim Ramon, were close to our political thinking, and we had open access to them.

We knew that Barak was committed to reaching a Permanent Status
Agreement with the Palestinians, concluding peace with Syria, and
withdrawing from Lebanon. We fully identified with these policy aims.
Though we applauded his intentions, we questioned many of his policy
assumptions: Barak believed that the closure of all outstanding core issues
of conflict between Israel and the PLO was the only way forward. In other
words, he adopted an "everything or nothing" approach, and he was convinced that the more concessions made during any interim period, the
weaker his position would become in negotiating the final status issues.[12]
Hence he believed that he had to keep the settler movement comfortable
and would only confront them after "end of conflict" and "end of claims"
had been achieved; then and only then, he believed, he could demand the
evacuation of settlements and their relocation to the agreed-on sovereign
territory of Israel. To keep the settler movement on board, Barak decided

to include the NRP (the representatives of the settler movement) in his government. According to Grinstein, Barak's inner circle soon discovered that every concession to Arafat would be blocked by Yizchak Levy, the NRP member in Barak's government.[13]

I personally opposed the entire "everything or nothing" approach and wanted Yossi Beilin and the peace team to consider three major questions:

1. What if a full agreement on all outstanding core issues was not achievable?
2. What if the Palestinian leadership needed to show some tangible achievements to the Palestinian public before being able to make decisive concessions on the Permanent Status issues?
3. Did the government understand that Arafat and the Palestinian leadership at large tended to be forthcoming to Israel on tactical issues but had little maneuvering space with regard to any proposed solution of the core issues of conflict, such as borders, Jerusalem, and refugees?

We quickly learned that it would be nearly impossible to change Barak's mindset. Accordingly, we sought the best way to promote the "everything or nothing" approach. Motti Kristal proposed to Barak that he should inform the Palestinians that the Beilin–Abu Mazen Understanding would be a reference document for the start of negotiations. However, Barak rejected this idea, as it suggested offering the Palestinians a state based on 100 percent of the territories occupied in June 1967, with a one-for-one swap that would permit 80 percent of the settlers to be incorporated into sovereign Israeli territory.[14] When Beilin, who was appointed minister of justice in Barak's government, presented the Beilin–Abu Mazen Understanding to Barak, Barak listened politely and commented that he would conclude a far better deal, and reach an agreement with the Palestinians whereby Israel would keep 35 percent of the West Bank territory for Israel and the Palestinians would establish their state in 65 percent of the West Bank territory.[15]

Although the ECF had full access to Barak, we had no common understanding on how to negotiate or what would be achievable. The gap in thinking related not only to issues of substance but also to the technique of track-two and back-channel diplomacy. At the beginning of his term, Barak announced that he would not allow anyone "in the woods of Norway" to negotiate on his behalf, evidently referring to Ron Pundak and me. Negotiations should start only when he and Arafat sat down and discussed the final give and take. He did not understand that Arafat thought and functioned very differently and would only become involved once a basic deal had been concluded by his advisers and a supportive coalition had been created.

Confidence Breaks Down: May 1999 to March 2000

The very first telephone call from Barak to Arafat—on May 18, 1999, immediately after the election results became known—irritated the Palestinian leader. Hussein Agha and Ahmed Khalidi told us that Arafat's first reaction to Barak was to fear that the asymmetry of power between Israel and the Palestinian Authority (PA) would maneuver the Palestinians into a no-win position.[16] Nevertheless, the wider Palestinian leadership had hoped for an ILP victory and knew that several channels to Barak's government were open to them.

Throughout most of the summer, Sher negotiated with Saeb Erekat and reestablished Palestinian confidence in Barak's honest intentions to conclude a Permanent Status Agreement. The outcome was the conclusion of the September 4, 1999, Sharm el-Sheikh Agreement.[17] It was more detailed than the Six Point Plan that we had prepared, but some of the plan's suggestions were co-opted and put to use. The agreement lacked reference to the points we had made on economic growth and civil society, but was more specific with regard to confidence-building measures. More important, however, it established working committees on the third Further Redeployment and the other committees provided for in the 1995 Interim Agreement, and it set clear dates for concluding Permanent Status negotiations: a Framework Agreement by February 13, 2000, and a Comprehensive Agreement on Permanent Status by September 13, 2000 (seven years to the day after the Oslo Accords signing ceremony on the White House lawn).[18] The Palestinians went along with Barak's suggestion to create relatively short-term deadlines for concluding the negotiations, but they would become suspicious about Barak's intentions as the negotiations proceeded only slowly.[19]

After the conclusion of the Sharm el-Sheikh Agreement, confidence was largely though not fully restored. To get negotiations going, the Norwegians invited President Clinton, Prime Minister Barak, and Chairman Arafat to a trilateral summit in Oslo at the end of October. At the summit, the decision was made to renew negotiations on Permanent Status and on Further Redeployments separately, along with a series of American visits to the region to permit the United States to push the process forward. However, the Palestinians left the summit with unease because they had hoped to achieve different understandings on both the process of negotiations and the substance of possible agreed-on solutions. According to my longtime American contact, Daniel Kurtzer, the atmosphere at the summit was very bad, as the US and Israeli teams did not hide the fact that all their attention was directed at Israeli-Syrian negotiations and that they viewed negotiations with the Palestinians as nothing more than a sideshow.[20]

Regarding the preferred process for negotiations, Mahmoud Abbas wanted a deniable and secret channel, preferably in Sweden, based on his experiences with Agha, Khalidi, Pundak, and me. He hoped to base the secret dialogue on the Beilin–Abu Mazen Understanding. To understand Abbas's approach, US Middle East coordinator Dennis Ross asked him to send Agha and Khalidi to Washington to present the understanding to the American peace team. They did so, and on their return to London, Ross arranged for a secret meeting between the Palestinians and Sher. According to Agha, Sher's first remark was that the understanding was not acceptable to Barak. Grinstein later suggested that the basic difficulty was the conceptual gap over the status of the West Bank; the understanding regarded the West Bank as occupied territory, whereas Barak viewed the West Bank as disputed territory, and would not agree to a one-for-one territorial swap.[21] The meeting was later leaked to the press, jeopardizing a potential continuation of dialogue between Agha, Khalidi, and Sher.

The Palestinians were upset about the Israeli opening position on territory, which offered 65 percent of the West Bank. The Israeli proposal was not merely rejected; it was seen as an indication that no deal could be made.[22] Emerging Palestinian fears were expressed by Miftah, a Palestinian nongovernmental organization led by Hanan Ashrawi. Under the title "Unilateral Peace," Miftah stated that

> very few people question Barak's determination to pursue and achieve a peace treaty with the Palestinians (and even the Syrians for this matter). The question is in his vision of "peace" and his misguided notion that he can single-handedly design a process, control the conduct of negotiations, select the Palestinian negotiators, dictate the substance and the time frame, redefine the role of the sponsors (the US) and the international community, and impose the outcome unilaterally. . . . The vast gap between Barak's concept of peace and the minimal level of Palestinian rights and legality cannot be solved by a forced or dictated version.[23]

Reports from Nimrod Novik and the presentation of a Palestinian Concept Paper on the Framework Agreement on November 18 did not change the basic picture of a prevailing substantial gap between the positions of the parties.[24]

In a mid-January meeting with Agha and Khalidi, Pundak and I received our first alarming message: "In case the Palestinian leadership will reach the conclusion that there will not be a general PSD [Permanent Status Deal], they will freeze security cooperation with Israel."[25] We were told that Palestinian leader Muhammad Dahlan had become the prime actor. He was supported by Abu Ala' and Hassan Asfour and would discuss with US national security adviser Sandy Berger how best to proceed. This was bad news for three reasons. First, Dahlan, together with Asfour, represented Gaza rather than the West Bank; although Abu Ala' came from Abu Dis (in the West Bank), the entire West Bank PLO leadership viewed Abbas and Yasser Abed Rabbo as their representatives, and not Abu Ala'. Second, after the 1998 Wye River Agreement was signed, Dahlan and Asfour had engaged in an ugly power struggle against Abbas, causing much resentment and a deep rift between Abbas and Dahlan and their supporters.[26] Worse, we remembered that in February 1998, Dahlan had argued that only Palestinian violence could bring about a breakthrough in the negotiations.[27] We were soon to learn that the power struggle between Abbas and Rabbo on one side, and Dahlan, Asfour, and Muhammad Rashid on the other, would only worsen over the months to come. We also worried that the idea of violence instigated by the PA would gain ground. If negotiations failed, it was possible that the vicious circle of violence would be renewed.

Another possible negative outcome was a unilateral declaration of the State of Palestine. We were told that the Palestinian leadership was determined to establish a state and that it would happen no later than December 31, 2000. Arafat had obtained overt European and passive US approval for this plan, and the Palestinians insisted that they would not negotiate the establishment of the state, but that its establishment could be carried out in full agreement with the Government of Israel and become the first step toward a wider solution.[28] Although this did not sound too bad, it indicated that the Palestinian commitment made in the Oslo Accords not to take unilateral action was eroding. In my mind, this was a lesser evil, and it did open the option of a rational fallback position.

A blow to Palestinian expectations came early in February 2000. To avoid confronting his own coalition, Barak informed Arafat that he was unwilling to hand over three villages on the outskirts of Jerusalem (Abu

Dis, al-Eizariya, and Sawah al-Sharqiyeh) that Israel had committed to transfer to Palestinan control. To discuss this move ahead of time, Barak invited Nimrod Novik and Shimon Shamir, who had been Israel's ambassador to Egypt, to his home and asked Novik to speak to Osama al-Baz about postponing the transfer of the three villages and to receive al-Baz's backing and blessing. During the subsequent telephone conversation with al-Baz, Novik argued that the political effort needed to obtain support from Barak's coalition for handing over control of these villages to Arafat could be better used for a more far-reaching agreement.[29] Barak, who had listened in on the conversation, was annoyed. He accused Novik of displaying his political weakness and insisted that Novik phone al-Baz a second time and change the argument.[30] Legally, Barak understood that he was acting in full accordance with the "Note of Record" that Netanyahu had signed in mid-January 1997. Then, Further Redeployment was categorized as one of the "issues for implementation" and not one of the "issues for negotiations." Accordingly, Barak understood that the village handover was not an issue to be negotiated, and thus he could decide unilaterally not to transfer the three villages that he had promised to hand over.[31]

When Barak presented Arafat with his proposal for Further Redeployment without the transfer of the villages, it caused anger. It seemed to prove what Miftah had written at the end of October:

> Having modified the transitional agreements, he [Barak] is maneuvering the implementation in such a way as to maintain control and guarantee consistency with his own version of the outcome of Permanent Status talks. Thus the implementation is grudging, excruciatingly painstaking and slow, and minimalist in terms of tangible Palestinian benefits.[32]

On March 6, Nimrod Novik wrote to Barak, proposing that the crisis with the Palestinians be overcome on the basis of work that had been done in the ECF and on the basis of ten hours of discussions with Abbas and Saeb Erekat over the previous two weeks. The two proposals were to secretly and deniably negotiate a "Roadmap to a Comprehensive Agreement on Permanent Status" and to agree on an interim action that would create public positive momentum. Novik argued that restoring the partnership with Arafat that had been created by Rabin, defining the way toward Permanent Status, and creating the necessary grassroots support were more realistic than seeking to identify compromise conditions for a final agreement.

What was worse for the Palestinians than being pressured into an agreement that they could not sustain was their worry about the immediate implications of the ongoing Israeli-Syrian peace negotiations. The Palestinians feared that success in concluding an Israeli-Syrian peace agreement would consume all of Barak's political capital and would not leave enough space to make progress on the Palestinian track. They feared that peace between Israel and Syria would take up all the time and energy that President Clinton could dedicate to the Middle East and that the PA would be left with the growing friction from Israeli settlers in the West Bank, who might accelerate settlement expansion in order to make up for the evacuation of settlements from the Golan Heights. At the same time, the Palestinians feared radical action from Palestinian sources as much as they feared provocation from radical Jewish sources, leaving the PA with few means to defend both its legitimacy and its peaceful relations with Israel.[33]

Renewed Hope: March 2000 to Mid-May 2000

At the end of March, the Israeli-Syrian track broke down over a difference of several tens of meters of territory on the northeastern shore of the Kinneret, also known as the Sea of Galilee or Lake Tiberias. Israel claimed that the legally accepted international border had been determined by the 1923 Lausanne Treaty (which had granted the shore of the lake to the British Mandate over Palestine—and thus, accordingly, to Israel, as the successor of British Mandatory Palestine), whereas Assad demanded the return to the June 4, 1967, situation, when the Syrians controlled that stretch of the lake shore.[34] Now aiming to intensify work on the Israeli-Palestinian track, the Americans summoned first Barak and then Arafat for talks in mid-April. Novik reported that Arafat anticipated that, considering the failure of Israeli negotiations with Syrian president Hafez al-Assad, substantial headway could be achieved on the Israeli-Palestinian track.

Novik and I had reason to believe that Arafat's main interest was the establishment of the State of Palestine. Our small group contemplated that a Framework Agreement that would proclaim the State of Palestine, obtain its official recognition of the state from Israel (and hence from the entire international community), and continue negotiations on all outstanding issues of conflict was achievable. Novik discussed this idea with Barak and understood that Barak was supportive, though he did not ask for greater detail on how this outcome should be achieved.[35] We did not understand at the time that Barak viewed such an agreement as the final outcome of negotiations, rather than a step toward achieving such a result.[36] In his memoirs, Dennis Ross explains Barak's thinking:

> He [Barak] wanted to keep the Jerusalem issue open in a way that would allow both sides to preserve their claims. . . . On territory, he had a 66–22–12 formula in mind: The Palestinians would get 66 percent of the territory quickly: 22 percent would be areas involving important security areas, but nearly all of the 22 percent would become Palestinian over a five- to ten-year period; and Israel would annex the 12 percent to meet their needs for settlement blocs. He [Barak] felt this was eminently fair and met the needs of both sides.[37]

Two weeks later, on April 20, 2000, Clinton met with Arafat. From his American contacts, Novik received a detailed account of the Clinton-Arafat meeting, which he then submitted to Barak. According to the briefing received, Clinton told Arafat that he did not know whether or not his successor (who would come into office in the following January) would be interested in dealing with the Palestinian issue. Clinton insisted, however, that he was willing to invest a major effort "even beyond my own capability" in order "to bring peace during my incumbency," and added, "I will not agree to divide the issues, or postpone any issue. I will make an effort to bring a solution to all outstanding (core) issues."[38]

Nimrod's report of the Clinton-Arafat meeting also included a detailed account of the positions outlined by Arafat. On Jerusalem, Arafat said that he could not accept Israeli sovereignty over Jerusalem as a whole or even East Jerusalem, because "East Jerusalem is the capital of Palestine." However, he was willing to discuss arrangements to keep Jerusalem an open city, in which "movement to the Holy Places will be assured." On borders, he said, "We have to fix the June 4, 1967, lines as the borders of the State of Palestine, with long-term security arrangements that have no territorial-geographic aspect." He mentioned the possibility of having international forces under US administration along the Palestinian borders. On refugees, he said:

> The "right of return" has to be made possible. Thereafter, we can seek arrangements to establish an international fund for compensation, or for the return to Israel, or the return to Palestine. This is the mother of all issues, as 70 percent of the population in Gaza and 45 percent in the West Bank are refugees.[39]

Reading the report of the Clinton-Arafat meeting in hindsight, the nucleus of the unfolding calamity is recognizable. From an Israeli point of view, Arafat's position was a nonstarter; from the Palestinian point of view, Barak's position was equally implausible.[40] At the time, however, our reading was far more optimistic, and it appeared that the compromises of the Beilin–Abu Mazen Understanding and additional agreements seemed achievable. The Americans, Barak, and the ECF all tended to adopt the most optimistic interpretation of Arafat's statements. It was not unusual for leaders to lay out their most far-reaching demands before engaging seriously in a negotiating effort that would be overseen and driven by the president of the United States. It was conceivable that Arafat would tone down his demands to more realistic positions during the negotiating process. However, with regard to the suggested negotiating strategy, the ECF and Barak differed. Barak believed that in order to get to Permanent Status, all other options had to be taken off the table, whereas we in the ECF were convinced that Permanent Status negotiations were only possible if three conditions were met: (1) a deal maker that would turn Arafat into the *demandeur*, (2) clearly defined red lines to be laid out on other issues, and (3) a fallback concept that would allow us to stick to the red lines. In preparing for the Beilin–Abu Mazen Understanding, the deal maker had been a commitment to a one-for-one swap on the basis of the June 4, 1967, lines. However, as Barak was not willing at that time to suggest such a swap, we prepared the "Principles for a Coordinated Unilateral Declaration of Independence by the Palestinians and a Unilateral Declaration of Annexation by Israel."

We proposed that on September 13, 2000—the date given in the September 1999 Sharm el-Sheikh Agreement—two coordinated unilateral actions would be taken and supported by six agreements. Arafat would be given the green light to unilaterally declare the State of Palestine within the June 4, 1967, borders, while Israel would unilaterally declare the annexation of 5 percent of Judea and Samaria in areas of settlement blocs. Following such unilateral actions, six understandings would be concluded between the Palestinians and the Israeli government:

- A security agreement would be developed to define the necessary security arrangements and permit a continued presence of Israeli security forces within Palestinian territory for twelve years, during which time Palestinian security capacities and Israeli-Palestinian security cooperation would be developed.
- The economic relationship between the two states would be governed by the Economic Permanent Status arrangements prepared by the ECF.

- A substantial third Further Redeployment would allow for contiguous Palestinian territory without Israeli presence in most of the West Bank.
- An agreement would be signed regarding the status of the remaining settlements in Palestinian territory.
- A three-year rehabilitation program would be introduced for 60,000 refugees residing in camps in the West Bank and Gaza.
- An Israeli-Palestinian negotiating plan would be concluded to deal with all outstanding issues.[41]

We had not given up hope for a more ambitious agreement on all outstanding core issues. We were simply proposing to move forward in two phases: the establishment of the Palestinian state and the annexation of 5 percent of territory, followed by continued negotiations.

To plan for Permanent Status negotiations, the American peace team—Rob Malley, Aaron David Miller, Jonathan Schwartz, and Gamal Helal—met with us to hear possible solutions to the core issues of conflict.[42] On territory, we suggested that the Israeli side define its concerns over three issues: security, settlements, and religious sites (particularly in Hebron). We suggested that the American team ask the Palestinian side to present a countermap to the Israeli one while addressing Israeli concerns. What seemed necessary to us was the definition of four categories of territory: (1) territories under full Palestinian sovereignty, (2) territories to be annexed by Israel, (3) "green" or "gray" areas in which Israel would have special rights for a limited time before being transferred to full Palestinian sovereignty, and (4) land given as compensation for annexed territories.[43] On security, we referred to the work we had carried out bilaterally with the Palestinians and trilaterally with the Palestinians and Jordanians; a trilateral coordinated security approach to diminish possible threats from Iraq and/or Syria, enable more effective coordination against potential terror threats, and create an effective nucleus for a wider regional security structure.[44] On Jerusalem, Pundak presented a stage-by-stage approach providing the Palestinians with sovereignty over Arab villages on the outskirts of Jerusalem. This would be followed by the recognition of Palestinian sovereignty over Palestinian areas within Jerusalem's municipal boundaries. Finally, after Israeli-Palestinian cooperation over Jerusalem was established, sovereignty over the holy places would be negotiated. We informed the Americans about the ongoing efforts for joint urban planning of Jerusalem and the plans to agree on a security regime for Jerusalem. In addition, we discussed the economic

Permanent Status concept, issues related to cross-border cooperation, and people-to-people activities.

The American team appeared to like our ideas, particularly on Jerusalem. In the same meetings, they nonetheless raised doubts about the likelihood or sustainability of an agreement on the "end of conflict." Gamal Helal, who originally was from Egypt and had been on the peace team first as a translator and then as a full member, asked us what would happen if Palestinian Diaspora groups took action against the agreement.[45] Although we had concentrated our efforts on talking and listening to the Palestinian inside leadership, not to the Palestinian Diaspora, we also feared that an "end of conflict" agreement was an unachievable goal. However, we refrained from seriously discussing alternatives to an "end of conflict" agreement, to avoid undermining Barak's efforts on the Permanent Status Agreement. In hindsight, this reticence was a mistake. Out of consideration for Barak and fear of undermining his negotiating effort, we missed the opportunity to put a more realistic aim for negotiations on the American agenda, even though we had done all the necessary preparatory work.

Dwindling Hopes and the Camp David Summit: May to July 2000

Following the April 20 Arafat-Clinton meeting, developments unfolded, as we saw it, on four different levels. At the top level, President Clinton and Prime Minister Barak were pursuing, with great passion and determination, a full agreement on achieving an end of the conflict. On the official negotiation level, ongoing contacts were being pursued in Israel and elsewhere, particularly in Sweden. The emerging difficulties were recognized, even as the negotiators continued to seek an agreement on all outstanding core issues of conflict. However, two fallback options were also being explored: The more ambitious Plan B would establish a Palestinian state and afterward negotiate the outstanding issues of conflict between two sovereign states, and Plan C contemplated an agreed-on third Further Redeployment combined with a more comprehensive additional Interim Agreement.[46] Because the Israeli negotiating team was being directed by Prime Minister Barak and the Palestinian negotiating team was reacting to strong pressure from the United States, the negotiators sensed that despite evident difficulties, headway was being made.

On the third level were the inside observers, like myself, who saw that we were moving toward a disaster. The fourth level was the unfolding reality of anger and despair of large sections of the Palestinian public and rising opposition within the Knesset against Barak's rumored concessions. Preparations for Palestinian violent action had begun after the end of Pope John Paul II's visit to Israel in March 2000. On May 14, the Palestinians planned and initiated five days of violence,[47] and on June 8, the Israeli Knesset voted in favor of a preliminary call for early elections.[48]

For us at the ECF, the emerging picture became even more apparent when we received our first alarming report from Agha and Khalidi. Abbas, who was in charge of the portfolio of negotiations with Israel, had found out that secret negotiations led by Dahlan had been held in Sweden behind his back, with Shlomo Ben Ami, Sher, Abu Ala', Asfour, and Ross participating. The Londoners said that Abbas was "exploding" with anger, as his position of overseeing the entire negotiating effort had been undermined. Beilin, Boaz Karni, and Pundak, in a meeting with the leadership of the Fatah movement in the territories, Marwan Barghouti and Qadura Fares, were also told how angry Abbas was.[49] To mollify the Palestinians, Barak succeeded in getting the Knesset to pass a law that would enable the government to transfer Abu Dis, al-Eizariya, and Sawah al-Sharqiyeh—the three villages near Jerusalem—to Palestinian control.[50]

Barak's gesture of willingness to transfer the villages was well intended, but it was too little, too late and did not deal with the internal rift that was causing substantial opposition to progress on the Palestinian side. Given that Dahlan was leading the secret negotiations in Stockholm and Abbas was being excluded, the transfer was viewed as Dahlan's achievement rather than Abbas's. However, the power to negotiate and make concessions still rested with Abbas, who was offended and irritated that too much attention was given to Dahlan.

The Berger–Dahlan channel had given the Americans the impression that Dahlan, Abu Ala', and Asfour were the prime movers on the Palestinian side. The Americans either did not understand or chose to ignore what the Londoners repeated to us time and again: Arafat would not negotiate without Abbas's knowledge and his prime involvement.[51] Thus, out of an eagerness to achieve progress, Abbas was crossed thrice: His demand to create a deniable track-two negotiating channel in Sweden was denied or ignored; secret official negotiations had started in Sweden without his knowledge; and worst of all, the negotiating team was, with the exception of Abu Ala', purely Gazan and publicly trying to undermine Abbas.[52] (Arafat might at times back Dahlan in order to make a point to Abbas and demonstrate that he could act behind the latter's back, but when push would come to shove and a final decision had to be made, Arafat still needed Abbas's full support.)

Agha and Khalidi let us understand that the way negotiations were being pursued in Stockholm made any successful outcome impossible. Agha said, "At first Abu Mazen wanted to kill it [the Swedish channel], but then he decided that it would be better to let it die slowly."[53] In our discussions with them, Novik explained Barak's strategy:

> Barak wants the deal to be done. It is only doable with Clinton. "Ehud and Arafat" does not work; bilateral, on a lower level, does not work. They need the pressure cooker of Camp David, with the burden of the danger of a breakdown; and they need Clinton to get the deal and market it. It is not money; it is engagement and commitment.[54]

Agha and Khalidi could not see how this would work with both the Palestinian inside and outside participants. To reach at least a minimal understanding on the negotiations and seek a possible way out, we suggested a meeting between Barak and Abbas.[55] In the following three weeks, Barak postponed his meeting with Abbas three times without giving any specific reason, most probably because his own working agenda was overloaded. However, it indicated how little Barak understood the internal Palestinian power constellation.[56]

On May 19, we heard from Novik about a meeting of Israeli and Palestinian negotiators at Egyptian ambassador Bassiouni's residence. At the meeting, internal affairs minister Haim Ramon argued forcefully that the Israeli public would not accept a final agreement on Jerusalem and borders, and that those two issues had to be postponed. With regard to a territorial deal, Ramon stressed repeatedly that the final agreement should offer the Palestinians 92 percent of the West Bank territory.[57] I knew that although the deal maker for the Palestinians was an agreement on 100 percent of the territory with agreed-on swaps, additional understandings on Jerusalem and refugees would also be necessary. I also understood that neither Barak nor Ramon was willing to agree to such a deal, and I knew that Ramon's judgment regarding the lack of Israeli public legitimacy for the attainable deal was accurate.

To overcome Abbas's annoyance at the Stockholm talks, I wrote to Sher that Abbas demanded that all preparations for a Camp David summit be fully coordinated and prepared with him. Provided that he was in control, Abbas would support another "Stockholm meeting," which would take place in Washington and last for seven to ten days. This preparatory meeting should enable Barak, Arafat, and Abbas to establish a team to prepare for the envisaged summit conference.[58] Sher told me that these conditions would be respected, but they were not. Barak ignored Abbas's proposal, causing further annoyance to his Palestinian negotiating partners.

In protest against the unfolding negotiations, on June 8, 2000, the Knesset voted sixty-one to forty-eight against the government. Barak had effectively lost his majority in the Knesset, but as long as the opposition was not able to form an alternative majority, the incumbent government would remain in power. Nevertheless, the public effect of the erosion of his majority sent a warning signal. If this was not clear enough, five of the parties in Barak's coalition left his government between June 24 and August 4. Hoping to keep Shas in his government, Barak agreed to offer them control over the Ministry of Education, which at the time was being led by the left-wing Meretz party. Barak's offer to Shas caused Meretz to leave the government on June 24. When summit negotiations started at Camp David on July 11, three right-wing parties (Shas, NRP, and Yisrael B'Aliyah) left the government, followed by Gesher on August 4.[59] As the legitimacy for reaching a Permanent Status Agreement was eroding on the Israeli side, those who were planning to return to violence on the Palestinian side were gaining strength.

On June 8, in a meeting with the Londoners, Agha remarked that the "events of Lebanon give a wrong message."[60] Viewing, together with Pundak and me, the disorganized Israeli withdrawal from Lebanon on TV, Agha and Khalidi became worried. Agha did not beat around the bush, and explained that he feared that Hezbollah violence against Israeli security forces would provide a dangerous precedent that many Palestinian groups would want to imitate.[61] At the same time, Israeli intelligence and security forces were gathering information that groups within Fatah were preparing the ground for short and controlled violent action.[62] Although Palestinians such as Abbas warned in their internal discussions against any such action, they also argued that Hezbollah could not and would not teach Fatah how and when to employ it. Fatah had applied violent action to serve political aims for many years and could teach others how to use or not use it. Under present conditions, however, it would be a fatal mistake for the Palestinians to engage in violence against Israel.[63]

Irrespective of the internal Palestinian discussion, Israeli security forces had already recorded internal Palestinian preparations to launch acts of violence.[64] I discussed the unfolding situation in a long and heated phone conversation with Beilin on June 10, 2000. My main point was that "having to choose between a workable Interim Agreement for Permanent Status, or open confrontation and violence, I still opt for an interim arrangement as the lesser evil." Beilin's answer both irritated and comforted me:

> Let us assume that everything you say is accurate. We still have to deal with the question of whether an Interim Agreement on Permanent Status would actually help to prepare a breakthrough for Permanent Status, or if it would rather postpone it for a long time to come and thereby actually contribute to the perpetuation of the conflict. . . . Maybe we can find a formula that would permit movement gradually on the basis of a two-step approach toward a Permanent Status Agreement, while maintaining enough causes to force the GOI [Government of Israel] to not stop halfway. If you could put something like this together, we should go for this as quickly as possible.[65]

Within a week, I prepared two papers.[66] The first, "Two-Step Permanent Status Understanding," intended to get as close as possible to Barak's strategic approach.This paper suggested the establishment of the State of Palestine on January 1, 2001, and provided for negotiations between the two states on all outstanding issues, much in line with ideas that we had prepared and worked on earlier.[67] The second paper, "Preliminary Guidelines for a 1,000-Day Program for a Barak-Led Government," was aimed to convince Barak to look beyond the end of the Clinton administration (January 2001) and to develop his own four-year plan for a full term in office.[68] This paper referred to four different issues. Following Israel's withdrawal from Lebanon, the first point proposed measures to stabilize Israel's northern border with international assistance. The second point was to create the reality of a two-state solution without finalizing all core issues of conflict. The third point proposed a program for National Unity (i.e., bridging religious, ethnic, and socioeconomic gaps within Israel), which I thought essential to help solve all outstanding central issues of conflict with the Palestinians. The final point suggested developing an agreed-on trilateral United States–Egypt–Israel understanding on a long-term strategy for comprehensive peace in the Middle East.[69]

At the time, I did not know that Barak had asked Othniel Schneller, former secretary-general of the settlers' movement and then director-general of the Ministry of Transport, to prepare proposals for dealing with all civilian matters under a two-state solution. By June 2000, Schneller had worked for more than eight months with all relevant Israeli government authorities on the one side, and with Jamil al-Tarifi, who was in charge of civilian affairs and the necessary coordination with Israeli authorities on the Palestinian side, to prepare an agreement. Schneller's and Tarifi's proposals complemented the ECF proposal to announce the State of Palestine on January 1, 2001, and continue negotiations on all the core issues thereafter, leaving sufficient time to work internally in Israel on the envisioned National Unity program.[70] The Schneller-Tarifi proposal did not relate to the question of statehood, but permitted the Palestinians of the West Bank and Gaza to experience the advantages and obligations of upgraded statehood-like powers of the PA and minimize the hardship of occupation. Such a development had the potential of creating the necessary social capital and regional support to enable both Barak and Arafat to deal successfully with the outstanding core issues of conflict.[71] If they had been concluded, the proposals would have created the foundations for a two-state solution without immediately solving all outstanding core issues of conflict. Schneller was nominated as a member of the official negotiating team. Because he did not agree with Barak's negotiating approach, he threatened to leave the negotiating team and return to Israel. In the end, he went along with the team, but he was left outside Camp David and did not get the opportunity to discuss with Palestinian counterparts the proposals he had prepared with full authority from the Israeli government.[72] (Many of Schneller's proposals are discussed as suggested proposals for Palestinian state building in chapter 10.)

Several days later, on June 20, the Israeli "Peace Administration" prepared a proposal for an Interim Agreement with the Palestinians providing for the establishment of a Palestinian state recognized by Israel and for the continuation of negotiations on Permanent Status.[73] I submitted papers to Barak, but did not receive any indication as to whether they had been read. The Peace Administration did receive a response from Barak; he rejected the "Palestinian state first with further negotiations" approach and ordered work on the concept of "separation" (which would not require Palestinian consent), instead of planning for an agreed-upon step. The idea of a unilateral Israeli withdrawal from different parts of the West Bank and Gaza had been pursued under Yitzhak Rabin in 1995, but had stalled because of the high financial costs that would be involved in such a move. Shaul Arieli, the head of the Peace Administration, and Motti Kristal were ordered to prepare the concept of an Israeli unilateral disengagement.[74]

In May, Clinton had stated that he wanted to convene a summit "before the end of June."[75] Despite all the contrary indications, Barak and Clinton were convinced that the idea of a "pressure cooker" summit made sense. In late June, Arafat went to Cairo and gave President Mubarak three reasons why he did not want to attend a summit conference: (1) the secret negotiations in Stockholm with Muhammad Dahlan on the Palestinian side had not yet reached the understandings necessary to enable the United States to bridge the gaps between the Israeli and Palesinian positions on Jerusalem, territory, and refugees; (2) Arafat was afraid that the Americans would put a paper on the table that he would have to reject; and (3) he feared that, as a result, he would be blamed for the failure of the summit.[76] In a direct message to Clinton, Arafat said that he would "prefer to quit" rather than give in on Jerusalem and the right of return.[77] Arafat's concerns were disregarded.

At the end of June, US secretary of state Madeleine Albright was sent to the region to make the summit happen. Aaron David Miller describes the outcome of the visit:

> We bought a little more time with Secretary Albright's trip in late June to assess the situation. She found an eager Barak, a reluctant Arafat, and no real information on what either would give on substance, once they got to a meeting with the president.[78]

Listening to both the Israeli and Palestinian interlocutors, it was obvious that an "end of conflict" agreement could not be achieved then. By the end of June, both Beilin and Novik were as convinced as I was that it would not be possible to reach a full agreement. Novik prepared another fallback concept for Barak, titled "Corridor to Permanent Status," and sent it to Barak's personal facsimile machine late in the evening. Several minutes later, he received a phone call from the agitated prime minister, prohibiting Nimrod from taking any action on the proposed fallback concept. Barak explained that he had worked out his strategy in every detail; he knew Arafat, he argued, and he would offer Arafat substantial concessions on the relevant core issues to make "an offer Arafat cannot refuse." It was essential, therefore, that no one else offer the slightest way out (*sedek*) for Arafat. Furthermore, Barak added, "The paper you prepared would offer him such a 'way out'; this is exactly what I have to prevent." Novik asked what would happen if Arafat refused to accept the Israeli offer or an American bridging proposal. Barak answered that it would not happen; the price of rejection would be too high.[79]

On July 6, despite all the odds against it, the proposed summit was announced.[80] Learning a lesson from Barak's response to Novik, Beilin adopted a psychological approach. Shortly before Barak left for Camp David, Beilin handed him a closed envelope and said, "If matters should go bad at Camp David, please open the envelope and take action in line of what is being suggested there."[81] In the meantime, I wrote a letter to

American peace team member Rob Malley with my suggestions for the structure of the summit:

> From the beginning, discuss the necessary Confidence Building Measures such as the release of prisoners and related "stage management." If necessary, Day 7, could be dedicated to guidelines between Barak and Arafat on a proposed fallback plan, thereby providing enough time to wrap up the fallback and to turn the gathering into something of a success.[82]

I learned later that just before the summit on July 10, the Americans had begun preparing a fallback concept. They were thinking of a concept very much in line with the suggestions made by Novik and me; namely, that Israel should recognize a Palestinian State and withdraw from the territories as part of the third Further Redeployment and that discussion on all the other outstanding issues would be postponed.[83]

The hope that the Camp David Summit would function as a "pressure cooker" and thus create an agreement was irrational. The minimal conditions for the summit's success had not been created. Arafat needed the support of the second echelon of the Palestinian leadership and similar support from the Arab world. Instead, Abbas and the coalition of West Bank Palestinian leaders who supported him were still at loggerheads with the Gazans: Dahlan, Rashid, and Asfour. Worse, on the eve of the summit, Barghouti and the Fatah movement called upon Arafat not to give up the right of return.[84] Neither the Americans nor the Israelis did anything to deal with the ramifications of the internal Palestinian rift, and nothing was done to obtain support from Egypt, Jordan, or Saudi Arabia. Eight and a half months earlier, Miftah, Ashrawi's nongovernmental organization, had described such a scenario as a Palestinian nightmare: Arafat went to Camp David to conclude a deal with little or no legitimacy from home. (This was also true for Barak, as he and the ILP had already lost the majority of support in the Knesset in June.) Novik had suggested that Barak obtain President Mubarak's support for an agreement, but Barak declined for reasons he kept to himself. Apparently, being aware of the most substantial gaps between the minimal Palestinian demands and the optimal Israeli positions, Saeb Erekat was anticipating that the negotiations would break down. To ensure that Arafat would not be isolated if this should happen, during the summit Erekat sent pessimistic reports to Cairo, Amman, and Riyadh. Based on this information, the Egyptian, Jordanian and Saudi leadership lost confidence in the possibility of success.[85]

At the summit, there was bad chemistry between Barak and Arafat. The negotiating teams had not prepared any agreed-on concepts, and even the conceptual give and take was unclear. The Israeli team believed that the give and take would be Israeli concessions on Jerusalem in return for a territorial deal that was less than 100 percent and the de facto exclusion of the right of return. None of this was acceptable to the Palestinian side.[86] Arafat's unwillingness to address Israeli concerns was probably best expressed when, at an informal get-together with the Israeli negotiating team, he argued that Jews had never been in Jerusalem and that the real Jerusalem was probably in Yemen.[87] In the meantime, the rift between Dahlan and Abbas caused further trouble. Dahlan agreed to concessions, claiming that he had backing from Arafat. The imagined concessions were soon withdrawn by the Palestinian team. This misled the Israeli delegation and created a perception among the Israeli delegation that no Palestinian commitment would be sustainable.[88]

On the sixth day at Camp David, it appeared that everything was falling apart, causing President Clinton to take a very tough stand against Arafat. In response, the Palestinians came up with two different proposals. The first reflected willingness to compromise on the territorial issue, conditioned upon a far-reaching demand with regard to Jerusalem;[89] the second, reported by Grinstein, suggested that the framework agreement determine only one issue: the establishment of a Palestinian state on September 13, 2000, thus allowing the parties to continue to negotiate and prevent the situation from exploding.[90] However, Barak's mindset was not to go for anything but a full Permanent Status Agreement, whatever the consequences might be.[91] Barak's strategic thinking was based on a binary approach: It was either the "end of conflict" or, as he wrote in a message to the US peace team, "to lead the people of Israel . . . to stand together unified, in a struggle, however tough it will become, even if we will be forced to confront the entire world."[92]

The Way to Calamity: July to September 2000

After the summit failed, Barak returned home and handed Beilin the envelope with the fallback proposals, unopened. Barak continued to reject any agreement based on such concepts.[93] However, the work on unilateral separation, which he had ordered toward the end of June, was continuing. Fourteen committees were established to prepare relevant maps, a security fence, legal questions, Knesset legislation, transportation routes, and a way back from unilateral action to renewed negotiations.[94] At the same time, negotiations on Permanent Status and the "end of conflict" were continuing. The day after the summit had failed, Barak also announced that "the dream of peace" had not died and that he would not implement a third Further Redeployment.[95] Thus, the dialogue of the deaf accelerated. Barak was determined to reach a Permanent Status Agreement, even though Arafat was unwilling to make minimal concessions because he did not have either internal Palestinian or external Arab legitimacy to do so. However, Arafat would have been willing to go for an interim move that would allow him to establish the State of Palestine and become its head of state, as such a move would have enhanced his personal prestige and his legitimacy.

On August 11, 2000, acting foreign minister Ben Ami (who had been appointed following David Levy's resignation on August 4) started a detailed dialogue with Abu Ala' on Jerusalem and the Holy Places and moved substantially beyond the directives he had obtained.[96] At the same time, Sher and Erekat engaged in an intense effort to prepare an "I and P" (Israeli and Palestinian) position document on Permanent Status. This technique, which Abu Ala' and I had applied in Norway in February 1993, would permit the Americans to suggest a bridging proposal. Thus, the contours of a possible Permanent Status Agreement became clearer.

This state of affairs appeared encouraging to Barak and the dovish wing of the Israeli government—Beilin, Ben Ami, and Lipkin-Shachak—who became more eager to finalize the Permanent Status Agreement, ignoring the fact that they possessed very little internal legitimacy for moving forward. This time around, an effort was made to get the Egyptians and Jordanians on board, while attempting simultaneously to prevent Arafat from taking unilateral action. Barak, Ben Ami, and Israel Khasson (who had been second in command of Israel's General Security Services, Shabak, and had joined the Peace Administration from its very beginning in September 1999) all engaged in an effort to obtain Mubarak's proactive support. Barak also tried to get King Abdullah of Jordan on board. In a meeting with the king, a trilateral Israeli-Palestinian-Jordanian security concept (developed by the ECF) was discussed.[97] Israel also successfully convinced the European Union to oppose any unilateral declaration of independence by the Palestinians, and the Palestinians announced that they would postpone their planned Unilateral Declaration of State on September 11, 2000. Barak perceived these responses as an indication that movement toward a Permanent Status Agreement was still achievable.[98]

All this was bad news from Arafat's point of view. It seemed as if Israel was mobilizing not only the United States but also Europe and even Egypt and Jordan on its side. Though Arafat was unwilling to make the necessary concessions on Jerusalem and refugees that Israel needed to reach an agreement, he was afraid that pressure would make it very difficult for him to reject a US proposal (as he had told Mubarak at the end of June 2000).[99]

In September, Abbas publicly renounced the 1995 Beilin–Abu Mazen Understanding, indicating that Palestinian concessions, particularly over Jerusalem, were no longer acceptable to the Palestinian side. At this decisive moment, Abbas thus delegitimized the work of our small group, which we had pursued in coordination with him and his two advisers, Agha and Khalidi, throughout the four preceding years. Abbas was still committed to concluding peace with Israel, but the political legitimacy he needed to provide the necessary backing and support to the understanding we had concluded on October 1995 (see chapter 5) had been diminished due to the pressure-cooker tactics of Barak and Clinton, which disregarded Palestinian concerns. The internal power rifts within the Palestinian political system and the reduced legitimacy on the Israeli side to reach an agreement, signified by the departure of several parties from the government coalition, substantially reduced the chance to reach an agreement. Soon, we heard that substantial additional Israeli concessions, far beyond the Beilin–Abu Mazen Understanding, were needed in order to continue. Still hoping to bridge prevailing gaps, Beilin called upon Abbas, saying that "today, we both know that our dream is within reach."[100] In reality, the dream had already dissolved.

The members of the American peace team had cautiously expressed their doubts about whether an "end of conflict" agreement would be attainable in May, 2000. Now they gradually doubted whether the hoped-for outcome could ever be achieved. Until the Camp David Summit, the American peace team had almost blindly supported Israeli positions for an agreement. After the summit, however, the psychological setup changed. Barak and his government became the *demandeurs*, who were willing to go a very long way to reach an agreement, and Arafat was the one who had to be convinced to come on board. From the American peace team's perspective, this meant that it made sense to be far more attentive to Palestinian rather than Israeli needs.

Toward the end of August 2000, I first felt the change in American tactics. Pundak and I went to see Malley during his holiday in eastern France, and we discussed possible bridging formulas in regard to the refugee issue. Malley explained the formula on refugees that the American peace team was contemplating, one that effectively opened the door for increasing Palestinian demands to allow refugees to return to their former homes in Israel. From my point of view, this was a recipe for continued friction and conflict; no Palestinian government would be able to oppose Palestinian Diaspora pressure to minimize demands for return to Israel, and no Israeli government would be willing to comply. I made it clear that the acceptance of such a formula would cause me to call publicly upon Barak *not* to sign an agreement. I argued that the Americans had uncritically endorsed Israeli positions on the Permanent Status issues during the first half of 2000, and had thus put the Palestinians in a no-win position. It would make no sense now, I continued, to adopt the reverse position and put proposals on the table that would cross the most essential of Israeli red lines.[101]

Aware of Barak's determination to close a deal, the Americans understood that a bridging proposal was needed. On September 20, Novik sent Malley a suggested bridging proposal that went a long way toward accommodating Palestinian demands. It suggested the June 4, 1967, lines as a basis for territorial negotiations "with amendments reflecting the spirit of the new era, as well as realities on the ground since," and included language from the Beilin–Abu Mazen Understanding on equivalent exchanges of land and on the issues of refugees and Jerusalem.[102] However, it deleted the demand for a two-thirds Jewish majority in Jerusalem and other items that appeared to be hard for the Palestinian side to accept. At the same time, the Palestinians submitted their proposals to the Americans, which echoed what Erekat had told President Clinton at Camp David: "President Arafat instructed me not to accept anything less than Palestinian sovereignty on all areas of Jerusalem, occupied in 1967 and at the forefront, Al Haram al-Sharif."[103] Seeing that the Palestinians were unwilling to advance, Barak instructed Sher to stop negotiations.[104]

At that point, Karni and I spoke to Ashrawi. After having had several meetings, in order to conclude our discussions we met on the morning of September 26, 2000, at her home in Ramallah. She reported that Arafat had given her a document with his conditions and demands. He asked for an understanding that would allow him to declare the State of Palestine, optimally on November 15, 2000, but no later than January 1, 2001. The Palestinians would view the 1967 cease-fire lines as the temporary border, but understood that the final border would only be defined by negotiations and by agreement with Israel. It was essential that Israel recognize the Palestinian State. However, the Palestinians would not commit themselves to the "end of conflict," but rather to "resolve all outstanding issues peacefully, being committed to nonviolence."[105] Three more substantial demands and several smaller demands were added, including municipal elections in Jerusalem, an end to financial support for the Israeli settlements, and a minimum of an 11 percent Further Redeployment. He also suggested that the passages to Jordan and Egypt be controlled and monitored by an international peacekeeping force, not by the Palestinians themselves.[106]

This message was immediately reported to Barak via Beilin. We knew that the same evening, on September 26, 2000, Arafat was invited to Barak's home for a private encounter. The following day, Ashrawi told me that Arafat had approached Barak directly with the ideas that she had shown to us, and Barak had rejected them.

Following this meeting, the two negotiating teams convened in Washington to conclude a joint text of an agreement and actually produced such a paper with "I" and "P" positions, representing differences on specific issues. The paper left little doubt as to what the US bridging proposals would be. Sher and Grinstein sent an upbeat report back to Jerusalem, claiming that the "point of no return on the way to a Permanent Status Agreement" had been reached.[107] But the reality was very different. On September 28, 2000, Sharon visited the Temple Mount / Haram ash-Sharif, and the next day, demonstrations against Israel turned violent, signaling the outbreak of what became known as the Intifada al-Aqsa (the Jerusalem Uprising). It was a disastrous turn of events that we had feared for quite some time. In the following couple of weeks, we learned how easy it is to destroy the fabric of peacemaking and reconciliation.

Brigadier General Dov Sedaka, the head of the Israeli Civil Administration for the West Bank and in charge of coordination with the Palestinians, described the events of violence to me as they unfolded. After violence had erupted on September 29, the mechanism of Israeli-Palestinian security coordination continued to function. To deal effectively with the violence, the official Israeli team in charge of coordination with the Palestinian security services was very senior and included Sedaka, Israeli Defense Forces chief of staff Lieutenant General Shaul Mufaz, West Bank Israeli Defense Forces Central Command head Major General Izchak Eitan, and the responsible Shin Bet commanders. On the Palestinian side, the main point of contact was Jibril Rajoub, commander of the Palestinian security forces.[108] Evidently, both sides intended to maintain the fabric of security coordination, but their efforts were halfhearted. On the Palestinian side, no central and top-level effort was made to stop the violence, whereas on the Israeli side the use of massive firing power as a deterrent only added oil to the fire.

The first visceral shock came at the outbreak of the intifada, when a Palestinian member of a joint patrol team shot his Israeli colleague, Eli Tabeka. The joint patrols were the symbolic political and security elements of Israeli-Palestinian security cooperation.[109] The fact that one side of the joint patrols would shoot to kill his partner shattered any concept of cooperation. Nevertheless, the Israeli side decided to view this incident as an isolated event and hence continue joint patrols and security coordination.

On September 30, violence spread to different areas of the West Bank. The four main areas of confrontation were Hebron, Gush Etzion, east of Ramallah close to the location of the Israeli Civil Administration in Beit El, and close to Joseph's Tomb near Nablus. Massive shooting persisted while dialogue and coordination on security continued. However, the next blow to cooperation came at Joseph's Tomb, which was in the middle of an urban Palestinian area and very close to the refugee camp of Ballata. Armed Palestinian groups from the Ballata refugee camp persistently fired at the tomb. The small Israeli border police unit guarding the tomb was not equipped to defend itself against the onslaught. According to a prior agreement, the Palestinian security forces under Rajoub were responsible for the security of this holy site, its surrounding area. and the small Israeli force there. The Palestinians assured the Israeli army that no harm would come to the Israeli border police stationed at the tomb, and to avoid further damaging the security coordination Israeli reinforcements (which were ready to move in) were not sent to safeguard the border police unit. However, the Palestinian Security Forces evidently feared confronting the Palestinian groups, and an Israeli border policeman, Madhat Yussuf, bled to death, causing a major public outcry in Israel.[110]

After Yussuf's death, the Palestinian security forces went into Joseph's Tomb and handed the policeman's body to the Israelis. Still hoping to maintain the fabric of cooperation, on October 6, 2000, Prime Minister Barak decided to order the Israeli withdrawal from Joseph's Tomb and hand it over to the Palestinians. General Eitan and General Sedaka had to coordinate this move with Rajoub. Under Rajoub's command, a small group of Israelis drove from his headquarters in Bethunia to Nablus, constantly exposed to gunfire. The Israelis entered the tomb and succeeded in evacuating it, taking the Torah scrolls and prayer books but leaving almost everything else behind. For the time being, Israel's presence at Joseph's Tomb had come to an end.

Security coordination continued until the next traumatic event on October 12, 2000. Palestinian security forces informed the Israeli side that two Israeli soldiers had lost their way in Ramallah, and promised to get them out of there unharmed and hand them over to the Israel security forces. Instead, the two soldiers were lynched in front of live television cameras.[111]

Among the Israeli security forces, a bitter discussion ensued as to whether the Palestinian violence was being directed from above or was a genuine popular uprising. General Moshe Ya'alon and General Amos Gilead argued that Arafat had planned the violence before September 2000. They stated that the first early signs had been identified as early as April 2000, after the pope's visit. Furthermore, in May of that year, Fatah leader Marwan Barghouti had been ordered (presumably by Arafat) to fire at Israeli soldiers. Thus, the events at the end of September were nothing more than the continued implementation of an original plan to once again adopt a policy of violence against Israel.[112] Colonel Efraim Lavie, the head of the Palestinian desk in Israeli military intelligence, gave a very different interpretation. According to evidence that he gathered, Arafat himself was surprised by the popular outbreak of violence and even tried to put an end to it, giving orders to post Palestinian security officials between militant Palestinian demonstrators and the Israeli security forces. This turned out to be an ineffective measure because, from the Israeli vantage point, they were shot at by civilians who were hiding behind the Palestinian security forces.[113] After several days, the Palestinian security forces took off their uniforms and joined the fighting.[114]

My own view, gleaned from ECF information, was that the violence probably erupted without a clear order from above. However, the moment the violence erupted, Arafat made no serious effort to put the "jinni back in the bottle" and decided to "ride with the wave," as Dennis Ross later put it.[115] Maher el-Kurd told me that "when the tiger [of violence] has gotten out of the cage, almost nobody can put him back into the cage."[116] Beilin had warned Fatah in the past that the use of violence would make it impossible for the Israeli peace camp to mobilize sufficient support within Israeli society for a two-state solution. His prophecy came true.

Attempting to Put Humpty Dumpty Together Again: October 2000 to February 2001

The period from late September through late December 2000 was dominated by violence. All attempts to reach a cease-fire and return to negotiations failed due to Arafat's unwillingness to move forward.[117] Barak was still driven to achieve a Permanent Status Agreement. However, in the face of continuing violence, he offered more interest and support for the Peace Administration's Plan C: unilateral steps for separation along the lines of Israel's territorial proposals, leaving full Israeli control over the entire Jerusalem area. At the end of October, the government voted in favor of the unilateral separation plan.[118] At the end of November 2000, Barak was willing to go for what had been Plan B: a Palestinian Declaration of State coordinated with Israel, with a third Further Redeployment that would permit Palestinian territorial contiguity. Evacuation of isolated settlements would be considered if the PA agreed that the settlement blocs would remain under Israeli sovereignty.[119]

At this point in time, Barak was starting to understand that his "everything or nothing" strategy was falling apart, but he was still determined to seek a way out of the calamity that had developed. His first choice remained to conclude an agreement on all outstanding issues and achieve a Palestinian commitment for "end of conflict" and "finality of claims," and thus the negotiating process continued. On December 23, 2000, President Clinton submitted the parameters for a deal to the parties. It was published immediately and was received negatively by the Palestinians.[120] Various Palestinian negotiators asked for further Israeli concessions. Dahlan wanted more on security; Abbas wanted more on refugees; Abu Ala' wanted more on territory; Rabbo presented the entire proposal as "a cheat" (*maasej hona'a*); and Erekat explained that the Clinton proposal asked the Palestinians to give up the right of return and commit to end the conflict, even though they were not "getting anything in return."[121] The Israeli government, however, responded positively to Clinton's points, and in a letter to Clinton on January 5, 2001, it asked only that a Special Status Regime for the entire Old City of Jerusalem be established instead of dividing it into separate quarters.[122]

Despite the ongoing violence and the Palestinian rejection of the Clinton proposals, negotiations were renewed and the two sides convened in Taba, Egypt, on January 12, 2001. There, the Palestinians adopted a strategy of increasing demands that they must have known would not be acceptable to the Israeli side. Erekat rejected Israel's suggestion of a "special regime" in the Holy Basin (the holy places in the center of Jerusalem), adding that "as long as Israel insists on Israeli sovereignty over the Wailing Wall, the Mount of Olives and the Jewish Quarter, there is nothing to talk about."[123] From the Israeli point of view, this was equal to saying that there was no place for an agreement.

At the end of January, Novik, Pundak, and I met with Agha and Khalidi in a last-minute effort to clinch a deal. Barak had empowered Novik and me to offer a 100 percent deal on territory, if the Palestinians were willing to make the necessary concessions in regard to the refugee question.[124] However, the negotiating positions presented to us—often against Agha's and Khalidi's better judgment—were nothing more than an absolute denial of any Israeli interests, particularly on Jerusalem and refugees.[125]

The failure of negotiations with Syria, the unilateral withdrawal from Lebanon, and the failure of the negotiations with the Palestinians was Barak's grievous legacy. In less than two years of government, Barak had raised expectations without being able to conclude an agreement or show a constructive way forward. He left despair and mutual mistrust behind. On February 6, 2001, the Israeli people went to the polls and voted Barak out of power.

Failures, Implications, and Lessons Learned

The outbreak of violence at the end of September 2000 and the ensuing breakdown of Permanent Status negotiations was far more than a temporary failure. It was a watershed in the history of Israeli-Arab relations that, together with the failure of peace negotiations with Syria and the unilateral withdrawal from Lebanon, opened a dangerous new chapter of radicalization, mistrust, hate, and despair.

The failure of negotiations created two contradictory narratives on the Israeli and Palestinian side, causing further friction. The Israeli narrative was that Barak had gone all the way and beyond to reach an agreement and had thus exposed Arafat's unwillingness to make even the most minimal concessions. This narrative, which contained a great deal of truth, convinced most of the Israeli public that a Permanent Status Agreement was not achievable. The Palestinian narrative was that Barak had attempted to cheat the Palestinians into a dictated agreement and had ignored earlier commitments. Thus, the Palestinian public was convinced that Israel never intended to end the occupation. This narrative also contained some truth.

The most destructive development was the outbreak of Palestinian violence. Violence shattered more than the belief in the possibility of peace; it destroyed a great part of the fabric of Israeli-Palestinian coexistence. In the years to come, it would also cause a substantial decrease in the Palestinian national income, as well as great economic loss to Israel. In the political arena, it illustrated the powerlessness of Fatah and the PLO while simultaneously preparing for the rise of the Hamas and Jihadist movements. On the Israeli side, Palestinian violence not only destroyed the Israeli Peace Camp but also created a general public sentiment of support for the Israeli right-wing parties and even radical right-wing groups. The situation was compounded by the breakdown of the Israeli-Syrian peace negotiations and the rise of Hezbollah in Lebanon.

Two Strategic and Four Tactical Causes of Failure

Much has been written elsewhere about the causes of failure of the Barak-Arafat-Clinton negotiating effort, and there is no need to repeat arguments or ascribe blame. What is necessary, however, is to identify the strategic and tactical causes of failure and identify lessons to be learned in order to achieve a more circumspect strategy toward a peaceful two-state solution.

STRATEGIC FAILURE ONE: THE GAP OF EXPECTATIONS AND THE "PRICE FOR PEACE"

The legitimacy for peacemaking on the Palestinian side was based upon the decisions made by the Palestinian National Council in November 1988. Three very clear demands were expressed: the need for an Israeli withdrawal to the June 4, 1967, cease-fire lines, the establishment of a Palestinian capital in East Jerusalem, and the right of the Palestinian refugees to choose to either return to their homes or receive compensation.[126] Not to obtain these demands meant accepting defeat to the Palestinians.

The legitimacy for peacemaking on the Israeli side was based on the ILP's political platform agreed to by the Sixth Party Congress of May 1997, which requested a territorial compromise, maintenance of the unity of Jerusalem, and a solution to the Palestinian refugee problem outside of Israel.[127] The substantial gaps between the two diverging positions meant that the leadership on both sides would have to pay the price for achieving less than what was perceived on each side as the minimal demands for end of conflict.

Worse, the "price for peace" that had to be paid was very substantial on each side: The Palestinian refugees were asked to give up their dream of returning to their former homes; the Israeli settlers were asked to give up their dream of residing in Judea and Samaria and fulfilling what they believed was God's demand. On security issues, the Palestinians were asked to give up substantial components of their own sovereignty, while Israel was asked to withdraw from territories that offered a certain strategic depth for the defense of Israel's population centers between Ashdod and Haifa, which would be vulnerable to attack if the violence recurred.

STRATEGIC FAILURE TWO: THE DESTRUCTIVE REPERCUSSIONS OF A
DOUBLE ASYMMETRY

The Israeli-Palestinian conflict is burdened by a double asymmetry. The first asymmetry relates to the uneven power relationship between Israel and the PLO/PA. Israel's government institutions, military power, $30,000 per capita annual income, ability to obtain substantial support from the United States and the international community, and presence in the West Bank and Gaza in combination constitute a dangerous power equation, with a sense of Israeli superiority and Palestinian inferiority. As a result, the Israeli leadership is all too easily tempted to dictate negotiating conditions, or even conditions on the ground, which the Palestinian side perceives as bullying. The resulting Israeli strategic logic reasons that sooner or later, if an "iron wall" of deterrence is built,[128] the Palestinians will have to acknowledge the reality and settle for an agreement that Israel offers to them.[129]

However, it is a double asymmetry, because the Palestinian people and leadership are capable of mobilizing not only the Arab world but most of the world's Islamic population. Second, Palestinians believe that current demographic developments (if they persist) will permit them to outnumber Israelis in the area west of the Jordan River in the not-too-distant future. Accordingly, the Palestinians are convinced that time is on their side, and that with the help of the Arab and Islamic world it might be possible to defeat Israel through war, terrorism, or diplomacy. Furthermore, the demographic developments will eventually make it possible to defeat Israel from within.

This double asymmetry creates a dangerous dynamic. The Israeli side is afraid of Palestinians switching repeatedly from negotiations to violence. It is aware of the wider regional support for the option of violence and armed conflict, and is thus hesitant about making far-reaching concessions and giving up strategic assets that would be needed in conflict. Those on the Palestinian side, aware of their power to withstand pressure, do not see the need to settle for less than what they perceive to be minimally fair. The Israeli side perceives the Palestinian demand to offer the Palestinian refugees a choice to return to their former places of residence in Israel as an attempt to undermine the very existence and identity of Israel. In addition to the prevailing gap between the minimalist negotiating positions on both sides, neither side has the power to impose a compromise solution upon the other.

TACTICAL FAILURE ONE: THE UNREALISTIC EVALUATION OF THE ZONE OF POSSIBLE AGREEMENT

In April 2000, Israel, the PLO/PA, and the United States were turning to Permanent Status negotiations. Both Barak and Arafat laid out their negotiating aims to Clinton.[130] It did not require much to understand that the gap was tremendous. However, no serious effort was undertaken to investigate what a realistic zone of possible agreement would be, even though one was effectively available: an agreement on proclaiming the State of Palestine, creating understandings on all civilian issues (as prepared by Othniel Schneller and Jamal Tarifi), and committing to continue negotiations on all outstanding issues of conflict.

TACTICAL FAILURE TWO: THE RISKY "EVERYTHING OR NOTHING" APPROACH OF A TARGET-DRIVEN LEADERSHIP

Clinton, in his meeting with Arafat on April 20, 2000, told the Palestinian leader, "I will not agree to divide the issues, or postpone any issue. I will make an effort to bring a solution to all outstanding (core) issues."[131] This line of thinking was shared by Barak, materializing in an "everything or nothing" approach that resulted from political and tactical considerations. Politically, Barak was aware that in response to any agreement that might be obtained, he had to expect strong opposition from Israel's right-wing and religious parties. He therefore wanted a one-time political struggle, where he would put peace and the end of conflict on one side of the scale and concessions on the other. Barak's tactical thinking was based on the "realist" orthodox school of conflict resolution: to reach an optimal outcome of negotiations, the principle "nothing is agreed upon until everything is agreed upon" seemed to make much tactical sense.

From May 2000 on, however, it became clear to the negotiating teams that the intended "everything or nothing" approach was a dangerous fallacy, and that Barak was rejecting the more realistic proposals of an achievable zone of possible agreement that were being submitted to him.

TACTICAL FAILURE THREE: THE DANGER OF IGNORING OR MISINTERPRETING THE IMPACT OF INTERNAL PALESTINIAN POLITICS

During the negotiations in Norway in the early 1990s, Rabin, Peres, Beilin, and I understood that in order to achieve agreement, it was essential to gain first the support for the proposed concept from the entire second echelon of PLO leaders. Only when Abbas, Abu Ala', Abed Rabbo, and Asfour all asked to conclude the proposed agreement was Arafat capable and willing to go for it. This simple truth was later disregarded. The United States–led attempt to promote negotiations with Dahlan and his allies, instead of Abbas, was a recipe for failure. Adding to Palestinian divisiveness is not a sound recipe for advancing toward a lasting peace. Going to Camp David in spite of Arafat's opposition to holding a summit made matters worse.

Barak's strategic thinking was rational, yet at the same time it was detached from reality. Rationally, it made sense to prepare a substantial offer built around US, European, Egyptian, Jordanian, and further Arab support. Barak's assumption that the price for rejection would be very high was also accurate. However, he did not understand that these two components did not necessarily add up and provide sufficient ground to reach the hoped-for agreement. Barak lacked a deeper understanding of Arafat's thinking, of his modus operandi, and of the internal working of Palestinian politics and decisionmaking. Arafat would refuse an offer that he believed would portray him as a weak and defeatist leader before the Palestinian people and before history.

TACTICAL FAILURE FOUR: COUNTERPRODUCTIVE NEGOTIATING TACTICS

Barak's negotiating tactics turned out to be counterproductive. Instead of building confidence at the beginning of his term as prime minister, he made requests to Arafat to postpone the implementation of agreements reached at Wye River in October 1998, and this caused frustration. In September 1999, in the Sharm el-Sheikh Agreement, he determined a first deadline to reach a Framework Agreement with the Palestinians by February 2000, but instead of pursuing these negotiations he dealt almost exclusively with Syria, enhancing Palestinians' fears that they would not be able to conclude an agreement while Barak was otherwise occupied. Moreover, Barak's dialogue with Arafat created a sense among the Palestinians that Israel was trying to impose a peace entirely on Barak's terms, without reflecting Palestinian demands and sensitivities, as expressed in the October 1999 Miftah article. This feeling of trying to enforce an agreement on Israeli and American terms was reinforced by obliging the Palestinians to attend the July 2000 Camp David Summit against their specific reservations. Worse, Abbas's constructive suggestion to prepare such a summit carefully was ignored. Last but not least, starting negotiations by offering 65 percent of the West Bank territories and claiming 35 percent for Israel, and then increasing the Barak offer after each Palestinian rejection, was a clear recipe for trouble. Barak made it obvious that he was rewarding Arafat's rejections; and even worse, it seemed that Barak had no red lines.

A more effective negotiating tactic would have been to create confidence at the beginning, to listen carefully to Palestinian demands and political needs, to identify the zone of possible agreement, and then to make a substantial conditional offer on what was most important to Arafat and turn him into the *demandeur*. Having achieved this, the Israeli peace team could have negotiated the necessary concessions that Israel had to receive from the Palestinians in order to provide Arafat with what he wanted to achieve. Barak rejected this negotiating approach, as it probably would not have brought about a solution to all outstanding issues of conflict. The more moderate approach that the ECF had suggested would not have brought both sides to "end of conflict" or to "finality of claims," but it had the potential to substantially move the Israeli-Palestinian two-state solution peace process forward.

Lessons Learned

LESSON ONE: TEST THE WORKABILITY OF YOUR PARADIGM

The September 1978 Camp David Accords defined the paradigm within which all sides were working: Negotiations on Palestinian self-government had to be followed by an agreement on Palestinian self-government, which after five years would be followed by a Permanent Status Agreement. Based on this paradigm, our small group prepared the Beilin–Abu Mazen Understanding in October 1995, a proposal that appeared to illustrate that an agreement on all outstanding core issues of conflict was possible. From 1999 through 2001, the Israeli, Palestinian, and American leaderships followed the Camp David paradigm and sought to conclude a Permanent Status Agreement.

We will never know whether it was a realistic option to start negotiations in 1999 on the basis of the Beilin–Abu Mazen Understanding and bring them to a successful conclusion in line with the mutually accepted paradigm. What we do know is that the once-accepted paradigm fell apart in the time between April 20, 2000 (when Arafat described to Clinton his conditions for a Permanent Status Agreement), and July 25, 2000 (when the Camp David Summit ended in failure). During the same three-month period, two other paradigms had been developed. Israel's "Peace Administration" had received Barak's approval to plan for Israeli unilateral disengagement. The idea was to build a security fence east of the major Israeli settlement blocs, while keeping close to the June 4, 1967, cease-fire lines elsewhere. This way, about 6 percent of West Bank territory would have been cut off by the planned line of the fence. The idea was to relocate settlements that were located east of the fence line, rebuild them within the areas of the settlement blocs, and ask the international community to support the PA in a concerted effort of Palestinian state building as well as possible security coordination. The ECF, as well as Schneller and Tarifi (independently from each other) prepared another paradigm, which we then called "transition to state." The key idea was to permit the proclamation of the State of Palestine, and to build all the elements necessary for good neighborly relations between the two states, as a step toward resolving all outstanding core issues of conflict by creating the enabling conditions.

Historians tend to oppose the "what if?" question, because no one can convincingly describe a possible alternative development to what actually did happen. However, I believe that in the summer of 2000 the various components for a "transition to state" paradigm were at hand. Arafat's main concern at the time was to become head of state. At Camp David, and again later in September 2000, in the proposal he asked that Ashrawi to share with me and by proxy with Barak, he proposed a "transition to state" concept. Without accepting all his demands, it provided a zone of possible agreement, which when combined with the Schneller-Tarifi proposals offered an agreement that might have been concluded in the summer or autumn of 2000.

The "unilateral disengagement" concept prepared by the Israeli Peace Administration offered another realistic option for a concept that the Government of Israel might have successfully negotiated with the US government, as well as with Arafat. I am convinced that these reflections are not purely academic, nor "crying about spilt milk." Rather, this hindsight analysis should be taken into account while planning and leading Secretary of State John Kerry's ongoing peace initiative (see chapter 10).

LESSON TWO: BE AWARE OF THE PRICE OF THE BREAKDOWN OF NEGOTIATIONS

On June 10, 2000, I had told Beilin that moving forward to Permanent Status under given conditions would cause violence to erupt, and that I would prefer a workable Interim Agreement as the comparatively lesser evil. In my letter to Malley of July 7, 2000, I suggested an alternative approach to the planned discussions at the Camp David Summit, one that included confidence-building measures such as the release of prisoners and related "stage management" that might help prevent a breakdown in negotiations. Beilin's letter to Barak shortly before the summit—which Barak left unopened—was also aimed at preventing the failure of the Camp David Summit. Analyzing the cost of failure, Kurtzer and his colleagues later described the price that all paid for the failure of the July 2000 Camp David Summit:

> For more than four years, both Israelis and Palestinians suffered under the impact of terrorism and reprisals. . . . Mutual trust collapsed and the Israeli "peace camp" virtually disappeared. . . . The paradigm of the inevitability of the two state solution collapsed. . . . The Jerusalem issue, as well as the rising power of Hamas as an Islamist organization putting forth a militant alternative to the failed negotiations, helped change the discourse from a nationalist discourse to a religious one. . . . The expansion of suicide bombings propelled the Israelis into the mode of confronting what was perceived to be an "existential" threat. . . . The events essentially assured the election of a right-wing Israeli government led by Ariel Sharon in February 2001.[132]

Moreover, they added, the American peace team was not aware that the breakdown of negotiations would have a far-reaching impact on US national security interests—an additional price of that failure.[133]

The logical conclusion of these observations is simple: In any presently ongoing or future negotiation effort, the consequences of failure have to be carefully calculated, and a workable Plan B must be prepared.

LESSON THREE: UNDERSTAND THE LIMITS OF US POWER TO ACHIEVE AN AGREEMENT

Bruce Riedel, who in this period was special assistant to President Clinton and the US National Security Council's senior director for Near East affairs, reflected on his president's limits during the negotiations: "Clinton had incredible strengths as a negotiator, but not the ability to twist arms thoroughly and you could not get a final deal without really hammering people."[134] This statement implies that some more US pressure might have done the job—yet I beg to differ with this assessment. The political consequences of agreement or failure are carried first and foremost by the political leadership of the parties involved, and thus each side is capable of rejecting (and at times determined to reject) "an offer you cannot refuse." Even if the United States offers substantial aid in the negotiating process, the immediate repercussions for the US leadership and people are minimal. I conclude, therefore, that without identifying a workable paradigm for conflict resolution and creating together an understanding on the achievable zone of possible agreement that is acceptable to all parties, US pressure will remain ineffective. Ambassador Ed Djerejian explained this philosophy in another way: "The parties—that is, the Israelis and Palestinians—need US adult supervision. Yet it is similarly essential to understand the limits of parental guidance."[135]

LESSON FOUR: PLAN FOR THE "FLIGHT OF THE FLAMINGOS" SCENARIO—
NOTHING MORE, NOTHING LESS

It is essential to avoid three of the four scenarios developed at Mont Fleur in South Africa. The "ostrich" scenario, which would mean ignoring reality; the "Icarus" scenario, which would mean reaching for the sky and falling into an abyss (this is what happened in 2000); and the "lame duck" scenario, which would mean maintaining business as usual. Instead, it is essential to plan for a fourth scenario: "the flight of the flamingos," which would mean aiming to gather a sufficient majority on both sides in order to make real progress. This logic influenced the ECF to prepare a paper on the suggested "Preliminary Guidelines for a 1,000 Day Program for a Barak-led Government." We thus referred to four elements: (1) create a stable security environment; (2) define phased progress on the way to an Israeli-Palestinian two-state solution; (3) permit a concomitant process of creating national unity on the Israeli side to be paralleled on the Palestinian side; and (4) create a regional roadmap toward a comprehensive Israeli-Arab peace. Even though the June 2000 ECF paper was only a beginning and needed to be followed up by more in-depth policy planning, the lesson to be learned is that for future negotiations, such a comprehensive planning approach is essential.

LESSON FIVE: ACCEPT THE LIMITATIONS OF TRACK-TWO AND
MULTITRACK DIPLOMACY

It seemed that the ECF had achieved impressive initial successes in preparing for Permanent Status negotiations. On each and every negotiating issue, we had developed comprehensive files and understandings with the Palestinian side. We had also proposed concepts of how to manage the negotiations; maintained close contact with Barak and with the Israeli,

Palestinian, and US negotiating teams before and during the negotiations; prepared guidelines and principles for negotiations (i.e., the "logic of peace" concept); and prepared fallback concepts ahead of time.

We brought all this knowledge into the Peace Administration.[136] We also forewarned the negotiators about emerging difficulties and suggested realistic fallback concepts in time for them to be useful. Furthermore, we were successful in convincing the Israeli Peace Administration, and later the US peace team, that it was necessary to develop a fallback concept instead of hastening toward an unachievable Permanent Status Agreement. However, none of our efforts helped, as we did not have the power or means to convince Barak to adopt our policy suggestions and go for a transition-to-state agreement, rather than try against all odds to solve all outstanding issues of conflict.

This account illustrates the potential and the limitations of track-two and multitrack diplomacy actors. Our work was comparable to the Global Positioning System. We could describe different routes to reach the envisaged targets; we could identify the obstacles on the way and prescribe ways to circumvent them; and we could seek, if necessary, a different, less ambitious target. However, we did not have the capacity to prevent the leadership from ignoring our warning and advice.

Chapter 8

Life after Failure: The ECF in Search of a Strategy, February 2001–February 2003

This chapter describes the events following the breakdown of Israeli-Palestinian Permanent Status negotiations between early 2001 and early 2003. It elaborates on the Economic Cooperation Foundation's (ECF's) attempts to adapt to changing strategic conditions. As this is a study on track-two and multitrack diplomacy, the strategic reorientation process of track-two agents such as the ECF offers insight into the available tools of defining and redefining strategies according to changing circumstances.

Historical Background

On February 6, 2001, the Israeli people voted Ehud Barak and the Israeli Labor Party (ILP) out of government, permitting Ariel Sharon and Likud to achieve a landslide victory. Upon leaving office, one of the first things Barak did was send letters to all the relevant leaders involved in the peace negotiations—US president George W. Bush, PLO chairman Yasser Arafat, Egyptian president Hosni Mubarak, King Abdullah of Jordan, Swedish prime minister Göran Persson, and UN secretary-general Kofi Annan—taking off the table both his government's proposal for a Permanent Status Agreement with the Palestine Liberation Organization (PLO) and also the proposal made in negotiations with Syria.[1] President Bill Clinton had done the same before leaving office earlier in the year. In his memoirs, Clinton explains his decision:

... the deal was so good I couldn't believe anyone would be foolish enough to let it go. Barak wanted me to come to the region, but I wanted Arafat to say yes to the Israelis on the big issues embodied in my parameters first. . . . Nothing came of it. As a backstop, the Israelis tried to produce a letter with as much agreement on the parameters as possible, on the assumption that Barak would lose the election and at least both sides would be bound to a course that could lead to an agreement. Arafat wouldn't even do that because he didn't want to be seen conceding anything.[2]

Having experienced Arafat's negativism, Clinton had told incoming president George W. Bush to keep away from Arafat.[3] All concerned parties understood that an impasse had been reached; how to overcome it remained unclear.

As prime minister, Sharon's strategic goal was to conclude a long-term Interim Agreement and to prevent the establishment of a fully sovereign Palestinian state. He believed that such a state would turn against Israel sooner or later.[4] Sharon's tactical goal was to put an end to Palestinian violence by making it absolutely clear that violence would not serve Palestinian interests. Because Sharon saw Arafat as responsible for the use of violence against Israel, he intended to incapacitate Arafat politically.[5]

Early in March 2001, Sharon sent his son Omri to Mahmoud Abbas to suggest an envisaged interim step of establishing a Palestinian state in Gaza and 42 percent of the West Bank territory, with negotiation on all the outstanding core issues over a seven-year period in order to reach a Permanent Status Agreement. However, Abbas refused, remarking that "you do not want peace."[6] The West Bank partial territory offer, with all the other issues left open, was intended to enable further settlement expansion in the remaining West Bank areas. For this reason, Sharon and Likud opposed the ILP's proposal to construct a security fence close to the June 4, 1967, cease-fire lines. This fence would indicate a possible future border on the ground, and would thus "out-fence" many potential settlements.

To pursue his intended long-term Interim Agreement, Sharon adopted several dialogue and confrontation tactics. Stressing his willingness to negotiate, he asked the ILP to join the government, and he offered Shimon Peres (as the ILP's leader) the post of foreign minister. Peres was granted some leeway to negotiate an Interim Agreement with Abu Ala' in the presence of Javier Solana and Miguel Moratinos, two senior European officials.[7] Sharon also encouraged the creation of multiple channels to the Palestinian leadership, the most important of which was led by Omri

Sharon.[8] Sufficient behind-the-scenes room for nongovernmental organizations such as the ECF was also ensured.

Despite such developments, Sharon opposed both the construction of a security fence and the internationally demanded freeze of new settlement construction, thereby strengthening his political and electoral power base with the settler movement. To turn international demands away from Israel and toward the Palestinian Authority, Sharon insisted that the Palestinians observe a seven-day complete cease-fire. In the face of continuing violence, the Israeli Defense Forces (IDF) moved into most parts of Area A—where, according to the Oslo II Agreement, the Palestinian Authority had full administrative and security control—aiming to defeat the intifada and make evident to the Palestinians that violence would defeat rather than serve their interests. At the same time, Sharon listened carefully to Brigadier General Eival Gilady, the newly appointed head of the IDF's strategic planning department, who asked him, "In case you achieve your military aim of defeating the intifada, what is the political aim that you would like to achieve, particularly if an agreement with the Palestinians cannot be concluded?"[9] Sharon eventually answered Gilady's simple question by asking him to plan for unilateral disengagement. However, the decision to go ahead with this objective was made only after sufficient internal and external pressure, when it was clear that a "business as usual" policy was no longer sustainable.

The emerging Palestinian strategy after the breakdown of negotiations was to pursue two seemingly contradictory but complementary positions: the continuation of violence in cooperation with the Jihad-al-Islam group and Hamas on one hand, and the request to resume the interrupted negotiations on the other.[10] Chairman Arafat and the Tanzim, the militant organizational arm of the Fatah movement, contemplated the use of violence as a strategic tool. The Tanzim leader, Marwan Barghouti, told Rob Malley, President Clinton's former Middle East national security adviser, that "violence will continue until the end of occupation."[11] Abbas, by contrast, opposed the strategy of violence but was unable to stop it. He wanted to renew the negotiations and reach an agreement along the lines laid out in the Palestinian National Council's Algiers meeting in November 1988, and accordingly he opposed Sharon's proposed long-term Interim Agreement as vehemently as did Arafat and Barghouti.[12]

The Israeli political and military leadership perceived that the combination of the Arafat/Tanzim and Abbas strategies pursued two aims for the PLO. First, the ongoing violence made it possible for the PLO to obtain support from militant regional state and nonstate actors—particularly

Iran, Syria, the Lebanese Hezbollah and the Palestinian Jihad al-Islam and Hamas movements—because all these actors advocated the policy of armed resistance. This support for the violence would be countered by US and European support for continued negotiations. Second, both the violence and the negotiations would prepare the ground for an agreement that would not only be in line with Palestinian demands but also would be imposed on Israel by the global and regional players involved. However, the complementarity of the PLO's two different strategic approaches did not hide the fact that the organization itself was deeply divided, as the existing high tensions between Arafat and Abbas were augmented by other PLO members' efforts to weaken Abbas's position.[13]

Altogether, the breakdown of Israeli-Syrian and Israeli-PLO negotiations, as well as the unilateral withdrawal from Lebanon, created a strategically precarious situation. The Israeli strategic aim of getting the PLO, Syria, and Saudi Arabia to join the Middle Eastern peace camp had failed. In Syria, President Hafez al-Assad had died and had been replaced by his inexperienced son, Bashar. Unlike his father, who had been careful not to give too much leeway to nonstate actors such as Hamas, the Jihadist movement, and the Lebanese Hezbollah, Bashar al-Assad substantially eased the flow of arms to them and did not limit their action in the ways that his father had done.[14] Saudi Arabia also offered substantial financial and other assistance to Muslim radical militants in the Middle East and Africa, while private Saudi sources financed al-Qaeda and other groups.[15] Added to the above was the Iranian threat against Israel: questioning Israel's right to exist and demanding its annihilation;[16] training, arming, and encouraging Hezbollah, Jihadist groups, and Hamas to launch terrorist acts against Israel; supplying these groups with rockets to be launched against civilian targets; and enriching uranium and seeking to develop mid- and long-range missiles that could threaten Israel and elsewhere.[17]

In the United States, the new administration led by President George W. Bush was afraid to repeat the mistakes made by President Clinton and decided to pursue a policy called "ABC" (Anything But Clinton). In practice, this meant that the United States refrained from taking any initiative for the renewal of the Israeli-Palestinian or the wider Israeli-Arab peace process for as long as possible. It also limited its activities mainly to conflict management rather than conflict resolution. The peace process that had been initiated by President Anwar Sadat—which had been directed along the guidelines laid out in the September 1978 Camp David Accords, and had led the way to the October 1991 Madrid Conference and intense bilateral and multilateral negotiations during most of the 1990s—had come to an end.[18]

The Israeli-Palestinian front had reached an impasse. The Palestinians' de facto rejection of the Clinton parameters and the conditions for an agreement outlined by Arafat made the large gap between the positions of both sides evident. Similarly evident was that both presidents, Clinton and Bush, felt that the Israeli government had gone a long way toward reaching an agreement, while Arafat had played an obstructive role.[19] Seeking a way to overcome the impasse, Israel had gained an important advantage over the Palestinians: US perception and goodwill went beyond the practical political interests related to the Jewish vote, or the influence of the American-Israeli Public Action Committee. In Prime Minister Sharon's point of view, this was an important asset. He could speak freely with President Bush and obtain his support for a strategy to overcome the impasse.[20] The problem was that nobody knew what an effective strategy for breaking the impasse could be.

The ECF's Search for a New Strategy

Different Approaches within the ECF

At the ECF, both the older and younger generations knew that former policy assumptions had to be revisited in order to seek a new strategic approach. However, we all interpreted what had happened differently, and we drew different conclusions.

Yossi Beilin's thinking was guided by the leading strategic idea that it was essential for Israel to conclude a Permanent Status Agreement with the Palestinians that would solve all the outstanding core issues of conflict and establish mutually recognized borders. He believed that the key to breaking the impasse would be to achieve a detailed blueprint for Permanent Status with a Palestinian counterpart. This would help to convince the Israeli public that the Israelis had a partner for peace and that the solution of all the outstanding core issues leading to the "end of conflict" was available. The next step would be to build an internal Israeli and an external international and regional coalition in support of the Permanent Status blueprint and to work on turning the track-two blueprint into a track-one agreement. Looking back at the achievements and failures of his 1995 understanding with Abbas, Beilin concluded that the ECF had made a major mistake. By keeping the understanding confidential, we had been unable to gain the support of Israeli and Palestinian stakeholders, strategists, intellectuals, and others, or to fight for its implementation. A common Israeli-Palestinian document signed by well-known public figures on both sides would raise a public argument for concluding a track-one agreement.[21]

Nimrod Novik's thinking was different. He developed, formulated, and pursued what he called the "lemon juice" approach. His argument was simple and well illustrated: We all wanted a Permanent Status Agreement, or what Novik called "the tasty orange juice." It was unrealistic to assume that anyone could extract an "orange juice" agreement on Permanent Status under a Sharon government, but it was essential that we not allow the period of Sharon's government to go by without achieving headway toward a two-state solution. Therefore, Novik argued that much could be achieved with the help of an efficiently planned multitrack diplomacy effort, which would give us some "less tasty lemon juice." (Novik's close connection to most senior stakeholders in the US, Egyptian, and Israeli governments made it possible to prove the validity of the lemon juice theory, which is described later in this chapter.)

IDF brigadier general Baruch Spiegel joined the ECF in 1999 after he retired from active service. His strategic approach was simple: Whatever the fate of negotiations for Permanent Status or for an Interim Agreement might be, Israel's essential and vital interest was to diminish hate and create a wide spectrum of common interests with all our neighbors. This meant developing, as widely as possible, security, economic, and civilian cooperation with the Palestinians, as well as with Jordan and Egypt. Back in 1991, when Spiegel was in charge of international relations within the IDF, he developed a close working relationship with his Jordanian counterpart, General Mansur Abu Rashed. This partnership became an important building block in preparing a supportive environment for the Israeli-Jordanian peace negotiations, and it was with the help of Spiegel and Abu Rashed that the ECF had organized trilateral Israeli-Jordanian-Palestinian discussions on a joint security concept (see chapters 6 and 7). The Jordanian connection also offered important opportunities to pursue and achieve a variety of supportive understandings with the Palestinians. Furthermore, Spiegel's prestige and network among Israel's security authorities and beyond provided the ECF with important access to decisionmakers that would be of pivotal importance for our work.

Eylon Javetz and Yael Banaji, who were members of the ECF's younger generation, argued in a paper that the central issue in reaching a Permanent Status agreement was Jerusalem. By concentrating efforts on Jerusalem, it was possible to deal with the symbols, beliefs, goals, and norms that could become a source of tolerance, mutual understanding, and coexistence. As they argued, a significant part of what had to be done was "the task of reeducating the Israeli and Palestinian public to alter the way they perceive the well-known symbols and issues, and thus to create a new perceived and alternative reality."[22] This process of reeducation would "add an ideational and symbolic dimension to the agreement and the necessary legitimacy and represent a tool which can and will be used to create long-lasting and widespread support for the spirit of the agreement."[23] The working concept they described was to develop two alternating agreed-upon narratives with our Palestinian partners.

After the first year under the Sharon government, Javetz prepared a different paper titled "Deficiencies in the Israeli 'Permanent Status' Strategy and Some Initial Recommendations." He argued that the different narratives that developed during one hundred years of conflict (as described in chapter 5) made it almost impossible to bridge the gap. Worse, both the Israeli and Palestinian people were still locked into the daily reality of occupation and terrorism, and had witnessed hardly any improvement in their condition throughout the duration of negotiations. The pendulum would devastatingly swing from celebration to depression, from expectation to crisis, and from negotiations to violence. Therefore, instead of a complete conflict-resolution approach, Javetz suggested a process-oriented approach that would lead to gradual partition, physical separation, capacity building, confidence building, economic packages, security arrangements, and educational programs.[24] Following Javetz and Banaji's conceptual lead, and with full cooperation from Faisal Husseini and his associates at the Orient House, the ECF intensified its track-two work on Jerusalem, and this collaboration produced several important policy papers.[25]

Other junior members of the ECF had different approaches. For Orit Gal, the central issue in promoting the process toward an agreed-on two-state solution was to involve the international community in all spheres: political, security, and economic. This was in line with the original concept of providing for an international trusteeship over Gaza that had been negotiated in Sarpsborg in the early 1990s (see chapter 4). After the negotiations failed in January 2001, this concept became popular again among both Israeli strategists and the Palestinians and other Arab actors.[26] Ron Shatzberg, who joined the ECF in 1999, focused on conflict transformation rather than conflict resolution. He concentrated on issues that would contribute to a bottom-up strategy for a two-state solution: cooperation with the Red Cross aimed at minimizing human pain, improving access and movement for Palestinians to ease Palestinian economic development, cultural issues with the aim of creating an atmosphere of mutual Israeli-Palestinian empathy, and attempting to humanize security measures within the Israeli security system.[27]

My own strategic thinking was to focus our efforts on achievable targets. Negotiations and an agreement on Permanent Status were an important means to an end, but nothing more. The strategic aim was to move toward a peaceful, two-state solution, with Palestinian state building and settlement evacuation being the most immediate concerns. In order to address these, what was needed was a US and European advocacy and facilitation concept on a phased approach to reaching a two-state solution. Bilaterally, on the Israeli-Palestinian level, we had to work to end the violence and to establish an economic base for Palestinian state building. Within Israel, it was essential that we form a coalition that was as wide as possible against settlement expansion and in favor of a policy that would eventually prepare for settlement evacuation. To develop this supportive internal coalition within Israel, I hoped to build bridges with the Israeli right wing, particularly toward the settler community. In the autumn of 2000, I met Othniel Schneller, former secretary-general of the Settlers' Movement, and we began a dialogue that has continued until today.[28]

Boaz Karni resented Javetz's paper on the shortcomings of Permanent Status. He wanted to combine Beilin's comprehensive approach with the more incremental approach supported by Novik, Spiegel, the ECF's younger generation, and me. Observers of the ECF's work were strongly impressed by the fact that the voices of the younger, junior members of our think tank had as much legitimacy as the opinions of the senior members—the generals, senior academics, and senior experts who had held high government positions. This situation often caused fiery discussions, but at the same time it enabled innovative thinking, which, when funds were available, was translated into important project work.

The ECF's Policy and Political Concerns

The ECF's policy planning effort after the formation of Sharon's government had to be aware of the fact that on the three basic policy challenges—(1) defining a political concept to move toward a two-state solution, (2) reaching an end to violence, and (3) creating a supportive structure for stability—the gap between Arafat's and Sharon's positions was huge. For Arafat and the Tanzim leaders, this meant continuing the armed struggle and agreeing to cease violence only if the Israeli occupation were brought to an end.[29] For Sharon, this meant defeating Arafat and the Palestinians and demanding "seven days of quiet" before negotiations.

His aim was to make it absolutely clear to the Palestinians that violence would not achieve results.

The gap between the proponents was no less substantial on political issues. Sharon wanted a long-term Interim Agreement, while the Palestinians wanted a Permanent Status agreement in line with the Palestinian National Council's November 1988 decisions and argued that if Israel did not accept these conditions, demographics would eventually defeat Israel's quest for a Jewish and democratic state.[30]

With regard to the substance of a supportive stability structure, the Palestinians wanted an internationally imposed settlement. Otherwise, a stability structure would work against their interests and create a sense of normalization and "business as usual" that would be detrimental to ending the occupation. The Israeli government opposed "the internationalization of the conflict" and was extremely suspicious of any outside political or security intervention.[31] Because the Americans considered the Palestinians responsible for the failure of the peace negotiations, and because Prime Minister Sharon had established a strategic rapport with President Bush, it was highly unlikely that the gap could be bridged through either internal or external negotiations.

The ECF's Initial Policy Proposals

Novik was the first ECF member to put ideas to paper. In February 2001, his paper "Israeli Hopes: A First Comment" described the need to turn the policy of agreed-on and coordinated separation into the central driving force of the peace process. He suggested a three-phase strategic approach in which negotiations would be substantially supported by a third party, leading to an interim understanding and finally to an agreement with a detailed timetable to coordinate the separation. In substance, Novik's paper proposed a give-and-take that would permit the Palestinian Authority (PA) to control 60 percent of the West Bank in return for a Palestinian agreement to permit 80 percent of the settler community to be integrated into Israel within existing settlement blocs and without defining the percentage of these areas.

On a more tactical level, Novik proposed what we would call a "zipper approach." Like the teeth of a zipper closing one by one, this approach encouraged Israel to take the first step by ending the violence, enabling the Palestinians to respond accordingly and thus permitting movement toward the second step of mutual confidence building. For this second step, Israel would initiate the moves and the Palestinians would respond, allowing the negotiations to resume in an ongoing "we do, they do" sequence.[32] (In hindsight, this concept included important components that became part of the Performance Based Roadmap that was concluded two years later in the early spring of 2003.)

We tested some of these strategic and tactical ideas with our Palestinian interlocutors and quickly realized that the Palestinians were unwilling to permit 80 percent of the Israeli settlers to be integrated into sovereign Israel in existing settlement blocs before a Permanent Status Agreement was concluded. The Palestinians argued that all settlements were illegal and that the acceptance of our proposal would legalize the settlements.

In response to the Palestinian rejection of Novik's suggested approach, Peres engaged in an intense political dialogue with Abu Ala' and proposed the establishment of a Palestinian State, at first on 41 percent of West Bank territory. The Peres–Abu Ala' concept differed from the proposal that Sharon's son Omri had earlier submitted to Abbas in two major ways: It had a strict timeline, and a mechanism that would refer in clear but general terms to the endgame. Sharon opposed the concept.[33] Paradoxically, between 2000 and 2001 the tables had turned. Between 1999 and 2000, Arafat had demanded that a Palestinian state be established on parts of the West Bank and Gaza before negotiating all the outstanding core issues, and Barak had demanded full agreement on Permanent Status. As in the theater of the absurd, the positions had changed: Israel wanted what Arafat had demanded and the Palestinians now refused, while Sharon rejected conditions that might have softened the Palestinian opposition.

With Novik's first concept off the table, the second concept we prepared was (pretentiously) titled "International Stability Pact for the Middle East."[34] We envisioned a hybrid system, with a crisis management mechanism built conceptually on the example of the Multinational Force and Observers (the United States–commanded multilateral force supervising peace between Israel and Egypt) and a preliminary structure of a mini-trusteeship. (I suggested handing control of Gaza over to an international trusteeship in Oslo, an idea that appealed to more than a few of the Israelis involved in the negotiations.)[35] A special coordinator would be appointed, and working groups would be established on economic affairs (which would oversee investment, coordination, and the construction of economic developments), social affairs (which would promote civil society and local political infrastructure), and security issues (which would develop and coordinate security and law enforcement collaboration), as well as a monitoring group (to follow up on activities and help overcome deadlocks). However, neither the Government of Israel nor the PA was willing to accept such far-reaching international involvement in its affairs, and the international community was not willing to undertake such a responsibility. Nevertheless, a considerably watered-down concept was eventually adopted in April 2003, when the Quartet powers (the United States, the European Union, Russia, and the United Nations) created the position of a special envoy to the Middle East—a task that was first given to former US Foreign Service officer and ambassador John Wolf, then to former World Bank president James Wolfensohn, and later still to former British prime minister Tony Blair.

Our third concept was simpler and aimed at improving the PA's economic conditions and infrastructure. The paper made specific proposals on creating Palestinian employment opportunities in Israel; promoting trade, tourism, and industrial development; easing transportation, movement, and the transfer of tax revenues to the PA; increasing humanitarian aid; and improving Palestinian infrastructure networks and systems.[36] At the ECF, we did not expect all our suggestions to be implemented. Rather, we put together a list of issues that we wanted to pursue and kept lobbying the Israeli Office of the Coordinator of Government Activities in the Territories (COGAT), the relevant Israeli authority. Brigadier General Baruch Spiegel and Brigadier General Dov Sedaka had held senior positions in COGAT and were able to suggest policy changes to the officials in charge. As most of the issues referred to in our list were below the radar of political decisionmakers, it was the task of the professional IDF civil servants to make the relevant decisions. This approach provided room for maneuvering and allowed the ECF to play a role in improving security, as well as in the social and economic conditions in the Palestinian territories under confrontational and hostile conditions.

Having prepared the three complementary concept papers at the beginning of the Sharon government, we at the ECF made sure to also sustain and improve our access to decisionmakers. We succeeded in establishing and maintaining the multiple channels necessary to disseminate our ideas: Beilin and Novik had free access to Peres, who had become foreign minister. Beilin also met periodically with Arafat and Abbas, as well as with the most senior European leaders, particularly with the EU's foreign affairs and security representative, Javier Solana, from Spain; the EU commissioner, Chris Patten, from the United Kingdom; and the German foreign minister, Joschka Fischer. At the same time, Novik and I maintained a close dialogue with our various American, European, and Middle Eastern interlocutors, while Spiegel maintained full access to the most senior echelons of the Israeli military establishment. The most important among these was Spiegel's close relationship with Shaul Mofaz, who was later appointed minister of defense. At the same time, Sedaka had a particularly close relationship with former chief of staff Amnon Lipkin Shachak, whose opinion was highly valued by the Israeli security establishment. I worked closely with David Brodet, who was respected as Israel's most outstanding senior authority on economic affairs. The ECF also provided Brodet with up-to-date detailed information about the Palestinian economic situation and the policies pursued by the Israeli military authorities, thus permitting Brodet to discuss suggested changes with the Prime Minister's Office and the Ministry of Finance.

I also developed an important working relationship with Tzipi Livni. During the late 1990s, as a young member of the Knesset who belonged to Likud, Livni had participated in a political dialogue with our Jordanian counterparts, organized by the ECF. In Sharon's government, she was nominated minister for regional cooperation, in charge of cooperation projects with the Palestinian territories, Jordan, and Egypt. In this position, she benefited from the ECF's network, and access to her and to others in the Sharon government was important for the ECF. Unlike other politicians, who cared first and foremost for their own political advancement, Livni cared about the subject matter and thus refrained from making any leaks to the press, which was a precondition for gaining the confidence of our interlocutors. She kept the door open for discussions with the Palestinians, Jordanians, Egyptians, and international visitors, and I arranged meetings between her and Maher el-Kurd (who had become chairman of the Palestinian Higher Committee for Investment and Finance and deputy minister of economy), Zuheir el-Menasreh, Abu Rashed, and others. In all these meetings, she adopted a down-to-earth approach and followed up effectively.[37]

The ECF's Advice Is Not Heeded: The Mitchell Recommendations

At the Middle East summit at Sharm el-Sheikh on October 17, 2000, President Clinton announced the establishment of a fact-finding committee "on the (violent) events of the past weeks and how to prevent their recurrence."[38] Former US senator George Mitchell would chair the committee, which was composed of members from Turkey, Norway, the United States, and the European Union, and the ECF presented its recommendations to the committee in time for them to be incorporated into its final report in April 2001.[39] We suggested a five-point program:

1. Commitment to a 100 percent effort to prevent violence and reestablish cooperation between and among all levels of the security forces of the Government of Israel and of the Palestinian National Authority;
2. Commitment to promote and encourage an economic revival program in full coordination between the Government of Israel and the Palestinian National Authority;
3. Commitment to adhere to previously signed agreements and to draw up a timetable for implementation on all issues that have yet to be fully implemented;
4. Development of understandings on the proposed and agreed consecutive steps of stability building (the "zipper approach"), as agreed upon in the Wye Memorandum; and
5. Upon achieving full stabilization, Permanent Status negotiations shall be renewed and viewed as the appropriate channel to discuss interim arrangements.[40]

Although the Mitchell Commission's recommendations adopted the first, third, and fourth points, point five was the main issue at hand. We had aimed to bridge the gap between the Israeli willingness to discuss interim arrangements and the Palestinian demand to go back to Permanent Status negotiations. The suggestion to discuss interim arrangements within the framework of Permanent Status negotiations was not merely a face-saving device for the Palestinians; if accepted, it would make it evident that interim arrangements had to be linked to and followed by Permanent Status negotiations. Our recommendation was watered down to a nonobliging comment stating that "negotiations must not be unreasonably deferred."[41]

The ECF also discussed the need to severely restrict Israeli settlement activities, while refraining from demanding a complete settlement freeze. On this issue, the commission decided to take a very strong (and politically unwise) position, demanding that "the GOI [Government of Israel] should freeze all settlement activity, including the 'natural growth' of existing settlements."[42] This was not only a nonstarter; it was a major stumbling block. Instead of trying to win over the pragmatic leaders of the settler community, who were willing to restrict settlement activities and even prepare for settlement evacuation, the commission was alienating them. The commission evidently also did not understand that for political reasons, Prime Minister Sharon could not and would not deliver a complete settlement freeze. The phrase "freeze all settlement activity, including natural growth" was particularly unfortunate. According to Schneller, the pragmatic former secretary-general of the Settlers' Movement, the settler community interpreted the prohibition on "natural growth" as a racist measure aimed at preventing married couples from expanding their families, and thus the phrase hit a very sensitive nerve.[43]

We tried to explain to the Mitchell Commission's members that the demand for a complete settlement freeze would cause a detrimental chain reaction. The Government of Israel would not comply, the commission's recommendations would be seen as empty demands with little or no political clout, and the Palestinian leadership would be maneuvered into a no-win position because they could not be less demanding than the Mitchell Commission and thus would have no excuse to return to negotiations as long as the Israeli government left the settlements as they were. Instead, we suggested defining restrictions on settlement expansion and establishing an effective monitoring structure to oversee implementation.[44] Without such detailed understandings, the demand for a settlement freeze was nothing but an empty diplomatic formula, aimed at putting aside the issue without dealing with it seriously. To enforce the necessary restrictions, any Israeli prime minister also needed to obtain certain gains. The ECF called for such an approach, suggesting Israeli commitments to both "respect Palestinian sensitivities regarding settlement activities according to agreed criteria" and "end internal closures" by removing roadblocks in Palestinian areas. In return for these commitments, we suggested obliging the Palestinians to collect unauthorized weapons and to end incitement.[45]

A more careful formulation of the Mitchell recommendations might have caused less damage, but it would not have solved the problem. What was needed was political will on behalf of the US leaders to put their prestige and action behind their words. However, the political will to do so was not there. In addition, the specific reference to the settlement issue contributed to the failure of the Mitchell recommendations, and also of its various follow-up versions, which included the same phrases.[46] At the end of June 2001, knowing that the Mitchell recommendations had disregarded our advice with regard to the settlements, I discussed the issue with the US consul-general to the PA, Jeff Feltman. My advice was to establish a strict and effective monitoring structure to oversee the obligations of each side while at the same time adopting a less demanding approach with regard to the general command of a settlement freeze. Feltman replied, "We feel the opposite; we are more willing to be tough on the settlements, and easy on the monitoring."[47]

Officially, both the Government of Israel and the PA seemed to accept the Mitchell recommendations. There was diplomatic pressure to acknowledge acceptance, and there was no political pressure to oversee their implementation. Parallel initiatives followed, such as the

Egyptian-Jordanian Initiative, which suggested a meaningful third-power intervention, and the Tenet security plan, which aimed to describe how the Mitchell recommendations could best be implemented by calling upon the parties to renew security cooperation and enforce a cease-fire.[48] All these plans would fail. In practice, business as usual and a continuation of the stalemate situation seemed to be the undeclared common approach of all concerned parties.[49]

The Impact of September 11, 2001

Operation Defensive Shield (September 2001–April 2002) and Greater International Involvement

The terrorist attacks of September 11, 2001, came as a terrible shock to everyone and had numerous repercussions. The war against terrorism became the focal point of President George W. Bush's foreign and domestic policy, and most nations joined in the endeavor, although advocating a different style and substance on some essential issues. To fight terrorism worldwide, the UN Security Council accepted Resolution 1373, a comprehensive toolkit against terrorists, their movement, the smuggling of weapons, the supply of monies, and more.[50]

The events of September 11 also reinforced the need for a close US-Saudi relationship.[51] The United States needed Saudi support to fight the Taliban in Afghanistan and al-Qaeda elsewhere; the Saudi kingdom needed, more than ever before, American backing and support to maintain security in the Persian Gulf against potential Iranian or Iraqi aggression. Nabil Shaath told us that Prince Bandar of Saudi Arabia had exchanged letters with President Bush before September 11. The Saudi message was that the Americans should overrule Sharon's demand for "seven days of quiet," take care to implement the Mitchell recommendations, and help renew the peace-finding process. President Bush's response was reported to be very different from his public statements; he agreed to get involved in political issues and supported the Palestinians' right to a state.[52]

However, the events of September 11 did bring about change. Chairman Arafat understood that under the aftershock of the al-Qaeda terrorist attacks, he had to appease the Americans and could not afford to repeat the mistake he had made in August 1990, when he sided with Iraq's Saddam Hussein against the United States after the Iraqi invasion of Kuwait. Furthermore, Arafat was exposed to European pressure to prevent Palestinian acts of violence. Throughout that September, Arafat repeatedly broadcast nine-point instructions against the use of violent action, and he also had them printed in the Palestinian press. Furthermore, he phoned senior officials in various governorates and repeated the same instructions in front of Western observers, and then he oversaw the enforcement of these instructions by the officials under his command. However, he simultaneously refrained from confronting oppositional forces within the PLO.[53] One such group, belonging to the Popular Front for the Liberation of Palestine, assassinated Israeli tourism minister Rehevam Zeevi on October 17, in a serious breach of the unwritten rules on the employment of violence.[54]

Afraid of further escalation, the Europeans took action and demanded that Arafat undertake an eleven-point action program against Palestinian terrorism. German foreign minister Fischer made Arafat sign and commit to the program on October 26, 2001.[55] Arafat's eleven points not only committed him to take effective antiterrorism action—such as by issuing warrants for, arresting, and detaining individuals involved in terror actions, including the Zeevi assassination—but also laid out guidelines for a European-led monitoring system and prepared the way for Palestinian security reform. To oversee ongoing Palestinian efforts, Solana appointed former British MI-5 agent Alastair Crooke as his regional security expert, with a focus on verifying PA arrests and imprisoning terrorist suspects. Eventually, Crooke's mission was reinforced into what would become the European "security group." This was the first nucleus of a more substantial European and US security presence on the ground, which eventually would make Palestinian security reform a reality.[56]

At this time, Arafat did take proactive measures to curb possible Palestinian acts of terrorism against Israel. He appointed Marwan Barghouti and Raed Karmi, two leading members of the Tanzim, to this task and apparently instructed them to disarm Palestinians who would not follow his orders to refrain from acts of violence.[57] Arafat's action against terrorists resulted in one notable incident in mid-October 2001, when Palestinian armed terrorists, who had become fugitives in the Palestinian territory, took refuge in the Church of the Nativity in Bethlehem. ECF members Boaz Karni and Ron Schatzberg, as well as former IDF consultant Motti Kristall, worked with Crooke's support to negotiate with the fugitives, agreeing to give them free passage provided they handed in their weapons.[58]

Prime Minister Sharon was faced with increasing pressure to resume negotiations, as the Saudis increased their own pressure on President Bush to overrule Sharon's negotiating conditions and Arafat made his initial moves to stop violence against Israel. We at the ECF learned from German foreign minister Fischer that Sharon had told the Europeans that he was making a serious effort to renew the negotiations. (According to Fischer, however, Sharon had added that the Zeevi assassination created clear constraints on what he as prime minister could do, as he was no longer able to take steps that would be interpreted as a concession to the Palestinians.)[59] In November, US secretary of state Colin Powell made a major speech in which he asked Israel to "accept a viable Palestinian state in which Palestinians can determine their own future on their own land and live in dignity and security."[60] At the same time, US general Anthony Zinni was appointed to follow Senator Mitchell and US Central Intelligence Agency director George Tenet to seek a way out of the ongoing Israeli-Palestinian violence. It seemed as though Israel and the Palestinians might get back on to the negotiating track.

However, on January 3, 2002, the Israeli navy captured the MV *Karine A*, a Palestinian ship full of weapons from Iran. For almost a year, Israeli intelligence had observed the Palestinians who had contacted Iran and purchased these arms, and had been aware that the preparations to purchase the arms had been in place for some time. These arms shipments could change the existing military equation and lead to a dangerous escalation of violence. The message from Arafat seemed clear: The measures that he had taken against those engaged in armed resistance were nothing but temporary tactics aimed at gaining time and preparing for the next round of violence.[61]

Initially, the US Department of State denied the political relevance of this incident, so as not to undermine the hope for a diplomatic initiative. In response to the denial, a special Israeli intelligence mission went to the United States to present the information gathered to President Bush. Upon seeing the evidence, Bush began to call—at first secretly, and later publicly—for Arafat's replacement.[62] On January 14, the Israeli General Security Services killed Raed Qarmi, who was responsible for handling the financial affairs related to Palestinian arms purchases.[63] The Palestinians saw his assassination as a breach of understanding, leading to a series of terrorist acts. Although several joint sessions between Israeli and Palestinian security officials had led to a cease-fire proposal, submitted by General Anthony Zinni on March 26, the Israeli side under Eival Gilady, immediately accepted the proposal while the Palestinian side rejected it.[64] On the following day, March 27, the latest Palestinian terrorist activity culminated in the murder of twenty-nine Israelis who were reading the Haggadah during Passover observations at the Park Hotel in Netanya.[65]

Several days later, the IDF launched Operation Defensive Shield, lead-ing military incursions into the Palestinian cities of Ramallah, Tulqarem, Qalqilya, Bethlehem, Jenin, and Nablus. The IDF's attacks destroyed most of the PA's physical facilities and seriously diminished the capacity of the Palestinian security forces. They did not, however, destroy the political power of the Palestinian leadership, nor did they undermine President Bush's support for Israel.[66] According to George W. Bush's memoirs:

> I was appalled by the violence and loss of life on both sides, but I refused to accept the equivalence between Palestinian suicide attacks on innocent civilians and Israeli military actions intended to protect their people. My views came into sharper focus after 9/11. If the United States had the right to defend itself and prevent future attacks, other democracies had those rights, too.[67]

The United States' empathy for Israel matched its growing willingness to work together with the Russian Federation, the EU, and the UN to develop a two-state solution. This interest was expressed in US support for UN Security Council Resolution 1397 in March 2002, which affirmed "a vision of a region where two States, Israel and Palestine, live side by side within secure and recognized borders."[68]

The Impact of Operation Defensive Shield

Operation Defensive Shield had a far-reaching effect on the unfolding his-torical process. Although the work of the Palestinian health and education ministries remained intact, the PA's power and ability to provide further basic services for the Palestinians' social and economic well-being were seriously impaired. The IDF had destroyed or damaged several Palestinian government buildings and had confiscated their records, mainly to inves-tigate financial activities aimed at arms purchases.[69] Finally, different security groups that served the PA were partially dismantled. The general effect was a substantial loss of power and reduced government capacity for the PA. Instead, local power holders, mainly small armed groups, gained control. In some areas, such as the Jenin Governorate, this power vacuum led to near-anarchy. Chairman Arafat found that his security could not be guaranteed during a planned trip to Jenin in May 2002, and he finally postponed the trip. Later, the emergence of irregular armed groups called into question the security of the officials appointed from Ramallah, and

Governor Zuheir el-Menasreh was also obliged to leave the Jenin area. The best illustration of the dire internal situation at the time involved a German assistant to the EU security group, who was attacked by a group of gunmen while driving in his bulletproof car. From inside his car, he was forced to call General Spiegel at the ECF, who helped to get him out of the area with support from the Israeli army.

From the beginning of the intifada at the end of September 2000, continued closures impaired the functioning of the Palestinian economy and of life in general, resulting in the impoverishment of the population. According to IDF sources, 66 percent of the West Bank and 85 percent of Gaza's population lived in poverty at the time, while unemployment rates reached 39 percent and annual per capita income fell by more than half, from $1,900 in September 2000 to about $900 by the end of 2002.[70]

Despite the serious damage inflicted upon the Palestinian infrastructure, the external political and diplomatic power of the PA and the PLO was not affected. Almost to the contrary, the devastating effects of Operation Defensive Shield mobilized the pro-Western Arab world and the international community to action in support of the interests of the PLO/ PA, leading the way to the Performance-Based Roadmap backed by the Quartet (the United States, the EU, Russia, and the UN). It also prepared the way for Sharon's eventual unilateral disengagement from Gaza and the Northern West Bank.[71]

Developing a Performance-Based Roadmap

On March 26, 2002, one day before the Netanya suicide attack, the Arab Peace Initiative was announced at the Arab Summit Conference in Lebanon.[72] This was an attempt to overcome the impasse that had been created in 2000–2001 by offering regional support to both Palestinian demands from and concessions to Israel. The initiative offered support for a two-state solution, as well as for the normalization of relations with Israel, but only following Israel's withdrawal from all territories occupied in June 1967 (including East Jerusalem), evacuation of the settlements, and recognition of Al-Quds as the capital of the State of Palestine. With regard to the Palestinian refugee problem, an "agreed solution" was proposed.

The initiative left little space for compromise with regard to the core issues of conflict. It did not propose a joint Arab-Israeli peace-building effort, but postponed any Arab concession to the time when Israel would have implemented all Arab demands. It was a far cry from Prime Minister

Sharon's strategy of reaching an Interim Agreement. However, it was a successful move in mobilizing the international community, followed by Arab pressure to move on the Israeli-Palestinian track. On April 5, while Operation Defensive Shield was still ongoing, the newly appointed Jordanian foreign minister, Marwan Muasher, discussed the emerging situation with US secretary of state Colin Powell. Muasher's account of the meeting reads as follows:

> During that April 5 meeting, I told him [Powell] that the Arab street was boiling. I emphasized that a political process, overall parameters, and a time frame to implement all the visions for a solution was needed; the incremental approach had lost credibility, and the time had come for an endgame within a specified timeline. This would be the first of many discussions with the US administration on this issue and the birth of what later became known as the Road Map.[73]

At first, Egypt, Jordan, and Saudi Arabia insisted that President Bush lay out his vision for reaching a two-state solution. In line with this idea, Novik prepared a concept proposal in a paper titled "From Crises to Process":

> Israeli-Palestinian negotiations (1) shall feature the President's vision as an eventual and agreed outcome. (2) It shall launch—and set a roadmap for—a "Transition to Permanent Status," via a long-term Interim Agreement, defined as "Corridor." Here, both the transition from one phase of the agreement to another, and progress within the "Corridor" shall not be "automatic," based on a rigid time-line, but via performance "benchmarks," where the referee is not the parties but a US-dominated mechanism. (3) . . . It shall cover all issues yet to be addressed from Tenet and Mitchell, coupled with the upgrade of the PA to an interim-statehood status. Settlement freeze should include the removal of one or two isolated settlements from Gaza and the West Bank.[74]

Novik's formula was based on several assumptions. President Bush's hoped-for vision of reaching a two-state solution needed an attached mechanism for getting there. The "corridor" concept aimed to take care of Sharon's request for a long-term Interim Agreement, as well as the Palestinian request to get to the endgame. To bridge the gap between those two positions, a strong, United States–dominated oversight and monitoring mechanism to judge performance-based benchmarks was necessary. Once

Sharon was in agreement, the funnel concept to move gradually toward Permanent Status would have been created, and the United States and other powers could bring the Palestinians and the Arab states on board. (This approach had worked twice before: first with Yitzhak Shamir in 1991, in getting to the Madrid Conference, and then with Benjamin Netanyahu in 1998, in getting to the Wye River Agreement.) Such an approach would normally have required American diplomatic leadership, but in this instance the initiative was led by Egypt, Jordan, and Saudi Arabia.

At the end of May, Egyptian president Mubarak's senior foreign policy adviser, Osama al-Baz, visited Israel. He argued that for an American initiative to be credible in the Arab world, and in order to justify Egyptian-Jordanian and Saudi pressure on Arafat, a US initiative had to include the promise to reach Permanent Status and establish a Palestinian state within a realistic time frame. The components of an Egyptian-suggested US plan needed to include a commitment to establish a Palestinian state; security, political, and institutional reforms for the PA; economic rehabilitation for the West Bank and Gaza supported by the international donor community; and possibly a parallel Israeli-Palestinian and a wider Israeli-Arab negotiating track. Egypt was unwilling to accept a long-term Interim Agreement, but it was willing to support the idea of a transitional period toward Permanent Status, with two conditions. First, progress from phase to phase would depend not upon the agreement of either side, but upon an American and European decision, or a Quartet decision; and second, the parties should give a clear guarantee to reach a Permanent Status Agreement.[75]

On the Palestinian side, the idea of internal reform was welcome. In an interview with the Palestinian newspaper *Al-Ayyam*, Mahmoud Abbas spoke of the need for reform in the Fatah movement, the need to create an effective security system that would unify the security apparatuses under one command, the need for control in all budgetary and fiscal matters, and reform of existing institutions. On political issues, Abbas repeated his opposition to any interim arrangement and described the known hard-line Palestinian positions.[76]

The coordinated Egyptian-Jordanian-Saudi pressure on the United States, and the desire to balance US policy with what Sharon could accept, paved the way for President Bush's political vision, expressed in his Rose Garden speech on June 24, 2002:

> And when the Palestinian people have new leaders, new institutions and new security arrangements with their neighbors, the United States of America will support the creation of a Palestinian state

whose borders and certain aspects of its sovereignty will be provisional until resolved as part of a final settlement in the Middle East.[77]

Two days later, the German Ministry of Foreign Affairs prepared a confidential document that provided for three phases: an emergency phase, a transitional phase, and a state creation phase. The emergency phase would begin with the appointment of a caretaker Palestinian prime minister and end with elections at the beginning of 2003; the transitional phase would end with the final negotiations on a provisional state by the end of 2003. The final phase would begin with the proclamation of a state on a provisional basis, one that kept final status issues such as borders and Jerusalem open until around the end of 2003, and it would end with the proclamation of a final state, the target date for which was 2005. The document also spoke of the need for an international representative, appointed by the UN Security Council, who would have executive powers in the civilian areas and whose mandate would end with the proclamation of a final state.[78]

In response to international pressure, by the end of June 2002 the PA had prepared a "100 Days Plan" for reform. The plan defined the reform program and indicative benchmarks, and suggested donor monitoring and support proposals. The reforms included general legislation of a "Basic Law" and elections for president in January 2003 and for the municipalities in March 2003; an interior affairs command chain for public security; and greater transparency and accountability for the PA's financial administration.[79] The plan was prepared in time to impress the Quartet powers, who met in mid-July with the Egyptian and Jordanian foreign ministers.[80] Thus, preparatory diplomatic work for defining the concept of the roadmap was under way. On August 1, 2002, at a meeting with King Abdullah II of Jordan, President Bush gave his go-ahead to finalize the roadmap.[81] It took several more months for the details to be worked out, but on April 30, 2003, the "Performance-Based Roadmap" was published with the full support of the Quartet powers.[82]

Sharon had a mixed reaction to the roadmap. He clearly supported the three-phase approach, and conceptually was not opposed to a two-state solution as long as he could achieve his two main terms: the acceptance of Israel's security demands, and permission for the majority of settlements to be annexed to Israel. Accordingly, Sharon strongly opposed a complete settlement freeze, although he was willing to seek a compromise. In 2001, he had empowered Peres to reach an understanding with Secretary of State Powell, committing the Government of Israel to limit settlement construction by preventing government subsidies and land sequestration for settlement purposes, not allowing new settlements, and limiting construction in existing settlements to meet only the "natural growth" needs.[83] Sharon assumed that if his terms would not be accepted, the process would get stuck in the interim phases. Thus, the Government of Israel offered its nominal support for the roadmap, yet added fourteen reservations, which described in some detail the Israeli conditions for the establishment of a Palestinian state with provisional borders, as well as the conditions for negotiations on phase three, (i.e., the conclusion of a Permanent Status Agreement). At this point, there was no need for the Bush administration to either accept or reject the fourteen Israeli reservations.[84]

The Concept of Unilateral Disengagement Reemerges

From the Israeli government's perspective, Operation Defensive Shield seemed to have paradoxically strengthened Arafat's strategy of employing violence and terrorism to bring about a settlement imposed by regional and global powers. Operation Defensive Shield, launched as a reprisal against Palestinian terror, had mobilized Saudi Arabia, Egypt, and Jordan, along with the international community in general, against Israel. Thus, the political and diplomatic legitimacy and capabilities of the PLO and the PA were reinforced, even though Arafat's personal standing had weakened.[85] The emerging Quartet-supported roadmap appeared to further enhance the internationalization of the conflict.

In addition to external pressures, Sharon had to simultaneously deal with rising internal demands for change. The IDF's review of the lessons learned from Operation Defensive Shield, prepared by a team headed by General Spiegel, referred to the need to rely upon and increase international involvement in supporting the PA. This approach was seen as essential in order to prevent a humanitarian crisis and to rebuild the PA's service capacities. To prevent anticipated acts of terrorism, Israel's security authorities demanded the construction of a security fence, which Sharon had originally opposed.[86] At that time, Eival Gilady had already started to plan, together with Dov Weissglas, what would become Sharon's Disengagement Plan.[87]

In August 2002, Uri Sagie and Gilead Sher, Barak's two chief negotiators on the Syrian and Palestinian tracks, published a policy paper suggesting a two-phase Israeli unilateral disengagement from Gaza and the West Bank. The paper drew upon the work that had been carried out by the Peace Administration during the second half of 2000. During the first phase, Sagie and Sher suggested three complementary policies: (1) to construct a security fence along the suggested provisional border, permitting 80 percent of the settler population to be included in the area west of the fence; (2) to prepare to relocate settlements that would remain east of the fence; and (3) to encourage international involvement to support and strengthen the PA's authority east of the fence. The paper stressed the importance of respecting the green line for the purpose of achieving both regional and international legitimacy, as well as reaching a national consensus in order to obtain internal legitimacy for future settlement relocation and evacuation. During the proposed second phase, the relocated (evacuated) settlements were to be reintegrated into their places of final residence, and the physical infrastructures between Israel and Palestine would be separated, creating the physical infrastructure to enable the establishment of a viable Palestinian state. An effective border security and cooperation system had to be prepared in a dialogue with the Palestinians, and a mandate for permitting an international military-civilian role in the Palestinian territories had to be defined. Last but not least, it was necessary to define the Israeli-Palestinian relationship in the Jerusalem area and to permit the Palestinians to establish their own institutions on the Arab side of the city.[88]

Between September 2000 and March 2004, the death toll from terrorist acts was more than 900 on the Israeli side and more than 2,700 on the Palestinian side.[89] The national economic loss was estimated in June 2002 to amount to more than $5 billion, or 3 to 4 percent of Israel's gross domestic product. The terrorist attacks and reprisals had broad consequences: Malls and hotels were often empty, a Tel Aviv university research study found that 40 percent of the children it surveyed were suffering from symptoms of trauma, and up to 40,000 cars a year were stolen through Israeli-Palestinian criminal cooperation. The establishment of a security fence was thus publicly regarded as the most important national project.[90] Public pressure for its construction increased most substantially in the spring and summer of 2002, and construction began in mid-June 2002.[91] An important component of the comprehensive proposals prepared by Sagie and Sher was being implemented. The logic of the emerging new paradigm tended to indicate that the other components would need to follow.

At the same time, however, Beilin and Yasser Abed Rabbo were still advocating the paradigm that had already failed under Barak and Clinton. A track-two exercise concluded in the autumn of 2003 created the "Geneva Accord," which was a detailed blueprint for a Permanent Status Agreement negotiated between Israeli and Palestinian teams, led on the Israeli side by Beilin and on the Palestinian side by Abed Rabbo, who signed the document in his personal capacity. His political standing and prestige resulted from the fact that he was a close adviser to Abbas. The exercise aimed to demonstrate that a Permanent Status Agreement on all outstanding issues of conflict could be concluded and that a Palestinian partner for such a strategy was forthcoming.[92]

The ECF was also busy developing a third paradigm for unilateral disengagement, in preparation for the Israeli elections at the end of January 2003. Gidi Grinstein and I joined a committee that had been asked to prepare a policy concept for an ILP-led government. Danny Yatom, who had been personally close to prime ministers Rabin and Barak, chaired the committee.

This third concept combined the unilateral disengagement approach proposed by Sagie and Sher, and the "transit to state" concept that the ECF had developed in 1999 and 2000. We suggested that according to the January 1997 "Note for the Record," which had been followed the January 1997 Hebron Agreement, an Israeli Further Redeployment would be unilaterally determined by Israel. We suggested handing over control of 55 to 60 percent of the West Bank territory and of all of the Gaza Strip to the PA, while engaging in negotiations on all Permanent Status issues based on the Clinton proposals of December 23, 2000 (see chapter 7).

A special annex to our concept dealt with the suggested Gaza withdrawal in four different scenarios: (1) on the optimal basis of a trilateral agreement of Israel, the Palestinian, and the international community; (2) on the basis of a possible bilateral Israeli-Palestinian agreement; (3) on the basis of an understanding between Israel and the international community understanding; or (4) a fully unilateral withdrawal as a last resort. The underlying assumption was that the suggested proposal was in line with the agreements that had been signed. We were convinced that our suggestion to withdraw from substantial territories and negotiate a Permanent Status Agreement on the basis of the December 2000 Clinton proposal would achieve wide international support. We had no difficulty in convincing the ILP's prime ministerial candidate, General Amram Mitzna, to pursue the suggested approach. However, the ILP was not successful at the polls, and Sharon was the winner of the January 28, 2003, elections.[93]

Analytical Implications: Searching for a Workable Paradigm

After the terrorism brought about by the failure of negotiations and the start of the second intifada, the three major actors in the Israeli-Palestinian drama all turned away from the negotiations. George W. Bush wanted to have as little as possible to do with the Israeli-Palestinian conflict and pursued his Anything But Clinton policy; Sharon was determined to teach Arafat and the Palestinians a lesson that terrorism and violence would not get them anywhere; and Arafat and Barghouti believed that by continuing the violence, they would be able to obtain further concessions, either directly from Israel or indirectly by creating regional and international pressure. Yet the September 11 terrorist attacks on New York and Washington made the US administration aware that the ongoing Israeli-Palestinian fighting had to be addressed more visibly in order to garner significant regional support for the US and international counterterrorism efforts.[94]

In seeking a more effective approach to deal with the complex Israeli-Palestinian relations, three different paradigms emerged. As a spillover from the Israeli Peace Administration's work in the summer and autumn of 2000, in 2001 Sagie and Sher prepared the concept of Israeli unilateral disengagement. Although Sharon initially opposed the concept, the increasing violence and the great human and material loss caused by the intifada, and the subsequent mounting public pressure in Israel, obliged him to adopt the proposed paradigm. The April 2003 announcement of the Benchmarked Roadmap to Peace in the Middle East represented a second paradigm. In its concept, it followed the logic of the "transit to state" or "corridor to Permanent Status" that the ECF had developed long before. The Geneva Accords, a detailed blueprint for a proposed Israeli-Palestinian Permanent Status Agreement, offered a third paradigm. All three approaches supported a two-state solution.[95]

However, none of the three paradigms were developed enough to provide an effective recipe for conflict resolution. Sharon's unilateral disengagement concept was still in the planning phase. Sharon planned his security fence to literally fence the Palestinians out by grabbing 20 percent of West Bank territory, rather than building the fence where possible along the June 4, 1967, cease-fire lines and including only the settlement blocs (as the Peace Administration, as well as Sagie and Sher, were proposing). The Benchmarked Roadmap included important components necessary for a comprehensive conflict resolution approach, but no clear working concept had yet been developed on how to build the four essential foundations for a two-state solution: (1) Palestinian state and institution building; (2) effective Israeli-Palestinian security coordination; (3) comprehensive Israeli-Palestinian people-to-people and government-to-government programs to create a wider Israeli and Palestinian interest and commitment to peace; and (4) a regional supportive environment. Worse, whereas the roadmap looked good on paper, it was unclear whether there was sufficient political will in Washington to make the concept work. And although the third Geneva Accord paradigm aimed to keep the goal of reaching an Israeli-Palestinian Permanent Status Agreement alive, obliging both sides to the "end of conflict" and "finality of claims," its efforts represented only a small idealist section of Israelis on the left wing of the ILP and the Meretz party.

The search for an Israeli-Palestinian solution still needed to pass through a process of trial and error. What remained necessary was to use the three paradigms to create a coherent step-by-step conflict resolution strategy.

Chapter 9

Trial and Error in
Testing Three Paradigms,
January 2003–February 2009

Chapter 9 describes the policymaking process that led (under Prime Minister Ariel Sharon) to Israel's Disengagement Plan from Gaza and the Northern West Bank and—under Israeli prime minister Ehud Olmert and Palestinian Authority (PA) president Mahmoud Abbas—to a second attempt to reach a Permanent Status Agreement. The chapter also describes many achievements of track-two and multitrack diplomacy work. The concept of unilateral disengagement that was adopted by the Sharon government had been prepared by work carried out under the auspices of the Van Leer Institute in Jerusalem. The Economic Cooperation Foundation (ECF) played an important role in preparing the ground for Israeli-Palestinian security coordination, which was a precondition for a successful Israeli military withdrawal; the peaceful handover of the greenhouses in Gaza to the PA was similarly managed by the ECF. Later, under the Olmert government, a track-two effort to agree on Israeli-Palestinian terms of reference for negotiations was undertaken but failed. Successful track-two work enabled the Israeli government to relocate the line of the security fence substantially closer to the former cease-fire lines; and efforts to ease access and movement in the West Bank were successful, creating an important precondition for Palestinian economic development. Last but not least, a multitrack diplomacy effort assisted the work of US general Keith Dayton, who prepared the ground for the creation of a professional Palestinian security force.

Historical Background

Events in the Middle East were all overshadowed by the impact of the terrorist attacks on the United States on September 11, 2001, and by the growing polarization between pro-Western forces in the Middle East and an emerging powerful radical militant front of Islamic state and nonstate actors.

In 2002, US troops invaded Afghanistan; and in April 2003, US troops brought an end to Saddam Hussein's regime in Iraq. Inadvertently, the United States' invasions of Afghanistan and Iraq served the regional interests of Iran's Shi'ite Islamic fundamentalist regime. The fall of the Taliban's Sunni fundamentalist regime in Afghanistan lessened potential dangers from the east, whereas the fall of the Arab Sunni Ba'th regime in Iraq opened the door for Iran to assert its influence upon Iraq's majority Shi'ite population. Similar opportunities for Iranian influence emerged in the Muslim republics of Central Asia, which were now free of the former Soviet Union's control. In the Persian Gulf, Shi'ite population groups also offered possibilities for intervention, particularly in Bahrain and Dubai. However, Iran was effectively encircled by the US political and military presence. The logical gambit for Tehran was thus to try to undermine US influence in the region. A most effective way to do this would be to exploit the Israeli-Palestinian conflict to Iran's advantage, an approach in line with the ideological tendency of the Iranian ayatollah's regime.[1]

Iran's ideological, political, and security strategy relied in many ways upon the development of a close proxy relationship with the terrorist non-state actors Hezbollah in Lebanon and Hamas in Palestine. Iranian support for and instigation to pursue a militant anti-Israeli policy included sup-plying arms to Hezbollah and Hamas and training their militants. These efforts improved the militants' fighting capacities, and at any given moment Iranian-supplied missiles could provoke a vicious circle of vio-lence between Israel and its neighboring nonstate actors. These Iranian interventions caused the breakdown of Israeli-Palestinian negotiations in August 2003, undermined the potential success of Israel's disengagement from Gaza and the West Bank after September 2005, abruptly terminated the early peace moves of the Olmert-Livni government in June 2006, and unleashed both the Israel-Lebanon War of July 2006 and the Israeli invasion of Gaza in December 2009. In all these cases, Iran's popularity skyrock-eted among the Arab public throughout the Middle East. Moreover, the arsenal of rockets and missiles delivered to Hamas and Hezbollah showed both Jerusalem and Washington that any attack on Iran would have a very high cost for Israel's civilian population. Simultaneously, Iran was making a major effort to acquire nuclear capabilities and was openly speaking of the need to "end the Zionist occupation of Palestine of 1948"—in other words, demanding the end of the State of Israel.[2]

Thus, a complex power puzzle dominated the Middle Eastern scene during the first decade of the twenty-first century. On the militant radical side of the equation, al-Qaeda outflanked Iran, Hezbollah, and Hamas in its militant extremism. Saudi Arabia and the Palestine Liberation Organization (PLO) under Arafat's leadership, as well as Turkey, could swing either way: at times, all three took a very constructive approach in supporting the peace process, while at other times they would tend to side with the militant Islamic actors in the Middle East. Even though Egypt, Jordan, and the PLO under Mahmoud Abbas's leadership wanted the peace process to be renewed and succeed, they were wary of making any modestly pro-Israel concessions and became politically and diplomatically incapacitated in the face of Israeli-Palestinian violence.

This power puzzle created a potential schism between Washington and Jerusalem. Militarily, the US troops in Iraq and Afghanistan were exposed to Islamic hostility, which tended to increase when Israeli-Palestinian or Israeli-Lebanese relations turned violent. Thus, the US military leadership, as General David Petraeus testified to the Senate Armed Services Committee in April 2008, wanted to put an end to the Israeli-Palestinian conflict or at least continue the peace process.[3] The US State Department also needed to obtain substantial support from Saudi Arabia, the Arab Gulf states, Egypt, Jordan, and Turkey in order to be able to stabilize the situation in Iraq, Afghanistan, and elsewhere in the Middle East, as well as to confront Iran, and so the American diplomatic community wanted progress on the Israeli-Palestinian peace front. As a result, Israel felt isolated, "squeezed" between the demands of the pro-Western Arab camp and the radicals, and it vacillated between initiating steps toward seeking peace and procrastinating. Between 2003 and 2009, three different peace-seeking paradigms were being tested: the Three-Phase Benchmarked Roadmap for Peace in the Middle East, the idea of Israeli unilateral disengagement, and the concept of renegotiating a Permanent State Agreement to achieve an "end of conflict" and finality of claims.

Testing the First Paradigm: The Benchmarked Roadmap

The Benchmarked Roadmap was largely in line with ideas that the ECF had developed and had named "The Transit (or Corridor) to State

Approach" (discussed in chapter 7). It was also similar to the proposal described in a paper issued by the German Ministry of Foreign Affairs at the end of June 2001 (discussed in chapter 8). The diplomatic pull and push over the final roadmap text took ten months, between President Bush's June 2002 Rose Garden speech and the final announcement of the roadmap on April 30, 2003.[4]

The idea behind the roadmap concept was to pursue a three-phase approach toward a Permanent Status Agreement. The first phase prescribed the conditions for creating a stable environment for negotiations, including a demand for PA reform and institution building, an end to Palestinian violence, an Israeli settlement freeze, an end to incitement by official institutions, and Israel's withdrawal from Palestinian cities. The second phase would use conflict transformation steps to create public legitimacy for the negotiations, which would enable the Israeli and Palestinian leadership to offer the concessions needed for negotiations. This phase called for the establishment of an independent Palestinian state with provisional borders, the renewal of regional multilateral talks, and the restoration of Arab states' pre-intifada links to Israel. The third and final phase would then involve a comprehensive peace deal, including a final agreement on all outstanding issues.[5]

Originally, in June 2001, the German Foreign Ministry's paper demanded that the three-phase approach be led by an international representative who had executive power to enforce the rule of law and order; to enable economic and financial reform; and to have some influence on the media, schools, and the penal system. In the meantime, the Palestinians had independently introduced government reforms, such as adopting a provisional Constitution. Giving in to international pressure, Arafat agreed to create the position of prime minister, to which he appointed Abbas. Simultaneously, the Quartet had created a working group to support the Palestinian reform effort, and the European Commission had appointed Alastair Crooke to help the Palestinians with their security reforms. However, President Bush disregarded the original German proposal to permit an international representative with extensive powers to oversee the roadmap's implementation, and instead nominated John Wolf, a little-known professional diplomat who had had no experience in the Middle East and was not given any meaningful powers to be able to succeed in his task.[6]

More important at this time, both Ariel Sharon and Abbas faced the roadmap's challenge. Although the Israeli government added fourteen reservations to the roadmap, the government's decision clearly referred to the concept of a two-state solution.[7] The PA accepted the roadmap without reservations.[8] Two weeks after the roadmap was published, Sharon and Abbas met to discuss it and the related phases. In the meeting, Sharon proposed to Abbas that the Israeli government, following the roadmap's prescriptions, would withdraw Israeli Defense Forces (IDF) troops from all Palestinian cities—and he was impressed that Abbas asked him to wait until the Palestinian security forces were ready to take over.[9] In June 2003, Bush, Sharon, and Abbas held a summit meeting in Aqaba, Jordan. Following the meeting, Israeli-Palestinian committees on security, the economy, trade, and prisoners were formed. In mid-August, Israel offered to withdraw from Jericho, Qalqilya, Ramallah, and Tulqarem, but Israeli defense minister Shaul Mofaz expressed his fears that this withdrawal offer would be too great an achievement for the PA, and Hamas would put an end to its rival's success. As it happened, on August 23, 2003, a suicide bomber attacked a bus in Jerusalem, killing twenty-three Israelis.[10] Israeli intelligence followed the internal Palestinian dialogue. Abbas and his people demanded effective action against Hamas, and they asked Arafat to delegate the necessary powers to allow Abbas to take control of the Palestinian security forces. Arafat denied this request, and Abbas resigned as Palestinian prime minister on September 8, 2003.

Abbas's resignation marked the end of the first attempt to make the Israeli-Palestinian roadmap concept work.[11] Yet when Sharon proposed a second paradigm—unilateral disengagement—to the Americans, important elements of the roadmap concept were adopted.

Testing the Second Paradigm: Unilateral Disengagement

Sharon's Disengagement Plan

Following Abbas's resignation, the American and Israeli leaders were seriously upset about the return to business as usual, in which Abbas was isolated and Arafat would lead the PLO as before. This meant that no headway could be made on creating the stable environment that had been the precondition for the roadmap to get under way. Dov Weissglas recounted that shortly after Abbas's resignation, US secretary of state Condoleezza Rice told him that the US government would not permit the achievements made after the announcement of the roadmap simply to evaporate.[12] Sharon and Weissglas's conclusion was to seek a way forward: Instead of negotiating roadmap implementation on Israeli terms with the Palestinian leadership, Israel would consider unilateral moves and negotiate with the United States in order to obtain approval from Washington. In November 2003, the concept of unilateral disengagement was discussed for the first time with the Americans.[13] At the beginning, it was not clear whether the idea was to disengage only from Gaza or also from the West Bank. The Israeli National Security Council would be asked to prepare four plans: (1) disengagement only from the Gaza Strip; (2) disengagement from Gaza and the evacuation of three settlements in the northern West Bank; (3) disengagement from Gaza and the evacuation of seventeen West Bank settlements, with altogether 15,000 settlers; and (4) identification of areas for a final Israeli withdrawal. The Israelis and Americans discussed the different plans in February 2004.[14] Shortly afterward, in a meeting with Weissglas and Baruch Spiegel, Sharon remarked, "Sometimes it is necessary to cut off a part of one's own arm in order to save the entire body."[15] Sharon had three aims in mind: to create optimal security for Israel, to save as many settlements as possible in any political deal that appeared to be achievable, and to agree to a two-state solution on his terms.[16]

On December 18, 2003, at the Herzliya Conference, an annual international gathering of senior experts and policymakers organized by the Center for Inter-Disciplinary Studies in Herzliya, Sharon announced his intention of designing and implementing a unilateral disengagement plan. The plan would include the redeployment of both IDF forces and settlements along new security lines, "which will reduce as much as possible the number of Israelis located in the heart of the Palestinian population."[17] Sharon added that he was committed to the roadmap and that he would "fully coordinate with the United States" all unilateral steps that Israel would take. Under the disengagement plan, Israel would also coordinate with Jordan and Egypt to enable the free and secure passage of people and goods through international border crossings.[18]

Sharon's main concern was to coordinate this move with the US government, opening it to adjust to US suggestions and demands. In a discussion between the Israelis and Americans, the key phrase used would be to meet "boldness for boldness"—that is, provide for substantial Israeli moves in return for meaningful US concessions.[19] Thus both the concept and substance of the unilateral disengagement plan were hammered out in an intimate US-Israeli dialogue that started in November 2003 and continued until its implementation early in September 2005. The unfolding dialogue culminated in an US-Israeli understanding reached in April 2004, during Prime Minister Sharon's visit to the United States. A letter from President

Bush to Sharon gave two American concessions to Israel for the Permanent Status negotiations: an envisaged territorial settlement that reflected the current reality on the ground (rather than the 1949 armistice lines), and the resolution of the refugee problem through the settlement of Palestinian refugees in a Palestinian state.[20] In a return letter from Weissglas to Rice, Israel committed not to build outside the existing construction line of settlements in the West Bank, to remove unauthorized outposts, and to ease mobility restrictions in the West Bank. Sharon further expressed his commitment to the two-state solution, to the roadmap, and to negotiations between the parties of a final status resolution of all outstanding issues.[21] The Government of Israel then published the "Overall Concept of the Disengagement Plan."[22]

At the end of 2003, the Israeli National Security Council (NSC) was tasked to prepare the Israeli Disengagement Plan from Gaza and the Northern West Bank. Giora Eiland, the head of the Israeli NSC, delegated most of the work to his deputy, Itamar Yaar.

The Emerging Cooperation between the Israeli NSC and the ECF

The Israeli NSC under Eiland and Yaar's leadership was initially concerned with developing a workable dialogue with the potential opposition from within Likud and from the settler community. Sharon mainly feared the potential opposition from Benjamin Netanyahu. Netanyahu finally agreed to support the disengagement under four conditions: (1) the establishment of security arrangements, particularly for continued Israeli control of border crossings; (2) US backing for Israeli freedom in regard to security action; (3) no Palestinian "right of return" to Israel; and (4) a government obligation to complete the security fence.[23] The settlers took a more radical position. Even the moderate and pragmatic settler leaders left no place for compromise; they argued that God would not permit settlements to be evacuated. The influence of the settlers in the Likud Central Committee persuaded the party to reject the disengagement plan in a referendum held on May 2, 2004.[24]

Thus, Yaar and his NSC team had to prepare a detailed plan of action based on the assumption that the government would proceed despite strong opposition from the entire settler community.[25] The NSC reached basic policy conclusions that were in line with the ECF's thinking. Disengagement could not be fully unilateral, but had to be coordinated with the international community and the Palestinians; withdrawal from

Gaza had to be complete, even though the IDF strongly opposed a withdrawal from the Gaza-Egypt border; and most of the immovable real estate assets that were to be left under Palestinian control should be transferred to the international community in order to benefit Palestinian economic development.[26] We discussed the emerging concept and the ECF's potential contribution to the process, and Yaar agreed with our assessment of the importance of working with nongovernmental organizations like the ECF on policy initiatives.[27] Figure 9.1 presents the outcome of the NSC-ECF discussions.

Figure 9.1 shows the strategic thinking that the ECF shared with Yaar and his team behind the disengagement plan. As members of the ECF, to proceed with this line of thinking, we organized into teams on peacebuilding strategy, public support for cooperative disengagement, international support, and action planning.[28] We also convinced US Ambassador Edward Djerejian, director of the Baker Institute for Public Policy, to cooperate with us in order to make the necessary impact on the US government. With our help, Djerejian organized several workshops to coordinate policies with the participation of leading track-two strategists from the United States, Canada, Israel, Egypt, and the PA. In February 2005, the Baker Institute published a report with its findings: "Creating a Roadmap Implementation Process under United States Leadership."[29]

The Effort to Implement the Components of the Strategic Diagram

The June 2004 diagram, shown here as figure 9.1, represented the ECF's and NSC's mutual understanding of how to proceed. Four sections of the diagram—the legal, political, security, and economic concerns—are worthy of further elaboration.

LEGAL RESPONSIBILITY

The legal category indicated the political aims of the entire move, as Sharon had expressed them in May 2004:

> Upon completion of the move, no permanent Israeli civilian or military presence in the areas that are evacuated in the continental expanse of the Gaza Strip will remain. As a result, there will be no basis for the claim that the Gaza Strip is occupied territory.[30]

Figure 9.1. NSC-ECF Strategic Discussion Diagram, June 2004

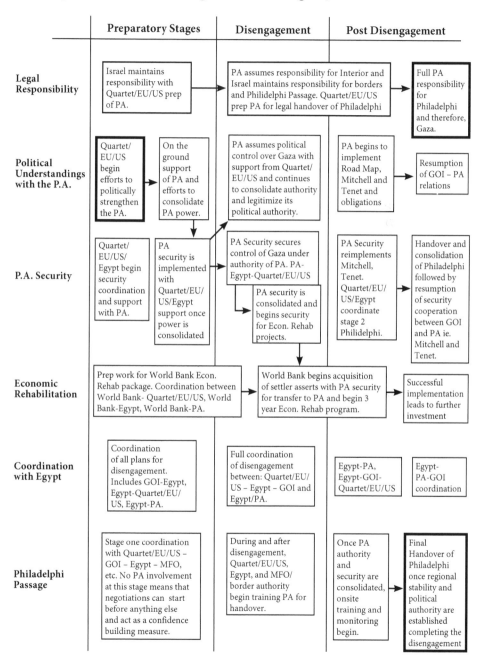

To achieve this goal of defining the Palestinians' legal responsibility for Gaza, it was understood that Israel would have to withdraw from the 14-kilometer border between the Gaza Strip and Egypt, known as the Philadelphi Axis. The ECF sought ways to enable this withdrawal, and wrote several papers on the matter.[31] Despite serious opposition from Israeli security sources, Sharon chose to withdraw from the Philadelphi Axis—though whether the ECF's work affected his decision is unknown.

POLITICAL UNDERSTANDINGS

The preparatory stage would require efforts to consolidate the PA's political power on the ground. This was easier said than done, because the Quartet powers were afraid of getting involved on the ground, fearing that they would become entangled in skirmishes with Palestinian militant groups or with the IDF, and the PA was too weak to undertake the task alone. Most important, local Palestinian power brokers had grown too strong and were unwilling to give up their control of local affairs. The ideological opposition of Hamas and the Jihadist movements in Gaza had effectively exploited the existing power vacuum in Gaza, and the PA itself avoided confronting the issue by claiming that everything was all right. In a February 2004 meeting, Daniel Kurtzer (who by then had become the US ambassador to Israel) provided a realistic but disturbing assessment of the situation: "The Palestinians do not assess their capabilities as low as the US does. They never show a security plan with tactical thinking on the ground. In order to ensure law and order the PA has 65,000 people receiving salaries; although even 9,000 people could do it. The problem was that they were given double messages."[32] To overcome the power vacuum, we advocated a strong international role on the ground.[33] These suggestions remained on paper.

In hindsight, the ECF's proposal for a greater international role aimed at changing the power balance on the ground in favor of the PA was both unrealistic and premature. What was needed then was what happened later under US general Keith Dayton's command: a protracted process of building Palestinian security capacities, combined with increased Israeli-Palestinian security cooperation.[34] The disengagement time frame left no room for the necessary rebuilding of the PA's political power on the ground in the Gaza Strip. Understanding that neither political understandings nor an increased international role on the ground were achievable, the ECF turned its efforts to security and economic channels.

THE SECURITY CHANNEL

In June 2004, we commissioned a paper that pointed out potential security threats from the Gaza Strip.[35] It referred to three dangers: (1) infiltration attempts into Israel by suicide bombers, either through the fence or by sea; (2) attacks on Israeli forces along the Palestinian-controlled border; and (3) the firing of missiles toward Israeli towns. Under Israeli occupation and control, arms had been smuggled through tunnels in the Rafah area in southern Gaza, near the border with Egypt. The IDF had managed only to limit the scope of smuggling, and the Palestinians had been unable to smuggle significant quantities of longer-range rockets and antiaircraft and antitank missiles into Gaza. We feared a leap in the capacities of armed Palestinian groups with longer-range missiles threatening Israeli towns, whereas antiaircraft and antitank missiles would limit the IDF's ability to operate. The ECF paper suggested several means of dealing with these dangers:

- Egypt would commit to taking action to prevent the smuggling of arms from the Egyptian side to the Palestinian side, even if these actions might require a change of the military annex of the Israeli-Egyptian peace agreements in order to enable further Egyptian deployment along the border.
- For international monitoring, we suggested using the US-led Multinational Force and Observers (MFO), which was on the ground in Sinai and had gained much experience in crisis prevention after the conclusion of the 1979 Israel-Egypt Peace Treaty.
- Israel, Egypt, and the MFO would establish a mechanism to coordinate and exchange information to prevent smuggling.
- An international force would be stationed on the Philadelphi Axis and at the Rafah checkpoint between Egypt and the Gaza Strip, monitoring Palestinian activities to prevent smuggling.
- To prevent massive arms smuggling from the sea, without having a negative economic effect on the income from fishing in Gaza, the Gaza-area fishing zones would be widened, even if larger marine forces were required to monitor these areas.[36]

As a result of these proposals, the ECF developed a long-standing dialogue with the MFO. Few of our suggestions were actually implemented, but the demand for an international monitoring force eventually led to the Access and Movement Agreement of November 2005 and the establishment of the EU Border Assistance Mission (EUBAM).[37]

The June 2004 paper also described the prospective situations that could evolve in Gaza after disengagement. Four scenarios were envisaged: (1) stability created by a rehabilitated PA with security capacities in the Gaza Strip, (2) a Hamas takeover, (3) the failure of state creation and a lapse into anarchy, or (4) an understanding between the Fatah and Islamist forces in Gaza to share power and enforce law and order together. Though the first option appeared to be optimal, it was unrealistic as a stand-alone possibility. Thus, the paper recommended that the PA be permitted to reform and build the capacities of its security forces under the strict supervision of third parties, that the Palestinians commit to prevent arms smuggling and act decisively against armed forces outside the PA's command under strict international supervision, and that an effective coordination mechanism be created if necessary with other Palestinian forces in Gaza.[38]

The same policy paper argued that for the disengagement plan to succeed, the Palestinians had to perceive this move "as a first step in a political process that has a chance to fulfill their basic needs." The Quartet and the international community at large were interested in creating a stable situation after Israeli withdrawal, but would "need guarantees that this plan is not an isolated step, but rather one step in the Roadmap that will lead to the creation of a Palestinian state and the resumption of Permanent Status negotiations." However, the paper added, because "the Israeli government had climbed a high tree on the issue of the lack of a Palestinian partner . . . the government will find it hard to veer sharply from this policy, and therefore all coordination vis-à-vis the Palestinians will have to be done in a partial manner, via intermediary organizations and in a relatively low level of participants."[39]

THE ECONOMIC CHANNEL

On the economic development issue, the ECF had a threefold strategic aim: Initiate an international plan for Palestinian economic rehabilitation, mainly to strengthen the PA politically; provide for the orderly transfer of nonmovable properties and the assets of the settlements that would be left behind; and create an impetus for substantial Palestinian economic growth in Gaza and the West Bank. At the end of October 2003, before the announcement of Sharon's Disengagement Plan, the US Agency for International Development had asked us to arrange informal talks with Israeli officials, which we did.[40] At the May 4, 2004, Quartet meeting, when Sharon's disengagement plan was conditionally welcomed, the

Quartet stated that it "will work with the World Bank to assess reconstruction and development needs for Gaza and parts of the West Bank, and to explore assistance needs and convene a donors meeting."[41] Nine days later, the ECF organized another meeting of the World Bank, the EU head of the Local Aid Coordination Committee, the UN special coordinator for the Middle East peace process, and the United Nations Development Program. This time, the official Israeli side was represented by a delegation from the Israeli NSC and the ministries of finance, foreign affairs, justice, agriculture, and the Office of the Coordinator of Government Activities in the Administered Territories.[42] It seemed that the foundations for Israeli-international-Palestinian coordination—possibly even on a back-to-back basis, where Israel would coordinate with the international actors, which then would coordinate with the PA—aimed at turning Israeli disengagement into a stepping-stone for Palestinian state building had been laid.

Emerging Conditions for Coordinating the Disengagement Plan

Following US president George W. Bush's reelection in November 2004, the opportunities for progress and achievement of a fully coordinated Israeli Disengagement Plan in line with the roadmap grew infinitely. Just a week after the election, Yasser Arafat died in a hospital in Paris, following an illness that had left him in a coma for more than a week. In January 2005, the Labor Party joined Sharon's government, and Shimon Peres was made deputy prime minister in charge of coordinating the disengagement plan with the international community and the Palestinians. Shortly thereafter, Mahmoud Abbas was elected president of the PA by a comfortable majority.[43] The way for a renewed dialogue had opened.

Shortly thereafter, in February 2005, official direct talks between the Israel government and the Palestinians were initiated at a summit in Sharm el-Sheikh. At the summit, both Sharon and Abbas committed to pursue roadmap obligations. Abbas expressed the need to create "appropriate mechanisms that will ensure [the roadmap's] implementation,"[44] and Sharon said "the disengagement plan paves the way to the implementation of the roadmap" and creates "a new starting point for a coordinated successful process."[45] Unfortunately, the newly emerged opportunity required hands-on US engagement, which was only halfheartedly forthcoming.[46] To follow up on security coordination and reform issues, US lieutenant general William Ward was appointed head of a new US security mission that would prepare Palestinian security reform as well as Israeli-Palestinian security coordination. The PA discussed possible reform measures with third-party actors in London on March 1. To carry out his task, General Ward hired the Strategic Assessments Initiative, a group of American, British, and Palestinian security experts.[47] The way for direct Israeli-Palestinian security coordination with outside assistance had been opened. Yet what was not really understood at the time was that, following the damage to the fabric of Israeli-Palestinian security cooperation after September 2000 (described in chapter 7), and after the defeat of most of the Palestinian security forces during and after "Operation Defensive Shield" in the spring of 2002 (described in chapter 8), it would take time to rebuild both a functioning Palestinian security force and a working Israeli-Palestinian security relationship.

At the same time, Deputy Prime Minister Peres started to plan for economic revival in the West Bank and Gaza and an orderly transfer of assets to the Palestinians. Peres worked with the World Bank, as representative of the entire donor community, and the newly appointed Quartet representative James Wolfensohn (who was replacing John Wolf). Working groups were established to discuss crossing points, trade relations, the transfer of assets (immovable settlement property), industrial estates, and the improvement of roads in the West Bank. Each of these joint Israeli–World Bank committees made substantial proposals aimed at strengthening the PA. The crossing points committee prepared parameters for upgrading passages and suggested service improvements, as well as the linking of passages to the Israeli railway system. The trade relations committee suggested an update of the April 1994 Paris Agreement that regulated the economic relationship between Israel and the PA, considered assistance to encourage Palestinian exports to third markets as well as to Israel, and requested limiting and decreasing Palestinian employment in Israel. The asset transfer committee distinguished between infrastructure services, public buildings, private and sensitive buildings, business outfits, and military assets. The idea was to continue coordinating activities and services for water, sewage, gas, electricity, and the like, while handing public buildings over to a third party. On private and sensitive buildings, no decision was made. However, several business outfits, such as greenhouses, were to be transferred to the Palestinians as functioning enterprises, and the IDF contemplated leaving buildings behind as well for Palestinian use.[48]

On the level of an ongoing diplomatic dialogue, it was easy to discuss these issues and reach reasonable understandings. However, implementation would require the existence of functioning Palestinian national institutions and the willingness of the international community to take responsibility for sustainable management and development. Neither the first nor the second was at hand. Instead, the United States' de facto "hands-off" policy and relative anarchy on the Palestinian side (characterized by infighting among various sections of Fatah, Hamas, and Jihadist groups) made the disengagement plan's success an unlikely proposition.

The ECF's Track-Two Input

In February 2005, under the leadership of Ambassador Djerejian, the Baker Institute policy paper (produced with ECF assistance) stressed that a paradigm change had taken place. Instead of an "agreements first, peace later" approach, change on the ground was a necessary precursor to the negotiating process.[49] To achieve this goal, an intense trilateral US-Israeli-Palestinian cooperation was asked for, as well as the strong support of international actors.[50] Both reports covered the political, security, and economic spheres.

The ECF directed much of its attention to the relevant security issues. Fearing the repercussions of the internal Palestinian anarchy-like conditions, we developed an intense dialogue with the Palestinians in charge of security. IDF brigadier general Shlomo Brom and brigadier general Dov Sedaka, as well as Ron Schatzberg and I, held preparatory meetings with our Palestinian partners, preparing the homework for IDF lieutenant general Amnon Lipkin Shachak. Shachak enjoyed the full confidence of both the Palestinian and Israeli sides, particularly of Palestinian interior minister Nasr Yussuf and Israeli defense minister Shaul Mofaz. In the dialogue, all the anticipated difficulties were put on the table. The following exchange between Yussuf and Shachak in early February 2005 presents a sample of the potential pitfalls. During a request for arms, Yussuf remarked:

> The security structure is the key. The street has a lot of weapons. In Gaza we have two battalions, each with 400 men. Each of the battalions has 70 Kalashnikovs. In every family they have more arms. The soldiers have little income and they sell their weapons. . . . We have no security institutions today and in our backyard we have gangs. . . . We will need financing and can build all the structures of cooperation.[51]

Shachak replied:

> I want to describe the situation to you as I see it. Israel has an interest
> in strengthening Fatah. At the same time, those who have betrayed
> us have been Fatah, not Hamas. We gave to your people 30,000
> weapons and you used some of them to shoot at us.[52]

The conclusion reached at this meeting was clear: The time for straightforward Israeli-Palestinian bilateral security cooperation was over. At the
ECF, we needed to either proceed in full cooperation with a third party or
take time for a longer process of rebuilding Palestinian security capacities
in coordination with Israel. Together with the Baker Institute's Israeli-
Palestinian Working Group, we prepared detailed proposals that described
a suggested Israeli-PA security coordination mechanism, a US-PA security
plan and related implementation structure, and the conditions necessary
to enable Israeli withdrawal from the Philadelphi Axis.[53] To try to convince the US government to adopt at least some of our proposals, upgrade
the Israeli-Palestinian security dialogue, and encourage a more intense
US-Palestinian dialogue, the ECF intensified existing links to the General
Ward mission and to the Strategic Assessments Initiative.[54]

On April 25, 2005, in response to international insistence and possibly also to the sense of confidence created by the ECF and Shachak, the
Palestinian Ministry of Interior Affairs was charged with "developing
security plans and coordinating them with the Israeli side."[55] Because the
Israeli side preferred not to create any formal joint planning mechanisms
with the PA, the ECF team held back-to-back consultations with both the
Strategic Assessments Initiative and Israeli security officials.[56] Through
these channels, the ECF commissioned Brigadier General Shmuel Sakai,
a former deputy commander in chief of the Israeli Southern Command, to
prepare guidelines for a strategic coordination plan between Israeli and
Palestinian security forces and a detailed coordination plan with General
Ward's team, which was organizing a table exercise planning for coordination between the Israeli and the Palestinian security forces. The plan
contained sixteen principles for coordination, including the following specific points:

- Israeli settlements will be evacuated from north to south, preferably
  in stages, while responsibility will be transferred to the Palestinians
  from south to north. Areas will be transferred to the Palestinians only
  after all settlements are evacuated.

- Armed forces of the two sides will not stay in the same specified areas during the evacuation. Each force will work with its own population.
- Once the evacuation is concluded, the IDF will transfer the territory to Palestinian responsibility as quickly as possible.
- The Palestinian police will complete its deployment and distribution of forces as early as possible, but not near the time of the beginning of evacuation. Palestinian forces should not be given responsibility over areas in which they are unable to prevent hostile activities.
- Third parties will not be active on the ground during the evacuation. Palestinian needs regarding local movement, health services, work, and other services during the evacuation period should be guaranteed, so as to avoid Palestinian outbursts against the IDF or the Palestinian police.[57]

This work was successful. The coordination between the Israeli and Palestinian security forces enabled an orderly and almost undisturbed evacuation of the Israeli settlers from the Gaza Strip. The withdrawal itself and the handover of Gaza happened without violence, and the Palestinian security forces sensed, at first, that they were being received by the population of Gaza as liberators from Israeli occupation.[58]

Parallel to these developments, the ECF prepared an additional document in an ongoing dialogue with the Israeli security authorities, the US Embassy in Tel Aviv, General Ward's team, and the Strategic Assessments Initiative. The document aimed not merely at addressing immediate concerns on the ground but also at linking them to the long-term strategic aims of both sides. The tasks identified included many of the reform, cooperation, coordination, and control transfer tasks that we had considered before. Our work outlined responsibilities and coordination measures to take before, during, and after the disengagement, including security arrangements and construction and the rebuilding of infrastructure such as the Gaza airport and seaport.[59]

To plan beyond the disengagement, we organized another meeting between IDF lieutenant general Shachak and Palestinian interior minister Yussuf. The discussion centered mainly on the question of how the PA could achieve stability in the Gaza Strip, put an end to *fauda* (anarchy), and control Hamas. Yussuf made it clear that although he had 14,000 soldiers under his command at the time, he did not have the power to establish stability through police action. Instead, Abbas was negotiating an agreed-on solution with Hamas; police action would be planned only if this did not work. The disunity and weakness of the

Fatah forces were discussed in a frank manner. In practice, this meant that Yussuf suggested that the IDF remain in the area until he had built up the capacity to take over, although to my knowledge no such request was made officially.[60]

The last Israeli soldier left the Gaza Strip on September 12, 2005.[61] However, neither Israel nor the PA—nor the international community— had created the necessary preconditions on the ground to ensure stability in Gaza after Israeli withdrawal. On September 7, Mussa Arafat, a cousin of Yasser Arafat and one of the Fatah-supported security lords, had been assassinated. The Al-Nasir Salah ed-din Brigade, which was apparently the military arm of the Popular Resistance Committees, had claimed responsibility.[62] The result was anarchy, which eventually led to the Hamas takeover in June 2007.

Knowing that the disengagement plan's political success or fail- ure also depended on developments in the Northern West Bank, we prepared a series of papers on the subject.[63] The papers related to civil- ian affairs as well to water and sewage issues. We understood that Palestinian control in the Northern West Bank would not be achieved solely through security measures, but rather through a buildup of the political control of the PA on the ground through economic and civilian affairs.[64] On track two, we proposed an international plan for Palestinian Economic Rehabilitation that included the rehabilitation of destroyed infrastructure such as roads and electricity; a community rehabilita- tion program to reinvigorate social welfare networks and rebuild civil society spaces such as schools, houses of religion, and public spaces; and the provision of the physical, technical, and professional facilities necessary to create trade.[65]

Unofficially, we prepared a comprehensive concept and detailed work plan for the transfer of assets with a former Palestinian deputy minister for planning. The Gush Katif settlements would become a Palestinian tourism resort; Netzarim, close to the town of Gaza, would become the wing of the University of Gaza's agricultural facility; the settlement of Homesh in the West Bank would become a center for promoting Palestinian agriculture; and Ganim and Kadim, also in the West Bank, would become Palestinian recreation centers.[66] Similarly detailed proposals were prepared for an effective border plan that would offer some sovereignty to the PA, coor- dinate the struggle against possible terrorist action, and oversee the legal movement of people and goods.[67]

At first, it seemed that our efforts to bring about an orderly transfer of assets and create a strong impetus for economic growth in Gaza and the Northern West Bank might be successful. The Israeli government, under Peres's leadership in this sphere, was in favor of it. In April 2005, the PA responded positively, and discussions fully in line with the earlier Israel–World Bank dialogue got under way.[68] The Israeli NSC collected all the necessary data on the assets that were being left behind by Israel, describing former and present landownership,the management and maintenance of agricultural and industrial equipment, private homes, public buildings, and more. NSC deputy head Yaar personally wanted to hand over all the matériel to Muhammad Dahlan, the PA minister responsible for dealing with the transfer of assets. Although the assets intended for transfer amounted to more than $4 billion, Dahlan ordered his subordinates to reject the Israeli offer.[69] The reason behind this strange move was Dahlan's fear that he would not be able to control the situation on the ground and that rivalries between the different power brokers in the Gaza Strip would cause looting and a violent power struggle over the control of these assets.[70]

In the meantime, the settler movement's struggle against the disengagement was reaching its peak. Part of the antigovernment campaign was a public demand not to leave the houses of the settlers behind "for terrorists" to live in.[71] In response, Sharon asked for an official Palestinian request to leave the properties behind. Such a request was never submitted. The international community did not suggest a diplomatic strategy that would have permitted a constructive way out. On the contrary, it made no effort to preserve the $4 billion in assets, and joined the radical choir that was calling for the destruction of the property left behind. Instead of permitting the available properties to serve as an impetus for Palestinian economic development and growth, Special Envoy James Wolfensohn and the United Nations Development Program effectively coordinated the destruction of the properties left behind with both the Government of Israel and the PA.[72]

The ECF Transfers the Greenhouses to the Palestinians

By the summer of 2005, it had become evident that the intended general transfer of assets would not take place, as the World Bank had no means to protect assets that the Government of Israel might have transferred to it. What remained was to take care of an orderly transfer of the greenhouses in the Gaza Strip to the Palestinians. Boaz Karni took it upon himself to organize the entire transaction.

First, the ECF under Karni's leadership prepared a paper indicating that the transfer of the greenhouses created a potential leverage for the development of the Palestinian economy in Gaza and could provide up to 5,000 jobs.[73] Next, the security of the transfer of the greenhouses had to be guaranteed and the necessary support from the IDF and the Palestinian security forces had to be ensured.[74] On this basis, and with Special Envoy Wolfensohn's help and personal donations, the necessary sum of $15 million was raised from among American Jewish donors.[75] (Wolfensohn, who had not been able to prevent the destruction of the more than $4 billion in assets left behind, donated more than $500,000 of his own money to secure the greenhouses.) This enabled the ECF, with the aid of the legal office of Herzog Fox Neeman, to sign agreements with all the settler entrepreneurs and their leaders, obtaining a commitment to hand over the greenhouses to the Palestinians in an orderly manner and with all the necessary equipment. Finally, all the practical arrangements with regard to water, electricity, technology transfer, and the like had to be put in place.[76] By November 2005, the greenhouses had been transferred to the PA, in an orderly manner with some relatively minor disturbances, and provided 3,000 Palestinian jobs and a projected yearly revenue of more than $50 million.[77]

After the Disengagement: Preparing for the Next Step

Throughout 2005, Othniel Schneller, Aviad Friedman (then director of the *Maariv* daily newspaper, and responsible for organizational matters), Pini Meidan (Ehud's Barak's former adviser on security and foreign affairs), and I worked on an ECF postdisengagement plan. Both Schneller and Friedman had open access to Prime Minister Sharon, who regularly consulted with Schneller on settlement affairs. Friedman had an even closer relationship with the prime minister, as well as with his son, Omri. Friedman belonged to Israel's national-religious camp and came from a settler family. After his military service, he had volunteered to work in the former Soviet Union with the Jewish community, where he developed a close friendship with Nathan Sharansky, who had been arrested by the Soviet police in 1977 on charges of spying for American intelligence and became known as a "prisoner of Zion" during his time in the gulag. Sharansky immigrated to Israel following his release in early 1986, and in the mid-1990s he established a political party in order to represent Russian immigrants in Israel. Friedman, who had helped Sharanksy establish his party, came into contact with Sharon, and the two became friends. In 2005, when we were working together, Sharon would phone Friedman and ask him to come and meet him late at night to talk about "God and the world," rather than about politics.[78]

Our strategic idea was to prepare a disengagement map for the West Bank for Sharon. Guided largely by Schneller's involvement with the settler community and his familiarity with the thinking of the pragmatists among them, we prepared a map with four categories of settlements: (1) the blue settlements, located west of the fence, which were intended to be annexed to Israel sooner rather than later; (2) the yellow settlements, east of the fence but close to it, which were intended to be annexed by Israel when a final agreement was concluded; (3) the green settlements, located near Palestinian towns or villages mainly along the north-to-south West Bank mountain ridge, which were to be evacuated and relocated within the June 4, 1967, borders or in "blue" settlement blocs; and (4) the red settlements, which would remain temporarily under Israeli control and would be viewed as negotiable with the Palestinians.[79] At the time, we did not know that our work at the ECF was part of a far more comprehensive planning effort that was being carried out by IDF brigadier general Baruch Spiegel in the Ministry of Defense, in cooperation with Prime Minister Sharon, Weissglas, and Brigadier General Eival Gilady of the IDF's Strategic Planning Department. Their intention was to create an effective mechanism to prevent a further expansion of settlements, in line with the obligations made in the April 2004 Weissglas letter to Rice. Spiegel's team analyzed air photographs of 120 settlements and 87 outposts with two aims in mind: to identify illegally built houses or caravans that had to be removed, and to locate places within the legal settlement areas where additional construction was possible. The idea was to resettle to these places the settlers who would have to be evacuated from settlements in Palestinian territories.[80]

Gilady reported that parallel to our four-person group work and Spiegel's work, the IDF Strategic Planning Department (under Gilady's leadership and in full coordination with Sharon) prepared a more far-reaching plan directed at improving relations with all of Israel's neighbors through 2025.[81] The plan, which was prepared in cooperation with Elliott Abrams of the US National Security Council, provided for a three-phase approach to relocate settlements. In the first phase, incentives for settlers to leave voluntarily would be offered, but disincentives would be given to those who chose to stay. In the second phase, obligatory settlement relocation would be carried out, leaving the IDF behind to maintain stability during the third phase. Here an important lesson from the events of September 2005 had been learned. It did not make sense for Israel to withdraw and leave an anarchic situation behind.

Schneller discussed the final ECF map with Sharon at noon on January 4, 2006. Sharon expressed his full support, and he made a commitment to implement the proposed plan.[82] But that same day, he had a stroke and fell into a coma. He remained severely incapacitated until his death in January 2014. Although we will never know whether Sharon would have implemented the second disengagement plan for the West Bank, we do know that he had committed to doing so.[83]

Testing the Third Paradigm: Returning to Permanent Status Negotiations during the Olmert Government, January 5, 2006–February 10, 2009

Prime Minister Olmert's Offer of a Permanent Status Agreement

Following Sharon's stroke and incapacitation, his deputy prime minister, Ehud Olmert, became acting prime minister in January 2006 and was formally declared prime minister in May 2006. Three weeks after Sharon's stroke, on January 26, 2006, the Palestinian elections resulted in a dramatic victory for Hamas, which seriously complicated matters.[84] Under Olmert's premiership, the option of reaching a Permanent Status Agreement with Abbas was tested again. Although Olmert's party was confirmed as the governing party in the March 2006 Israeli elections on the platform of a second disengagement plan, immediately after the government was formed a small committee headed by Ahron Abramovitch, director-general of the Ministry of Foreign Affairs, with the participation of Daniel Reisner, legal adviser to the Israeli government, strongly opposed the concept of pursuing a second disengagement. Learning from the mistakes that Ehud Barak had made, Olmert proceeded carefully. During the first twenty months of his government, between January 2006 and October 2007, he attempted to agree on the terms of reference for the negotiations on a Permanent Status deal through back-channel negotiations. Although this approach failed, he worked with the Americans, the Palestinians, and the pragmatic Arab nations to prepare the November 2007 Annapolis Conference. Aimed at reaching a Permanent Status Agreement, three parallel complementary efforts were pursued:

- An intimate and intensive personal dialogue between Olmert and Abbas on all outstanding core issues of conflict;
- A comprehensive negotiating effort led on the Israeli side by Foreign Minister Tzipi Livni and on the Palestinian side by Abu Ala'; and
- Twelve working groups dealing with the various aspects of present and future relations between Israel and an emerging Palestinian State.

In the autumn of 2008, Olmert's final proposal was submitted to Abbas. In it, Olmert accepted Abbas's demand for a one-for-one territory swap based on the June 4, 1967, lines. Knowing that on 6 percent of the West Bank territory, 95 percent of the residents were Israelis living in settlement blocs, Olmert asked for a 6.3 percent exchange in which Israel would incorporate settlement blocs on 6.3 percent of the West Bank territory. The Palestinian State would be established on all of the Gaza Strip and on 94 percent of the West Bank territory, where 97 percent of the residents were Palestinians and only 3 percent were Israelis. In return for annexing the settlement blocs, Olmert would offer to swap 5.8 percent of territory from Israel proper, as well as a passage from the West Bank to Gaza through Israeli territory that would be calculated (due to its great strategic and practical value) as the additional 0.5 percent of the swap. Settlers living in the areas that would become part of Palestine would be relocated to permanent places of residence in Israel's sovereign territory. Furthermore, the Palestinian state would be able to establish its capital, Al-Quds, in the Arab neighborhoods of Jerusalem, while the Olmert proposal suggested a Special Regime for the Holy Basin to be managed by a joint committee formed by three Arab states, the United States, and Israel. The committee designed to manage the Holy Basin in Jerusalem would be obliged to only make unanimous decisions. On refugees, the issues of compensation and rehabilitation were all dealt with in line with understandings that had emerged over the years. Taking no small political risk, Olmert was willing to grant a symbolic number of Palestinians the right to return to Israel.[85]

However, Abbas rejected this offer.[86] When Abbas paid his last visit to President Bush after the November 2008 US presidential elections, the presidents and Secretary of State Rice asked the Palestinian president to at least consider the proposal. Rice describes the outcome in her memoirs: "The President took Abbas into the Oval Office alone and appealed to him to reconsider. The Palestinian stood firm, and the idea died."[87]

Asher Susser explains Abbas's resistance as his belief that in the proposed deal, the refugee issue was unacceptable to the Palestinians.[88] The Palestinians explained to us in a track-two exercise that even if Israel accepted the principle of a one-for-one swap along the 1967 lines, a "maximum" swap as proposed was not acceptable.[89] In an "everything or nothing" approach, the gap between the most minimalist Israeli and Palestinian positions remained unbridgeable. Once again, the existing impasse became manifest.[90]

Was There a Fallback to Maintain the Paradigm of a "Permanent Status Agreement First"?

It might be argued that a less detailed agreement on the terms of a Permanent Status Agreement, referring to principles rather to the details, might have shown the viability of the "Permanent Status first" paradigm. Olmert and his deputy prime minister, Haim Ramon, tested this option with the help of back-channel diplomacy. One of the back channels included David Brodet and me on the Israeli side and Hussein Agha and Ahmed Khalidi on the Palestinian side.

Because the ECF enjoyed open access to central decisionmakers in the Olmert government, particularly to Haim Ramon and Foreign Minister Tzipi Livni, David Brodet and I were able to reestablish (at first on our own) a track-two channel with our Palestinian partners. Brodet, who had negotiated the 1994 Paris Agreement, and I started to meet with Agha and Khalidi, who enjoyed President Abbas's full support and confidence. During meetings held in the spring of 2006, we agreed on a draft describing an Israeli-Palestinian political horizon. It included the following seven points:

1. The ultimate goal of the political process is the creation of a free, independent, democratic, sovereign, viable, secure and contiguous Palestinian state, living side by side with Israel in peace and security.
2. Future Israeli withdrawals from the West Bank are part of a process of ending the occupation.
3. The final borders between the two states and other outstanding issues will be determined by negotiations. This will include agreed-upon land swaps.
4. No progress in the political process is possible without mutual and reciprocal security for the Israeli and the Palestinian peoples.
5. Progress in the political process should include measures to provide for economic viability and independence for the Palestinian people.
6. Jerusalem is a city holy to all three monotheistic faiths, and freedom of access to holy sites shall be guaranteed. The political future of Jerusalem will be determined by demographic considerations.

7. A fair and equitable resolution of the Palestinian refugee problem shall be agreed upon with due consideration for the concerns of both parties.[91]

Khalidi and Agha discussed this text with Abbas in May 2006 in Strasbourg, and they received his full support. The same text was subsequently submitted to Prime Minister Olmert and Foreign Minister Livni. They agreed to the first five points and asked that points six and seven be deleted. The Israeli response was relayed to Abbas, who responded that "the agreed process was important, not the words."[92] The emerging understanding and the goodwill that the Israeli and Palestinian leadership demonstrated during our track-two work helped to create a favorable atmosphere at the first meeting between Abbas and Livni in Sharm el-Sheikh in June 2006. However, the abduction of an Israeli soldier, Gilad Shalit, on June 25, followed by the outbreak of war between Israel and Lebanon in the summer of 2006, ensured that headway based on these preliminary understandings was now impossible.[93]

Despite the bad general atmosphere, neither Olmert nor Abbas was willing to give in to the forces of radicalism. Instead, they decided to proceed secretly, away from the media limelight. Over an entire year, they pursued a close dialogue and discussed three major "baskets": territorial issues, Jerusalem, and refugees. They then intended to prepare a very short joint paper defining the political horizon. To prepare the paper and keep the content deniable, Deputy Prime Minister Ramon asked David Brodet and me to renew our collaboration with Hussein Agha and Ahmed Khalidi. Receiving policy ideas from our meetings, Ramon would meet with Yasser Abed Rabbo and discuss additional conceptual compromise formulas. Alas, this effort failed. Early in the summer of 2007, Agha prepared a text that contained many of the familiar requests, include permanent borders based on the June 1967 lines, a one-for-one exchange of territory, withdrawal of Israeli settlers, secure passage between the West Bank and Gaza, an agreed-upon solution to the refugee problem, the division of Jerusalem by neighborhoods, and protection of holy sites. Ramon rejected this text, as it most severely narrowed the Israeli negotiating space. Our counterproposals, which demanded Palestinian recognition of Israel as the "state of the Jewish people," were also rejected by the Palestinians. Yet in hindsight, Prime Minister Olmert's 2008 proposal to President Abbas for a detailed Permanent Status Agreement was fully in line with the principles that Agha had laid out in the summer of 2007.[94]

The lesson to be learned from this experience is important. In seeking to agree on principles (or terms of reference) for negotiations, the

Palestinian side viewed it as necessary to obtain formulations to limit the Israeli negotiating space and ensure an optimal Palestinian outcome. As a result, the Israeli side had difficulties in accepting far-reaching terms of reference. However, when Olmert suggested a Permanent Status Agreement, in line with the principles laid out by the Palestinian side (in the Hussein Agha paper), the details that were acceptable to Israel turned out to be not acceptable to the Palestinian side. Only very generally described guidelines—similar to the seven-point draft that Agha, Khalidi, Brodet, and I had produced in the late spring of 2006—appeared to be useful.

The Annapolis Input for Understanding the Needs of Palestinian State Building

At the end of November 2007, an international conference was held in the United States in Annapolis, Maryland, to officially renew the Israeli-Palestinian Permanent Status negotiations. A joint statement was produced, and the decision was made to pursue negotiations in twelve committees covering topics such as the economic relationship, the environment, state-to-state relations, border crossings, legal issues, prisoners, and the culture of peace. In a parallel fashion, negotiations on the core issues of conflict were pursued, being managed confidentially by Tzipi Livni on the Israeli side and Abu Ala' on the Palestinian side, while Prime Minister Olmert and President Abbas were continuing an in-depth one-to-one dialogue. Unfortunately, the principle that "nothing is agreed upon until everything is agreed upon" was applied, not only for negotiating the core issues but also for establishing the necessary understandings on Palestinian state building. The implementation of the committee's understandings would have created important legitimacy for the peacemaking effort, but these efforts were once again postponed until a comprehensive agreement might theoretically be achieved.[95]

Back to the Roadmap Paradigm of Transit to State

As mentioned above, the roadmap's phase one provisions had outlined the need for Palestinian reform, an end of violence, Israeli-Palestinian security cooperation, Palestinian access and movement, and a settlement freeze. Some of these activities had been pursued since April 2003, but the weakness of the PA caused an internal Palestinian rift and an anarchy-like situation. The January 2006 Palestinian elections, which created a Hamas majority, only complicated the situation. A Palestinian unity government combining Fatah and Hamas was ineffective. Saudi efforts to bridge the gap between the two rival Palestinian factions in the so-called Mecca Accord also failed, and in June 2007 Hamas launched a coup in Gaza.[96] The outcome was both a geographical and a political-ideological Palestinian split. Hamas had control of Gaza, but the West Bank remained under Fatah and the PLO, where President Abbas had appointed Salam Fayyad as prime minister.

Prime Minister Fayyad's appointment was followed by a bottom-up Palestinian state-building effort, largely in line with the roadmap's first-phase provisions. Fayyad's first decisive move was to change the existing system of financing the work of Palestinian security groups. To unify the Palestinian security forces and obtain effective government control over them, Fayyad insisted that the government pay all Palestinian security agents and that their salaries be transferred to their personal bank accounts. Until that point, different Palestinian security lords had possessed independent sources of income (e.g., Muhammad Dahlan received income from payments at the Karni crossing). What seemed to be a mere technical-administrative change laid the foundations for both the PA's monopoly over the use of force and comprehensive security reform. Having achieved this, Fayyad dedicated his time to building and reforming the Palestinian state's institutions and attempted to get the Palestinian economy back on track.[97] His approach was to improve the situation on the ground, creating the social capital necessary to provide the leadership with the legitimacy for conflict resolution.[98] Shortly after Fayyad's nomination as prime minister, President Bush also offered strong conceptual support:

> We can help them show the world what a Palestinian state would look like and act like. We can help them prove to the world, the region, and Israel that a Palestinian state would be a partner—not a danger. We can help them make clear to all Palestinians that rejecting violence is the surest path to security and a better life. And we can help them demonstrate to the extremists once and for all that terror will have no place in a Palestinian state. . . . First we are strengthening our financial commitment.[99]

The logic of the Bush statement emphasized the necessity of creating a nonviolent relationship between Israel and the Palestinians. This was no small challenge. Three different high-ranking military assignments were made in order to do the job. In 2005, General Keith Dayton succeeded General Howard Ward as US security coordinator, responsible for training the Palestinian security forces and enabling Israeli-Palestinian security cooperation. Shortly after the Annapolis Conference, Secretary of State Rice appointed a special mission (first under the command of General William Frazer, and then under General Paul Selva) to monitor roadmap implementation. Rice also appointed General James Jones as special envoy for Middle East regional security, to comprehensively assess the current Israeli-Palestinian security situation (including, threats, capabilities, security arrangements, and assistance); to identify ways to foster security cooperation, strengthen Palestinian security institutions, and engage the neighbors on how best to ensure security in a two-state solution; and to advise the secretary of state on how best to implement this plan.[100]

This support was tremendously important but not an easy challenge. Both the Sharon and Olmert governments had adopted a tough approach in the struggle against terrorist attacks. The Israeli strategy applied was based on a conceptual triangle: The first side of the triangle was the construction of the fence as a security barrier to impede entrance from Gaza and the West Bank into Israel; the second side was roadblocks and other impediments to movement, slowing Palestinian movement from one place to the other and thus offering Israeli security forces more time to identify and impede the movement of terrorists; and the third side involved "cutting the grass," which meant purging terrorists whenever and wherever they were found. This triangular approach was a classic antiterrorism strategy and was effective in preempting terrorist acts, so the Israeli security authorities tended to maintain this seemingly successful approach, on the basis of "do not fix what is not broken." However, the strategy also made the everyday lives of innocent civilians unbearable and pushed them toward support of radical groups in the West Bank. It was no small challenge for General Jones and General Dayton to overcome the initial suspicion of the Israeli security authorities. In this niche, the members of the ECF could assist in trust building because of our close connection with both the Israeli security authorities and the Palestinian leadership.

Promoting the Economic Corridors Concept

To revive the Palestinian economy, the first concept we at the ECF developed was one that created three economic corridors, as shown in figure 9.2.

Figure 9.2. Draft Design of Palestinian Economic Corridors

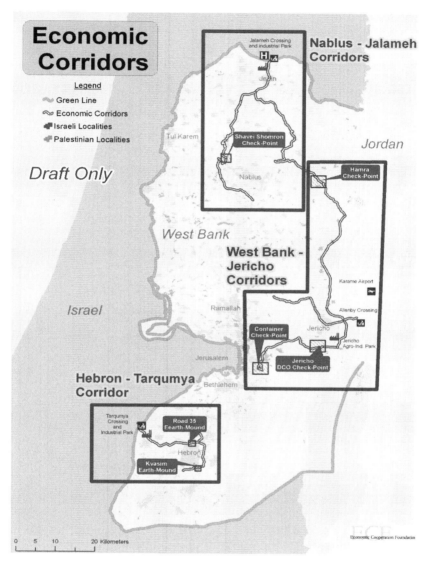

Source: Economic Cooperation Foundation, December 2007.

The Nablus-Jalameh corridor would serve the northern West Bank. The Hebron-Tarqumya corridor would serve the area of Bethlehem and Hebron. The West Bank–Jericho corridor would serve the eastern West Bank, along the Jordan Valley.

The concept of the economic corridors had four components. The first was to reintegrate so-called fugitives—those individuals and groups that had carried arms and terrorized the local population by demanding protection money for economic activities. Fearing apprehension by Israeli security forces, these fugitives violently opposed the Palestinian security forces and were a major threat to law and order. We suggested that fugitives who were willing to give up their arms should be granted clemency by the Israeli security forces, and the PA would arrest them for several more months in order to keep them off the streets for a transitional period, while offering their families a minimal degree of social security. Both the relevant Israeli and Palestinian authorities accepted this concept, which enabled the Palestinian security forces to disarm the fugitives and start to restore law and order. The agreement that the ECF planned between the Israeli and the Palestinian security forces prepared the way for further cooperation beyond the immediate effort of the economic corridors.[101] The second component was to remove roadblocks and other impediments to movement. This activity was further expanded to improve access and movement. The third component was to foster the establishment of border industrial parks. In the north, in Jenin, substantial support for the establishment of such a park was obtained from the German government. In the east, near Jericho, the Japanese government supported the establishment of an agroindustrial park that would permit agricultural exports, particularly to Jordan and the east. The third industrial park was planned for Tarqumya. There, no outside actors were permitted to be involved, because the influential Palestinian merchants of the Greater Hebron area wanted to control trade and industry in the area themselves.[102] The fourth and final component was to ease procedures at the crossing points into Israel.

To make the concept of the economic corridors work, we convened a workshop with support from the Crown Center for Middle East Studies at Brandeis University, and invited the relevant Israeli, Palestinian, and international actors (particularly those in charge of supporting the industrial parks from Germany, Turkey, and Japan) to work on a coordinated concept. We also invited Peres (who had become president of Israel in July 2007) and Palestinian prime minister Fayyad and submitted the concept of the economic corridors to them. Fayyad endorsed the concept, and Peres decided to present the ECF map to President Bush. (Because the map shows the June 4, 1967, line as the border, it was important that it was made clear that this was not an official map. Therefore, the map that was given to President Bush had the ECF's insignia deliberately left in its right-hand lower corner.)

Solving the fugitive problem became the key to success. The PA was able to create a regained sense of law and order, and the strategy opened Palestinian areas for trade and other economic activities. The success demonstrated that a bottom-up strategy could be successfully implemented. In hindsight, these seemingly minor steps prepared the ground for Fayyad's Palestinian state building.

Promoting the Jenin-First Concept

The success in promoting the economic corridor concept offered the opportunity to take the next step. In early 2008, the ECF prepared a Jenin-first paper, outlining four crucial issues: (1) demarcating the area for a Jenin-first approach, (2) defining important security issues, (3) providing for law and order and increased PA government and administrative capacities, and (4) promoting economic development.[103] The basic idea was to enable the Palestinian security forces to create a secure and stable environment, enforcing law and order and enabling economic development in a specified area that was as large as possible, in full coordination with the Israeli security forces. This strategy was based on the assumption that there would be less of a need for an Israeli security presence if the Palestinian forces were able to develop their capacities. In describing the envisaged area, we presented a proposed security map of the Jenin district (figure 9.3).[104]

We then suggested various options for security cooperation. Regarding military coordination, we suggested preparing an agreed-upon procedure to accompany the Palestinian security forces between different areas. With regard to police coordination, we asked whether this should be continued through the Civil Administration or whether the pre–second intifada pattern of coordination outside the Civil Administration should be reinstituted. In the same context, we suggested developing three different agreed-on procedures: one for addressing reciprocal police complaints, one for addressing Israeli misdemeanors inside Palestinian territory, and one for ensuring the return of Israelis on the Palestinian side of the border to Israel. We suggested checking the possibility of reinstating Israeli-Palestinian intelligence coordination, and we proposed that General Dayton and his team take upon themselves four tasks: instruction and training, monitoring, involvement in coordination and problem solving, and crisis management. Furthermore, we suggested defining the type of arms and vehicles that the Palestinian police would

Figure 9.3. Jenin District Security Plan, January 2008

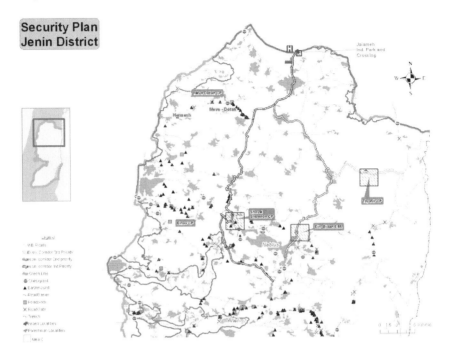

Source: Economic Cooperation Foundation.

use, and referred to the need to rehabilitate Palestinian security institutions and defined how best to protect them. We also asked to check
authorization for Palestinians to have live training exercises and to limit
areas east of the fence that the Palestinian security forces would be for-
bidden from entering. Finally, we suggested defining a procedure for the
IDF's entry into Palestinian territory if needed to foil terrorist activities.[105] We also produced a paper suggesting that the PA, rather than the
Civil Administration, carry out land registering and other administrative
duties.[106] On economic development, we referred to the need to promote
the industrial park at Jalameh, as well as a variety of economic development projects inside the Jenin Governorate.[107]

Both General Jones and General Dayton supported the project and
worked to make it happen.[108] At first, the Israeli security authorities opposed
these developments. In 2008, when only slight progress had been made,
General Jones complained about the lack of cooperation from the Israeli
security authorities to Gilead Sher, Baruch Spiegel, and me. Sher phoned

Ehud Barak, who was serving as minister of defense, and arranged for a meeting with Jones that same day. This meeting was a turning point, and several weeks later both Barak and Israeli chief of staff Gabi Ashkenazi visited Washington. After the US visit, both the Jenin-first approach and the entire bottom-up approach became accepted US-Israeli-Palestinian policy. Ashkenazi provided a straightforward summary: "The Palestinians do more, so we can do less."[109]

Easing Access and Movement

The success of our efforts to create the economic corridors reinforced our commitment to expand freedom of movement and access beyond the areas of the corridors and attempt to create a West Bank–wide change. However, the Israeli security authorities told us that they would oppose further easing of access and movement, as this would provide greater freedom to terrorists. (In practice, the opposite tended to be true, as the roadblocks tended to provide clear targets for terrorist attacks, and in several cases, the removal of the roadblocks brought stability rather than unrest.)[110] Nonetheless, we needed a comprehensive concept that the Israeli security authorities would regard as sufficiently reliable in the struggle against terrorism in order for them to permit the necessary easing of movement.

We thus pursued a three-step approach. First, we researched the major blockages to access and movement that hindered Palestinian economic development, as well as the PA's capability to perform basic administrative and police functions. Following our background research, we brought together a small group of very senior reserve officers, led by Brigadier General Avraham Ben Ami, who prepared a six-point approach:

- Finishing the security barrier/fence, particularly in the Jerusalem and the Gush Etzion and Southern Hebron areas.
- Substantially reducing the number of roadblocks while introducing rapid deployment checkpoints at unpredictable places and times.
- Transferring control of areas to Palestinian security forces, while making it clear that they were responsible for preventing violence.
- Enhancing bilateral security coordination.
- Abolishing blockages at the entry and exit points of the economic corridors.
- Providing for joint Israeli and Palestinian traffic along the main roads.

The proposals were submitted to the IDF, the Ministry of Defense, the Knesset committee on security and foreign affairs, several university-based research institutes, the US Agency for International Development, the World Bank, and the UN Organization for the Coordination of Humanitarian Activities. To create an effective follow-up, we encouraged the US Agency for International Development to establish a forum to monitor progress, identify obstacles, and suggest how to overcome them. All relevant parties from Israel and the international community were invited to attend these brainstorming meetings every two months.

Considerable impact was made. The improved flow of Palestinian traffic enabled economic development and simultaneously boosted the PA's prestige and standing, thus increasing the Palestinian security forces' interest in intensifying their coordination with the Israeli security authorities.[111] In many ways, this work created the necessary preliminary conditions for what became the Fayyad Plan for Palestinian state building and enabled Fayyad to achieve some of his remarkable successes.

Prime Minister Fayyad's state-building effort would continue beyond the Bush presidency. However, the political scene changed early in 2009. President Barack Obama started his first term, largely on an ABB (Anything But Bush) ticket. In Israel, the February 2009 elections were won by Benjamin Netanyahu. It was still unclear what the new leadership would do.

Analytical Implications

The Causes of Failure of the Permanent Status Paradigm

Testing the three paradigms discussed in this chapter, the outstanding finding is the repeated failure of Permanent Status negotiations. It should be remembered that the first track-two attempt, the Beilin–Abu Mazen Understanding, was rejected by Peres in 1995 and withdrawn by Abbas in the summer of 2000. Barak's offers were rejected at the 2000 Camp David Summit conference. Arafat rejected the Clinton Parameters in 2001, and Maher el-Kurd called the Israeli offers at Taba in 2001 "insulting and ridiculous." Last and most important, Olmert's autumn 2008 proposal was similarly rejected. The causes of failure have been discussed in previous chapters, but four additional observations may add to a better understanding of the problems with this paradigm:

1. To commit to "end of conflict" and "finality of claims," Abbas had to satisfy the essential demands of four different Palestinian groups: the Palestinian inhabitants of the West Bank and Gaza, the Palestinian communities in other Arab states (who often held passports from their host countries), the Palestinian Diaspora, and the Palestinian Arab citizens of the State of Israel. To obtain the support of the West Bank and Gaza Palestinians, any territorial concession was conceived as failure; to obtain the support of the Palestinian communities in other Arab states, the support of the host countries was important. To obtain minimal support from the Palestinian Diaspora, Abbas could not compromise on the "right of return," and in order to take care of the interests of the Palestinian Arab citizens of the State of Israel, he could not accept the Israeli demand to recognize Israel as the state of the Jewish people.

2. On the Israeli side, the picture was not much different. To agree on a two-state solution on the basis of a Permanent Status Agreement, the Government of Israel had to obtain support from the pragmatist settler leadership and rank and file, as well as Israel's security establishment. According to the Clinton Parameters, 20 percent of the settler population—somewhere between 40,000 and 100,000 people—had to be evacuated. This would be only possible under two conditions. First, it was essential to obtain in negotiations the Palestinian agreement to incorporate the major settlement blocs into Israel's sovereign territory, guaranteeing a secure livelihood for 80 percent or more of the settler community. Second, the sacrifice of giving up residence in parts of Judea and Samaria could only be justified if Israel was recognized as the Jewish homeland since ancient times, or at least as the state of the Jewish people. For the Israeli security establishment, extensive security provisions in an increasingly unstable area were crucial.

3. To bring about a "flight of the flamingos" scenario, it was and is essential for the Israeli and Palestinian leadership to have their ideological opposition on board: the settler movement on the Israeli side and Hamas on the Palestinian side. There is no way that either the one or the other could or would ideologically accept the logic and the provisions of a two-state solution up front. However, both the settler movement and Hamas could accept an emerging reality on the ground. Both movements could be brought on board for a roadmap-like state-building effort, but both would do everything

in their power to prevent a ready-made political concept during the negotiation period, at the conclusion of an agreement, or during the subsequent implementation.[112]

4. Iran, al-Qaeda, Hezbollah, and Hamas view an Israeli-Palestinian peace—and the possibility of a more comprehensive Arab-Israeli peace—as a threat to their interests, as it would isolate them and undermine their popular support. Incitement, terrorist acts, and rockets have provided the Islamic militant state and nonstate actors with sufficient power to undermine and spoil the Permanent Status Agreement efforts. Nonetheless, an ongoing state-building process has been shown to overcome periodic spoiler action.

The Sustainability of the Roadmap Paradigm

The second paradigm, the roadmap, took the shortcomings of a direct Permanent Status approach into consideration and provided for a three-phase approach. At first, this paradigm also appeared to be a failure. The renewal of Israeli-Palestinian negotiations that started shortly after the roadmap was announced at the end of April 2003 came to a sudden end early in September 2003, when Abbas was forced to resign. As Kurtzer and his colleagues have commented tersely, "Perhaps the entire venture was doomed from the outset."[113]

However, remarkably enough, the roadmap paradigm was soon revitalized. Under Sharon and Olmert, the Israeli government committed itself to the roadmap, and the Quartet continued to support Palestinian reform efforts. Most important, the Palestinian security reform being overseen by General Dayton made important headway. After the failure of the Israeli-Palestinian Permanent Status negotiations in 2008, Prime Minister Fayyad, in cooperation with the international community, achieved substantial headway in implementing state-building activities in line with the letter and spirit of the roadmap.

The Logic and Shortcoming of the Disengagement Paradigm

After the failure of the Permanent Status negotiations under Barak, Sharon's first political move as prime minister was to suggest to the Palestinians a long-term Interim Agreement and agree to a two-state solution on his terms. Abbas rejected this proposal. From an Israeli point of view, this meant that the Palestinians were not willing either to pay the necessary price for a Permanent Status Agreement or to follow a step-by-step approach without finalizing the endgame beforehand. Unilateral action toward to a two-state solution, fully coordinated with the United States, appeared to be the only way forward.[114]

The June 2004 ECF-NSC diagram of the necessary legal, political, security, and economic understandings and the interaction among them (see figure 9.1 above) described the actions that were required by all involved parties—Israel, Egypt, the PA, and the international community—to turn an Israeli disengagement into an important step toward a negotiated two-state solution. At the ECF, we hoped that the Quartet powers in cooperation with the PA would be able to consolidate the political power of Abbas's leadership and translate it into PA security capabilities that would enable the PA to control the situation on the ground in the Gaza Strip, with substantial Quartet support if needed. Through security control, the path to promote economic rehabilitation and growth could be opened. Evacuating Israeli settlements from Palestinian territories while permitting other settlements to remain would set the stage for renewed Israeli-Palestinian bilateral negotiations toward Permanent Status and an agreed-on "end of conflict."

As a matter of fact, the roadmap concept, permitting the Quartet to lay out a phased conflict resolution program, opened the way for coordinated unilateral moves on all sides. However, the shortcomings of the concept were very substantial. Because unilateral action was possible, no serious effort was undertaken to develop a coordinated working concept with all the concerned parties. The time factor needed to develop the PA's necessary political, security, and economic capacities was underestimated. Neither the United States nor the other three Quartet powers were willing to be sufficiently involved to offer the backing necessary for the PA to build these capacities for an orderly takeover. Last but not least, no public relations effort was undertaken to explain the concept to both the Israeli and Palestinian people.

These shortcomings explain the failure of Sharon's unilateral disengagement plan. However, looking at the experience gained and the capacities built by the PA since 2005—in institution building, the creation of a professional Palestinian Security Force with a clear chain of command, and the development of the Palestinians' financial and economic capacities—a coordinated and well-planned Israeli disengagement concept does offer a potential path toward an agreed-on two-state solution.

Successes, Failures, and Lessons Learned

Successes

In the period under review (2001–9), seven important building blocks toward the construction of a peaceful Israeli-Palestinian two-state solution were developed:

1. The roadmap made it clear that the final outcome would be the establishment of a Palestinian State and defined the way to get there.
2. Palestinian prime minister Fayyad created essential steps in a well-thought-out Palestinian state-building effort.
3. General Dayton and his mission succeeded in pursuing Palestinian security reform while simultaneously rebuilding Israeli-Palestinian security cooperation.
4. Substantial headway was achieved in easing access and movement, thereby creating supportive conditions for renewed Palestinian economic growth.
5. International monitoring structures were established by General Frazer and General Selva to oversee roadmap implementation, and by EUBAM to implement the agreement on access and movement that was signed in November 2005 (although the powers given to them were substantially truncated).
6. Sharon's disengagement plan evacuated seventeen settlements from Gaza and four from the Northern West Bank, creating the preconditions for Palestinian empowerment in the entire Gaza Strip as well as in the Northern West Bank.
7. Although the Olmert-Abbas negotiations process did not succeed in resolving the core issues of conflict, its working groups created an understanding of what would be necessary in order to pursue a coordinated effort for Palestinian state building and the creation of good neighborly relations between Israel and the emerging State of Palestine.

Failures

The failure of the Permanent Status negotiations is self-evident, though further elaboration is needed on the failure of to develop the roadmap paradigm and promote the disengagement paradigm. The basic task of the roadmap was to provide both Israel and the Palestinians with the necessary assurance that the international community was determined to assist the parties on their way to a two-state solution and to request a commitment for implementing realistic obligations. However, too little attention and political support were being offered at the time, even though political support would be more forthcoming in the second term of the George W. Bush administration.

In designing the roadmap, the time factor was underestimated and too little attention was paid to the necessary sequencing in creating the PA's institutional, security, economic, and political capacities. Several important mistakes were also made in dealing with the settlement issues. Although US secretary of state Colin Powell concluded an understanding on settlement activity limitation with his Israeli counterpart, Shimon Peres, in 2001, these understandings were ignored. Thus in 2003, the roadmap included the nonachievable demand for a settlement freeze including "natural growth" that set up all sides for failure. Also, a serious commitment to the roadmap would have necessitated the establishment of a monitoring structure from the very beginning. When General Frazer's monitoring group was finally established after the Annapolis conference in November 2007, it was given too few powers.

Sharon's disengagement plan would have opened up important opportunities if only four of the major elements of the plan would have been sustained: (1) the evacuation of settlements preparing the way for further settlement evacuation as well as for the incorporation of Israeli settlement blocs to Israel; (2) the orderly transfer of assets; (3) the unfolding of an effective security cooperation; and (4) agreed-on terms to return to further negotiations in line with roadmap provisions, first for a state with provisional borders and finally for Permanent Status. However, matters were mishandled. The Israeli disengagement from the Gaza Strip created havoc, and the international community preferred to destroy assets rather than take responsibility for keeping them. Furthermore, Permanent Status negotiations were restarted when both the Palestinians and the Israelis had mindsets full of hate and resentment, with neither side believing that substantial progress would be possible. Ignoring this, no serious effort had been made to invest in the social capital that would be essential to provide the leaders on both sides with the legitimacy that would allow them to make those concessions that would be indispensable for concluding a peace agreement.

Lessons Learned

LESSON ONE: COMBINE THE FORMULA "NOTHING IS AGREED UPON UNTIL
EVERYTHING IS AGREED UPON" WITH "WHAT HAS BEEN AGREED UPON SHALL BE
IMPLEMENTED."

Negotiating the core issues of conflict—Jerusalem, refugees, borders,
settlements, security, end of conflict, and finality of claims—the negotiators need to balance concessions on one issue with concessions on
another issue. Hence, it is essential for both sides to maintain the formula that "nothing is agreed upon until everything is agreed upon."
However, this formula does not contradict the option of adopting a different approach to Palestinian state building and the entire complex of
Israeli-Palestinian state-to-state relations. There, the principle of "what
has been agreed upon shall be implemented" needs to be adopted. ***The
basic conclusion of my study is that without prior state building and
the development of good neighborly state-to-state relations, no party
will possess sufficient legitimacy to solve the outstanding core issues
of conflict.***

LESSON TWO: PERMIT THE UNITED STATES AND THE OTHER QUARTET POWERS TO
DEFINE THE ENDGAME.

The failure to reach a Permanent Status Agreement created a dilemma. On
one hand, neither side was willing to accept (and, politically, was hardly
capable of accepting) the minimal demands of the other side; nor was it
possible to agree on common terms of reference. On the other hand, it
is essential to have a common understanding, albeit not necessarily an
agreement, on where the endgame is. (As the old Greek seafarers said,
"When you have not decided where to go, no wind can take you there.") It
is the task of the United States and the other Quartet powers to solve this
dilemma, discussing with each side the essentials that have to be reflected
in defining the endgame, and accordingly prescribing the endgame in a
way that accounts for the needs of both parties. This means that the United
States and the other Quartet powers could and should lay out the guidelines for an Israeli-Palestinian peace agreement, without obliging either
side to fully accept the prescribed conditions. Moreover, as the solution
of the Israeli-Palestinian conflict is not merely in the interest of the parties but also reflects a vital international strategic interest, the proposed
endgame concept might well be anchored in a Quartet statement that then
turned into a UN Security Council resolution.

LESSON THREE: EXPECT FURTHER SPOILER ACTION AND MOVE TO MINIMIZE AND NEUTRALIZE ITS IMPACT.

The present power equation in the Middle East will not tend to permit a sustainable and uninterrupted stable and secure environment for peacemaking. Further Iranian instigation to renew the vicious circle of Israeli-Palestinian violence—and also terrorist acts committed by al-Qaeda, by the Jihadist or Salafist movements, and by Hezbollah or Hamas—remain real threats. There is political interest in spoiling the peace process, and also the capacity to commit a terrorist act that would dispatch rockets, missiles, or bombers against Israeli targets. On the Israeli side, radical Jewish fundamentalist violence against Palestinian targets that would provoke Palestinian counteraction also remains a serious threat.

Being aware of this danger makes it necessary to plan the peace process accordingly. Experience gained during the first decade of the twenty-first century shows that Palestinian state-building efforts (following the roadmap) can advance even in the face of renewed violent action. Evidently, a most serious international, regional, and bilateral Israeli-Palestinian, Israeli-Egyptian, and Israeli-Jordanian effort is necessary to minimize the dangers of a possible cyclical violent flare-up. I believe that the following measures are imperative:

- To deter Iran, its formula that "regime safety can be secured by developing a military nuclear capacity and by instigating violence against Israel and other regional players" (e.g., Bahrain and Dubai) must be turned around. It is crucial to ensure Iran's regime safety in exchange for its commitment to verifiably and effectively give up nuclear enrichment, and ending the instigation of acts of violence against Israel and the region.[115]
- To minimize the potential of terrorist acts, it is essential to ensure United States–led coordination of regional intelligence sharing, action to prevent arms smuggling and the movement of terrorists and their funds, and a limiting of incitement. In this context, it is important to strengthen bilateral Israeli-Jordanian and Israeli-Egyptian security coordination.
- Building on the positive experience of Israeli-Palestinian security coordination, improved Palestinian security capacities should expand hand in hand with Palestinian state-building efforts.
- To limit the incentive for Hamas terrorist action, measures to build the economic stability of Gaza are necessary, concomitant with the demand upon Hamas to suppress any terrorist activities by rival groups.

LESSON FOUR: ENCOURAGE BOTTOM-UP AND TOP-DOWN PALESTINIAN STATE BUILDING.

Fayyad's state-building efforts from 2007 through 2010 were impressive. However, it is important to understand that the bottom-up approach has serious limitations. It is by and large restricted to Area A and Area B, which make up about 40 percent of the West Bank territory. Palestinian state building definitely must expand substantially into Area C, which is only possible if negotiated with the Israeli leaders, who will demand understandings on security issues in return. The way to connect the bottom-up Palestinian state-building process with top-down understandings achieved through negotiations is to create a fast-track negotiating process, operating on the principle that "what has been agreed upon shall be implemented." Much negotiating work has already been done. In preparation for the July 2000 Camp David Summit, Othniel Schneller and Jamil Tarifi developed far-reaching Palestinian state-building proposals that never materialized. During the 2007 Annapolis process, the parties negotiated further important understandings in committees. All this work provides important knowledge upon which the parties can draw, and ask for international and regional assistance for its implementation.

LESSON FIVE: KEEP EXPECTATIONS LOW.

The "Icarus" scenario referred to in chapter 5 describes the fall from high, caused by a too-ambitious plan and too-high expectations. High expectations of ongoing negotiations tend to create two detrimental effects: Actors that oppose the peacemaking effort will prepare for spoiler action, while those that support a peace outcome may all too easily despair over the failure to reach an agreement or unmet expectations even when an agreement is reached.[116] Keeping expectations low, paradoxically enough, is an important device to get the opponents of peace on board and to engage step by step. The "flight of the flamingos" does not necessarily have to reach a substantial height; as long the birds make progress on the way to their final destination, the main purpose of peace building is being achieved.

LESSON SIX: MAINTAIN AN OPTIMAL INTERNATIONAL CONTRIBUTION.

The United States and the international community at large undoubtedly have substantial vested interests in promoting Israeli-Palestinian peace. Pacification may help the West to build a stable and cooperative relationship with the entire Arab and Muslim world, while at the same time being able to fight effectively against radical Islamic terror. Moreover, regional development in the population-rich but otherwise poor Arab states may at least partially limit the flow of Muslim immigration to Europe, which has turned into a challenge to social tranquillity.

It is also evident that the United States' leadership, along with the support of the other Quartet powers and other members of the international community, is an essential factor in the Israeli-Palestinian peace-finding process. Neither the Israeli nor the Palestinian leaders enjoy enough political legitimacy to make peace without US and other international guidance and support. Nevertheless, the natural tendency of the US and European leaders is to avoid responsibility as much as possible and to put the onus of action upon the Israelis and Palestinians.[117] What is needed is what Ambassador Ed Djerejian called "a combination between parental guidance and adult supervision."[118] "Parental guidance" should include the following:

- Develop, in a dialogue with both parties, the next steps to the endgame, permitting for a variety of steps: by agreement, by coordinated unilateral action, or by moving cautiously with a bottom-up approach on the basis of negotiated (top-down) understandings. (It must be noted, however, that the eagerly anticipated photo opportunity of signing a negotiated agreement may under certain circumstances cause more damage than profit, as it may instigate violent spoiler reaction.)
- Provide the necessary support for regional security and work with both parties to develop crisis prevention and management capacities. This is of particular importance to keep the Israeli government and public on board.
- Mobilize substantial regional support from Egypt, Jordan, Saudi Arabia, and other Arab states to provide Abbas with the necessary political backing, and offer practical support for the Palestinian state-building effort.
- Develop—with the financial, economic, technical, and security support of multiple international actors—the necessary backing and involvement for Palestinian state building, regional security, and crisis prevention and management.

"Adult supervision" should include the following:

- Establish an effective monitoring structure to oversee the implementation of obligations of both parties, including the control of settlement expansion, measures to prevent violence, Palestinian state building, and the development of good neighborly relations.

• When spoiler action cannot be avoided, work to diminish the damage and prepare to renew the peace-building efforts.

• Make it evident that reaching a peaceful Israeli-Palestinian solution is a vital US national interest, and not merely the concern of the involved parties.

Evidently, progress toward a two-state solution has laid the foundations upon which the edifice of peaceful coexistence can be erected. The lessons learned from past successes and failures provide the necessary knowledge to design and construct an entire building over a realistically anticipated period of time, and withstand potential storms.

Chapter 10

The Kerry Initiative and Beyond

This chapter analyzes the causes of the United States' strategic interest in forging the way to an Israeli-Palestinian two-state solution, and it describes the political motivation behind US secretary of state John Kerry's Initiative and his drive to achieve peace between Israel and Palestine, along with Israeli and Palestinian fears and hopes that may support or impede the US efforts. As the immediate outcome of the Kerry Initiative is as yet unknown at the time of writing, this chapter concludes by describing the trial-and-error process, from 1978 onward, on the way to a peaceful two-state solution.

The Kerry Peace Initiative: Historical Context

Shortly after his second inauguration, US president Barack Obama decided to undertake a major effort to resolve the Israeli-Palestinian conflict through the efforts of newly appointed Secretary of State John Kerry. In a speech in Jerusalem and meetings in Ramallah in March 2013, President Obama reached out to his Israeli and Palestinian audiences. To the Israelis, he repeated his commitment to the security of Israel, the right of Israel to defend itself independently, and the need to maintain and strengthen strong US-Israeli security ties. He also reached out to the Palestinians, arguing in Jerusalem as well as in Ramallah that neither occupation nor expulsion was the answer, and he concluded that "just as Israelis built a state in their homeland, Palestinians have a right to be a free people in their own land."[1] Obama did refer to the various issues on the table, and he stressed that what was at stake was the need to make peace "between two peoples and not just governments" and that "progress with the Palestinians was a powerful way to begin sidelining extremists, who thrive on conflict."[2] The new approach appeared to be a resolute thrust toward an Israeli-Palestinian two-state solution.

The US Strategic Interest in a Two-State Solution

The resolute thrust evinced in President Obama's persistence to seek a path to solve the Israeli-Palestinian conflict is not a coincidental move. It is the result of the growing understanding in Washington—among policy strategists, senior military officers, and diplomats alike—that achieving peace in the Middle East is a most essential US strategic interest and need.[3] The United States cannot neglect the financial power of the Arab states, their supply of oil and natural gas, their political power as a bloc in the United Nations and in other international forums, and the geopolitical importance of the Arab and Muslim world over vast areas connecting Africa and Asia and on the southern flank of Europe. Nor would it be possible to denounce the United States' relationship and alliance with Israel, which is the only functioning democracy in the Middle East and offers important political and security assets both directly on a bilateral level and indirectly through strategic assistance to the other US allies in the region, particularly Jordan.[4] Without America's commitment and action to lead the way in resolving the Israeli-Palestinian conflict, militant forces in the Middle East could use the escalating vicious circle of violence between Israel and the Palestinians, Hamas, Hezbollah, and other state and non-state actors to incite enmity against America and undermine Washington's regional Arab allies.

The Emerging Historic Maturity of the Quest for a Two-State Solution

In addition to the United States' essential need to seek a solution, a relatively high degree of historical maturity has emerged. The substance of a potential Israel-Palestine Permanent Status Agreement is largely known, and enough experience has been gained throughout the past forty years to know what policies will and will not work. The situation can be illustrated with a Persian proverb: "You can apply heat to an egg, and if you act carefully a chick will come out of the broken shell; no heat whatsoever will be useful if you have a stone instead of an egg."

Many objective conditions for pursuing a two-state solution have emerged since the signing of the Oslo Accords on the White House lawn on September 13, 1993. At that time, only a small group of people supported an Israeli-Palestinian two-state solution. The United States had rejected that idea under the Reagan New Initiative of September 1982 (see chapter 2), and it only finally committed to the two-state solution in June 2002 (see chapter 8). In Israel, the ideological right wing, the security authorities, and even the leadership of the Labor Party opposed a two-state solution. And no less important, the Palestine Liberation Organization (PLO) under Arafat's leadership remained a revolutionary movement, preferring in September 2000 to renew its resistance rather than to lay the foundations for a state. But now this landscape has changed dramatically: The US government and the international community are committed to the concept of a two-state solution, and they have anchored the concept in UN Security Council Resolution 1515 of November 2003. In Israel, Prime Minister Netanyahu has committed himself and Israel to the two-state solution.[5] More important, the Palestinian leadership and its government have not only fully committed themselves to a two-state solution, but they have also taken a large leap forward in building state institutions in all spheres. In particular, the Palestinian Authority (PA) has replaced the old revolutionary system of rival security warlords, who controlled their own turf and maintained their own resistance, with professional security and police forces and a clear chain of command.

Understanding the Volatility of the Progress Achieved

Although the Palestinian state-building effort, particularly under the leadership of Prime Minister Salam Fayyad, has been very impressive, this process has not yet reached a point of no return. The proverbial example of the egg illustrates a basic truth: Renewed violence, extensive Israeli settlement expansion, and a hands-off US policy may cause the death of the chick that had emerged from the egg. The diverging Israeli and Palestinian narratives of despair, hatred, and resentment, along with the limited legitimacy experienced by both the Israeli and Palestinian leadership, has not yet made the march toward a peaceful two-state solution irreversible.

Lessons Learned from Earlier Successes and Failures

On the brighter side, the experience gained during the past thirty and more years provides sufficient knowledge about what to do and what not to do from diplomatic, economic, and implementation perspectives. For instance, US diplomacy was successful in convening the October 1991 Madrid Conference and in concluding the January 1997 Hebron Protocol and the October 1998 Wye River Agreement. The lesson learned was that when US leadership helped the parties to identify common ground and tirelessly pursued a well-designed diplomatic initiative, the parties would come to terms with each other.

Other lessons may be learned from mistakes that were committed. Bill Clinton's support for Ehud Barak's "everything or nothing" approach turned out to be disastrous (see chapter 7). The lesson is simple: Permit the peace-finding process to develop the supportive structures of state institutions, security cooperation, and reconciliation that will in turn create the necessary social capital over a realistic period in order to be able to resolve the outstanding core issues of conflict.

In the specific Israeli-Palestinian context, committing to an agreement on controlling Israeli settlement expansion (between Colin Powell and Shimon Peres in 2001, and between Condoleezza Rice and Dov Weissglas in April 2004), but not sticking to it, opened the way to further settlement expansion. The lesson we learned from this failure was to permit settlement expansion in an area that will be incorporated into the sovereign territory of Israel, and to insist on a freeze and encouragement to relocate settlements beyond that line. Moreover, the destruction of more than $4 billion in assets left behind during the evacuation of settlements (see chapter 9) associated a potentially important peacemaking device with waste and loss rather than with the creation of prosperity. The lesson learned was to permit the Israeli Defense Forces (IDF) to stay in the area of settlement evacuation and to hand the settlements' assets over to an international custodian, which would work with the PA to turn these assets into a catalyst for further Palestinian investment and economic development, instead of wasting them.

Serving the Essential Interests of the People of Israel and the People of Palestine

In the past, US policy was guided by the slogan "the United States cannot want peace more than the parties involved." Now, when it is evident that the United States has a vested self-interest in peace between the Israelis and the Palestinians, the adapted slogan could be "the United States will fully cooperate with the parties as they lead the way to peace, however long it may take." Most evidently, the US peace-building effort needs to respect and feed into the most essential interests of both the Israelis and the Palestinians, and the peace-building process needs to be designed to build support from majorities on both sides.

A Plan to Combine the Three Potential Paradigms

Chapters 8 and 9 described three potential paradigms: (1) the Permanent Status Paradigm, (2) the Roadmap or Transit to State Paradigm, and (3) the Unilateral Disengagement Paradigm. It will be essential for the United States to define the endgame and commit the parties to continue the peace-finding process until reaching a Permanent Status Agreement, solving all outstanding core issues of conflict. It should be possible to assist the parties to take coordinated unilateral action, on the way to a two-state solution, whereas the entire peace-finding process, based on action on the ground, as well as on negotiated understandings, will need to pursue the "transit to state" paradigm. The Palestinian leadership and public will need to see how to bring about the end of occupation and to establish an independent, internationally recognized state. The Israeli leadership and public will want to know the necessary concessions to make possible the withdrawal of Israeli forces, the relocation of settlements, the division of Jerusalem, and the commitment to pay compensation to Palestinian refugees that will create stability and prosperity rather than renewed demands and violence. If the Palestinians reject the United States' bridging proposals, the third paradigm of unilateral disengagement may offer an important way forward. If the Israelis reject the proposals, a United States–led public diplomacy campaign—which, regardless, will be needed for all scenarios—should prevent progress from stalling completely, while carefully crafted unilateral Palestinian action should not be excluded.

Kerry's Six-Pillar Approach

From the very beginning of his term as secretary of state, John Kerry has shown wisdom and determination to contribute to achieving a peaceful Israeli-Palestinian two-state solution. After the opening move of President

Obama's visit to Jerusalem and Ramallah, Kerry began to develop a six-pillar approach aimed at building the structure of an Israeli Palestinian-peace.

The first pillar was to concentrate on direct Israeli-Palestinian negotiations on all outstanding issues, including both the core issues of conflict (e.g., Jerusalem, refugees, borders, settlements, security, end of conflict) and the emerging state-to-state issues (e.g., economy, water, good neighborly relations, the culture of peace). Kerry successfully convinced both Mahmoud Abbas and Benjamin Netanyahu to return to negotiations on these issues and imposed strict rules to help prevent the process from derailing. Both the Israeli and Palestinian sides committed to keep the ongoing negotiations secret, and only Kerry would be permitted to inform the press of possible headway. To hammer out an agreement on these disparate issues, Kerry and his team pursued four complementary activities: (1) review understandings reached in earlier negotiations, as well as working concepts that had emerged from the vast amount of earlier track-two work; (2) insert some of these ideas into the ongoing negotiations; (3) identify and compile emerging Israeli-Palestinian understandings (and gaps) on various issues; and (4) based on these understandings, prepare a US bridging proposal to serve as a Framework Agreement. Kerry, aware that any United States–imposed concept might create opposition from either side, spent a tremendous amount of time speaking with Netanyahu as well as with Abbas in confidential bilateral meetings, as well as on the telephone from wherever he might be.[6]

The second pillar was to explore security issues. Kerry appointed US general John Allen, formerly commander of the International Security Assistance Force in Afghanistan, to quietly work with the IDF leadership to define Israel's security needs, explore ways to expand Palestinian security capacities, identify the security threats to Israel and Palestine, and test various solutions that would be in line with the political needs of all the concerned parties. General Allen had to provide security solutions to address Israeli fears about a possible overspill of violence from Syria to Jordan and via the Golan Heights to Israel, and to prevent both the movement of terrorists and arms and attacks from mortars, rockets, and missiles against Israel from anywhere in the Middle East. For the Palestinians, General Allen's challenge was that his ideas would take utmost care to protect Palestinian sovereignty, and to permit the Palestinians to develop a security doctrine that would fully meet their security needs through a functioning regional security structure.[7]

The third pillar was to concentrate on Palestinian state building. Kerry asked former British prime minister Tony Blair and Blair's friend Tim Collins to prepare an Eight-Point Plan that would enable the PA to create 300,000 new employment opportunities within three years. Ideally, these opportunities would propel economic growth and would contribute to Palestinian state building in coordination with Israel and the Arab states of the region.[8]

The fourth pillar was to build regional support for the emerging Israeli-Palestinian negotiations, as well as to promote hoped-for change on the ground. In a steady dialogue with the Arab leadership, Kerry could refer to and rely on the principles of the March 2002 Arab Peace Initiative. He convinced the Saudis, the Qataris, the Egyptians, and the Jordanians, as well as the Secretariat of the Arab League, to renew their commitment to the Arab Peace Initiative and offer Abbas full support in returning to the negotiating table. The next task would be to convince the Arab leadership to support Palestinian state building, to coordinate security against spoilers, and to begin regional cooperation on issues in which all sides share a vested interest with Israel.[9]

The fifth pillar was to prevent spoiler action in Gaza by Hamas or other radical Palestinian groups by pursuing a stability-building policy there. This policy is building stability by encouraging economic development—in full coordination with the Palestinian, Israeli, and Egyptian governments—and is being supported as far as possible by the Arab Gulf states.

The sixth pillar was to create public legitimacy for the agreement to be concluded, through a public diplomacy initiative aimed at three target audiences: (1) the wider circle of the political leadership on both sides of the divide, seeking their support for a top-down public campaign; (2) politically uninvolved academic, security, economic, business, and religious experts and leaders, asking them to speak publicly in favor of emerging understandings in a "middle-out" approach; and (3) the wider public, addressing their needs, hopes, and fears as part of a bottom-up strategy.

Kerry's Four Challenges

Secretary Kerry has committed himself publicly to reach a first agreement nine months after the beginning of negotiations. Although deadlines can be postponed, this commitment poses no small hurdle for the entire effort, because to meet it, four different interrelated challenges must be tackled.

The First Challenge: To Reconcile the (Apparently) Irreconcilable

Secretary Kerry is faced with the need to reconcile two seemingly irreconcilable positions. First, the Government of Israel and the Israeli public do not believe that any core issue is ripe for ultimate resolution within the designated time frame and do not believe in the feasibility of a comprehensive Permanent Status Agreement at this point in time. Second, the PLO is reluctant to get stuck with yet another Interim Agreement, and it is insisting on a clear and binding definition of the endgame as a prerequisite for its gradual implementation. The Palestinian people in the West Bank and Gaza desire mainly to end the hardships of occupation with a most substantial effort of Palestinian state building. However, they will simultaneously oppose measures that would have only medium- and long-term effects on their situation, without creating visible change in the short term, owing to their lack of trust in the possibility of current efforts to bring about the hoped-for change.

To reconcile these seemingly irreconcilable positions, I would suggest adopting some of the lessons learned from the Northern Ireland peace process. Jonathan Powell, former chief of staff to Prime Minister Tony Blair and a chief British negotiator during the Northern Ireland peace negotiations, has defined two major conditions as essential to achieve success in such a situation: First, the participants must understand that "peace is not an event but a process, whereby two warring sides come to trust each other over time"; and second, they must realize that "negotiations need to move in parallel and to be structured in such a way as to allow trade-offs between concessions in different areas."[10] Accordingly, the ECF's research and track-two diplomacy have proposed to the US peace team policy steps that take care of the sensitivities and the political needs of both the Israelis and the Palestinians—without, of course, fully satisfying all the demands of either side.

The Second Challenge: To Maintain the End-of-Conflict Momentum

To reach a US bridging proposal, Kerry and his team are working with both sides, particularly to reach an agreed-on definition of the endgame as a prerequisite for a gradual approach of a transit-to-state and end-of-conflict paradigm. This approach aims to take care of Palestinian interests by defining the conditions for the endgame. At the same time, it aims to take care of Israeli interests by proposing a gradual, phased transit-to-state process under optimally stable conditions. Although the logic in support of this approach is overwhelming, it creates no small problems and a very real danger that the negotiating effort may end in failure.

Intending to present a US bridging proposal by the end of April 2014, on the basis of inputs gained from negotiations held between end of July

2013 and the beginning of January 2014, Kerry and his team have submitted a first text for a suggested Framework Agreement to both sides, asking each side to comment on all the issues raised. Much coordinated work on the proposed document would enable Kerry and his team to achieve the optimally full support of the parties for the suggested agreement.[11] If this cannot be achieved (which appears to be as good as certain at the time of writing) the ECF's suggested game plan would be to present the Framework Agreement and ask the parties to accept its terms in general and permit each side to add reservations, while committing to the framework and to pursuing the peace-building effort prescribed by the US bridging concept. (This approach would mirror what happened after the Quartet powers submitted the Benchmarked Roadmap for Peace in the Middle East at the end of April 2003.) Preparing for the extended "moment of truth" period—which will start with the submission of the Kerry concept and will last until both Israeli and Palestinian societies have sufficient trust in the effectiveness and workability of the United States–proposed concept—Secretary Kerry and his team will need to anticipate two negative scenarios: Either the Israeli or Palestinian leadership, or both, will reject the US proposal; or, worse, growing popular opposition to the agreement will enable radical forces to rise to power and further destabilize the region.

Neither of these two negative scenarios should be neglected. Although it goes without saying that both Abbas and Netanyahu want the negotiations to succeed—not only to achieve an agreement and to obtain substantial US support but also to avoid the radicalizing repercussions of failure—in order to make progress they must be able to mobilize majority support. This is no small challenge, for a number of reasons. So far, low expectations for success have kept the political and ideological hard-liners on both sides relatively quiet. However, the moment the substance of the United States–proposed Framework Concept is known (and possibly even before it is officially made public), opposition forces will tend to raise their voices and take legal and probably also illegal action to foil any acceptance of the agreement. The work of the opposition will be eased by the fact that on the core issues of conflict, the gaps between the two sides are still very substantial.

To be able to either sustain progress or overcome a possible crisis, Secretary Kerry will need full and sustained support from President Obama and the leaders of the other Quartet powers. In addition, he will need to activate the six-pillar structure in order to maintain or re-create the necessary momentum over time.

The Third Challenge: To Obtain Majority Support in Israel

Any American bridging proposal, in order to be accepted, will need majority support from the Knesset. The best-case scenario would of course be an agreement supported by all the parties of the present Israeli government, with additional support from the Labor Party, the left-wing Meretz party, and the three Arab parties. Under a second scenario, Netanyahu would form an alternative coalition including the Labor Party and possibly also the Orthodox religious party Shas. A third, still-positive scenario would be to go to elections for or against the proposed agreement and to convince the Israeli electorate to vote for a peace government. To prepare for any of these three potentially positive scenarios, Secretary Kerry will need to be aware of some good and some bad news.

The good news is that Netanyahu has a potential majority coalition in support of the United States–proposed action plan, through the parties led by Yitzhak Herzog (Labor), Rabbi Arieh Der'i (Shas, the religious Orthodox party, mainly representing Jews who have immigrated to Israel from Arab states), Yair Lapid (Yesh Atid, a secular liberal party), and Tzipi Livni (Hatnuah, a secular liberal party), with or without the added support of Avigdor Liebermann (Yisrael Beiteinu, a secular nationalist party, supported mainly but not only by Jews from the former Soviet Union) or Naftali Bennett (the Jewish Home, a religious nationalist party). The Israeli pragmatic pro-peace camp potentially controls 59 of the 120 Knesset seats (Yesh Atid, 19 seats; Labor, 15; Hatnua, 6; Meretz, 6; Kadima, 2; and the three Arab parties, 11). These parties have a vested political interest in the peace agenda, and thus they can effectively counterbalance right-wing pressure on Netanyahu to oppose any Israeli concessions. As a matter of fact, President Shimon Peres has already said that when he steps down in June 2014, his first task will be to unite the 59-member bloc of the Knesset in support of promoting peace. Another potential source of good news is that the Israeli public at large tends to support a two-state solution and is definitely interested in pursuing an ongoing peace process.

The bad news is that during the recent years of stagnation in the peace process, the Israeli public has largely lost confidence in the process, and it will not be an easy task to translate their hope for a peaceful solution into necessary activist support. Worse, when the conditions of the proposed Framework Agreement are published, Israeli right-wing politicians and activists will lead a massive campaign addressing the most basic fears and traumas of all echelons of Israeli society. The threat of civil war— Jews fighting against Jews—will be written on the wall, and acts may be launched to illustrate such a possible development. Equally likely is a well-concerted campaign to show the "price tag" of such an agreement, in which acts of terrorism against Palestinian targets would unleash a vicious circle of violence against Israelis that would quickly bring the peace process to an end.[12]

To overcome these forces of ideologically motivated opposition to peace and to turn the potential Israeli public support for a two-state solution and the political clout of Israel's peace-oriented political parties into effective action, three complementary approaches need to be adopted:

1. Make it evident to the Israeli public that the strategic national interest of the United States is to achieve a peaceful Israeli-Palestinian two-state solution regardless of the political climate. The substance of the United States' envisaged endgame must be perceived as representing a vital US strategic interest that Washington will continue to support, no matter which party or alliance controls the Knesset.
2. At the same time, make it evident to the Israeli public that the conditions for a US envisaged endgame, defining necessary Israeli concessions, are in essence a request for a "deposit" for a final agreement. These concessions will be implemented only if the necessary enabling conditions to guarantee sustainable stability have been created. The proposal will define the contours of a final negotiated agreement, but the agreement itself will be obtained in a phased process, whereby sustained stability and bilateral and multilateral regional cooperation will create the enabling conditions to advance the negotiation and implementation process. It must be evident that Israel's identity as a Jewish and democratic state will be strengthened, and that Israel's security, economic, business, research, and cultural interests will be rewarded.
3. Undertake a comprehensive public diplomacy campaign to muster support from political parties, religious institutions, universities and other educational institutions, business associations, trade unions, and cultural icons and institutions.

The Fourth Challenge: To Obtain Majority Support in Palestine

The ECF, being an Israeli nongovernmental organization, did not work on how to obtain majority support in Palestine, although on this front there are also no small difficulties. A joint Israeli-Palestinian poll conducted between June 13 and 21, 2013, by the Palestinian Center for Policy and Survey Research and the Truman Center at the Hebrew University, Jerusalem, showed that support for a two-state solution was stronger in Israel than in Palestine. Sixty-two percent of Israelis supported the two-state concept, while 33 percent opposed it; in Palestine, support was at only 53 percent, with 46 percent opposed.[13] In dozens of confidential meetings with senior Palestinian interlocutors, the ECF team has been told the Palestinian leadership and public must obtain three major achievements. The first achievement will be a commitment from the United States, the Arab states, and the international community at large—underpinned by a concomitant Israeli commitment—to lead the way to end occupation. The second achievement will be visible change on the ground, enabling a dramatic leap forward in economic development and state building. The third, equally important achievement will be an agreed-on monitoring and oversight system to prevent procrastination.

The bad news is that Hamas and even some oppositional groups within Fatah will tend to oppose any feasible compromise with Israel and will seek to build their own political power by demanding that the anticipated US proposal be rejected. The good news is that these rejectionist forces do not offer any visible alternative to President Abbas's policy of seeking a peaceful solution. Even though the rejectionists may cause setbacks, a serious American, regional, and wider international commitment to a peaceful two-state solution has the power to overcome prevailing doubts and opposition among the Palestinians.

Concluding Remarks

This book has described a long process of trial and error. The aim of this study has not simply been to tell the story of unfolding events but also to reflect upon the experience gained and lessons learned in the hope of helping to create a better future for Israelis and Palestinians alike.

The conclusion of the September 1978 Camp David Accords set the framework for a proposed process to solve the Israeli-Palestinian conflict. During the next thirteen years, the political effort was directed at seeking ways to permit the Israelis and Palestinians to start negotiating with each other. Direct negotiations started on November 3, 1991, at the finale of the Madrid Conference. During the 1990s, the first phase of Palestinian self-government was achieved, while track-two preparations were under way to seek a Permanent Status Agreement. This track-two effort ended in October 1995 with the "Beilin–Abu Mazen Understanding," which was intended to solve, in one go, all the outstanding core issues of conflict. Although this track-two understanding seemed to create a blueprint for an Israeli-Palestinian Permanent Status Agreement, neither side's political leadership nor the general Israeli and Palestinian public was willing to undertake the mutual concessions necessary to reach an official agreement. Accordingly, track-one diplomacy efforts to conclude a Permanent Status Agreement failed time and again. In August 2000, Mahmoud Abbas withdrew his consent for the understanding that he and Yossi Beilin had concluded less than five years earlier, and Ehud Barak's and Bill Clinton's "everything or nothing" strategy ended in a complete disaster—forcing the Palestinian leadership to attend the July 2000 Camp David Summit without sufficient preparation and against their will, which broke the mutual confidence and trust that had started to develop between the parties. Years of violence and devastation followed.

Trying to put Humpty Dumpty together again, three different paradigms for conflict resolution emerged. The original paradigm, defined by the Camp David Accords, proposed to resolve all the core issues by negotiation, have a Permanent Status Agreement signed that would announce the end of conflict and finality of claims, and proclaim the State of Palestine based on these understandings. Ehud Olmert and Mahmoud Abbas undertook another attempt to reach such a Permanent Status Agreement through a serious, in-depth negotiating effort from 2006 to 2008, which again ended in failure. Around the turn of the century, Nimrod Novik, Baruch Spiegel, Ron Shatzberg, and I developed a second paradigm, suggesting a "transition to state" concept with an ongoing process of conflict transformation in order to prepare the groundwork for solving the core issues of conflict. A third paradigm of Israeli unilateral disengagement also was in operation, contemplated during Yitzhak Rabin's premiership (1994–95) and again under Barak (from June 2000 onward), and finally implemented by Ariel Sharon in 2005.

During these years of trial and error, the concept of a two-state solution became accepted by the international community at large, as well as by the Israeli and Palestinian leadership. Whether influenced by the ECF or not, in April 2003 the Quartet powers, by announcing the "Performance-Based Roadmap to a Permanent Two-State Solution to the Israeli Palestinian Conflict," adopted the "transit to state" paradigm.[14] Although the time frame laid out in the suggested Performance-Based Roadmap turned out to be totally unrealistic, the process of Palestinian institution building and state building was set in motion. Under the leadership of President Abbas and Prime Minister Salam Fayyad, substantial headway was achieved in a largely unilaterally performed Palestinian state-building effort. Yet the limits of unilateral Palestinian state building became evident by 2010 and 2011: The division of the West Bank into different areas under varying degrees of Israeli control, as provided for in the September 1995 Oslo II Agreement, unduly limited Palestinian economic development and state-building efforts. Moreover, the expansion of Israeli settlements altogether questioned the concept of achieving an agreed-on two-state solution, and continuing security threats against Israel and its civilian population tended to enhance an Israeli policy of entrenchment. It became evident that progress could be achieved only through a well-thought-out negotiation and implementation process.

Over time, the repeated failures and intervals of violence had eroded the legitimacy of the peacemaking effort both in Israel and Palestine, even though a peaceful, two-state solution would offer both sides a chance to obtain their most essential demands: permitting the Palestinians to end Israeli occupation and establish an independent state of their own, and permitting Israel and the Jewish people at large to create a successful Jewish and democratic state that could enjoy substantial regional and international support. Because the legitimacy of Israeli and Palestinian peacemaking had eroded so greatly, US leadership became the most decisive factor in the entire power equation. When John Kerry was appointed secretary of state in January 2013, the United States recognized its strategic self-interest in forging the way toward a two-state solution. The historical maturity of events, as well as the lessons learned from successes and failures, has provided the United States and all the other concerned parties with the necessary knowledge and instruments to pursue negotiations and action on the ground.

This is not to say that the United States has the power to impose an agreement. It does not. Yet it has the power to define, in an intense dialogue with all the concerned parties, sooner or later, the contours of the endgame. Washington's support is also a catalyst for mobilizing a supportive coalition for the peace process within Israel and Palestine, among regional powers such as the Arab states and Turkey, and in the broader international community. In addition, Secretary Kerry's six-pillar structure not only allows for mutual trade-offs and concessions but also provides the opportunity to work on different pillars if progress on one pillar is being blocked.

It is beyond doubt that the way to a peaceful, two-state solution is stormy and the historical process may still experience major setbacks. However, if President Obama and Secretary Kerry desire to establish for themselves an important legacy by having promoted Israeli-Palestinian peace, they may achieve two major targets: first, conclude an Israeli-Palestinian agreement on Palestinian state building and the promotion of good neighborly relations; and second, announce a US Framework proposal, defining the endgame and the path needed to get there, and provide international and regional backing.

This does not mean that everything will happen according to plan. Yet if sufficient political determination can be developed in Washington and sustained over time, the concerned parties will want to come along. Peace between Israel and Palestine will never be a single event, or be written on a piece of paper that describes a more-or-less-brilliant plan. Instead, it will be an ongoing process of developing mutual trust over time and pursuing joint interests. Committing to a joint state of mind—saying "yes, we can"—will be essential, but this process will pose no small challenges in the years to come.

Notes

Chapter 1

1 For the text of the September 1978 Camp David Accords, see William B. Quandt, *Peace Process: American Diplomacy and the Arab-Israeli Conflict since 1967* (Berkeley and Washington, DC: University of California Press and Brookings Institution Press, 1993), appendix E, 445–56.

2 Returning from his historic visit to Jerusalem, President Sadat said in his statement before the Egyptian People's Assembly on November 26, 1977, "The balance of the Arab nation, as recognized by one and all, is Egypt; the key to war and peace is Egypt." See http://sadat.umd.edu/archives/speeches/AADK%20Sadat%20 Speech%20after%20Jersusalem%2011.26.77.pdf.

3 "Sadat Addresses the Knesset in Jerusalem, November 20, 1977," in *Peace in the Making: The Menachem Begin–Anwar el-Sadat Personal Correspondence*, ed. Harry Hurwitz and Yisraek Nedad (Jerusalem: Gefen, 2011), 26.

4 Camp David Accords, September 17, 1978, cited by Quandt, *Peace Process*, 445–56.

5 Ibid. The text relating to this issue reads: "(c) When the self-governing authority (administrative council) in the West Bank and Gaza is established and inaugurated, the transitional period of five years will begin. As soon as possible, but not later than the third year after the beginning of the transitional period, negotiations will take place to determine the final status of the West Bank and Gaza and its relationship with its neighbors, and to conclude a peace treaty between Israel and Jordan by the end of the transitional period."

6 See the full text of the Camp David Accords, in ibid.

7 Martin Gilbert, *Israel: A History* (London: Black Swan, 1998), 469.

8 Interview with Ambassador Yizchak Meir, July 22, 2013. Meir was one of the leaders of MAFDAL's moderate wing.

9   Rabbi Shlomo Goren, "The Holy Land and the Value of Life," *Jerusalem Post*, October 6, 1989.

10   For a description of Israeli right-wing opposition to the Camp David Accords, from within Likud and from groups and parties to its right, see Gilbert, *Israel*, 493–96.

11   Interview with Dan Meridor, January 13, 2013.

12   Shimon Peres, *Battling for Peace: A Memoir*, ed. David Landau (London: Weidenfeld & Nicolson, 1995), 352–53.

13   Ibid.

14   Yitzhak Rabin, speech to the Knesset, October 5, 1995, http://www.mfa.gov.il/mfa/mfa-archive/1995/pages/pm%20rabin%20in%20knesset-%20ratification%20of%20interim%20agree.aspx.

15   See letter from President Jimmy Carter to Prime Minister Begin, September 22, 1978, quoted by Quandt, *Peace Process*, 455–56. (The English term "Palestinian Arabs" is less politically charged than the Hebrew expression "Arawej Eretz Yisrael," properly translated as "Arabs of the Land of Israel.") On the settlement issue, see President Carter's answers to King Hussein's questions given by Quandt, *Peace Process*, 461–62.

16   Hurwitz and Medad, *Peace in the Making*, 85; for the entire speech, see 83–92.

17   Ibid., 86.

18   Responding to a question from King Hussein, President Carter described the area of the West Bank and Gaza as follows: "In the view of the United States, the term 'West Bank and Gaza' describes all of the area west of the Jordan River under Jordanian administration prior to the 1967 war and all of the area east of the western border of the British Mandate of Palestine which, prior to the 1967 war, was under Egyptian control and is known as the Gaza Strip." Quoted by Quandt, *Peace Process*, 458.

19   See "Reagan Plan and Attached Talking Points, September 1, 1982," in *The Arab-Israel Conflict and Its Resolution: Selected Documents*, ed. Ruth Lapidoth and Moshe Hirsch (Boston: Martinus Nijhoff, 1992), 287–92, 293–95.

20   See William Davidson and Joseph Montville, "Foreign Policy According to Freud," *Foreign Policy* 45 (Winter 1981–82): 145–57.

21   Immediately after the October (Yom Kippur) War of 1973, Kreisky led a delegation of the Socialist International to the Middle East, where he reported that Sadat wanted to move toward peace "bit by bit." "Socialist International Fact-Finding Mission to the Middle East," SI Circular B32/74, March 8, 1974. See also Peres, *Battling for Peace*, 233–41.

22   "Sartawi to Kreisky, Hotel Imperial Wien, Vienna," SI Circular B14/77, January 27, 1977, attached as annex I to Report of a Socialist International Fact-Finding Mission to the Middle East, Israeli Labor Party Archives, Beith Berl.

23   Interview with Yossi Beilin, February 29, 2012.

24   Efraim Lavie, "HaPalestinim b'gada hama'aravit: Dfussej hitargenut politit tachat kibush vebshilton azmi" [The Palestinians in the West Bank: Political patterns under occupation and under self-government] (PhD thesis, University of Tel Aviv, 2009), 142–45.

25   The Arab Industrial Committee that was formed as a result was officially authorized by Amman to represent the industries in the West Bank. Letter of Muhammad Masrouji (Secretary-General) to Dr. Otto Gatscha, Prime Minister's Office, Vienna and Jerusalem, August 3, 1980.

26   "Some Suggestions for Aiding the West Bank Economy," September 30, 1980. This policy paper was written by Crown Prince Hassan of Jordan specifically for Austrian chancellor Kreisky's visit.

27   Ibid.

28   An excellent, precise account of Ben Gurion's political thinking, particularly on international relations, is given by Uri Bialer, "Facts and Pacts: Ben Gurion and Israel's International Orientation, 1948–1967," in *David Ben Gurion: Politics and Leadership in Israel*, ed. Ronald W. Zweig (London: Frank Cass, 1991), 216–35. Other essays in the same book provide a coherent and comprehensive overview of Ben Gurion's political thinking.

29   Clausewitz, quoted by Rupert Smith, *The Utility of Force: The Art of War in the Modern World* (London: Penguin Books, 2006), 57–58.

30   Rupert Smith discusses this at length; see Smith, *Utility of Force*, 267–331. See also B. H. Liddle-Hart, *Strategy* (New York: Penguin, 1991), 353–60.

31   For this purpose, Ben Gurion hoped to achieve a defensive alliance with the United States, as he was convinced that this would not merely serve Israel's security but lead the way to peace with the Arabs. See Bialer, "Facts and Pacts"; and Ben Gurion's remarks in "Reports to the State Council by the Prime Minister and Foreign Minister, 27 September 1948," in *Israel's Foreign Relations: Selected Documents, 1947–1974*, vol. 1, ed. Meron Medzini (Jerusalem: Ministry of Foreign Affairs, 1976), 157–59.

32   Senior Israeli Defense Forces officers had all studied Yehoshafat Harkabi's thoughts on strategy, which argue (in line with Clausewitz's teaching) that victory is made possible by war but only achieved by political and diplomatic means. See Yehoshafat Harkabi, "War and Strategy" [in Hebrew], in *Milhamah ve-astrategyah* (Tel Aviv: Tsahal–Hotsaat Maarakhot / Misrad ha-bitahon, 1992), 593–605.

33   See, e.g., "The Truth About the 1948 Battle for Jerusalem," *Israel Matzav*, June 2, 2008, http://israelmatzav.blogspot.com/2008/06/truth-about-1948-battle-for-jerusalem.html.

34   See Bialer, "Facts and Pacts." In this context, Ben Gurion referred particularly to the issue of the Palestinian refugees.

35   Regarding Sadat's proposal of February 1971, see Anwar el-Sadat, *In Search of Identity: An Autobiography* (New York: Harper & Row, 1978), 219–22; for the agreement signed, see *Arab-Israel Conflict*, ed. Lapidoth and Hirsch, 161–76.

Chapter 2

1   Avi Shlaim, *Lion of Jordan: The Life of King Hussein in War and Peace* (London, Allen Lane, 2007), 172 ff.

2   See "Carter's Answers to King Hussein, October 1978," appendix F in *Peace Process: American Diplomacy and the Arab-Israeli Conflict since 1967*, by William B. Quandt (Berkeley and Washington, DC: University of California Press and Brookings Institution Press, 1993), 457–65.

3   See "Proposed Model of Full Autonomy for the West Bank and the Gaza Strip, submitted by Egypt on January 28, 1980," in *The Egyptian Position in the Negotiations Concerning the Establishment of Transitional Arrangements for the West Bank and Gaza, 1979–1980* (Cairo: State Information Service, Ministry of Foreign Affairs), 107–12; reprinted in *The Arab-Israel Conflict and Its Resolution: Selected Documents,*

ed. Ruth Lapidoth and Moshe Hirsch (Boston: Martinus Nijhoff, 1992), 207–14; and "Israel's Autonomy Proposals, January 1982 (Briefing No. 135/2.7.82/3.08.10 of the Israel Ministry of Foreign Affairs, Information Division)," in *Arab-Israel Conflict*, ed. Lapidoth and Hirsch, 214–17.

4   "Proposed Model of Full Autonomy for the West Bank and the Gaza Strip," in *Egyptian Position*; Steven Spiegel, *The Other Arab-Israeli Conflict: Making America's Middle East Policy from Truman to Reagan* (Chicago: University of Chicago Press, 1985), 379. Compare this with Harvey Sicherman, *Palestinian Self-Government (Autonomy): Its Past and Its Future* (Washington, DC: Washington Institute for Near East Policy, 1991), 21–34, and appendixes 6 and 7.

5   Historical developments after World War I had allowed various emerging national movements in Egypt, Syria, Iraq, and Lebanon to build up effective government power structures under French and British auspices. The Palestinians refused to obtain these powers in order not to have to share governmental powers with the Yishuv, the Jewish population of Palestine. The Palestinian revolt of 1936–39 heavily impaired the carefully constructed Palestinian leadership structure and caused further internal divisions. See Yehoshua Porath, *The Emergence of the Palestinian National Movement, 1918–1929* (London: Frank Cass, 1974); and Yehoshua Porath, *The Palestinian National Movement; From Riots to Rebellion, 1929–1939* (London: Frank Cass, 1977).

6   There is some dispute over the actual number of Palestinian refugees at the time. The State Department estimated a total of 725,000 refugees, according to "Policy Paper Prepared in the Department of State, Palestine Refugees, Washington, March 15, 1949," in *Foreign Relations of the United States, 1949*, vol. VI (Washington, DC: US Government Printing Office, 1977), 828–42. Yoav Gelber, in his research, argues that the number of Palestinian refugees was 550,000. Normally, the number 800,000 is quoted. Yoav Gelber, *Palestine 1948: War, Escape and the Emergence of the Palestinian Refugee Problem* (Eastbourne, UK: Sussex Academic Press, 2006).

7   The best description of the establishment of Israeli policies in the West Bank and Gaza and the means of control is given by Shlomo Gazit, *The Carrot and the Stick: Israel's Policy in Judea and Samaria, 1967–1968* (Ann Arbor: B'nai Brith Books, digitized by University of Michigan, 1995).

8   Naseer Hasan Aruri, *Jordan: A Study in Political Development, 1921–1965* (Ann Arbor, MI: University Microforms, 1970), 31–53; Clinton Bailey, *Jordan's Palestinian Challenge, 1948–1983: A Political History* (Boulder, CO: Westview Press, 1984); Avraham Cohen, *The Economy of the West Bank and Gaza Strip 1922–1980* (in Hebrew) (Givat Haviva: Institute for Arabic Studies, 1986), 88 ff.

9   Asher Susser, "Jordan, the PLO and the Palestine Question," in *Jordan in the Middle East, 1948–1988*, ed. Joseph Nevo and Ilan Pappe (Newbury, UK: Frank Cass, 1994), 211–28.

10   The term "disappearance" of the Palestinian identity is taken from Rashid Khalidi, *Palestinian Identity: The Construction of Modern National Consciousness* (New York: Columbia University Press, 1997), 177–80; and Efraim Lavie, "HaPalestinim b'gada hama'aravit: Dfussej hitargenut politit tachat kibush vebshilton azmi" [The Palestinians in the West Bank: Political patterns under occupation and under self-government] (PhD thesis, University of Tel Aviv, 2009).

11   Herbert Pundik is Ron Pundak's father; the name is spelled "Pundik" in Denmark and "Pundak" in Israel.

12   Interview with Yossi Beilin, February 29, 2012.

13 Immediately after the conclusion of the Israel-Egypt Peace Treaty, Tel Aviv University arranged to lead the way in developing regional cooperation projects with Egyptian partners. After a joint conference, work for sixteen projects—partly bilateral and partly multilateral, mainly with US, Canadian, and other international support—got under way. Tel Aviv University/Research Project on Peace, Promoting Academic Regional Cooperation, December 1979.

14 Yair Hirschfeld to Shimon Peres, January 31, 1982.

15 The March 1979 Israel-Egypt Peace Treaty provided for a final and complete Israeli withdrawal from Sinai in April 1982, a commitment that the Israeli government kept in full. The anticipation of the Israeli withdrawal made it possible to plan the Israeli-Egyptian cooperation projects in detail and offered the opportunity to ask for international help. Furthermore, if economic support were to be prevented by the PLO or Jordan in the West Bank, action in Gaza might still be possible with Egyptian assistance.

16 Elias Freij, "A Palestinian Initiative for Peace," *Washington Post*, February 14, 1982.

17 Letter from Yair Hirschfeld to Yossi Beilin, March 19, 1982.

18 For the American view in this context, see Spiegel, *Other Arab-Israeli Conflict*, 412–18.

19 On the emerging 1983 Israel-Lebanon Agreement, see Laura Zitrain Eisenberg and Neil Caplan, *Negotiating Arab-Israeli Peace: Patterns, Problems, Possibilities*, 2nd ed. (Bloomington: Indiana University Press, 2010) 54–72.

20 Martin Gilbert, *Israel: A History* (London: Black Swan, 1998), 496 ff.

21 Only in the Israeli army is it possible for lecturers to present the troops with such a critical, analytical approach during war. I told the troops that they had to follow orders, but a positive outcome of the struggle could only be achieved by political means.

22 For a description of Karl Lueger's political anti-Semitism, see Brigitte Hamann, *Hitler's Vienna: A Dictator's Apprenticeship* (Oxford: Oxford University Press, 1999).

23 Spiegel, *Other Arab-Israeli Conflict*, 419; compare with Quandt, *Peace Process*, 344–48.

24 Spiegel. *Other Arab-Israeli Conflict*, 419.

25 Quandt, *Peace Process*, 344–45.

26 Lapidoth and Hirsch, *Arab-Israel Conflict*, 287–95.

27 Shimon Peres, *Battling for Peace: A Memoir*, ed. David Landau (London: Weidenfeld & Nicolson, 1995), 347–65.

28 Protocol of Peres and Rashad Shawwa meeting, November 21, 1982.

29 Quoted from "Protocol: Meeting between Shimon Peres and Rashad Shawwa," November 21, 1982. Nine years later, I prepared a study of possible models for negotiations for the European Union. One of the models that I proposed suggested 50:50 control over land and water. In 1991, the Palestinians, including PLO supporters in the West Bank, were very willing to accept this proposal, which had been pushed aside as insignificant in 1982.

30 "Hussein's Decision: Fears for His Kingdom, Sense of History Drove Monarch to Seek Talks," *Wall Street Journal*, April 15, 1983.

31 Ibid.

32 Yair's diary, 161.

33 Protocols of two meetings with Dan Kurtzer, November 9 and 17, 1983.

34 Secretary of State George Shultz, address to the Council of Jewish Federations and Welfare Funds, Atlanta, November 21, 1983.

35 Meetings with Dan Kurtzer, November 9 and 17, 1983.

36 Protocols of meetings with Dan Kurtzer, November 9 and 17, 1983; interview with Shalom Harari, March 29, 2012. Brig. Gen. Shalom Harari, who at that time advised the Israeli Civil Administration on Arab Affairs, said that eventually the Israeli government gave in to US pressure to permit the construction of a cement factory in Hebron. He added that the idea was finally foiled due to internal Palestinian opposition led by Bassam Shakaa from Nablus. Shakaa had been a member of the Ba'th Party and was influenced by Syrian interests and motivated by the long-standing rivalry between Nablus and Hebron.

37 See Shlaim, *Lion of Jordan*, 433; interview with Shalom Harari, March 29, 2012.

38 "Sicha im Karim Khalaf" [Discussion with Karim Khalaf], December 30, 1983; the same message was given at times with different words, changing the political message only marginally.

39 The interview was demonstratively given during the meeting with us. "Protocol of Meeting with Rashad Shawwa," December 30, 1983.

40 Meeting with Rashad Shawwa, December 30, 1983.

41 The list of recommendations is a partial summary of the proposals that were based on the work of two different groups: the Mashov Committee on the West Bank and Gaza Strip, and the Blumental group. For Mashov Committee, see "Approved Text of Mashov Council of January 25, 1984"; for the work of the smaller group headed by Naftali Blumenthal, see "Sheelot Politiot merkasiot hakshurot lapituah hakalkali bshtaschim," paper prepared for a meeting of the Blumenthal group, February 16, 1984, n.d. This included summaries of meetings with Shlomo Gazit, December 15, 1983; Brig. Gen. Benjamin Ben-Eliezer, November 17, 1983; and Rashad ash-Shawwa, December 1983; as well as various meetings with Elias Freij.

42 Interview with Amnon Neubach, March 15 2012. Neubach, a member of Mashov, was appointed adviser to Prime Minister Peres on economic affairs and put in charge of negotiating the establishment of an Arab Bank in the West Bank with the head of the Jordanian Central Bank, a grandson of the former Arab mayor of Haifa, Hassan al-Shukri. The Jordanian's first remark to Neubach was that Jordan needed regulations that would prevent the money from going to finance any terrorist action.

43 Interview with Efraim Lavie, March 14, 2012; interview with Shalom Harari, March 29, 2012. COGAT policy was strongly influenced by its observation that, in the decade between 1975 and 1985, the various branches of the PLO in the territories had succeeded in establishing deep organizational roots among the inhabitants. COGAT was determined to counteract this development and limit, wherever possible, the PLO's influence.

44 Israeli Government Decree 145, November 11, 1979: "We decide (unanimously): to expand the settlements in Judea, Samaria, Jordan valley, Gaza Strip and the Golan heights by adding population to existing settlements and by building new settlements on 'state land' (possessed by the state)."

45 Usama Halabi, Aron Turner, and Meron Benvenisti, *Land Alienation in the West Bank: A Legal and Spatial Analysis* (Jerusalem: West Bank Data Project, 1985).

46 Interview with Efraim Lavie, March 14, 2012. Shmuel Goren legalized the socioeconomic activities of the established endowment created by Sheikh Ahmed Yazzin, who became the founder of the Hamas movement. Interview with Shalom Harari, March 29, 2012. Harari added, in 2012, that Jordan had indirectly supported the Muslim Brotherhood movement, particularly in the West Bank. See Lavie, "HaPalestinim b'gada hama'aravit," 165–67.

47   Interview with Dan Kurtzer, September 10, 2013.

48   These points are taken from the 100-Day Program for 1984, in the section on suggested policies in the occupied territories. "Tochnit hapeula bshtachim i mea hayamim harishonim" [Action program in the territories for the first hundred days], n.d. (approximately February 1984).

49   Yossi Beilin and Efraim Lavie each explained this to me independently. Interview with Yossi Beilin, February 29, 2012; interview with Efraim Lavie, March 12, 2012.

50   The 1984 elections preserved the delicate balance in the Knesset. The ILP had forty-four seats and the Likud had forty-one, but Labor was unable to establish a new government without the support of the religious parties. The subsequent coalition included a few other small parties, allies of the ILP and the Likud, and the government consisted of twenty-five ministers—the largest ever by that point in time.

51   The radical right-wing Kach movement, established by Rabbi Meir Kahane in 1971, wanted to evict all Arabs from Israel and take away their civil rights, on the claim that Arabs were not loyal to the Jewish state. The Israeli central elections committee barred Kach from running in the 1984 Knesset elections because of the movement's racist platform, but on appeal the Supreme Court struck down the committee's decision and ruled that the Knesset elections laws do not allow a party to be barred on the grounds of racism and suggested that the law be amended. Kach won one seat, and Kahane became a member of the Knesset in 1984. In 1985, the law was changed to prevent parties with racist platforms from running for the Knesset, and in October 1988 the Kach movement was barred from running in the upcoming election because of its platform, which called for limiting marriage between Arabs and Israelis. The Israeli Supreme Court upheld this decision in light of the change in the Knesset law. In 1990, Kahane was assassinated in the United States; and in 1994, following a massacre in Hebron's Cave of the Patriarchs by a member of the movement, the Kach movement was declared a terrorist organization in Israel, the EU, Canada, and the United States.

52   Meron Benvenisti and the West Bank Data Projects, *1987 Report: Demographic, Economic, Legal, Social and Political Developments in the West Bank* (Jerusalem: West Bank Data Project, 1987).

53   Akiba Eldar and Idit Zartal, *Lords of the Land: The War over Israel's Settlements in the Occupied Territories, 1967–2007* (New York: Nation, 2007), 101–4.

54   Interview with Amnon Neubach, April 19, 2012; Mandelbaum was opposed to the development of an Arab Bank. Headway was made only when Arnon Gafni replaced Mandelbaum as head of the Bank of Israel.

55   Road construction, easing the commute for settlers living in the West Bank to places of employment in the wider Tel Aviv area, was mainly carried out later under Prime Minister Yitzhak Rabin. In reaction to increasing terror, Rabin's roads circumvented the Palestinian villages. Interview with Othniel Schneller, March 4, 2012; interview with Shaul Arieli (who was involved in the planning), August 8, 2012.

56   At first, Schneller tried to mobilize Yitzhak Shamir's support, but Shamir did not "want to rock the boat, with the ILP." Having been rejected, Schneller, with the help of some Labor members of the Knesset, arranged a long filibuster. Because the annual budget had to be passed, further budgetary means were allocated for additional settlement activities for the next year. Interview with Othniel Schneller, March 4, 2012.

57   Shimon Peres, *Battling for Peace*, 274–82.

58   Interview with Yossi Beilin, February 29, 2012; interview with Amnon Neubach, April 19, 2012.

59   Peres was particularly interested in impressing upon Najaf Halaby his determination to make the Reagan Plan work. At a meeting in New York in the early autumn of 1984, Peres asked Halaby whether he had a strong influence upon his son-in-law. Najaby replied, "Like any other son-in-law, he sometimes listens to me, and sometimes not."

60   Interview with Amnon Neubach, April 19, 2012.

61   Italy, as an EU member state, was the state where the Venice Declaration of 1980 demanding the establishment of a Palestinian state was concluded. Lapidoth and Hirsch, *Arab-Israel Conflict*, 253–54.

62   Interview with Yossi Beilin, February 29, 2012; interview with Nimrod Novik, June 24, 2012. Nimrod Novik remembered that at every meeting, Ambassador Tarasov would tell him that the Soviet Union was pressuring the PLO to permit King Hussein to move forward. Novik did not take this account literally at the time. However, many years later, Hassan Asfour told him that whenever they went to Moscow, or whenever Tarasov came to Tunis, he would push them heavily to support Jordanian leadership in the peace process.

63   At the decisive meeting between Shimon Peres and King Hussein on April 11, 1987, Yossi Beilin was given one hour to put the conditions to rule an international conference on paper. The preparatory work had been carried out two years earlier. For a description of the London meeting, see Shlaim, *Lion of Jordan*, 443–44.

64   Interview with Nimrod Novik, June 24, 2012.

65   Lapidoth and Hirsch, *Arab-Israel Conflict*, 304.

66   Shlaim, *Lion of Jordan*, 422–39.

67   Interview with Yossi Beilin, February 29, 2012.

68   Shlaim, *Lion of Jordan*, 426 ff.

69   Ibid., 428–31.

70   Yehuda Litani, "Signed Bank Pact May Presage Israel-Jordanian Condominium, Hussein's W. Bank Push," *Jerusalem Post*, October 3, 1986; Robert Lustig, "After the Carrot, Jordan Tries the West Bank Stick," *The Observer*, June 29, 1986.

71   See a description of this paper in chapter 4 below.

72   Interview with Shalom Harari, March 29, 2012.

73   Trudy Rubin, "Israel Tries to Outflank West Bank Leadership," *Christian Science Monitor*, August 28, 1981. Compare with Daniel C. Kurtzer, Scott B. Lasensky, William B. Quandt, Steven L. Spiegel, and Shibley Z. Telhami, *The Peace Puzzle: America's Quest for Arab-Israeli Peace, 1989–2011* (Ithaca, NY, and Washington, DC: Cornell University Press and US Institute for Peace Press, 2013), 19.

74   In his doctoral thesis, Efraim Lavie describes the PLO and Fatah's lack of effective means of control over the Palestinian inhabitants of the West Bank. He further describes the ways and means that the Palestinians successfully asserted pressure on the PLO leadership in Tunis; see Lavie, "HaPalestinim b'gada hama'aravit," 136–76. Shalom Harari, however, explains that due to a delicate balance of power, various groups within the PLO would each employ small groups of thugs in order to assert the necessary pressure to prevent action that would undermine the political standing of the other PLO groups. Interview with Shalom Harari, March 29, 2012.

75   Shlaim, *Lion of Jordan*, 431.

76   Ibid.

77   Ibid., 433.

78   Shalom Harari argues that the assassination of Zafer al-Masri was engineered by members of the Popular Front for the Liberation of Palestine from within the Jenin prison who effectively ordered the assassination. Interview, March 29, 2012.

79   Shlaim, *Lion of Jordan*, 433.

80   Litani, "Signed Bank Pact," *Jerusalem Post*, October 3, 1989.

81   Shlaim, *Lion of Jordan*, 435.

82   Ibid., 433–34.

83   Ernest Gellner and John Waterbury, eds., *Patrons and Clients in Mediterranean Societies* (London: Duckworth, in association with the Center for Mediterranean Studies of the American Universities Field Staff, 1977).

84   Yossi Beilin speculated, in hindsight, that King Hussein either preferred dealing with the Likud rather than with the ILP, or that he wanted Shamir to sense that he had been a full partner to the deal. Interview with Yossi Beilin, February 29, 2012.

85   Interview with Yossi Beilin, February 29, 2012. Micha Goldmann, a member of the Knesset who was close to Yitzhak Rabin, remembers that Rabin's first question to Peres was whether Prime Minister Shamir had been informed. Interview with Micha Goldmann, September 4, 2013.

86   Shlaim, *Lion of Jordan*, 444.

87   Ibid., 450–52. Dan Kurtzer recounts that Secretary of State George Shultz did not trust Shimon Peres and, worse, resented the fact that Peres, as minister of foreign affairs, had acted behind Prime Minister Shamir's back. Two years later, Secretary of State James Baker understood that in order to achieve headway in the peace process, the United States could rely on policy understandings reached by the ILP in order to convince Shamir to go along. Interview with Dan Kurtzer, August 7, 2012.

88   Yaakov Katz, "Analysis: Jewish Terrorism Gaining Steam," *Jerusalem Post*, October 4, 2011.

89   "Daily Report" (in Arabic), Radio Monte Carlo, July 30, 1988.

90   King Hussein, speech to the Arab Nation (in Arabic), "Daily Report," Amman Domestic Service, July 31, 1988.

91   Shlaim, *Lion of Jordan*, 457–74; Adnan Abu Odeh, *Jordanians, Palestinians and the Hashemite Kingdom in the Middle East Peace Process* (Washington, DC: US Institute of Peace Press, 1999).

92   Marwan Muasher, *The Arab Center: The Promise of Moderation* (New Haven, CT: Yale University Press, 2008), 10–71.

93   Shlaim, *Lion of Jordan*, 422–39.

Chapter 3

1   See Israel Central Bureau of Statistics, *Year Book for 1990* (Tel Aviv: Israel Central Bureau of Statistics); and M. Harnoi, "Trends of Settlement of Judea, Samaria and Gaza Regions" (in Hebrew), in *Judea and Samaria Research Studies: Proceedings of the Second Annual Meeting 1992*, ed. Zeev H. Erlich and Yaakov Eshel (Ariel: College of Judea and Samaria, 1992), 369–75.

2   Mark Matthews, "US, Soviets Agree to Pact on Arms Cuts," *Baltimore Sun*, October 4, 1990.

3   My US Embassy contact, Daniel Kurtzer, gave me a report on this very first US-Russian peace team meeting, as did Alexej Chiastokov, a member of the Russian team. Kurtzer took upon himself the task of telling the Russians that they had to let the

American team lead the negotiations. As Kurtzer presented it, the United States had gained most relevant experience on promoting the peace process between 1970 and 1987, whereas the Russians had voluntarily excluded themselves from the negotiations until that point.

4   For a more general theoretical discussion of the limits of military power, see Rupert Smith, *The Utility of Force: The Art of War in the Modern World* (London: Penguin Books, 2006).

5   "PLO View: Prospects of a Palestinian Israeli Settlement," Palestinian Dossier, Arab Summit Conference, June 1988. See also Elaine Sciolino, "PLO Aide's Plan Has US Intrigued," *New York Times*, June 28, 1988.

6   See Daniel C. Kurtzer, Scott B. Lasensky, William B. Quandt, Steven L. Spiegel, and Shibley Z. Telhami, *The Peace Puzzle: America's Quest for Arab-Israeli Peace, 1989–2011* (Ithaca, NY, and Washington, DC: Cornell University Press and US Institute for Peace Press, 2013), 20–22.

7   Interview with Yossi Beilin, February 29, 2012.

8   Ruth Lapidoth and Moshe Hirsch, eds., *The Arab-Israel Conflict and Its Resolution: Selected Documents* (Boston: Martinus Nijhoff, 1992), 337–38.

9   "For a discussion of the "Shultz Initiative," see William B. Quandt, *Peace Process: American Diplomacy and the Arab-Israeli Conflict since 1967* (Berkeley and Washington, DC: University of California Press and Brookings Institution Press, 1993), 364–75.

10   Dan Kurtzer told me this story in one of our meetings in Washington when I was there on a sabbatical in 1989. He repeated it to me on August 7, 2012.

11   Henry Kissinger, *Years of Upheaval* (Boston: Little, Brown, 1982), 626–27. Kissinger recounts how the PLO took the initiative in July 1973 and suggested a dialogue with the United States on the basis of two premises—that "Israel is here to stay," and that Jordan should be "the home for the Palestinian state" (i.e., that King Hussein should be overthrown). Kissinger rejected Arafat's suggestion. Another attempt was initiated by US president Jimmy Carter in 1977, who asked the king of Saudi Arabia to bring a message to Arafat that the United States was willing to recognize the PLO if the PLO would recognize and accept UN Security Council Resolution 242 as a basis for negotiations. The Saudis viewed this as a big gesture toward them and invited Arafat to Riyadh, where they made him the offer. Arafat went out of his way to thank the king and reportedly "jumped full of joy." He said he would consult with his people and never sent word back to the Saudis. Prince Turki al-Faisal of Saudi Arabia told this anecdote to Nimrod Novik. It clearly elucidates that Arafat was not willing to accept UN Security Resolution 242 as long as the territory from which Israel would withdraw would be returned to Jordan. Only King Hussein's July 31, 1988, decision not to engage in peace negotiations with Israel in regard to the West Bank and Gaza and to separate Jordan from Palestine allowed Arafat to accept UN Security Council Resolution 242 in December 1988.

12   "Memorandum of Agreement between the Governments of Israel and the United States—The Geneva Peace Conference," point 2, September 1, 1975, in *Arab-Israel Conflict*, ed. Lapidoth and Hirsch, 174.

13   In a speech given at the Washington Institute for Near East Policy at Wye Plantation on September 16, 1988, Shultz said: "To expect the PLO to accept Resolutions 242 and 338 as the basis for negotiations is not to ask it to make a concession. Those resolutions lay out basic principles, which the international community has decided must be reflected in a peace settlement. In addition to these,

the legitimate rights of the Palestinian people—including political rights—must also be addressed. It is through acceptance of these principles—not through any action by the United States—that the Palestinians can participate fully in determining their own future." Speech and Q&A Session, the Honorable George P. Shultz, Secretary of State, before Washington Institute for Near East Policy, Wye Plantation, MD, September 16, 1988.

14   "Official Translation of the Final Statement of the Nineteenth Session of the Palestine National Council, Algiers, November 12–14, 1988," in *Arab-Israel Conflict*, ed. Lapidoth and Hirsch, 344–52.

15   "United States Dialogue with the PLO," December 14, 1988, in *Arab-Israeli Conflict and Conciliation: A Documentary History*, ed. Bernard Reich (Westport, Conn.: Praeger, 1995), 218–20.

16   Interview with Eitan Haber, August 27, 2012; meeting with Rabbi Yuval Sherlov, June 2011. Rabbi Sherlov recalled that in a meeting he and other rabbis had with Rabin early in the summer of 1990, Rabin explained this concept to them by drawing a map of the Middle East on a piece of paper. Rabin then explained that in order to get the necessary support from the United States against faraway threats— referring to Iran and Pakistan—Israel had to agree to important concessions with regard to the West Bank and Gaza.

17   Interview with Eitan Haber, August 28, 2012.

18   Eitan Haber remembered that the two leaders of the intifada were sitting close to the kitchen, peeling potatoes. Although Haber was afraid that they might attack Rabin, Rabin sat down near them and talked with them. Interview with Eitan Haber, August 28, 2012. One of the two Palestinians was Khalid Yazdji, a member of a leading Gaza family who own a Pepsi-Cola factory. Yazdji remembered the meeting and said, "At the time we thought that we in Palestine were small, whereas the leadership of PLO in Tunis were great. Today, we know that the opposite was true." Meeting with Khalid Yazdji, June 8, 2006, quoted from memory.

19   Interview with Eitan Haber, August 27, 2012.

20   The concept was based on four subjects "to be dealt with in the peace process": (1) The Camp David Accords should serve as a cornerstone for enlarging the circle of peace in the region, through continued consultation; (2) Israel calls for the establishment of peaceful relations between it and those Arab states that still maintain a state of war with it, to include recognition, direct negotiations, ending the boycott, diplomatic relations, cessation of hostile activity in international institutions or forums, and regional and bilateral cooperation; (3) Israel calls for an international endeavor to resolve the problem of the residents of the Arab refugee camps in Judea, Samaria, and the Gaza district, and Israel is prepared to be a partner in this endeavor; and (4) free and democratic elections in the territories of Judea, Samaria, and the Gaza district should be held in order to choose a representation to conduct negotiations for a transitional period of self-rule. At a later stage, negotiations will be conducted for a permanent solution, during which all the proposed options for an agreed-on settlement will be examined, and peace between Israel and Jordan will be achieved. In addition to these four suggestions, the Shamir Plan included three "no's": no to the establishment of "an additional Palestinian state," no to negotiations with the PLO, and no change of status of "Judea, Samaria, and Gaza." As described in *Arab-Israel Conflict*, ed. Lapidoth and Hirsch, 357–60.

21   Meeting on January 6, 1989, with Mayor Mustafa Abdel Nabi Natche and Kamal Hassouneh from Hebron, Immanuel Halperin, and Yair Hirschfeld.

22   Halperin's statement was apparently a quotation from the Camp David Accords. However, whether intentionally or not, he spoke merely of "the legitimate rights of the Palestinians" instead of the phrase in the agreement that read that Israel would "recognize the legitimate rights and just requests of the Palestinian people." He had omitted the phrase that referred to "the Palestinian people" and instead spoke merely about "the Palestinians."

23   Meeting with Hana Siniora, December 27, 1988.

24   Meeting on January 6, 1989, with Mayor Mustafa Abdel Nabi Natche et al.

25   Ibid.

26   Ibid.

27   Rashid Khalidi, *Palestinian Identity: The Construction of Modern National Consciousness* (New York: Columbia University Press, 1997), particularly 232n17 in chap. 4; Butrus Abu Manehs, "The Husaynis: The Rise of a Notable Family in 18th-Century Palestine," in *Palestine in the Late Ottoman Period: Political, Social, and Economic Transformation*, ed. David Kushner (Jerusalem: Yad Yizchak Ben Zvi, 1986), 93–108. In later years, Faisal Husseini became very emotionally tied to the Israeli Peace Now movement, and members of the movement would build human chains around him in order to shield him from physical attacks by Israeli radical right-wing extremists. Later, Uzi Narkiss, who had been the commanding officer in the Battle of the Qastal and had fought against Faisal Husseini's father, suggested that I ask Faisal Husseini if he would be willing to receive the Qur'an that Narkiss had taken from Husseini's fallen father in a small ceremony. Husseini's response was that he would like to receive the Qur'an in a public ceremony, but only after the establishment of the independent State of Palestine.

28   Yair Hirschfeld, "Negotiations on Elections in the Territories: The First Move," February 1, 1989.

29   When Arafat had an airplane accident and disappeared for several days in the Libyan desert, Ashrawi made a public remark that it was time to choose a successor to Arafat. From then until his death, she continued to try to mend her relations with him. I owe this information to Shalom Harari; interview with Shalom Harari, September 11, 2013.

30   Nusseibeh would later lead the so-called Palestinian technical committees, an organizational setup to prepare for the transfer of authority from the Israeli military government to Palestinian self-government. Sari Nusseibeh (with Anthony David), *Once Upon a Country: A Palestinian Life* (London: Halban, 2013).

31   Protocol: Meeting of February 15, 1989, 20.00–22.15, Notre Dame (Jerusalem).

32   Ibid.

33   Ibid.

34   "Beilin, Novik, and Sneh Met Faisal el Husseini" (in Hebrew) *Maariv*, February 16, 1989.

35   The Mashov is the left-wing political circle of the ILP, led by Yossi Beilin.

36   Handwritten notes on a meeting between Dan Kurtzer and Yair Hirschfeld, May 17, 1989.

37   Throughout this book, "Abu Mazen" is used only in specific circumstances where the nom de guerre is common, as in the "Beilin–Abu Mazen Understanding," whereas "Mahmoud Abbas" is used as his official name.

38   See the details of the assassination in chapter 2.

39   The Americans had asked the Soviet Union to use its influence to prevent the PLO's November 15, 1988, Declaration of Independence. Though Moscow did not do

anything to prevent the Declaration of Independence, the Russians told Washington that they had effectively used their influence in convincing Arafat to recognize the State of Israel's right to exist, which he did in Geneva on December 14, 1988.

40   Handwritten note by Yair Hirschfeld, "The Meeting in (the Dutch) Ministry of Finance," June 27, 1989.

41   In my notes on the meeting, I wrote that it is "not clear who he is." He was a member of the Communist Party, and as such he had been supportive of the recognition of Israel. He was also very close to Mahmoud Abbas at the time, something that changed later on. Asfour later became one of the three members of the PLO delegation to Norway.

42   Afif Safiyeh was a Catholic who later served as the PLO ambassador to the Vatican. In The Hague, he was one of the most outspoken advocates of the Palestinian peace camp. Due to his diplomatic achievements, he was later upgraded to PLO representative to London, where he had to compete with several other Palestinian political stakeholders who would bring about his marginalization within the internal system. He gradually adopted a very cynical and destructive approach to peace negotiations with Israel. The pattern that we witnessed in Safiyeh—moving within the Palestinian system from peace supporter to peace opponent—was one that occurred again and again with others among our Palestinian interlocutors. On the Palestinian side, far more so than on the Israeli side, personal involvement in a prominent or less prominent position determined their political agitation and advocacy in support or against peace. This did not bode well for the peace process, because it was indicative of two negative tendencies: First, Palestinian political stakeholders moved, often very quickly, from being a part of the peace camp to the opposing camp; and second, opposition to progress often originated from within Fatah's political structure.

43   Handwritten note of Yair Hirschfeld, June 26 and 27, 1989.

44   King Hussein had proposed a federation in 1972, only relatively shortly after September 1970, when the PLO was expelled from Jordan as a result of a bitter civil war between Jordanians and Palestinians. See "King Hussein's Plan for a Federation," March 15, 1972, in *Arab-Israel Conflict*, ed. Lapidoth and Hirsch, 143–44. In February 1985, King Hussein and Chairman Arafat had agreed that eventually a Jordanian-Palestinian Confederation would be established. The decisions made by the Palestinian National Council of November 1988 "confirmed that the future relationship between the two states of Jordan and Palestine will be established on a confederal basis" (as quoted above in the text). In meetings between King Hussein, Shimon Peres, and Yossi Beilin, King Hussein said that he would not permit the establishment of a Palestinian state, even only for 10 minutes, before the formation of the Confederation. Interview with Yossi Beilin, February 29, 2012.

45   Interview with Yossi Beilin, February 29, 2012

46   The text offers both versions to make it easier for the reader to understand. (P) refers to the version suggested by the Palestinians, and (I) to the version suggested by us.

47   Attached to a letter from Max van der Stoel to Yair Hirschfeld, July 19, 1989; facsimile sent to Boaz Karni. Yossi Beilin made an effort to achieve wider support within the ILP for the document, and received positive reactions from Uzi Baram and Haim Ramon.

48   "Proposed Model of Full Autonomy for the West Bank and the Gaza Strip, Submitted by Egypt on 28 January 1980," in *Arab-Israel Conflict*, ed. Lapidoth and Hirsch, 207–13.

49   Interview with Nimrod Novik, January 12, 2012.

50   Nimrod Novik, policy paper, October 4, 1989.

51   Protocol of ILP Secretariat Meeting of July 10, 1989, and the thereto-attached decision made. Also see the letter from Yair Hirschfeld to Max van der Stoel, July 13, 1989; in this letter, I suggested to Max van der Stoel that an ongoing dialogue mechanism with the PLO should be created, one quite similar to what was later done by the Norwegians.

52   Handwritten protocol by Yair Hirschfeld, July 30, 1989.

53   Ibid.

54   See ILP decision, August 8, 1989.

55   "Political Program," unofficial translation, adopted by the Fifth General Congress of the Palestinian National Liberation Movement (Fatah), August 8, 1989.

56   Meeting with Hanan Ashrawi, and later with Faisal Husseini, August 24, 1989.

57   Meeting with John Becker, August 18, 1989.

58   Ibid.

59   Ahmed Asmat Abdel-Meguid served as Egypt's minister of foreign affairs from 1984 to 1991, and as the secretary-general of the Arab League from 1991 to 2001.

60   Nimrod Novik. "Yosmat Baker" (The Baker Initiative), Nimrod Novik to M. K. Micha Harish; October 8, 1989.

61   Telephone call from Max van der Stoel to Yair Hirschfeld, September 4, 1989; 7.45, p. 2.

62   Ambassador Bassiouni at first informed Nimrod Novik that Arafat had agreed to offer support to the unfolding peace initiative. Novik mentioned this in a meeting with Rabin, who in his deep voice reprimanded Novik, saying "Young man, you are mistaken." When it turned out that Novik's information was accurate, Rabin took the lead in promoting the unfolding peace initiative. Interview with Nimrod Novik, February 7, 2014.

63   Yossi Beilin remembers that Rabbi Arieh Der'i took a very proactive position in support of the initiative and wanted to turn it into a success, even if it meant breaking up the coalition and forming an alternative government. Interview with Yossi Beilin, February 27, 2012.

64   Meeting of Yair Hirschfeld and Nimrod Novik, September 14, 1989.

65   "Rabin yoze haboker lepgischa im Mubarak" (This morning Rabin is going to Cairo to meet Mubarak), *Haaretz*, September 28, 1989; Novik, policy paper, October 4, 1989.

66   Novik, policy paper, October 4, 1989.

67   "Interview: The Americans Are the Critical Link," *Jerusalem Post*, September 15, 1989. Two years later, this formula defined the PLO's role for the Palestinian delegation that was to participate in negotiations at the Madrid Conference. The PLO itself would not be present at the negotiating table, but the Palestinian delegation would consult on an hourly basis—outside the negotiating room—with the PLO officials present; and every second or third day, the Palestinian delegation would fly to Tunis for direct instructions from Chairman Arafat. Eventually, this almost ridiculous state of affairs led to direct talks with the PLO.

68   Lapidoth and Hirsch, *Arab-Israel Conflict*, 362. Although the date given there is July 5, 1989, this is incorrect; the 10-Point Mubarak Initiative was actually announced on September 11, 1989.

69   Meeting with Jan Revis (deputy chief of mission, Embassy of the Netherlands in Tel Aviv) and Yair Hirschfeld, September 26, 1989.

70   "Neum sar habitachon bfnej merkaz mifleget ha'awoda b 21.9.1989" [Speech of the minister of defense before the central committee of the ILP, September 21, 1989], *Haaretz*, September 24, 1989.

71   "Shamir: Efarek et hamemshala im Rabin ve Peres yitmechu byosmato shel Mubarak" [Shamir: I will break up the government if Rabin and Peres will support Mubarak's initiative], *Haaretz*, September 24, 1989.

72   Jackson Diehl, "Israelis Ease Opposition to Cairo Plan," *Washington Post*, October 3, 1989.

73   Nimrod Novik to M. K. Micha Harish, October 18, 1989; notes on telephone conversation between Nimrod Novik and Ambassador Bassiouni, October 4, 1989, 12:30.

74   See *Arab-Israel Conflict*, ed. Lapidoth and Hirsch, 364–65.

75   "Hamagama blikud: Lalechet lebchirot" [The tendency in Likud: To go to elections], *Haaretz*, September 18, 1989.

76   Dan Petreanu, David Makovsky, and Wolf Blitzer, "Shamir Seen Ready to Accept Baker Plan—but Likud Hardliners Balk," *Jerusalem Post*, November 3, 1989.

77   Meeting with Radwan Abu Ayyash November 28, 1989; "Moezet ashaf niftacha bbaghdad bsiman hilukiej de'ot charifim" [The PLO Council opened in Baghdad under heavy differences of opinion], *Haaretz*, October 15, 1989.

78   Meeting with Yossi Beilin, Yair Hirschfeld, Boaz Karni, and Radwan Abu Ayyash, November 28, 1989; meeting with Nimrod Novik, Yair Hirschfeld, Boaz Karni, and Faisal Husseini, January 14, 1990.

79   Nimrod Novik to M. K. Benjamin Fuad Ben Eliezer (deputy chairman of the Knesset Committee for Foreign Affairs and Security), February 26, 1990.

80   Ibid.

81   "Leil hamikrofonim harishon: Kach ze haya" (The first microphone night: This is how it went), YNet News, November 30, 2004.

82   Ibid.

83   Interview with Yossi Beilin, February 29, 2012; Shimon Peres, *Battling for Peace: A Memoir*, ed. David Landau (London: Weidenfeld & Nicolson, 1995), 323–36.

84   Rabbi Ovadia Yossef, "Nothing Must Stand in the Way of Saving a Life," *Jerusalem Post*, October 6, 1989.

85   Joel Greenberg, "Rabbi Eliezer Schach, 103, Leader of Orthodox in Israel" (obituary), *New York Times*, November 3, 2001; Peres, *Battling for Peace*, 334–35.

86   Protocol of Meeting in Nijmegen, April 18, 1990; and list of the participants.

87   Ibid.

88   In September 1996, after the opening of the Hasmonean Tunnel in Jerusalem, the Palestinians reengaged in violent action against Israel (see chapter 6) At the end of September 2000, the second intifada brought about a terrorist war against Israel, causing more than a thousand Israeli casualties (see chapters 7 and 8).

89   Leigh Thompson, *The Mind and Heart of the Negotiator* (Upper Saddle River, NJ: Prentice Hall, 1998), chap. 2, "Preparation: What to Do Before Negotiation," 14–29.

90   James A. Baker III, *The Politics of Diplomacy: Revolution, War, and Peace, 1989–1992* (New York: G. P. Putnam's Sons, 1995), 443.

91   Thompson, *Mind and Heart of the Negotiator*, 14–29.

92   Meetings in November 1989 and January 1990.

93   Faisal Husseini was willing to meet and speak with Likud and Shas supporters. Rabbi Ovadia Yosef actually was willing and took a clear public position in favor of a peace move. Peres, *Battling for Peace*, 333–34.

94   Letter from Yair Hirschfeld to Molly Williamson, October 18, 1989.

Chapter 4

1   Avi Shlaim, *Lion of Jordan: The Life of King Hussein in War and Peace* (London, Allen Lane, 2007), 507–8.

2   Ibid.

3   James A. Baker III, *The Politics of Diplomacy: Revolution, War, and Peace, 1989–1992* (New York: G. P. Putnam's Sons, 1995), 411.

4   Ibid., 411–69; Dennis Ross, *The Missing Peace: The Inside Story of the Fight for Middle East Peace* (New York: Macmillan, 2005), 46–87; Daniel C. Kurtzer, Scott B. Lasensky, William B. Quandt, Steven L. Spiegel, and Shibley Z. Telhami, *The Peace Puzzle: America's Quest for Arab-Israeli Peace, 1989–2011* (Ithaca, NY, and Washington, DC: Cornell University Press and US Institute for Peace Press, 2013), 22–30.

5   Joel Peters, *Pathways to Peace: The Multilateral Arab-Israeli Peace Talks* (London: Royal Institute of International Affairs, 1996); Shai Feldman, *Nuclear Weapons and Arms Control in the Middle East* (Cambridge, MA: MIT Press, 1997).

6   Daniel Kurtzer, presentation to the US Institute for Peace–Baker Institute for Public Policy Conference on Twenty Years since Madrid, November 2, 2011.

7   The speeches of President George H. W. Bush and President Mikhail Gorbachev at Madrid on October 30, 1991, are reprinted by Mahdi F. Abdul Hadi, ed., *Documents on Palestine: From the Negotiations in Madrid to the Post–Hebron Agreement Period* (Jerusalem: PASSIA, 1997), vol. 2, 11–15.

8   Interview with Ambassador Edward Djerejian, January 22, 2012.

9   Procedural Ground Rules, Israeli Delegation and Joint Jordanian-Palestinian Delegation, January 13, 1992, in *Documents on Palestine*, ed. Abdul Hadi, vol. 2, 58–59.

10   Yehoshua Porath, *The Palestinian Arab National Movement, 1929–1939: From Riots to Rebellion* (London: Frank Cass, 1977).

11   Kurtzer et al., *Peace Puzzle*, 32.

12   Yair Hirschfeld, "Israel, the Palestinians, and the Middle East: From Dependence to Interdependence," unpublished ECF paper, Ramat Yishai, 1992, 4.

13   This was Shimon Peres's proposal to Mayor Rashad Shawwa in November 1982; see chapter 2 above.

14   Ruth Lapidoth and Moshe Hirsch, eds., *The Arab-Israel Conflict and Its Resolution: Selected Documents* (Boston: Martinus Nijhoff, 1992), 337–38.

15   Hirschfeld, "Israel, the Palestinians, and the Middle East," esp. chap. 8, "Building Interdependence: The Long Term," and subchap. II, "The Threat of Arab Radicalism and Militant Islamic Fundamentalism," 142.

16   Ibid., 142.

17   Ibid., 148; I also referred to other activities that were necessary in this context, such as a social charter, social development funds, investment in community work, the development of rural-based industries strengthening tradition in the context of modernity, deepening and widening citizen's rights, and strengthening the institutionalization of democratic procedures.

18   ILP platform, 1992 (in Hebrew).

19   Shimon Peres, *Battling for Peace: A Memoir*, ed. David Landau (London: Weidenfeld & Nicolson, 1995), 378.

20   Brig. Gen. Shalom Harari told me that it was originally planned to split up the Hamas activists and take different groups by helicopters to various destinations. However, due to bad weather the decision was made (hastily) to take the entire group in buses to Southern Lebanon. Interview with Shalom Harari, January 18, 2013.

21   I have told the story of two meetings in London, on December 3 and 4, in *Oslo Nushat Shalom*, by Yair Hirschfeld (Tel Aviv: Am Oved, 1999).

22   Yair Hirschfeld and Ron Pundak to Yossi Beilin, "Pgisha im mishlachat ashaf" [Report of meeting with a PLO delegation], January 24, 1993.

23   In 1946, the Kingdom of Saudi Arabia had already decided to construct a pipeline from the Persian Gulf to the Mediterranean circumventing Israel and the Palestinian areas, although geographically it would have been shorter to have the pipeline reach Gaza as the exit point to the Mediterranean.

24   Abu Ala' [as Ahmed Qurei], *From Oslo to Jerusalem: The Palestinian Story of the Secret Negotiations* (London: I. B. Tauris, 2006), 63–64.

25   Ibid., 64.

26   Yair Hirschfeld and Ron Pundak to Yossi Beilin, "Pgisha im mishlachat ashaf."

27   "The Principles of an Israeli-Palestinian Negotiating Plan," paper submitted in Sarpsborg, February 12, 1993.

28   The statement by Abu Ala', saying that we concluded the Sarpsborg Agreement during the February meeting, is not correct. Abu Ala', *From Oslo to Jerusalem*, 77–96; Peres, *Battling for Peace*, 382–83.

29   "Principles of an Israeli-Palestinian Negotiating Plan."

30   Yair Hirschfeld and Ron Pundak to Yossi Beilin, Report on the Meetings with a PLO Delegation, Ramat Yishai, February 13, 1993; Yair Hirschfeld to Yossi Beilin, Evaluation of the Sarpsborg Proposals, February 18, 1993; Peres, *Battling for Peace*, 382–83. Peres writes that I sent a report directly to him.

31   Minutes of the meeting between Faisal Husseini and Shimon Peres, February 21, 1993.

32   Ross, *Missing Peace*, 102–3. According to Ross's account of the Oslo negotiations, the idea of an American shuttle diplomacy effort after the first two meetings in Norway was never contemplated and never even suggested.

33   Summary Report on Meeting with Faisal Husseini and Hanan Ashrawi, February 27, 8:00–10:00 a.m., and with Faisal 12:30–12:50 p.m.

34   Text of the US-Russian announcement, March 10, 1993.

35   Interviews with Yossi Beilin, February 29, 2012, and June 4, 2012.

36   The Principles of an Israeli-Palestinian Understanding, version 3, March 21, 1993; Summarized Report of the Third Sarpsborg Meeting (the report is undated, reporting about the meeting in Sarpsborg, March 20–22, 1993).

37   Principles of an Israeli-Palestinian Understanding, version three, March 21, paragraph 4.

38   See chapter 1 and Protocol of Meeting between Shimon Peres and Faisal Husseini, January 9, 1993.

39   Hirschfeld, "Israel, the Palestinians, and the Middle East."

40   Peres, *Battling for Peace*, 383; Peres opposed this concept. However, in his autobiography he does explain the logic of the proposed concept.

41   Ibid., 390.

42　Ibid., 381–90.

43　Ron Pundak was so upset and afraid that his career would be compromised that he refused to sign the report regarding the Sarpsborg Document with me. As a result, I took full "blame" and responsibility. When matters calmed down, Pundak asked to come back onboard.

44　Clinton, in his memoirs, says that he was informed of the Oslo talks "shortly before I took office"—i.e., before the first meeting in Norway; he continues: "On a couple of occasions, when the talks were in danger of being derailed, Warren Christopher had done a good job of keeping them on track." Bill Clinton, *My Life* (New York: Random House, 2005), 541.

45　Kurtzer remarked that, in this context, the Americans were "more Catholic than the Pope." See also his more analytical account: Kurtzer et al., *Peace Puzzle*, 35–41.

46　Yair Hirschfeld and Ron Pundak to Yossi Beilin, April 13, 1993.

47　Ron Pundak, meeting between Larsen and Beilin, April 11, 1993. The meeting took place in the Tel Aviv office of the Ministry of Foreign Affairs. Peres was present in the office but intentionally did not meet with Larsen, though the two men did see each other and it was clear that Peres endorsed the meeting even though he was not willing, at that point in time, to discuss it with Larsen, in order for the time being to keep deniability and influence the PLO to renew the Washington channel.

48　Statements made by Abu Ala' in Oslo, April 30 and May 1, 1993.

49　Later, when Uri Savir and Yoel Singer joined the meetings in Norway, we explained this repeatedly to Abu Ala' and his team and we achieved full understanding and acceptance on this point. When, after the conclusion of the DoP, negotiations for what became the May 4, 1994, Cairo Agreement started, the Palestinians once again made the same demands that they had previously given up. Ross, *Missing Peace*, 133–36.

50　Peres, *Battling for Peace*, 387.

51　Interview with Nimrod Novik, June 24, 2012.

52　Minutes of the meetings with Shimon Peres, April 25 and April 27, 1993.

53　This is Peres's figure.

54　Minutes of the meetings with Shimon Peres, April 25 and 27, 1993.

55　Report of meetings in Oslo, April 30 and May 1, 1993.

56　Ibid.

57　Briefing to Shimon Peres and Yossi Beilin, Meeting with the PLO Delegation, May 11, 1993.

58　Peres, *Battling for Peace*, 388.

59　Uri Neeman, *Hachra'ot Gvuliot* [Borderline choices] (Tel Aviv: Yedioth Ahronoth, 2011), 200–211.

60　Compare with Peres, *Battling for Peace*, 391; For a discussion of the arguments in favor of and against the idea of a trusteeship, see the section below titled "Successes, Failures, and Lessons Learned."

61　See "Report of Meeting in Norway" (in Hebrew), Yair Hirschfeld and Ron Pundak to Shimon Peres, Yossi Beilin, and Uri Savir, July 13, 1993. As the content of the Palestinian demands had to remain secret, they were not included in the account given to British journalist Jane Corbin, and in her description in chapter 9 of her book, she describes Abu Ala's nervousness and the way he dealt with Terje Larsen, rather than the actual events. See Jane Corbin, *Gaza First: The Secret Norway Channel to Peace Between Israel and the PLO* (London: Bloomsbury, 1994), 127–36. The account by Abu Ala' relates more to the sensed crisis situation than to the substance that had been discussed. See Abu Ala', *From Oslo to Jerusalem*, 194–209.

62   "The Final Palestinian Proposal," unofficial draft, August 7, 1993, also quoted above.

63   Declaration of Principles on Interim-Self Government Arrangements, August, 1993. Abu Ala' signed for the Palestinian side and Uri Savir for Israel, with Shimon Peres present at the signing ceremony. Each member of the two negotiating teams possesses a copy of the document signed by all of us.

64   See "Israel-PLO Recognition," September 9, 1993, and "Israel-PLO Declaration of Principles," September 13, 1993, both in *Arab-Israeli Conflict and Conciliation: A Documentary History*, ed. B. Reich (Westport, Conn.: Praeger, 1995), 229–34.

65   The material about these efforts is to be found in the Mapam Archive in Givat Haviva.

66   Uri Avnery, *My Friend, the Enemy* (London: Zed Books, 1986). In order not to oblige the PLO, the policy proposal was written on the letterhead of the Hotel Imperial in Vienna. In the letter, there was a hardly disguised threat that Israeli peace efforts toward Egypt would lead to a renewed conflagration. For a more detailed description of the substance of Sartawi's letter to Kreisky, see chapter 1 above, esp. note 22.

67   Rabin, rather naively, wrote a letter to Kreisky thanking him for the back-channel effort. The entire file is catalogued in the Mapai Archives in Beit Berl under the number B/52, Correspondence with the Socialist International.

68   Mahmoud Abbas (Abu Mazen), *Through Secret Channels: The Road to Oslo— PLO Leader Abu Mazen's Story of the Negotiations* (London: Ithaca Press, 1995), 113.

69   Abu Ala', *From Oslo to Jerusalem*, 111.

70   Meeting between Shimon Peres and Faisal el-Husseini, Jerusalem, January 9, 1993, 9:30–10:00 am. Present: Avi Gil, Ron Pundak, and Yair Hirschfeld.

71   Peres, *Battling for Peace*, 380–402.

72   Kurtzer et al., *Peace Puzzle*, 38.

73   Interview with Dan Kurtzer, May 11, 2012.

74   Meeting between Shimon Peres and Faisal Husseini, January 9, 1993.

75   "Principles of an Israeli-Palestinian Negotiating Plan."

76   Meeting between Shimon Peres and Faisal Husseini, January 9, 1993; the first part of the quotation here is taken from page 5 of the protocol; the second part (after the dots) is taken from page 12.

77   "Principles of an Israeli-Palestinian Negotiating Plan."

78   Minutes of meeting between Shimon Peres, Faisal Husseini, and Hanan Ashrawi. January 23, 1993, 9:30 a.m. Present: Dr. Yair Herchefeld [*sic*.; this time, the Palestinians wrote the protocol and misspelled my name].

79   "Principles of an Israeli-Palestinian Negotiating Plan."

80   Meeting between Shimon Peres and Faisal Husseini, January 9, 1993, 7.

81   Report on a Meeting with a PLO Delegation, Yair Hirschfeld and Ron Pundak to Yossi Beilin, January 24, 1993.

82   Report of Meeting with PLO Delegation, Yair Hirschfeld and Ron Pundak to Yossi Beilin, January 24, 1993.

83   Peres, *Battling for Peace*, 408. At the initialing ceremony of the Declaration of Principles in Oslo, during the night between August 19 and 20, 1993, Abu Ala' informed Peres that "all the major figures in the PLO" supported the agreement, although Faisal Husseini and Hanan Ashrawi had not yet been informed.

84   This rule had a clear downside. On the way back from Norway to Tunis, the Palestinian delegation would, as a rule, stay over in Geneva and rewrite the protocol in order to please Chairman Arafat.

85 More humorously, I referred to this rule as the "Katharina principle." To prepare Abu Ala' and his team for changes that the Israeli side would insist upon if negotiations moved to the official channel, I told him a joke about Czarina Katharina of Russia, who had committed one of her Cossacks to please her sexually one hundred times. The Cossack kept count by making marks on his boots. One morning, the czarina and the Cossack disagreed on the number in the tally. To please his queen, the Cossack wiped all the marks off his boots and simply suggested that they start again from the very beginning—or, in context, that the Palestinians might have to expect substantial demands for changes when the official Israeli negotiators took over.

86 This happened in Permanent Status negotiations between Barak and Arafat; see chapter 6 below.

87 See chapter 5, where Benjamin Begin is quoted in an interview he gave to *The New Yorker*.

88 These documents can be found in the "Guide to the Mideast Peace Process," Israel Ministry of Foreign Affairs, accessed March 10, 2014, http://www.mfa.gov.il /MFA/ForeignPolicy/Peace/Guide/Pages/GUIDE%20TO%20THE%20MID EAST%20PEACE%20PROCESS.aspx.

89 "Recent Platform, as approved by the 6th Party Congress, May 1997," Zionism and Israel Information Center, 2005, http://www.zionism-israel.com/dic/Labor_Party .htm.

90 Peres, *Battling for Peace*, 390.

91 See "Recent Platform, as approved by the 6th Party Congress, May 1997"; and Idith Zertal and Akiva Eldar, *Lords of the Land: The War Over Israel's Settlements in the Occupied Territories, 1967–2007* (New York: Nation Books, 2014), 134–36.

92 See "Cairo Agreement," May 4, 1994, in *Arab-Israeli Conflict*, ed. Reich, 240–49.

93 Lev Grinberg, *Imagined Peace, Discourse of War: The Failure of Leadership, Politics, and Democracy in Israel, 1992–2006* (in Hebrew) (Tel Aviv: Resling Publishing, 2007).

94 Kurtzer et al., *Peace Puzzle*, 51–58.

95 Ibid., 13–14.

96 Secretary of State John Kerry, in establishing his peace team to support Israeli-Palestinian peace negotiations, has appointed Laura Blumenthal to fill this spot and manage public expectations on both the Israeli and Palestinian sides.

97 Kurtzer et al., *Peace Puzzle*, 54–55.

98 Ibid.

99 Compare with John Paul Lederach, *Building Peace: Sustainable Reconciliation in Divided Societies* (Washington, DC: US Institute for Peace Press, 1997), 81 ff.

100 Ibid. See chapters 9 and 10 for achievements in Palestinian state building, and empirical descriptions of the time needed for these developments.

Chapter 5

1 Dennis Ross, *The Missing Peace: The Inside Story of the Fight for Middle East Peace* (New York: Macmillan, 2005), 133–36.

2 Daniel C. Kurtzer, Scott B. Lasensky, William B. Quandt, Steven L. Spiegel, and Shibley Z. Telhami, *The Peace Puzzle: America's Quest for Arab-Israeli Peace, 1989–2011* (Ithaca, NY, and Washington, DC: Cornell University Press and US

Institute for Peace Press, 2013), 112–13; Ministry of Foreign Affairs, Jerusalem, "Israeli-Palestinian Interim Agreement of the West Bank and the Gaza Strip," Washington, September 28, 1995.

3 For a critical account, particularly with regard to American diplomacy, see Kurtzer et al., *Peace Puzzle*, 58–104.

4 Ehud Sprinzak, *Brother Against Brother: Violence and Extremism in Israeli Politics from Altalena to the Rabin Assassination* (New York: Simon & Schuster, 1999).

5 Y. Shabath, *Hamas and the Peace Process* (Jerusalem, 2010), 1–26, 63–87.

6 Ibid.

7 See chapter 1 above and notes 8, 9, and 10.

8 Sprinzak, *Brother Against Brother.*

9 Kurtzer et al., *Peace Puzzle*, 113.

10 Private copy of "Final Agreed Draft of August 19, 1993: Declaration of Principles on Interim Self-Government Arrangements," cosigned by all participants; the date of the document refers to August 19, 1993; the signing ceremony actually took place after midnight, and hence was de facto on August 20, 1993.

11 "Israel-PLO Recognition," September 9, 1993; Bernard Reich, ed., *Arab-Israeli Conflict and Conciliation: A Documentary History* (Westport, CT: Praeger, 1995), 229–30.

12 Interview with Shalom Harari, June 13, 2012.

13 Shabath, *Hamas*, 215–16; interview with Brig. Gen. Shalom Harari, June 13, 2012.

14 See Arafat's remarks immediately after the assassination of Rabin, recounted in chapter 6 below.

15 Quoted by Martin Gilbert, *Israel: A History* (London: Black Swan, 1998), 468.

16 Yair Hirschfeld to Yossi Beilin, Preparing for Israeli-Palestinian Final Status Negotiations, April 18, 1994.

17 The Jerusalem Khalidis were one of the leading Palestinian aristocratic families in the area, having received an endowment from the Mamluks in the fourteenth century. Ahmed's father, Walid Khalidi, is a respected Palestinian historian, and Ahmed's mother was the sister of former Lebanese prime minister Riyad as-Sulh.

18 Hussein Agha's family descends, on one side, from the Qajar Dynasty that ruled Iran between 1796 and 1925 and on the other side from Ayatollah Khorassani, one of the most revered Shi'ite ayatollahs of the late nineteenth and early twentieth centuries. Hussein's grandfather had an important government position in Iraq where, due to his high rank—or so the story goes—he was the only person permitted to ride a white horse.

19 The relevant text read: "The negotiations shall be based on all the provisions and principles of UN Security Council Resolution 242. The negotiations will resolve, among other matters, the location of the boundaries and the nature of the security arrangements. The solution from the negotiations must also recognize the legitimate rights of the Palestinian people and their just requirements." The Camp David Accords, September 17, 1978, as cited by William B. Quandt, *Peace Process: American Diplomacy and the Arab-Israeli Conflict since 1967* (Berkeley and Washington, DC: University of California Press and Brookings Institution, 1993).

20 For Arafat's December 14, 1988, statement and the US response, see "United States Dialogue with the PLO, December 14, 1988," quoted by Reich, *Arab-Israeli Conflict*, 218–20.

21 Rashid Khalidi, *Palestinian Identity: The Construction of Modern National Consciousness* (New York: Columbia University Press, 1997), 192–201. Palestinian thinking and emotions in regard to 1948 are strongly reflected in Palestinian poetry, which expresses the need to rectify the perceived injustice committed against them. The Covenant of Hamas is clear on the issue. In article 6, it says, "[Hamas] is a unique Palestinian movement. . . . It strives to brandish the flag of Allah on every inch of Palestine's land." And in Article 7 it reads, "It is a lion in the chain of Jihad against the Zionist occupier which has endured since the revolt of the martyr Izz al-Din al-Qassam." It also quotes a Hadith: "The hour (for resurrection of the dead) will not arrive until the Muslims fight the Jews and kill them to the extent that where a Jew was hidden behind a tree or a stone, these (the tree or the stone) would say to the Muslim: Oh, servant of Allah, there is a Jew behind me, come and kill him." Article 7, quoted by Shabath, *Hamas*, 5; for the entire text of the Hamas Charter, see Avalon.law.yale .edu/20thcentury.hamas.asp.

22 Aharon Klieman, *Compromising Palestine: A Guide to Final Status Negoti*ations (New York and Tel Aviv: Columbia University Press and Jaffe Center for Strategic Studies, 2000), chaps. 5, 8, and 10.

23 Meir Rosenne, "The Legal Perspective: Understanding UN Security Council Resolution 242 of November 22, 1967 on the Middle East," in *Defensible Borders for a Lasting Peace*, ed. Dan Diker (Jerusalem: Jerusalem Center for Public Affairs, 2008), 45–53. Rosenne presents three main arguments: that the acquisition of territory captured in a war of self-defense is different from a war of aggression, that UN Security Council Resolution 242 is not self-enforcing, and that Israel is not expected to unilaterally withdraw from territories to fulfill its terms. It requires direct negotiations between Israel and its Arab neighbors and, according to Resolution 242, there is no requirement for Israel to withdraw fully from the territories it captured in 1967.

24 See "Recent Platform, as approved by the 6th Party Congress, May 1997"; and Idith Zertal and Akiva Eldar, *Lords of the Land: The War Over Israel's Settlements in the Occupied Territories, 1967–2007* (New York: Nation Books, 2014), 134–36.

25 Alan Baker, "Israel's Rights Regarding Territories and the Settlements in the Eyes of the International Community," in *Israel's Rights as a Nation-State in International Diplomacy*, ed. Alan Baker (Jerusalem: Jerusalem Center for Public Affairs and World Jewish Congress, 2011), 65–74; Klieman, *Compromising Palestine*, 69–82.

26 Statements on Jerusalem made by religious personalities before the Subcommittee on the Near East of the US House of Representatives, July 28, 1971, in *The Jerusalem Question and Its Resolution: Selected Documents*, ed. Ruth Lapidoth and Moshe Hirsch (Boston: Martinus Nijhoff, 1994), 252–61. Also see Karen Armstrong, *A History of Jerusalem: One City, Three Faiths* (New York: Harper Perennial, 1996), 37–55; Dore Gold, *The Fight for Jerusalem* (Washington, DC: Regnery, 2007), chap. 1; and Lee I. Levine, "Jerusalem in Jewish History, Tradition, and Memory," in *Jerusalem: Idea and Reality*, ed. Tamar Mayer and Suleimnan Mourad (London: Routledge, 2008), 27–46.

27 For a compilation of sayings, stories, and legends on Jerusalem, see Zev Vilnay, *Legends of Jerusalem* (Philadelphia: Jewish Publication Society of America, 1973). According to legend, when Jerusalem was burned and the Second Temple was destroyed in 70 CE, all the Jewish kings who had ruled until that point in time sat on the Western Wall and their tears saved it from being destroyed. Following the destruction of the

Temple by the Romans, the Jewish zealots, led by Bar Kochva, prepared for a revolt. In the meantime, the moderate wing of Judaism at the time, led by Rabbi Yochanan Ben Zakkai, accepted the foreign conquest of Jerusalem by including Jerusalem in every prayer and every Jewish religious and traditional ceremony.

28 Dore Gold quotes a Hadith that says "one prayer in my Mosque (Medina) is worth ten thousand prayers, and one prayer in the Aqsa Mosque (Jerusalem) is worth one thousand prayers, and one prayer in the Sacred Mosque (of Mecca) is worth one hundred thousand prayers"; Gold, *Fight for Jerusalem*, 88. For Jerusalem under Ottoman rule, see Armstrong, *History of Jerusalem*, 323–46. Compare with Issam Nassar, "Jerusalem in the Late Ottoman Period: Historical Writing and the Native Voice," in *Jerusalem: Idea and Reality*, ed. Mayer and Mourad, 205–23. Issam Nassar deals with the entire question of how conflicting parties use different historical narratives to strengthen their own cause and delegitimize the cause of the opponent. "Introduction," in *Jerusalem Question*, ed. Lapidoth and Hirsch, xix–xxix.

29 Quoted from memory.

30 Sari Nusseibeh refers to this in his book *Once Upon a Country*, saying that he publicly rejected Arafat's denial of any former Jewish presence in Jerusalem. Sari Nusseibeh (with Anthony David), *Once Upon a Country: A Palestinian Life* (London: Halban, 2013), 426. For more extensive descriptions, see Gilead Sher, "Negotiating Jerusalem: Reflections of an Israeli Negotiator," in *Jerusalem: Idea and Reality*, ed. Mayer and Mourad, 303–20; and Sari Nusseibeh, "Negotiating the City: A Perspective of a Jerusalemite," in *Jerusalem: Idea and Reality*, ed. Mayer and Mourad, 198–204.

31 Dr. Muhammad Abdul Rauf, "Meaning of Jerusalem to Muslims and the Holy City's Future," Hearing before the Subcommittee on the Near East, July 28, 1971, quoted by Lapidoth and Hirsch, *Jerusalem Question*, 261–67.

32 Yoav Gelber, *Palestine 1948: War, Escape and the Emergence of the Palestinian Refugee Problem* (Brighton, UK: Sussex Academic Press, 2001).

33 Khalidi, *Palestinian Identity*, esp. 203–9, and the footnotes on 264–65. Also see Salman Abu Sitta, "The Right of Return: Sacred, Legal and Possible," in *Palestinian Refugees: The Right of Return*, ed. Naseer Aruri (London: Pluto Press, 2001), 195–207; and Michael R. Fischbach, *Records of Dispossession: Palestinian Refugee Property and the Arab-Israeli Conflict* (New York: Columbia University Press, 2003). Compare with Meron Benvenisti, *Sacred Landscape: The Buried History of the Holy Land since 1948* (Berkeley: University of California Press, 2000); and Lex Takkenberg, *The Status of Palestinian Refugees in International Law* (Oxford: Clarendon Press, 1998).

34 Lapidoth and Hirsch, *Jerusalem Question*, 344–56.

35 Israel Labor Party Platform 1992 (in Hebrew). For a description of the relevant issues, see chapter 3.

36 Compare with Maher el-Kurd, Israeli-Palestinian Relations: An Appraisal and Background for a Position Paper, attached to letter from Maher el-Kurd to Yair Hirschfeld and Ron Pundak, April 19, 2001. For a more detailed discussion, see chapters 7 and 8.

37 See Asher Susser, "Jordan, the PLO and the Palestine Question," in *Jordan in the Middle East, 1948–1988*, ed. Joseph Nevo and Ilan Pappe (Newbury, UK: Frank Cass, 1994), 91.

38 This description is based largely on an interview with Maj. Gen. Oren Shachor who, on February 2, 1995, was appointed head of the Office of the Coordinator of Government Activities in the Territories (COGAT). In this position, Shachor was in daily contact with Rabin, and he would have at least one full hour a week alone with

him in which they discussed strategy, tactics, and operational issues related to the Palestinian Authority. Interview with Oren Shachor, August 21, 2012.

39   Interview with Nimrod Novik, August 16, 2012. Yitzhak Rabin, "Bli hafrada ein bitachon" [Without separation there is no security], April 8, 1993, in *Pursuing Peace: The Peace Speeches of Prime Minister Yizchak Rabin* (in Hebrew) (Tel Aviv: Zmora-Bitan, 1995), 83–85; Yitzhak Rabin, "Ein Heskem shekulam merozim mimeno" [There is no agreement everybody is pleased with], May 11, 1994, ibid., 112–20.

40   Interview with Nimrod Novik, August 16, 2012.

41   Shimon Peres, *Battling for Peace: A Memoir*, ed. David Landau (London: Weidenfeld & Nicolson, 1995), 388.

42   Ibid., 388–89.

43   As described above in chapter 4, Peres was adamant in insisting that the Palestinian Diaspora would not be given a role in the negotiations with Israel. Arafat, or other Palestinians, could be given Israeli approval to return to Gaza or the West Bank, but not back to Israel.

44   Interview with Yossi Beilin, February 29, 2012.

45   Ibid.

46   Sprinzak, *Brother Against Brother.*

47   Yair Hirschfeld to Yossi Beilin, Preparing for Israeli-Palestinian Final Status Negotiations, April 18, 1994.

48   Interview with Baruch Spiegel, August 17, 2012.

49   Interview with Baruch Spiegel, August 12, 2012; in COGAT, Baruch Spiegel was in charge of planning the comprehensive separation approach. Shaul Arieli was in charge of planning the fence.

50   When Netanyahu became prime minister in May 1996, he viewed the construction of the fence as an attempt to draw the border between Israel and the Palestinian Authority and he ordered that the work be stopped. Interview with Shaul Arieli, August 8, 2012.

51   Israeli Labor Party platform, 1992.

52   See Moshe Yaalon, "Introduction: Restoring a Security-First Peace Policy," in *Israel's Critical Security Needs for a Viable Peace*, ed. Dan Diker (Jerusalem: Jerusalem Center for Public Affairs, 2010), 12–21; and Uzi Dayan, "Defensible Borders to Secure Israel's Future," ibid., 22–33.

53   The common understandings reached referred to procedural issues of the work of the group, broad guidelines for a final status agreement, items to be included in such an agreement, and the need for further steps toward a peaceful regional environment for all the peoples of the area. "First Progress Report," November 1994; Yair's diary, October 4, 1994, 55–58, October 12, 1994, 103–4, and May 11, 1995, 430–31.

54   The reader should note the difference between East Jerusalem and Arab Jerusalem: East Jerusalem describes the territories beyond the June 4, 1967, lines; Arab Jerusalem describes the Arab neighborhoods of Jerusalem.

55   Klieman, *Compromising Palestine*, 137–57.

56   Yair's diary, November 13, 1994, 146–49.

57   Ibid., 149–50.

58   Ibid., February 16, 17, and 18, 1995, 327.

59   Ibid., March 3, 1995. 331.

60   Ibid., May 12, 1995, 437.

61   See chapters 6 and 8, where the logic of Nusseibeh's argument is described and analyzed in some detail.

62 Yossi Beilin discussed this with Faisal Husseini, and they agreed that the second phase of Permanent Status should be postponed for ten years.

63 Yair's diary, March 16, 1995, 341, 343. When the same question came up, years later, under Barak's premiership, the Palestinian position had changed and demanded that they be dealt with first. See chapter 7.

64 Meeting between Yossi Beilin and Abu Mazen, September 6, 1995.

65 Suleiman told me, for example, that he had helped Bashar Assad obtain an internship in an ophthalmologist's clinic in Britain, enabling Bashar Assad to become an eye doctor. When Bashar's brother, Bazil, died in a car accident and Bashar was ordered to become his father's successor, Abe told me that Bashar cried on his shoulder, saying, "Uncle Abe, I do not want to become a politician."

66 See Kurtzer et al., *Peace Puzzle*, 59–104, esp. the map on 66, of the "Syrian-Israeli Frontier, Relevant Lines: 1923, 1949, 1967." I knew that President Assad, who was Syrian minister of defense during the Six-Day War when Syria lost the Golan Heights to Israel, insisted on getting every inch of territory back.

67 When Uri Sagie became Israel's chief negotiator on the track with Syria, he convinced his counterpart, Rifaat Daud, and eventually Hafez el-Assad as well, that the June 4, 1967, line had to be reworked in a common effort. Uri Sagie, *Ha Yad she Kafa* [The frozen hand] (Tel Aviv: Yedioth Ahronoth, 2011), 37–46, 55–68.

68 Israeli Government Decision 563 of June 19, 1967, states: "Syria: Israel proposes the conclusion of a Peace Treaty with Israel on the basis of the international border and the security needs of Israel. A peace treaty will need: the demilitarization of the Syrian Height which is presently kept (*muchseket*) by Israel; an absolute commitment for the flow of water from the Jordan sources to Israel; Until the conclusion of the Treaty of Peace with Syria, Israel will continue to keep the territories presently under its control." Government Secretariat, Hachlata 563 shel hamemshala myom 19.6.67 (decision 563 of the Government on June 19, 1967).

69 "Preparing for Negotiations with Shlomo's Boss," December 8, 1995 ("Shlomo" was the code name for Abe Suleiman).

70 Martin Indyk, *Innocent Abroad: An Intimate Account of American Peace Diplomacy in the Middle East* (New York: Simon & Schuster, 2009), 82. See also Kurtzer et al., *Peace Puzzle*, 59–104.

71 Nimrod Novik, "Ikarej hadvarim im Martin Indyk" [The main issues with Martin Indyk], October 12, 1995; Indyk added that Christopher was extremely keen to achieve a breakthrough on the Syrian front.

72 Yair's diary, March 16, 1995, 347.

73 At Queen Beatrix's reception for the Israeli guests, her husband was far more interested in speaking to my wife Ruthie than to me. They discussed the Netherlands' role in World War II and its policies in regard to its Jewish citizens.

74 Yair's diary, April 27, 1995, 393–95 (the pages describe the visit to Jordan altogether; the quotation is from the end).

75 See Susser, "Jordan," 76; Sapir illustrated this by saying that keeping the territories could be compared with a child who bound himself to a tree and then would cry that the tree would not let him go. The protocols of these discussions are all kept in the Archive of the Israeli Labor Party, Beith Berl.

76 Susser, "Jordan," 76.

77 Ibid.

78 Note written by Ron Pundak, "Dan Abram's Group with Shimon Peres," June 25, 1995; compare also with my notes in the diary entry of June 27, 1995, 472–75.

79 Yair's diary, February 21, 1995.

80 Ibid., June 27, 1995, 475–76.

81 Interview with Yossi Beilin, December 22, 2011.

82 "Roundtable Discussion of an Interim Proposal: A Palestinian State with Sovereignty over Gaza/Jericho and Administrative Authority over the West Bank," 110–11.

83 Yair's diary, Vienna airport, February 21, 1995, 324–26.

84 Yonathan Lerner was Shlomo Brom's predecessor in the Strategic Planning Department.

85 Shlomo Gazit wrote about his experience establishing the Israeli administrative structure over the West Bank after the Six-Day War. Shlomo Gazit, *Ha-Makel veha-gezer: Ha-mimshal ha-Yisreeli bi-Yehudah ve-Shomron* [The stick and the carrot: The Israeli administration in Judea and Samaria] (Tel Aviv; Zmora Bitan, 1985).

86 Yair's diary, 335, report on the Caeserea meeting, 1995.

87 This concept was actually discussed at the Camp David Summit of July 2000 in great detail, when General Shlomo Yanai and Muhammad Dahlan were close to concluding an understanding along these lines. See Indyk, *Innocent Abroad*, 331.

88 Ze'ev Schiff, "Israeli Preconditions for Palestinian Statehood, Policy Focus: Special Studies on Palestinian Politics and the Peace Process," Washington Institute for Near East Policy; Research Memorandum 39, May 1999. ECF, "Jordan-Israel-Palestine Trilateral Security Regime," December 2, 1999; the paper referred to the general concept, the anticipated security powers of the Palestinian state—its demilitarization, a strong Palestinian police force, guarantees as part of the security regime—the peacekeeping force, monitoring and verification, the role of guarantors, the role of facilitators of confidence- and security-building measures, early warning arrangements, intelligence cooperation and sharing, and the building of a regional security system.

89 Interestingly enough, Rabin discussed this with Oren Shachor and said that with the responsibility of a state, any Palestinian government would have to take care of the security of Jewish settlers who would stay behind in a Palestinian state. Interview with Oren Shachor, August 21, 2012.

90 Meeting between Abu Mazen [Mahmoud Abbas] and Yossi Beilin, September 6, 1995.

91 Yair's diary, April 27, 1995, 409–10.

92 Fredy Zach and Gadi Zohar were hired by Daniel Abram, an American donor who was the former owner of the Slimfast corporation, to work on the Jerusalem issue, and we cooperated in studying all the relevant issues. Both groups also worked in full cooperation with Faisal Husseini and the Orient House, which belonged to the Husseini family and had become the symbol of Palestinian presence in Jerusalem.

93 The Israeli team at the seminar comprised Dan Seidemann, a lawyer specialized on Jerusalem affairs; Izchak Reiter, from the Institute for Israeli-Palestinian Studies at the University of Jerusalem; and myself. The Palestinian team comprised Mahdi Abdul Hadi, director of PASSIA Research Center; Sari Nusseibeh, director of the Palestinian Consultancy Group; and Bernard Sabella, professor at the University of Bethlehem. The French team was headed by Basma Kodmani-Darwish from the Middle East Studies Office at the Institut Français des Relations Internationales (IFRI), and comprised Dominique Moissi, assistant director at IFRI; Jean-Pierre Colin, professor of international law at University of Reims; and Simone Biton, cinema producer. Lucien Champenois and Roland Dubertrand from the French Ministry of Foreign Affairs participated as observers.

94 Report Re: Paris seminar on Jerusalem (May 13–14, 1995), May 17, 1995, 5.

95 Ibid., 6.

96 Letter from Faisal Husseini to Hans van Mierlo, July 6, 1995.

97 Amir Heshin, "Yerushalayim ir echat, rosh ir echad, stej rashuyot ironiyot ve iriyat gag" [Jerusalem one city, one mayor, two city administrations, one roof municipality], *Sivan Tashna*, June 1995.

98 Yair's diary, August 15, 1995, about the meeting on August 1, 1995, 543–44.

99 Ibid., 533–34. Yossi Beilin made this statement on July 16, 1995, at a meeting of the ILP at Beit Berl, which was originally convened to confirm his nomination as minister of economic planning. However, on the same day, a former chief of staff of the IDF, Motta Gur, had committed suicide, and the meeting was mainly dedicated to his memory.

100 Ibid., 508–10. My diary does not give the exact date. However, the discussion referred to took place early in July 1995, when Rabin informed Beilin that he was appointing him minister of planning in his government.

101 Interview with Oren Shachor, August 21, 2012.

102 Brig. Gen. Shlomo Brom, who was a member of the negotiating team for the Oslo II Agreement, remembered that the negotiators would meet with Rabin every Friday and would unsuccessfully attempt to obtain directives from Rabin. Interview with Shlomo Brom, January 5, 2012.

103 Interview with Maj. Gen. Danny Rothschild, January 4, 2012.

104 Gilbert, *Israel*, 468.

105 Rabin's speech to the Knesset, October 5, 1995; and ECF, "PM Rabin's Opposition to a Palestinian State," October 27, 1995. The aim of the paper was to convince our Palestinian interlocutors to adapt the proposed solutions to Rabin's concerns.

106 Interview with Oren Shachor, August 21, 2012.

107 The remark is a personal comment on a meeting we had in Stockholm July 4–5, 1995; Yair's diary, 514–15.

108 Ibid.

109 Ibid., September 6, 1995, 569.

110 Ibid., 568–69.

111 Yair's diary, July 23, 1995, 539–40.

112 Ibid., 540.

113 Author's notes, meeting, September 26, 1995. In a meeting I had with Arafat on September 11, 1995, together with Patricia Kahane and Ferdinand Lacina, Arafat remarked that final status issues "were too difficult and too complicated" and that one could not deal with all of them before the Israeli elections, but that "maybe" a Framework Agreement was feasible. Yair's diary, 598.

114 See also Idith Zertal and Akiva Eldar, *Lords of the Land: The War Over Israel's Settlements in the Occupied Territories, 1967–2007* (New York: Nation Books, 2014), 152–58.

115 Shabath, *Hamas*, 201–2.

116 Ibid., 232.

117 For the Israeli side, this was a frightening déjà vu. More than a year earlier, Rabin had asked Arafat to arrest Muhammad Deiff and had also received an evasive answer. See note 10 above. Samuel Katz, *The Hunt for the Engineer* (Guilford, CT: Lyons Press, 2002).

118 In its editorial comment of February 23, 1996, *Haaretz* made the following remarks: "There is nothing in the contacts that have taken place that commits

either the Israeli Government, or the leadership of the Palestinian Authority. It is reasonable to assume that both sides will seek to make many changes to the agreed formula. Contacts between academics, even when they take place with the backing of a Minister, and with the knowledge of two Prime Ministers, do not take the place of formal, official, diplomatic negotiations that are designed to finalize matters. However, the Oslo experience demonstrates that putting out feelers like this are a pragmatic technique, in an era of mass communications, wherein Governments are cautious in taking upon themselves the responsibility for exploratory contacts that are undertaken at their behest. Tactical considerations caused the Prime Minister to express reservations about the Paper, and to reject it although it was presented to him. . . . In terms of the substance, it can already be established that the basis on which future Israeli-Palestinian discussions will be built offers both continuity and encouragement" [taken from an official translation of the original text in Hebrew].

119   "Terrorism Deaths in Israel, 1920–1999," Israel Ministry of Foreign Affairs, January 1, 2000, http://www.mfa.gov.il/mfa/foreignpolicy/terrorism/palestinian/pages /terrorism%20deaths%20in%20israel%20-%201920-1999.aspx.

120   Gilbert, *Israel*, 593.

121   Nusseibeh, *Once Upon a Country*, 378.

122   Interview with Nimrod Novik, August 12, 2013.

123   "Beilin–Abu Mazen Understanding," October 31, 1995.

124   Ibid.

125   Israeli Ministry of Foreign Affairs, annex VI, particularly article viii, Israeli-Palestinian Interim Agreement on the West Bank and the Gaza Strip, Washington, D.C., September 28, 1995, 301–12. The annex related to a plethora of cooperation programs. To pursue this, Ilan Baruch from the Ministry of Foreign Affairs was appointed head of the Palestinian desk with clear instructions to build cordial relations between Israel and the Palestinian Authority. A discussion as to whether the people-to-people programs should be managed and overseen by the government or rather by civil society followed between him and the ECF. The ECF's position was that it made sense to detach government involvement as much as possible and to permit the civil society on both sides to pursue people-to-people activities.

126   Connie Bruck describes Nasr al Qidwa's "disappointment" with the Oslo Accords. Connie Bruck, "The Wounds of Peace," *The New Yorker*, November 14, 1996.

127   The *Cambridge Dictionary* defines "tunnel vision" or "tunnel thinking" as "the fact that someone considers only one part of a problem situation, or holds a single opinion rather than having a more general understanding."

128   John Paul Lederach, *Building Peace: Sustainable Reconciliation in Divided Societies* (Washington, DC: US Institute for Peace Press, 1997), 38–55.

Chapter 6

1   See chapter 5 above, where the discussion with Sari Nusseibeh is described.

2   The ECU was the forerunner of the euro.

3   Yair's diary, May 1996, 975–82.

4   Nimrod Novik was not in charge of the official transfer of government files to the incoming government. Interview with Nimrod Novik, October 4, 2013.

5   Yair's diary, May 1996, 982–86.

6   Meeting between Abu Mazen, Hassan Asfour, Yossi Beilin, Yair Hirschfeld, and Ron Pundak, June 1, 1996.

7   Ibid.

8   Yair's diary, June 1996, 986–91.

9   Ibid., 991–93.

10   Ibid., 993–94.

11   As a matter of fact, Dore Gold invited Hussein Agha to come to a dinner with Netanyahu, still before the inauguration of Netanyahu's government, on June 18. Because the invitation was spontaneous and came relatively late, Hussein missed this first opportunity out of a sense of insecurity and politeness. Ibid., 998–1004; interview with Dore Gold, January 22, 2012.

12   Nimrod Novik's notes on the meeting with Osama al-Baz, June 5, 1996.

13   Ibid.

14   Yossi Beilin also ran for the leadership of the Israeli Labor Party but lost to Ehud Barak.

15   Yuval Frankl-Rotem would engage in a coordinated brainstorming effort about how to best promote and improve relations with the Palestinians.

16   Quoted by Nimrod Novik, interview, October 4, 2013.

17   Yair's diary, July 1996, 1024–26.

18   Interview with Brig. Gen. Dov Sedaka, December 8, 2013. Although we cannot know for sure, it was highly unlikely that the minister of defense, Yitzhak Mordechai, would have made such a decision.

19   Yair's diary, July 1996, 1029. The Palestinian perception was that Netanyahu had intentionally insulted Arafat. Journalists asked about the helicopter incident at a joint press conference between Netanyahu and Arafat; see "Press Conference of Prime Minister Netanyahu and Chairman Arafat," September 4, 1996, given by Mahdi F. Abdul Hadi, ed., *Documents on Palestine: From the Negotiations in Madrid to the Post–Hebron Agreement Period* (Jerusalem: PASSIA, 1997), vol. 2, 286–88.

20   Interview with Dore Gold, January 22, 2012

21   Yair's diary, July 1996, 1026.

22   See "The Western Wall Tunnel – Update," Israeli Ministry of Foreign Affairs, September 29, 1996, http://www.mfa.gov.il/MFA/MFA-Archive/1998/Pages/The%20Western%20Wall%20Tunnel%20-%20Update.aspx; and "Kotel Tunnel Incident, 1996," Palestine Facts, 2013, http://www.palestinefacts.org/pf_1991to_now_kotel_tunnel_1996.php.

23   Yair's diary, July 1996, 1032–33.

24   Interview with Shalom Harari, June 22, 2012.

25   See chapter 3.

26   Yair's diary, July 1996, 1035.

27   The television documentary *One Million Bullets* tells the story of the events of the autumn of 2000.

28   Nimrod Novik, "The Meeting of the Six" [Hamifgash ha meshusha], February 3, 1998.

29   All these declarations are given by Abdul Hadi, *Documents on Palestine*, vol. 2, 294–96.

30   Demonstrating their annoyance, they would not even serve coffee to the Israeli delegation, ostentatiously disregarding the basic rules of hospitality. Interview with Dore Gold, January 22, 2012.

31   Dennis Ross, *The Missing Peace: The Inside Story of the Fight for Middle East Peace* (New York: Macmillan, 2005), 266. Ross's description is fully in line with what Netanyahu said publicly coming back from Washington when he spoke about a prevailing national consensus. Netanyahu's address to the Knesset, October 7, 1996.

32   The William and Mary Declaration, draft, November 21, 1996.

33   "Azam Azam speaks out on his captivity in Egypt," YouTube video, 2:02, posted by "infolivetvenglish," January 3, 2010, http://www.youtube.com/watch?v=SKBqFsq5kCk.

34   Interviews with Nimrod Novik, January 12 and 13, 2012.

35   This was as agreed in the Cairo Agreement of May 4, 1994, when the five-year count started.

36   "The National Agreement Regarding the Negotiations on the Permanent Settlement with the Palestinians," January 22, 1997. See also Haggai Hubermann, "Beilin et Eitan yechalku et Yerushalayim" [Beilin and Eitan will divide Jerusalem], *HaZofe*, January 31, 1997.

37   "National Agreement Regarding the Negotiations on the Permanent Settlement with the Palestinians."

38   Ibid.

39   Ibid.

40   Herb Keinon, "Jordan Valley Settlers Fume over Labor-Likud Position Paper," *Jerusalem Post*, January 10, 1997.

41   Huberman, "Beilin et Eitan yechalku et Yerushalayim."

42   Ross, *Missing Peace*, 293–322.

43   Note for the Record, January 15, 1997, given by Abdul Hadi, *Documents on Palestine*, vol. 2, 322–23.

44   Interview with Dore Gold, January 22, 2012; the related wording strongly influenced Barak and had a negative impact on his relationship with Arafat; see chapter 7 below.

45   Interview with Dore Gold, January 22, 2012; see also the discussion of Barak's approach to the same issue in chapter 7.

46   Dore Gold interview, where he referred particularly to a discussion with Lally Weymouth, the daughter of the owner of the *Washington Post*, who apparently was asked by Arafat to draw the attention of the Israeli team to this fact. Interview with Dore Gold.

47   Shaul Arieli and Shlomo Brom, who are both closely associated with the ECF, had a leading part in preparing the "interest map" within the IDF in 1994. See also the next note.

48   Dore Gold interview; interview with Shlomo Brom, January 24, 2012; Shlomo Brom said that when preparing the map, he was asked by Netanyahu to graphically insert "threatening tanks from the East" in order to make the point that Israel could not afford to make any territorial concessions on the West Bank. According to Brom's account, neither Netanyahu nor Dore Gold understood that President Clinton had been given the same presentation many times before. However, at earlier presentations the same arguments had been applied to provide the background for a very different, far more forthcoming strategic approach.

49   Nimrod Novik to Danny Naveh; January 17, 1997.

50   Dore Gold remembers that on the next day, after the signing of the Hebron Protocol, he went to see Dennis Ross, informing him that in order to keep the settler movement on board, Netanyahu would build Har Homa. Ross responded that this

would be difficult, but that the US government "would have to swallow it." Interview with Dore Gold, August 23, 2012.

51 Interview with Dore Gold, January 22, 2012.

52 Report from Nimrod on meeting between David Levy and Mahmoud Abbas, March 9, 1997; Ross, *Missing Peace*, 349–50 ff; "Chronology" given by Abdul Hadi, *Documents on Palestine*, vol. 2, 392–95.

53 Nimrod Novik, draft of "The Mubarak Initiative," May 3, 1997. This was a repetition of tactics we had employed in the summer of 1989, when Nimrod Novik and Ambassador Bassiouni suggested a "Ten-Point Initiative" to President Mubarak; see chapter 3 above.

54 Nimrod Novik to Osama al-Baz, May 18, 1997.

55 They had read Benjamin Begin's statement to *The New Yorker*, where he openly admitted that Likud intended to derail the Oslo Process. Connie Bruck, "The Wounds of Peace," *The New Yorker*, November 14, 1996.

56 Baker uses and explains the expression of "putting the dead cat at the doorstep"—i.e., putting the blame for the deadlock on one side. See James A. Baker III, *The Politics of Diplomacy: Revolution, War, and Peace, 1989–1992* (New York: G. P. Putnam's Sons, 1995), 443. Also see Ross, *Missing Peace*, 350.

57 Erekat was a PLO representative, and Naveh was the government secretary at the time.

58 Nimrod maintained contact with Danny Naveh regarding talks with Saeb Erekat, and with Yuval Rotem regarding the discussions in the four committees led by David Levy; Yossi Beilin was informed by Uri Savir about the Abu Ala'–Yitzhak Molcho channel, and on the Palestinian side, Yossi Beilin, Nimrod Novik, and Haim Ramon met regularly with Abbas and Saeb Erekat. Ron Pundak and I would be in ongoing contact with Hussein Agha, Ahmed Khalidi, and various other local Palestinian interlocutors, such as Faisal Husseini.

59 Nimrod to Ehud (Barak) and Yossi (Beilin), "Hasarnu," January 7, 1998; Nimrod to Yuval (Rotem-Frankl), "Hahachanot Hapalestiniot" [The Palestinian preparations], January 18, 1998; Nimrod to Ehud and Yossi, "Emdot roshhamemschala lemachar" [The positions of the prime minister for tomorrow], January 19, 1998; Nimrod to Ehud and Yossi, "Ikarej hasicha Albright–Mel Salberg of January 16–January 19, 1998" [The main points of the meeting, Albright–Mel Salberg, of January 16–19, 1998]; Nimrod to Ehud and Yossi, "Pgisha im Osama" [Meeting with Osama], January 25, 1998; Nimrod to Ehud and Yossi, "Hamitveh ha amerikai idkun" [The American approach—update], February 3, 1998; Yossi Beilin to Ehud Barak, "The February 5 Meetings in Cairo," February 10, 1998; Nimrod to Yair (Hirschfeld), "The Involvement of the European Union," February 15, 1998; Nimrod to Yair, Ron (Pundak), and Daniel Levy, "Update from Washington," February 15, 1998; Nimrod to Yossi, "The Return of the Host (Bassiouni)," February 23, 1998; Nimrod to Ehud and Yossi (and Yair and Ron), "Update: The Committees for the Interim Agreement and Permanent Status," February 25, 1998 (this report had papers attached on outstanding issues for safe passage, the Gaza Industrial Estate, and Gaza Airport); Nimrod to Ehud and Yossi, "Update," March 16, 1998; Nimrod to Ehud, "Update from Washington," April 15, 1998 (there is also a handwritten note from Nimrod offering additional oral explanations to Ehud Barak); Nimrod to Ehud, "Meetings in Cairo," April 29, 1998; Nimrod to Ehud, "The Dennis (Ross) Arafat Meeting (April 26), with Martin Indyk, Abu Mazen, and Saeb present," April 29, 1998; Nimrod to Yossi, "Update from London" (on the Albright-Arafat Meeting), May 5, 1998; Nimrod

to Yair, "Bibi-Lingo," May 6, 1998; Nimrod (to all), "Additional Information from London," May 8, 1998 (this report indicated that Netanyahu was already willing to accept the US suggestion of a 13 percent further redeployment but was still reluctant to go forward as long as Sharon insisted that Israel should not agree to more than a 9 percent further redeployment).

60 Nimrod to Yair and Ron, "Update on the Process," June 25, 1998; Nimrod to Ehud and Yossi, "Albright Fights Back," June 28, 1998.

61 Ross, *Missing Peace*, 415–59.

62 "Israeli-Palestinian Understanding Regarding Guidelines for Permanent Status Negotiations," second draft, March 30, 1999

63 "Yasir Arafat, Address to the Swedish Parliament, Stockholm, 5 December 1998 (excerpts)," *Journal of Palestine Studies* 28, no. 3 (April 1999): 143.

64 Ibid.

65 Ibid. In the text we had prepared, Arafat was asked to agree to the full demilitarization of the Palestinian territories. Arafat skipped this part, obviously not accidentally.

66 Yair Hirschfeld and Ron Pundik to Sten Andersen, "Three Weeks Later," December 24, 1998; Ze'ev Schiff, "A Very Careful Speech," *Haaretz*, December 6, 1998.

67 Document of the Stockholm group (Hussein, Ahmed, Ron, and me), "Israeli-Palestinian Understanding Regarding Guidelines for Permanent Status Negotiations," second draft, March 30, 1999.

68 ECF, "Aims and Strategies," February 21, 1999. This paper also said that it would be important to efficiently use the time period until the end of President Clinton's incumbency. We had no idea that this remark would be taken to the extreme by Barak to initiate what he thought were high-pressure tactics in negotiations.

69 Mari Fitzduff, *Beyond Violence: Conflict Resolution Process in Northern Ireland* (Tokyo: United Nations University Press, 2002).

70 Lena Endresen Fafo, "The People-to-People Program: Report by the Norwegian Secretariat in Jerusalem, 15 May 1996–31 July 1997."

71 See "Israel Health & Medicine: Israeli-Palestinian Health Cooperation, 1994–1998," Jewish Virtual Library, accessed March 10, 2014, https://www.jewish virtuallibrary.org/jsource/Health/pacoop.html. This report did not cover all activities and refers to 148 cooperative Israeli-Palestinian projects, involving 67 mainly nongovernmental organizations and 4,000 Israeli and Palestinian participants. See also "Palestinian-Israeli Cooperation: Building Bridges through Health" (annual report on ECF-PCH Health Cooperation Activities), Economic Cooperation Foundation and Palestine Council of Health, 1997, submitted by Hikmat Ajouri and Ron Pundik, February 3, 1998.

72 Sami Adwan, Dan Bar-on, Fidi Obeidi, and Julia Chaitin, "A Study of Palestinian and Israel Environmental Non-Governmental Organisations," Peace Research Institute in the Middle East, April 2000–August 2001, http://vispo.com /PRIME/palisenvngos.htm; and Michael J. Zwirn, "Promise and Failure: Environmental NGOs and Palestinian-Israeli Cooperation," *Middle East Review of International Affairs* 5, no. 4 (December 2001): 116–26.

73 Janet Aviad (CRB Foundation) and Sari Nusseibeh (Palestine Consultancy Group), "Belgian-Israeli-Palestinian Cooperation in Scientific Research and Education," December 4, 1996; for further activities, see CRB Foundation, "Proposal for Cooperation with Research Centers in Israel," February 1, 1999.

74 Sari Nusseibeh worked closely with Jibril Rajoub, who fully supported this approach. Sari Nusseibeh (with Anthony David), *Once Upon a Country: A Palestinian Life* (London: Halban, 2013), 411.

75 "Israeli-Palestinian Cooperation at the Municipal Level," presentation at FES EU Workshop, Brussels, December 10–14, 1997.

76 Cooperation North, "Agreement on Cross-Border Cooperation between the Israeli Municipalities of Haifa, Gilboa, and Emek Hamaayanot with the Governorate of Jenin," February 15, 1999.

77 The work on the industrial park was interrupted after the outbreak of violence in the area in 2001. Since then, a fence has been constructed on the Green Line in the area. However, cross-border trade has been renewed and is providing an important income to the Palestinian population of the Jenin governorate. At the time of writing, the Turkish Chambers of Commerce are investing $10 million to obtain the concession of the PA to develop the industrial park; the German government is providing a grant of the same amount to develop the onsite infrastructure, and the Government of Israel has committed to provide the necessary electricity and water.

78 On the basis of guidelines defined and agreed on by our working group on how to deal with the sewage issue, the German government offered the PA the financing required for the construction of a recycling plant. However, the outbreak of violence brought this project to an erstwhile end. In 2011, the renewal of the project was contemplated by the late governor of Jenin, Qaddura Mussa, and the mayor of the Gilboa Municipal Council, Dani Atar. The German municipality of Mannheim offered to sponsor the project. ECF is presently (as of the end of 2013) working on bringing about its implementation.

79 The Israeli Railway is presently constructing a railway line from Haifa to Beith Shean, and the connection to Jalameh is being studied largely on the basis of the concepts developed in 2000. Ali Shaath, who is responsible for the planning of the Palestinian transportation system, has told the author that it is essential that the line from Haifa to Jordan pass through Jenin.

80 At the time, agricultural thefts were substantially reduced. Governor Menasreh gave specific orders to his security teams to allocate stolen equipment and return it to Israel.

81 Presentation by Cooperation North to its European partners during a tour in Europe, March 14–20, 1999; protocol of meeting of the Steering Committee of Cooperation North, October 4, 1999.

82 Pinhas Yechezikieli, "Mitve letichnun astrategi b'nose' maarekhet ha lo-formaliim im ha palestiniayim" [Guidelines for strategic planning of cooperation with the Palestinians on the informal level], June 26, 2000.

83 Yossi Beilin's remarks, in Notes of Meeting with Fatah West Bank Leadership, A-Ram, April 2, 1997.

84 Interview with Avivit Hai, October 3, 2013.

85 A wonderful documentary film, *Dancing in Jaffa*, illustrates this; see http://www.dancinginjaffa.com.

86 See the analytical assessment under "Lessons Learned" below in this chapter, as well as in chapters 7 and 8.

87 Memorandum of Understanding, December 16–17, 1997.

88 These were in the incomplete draft titled "Israeli-Palestinian Framework Agreement on Security Permanent Status," May 26, 1999.

89 Article IV of the Israeli-Jordanian Treaty of Peace, October 26, 1994.

90 ECF, "Integrated Security Arrangements between Israel, Jordan and the Palestinian State: The Need, Main Characteristics, and the Possible Participation of Third-Party Forces," December 10, 1998; ECF, "Israeli-Palestinian Framework Agreement on Security Permanent Status," May 26, 1999; ECF, "Jordan-Israeli-Palestine Trilateral Security Regime," October 1999.

91 The first part of the agreement (articles 1–5) dealt with the trade regimen between the two parties, for which the idea was to permit the PA—during negotiations and after the declaration of the State of Palestine—to enjoy the comparative economic advantage necessary for economic growth. The concept would permit the Palestinians to preserve the benefit of the Customs Union (which had been established on the basis of the Paris Agreement) and to simultaneously enjoy the benefits of a Free Trade Agreement. The second part (articles 6–7) dealt with the Palestinian labor market and trade and investment. It assumed that trade with and through Israel was a significant factor for Palestinian economic growth, and thus provided for its necessary regulation. Article 8 dealt with monetary policies and the Palestinian financial market and defined conditions for the creation of an independent Palestinian currency without causing damage to the Israeli shekel or the Jordanian dinar. Articles 9 and 10 dealt with long-term planning and development cooperation and provided for a Joint Planning Team and cooperation—where requested (by the Palestinians)—in constructing the physical infrastructure of the State of Palestine. Article 11 dealt with refugee rehabilitation. It obliged the Palestinian side to grant priority to the economic rehabilitation of the refugees in the refugee camps in Gaza and the West Bank without undermining the economic stability of either the PA or Israel. Article 12 dealt with economic relations with Jordan. The other four articles dealt with various implementation mechanisms.

92 Pre-EPS model, February 1, 1998.

93 Report by Gidi Grinstein, March 7, 1999; "Sikum sadna al hesder hakeva hakalkali birgun habank ha-ulami vekeren hamadbea keren hamadbea habenleumit" [Summary of workshop on the Economic Permanent Status Arrangements with the World Bank and the International Monetary Fund], October 10, 1999; "Sikum bikur bwashington" [Summary of visit to Washington], October 10, 1999.

94 We produced papers that were given to the Peace Administration later on; see "Side Agreement on the Permanent Resolution of Palestinian Refugeeism," first draft, September 13, 1999; and "On Jerusalem," July 17, 2000.

95 In 1997, forty-one Israelis died as a result of Palestinian terror acts; in 1998, sixteen died; and in 1999, eight died. See "Terrorism Deaths in Israel, 1920–1999"; and "Report on Economic and Social Conditions in the West Bank and Gaza Strip" (Gaza: United Nations Office of the Special Coordinator in the Occupied Territories, April 1999).

96 As a matter of fact, I was tempted to call my account of the Oslo Process "Oslo: A Formula for Peace." When the second intifada started in September 2000 and peace negotiations were followed by an accelerating vicious circle of violence, the title "Oslo: A Formula for Peace" appeared to be not at all adequate.

97 Lev Grinberg, *Imagined Peace, Discourse of War: The Failure of Leadership, Politics, and Democracy in Israel, 1992–2006* [in Hebrew] (Tel Aviv: Resling Publishing, 2007), 204–8.

98 Interview with Yuval Diskin, October 6, 2013; the numbers are referred to above.

99 When one is writing history, the "what if" argument is always difficult, and needs somehow to be substantiated. In 1999 and early 2000, a former secretary-general of the settler movement, Othniel Schneller, prepared, together with Jamil

al-Tarifi, a file of civilian Israeli-Palestinian understandings, which—if they had been implemented—described, in much detail, the second phase of the "transit to state" that we had in mind. Its aim was to provide the Palestinian people with dignity and substantial components of statehood and create a situation where most components of Israeli occupation could be eliminated. See also chapters 8 and 10.

100   Nimrod Novik, report of February 3, 1998, where he notes that Dahlan and Asfour openly argued that a renewal of Palestinian violence against Israel was necessary to get the negotiating process back on track.

101   Interview with Efraim Lavie, who was in charge of the Palestinian desk in the Israeli intelligence forces.

102   Daniel C. Kurtzer, Scott B. Lasensky, William B. Quandt, Steven L. Spiegel, and Shibley Z. Telhami, *The Peace Puzzle: America's Quest for Arab-Israeli Peace, 1989–2011* (Ithaca, NY, and Washington, DC: Cornell University Press and US Institute for Peace Press, 2013), 116, 117.

Chapter 7

1   Ehud Barak received 1,791,020 votes, or 56.06 percent of the votes; Benjamin Netanyahu received 1,402,474 votes, or 43.92 percent of the votes.

2   The Economic Cooperation Foundation (ECF) was given a very clear lecture on this issue at a seminar we had organized in Milan at the beginning of July 1998. The Israeli Sephardic chief rabbi, Bakshi-Doron, had issued a statement saying that, from the religious Jewish point of view, it was important that the Temple Mount / Haram ash-Sharif should be managed by Islamic dignitaries, the Waqf. He wanted to meet the mufti of Jerusalem, who refused but instead sent his deputy to the workshop in Milan, causing Chief Rabbi Bakshi-Doron to send his confidant, Rabbi Shmuel Sirat from Saviyon. After having read Bakshi-Doron's statement, the vice mufti who attended the seminar asked to have a more private meeting with Bakshi-Doron's emissary, with Faisal Husseini, and with myself. In that meeting, the vice mufti asked whether it was true that according to Jewish belief, the Temple would descend from heaven. Rabbi Sirat's answer was" "Yes, this will happen on the Day of Judgment." The vice mufti asked, to reassure himself, "When?" and the rabbi repeated what he had said before: "On the Day of Judgment." With much relief, the vice mufti responded: "On the Day of Judgment is fine with me." However, Rabbi Sirat retracted: "I am not sure you understand. As God will replace the Temple on its place on the Day of Judgment, no Israeli government will have the legitimacy to sign away the sovereignty over Jerusalem."

3   This was explained to me by a member of the Shas Party in a rather amusing situation. My granddaughter Naama was born May 20, 1999, three days after Barak's election. When my daughter was in labor, my wife Ruthie, my second daughter Naomi, and I were sitting together in the waiting room of the hospital with a member of the Shas Party from Holon. To pass the time, we engaged in a longer conversation. Observing my beard and the "conservative" way that my wife and daughter were dressed, he assumed that the three of us were settlers, and told us that Shas would support Barak without hesitation in limiting settlement activities and even evacuating them.

4   See Lev Grinberg, *Imagined Peace, Discourse of War: The Failure of Leadership, Politics, and Democracy in Israel, 1992–2006* [in Hebrew] (Tel Aviv: Resling Publishing, 2007), 131–68.

5   Report of a meeting with Dan Kurtzer, Yair Hirschfeld, and Gidi Grinstein to Yossi Beilin, Nimrod Novik, Ron Pundak, Boaz Karni, and Daniel Levy, April 18, 1999 [in Hebrew].

6   See "Excerpts from the Statement Issued by the Palestinian Central Council," April 29, 1999.

7   Interview with Gidi Grinstein, August 21, 2012. Apparently no one among Barak's closest advisers made an effort to suggest to him that he think differently and follow Rabin's mode of reaching an agreement with the Arab parties in support of his government.

8   Interview with Nimrod Novik, January 24, 2012. See also chapter 6, particularly note 59.

9   Paper with the same title, May 22, 1999; and a final version that Nimrod Novik submitted to Barak, dated June 6, 1999.

10   The papers are being quoted, each separately, in this chapter.

11   ECF, "Contingency Planning for Permanent Status." Despite the ECF's excellent relations with the European Union and with several European governments, we did not succeed in achieving the necessary cooperation for such a European crisis prevention and/or crisis management role.

12   Reading Kurtzer et al., it appears that Barak succeeded in convincing the US peace team of the accuracy of this approach not merely at the time, but even after this concept had ended in disaster. See Daniel C. Kurtzer, Scott B. Lasensky, William B. Quandt, Steven L. Spiegel, and Shibley Z. Telhami, *The Peace Puzzle: America's Quest for Arab-Israeli Peace, 1989–2011* (Ithaca, NY, and Washington, DC: Cornell University Press and US Institute for Peace Press, 2013), 116.

13   Interview with Gidi Grinstein, August 21, 2012.

14   Interview with Motti Kristal; August 7, 2012; on the "Beilin–Abu Mazen Understanding," see chapter 5 above.

15   Interview with Yossi Beilin, February 29, 2012; interview with Efraim Lavie, Lavie said that a member of the peace team had convinced Barak that a 65 percent territorial deal would be possible. Interview with Shaul Arieli, August 8, 2012. Shaul Arieli, who was the secretary-general of the Peace Administration, was told by Barak that the aim of peace negotiations was to divide the West Bank between the Palestinians and Israel; interview with Gidi Grinstein, August 21, 2012. Grinstein explained that Barak viewed the West Bank as "disputed territory," which was in line with Israeli political thinking that had developed since 1967.

16   Remarks by Hussein Agha and Ahmed Khalidi in Stockholm, June 24, 1999.

17   See "The Sharm el Sheikh Memorandum on Implementation Timeline of Outstanding Commitments of Agreements Signed and the Resumption of Permanent Status Negotiations," The State of Israel, 1999, http://www.knesset.gov.il/process/docs/sharm_eng.htm.

18   Ibid. The timeline was influenced by the Palestinian argument that the interim period had ended on May 4, 1999, and that they intended—if negotiations failed—to proclaim unilaterally the State of Palestine.

19   Report of Hussein Agha to Yair Hirschfeld and Ron Pundak, January 18, 2000.

20   Interview with Dan Kurtzer, August 7, 2012.

21   Interview with Gidi Grinstein, August 21, 2012.

22   Nimrod Novik, "Oslo al pi Saeb" (Oslo according to Saeb), November 4, 1999.

23   Miftah, "Unilateral Peace," Jerusalem, October 30, 1999, http://www.miftah .org/KeyIssues/english/Oct30.htm.

24   Nimrod Novik, "Tmunat hamazav alpi Abu Mazen 7/11" [The picture of the situation according to Abu Mazen], November 8, 1999; Nimrod Novik, Mifgash Ehud-Arafat (Mozej 14/11) [the meeting with Ehud-Arafat]; Dennis-Arafat (15/11), November 17, 1999; Nimrod, Mu'm FAPS (Negotiations on a FAPS [Framework Agreement on Permanent Status]), November 29, 1999; Concept Paper: Framework Agreement, Prepared by the Legal Unit of the Palestine Liberation Organization's Negotiation Affairs Department, November 18, 1999.

25   Meeting with the Londoners, January 18, 2000; telephone call with H (Hussein Agha), January 22, 2000.

26   The immediate cause for their fight had to do with the way negotiations on a Palestinian prisoner release were led. The categories of the prisoners and the numbers related did not match, meaning that the prisoner release fell dramatically short of Palestinian expectations. A demonstration by the families of prisoners in front of Mahmoud Abbas's villa in Ramallah ended in stone throwing. Abbas understood, apparently wrongly, that the demonstrations had taken place at Dahlan's instigation. Interview with Sufyan Abu Saideh, February 24, 2013.

27   Nimrod Novik, Hamifgash Hameshusheh [The meeting of six], February 3, 1998.

28   Meeting with the Londoners, January 18, 2000.

29   Interview with Nimrod Novik, January 24, 2012.

30   Ibid. Apparently, Osama al-Baz sensed that Barak had scolded Novik and responded, "I understand." This was by no means an agreement to postponing the transfer of the three villages.

31   For further discussion of this issue, see chapter 5.

32   Miftah, "Unilateral Peace"; Novik, "Az ma haja lanu hayom? Pizuz b'erez" [What did we have today? A [negotiating] disaster at Erez], February 3, 2000.

33   Nimrod Novik to Prime Minister Ehud Barak, "Haaruz hapalestini" [The Palestinian track], March 6, 2000. It is interesting to compare these Palestinian statements with what they told us five years earlier in 1995, when they urged the Israeli side to move toward concluding peace with Syria first. See chapter 5.

34   For a more detailed description of the reasons of the breakdown of negotiations with Syria, see Uri Sagie, "Ha Yad she kafa" [The frozen hand]; Dan Yatom', *'Shutaf Sod* [The Confidant: From Sayyeret Matkal to the Mossad] (Tel Aviv: Yedioth Ahronot, 2009), 351; Dennis Ross, *The Missing Peace: The Inside Story of the Fight for Middle East Peace* (New York: Macmillan, 2005), 581–87; Aaron David Miller, *The Much Too Promised Land: America's Elusive Search for Arab-Israeli Peace* (New York: Bantam Books, 2008), 282–89; and Kurtzer et al., *Peace Puzzle*, 59–104.

35   Nimrod Novik, "Idkun tahalich" [Update of the process], April 9, 2000; Just as it had been important for Arafat to return to Gaza during Oslo, it became important for him to have the State of Palestine proclaimed now, permitting him to become a head of state rather than the chairman of the PLO. Ibid.

36   Nimrod Novik, "Tguva" [Response], April 10, 2000.

37   Ross, *Missing Peace*, 599–600.

38   Nimrod Novik to Prime Minister Ehud Barak, April 25, 2000; Gidi Grinstein, "May 17, 1999–February 6, 2001: The Permanent Status Negotiations," compilation; Grinstein quotes Hassan Asfour's comment: "We have nothing to add; we are the side that made a historical compromise in 1993." Unnamed Palestinian sources said that "Arafat is not expected to agree to Clinton's request to compromise on the issue of the size of the territory passed to the Palestinians in the PSA." Ibid.

39   Nimrod Novik to Prime Minister Ehud Barak, April 25, 2000.

40   Dennis Ross describes his own doubts and the way he overcame them, referring to a discussion he had with Muhammad Rashid and Yossi Ginossar, who described a possible compromise solution to him. Ross, *Missing Peace*, 610.

41   On March 7, 2000, Barak had made an offer to Arafat to try to reach a limited agreement. Israel would recognize the Palestinian State that would be established on 50 percent of the West Bank; 10 percent of the West Bank, including settlement blocs, would be under Israeli sovereignty, and the other 40 percent would remain in dispute; see Grinstein, "May 17, 1999–February 6, 2001," entry for March 7, 2000. At the ECF, it was understood that the 50:10:40 proposal had no chance of being accepted. The aim of the March 2000 ECF paper was to test the same concept—however, on more realistic terms.

42   As far as I can remember, the American team did not want—at that point in time—to discuss fallback options. By the end of June 2000, this would change. See below.

43   ECF, "Report on Washington Talks," May 11–12, 2000.

44   See chapter 5.

45   ECF, "Report on Washington Talks." We also informed the American team about EPS, joint urban planning of Jerusalem, the security regime in Jerusalem, cross-border cooperation, people-to-people activities, and macro financing.

46   Grinstein, "May 17, 1999–February 6, 2001"; the two negotiating teams in Stockholm decided to work on these three options, May 26, 2000.

47   Miller, *Much Too Promised Land*, 293–94; Ross, *Missing Peace*, 620–21.

48   Grinstein, "May 17, 1999–February 6, 2001," June 8, 2000, entry. It might be remembered that in January 2000, we already got a concealed indication that the Palestinians "would stop security cooperation with Israel," which was a coded way to say that violence might start.

49   In protest, Yasser Abed Rabbo resigned from the Palestinian negotiating team.

50   Nimrod Novik to Yossi Beilin, Yair Hirschfeld, Ron Pundak, and Boaz Karni, May 16, 2000. Novik added that Mahmoud Abbas's anger was directed at the Palestinians and not at the Israelis.

51   Hussein Agha's comment was, "The Americans played a dirty game," and Nimrod Novik corrected him, saying, "It was a stupid game"; Hussein Agha, Ahmed Khalidi, Nimrod Novik, Yair Hirschfeld, and Ron Pundak, May 18, 2000, handwritten minutes. The American peace team referred to Muhammad Dahlan as "our man." Interview with Dan Kurtzer, August 7, 2012.

52   Handwritten minutes of meeting on May 18, 2000.

53   Meeting on May 17, 2000, with Hussein Agha, Ahmed Khalidi, Yossi Beilin, Yair Hirschfeld, Boaz Karni, and Daniel Levy.

54   Handwritten report of the May 18, 2000, meeting with Hussein Agha and Ahmed Khalidi.

55   Handwritten report, May 18, 2000, meeting.

56   Handwritten report of a meeting between Yossi Beilin, Nimrod Novik, Boaz Karni, Ron Pundak, and Daniel Levy, June 8, 2000.

57   Nimrod Novik to Yair Hirschfeld, Ron Pundak, and Boaz Karni, May 19, 2000; at the same meeting, Yossi Ginossar stressed that action had to be taken to strengthen Arafat's position.

58   Yair Hirschfeld to Gilead Sher, June 6, 2000.

59   See Government of Israel, "Fifteenth Knesset: Government 28," The State of Israel, 2014, http://www.knesset.gov.il/govt/eng/GovtByNumber_eng.asp?govt=28.

60 Cited from memory.

61 Handwritten report meeting of June 8, 2000, after 2 p.m.

62 Interview with Efraim Lavie, March 14, 2012; interview with Shalom Harari, June 13, 2012; interview with Motti Kristal, August 7, 2012; interview with Shaul Arieli, August 8, 2012.

63 Interview with Efraim Lavie, March 14, 2012.

64 Interview with Shalom Harari, June 13, 2012.

65 Typed protocol of "Phone Conversation between YB and YH," Saturday, June 10, 2000; this was the first time in twenty years of cooperation that I thought it important to record a phone conversation with Yossi Beilin, indicating my awareness of the importance of the discussion and the emergence of a clear gap between our positions.

66 Framework Agreement on Permanent Status Between the State of Israel and the PLO, June 19, 2000.

67 Advantages of the Proposed Agreement, June 14, 2000.

68 ECF, "Preliminary Guidelines for a 1,000-Day Program for a Barak-Led Government," draft 1, June 15, 2000.

69 For a more detailed description, see note 71 below.

70 See ECF, "Preliminary Guidelines."

71 Here the idea was to work together with Presidents Mubarak and Clinton on a strategic understanding for the full implementation of all three parts of the Camp David Accords of 1978. Encourage a Donor Conference for Lebanon with Saudi, Syrian, Egyptian, and US support and renew Israeli-Syrian and Israeli-Lebanese peace negotiations.

72 Interviews with Othniel Schneller; September 28, 2013, and December 12, 2013.

73 Grinstein, "May 17, 1999–February 6, 2001," June 20, 2000, entry.

74 Ibid.; statement of Motti Kristal in a meeting at ECF, June 25, 2012.

75 Grinstein, "May 17, 1999–February 6, 2001," May 19, 2000 entry.

76 Interview with Dan Kurtzer (who at the time was US ambassador to Egypt); August 7, 2012.

77 Grinstein, "May 17, 1999–February 6, 2001," June 27, 2000, entry.

78 Miller, *Much Too Promised Land*, 294.

79 Interview with Nimrod Novik, January 25, 2012. Novik also wondered on what grounds Barak assumed that Arafat could not refuse his offer. Barak did not base his analytical assumption on "three hundred or more hours of discussions with Arafat" but rather "on reports of Israel's security services, written as a rule by twenty-year-old soldiers." Interview with Nimrod Novik, October 10, 2013.

80 Grinstein, "May 17, 1999–February 6, 2001," July 6, 2000, entry; according to Grinstein, Clinton's comment (obviously detached from reality) was, "This is the only way to make progress"; Barak's comment was, "This is an important moment in the attempt to solve the historical conflict."

81 Interview with Nimrod Novik, January 25, 2012; interview with Yossi Beilin, February 29, 2012.

82 Yair Hirschfeld to Rob Malley, July 7, 2000; I believe I added the proposal for a two-phase Permanent Status deal, but it is not attached to the letter in my archive.

83 Grinstein, "May 17, 1999–February 6, 2001," July 10, 2000, entry.

84 Ibid., July 12, 2000, entry.

85 Interview with Nimrod Novik, January 15, 2012; Miller, *Much Too Promised Land*, 305–7.

86   President Mubarak had told Barak that offering Arafat to establish his capital in Jerusalem would be the deal-maker and would make it possible to offer Arafat less than a 100 percent territorial deal. Interview with Nimrod Novik, October 10, 2013.

87   Gilead Sher, "Negotiating Jerusalem: Reflections of an Israeli Negotiator," in *Jerusalem: Idea and Reality*, ed. Tamar Mayer and Suleiman A. Mourad (New York: Routledge, 2008), 303–20. Sari Nusseibeh describes in his autobiography that "he shot down" Arafat's theory. Sari Nusseibeh and Anthony David, *Once Upon a Country: A Palestinian Life* (London: Halban Publishers, 2013), 430.

88   This became clear after the summit. Nimrod Novik described this in some detail in a report to Barak, saying that Mahmoud Abbas had asked Bassiouni to tell the Israeli side that whatever Dahlan, Hassan Asfour, and Muhammad Rashid said, they only represented themselves. Abbas's message said that "those 'youngsters' went to the Americans and said that Arafat might agree and this turned out to be wrong. Arafat never agreed to the positions that they presented. If anybody wants to meet them, this would be fine; but the Israeli side had to know that they had no authority." Nimrod Novik to Prime Minister Ehud Barak, August 14, 2000.

89   Ross, *Missing Peace*, 673–82; Martin Indyk, *Innocent Abroad: An Intimate Account of American Peace Diplomacy in the Middle East* (New York: Simon & Schuster, 2009), 312–15.

90   Grinstein, "May 17, 1999–February 6, 2001," July 17, 2000, entry; the Palestinian proposal was close to the various Plan B proposals prepared by the official Israeli negotiating team, as well as by the ECF. What would have made sense would have been to take the policy proposals that Othniel Schneller and Jamil Tarifi had developed as complementary steps to the establishment of the State of Palestine as an important milestone on the way to a Permanent Status Agreement.

91   Compare with Miller, *Much Too Promised Land*, 307–9.

92   The entire message of Barak to the US peace team is reprinted by Ross, *Missing Peace*, 676–77.

93   Interview with Nimrod Novik, January 25, 2012; Miller, *Much Too Promised Land*, 307–9.

94   Interview with Motti Kristal, August 7, 2012; interview with Shaul Arieli, August 8, 2012.

95   Grinstein, "May 17, 1999–February 6, 2001," July 26, 2000, entry.

96   Ibid., August 13, 2000, entry; Shlomo Ben Ami, *Scars of War, Wounds of Peace: The Israeli-Arab Tragedy* (New York: Oxford University Press, 2006).

97   Nimrod Novik to Prime Minister Ehud Barak, "Lepgishatcha im hamelech Abdallah" [On your meeting with King Abdallah], August 21, 2000. It should be remembered that Gilead Sher had headed the ECF team in 1998 and 1999.

98   Grinstein, "May 17, 1999–February 6, 2001," August 13, 2000, entry.

99   Interview with Dan Kurtzer, August 7, 2012.

100   Yossi Beilin's "private and personal" letter to Mahmoud Abbas, of September 20, 2000.

101   Rob Malley later told me that due to the discussions with me, the American peace team revised the concept and the text that they were preparing in order to deal with the refugee issue.

102   The paper suggested that Israel annex "no more than 6% of the territory of the West Bank and the yielding by Israel of territory of equal value." On refugees, Beilin–Abu Mazen language was adopted once again, going further to accommodate the Palestinians on some issues. It read: "The Parties thus agree to the full and agreed

implementation of UNGAR 194 (Article 11) as defined by the following arrangements," which were largely identical—only more specific—to what President Clinton would propose later on December 23. Altogether, the suggested US bridging proposal was what Mahmoud Abbas had called a "Beilin–Abu Mazen Plus Agreement." Nimrod Novik et al. to Rob Malley, enclosure, September 20, 2000.

103 Quoted by Akram Hanieh, "The Camp David Papers," *Al-Ayyam* (Ramallah), August 2000, 95–96, at 96. Clinton's four-point proposal on Jerusalem was more favorable to Palestinian demands than what had been concluded in the Beilin–Abu Mazen Understanding. In the understanding, Israel was to maintain a two-thirds majority in the joint municipality, a demand that was not repeated under Clinton's proposals.

104 Novik to Hirschfeld, Pundak, and Karni; cover note to "enclosure," September 20, 2000.

105 Meeting with Hanan Ashrawi, September 26, 2000.

106 Ibid. Arafat's paper also referred to a tacit understanding that the IDF would not enter 90 percent of Area B while the Palestinian security forces would be permitted to do so, and an arbitration clause with the appointment of the United States, the EU, and Egypt as arbitrators.

107 Interview with Gidi Grinstein, August 21, 2012.

108 Interview with Dov Sedaka, October 11, 2013.

109 See Article I, subparagraph 4, of the Israeli-Palestinian Interim Agreement on the West Bank and the Gaza Strip, Washington, DC, September 28, 1995, 38; the joint patrols would patrol twenty-four hours a day, and thus the teams became very close to each other.

110 Interview with Brig. Gen. Dov Sedaka, June 14, 2012.

111 Ibid.; compare also with the television program *One Million Bullets in October.*

112 Moshe (Bugi) Ya'alon, *Derekh Aruka Kzara* [The longer shorter way] [in Hebrew] (Tel Aviv: Yedioth Ahronot, 2008), 107–10.

113 Interview with Efraim Lavie, March 14, 2012.

114 Kurtzer et al. offer the following comment: "Although the Intifada was primarily spontaneous, Arafat embraced, it as he came to believe that it could serve as an instrument of pressure on the Israelis." Kurtzer et al., *Peace Puzzle*, 148.

115 Ross, *Missing Peace*, 730.

116 Quoted from memory. Aaron Miller, discussing the question of whether Arafat planned the outbreak of violence or not, writes, ". . . all agree that once the tiger of Palestinian violence was out of its cage, Arafat rode it, did little to moderate it, and in fact fed it to improve his own legitimacy." Miller, *Much Too Promised Land*, 308.

117 Ross, *Missing Peace*, 730–42.

118 Interview with Motti Kristal, August 7, 2012; interview with Shaul Arieli, August 8, 2012; When Sharon formed his government in February 2001, Motti Kristal handed all the details of the plan over to Omri Sharon and Uri Shani. The concept was later translated into a public plan prepared by Uri Sagie and Gilead Sher and published in August 2002 under the auspices of the Van Leer Institute. The plan created public pressure on Sharon to pursue a similar approach. When, eventually, Sharon planned his unilateral disengagement, Omri Sharon called Motti Kristal and asked for his help. Also see chapters 8 and 9 below.

119 Grinstein, "May 17, 1999–February 6, 2001," entry for November 28, 2000.

120 "Bpitaron hogen jesh lehakzot, 94–96% m'shetach hagada lamedina hapalestinait" [For a decent solution, 94–96% of the West Bank territory must be

given to the Palestinian State], *Haaretz*, December 31, 2000. For the English text, see Bill Clinton, *My Life* (New York: Random House, 2005), 936–37.

121   Nimrod to Prime Minister, "Markiwej Iska" [The components of the deal], December 31, 2000. Samih el-Abed, who was in charge of the territorial negotiations with Israel, told me that he wanted to convince Arafat to accept the Clinton proposals, but at the last minute refrained from doing so, understanding that Arafat had made up his mind and nothing could change it. Interview, October 11, 2013.

122   See Clinton, *My Life*, 938, 943–45.

123   Quoted by Grinstein, "May 17, 1999–February 6, 2001," January 24, 2001, entry.

124   Interview with Nimrod Novik, August 7, 2012.

125   Report on Meeting with Ahmed Khalidi and Hussein Agha in London and Follow-Up, January 29–30, 2001.

126   See PNC decisions, chapters 2 and 3.

127   See "Israel Labor Party Definition," *Zionism and Israel—Encyclopedic Dictionary*, www.zionism-israel.com/dic/Labor_Party.htm. On most issues, the wording was drafted very carefully to allow for compromise in the forthcoming negotiations; with regard to Jerusalem, the position that was outlined referred to a united Jerusalem under Israeli sovereignty, permitting Palestinian citizens to obtain a certain municipal autonomy.

128   The concept of the "iron wall" was first outlined in a centennial article written by Jabotinsky in the early 1920s. He was the leader of the Zionist revisionist movement, a teacher, and forerunner of the Israeli Likud movement. See: Yosef Heller, "The Positions of Ben Gurion, Weitzmann, and Jabotinsky in regard to the Arab Question: A Comparative Research" [in Hebrew], in *The Era of Zionism*, ed. Anita Shapra, Yehuda Reinharz, and Yaakov Harris (Jerusalem: Zalman Shazar Center, 2000), 203–40.

129   Ya'alon, *Derekh Aruka Kzara*, 230–51.

130   Meeting between Arafat and Clinton, April 20, 2000.

131   See note 36 above, and particularly Nimrod Novik to Prime Minister Ehud Barak, April 25, 2000.

132   Kurtzer et al., *Peace Puzzle*, 148.

133   Ibid., 151–53.

134   Ibid., 147.

135   Interview with Ed Djerejian, December 10, 2012.

136   Gidi Grinstein, who became a member of the Peace Administration and the Israeli negotiating team, remembers that he had an enormous advantage over the other officials due to the software he brought with him from the ECF and due to the fact that official government actors had not prepared themselves for Permanent Status negotiations. Interview with Gidi Grinstein, August 21, 2012.

Chapter 8

1   Barak's letter to Martin Indyk said, "At today's Government meeting, I brought to the Government's attention the contents of my letters of February 9, 2001 to President Bush and to Chairman Arafat, as well as letters to King Abdullah, President Mubarak, Prime Minister Persson and Secretary-General Annan. The Government took notice of the contents of these letters, reflecting the situation concerning the negotiations with the Palestinians. I alluded as well—and the Government took note

of it—to the negotiations with the Syrians, and ideas discussed in their framework. The rule nothing is agreed until everything is agreed applies to them as well. Copies of the letters to Chairman Arafat, King Abdullah, President Mubarak, Prime Minister Persson, and Secretary-General Annan are attached." Ehud Barak to Martin Indyk, February 11, 2001. The legal position was defined in a paper by the legal adviser of the Ministry of Foreign Affairs, "Hamamad hamishpati shel mazav ha massaumatan al mamad hakeva" [The legal situation of the negotiations on Permanent Status], Alan Baker (legal adviser) to Minister of Foreign Affairs and Director-General Ministry of Foreign Affairs, February 13, 2001.

2   Bill Clinton, *My Life* (New York: Random House, 2005), 944.

3   Interview with Daniel Kurtzer, August 7, 2012. Compare with Elliott Abrams, *Tested by Zion: The Bush Administration and the Israeli-Palestinian Conflict* (New York: Cambridge University Press, 2013), 5–7.

4   Interview with Aviad Friedman, April 19, 2012; Aviad Friedman is personally very close to both Ariel Sharon and his son Omri. Interview with Brig. Gen. Evval Gilady, June 17, 2012.

5   Interview with Eival Gilady, August 2, 2012; interview with Daniel Kurtzer, August 7, 2012. Also compare with interviews of Uri Shani and Yuval Diskin in *The Gatekeepers*, which is a 2012 documentary film that tells the story of the Israeli General Security Service (Shabak), as seen from the perspective of six of its former heads.

6   Protocol of meeting between Yossi Beilin and Mahmoud Abbas, Ramallah, April 30, 2001.

7   Report from Nimrod Novik, "Peres–Abu Ala' Meeting, September 3, 2001," September 5, 2001.

8   Alex Fishman, "Bzel ha intifada nimshach ha mum bein Israel lepalastinaim gam b'idan Sharon" [In the shadow of the intifada, Israeli-Palestinian negotiations continue], *Yedioth Ahronoth*, March 16, 2001.

9   Interview with Eival Gilady, June 17, 2012.

10   Arafat boycotted Abbas after Abbas met with US secretary of state Colin Powell without reporting to Arafat first. Hassan Asfour, who had enjoyed Abbas's support during the early 1990s, had become Abbas's worst enemy and demanded that Arafat take even further steps to ostracize Abbas, suggesting that the PLO reject funding from the US Agency for International Development as that money served to strengthen the Abbas camp. Nimrod Novik to Eylon Yavetz (ECF), July 25, 2001.

11   Report from Rob Malley on a meeting with Marwan Barghouti, April 26, 2001.

12   Meeting of Yossi Beilin and Mahmoud Abbas, April 30, 2001. On the Palestinian approach to negotiations, see Maher el-Kurd, "Israeli-Palestinian Relations: An Appraisal and Background for a Position Paper," attached to letter from Maher el-Kurd to Yair Hirschfeld and Ron Pundik, Ramallah, April 19, 2001.

13   Interview with Brig. Gen. Baruch Spiegel, March 5, 2012.

14   Interview with Brig. Gen. Ehud Dekel, March 14, 2012. The Syrian leadership even played with the idea of encouraging militant action against Israel in the Golan Heights. However, a very strong message from Jerusalem to Damascus made it clear that such action would result in a very powerful Israeli reprisal and convinced the Syrian leadership to refrain from provoking violence in the Golan Heights.

15   Dore Gold, *Hatred's Kingdom: How Saudi Arabia Supports the New Global Terrorism* (Washington, DC: Regnery, 2003).

16   The Iranian government supported and instigated demonstrators who carried slogans reading "Marg-e Yisrael," which means "Death to Israel." Alireza Jafarzadeh,

The Iran Threat: President Ahmadinejad and the Coming Nuclear Crisis (New York: Palgrave Macmillan, 2007), 192–93, 208–9.

17 Ibid., part IV, "March to the Bomb," 125–200.

18 Abrams, *Tested by Zion*, 6–7.

19 See, for instance, Dennis Ross, *The Missing Peace: The Inside Story of the Fight for Middle East Peace* (New York: Macmillan, 2005), 753–58; It was clear that President Clinton bitterly resented Arafat. Right before Clinton left office, he told Arafat, "I am not a great man. I am a failure and you have made me one." Clinton, *My Life*, 944.

20 Interview with Eival Gilady, June 17, 2012. The sense of confidence between Jerusalem and Washington was reinforced by the fact that any emerging strategy could be discussed with Elliott Abrams, who was in charge of the Middle East in the National Security Council. The two closest advisers to Prime Minister Sharon, Dov Weissglas and Eival Gilady, worked closely with him. See Abrams, *Tested by Zion*, 9–13.

21 Interview with Yossi Beilin, February 29, 2012.

22 Eylon Javetz and Yael Banaji, "Constructing a Mountain of Peace: Transforming the Meanings of the Temple Mount—Harem ash-Sharif towards an Israeli Palestinian Peace Agreement," paper written for the ECF, April 2001.

23 Ibid.

24 Eylon Javetz, "Deficiencies in the Israeli 'Permanent Status' Peace Strategy and Some Initial Recommendations," paper submitted to the ECF, twentieth draft, February 2002.

25 The policy papers were: Riad Malki, "The Future Administration of Jerusalem: The Municipality Aspect," Arab Studies Society, London, and Orient House, Jerusalem, April 2001; Riad Dajani, "Considerations for Future Economic Cooperation between East and West: Jerusalem—The Open City," Orient House, Jerusalem, April 2001; Manuel Hassassian, "The Palestinian/Israeli Security Arrangements in Jerusalem: An Open City, Jerusalem, 2001; unnamed author, "Legal Status and Regime for Jerusalem," draft; Rotem M. Gilady, "Jerusalem: A Capital City of Two States? An Introductory Survey of Legal and Practical Problems and Prospects," April 20, 2001 (Rotem Gilady is a fellow researcher, Jerusalem Institute for Israel Studies); Elinoar Barzaccchi, "Jerusalem in Peace: One City, Two Capitals—Organization of Municipal Services—Independent, Coordinated, Joint," April 2001; Shai Javetz, "Policing Jerusalem in Peace" (Yerushalayim-Al-Quds), February 2001; Issaschar Ben-Haim, "The Economy of Jerusalem," January 2001; Michael Karayanni, "A Legal Model for Jerusalem the Capital and Jerusalem City," February 2001; Menahem Klein, "Jerusalem as an Open City," April 2001; Riad Malki, "Jerusalem: Open City—London Track"; and Nazmi al-Jubeh, "The Holy Basin," April 2001.

26 Marwan Muasher gives an account of the Jordanian efforts to engage the United States and the international community in a more proactive role. Marwan Muasher, *The Arab Center: The Promise of Moderation* (New Haven, CT: Yale University Press, 2008), 134–75.

27 Interview with Ron Shatzberg, September 6, 2012.

28 Othniel Schneller publicly suggested unilaterally recognizing a Palestinian State, establishing a security fence, and relocating settlements into settlement blocs while simultaneously establishing good neighborly relations with the Palestinians. Othniel Schneller, "Shkenut weshituf peula b'header shalom: Tfisat hahafrada a terro-demografit hahadzdadit kmanof legibush heskem kewa b'atid" [Neighborhood and cooperation under no peace conditions: The concept of a territorial-demographic separation as a lever for a Permanent Status Agreement], *Yedioth Ahronoth*, June 2001.

29 Report from Rob Malley on meeting with Marwan Barghouti, April 26, 2001: Rob Malley stated that "Barghouti appeared very relaxed and open. He began the meeting with his central message: there will be no end to the intifada until an end to the occupation. I [R. M.] asked how he believed the intifada could produce this or any territorial gain; he claimed that the Israeli public would move, in fact had been moving, and would realize that was the price to an end of the uprising."

30 The Maher el-Kurd paper said, "It will take one, or at most two more generations for the Apartheid policy imposed by Israel to run its full course and reach its logical conclusion, an historical process that will avoid the partition of Palestine between the two peoples, and the eventual creation of a democratic and secular state for all its citizens west of the Jordan river." See also note 12 above.

31 Interview with Gen. Baruch Spiegel, March 5, 2012.

32 Nimrod Novik to Yossi Beilin, Yair Hirschfeld, Ron Pundak, Boaz Karni, Daniel Levy, Avrum Burg, and Yuval Rotem. "Tikvot Israel: Hityachsut rishonit" [Israeli hopes: A first comment], February 20, 2001. Also see Novik's two follow-up papers: "Action Plan for the Cessation of Violence, Rebuilding of Confidence, and Resumption of Negotiations," May 21, 2001, which already refers to Mitchell Report; and "Transition to Permanent Status (TPS)," May 22, 2001.

33 Interview with Eival Gilady, June 17, 2012.

34 ECF, "International Stability Pact for the Middle East," February 20, 2001.

35 As a result of my suggestion, my personal popularity increased and I received various suggestions to cooperate on preparing the concept for such a trusteeship.

36 ECF, "Economic and Infrastructure Conditions in the PA," February 13, 2001.

37 See, e.g., letter from Yair Hirschfeld to Daniel Kurtzer, April 11, 2002, reporting on a meeting with Tzipi Livni, where she proposed a donor relief program for the Palestinians that would be led by the US Agency for International Development, as well as several other steps to be discussed with US secretary of state Powell at his—then—forthcoming visit.

38 Report of the Sharm el-Sheikh Fact-Finding Committee, April 30, 2001.

39 The chairman of the committee was former Senator George J. Mitchell; the members were Suleyman Demirel, ninth president of the Republic of Turkey; Thorbjoern Jagland, minister of foreign affairs of Norway; Warren B. Rudman, former member of the US Senate; and Javier Solana, high representative for the European Union's Common Foreign and Security Policy.

40 ECF, "Recommendations to the Mitchell Commission," April 12, 2001.

41 The official text read: "In order to provide an effective political context for practical cooperation between the parties, negotiations must not be unreasonably deferred and they must, in our view, manifest a spirit of compromise, reconciliation and partnership, notwithstanding the events of the last seven months." Report of the Sharm el-Sheikh Fact-Finding Committee, 31.

42 Ibid.

43 At the time, Schneller was living in a settlement in northeast Jerusalem, but he would later work with Prime Minister Sharon on a plan to not only restrict but also evacuate/relocate settlements.

44 Daniel Kurtzer recollected that according to Secretary of State James Baker, detailed settlement restrictions had been negotiated in return for the US loan guarantee for which the Israeli government was asking in the early 1990s. Interview with Daniel Kurtzer, August 2, 2012.

45 ECF, "Recommendations to the Mitchell Commission."

46 Apparently, Senator Mitchell did not learn from this mistake. When President Obama appointed him peace envoy to the Middle East, he took the same approach, resulting in a failed mission. Mahmoud Abbas commented to Hussein Agha that "Senator Mitchell has put me up on a tree and I have no ladder to climb down." Meeting with Hussein Agha in Zurich, September 2010.

47 Handwritten protocol by Yael Banaji, "Meeting with Jeff Feltman and John Listen," June 28, 2001.

48 For the Egyptian-Jordanian Initiative, see Muasher, *Arab Center*, 108–11.

49 Protocol of Meeting of Yossi Beilin with Mahmoud Abbas, Ramallah, April 30, 2001.

50 UN Security Council Resolution 1373; see also Abrams, *Tested by Zion*, 20–22.

51 The dialogue between the Saudis and Secretary of State Powell started in June 2001, when the Saudis attempted to assert strong pressure on the United States to intervene in the Israeli-Palestinian conflict. See Abrams, *Tested by Zion*, 14–15.

52 "Protocol: Meeting with Nabil Shaath, at Gaza-Erez," September 6, 2001.

53 Monthly ECF Report to Labor ministers (Daliya Iziq, minister of trade and industry; Avram Burg, chairman of the Knesset; Benjamin Ben Eliezer, minister of defense; Matan Wilnai, minister of science, culture, and sport; Salah Tarif, minister without portfolio; Raanan Cohen, minister without portfolio; Efraim Sneh, minister of transport; Shimon Peres, minister of foreign affairs; and Shalom Simhon, minister of agriculture), "Subject: A Change?" September 23, 2001. See also an anonymous Palestinian paper, "The Road Ahead: Palestinian Policy in the Wake of the US Terror Attacks" (*sic*), September 16, 2001.

54 "Minister of Tourism Rehavam Zeevi Assassinated at Point-Blank Range in Jerusalem Hyatt," *Globes*, October 17, 2001.

55 Saeb Erekat described the "recent Euro visitors" (Solana, Fischer, et al.) as being "'more Catholic than the pope" in adopting the Sharon line of "don't let Arafat off the hook"; Report on Meeting between Yossi Beilin and Saeb Erekat, Jericho, October 26, 2001.

56 Report on Meeting with German Foreign Minister Fischer; Tel Aviv, October 26, 2001. The European "security group" was the forerunner of a more substantial European and US security presence on the ground. See chapter 9.

57 Interview with Admiral Ami Ayalon, in the film *The Gatekeepers*.

58 Interview with Boaz Karni, Ron Schatzberg, and Motti Kristal, August 7, 2012.

59 Report on Meeting with German foreign minister Fischer, Tel Aviv, October 26, 2001.

60 Quoted by Daniel C. Kurtzer, Scott B. Lasensky, William B. Quandt, Steven L. Spiegel, and Shibley Z. Telhami, *The Peace Puzzle: America's Quest for Arab-Israeli Peace, 1989–2011* (Ithaca, NY, and Washington, DC: Cornell University Press and US Institute for Peace Press, 2013), 163.

61 Interview with Shalom Harari, June 21, 2012; interview with Eival Gilady, August 2, 2012.

62 Ibid.; Bush speech, June 24, 2002; Kurtzer et al., *Peace Puzzle*, 164–67. See also Condoleezza Rice, *No Higher Honor: A Memoir of My Years in Washington* (New York: Random House, 2011), 131–35; and Abrams, *Tested by Zion*, 24–27.

63 Interview with Gen. Baruch Spiegel, March 5, 2012; "Bomb Kills Palestinian Military Chief," *Los Angeles Times*, January 15, 2002.

64   Interview with Eival Gilady, August 2, 2012. For the text of the Zinni proposal, see "Zinni's ceasefire plan: Israeli-Palestinian ceasefire plan proposed by US envoy Anthony Zinni on 26 March 2002," al-bab.com: An Open Door to the Arab World, last modified June 18, 2009, http://www.al-bab.com/arab/docs/pal/zinni2002a.htm.

65   "Terrorist Attack against the Park Hotel in Netanya (2002)," Israel Security Agency, 2010, http://www.shabak.gov.il/English/History/Affairs/Pages/theParkHotel inNetanya.aspx.

66   This was a conclusion reached by an internal IDF report written immediately after Operation Defensive Shield. The team writing the report was headed by Baruch Spiegel. See the documents quoted in notes 70 and 72 below.

67   Quoted by Kurtzer et al., *Peace Puzzle*, 167.

68   UN Security Resolution 1397, March 17, 2002; see note 78.

69   Ad Hoc Liaison Committee, informal donor meeting, Oslo, April 25, 2002; World Bank, "Two Years of Intifada, Closures, and Palestinian Economic Crisis: An Assessment," March 2003; interview with Shalom Harari, June 21, 2012.

70   IDF source, June 16, 2002; as well as World Bank, "Two Years of Intifada."

71   For the full text of UN Security Council Resolution 1397, see www.mideastweb .org/1397.htm.

72   See www.al-bab.com/arab/docs/league/peace02.Int_ and note 74; on the US reaction, see Abrams, *Tested by Zion*, 28–45.

73   Muasher, *Arab Center*, 135.

74   Nimrod Novik, "From Crises to Process," May 7, 2002.

75   Nimrod Novik, "Sikum bikur Osama: Emdat mizrayim" [Summary of Osama's visit: The Egyptian position], May 31, 2002.

76   He said: "Frankly, we want to go back to June 4, 1967, borders including (resolving) the refugees and Jerusalem issues. The solution is as the Arab initiative stipulated acknowledging the right of return (based on UN resolution 194) with an agreement on implementation and mechanism of such an implementation. In return, Israel gets normal relations (with the Arabs). Israel or the United States must not divide the initiative. . . . The Arab initiative is a full package; either accept it as a whole or nothing." Mahmoud Abbas, interview with *Al-Ayyam*, May 7, 2002.

77   White House Office of the Press Secretary, "President Bush Calls for New Palestinian Leadership," June 24, 2002, http://georgewbush-whitehouse.archives.gov /news/releases/2002/06/20020624-3.html.

78   German "Non-Paper," attached to RL 300, "US Plan Bush Rede und US Talking Points." Berlin, June 26, 2002 (the document was classified as "confidential"). It is difficult to overlook the conceptual similarity between the German proposal and the conceptual ideas that Nimrod Novik and I had launched before the Camp David Summit of July 2000.

79   "The Program of Reform," as prepared by the Ministerial Reform Committee and approved by President Arafat, "100 Days Plan of the Palestinian Government (with Reference to the Presidential Decree of 12 June 2002)," June 23, 2002; Reform Agenda of the Palestinian Government, July 9, 2002, 1–18; the latter document was prepared for the Quartet meeting in mid-July.

80   For a detailed description of the political action led by Egypt, Jordan, and Saudi Arabia, see Muasher, *Arab Center*, 134–75. Muasher describes meeting with Secretary of State Powell before the Quartet meeting. Powell assured him that "Sharon was ready to move forward" and that "the Arab Initiative would not be ignored and stressed the need for security reforms within the Palestinian Authority." Ibid., 157.

81   Ibid., 162–63. Compare also with Kurtzer et al., who give a more United States–centric account of the diplomatic moves leading to the acceptance of the Performance Based Roadmap to Peace in the Middle East; see Kurtzer et al., *Peace Puzzle*, 174–78.

82   "A Performance-Based Roadmap to a Permanent Two-State Solution to the Israeli-Palestinian Conflict" (press statement, US Department of State Archive), April 30, 2003, http://2001-2009.state.gov/r/pa/prs/ps/2003/20062.htm.

83   See Dov Weissglas, *Arik Sharon: Rosh Hamemshala—Mabat Ishi* [Arik Sharon: A prime minister] (Tel Aviv: Yedioth Ahronot, 2012), 180–84, 216. Compare with Rice, *No Higher Honor*, 280. Rice writes: "In accepting the Road Map for Peace in the Middle East and speaking forcefully about the need to make 'painful concessions,' in 2003, the Israeli prime minister (Sharon) had put himself firmly on the side of a two-state solution."

84   "Israeli Cabinet Statement on Road Map and 14 Reservations," May 25, 2003. The two most important reservations were "5. The character of the provisional Palestinian state will be determined through negotiations between the PA and Israel. The provisional state will have provisional borders and certain aspects of sovereignty, be fully demilitarized with no military forces, but only with police and internal security forces of limited scope and armaments, be without the authority to undertake defense alliances or military cooperation, and Israeli control over the entry and exit of all persons and cargo, as well as of its air space and electromagnetic spectrum"; and "6. In connection to both the introductory statements and the final settlement, declared references must be made to Israel's right to exist as a Jewish state and to the waiver of any right of return for Palestinian refugees to the State of Israel." See "Israel's Response to the Road Map, May 25, 2003," The State of Israel, 2003, http://www.knesset.gov.il/process/docs/roadmap_response_eng.htm. Parallel to the Israeli response was the Palestinian one, in which the roadmap was nominally accepted, with serious reservations, particularly with regard to phase two, which once again seriously impeded its possible implementation. See PLO Negotiations Affairs Department, *The Road Map Obligations: Road Map Status Report: Phase 1*, May 5, 2003, available at www.nad-plo.org.

85   See Weissglas, *Arik Sharon.*

86   Interview with Baruch Spiegel, March 5, 2012; IDF source, June 16, 2002.

87   Interview with Eival Gilady, August 2, 2012; and Weissglas, *Arik Sharon*, 208–30.

88   Uri Sagie and Gilead Sher, *Niyar Emda Medini* [A political position paper] (Jerusalem: Van Leer Institute, 2002).

89   Ibid., 65–66.

90   Yeshayahu Folman, *Sipura shel Geder Hafrada* [The story of the security fence] (Jerusalem: Carmel, 2003), 64–72.

91   Matthew Gutman and David Rudge, "Groundbreaking Begins for West Bank Fence," *Jerusalem Post*, June 11, 2002

92   "The Geneva Accord: A Model Israeli-Palestinian Peace Agreement—Draft Permanent Status Agreement—Full Text," www.geneva-accord.org/mainmenu/english.

93   See "Knesset Election Results: January 28, 2003," Israel Ministry of Foreign Affairs, 2013, http://mfa.gov.il/MFA/AboutIsrael/History/Pages/Knesset%20Election%20Results.aspx.

94   Compare with Kurtzer et al., *Peace Puzzle*, 161–64.

95   In his biography of Ariel Sharon, Dov Weissglas stresses that when the Government of Israel accepted the roadmap with fourteen reservations, the government decision clearly referred to and committed to the two-state solution.

Chapter 9

1 See Alireza Jafarzadeh, *The Iran Threat: President Ahmadinejad and the Coming Nuclear Crisis* (New York: Palgrave Macmillan, 2007), 39–58 (the chapter is titled "Iran's Grand Plan"). For a different view, see Hooman Majd, *The Ayatollah Begs to Differ: The Paradox of Modern Iran* (New York: Anchor Books, 2008). In a RAND Corporation study of Iran, the following is said in this context: "Although the US invasions of Afghanistan and Iraq eliminated Iran's most serious regional adversaries, it still faced serious threats with the potential to wreak internal havoc. The spread of crime, weapons and sectarian tensions from Iraq has animated ethnic activists in the provinces of Kurdistan and Khuzestan, and even in the eastern province of Baluchistan. . . . Finally, the Islamic leadership continues to perceive an existential threat posed to the Islamic Republic by the US." Frederic Wehrey, David E. Thaler, Nora Bensahel, Kim Cragin, Jerrold D. Green, Dalia Dassia Kaye, Nadia Oweidat, and Jennifer Li, *Dangerous but Not Omnipotent: Exploring the Reach and Limitations of Iranian Power in the Middle East* (Washington, DC: RAND Corporation, 2009).

2 On the Iranian asymmetric strategy, see Wehrey et al., *Dangerous but Not Omnipotent*, chaps. 3, 4, and 5. The Iranians had no difficulties using the UN platform for threats against Israel. I myself participated at the end of January 2009 in a panel discussion at the UN in Geneva with all the accredited ambassadors in the audience. In response to my remark saying that since 1967 I had fought against Israel's occupation of the Palestinian territories, the Iranian ambassador stood up and demanded that Israel "end the occupation of 1948."

3 See David Petraeus, "Gen. Petraeus' Testimony to the Senate Armed Services Comm.," *Real Clear Politics*, April 8, 2008, http://www.realclearpolitics.com/articles/2008/04/gen_petraeus_testimony_to_the.html.

4 Compare with Daniel C. Kurtzer, Scott B. Lasensky, William B. Quandt, Steven L. Spiegel, and Shibley Z. Telhami, *The Peace Puzzle: America's Quest for Arab-Israeli Peace, 1989–2011* (Ithaca, NY, and Washington, DC: Cornell University Press and US Institute for Peace Press, 2013), 174–78.

5 Ibid., 176. A completely unrealistic timeline of two years was being sought.

6 Kurtzer et al., *Peace Puzzle*, 178; compare with Elliott Abrams, *Tested by Zion: The Bush Administration and the Israeli-Palestinian Conflict* (New York: Cambridge University Press, 2013), 48 ff.

7 Dov Weissglas, *Arik Sharon: Rosh Hamemshala—Mabit Ishi* [Arik Sharon: A prime minister] (Tel Aviv: Yedioth Ahronot, 2012), 190. Abrams described the way he read Sharon's intention as follows: "Sharon's goals appeared to me to be to build the fence, stop the terrorism, and get to Phase II of the Roadmap. That would mean negotiations over the existence of a Palestinian state and of its provisional borders, and significant withdrawals in the West Bank and Gaza, but it would not mean dealing with all the most sensitive final status issues (including Jerusalem) or a full withdrawal to whatever the final borders would be." Abrams, *Tested by Zion*, 68.

8 Weissglas, *Arik Sharon*. However, Mahmoud Abbas would later refuse to accept phase two of the roadmap.

9 Ibid., 192–93.

10 Ibid., 192–207.

11 Abrams describes in some detail the unfolding dialogue between Sharon and Abbas as well as the developments that led to the resignation of Abbas. Abrams, *Tested by Zion*, 69–86.

12   Ibid., 87–92; Weissglas, *Arik Sharon*, 208.

13   Weissglas reports that he discussed the concept at the end of November with Condoleezza Rice and her team in Washington; Weissglas, *Arik Sharon*, 212; Kurtzer et al. report that Elliott Abrams in an interview told them that Sharon had discussed the concept with him. Kurtzer et al., *Peace Puzzle*, 179, 308n130.

14   See Weissglas, *Arik Sharon*, 226–28; The description by Kurtzer et al. gives the misleading impression that Israel was contemplating only disengagement merely from the Gaza Strip, although the US role in shooting down Plan C is mentioned, The US responsibility for defining the concept of the Israeli Disengagement Plan is hardly mentioned. Kurtzer et al., *Peace Puzzle*, 179–80.

15   Interview with Baruch Spiegel, June 9, 2013.

16   Weissglas, *Arik Sharon*, 200; There, Weissglas quotes Sharon's speech at the Aqaba Summit in June 2003, where Sharon said that he understood the importance of territorial contiguity for a sustainable Palestinian State.

17   See "Address by PM Ariel Sharon at the Fourth Herzliya Conference – Dec 18, 2003," Israel Ministry of Foreign Affairs, December 18, 2003, http://www.mfa.gov il/mfa/pressroom/2003/pages/address%20by%20pm%20ariel%20sharon%20at%20 the%20fourth%20herzliya.aspx.

18   Ibid.

19   Weissglas, *Arik Sharon*, 226–28.

20   The relevant paragraph on the resolution of the refugee issue reads as follows: "It seems clear that an agreed, just, fair and realistic framework for a solution to the Palestinian refugee issue as part of any final status agreement will need to be found through the establishment of a Palestinian state, and the settling of Palestinian refugees there, rather than in Israel." The relevant paragraph on territory reads as follows: "In light of new realities on the ground, including already existing major Israeli population centers, it is unrealistic to expect that the outcome of final status negotiations will be a full and complete return to the armistice lines of 1949. . . . It is realistic to expect that any final status agreement will only be achieved on the basis of mutually agreed changes that reflect these realities." Letter from US president George W. Bush to Prime Minister Ariel Sharon, April 14, 2004. Compare with Abrams, *Tested by Zion*, 98–118.

21   Letter from Dov Weissglas to National Security Adviser Condoleezza Rice, April 19, 2004.

22   Government of Israel, "Overall Concept of the Disengagement Plan," April 15, 2002; "Sharon's Disengagement Plan: Full Text, Key Principles," May 3, 2004.

23   Weissglas, *Arik Sharon*, 229.

24   Kurtzer et al., *Peace Puzzle*, 183.

25   Interview with Itamar Yaar, March 12, 2012.

26   Ibid.; "Tochnit Hitnatkut bshlavim: Haekronot hamerkazim" [Appendix A: A phased disengagement program—main principles], May 28, 2004, nonpublished appendix to the official program.

27   In an interview I held with Itamar Yaar in June 2007, he stressed that working with nongovernmental organizations (NGOs) "offered the professional echelons of the governmental establishment four important advantages: (1) It offered outside professional inputs to better oversee the anticipated unfolding of the envisaged strategy; (2) professionals in official positions needed support and effective arguments to be able to give the political leadership a second opinion and describe to them possible emerging difficulties and opposition; (3) an external NGO has the privilege to pursue

policy initiatives that could not be pursued by track-one actors; and (4) outside NGOs receive from the conflict or negotiating partners (i.e., the Palestinians, Jordanians, and others) a more comprehensive feedback that is not provided in official channels." Interview with Itamar Yaar, June 7, 2007.

28 Project Gildor, Comprehensive National Strategy and Action Plan for the Government of Israel, January 1, 2004.

29 Israeli-Palestinian Working Group, James A. Baker III Institute for Public Policy, Rice University, "Creating a Roadmap Implementation Process under United States Leadership," February 2005.

30 "Sharon's Disengagement Plan."

31 ECF, "Transferring the Philadelphi Corridor and Rafah Crossing," June 30, 2004; we were also aware that this would include the necessity of transferring the territorial waters of Gaza to the Palestinians. Also see ECF, "Preparing for the Transfer of the Territorial Waters of Gaza," June 30, 2005; ECF, "From Unilateral Disengagement to Trilateral Engagement"; and ECF, "Preparing for Israeli withdrawal from Philadelphi, Gaza Airport and Gaza Seaport," commissioned paper, August 26, 2004.

32 Meeting with Dan Kurtzer, Norman Olsen, Yair Hirschfeld, and Celine Touboul, February 18, 2004.

33 Orit Gal, Gidi Grinstein, Pini Meidan, and Yair Hirschfeld, "Using International Monitoring to Ensure the Success of the Disengagement Plan and the Day After," June 30, 2005.

34 For a description of Gen. Keith Dayton's work, see Steven White and P. J. Dermer, "How Obama Missed an Opportunity for Middle East Peace," *Foreign Policy*, May 18, 2012, http://www.foreignpolicy.com/articles/2012/05/18/how_obama _missed_an_opportunity_for_middle_east_peace.

35 ECF, "The Disengagement Plan: An Analysis of the Security Component," June 29, 2004.

36 Ibid.; this description is quoted from this paper.

37 The following official Israeli documents have been consulted: "Agreed Principles for Rafah Crossing," November 16, 2005; "Protocol on Security Implementation Procedures," November 24, 2005, and attached letter of Maj. Gen. Amos Gilad to Ambassador Jones, November 24, 2005; "Agreed Arrangement on the European Union Border Assistance Mission at the Rafah Crossing Point on the Gaza-Egypt Border," and attached letter of Deputy Prime Minister and Minister of Foreign Affairs Silvan Shalom to Jack Straw, Foreign Secretary and President of the EU Council of Ministers, November 24, 2005; "Agreement on Movement and Access (a)," November, 15, 2005, 3.18 p.m.

38 ECF, "Disengagement Plan."

39 Ibid.

40 Invitation for the meeting of the October 23, 2003, at Herzog-Fox-Neeman Office, Tel Aviv. The list of those present showed a strong international presence from the US Agency for International Development, UNESCO, the World Bank, the European Union, the International Committee of the Red Cross, the United Nations Relief and Works Agency for Palestine Refugees in the Near East, and the Friedrich Ebert Foundation. On the Israeli side, the Central Command and the Israeli National Security Council were present.

41 Talking Points attached to Text of May 4, 2004, Quartet Statement, New York.

42 List of participants, World Bank meeting, May 13, 2004, Herzog-Fox-Neeman.

43 Kurtzer et al., *Peace Puzzle*, 186.

44 "Transcript of Mahmoud Abbas' speech at Egypt summit," CNN.com, February 8, 2005. http://www.cnn.com/2005/WORLD/meast/02/08/transcript.abbas/.

45 Ibid.

46 Compare with the reporting by Kurtzer et al. that the US diplomats had submitted a variety of such proposals to the US leadership but were being either ignored or rejected. Kurtzer et al., *Peace Puzzle*, 186.

47 "Conclusions of the London Meeting on Supporting the Palestinian Authority," March 1, 2005, 11.

48 PMO and Israeli National Security Council, "Ptichat tium kalkali/ezrachi im hapalestinim swiw tochnit hahitnatkut: B'rashut hamshneh leroshhamemshala [The beginning of economic/civilian coordination with the Palestinians on the basis of the Disengagement Plan: Led by the vice prime minister], February 23, 2005.

49 Israeli-Palestinian Working Group, "Creating a Roadmap Implementation Process," 4.

50 We also produced a follow-up report: Israeli-Palestinian Working Group, James A. Baker III Institute for Public Policy, Rice University, "Trilateral Action Plan for Roadmap Phase I Implementation," December 2005.

51 Meeting Notes, February 8, 2005; the participants were Amnon Lipkin Shachak, Nasr Yussuf, Ibrahim Salame, Yair Hirschfeld, Dov Sedaka, and Ron Shatzberg.

52 Ibid.; Nasr Yussuf responded, "We only got 11,000 weapons," indicating that of the 30,000 arms sent to the Palestinians the rest—i.e., 19,000 weapons—had been stolen. Also see chapter 6.

53 Israeli-Palestinian Working Group, "Creating a Roadmap Implementation Process," 12–15.

54 Strategic Assessments Initiative, "Planning Considerations for International Involvement in the Palestinian Security Sector: An Operational Assessment," prepared by International Transition Assistance Group, Strategic Assessments Initiative, July 2005.

55 Ibid., 37.

56 Ibid., 39; ECF, "Making the Disengagement Plan Work: Progress Report, End of Phase Two," July 28, 2005.

57 ECF, "Principles for the Evacuation Plan of the Gush Katif Settlements," July 13, 2005.

58 Maj. Gen. Gadi Shamni recounts that the original IDF plan for the withdrawal provided for a three-month implementation. When the plan was submitted to Sharon, he insisted on carrying out the plan in no more than one week, in order to prevent the buildup of Jewish radical fundamentalist resistance. Meeting with Gadi Shamni, December 29, 2013. Brig. Gen. Ehud Dekel was in charge of coordinating the withdrawal from Gaza with the Palestinian security forces. Interview with Gen. Ehud Dekel, June 24, 2012.

59 "Institutionalizing Israeli-Palestinian Security Coordination," June 15, 2005.

60 Pgisha im Nasr Yussuf, yom shishi [Meeting with Nasr Yussuf], September 9, 2005; present: Amnon Lipkin Shachak, Yair Hirschfeld, Ron Schatzberg, Nasr Yussuf, and Ibrahim Salameh. Nasr Yusuf reported that in order to create a unanimous Fatah position, Mahmoud Abbas and he were planning to establish a Security Forum to advise Abbas and a Security Cabinet; with such a backing, it would be possible to confront Hamas. With regard to the delivery of arms, Nasr Yussuf reported that he knew exactly how much money Arafat had given to the security groups in Gaza to buy

weapons, whereas weapons were acquired for only 10 percent of the sums transferred, indicating that a substantial portion of the funds allocated for the Palestinian security forces was spent otherwise.

61 Government of Israel, "IDF to Leave Gaza by Monday morning," reliefweb.int, September 11, 2005, http://reliefweb.int/report/occupied-palestinian-territory/idf-leave-gaza-monday-morning.

62 This was reported by Al Jazeera, September 7, 2005; also see Pinhas Inbari and Dan Diker, "The Murder of Mussa Arafat and the Battle for the Spoils of Gaza," *Jerusalem Issue Brief* (Institute for Contemporary Affairs) 5, no. 6 (October 10, 2005), http://www.jcpa.org/brief/brief005-6.htm.

63 ECF, "Security Guarantees for a Sustainable Ceasefire: A Proposal for the West Bank," June 2, 2004; "North West Bank Disengagement: Security Issues" (n.d.); "Implications of the Disengagement from the Northern West Bank," August 31, 2005; "North West Bank Disengagement: Security Plan," November 6, 2005; Dov Sedaka and Celine Touboul, "Implications of the Disengagement from the Northern West Bank: Civilian Issues," October 16, 2005; Zecharya Tagar, "The Disengagement Plan: Implications and Opportunities in the West Bank, Water, Wastewater, and Solid Waste," July 2005.

64 Sedaka and Touboul, "Implications of the Disengagement." In hindsight, it appears that the working assumptions laid out by Sedaka and Touboul in October 2005 became relevant policy proposals in 2008 when, under Gen. Dayton's and Gen. Jones's leadership, the "Jenin-first" concept was developed and implemented.

65 Our November 2003 paper on the border regime, "Preparing an Israeli-Palestinian Good Neighborly Relations Accord (GNRA)," was updated and adapted to emerging conditions—see Israeli-Palestinian Working Group, "Creating a Roadmap Implementation Process," 16—and was further developed into ECF, "Cross-Border Regime and Israeli-Palestinian Cooperation for Palestinian Economic Rehabilitation in the Context of Disengagement," June 23, 2005.

66 "Transfer of Assets and Infrastructure," September 2004.

67 Israeli-Palestinian Working Group, "Creating a Roadmap Implementation Process," 18–20.

68 Office of the Vice Prime Minister and Israeli National Security Council, "The Disengagement Plan: Economic and Civilian Coordination with the Palestinian Steering Committee," presentation to James Wolfensohn, May 3, 2005.

69 Interview with Itamar Yaar, March 12, 2012.

70 Report of Strategic Assessment Initiative, which says: "Early efforts of the PA to deal with the issues of assets allocations, land use and land claims, however, did not materialize, as it was feared that arguments over assets distribution would trigger confrontation between families and other social units and due to existing tensions would result in armed conflict." See Strategic Assessment Initiative, "Planning Considerations for International Involvement in the Palestinian Security Sector."

71 Interview with Itamar Yaar, March 12, 2012.

72 James Wolfensohn to Minister Shaul Mofaz, August 23, 2005, copies to Prime Minister Ahmed Qurei and Prime Minister Ariel Sharon; James Wolfensohn to Muhammad Dahlan, August 24, 2005, countersigned by Muhammad Dahlan with copies to President Mahmoud Abbas, Prime Minister Ahmed Qurei, and Prime Minister Ariel Sharon. Also see "Trust Fund Agreement between the Government of Israel and UNDP [United Nations Development Program] Regarding the Management of the Funds for the Deconstruction and Removal of Rubble of the Houses Demolished

by Israel and the Evacuated Areas in the Gaza Strip." The document I saw was signed by the UNDP but not yet by the Government of Israel. Compare also with Abrams's account; the White House took the Palestinian demand to destroy the assets evidently as a given. At the same time, Abrams explains that Rice tried to induce Abbas to take action—without, however, really understanding the weakness of his situation on the ground, and the need to take supportive US action. Abrams takes a very critical view of Wolfensohn. Abrams, *Tested by Zion*, 134–37.

73   ECF, "Transfer of Israeli Greenhouses in Gaza as Leverage for Developing the Palestinian Economy," June 5, 2005

74   ECF, "Avtachat hahamamot bsman pinui betkufat habenayim" [Securing the greenhouses during the evacuation and the intermediary period], July 24, 2005.

75   Interview with Boaz Karni, August 21, 2012.

76   ECF, "Haavarat hamamot hahesder begush katif lyadei hapalestinim: Noss'im ikariim" [The transfer of the greenhouses, the agreement in the Gush Katif area for a handover to the Palestinians: The main issues], August 24, 2005.

77   "Report from the Office of the Special Envoy for Disengagement (James Wolfensohn)," October 17, 2005.

78   Interview with Aviad Friedmann, April 19, 2012

79   Interview with Othniel Schneller, April 3, 2012.

80   Interview with Baruch Spiegel, August 20, 2012.

81   Interview with Eival Gilady, June 17, 2012.

82   Interview with Othniel Schneller, August 19, 2012

83   Interview with Eival Gilady, June 17, 2012; interview with Othniel Schneller, August 19, 2012.

84   See Marwan Muasher, *The Arab Center: The Promise of Moderation* (New Haven, CT: Yale University Press, 2008), 264–5. Boaz Karni is the only person I know who accurately predicted the Hamas victory.

85   The details are based on a private meeting between Yair Hirschfeld and Ehud Olmert, when he was still prime minister, in January 2009. Those details have been reported, with small variations, by different sources. See, e.g., Condoleezza Rice, *No Higher Honor: A Memoir of My Years in Washington* (New York: Random House, 2011), 650–55; and Kurtzer et al., *Peace Puzzle*, 231.

86   See Rice, *No Higher Honor*, 723–24. George Hawatme, a friend of mine and a journalist living in Amman, as well as the nephew of the Palestinian leader of the Democratic Front for the Liberation of Palestine, Naif Hawatme, told me that when rumors about an agreement on Permanent Status leaked in the autumn of 2008, President Abbas visited Amman and asked journalists to visit him at what was known as the Palestinian Embassy. He told the journalists that whatever they might hear about a pending agreement on Permanent Status, they should know that this information was all unreliable and untrue. See also Asher Susser, *Israel, Jordan, and Palestine: The Two-State Imperative* (Lebanon, NH: University Press of New England, 2012), 64–71; Susser also refers to the documents with respect to the negotiations that were published by Al Jazeera in 2011.

87   Rice, *No Higher Honor*, 724; Kurtzer et al. offer a more supportive description in explaining the Palestinian rejection. Kurtzer et al., *Peace Puzzle*, 232.

88   Susser, *Israel, Jordan, and Palestine*, 64–68. Tamar Hermann explained that the Palestinian leadership did not have the legitimacy to give away—in one way or the other—the Palestinian Right of Return. Interview with Tamar Hermann, September 28, 2013.

89   Our track-two work was issued as follows: Edward Djerejian, "Getting to the Territorial Endgame of an Israeli-Palestinian Peace Settlement," James A. Baker III Institute for Public Policy, Rice University, February 2010.

90   Asher Susser discussed the great internal difficulty for the Palestinians to commit to finality. See Susser, *Israel, Jordan, and Palestine*, 37–43.

91   Yair Hirschfeld, "Second-Year Report," submitted to James A. Baker III Institute for Public Policy, Rice University, October 12, 2007, 8.

92   Ibid.

93   Ibid. The immediate cause for the outbreak of the war was a Hezbollah attack on Israeli soldiers and the abduction of three of them from within Israeli territory. This was one act among many of escalating violent provocations; see "Second Lebanon War: Background and Overview," Jewish Virtual Library, accessed March 10, 2014, http://www.jewishvirtuallibrary.org/jsource/History/lebanon2.html..

94   Hussein Agha, quoted by Hirschfeld, "Second-Year Report," 9–10.

95   Interview with Ehud Dekel, June 24, 2012. Dekel headed the Israeli teams for these negotiating committees.

96   See Kurtzer et al., *Peace Puzzle*, 213–19.

97   "Fayyad's State-Building Plan," *Bitterlemons*, March 15, 2010. This entire issue of *Bitterlemons* was dedicated to describing and commenting on Fayyad's state-building efforts and included contributions from Yossi Alpher, Ghassan Khatib, Yisrael Harel, and Ali Jarbawi.

98   Thania Paffenholz, "Exploring Opportunities and Obstacles for a Constructive Role of Social Capital in Peace-Building: A Framework for Analysis," in *Social Capital and Peace Building: Creating and Resolving Conflict with Trust and Social Networks*, ed. Michaelene Cox (New York: Routledge, 2009), 186–201.

99   Quoted by Kurtzer et al., *Peace Puzzle*, 220–21.

100   Mission Statement for Special Envoy for Middle East Regional Security, sent upon request to ECF, May 10, 2008.

101   ECF, "A Task-Oriented Approach to Israeli-Palestinian Security Coordination," June 6, 2005. This paper defined the responsibilities for task-oriented security cooperation. The Israeli government was responsible for providing a biweekly list of wanted fugitives to the PA, and refraining from arrest operations in areas under PA control unless the actions had been coordinated beforehand. The PA was responsible for disarming designated militants and arresting designated fugitives in areas under their jurisdiction. The international observers were responsible for mediating Israeli-Palestinian dialogue over the fugitive list, disarmament plans, arrest plans for fugitives with legal action, and detention requirements, and verifying arrest protocol and detention of fugitives.

102   Yair Hirschfeld to Karim Nashashibi, December 21, 2007; personal correspondence.

103   ECF, "Jenin-First Presentation," January 2008. Much of our work was based on earlier work; see ECF, "Task-Oriented Approach," where we include a table titled "Responsibilities of the Parties for Task-Oriented Security Cooperation."

104   Ibid.

105   ECF, "Task-Oriented Approach."

106   Sedaka and Touboul, "Implications of the Disengagement."

107   ECF, "Jenin-First Presentation."

108   Gen. Jones to Yair Hirschfeld, April 11, 2008; personal correspondence, framed in my office.

109 For Gen. Jones's evaluation of the Jenin-first effort, see Christopher J. Castelli, "Jones: New Team Must Build on Israeli-Palestinian Progress in Jenin," interview, *Inside the Pentagon*, October 30, 2008.

110 Interview with Brig. Gen. Dov Sedaka, August 20, 2012.

111 ECF, "ECF Activities and Outcomes: Report to USAID," delivered February 28, 2011, 41–49, where a nine-page table described original movement restrictions, their relevance to the Palestinian governance and the delivery of trade and services, ECF recommendations and priority, and the results of intervention.

112 The empirical evidence of the spoiler activities of both Hamas and the settler movement are abundant. Othniel Schneller would discuss this repeatedly with Sharon, Olmert, and Netanyahu. Interview with Othniel Schneller, October 19, 2013.

113 Kurtzer et al., *Peace Puzzle*, 178.

114 Interview with Eival Gilady, June 17, 2012.

115 After the election of President Rohani, there could be a realistic chance to achieve this, in case relevant negotiations will refer not only to the nuclear issue but also include, similarly, a clear demand for Iranian contribution to regional stability, while maintaining the necessary means of military and economic deterrence to prevent noncompliance.

116 I remember, in early 1995, the US secretary of state, Warren Christopher, returning from one of his many visits to Damascus. Although he had received nothing but a rejection from Syrian president Hafez al Assad, he asked Shimon Peres to make a statement that the trip had been successful. Christopher wanted such a statement in order to obtain from President Clinton some further leeway to continue his effort to reach an Israeli-Syrian peace. Yossi Beilin, Nimrod Novik, and I argued that any positive statement from Peres would have two detrimental repercussions, because the Israeli-Golan lobby would be warned that a deal on Israel's withdrawal from the Golan was imminent, and President al-Assad would be applauded for his rejection. Although Peres listened to us, he said that his personal relationship with Christopher was similarly important.

117 Aaron Miller, who was a member of the US peace team, has been quoted as saying that "the Roadmap, like the June 24 speech, became a convenient administration talking point and guidepost, pointing toward what the parties needed to do." Quoted by Kurtzer et al., *Peace Puzzle*, 178.

118 Meeting with Ambassador Djerejian, November 18, 2013.

Chapter 10

1 White House Office of the Press Secretary, "Remarks by President Barack Obama to the People of Israel," March 21, 2013, http://www.whitehouse.gov/the-press -office/2013/03/21/remarks-president-barack-obama-people-Israel

2 Ibid.

3 Compare with note 3 in chapter 9, referring to statements made by Gen. David Petraeus to the Senate Armed Services Committee, on April 8, 2008.

4 Avi Shlaim, *Lion of Jordan: The Life of King Hussein in War and Peace* (London: Allen Lane, 2007), chap. 9, "Arab Foes and Jewish Friends," 172–201.

5 See "Full Text of Netanyahu's Foreign Policy Speech at Bar Ilan," *Haaretz*, June 14, 2009.

6   This information as most of the information following is based on confidential briefings given to the author. I was told that Kerry having visited a Buddhist temple in East Asia, would immediately afterward phone Netanyahu and clarify several issues with him. This story indicates that the Israeli-Palestinian issue was uppermost in Kerry's mind, wherever he would go.

7   The initial reaction of both the Israeli and Palestinian sides was to reject the Allen proposals, while engaging in an in-depth discussion with him and his team to seek common ground. An ECF team headed by a very senior, recently retired IDF officer is working on track-two negotiations with all parties. The ECF's task here is mainly to explain the security concerns of one side to the other and help test possible minor adaptions to Gen. Allen's proposals.

8   See Office of the UN Special Coordinator for the Middle East Peace Process, "Closing the Gap: Palestinian State-building and Resumed Negotiations," Report to the Ad hoc Liaison Committee, New York, September 25, 2013.

9   Kerry would take care to brief the Arab leadership regularly. Doing so, Kerry would also explain to them the political considerations of Prime Minister Netanyahu and ask the Arab leadership to understand controlled settlement activities. See ECF, Newsletter 385, covering events from October 20 to 26, 2013.

10   Jonathan Powell, "Talking to Terrorists: How to End Armed Conflicts," unpublished manuscript, 209, 213 . In order to understand the full meaning of these two ground rules, it is advised to read Powell's account of the entire peace-finding process in Ireland as described in his book: Jonathan Powell, *Great Hatred, Little Room: Making Peace in Northern Ireland* (London: Vintage Books, 2009).

11   A similar approach was successfully applied in negotiations over Northern Ireland. See Powell, *Great Hatred, Little Room*, chaps. 3, 4, and 5, 59–119.

12   The ECF has prepared a paper proposing a comprehensive strategy aimed to deter Jewish hate crimes. The proposals made were discussed in detail with the IDF, the Israeli police, Shabak, and the Ministry of Justice. Given that Tzipi Livni is minister of justice, much followup work is quietly being carried out.

13   See Palestinian Center for Policy and Survey Research, "PSR Poll No. 48 – Joint Palestinian-Israeli Press Release," July 2, 2013, http://www.pcpsr.org/survey/polls/2013/p48ejoint.html; and Shaul Arieli, "Testing the Probability of a Two State Solution" [in Hebrew], Economic Cooperation Foundation; unpublished.

14   United States Department of State Archive, "A Performance-Based Roadmap to a Permanent Two-State Solution to the Israeli-Palestinian Conflict," Press Statement, Washington, DC, April 30, 2003, http://www.state.gov/r/pa/prs/ps/2003/20062.htm.

Bibliography

Manuscripts and Unpublished Sources

Archival Resources

Economic Cooperation Foundation Archives, Israel
(Internal Documents and Policy Papers)

A Ten Point Agenda for an Israeli-Egyptian Dialogue on Peace Consolidation. February 8, 1997.

Ad Hoc Liaison Committee. Informal Donor Meeting. April 25, 2002. Oslo.

Advantages of the Proposed Agreement. June 14, 2000.

Agha, Hussein. Report to Yair Hirschfeld and Ron Pundak. January 18, 2000.

Agreed Arrangement on the European Union Border Assistance Mission at the Rafah Crossing Point on the Gaza-Egypt Border. November 24, 2005.

Agreed Principles for Rafah Crossing. November 16, 2005.

Agreement on Movement and Access. November 15, 2005. 3:18 p.m.

Ajouri, Hikmat, and Ron Pundak. Palestinian-Israeli Cooperation, "Building Bridges Through Health." Annual Report on ECF-PCH Health Cooperation Activities for the 1997 Project Year. February 3, 1998.

al-Jubeh, Nazmi. The Holy Basin. April 2001.

Approved Text of Mashov Council. January 25, 1984.

Arafat, Yasser. Speech at the meeting in the Swedish Parliament building. December 5, 1998.

Arieli, Shaul. Bhinat hayitachnut rayon 'stey medinot lshney amim" b'eretz yisrael [Testing the probability of a two-state solution]. ECF Document.

Ashrawi, Hanan. Handwritten notes on negotiations on what to do to bring the deportees back home. February 27, 1993.

Aviad, Janet, and Sari Nusseibeh. Belgian-Israeli-Palestinian Cooperation in Scientific Research and Education. Aviad for the CRB Foundation, Nusseibeh for the Palestine Consultancy Group. December 4, 1996.

Baker, Alan [legal adviser to the Minister of Foreign Affairs and Director-General, Ministry of Foreign Affairs]. Hamamad hamishpati shel mazav ha massaumatan al mamad hakeva [The legal situation of the negotiations on Permanent Status]. February 13, 2001.

Banaji, Yael. Handwritten protocol of meeting with Jeff Feltman and John Listen. June 28, 2001.

Barzacchi, Elinoar. Jerusalem in Peace: One City, Two Capitals—Organization of Municipal Services—Independent, Coordinated, Joint. April 2001.

The Beilin-Abu Mazen Understanding. October 31, 1995.

Ben-Haim, Issaschar. The Economy of Jerusalem. January 2001.

Briefing to Shimon Peres and Yossi Beilin, Meeting with the PLO Delegation. May 11, 1993.

Conclusions of the London Meeting on Supporting the Palestinian Authority. March 1, 2005.

Confidential Proposed Draft. US-Israel Memorandum of Agreement. October 5, 1988. To Nimrod Novik.

Confidential Report. Re: Paris Seminar on Jerusalem (May 13–14. 1995). May 17, 1995.

Cooperation North. Agreement on Cross-Border Cooperation between the Israeli Municipalities of Haifa, Gilboa, and Emek Hamaayanot with the Governorate of Jenin. February 15, 1999.

CRB Foundation: Proposal for Cooperation with Research Centers in Israel. February 1, 1999.

Dajani, Riad. Considerations for Future Economic Cooperation between East and West: Jerusalem—Jerusalem: The Open City. Orient House, Jerusalem. April 2001.

Developing a Strategy for Peace. December 1, 1996.

Discussion about the Ongoing Negotiations. August 2, 1995.

Djerejian, Edward. Getting to the Territorial Endgame of an Israeli-Palestinian Peace Settlement. James A. Baker III Institute for Public Policy, Rice University. February 2010.

Economic Cooperation Foundation. Aims and Strategies. February 21, 1999.

———. Avtachat hahamamot bsman pinui betkufat habenayim [Securing the greenhouses during the evacuation and the intermediary period]. July 24, 2005.

———. Cross-Border Regime and Israeli-Palestinian Cooperation for Palestinian Economic Rehabilitation in the Context of Disengagement. June 23, 2005.

———. The Disengagement Plan: An Analysis of the Security Component. June 29, 2004.

———. ECF Activities and Outcomes: Report to USAID. Delivered February 28, 2011.

———. Economic and Infrastructure Conditions in the PA. February 13, 2001.

———. Final Status Project, Internal Memo. Update. February 4, 1997.

———. Five-Point Plan for the Promotion of the Peace Process. January 18, 1998.

———. From Unilateral Disengagement to Trilateral Engagement.

———. Haavarat hamamot hahesder begush katif lyadei hapalestinim: Noss'im ikariim [The transfer of the greenhouses, the agreement in the Gush Katif area for a handover to the Palestinians: the main issues]. August 24, 2005.

———. Implications of the Disengagement from the Northern West Bank. August 31, 2005.

———. Integrated Security Arrangements between Israel, Jordan and the Palestinian State: The Need, Main Characteristics and Possible Participation of Third Party Forces. December 10, 1990.

———. International Stability Pact for the Middle East. February 20, 2001.

———. Israeli-Palestinian Five-Point Plan of Action for the Promotion of the Process of Peace. April 28, 1999.

———. Israeli-Palestinian Framework Agreement on Security Permanent Status. Incomplete Draft. May 26, 1999.

———. Israeli-Palestinian Guidelines for the Prevention of Terror and for Security Cooperation. January 13, 1998.

———. Israeli-Palestinian Six Point Plan of Action for the Promotion of the Peace Process. Draft. May 22, 1999.

———. Israeli-Palestinian Six Point Plan of Action for the Promotion of the Peace Process. Final copy submitted to Ehud Barak by Nimrod Novik. June 6, 1999.

———. Jenin-First Presentation. January 2008.

———. Jerusalem. July 17, 2000.

———. Jordan-Israel-Palestine Trilateral Security Regime. Proposed Paper. December 2, 1999.

———. Making the Disengagement Plan Work: Progress Report, End of Phase Two. July 28, 2005.

———. Monthly Report to Labor Minister. Subject: A Change? September 23, 2001.

———. Newsletter 385, covering events from October 20–26, 2013.

———. North West Bank Disengagement: Security Plan. November 6, 2005.

———. Peace Education. December 17, 1997.

———. People-to-People Summary Report. December 11, 1998.

———. Preliminary Guidelines for a 1,000-Day Program for a Barak-Led Government. Draft 1. June 15, 2000.

———. Preparing an Israeli-Palestinian Good Neighborly Relations Accord (GNRA).

———. Preparing for Israeli Withdrawal from Philadelphi, Gaza Airport and Gaza Seaport. August 26, 2004.

———. Preparing for the Transfer of the Territorial Waters of Gaza. June 30, 2005.

———. Prime Minister Rabin's Opposition to a Palestinian State. October 27, 1995.

———. Principles for the Evacuation Plan of the Gush Katif Settlements. July 13, 2005.

———. Recommendations to the Mitchell Commission. April 12, 2001.

———. Report on Washington Talks. May 11–12, 2000.

———. Security Guarantees for a Sustainable Ceasefire: A Proposal for the West Bank. June 2, 2004.

———. A Task-Oriented Approach to Israeli-Palestinian Security Coordination. June 6, 2005.

———. Transfer of Israeli Greenhouses in Gaza as Leverage for Developing the Palestinian Economy. June 5, 2005.

———. Transferring the Philadelphi Corridor and Rafah Crossing. June 30, 2004.

Excerpts from the Statement Issued by the Palestinian Central Council. April 29, 1999.

Final Agreed Draft of August 19, 1993: Declaration of Principles on Interim Self-Government Arrangements. August 20, 1993.

First Progress Report. November 1994.

Framework Agreement on Permanent Status Between the State of Israel and the PLO. June 19, 2000.

Framework for the Conclusion of a Final Status Agreement Between Israel and the Palestinian Authority/PLO (Draft to be reviewed). May 18, 1995.

Framework for the Conclusion of a Final Status Agreement Between Israel and the Palestinian Liberation Organization. September 28, 1995.

Fundamental Israeli Assumptions for a Final Status Agreement with the Palestinians. June 15, 1995.

Gal, Orit, Gidi Grinstein, Pini Meidan, and Yair Hirschfeld. Using International Monitoring to Ensure the Success of the Disengagement Plan and the Day After. June 30, 2005.

German Non Paper attached to RL 300. US-Plan Bush Rede und US Talking Points. June 26, 2002. Berlin.

Gilady, Rotem M. Jerusalem: A Capital City of Two States? An Introductory Survey of Legal and Practical Problems and Prospects. April 20, 2001.

Grinstein, Gidi. May 17, 1999–February 6, 2001: The Permanent Status Negotiations.

———. Report. March 7, 1999.

———. Sikum sadna al hesder hakeva hakalkali birgun habank ha-ulami ve keren hamadbea habenleumit [Summary of workshop on the Economic Permanent Status Arrangements with the World Bank and the International Monetary Fund]. October 10, 1999.

Government of Israel. Overall Concept of the Disengagement Plan. April 15, 2002.

———. Sharon's Disengagement Plan: Full Text, Key Principles. May 3, 2004

Guidelines for Permanent Status Negotiations. Draft only. January 18, 1998.

Hasmonean Tunnel in Jerusalem Re-opened. September 25, 1996.

Crown Prince Hassan of Jordan. "Some Suggestions for Aiding the West Bank Economy." Prepared for the state visit of [Austrian] Bundeskanzler Kreisky to Jordan. September 30, 1980.

Hassassian, Manuel. The Palestinian/Israeli Security Arrangements in Jerusalem: An Open City. Jerusalem, 2001.

Hirschfeld, Yair. Developing an ILP Strategy: The Barak-Beilin Initiative. May 29, 1997.

———. Handwritten notes on a meeting with Katz Oz and Shaul Arlozorov, Yair Hirschfeld, Ron Pundak, and Daniel Levy. February 16, 1997.

———. Handwritten notes on meeting with Ehud Barak, Haim Ramon, Yossi Beilin, Baiga Shochat, Fuad ben Eliezer, Uzi Baram, Dalia Rabini, Eli Goldschmid, Ori Or on 19th May. May 20, 1998.

———. Handwritten notes on Meeting with Nabil Shaath. September 29, 1994.

———. Handwritten notes on meeting with Nimrod Novik, Abu Mazen and Ambassador Bassiouni. October 19, 1999.

———. Handwritten notes on meeting with Nimrod Novik, Ruth Riedel and Rob Malley. October 4, 1999.

———. Handwritten notes on meeting with the Stockholm Group. September 18, 1999.

———. Handwritten notes on Understanding for Rome. May 6, 1993.

———. Handwritten notes on various Israeli Daily Reports (chatsav's). April 25-May 2, 1985.

———. Israel, the Palestinians and the Middle East: From Dependence to Interdependence. Unpublished Draft of Final Research Report submitted to the European Commission. Ramat Yishai, September 1992.

———. Israeli-Palestinian Road Map Towards Permanent Status Negotiations. Pre-Draft Concept Only. October 8, 1997.

———. Jerusalem. In preparation for Stockholm. October 12, 1994.

———. National Reconciliation and the Promotion of the Peace Process, 100 Days. November 15, 1995.

———. Negotiations on Elections in the Territories: The First Move. February 1, 1989.

———. Notes on meeting between Dan Kurtzer and Yair Hirschfeld. May 17, 1989.

———. Notes on meeting in (the Dutch) Ministry of Finance. June 27, 1989.

———. Notes on June 26 and 27, 1989.

———. Notes on meeting. September 26, 1995.

———. Notes on meeting between Zuhair Mennasreh and Deputy Minister of Defense Eframi Sneh. April 23, 2000.

———. Personal diary of the author.

———. Plan and Timetable for (US-Proposed?) Israeli-Palestinian Negotiations. February 26, 1993.

———. The Principles of an Israeli-Palestinian Negotiating Plan. February 11, 1993.

———. Second-Year Report. Submitted to James A. Baker III Institute for Public Policy, Rice University. October 12, 2007.

———. Talking Points for Meeting with Nabil Shaath. March 31, 1995.

———. A 10-Point Security Plan. October 10, 1997.

ILP Decision. August 8, 1989.

ILP Platform [in Hebrew]. 1992.

ILP Platform approved by the Party Congress. May 1997.

Institutionalizing Israeli-Palestinian Security Coordination. June 15, 2005.

International Transition Assistance Group, Strategic Assessments Initiative. Planning Considerations for International Involvement in the Palestinian Security Sector: An Operational Assessment. July 2005.

Invitation to the parties of the Washington Negotiations from the US and Russia to bilateral meetings. March 10, 1993.

Invitation for the World Bank meeting of October 23, 2003, at Herzog-Fox-Neeman Office, Tel Aviv.

Israeli Cabinet Statement on Road Map and 14 Reservations. May 25, 2003.

Israeli-Palestinian Cooperation at Municipal Level. Presentation at FES EU Workshop. Brussels, December 10-14, 1997.

Israeli-Palestinian Final Status Agreement (draft no. 1). October 12, 1994. ECF document.

Israeli-Palestinian Final Status Agreement (draft no. 2). November 12, 1994. ECF document.

Israeli-Palestinian Five-Point Plan of Action for the Promotion of the Process of Peace. April 28, 1999. ECF document.

Israeli-Palestinian Six Point Plan of Action for the Promotion of the Process of Peace. May 22, 1999. Draft.

Israeli-Palestinian Six Point Plan of Action for the Promotion of the Process of Peace. June 6, 1999. Final version submitted to Barak by Nimrod Novik.

Israeli-Palestinian Understanding Regarding Guidelines for Permanent Status Negotiations. Draft only. January 7, 1998. ECF document.

Israeli-Palestinian Understanding Regarding Guidelines for Permanent Status Negotiations. Draft. April 21, 1999. ECF document.

Israeli-Palestinian Understanding Regarding Guidelines for Permanent Status Negotiations. Second Draft. March 30, 1999. ECF document.

Israeli-Palestinian Working Group, James A. Baker II Institute for Public Policy, Rice University. Creating a Roadmap Implementation Process under United States Leadership. February 2005.

Israeli-Palestinian Working Group, James A. Baker II Institute for Public Policy, Rice University. Trilateral Action Plan for Roadmap Phase I Implementation. December 2005.

Javetz, Eylon. Deficiencies in the Israeli 'Permanent Status' Peace Strategy and Some Initial Recommendations. Paper submitted to the ECF. Draft 20. February 2002.

——— and Yael Banaji. Constructing a Mountain of Peace: Transforming the Meanings of the Temple Mount-Haram ash-Sharif towards an Israeli Palestinian Peace Agreement. Paper written for the ECF. April 2001.

Javetz, Shai. Policing Jerusalem in Peace. Jerusalem. February 2001.

Karayanni, Michael. A Legal Model for Jerusalem the Capital and Jerusalem City. February 2001.

Klein, Menahem. Jerusalem as an Open City. April 2001.

Kurtzer, Daniel. Presentation to the US Institute for Peace–Baker Institute for Public Policy Conference on Twenty Years Since Madrid. November 2, 2011.

Legal Status and Regime for Jerusalem. Draft.

Main Points Raised at Meeting (present: Ghassan al-Khatib, Hanan Ashrawi, Samir Huleileh; Avrum Burg, Arie Ofri, Boaz Karni, Yair Hirschfeld). 9:30–10:30. April 11, 1991. Ramallah.

Malki, Riad. Jerusalem: Open City—London Track.

———. The Future Administration of Jerusalem: The Municipality Aspect. Arab Studies Society, London, and Orient House, Jerusalem. April 2001.

Malley, Rob. Report on a meeting with Marwan Barghouti. April 26, 2001.

Meeting between Abu Mazen, Hassan Asfour, Yossi Beilin, Yair Hirschfeld, and Ron Pundak. June 1, 1996.

Meeting between Arafat and Clinton. April 20, 2000.

Meeting between Hussein Agha, Ahmed Khalidi, Yossi Beilin, Yair Hirschfeld, Boaz Karni, and Daniel Levy. May 17, 2000.

Meeting between the Partners of Cooperation North and President Arafat. Internal document only. September 25, 2000.

Meeting between Shimon Peres and Faisal Husseini (present: Avi Gil, Dr. Ron Pundak, Dr. Yair Hirschfeld). 9:30–10:00. January 9, 1993. Jerusalem.

Meeting between Yair Hirschfeld and Nimrod Novik. September 14, 1989.

Meeting between Yossi Beilin and Mahmoud Abbas [Abu Mazen]. September 6, 1995.

Meeting between Yossi Beilin and Mahmoud Abbas [Abu Mazen]. April 30, 2001. Ramallah.

Meeting between Yossi Beilin and Eberhard Rhein (present: Yair Hirschfeld). Hotel Laromme, August 1, 1995.

Meeting between Yossi Beilin, Nimrod Novik, Boaz Karni, Ron Pundak, and Daniel Levy. June 8, 2000.

Meeting with Ambassador Bassiouni (present: the Egyptian Attache for Economic Affairs, Boaz Karni, Ron Pundak, and Yair Hirschfeld). Sunday, February 22, 1987. 9:30–10:30 a.m.

Meeting with Amnon Lipkin Shachak, Nasr Yussuf, Ibrahim Salame, Yair Hirschfeld, Dov Sedaka, and Ron Schatzberg. February 8, 2005.

Meeting with Dan Kurtzer. November 9, 1983.

Meeting with Dan Kurtzer. November 17, 1983.

Meeting with Dan Kurtzer, Norman Olsen, Yair Hirschfeld, and Celine Touboul. February 18, 2004.

Meeting with Hana Siniora. December 27, 1988.

Meeting with Hanan Ashrawi. September 26, 2000.

Meeting with Hanan Ashrawi and later with Faisal Husseini. August 24, 1989.

Meeting with Hanan Ashrawi, Yair Hirschfeld, and Boaz Karni. September 26, 2000.

Meeting with Hussein Agha. September 2010. Zurich.

Meeting with Jan Revis [deputy chief of mission, Netherlands Embassy in Tel Aviv] and Yair Hirschfeld. September 26, 1989.

Meeting with John Becker. August 18, 1989.

Meeting with the Londoners [Hussein Agha and Ahmed Khalidi]. January 18, 2000.

Meeting with Mayor Mustafa Abdel Nabi Natche, Kamal Hassouneh, Immanuel Halperin, and Yair Hirschfeld. January 6, 1989.

Meeting with Nimrod Novik, Yair Hirschfeld, Boaz Karni, and Faisal Husseini. January 14, 1990.

Meeting with Rashad Shawwa. December 30, 1983.

Meeting with Samih el-Abed. August 6, 1995.

Meeting with Yair Hirschfeld and Dan Kurtzer. 13:00–14:00, August 22, 1994. U.S. Department of State.

Meeting with Yossi Beilin, Yair Hirschfeld, Boaz Karni, and Radwan Abu Ayyash. November 28, 1989.

Middle East Peace Multilateral Talks Working Group on Economic Development. The Palestine Delegation. May 5, 1993. Rome.

Ministerial Reform Committee. The Program of Reform. June 23, 2002.

———. 100 Days Plan of the Palestinian Government (with Reference to the Presidential Decree of 12 June 2002). June 23, 2002.

Minutes of the 5th Steering Committee Meeting of Cooperation North. March 6, 2000. Haifa Municipality.

Minutes of the meeting with Hussein Agha and Ahmed Khalidi. May 18, 2000.

Minutes of the meeting with Shimon Peres. April 25 and April 27, 1993.

Minutes of the meeting with Mr. Shimon Peres (present: Dr. Yair Hirschfeld, Faisal Husseini, Hanan Ashrawi). January 23, 1993.

Minutes of the meeting with Shimon Peres and Faisal Husseini. February 21, 1993. 2:20 p.m.

Minutes of the meeting at the Arab American University-Jenin. Participants: Dr. Waleed Deeb, Dr. Ghassan A. Abu Hyleh, Dr. Mahmoud Haddad, Dr. Mamoud Abu-Mowais, Mr. Jim Thomas, Mr. Ayman Agbaria, Michal Schwazman. Arab-American University, Jenin. September 24, 2000.

Mission Statement for Special Envoy for Middle East Regional Security. May 10, 2008.

The National Agreement Regarding the Negotiations on the Permanent Settlement with the Palestinians. January 22, 1997.

Notes of Meeting with Fatah West Bank Leadership. A-Ram, April 2, 1997.

Notes on a conversation between Dan Kurtzer and Yair Hirschfeld. US Embassy, Tel Aviv, July 17, 1983, 14:30–16:00.

Novik, Nimrod. Action Plan for the Cessation of Violence, Rebuilding of Confidence, and Resumption of Negotiations. May 21, 2001.

————. The American Initiative. May 28, 1998.

————. Az ma haja lanu hayom? Pizuz b'erez [What did we have today? A [negotiating] disaster at Erez]. February 3, 2000.

————. From Crises to Process. May 7, 2002.

————. Guidelines for Permanent Status Negotiations. January 18, 1998.

————. Hamifgash ha meshusha [The meeting of the Six]. February 3, 1998.

————. Idkun tahalich [Update of the process]. April 9, 2000.

————. Ikarej hadvarim im Martin Indyk [The main issues with Martin Indyk]. October 12, 1995.

————. Mifgash Ehud-Arafat (mozej 14/11, 1999) [The meeting, Ehud-Arafat (14/11/1999)].

————. The Mubarak Initiative. Draft. May 3, 1997.

————. Mu'm FAPS [Negotiations on a FAPS (Framework Agreement on Permanent Status)]. Novermber 29, 1999.

————. Notes on the meeting with Osama al-Baz. June 5, 1996.

————. Oslo al pi Saeb [Oslo according to Saeb]. November 4, 1999.

————. Peres-Abu Ala Meeting, September 3, 2001. September 5, 2001.

————. Policy Paper. October 4, 1989.

————. Report on David Levy–Abu Mazen meeting. March 9, 1997.

————. Report of February 3, 1998.

————. Sikum bikur Osama: Emdat mizrayim [Summary of Osama's visit: The Egyptian position]. May 31, 2002.

————. Talking Points. June 2, 1998.

————. Tguva [Response]. April 10, 2000.

————. Tmunat hamazav alpi Abu Mazen 7/11 [The picture of the situation according to Abu Mazen on 7/11/1999]. November 8, 1999.

————. Transition to Permanent Status (TPS). May 22, 2001.

Office of the Vice Prime Minister and Israeli National Security Council. The Disengagement Plan: Economic and Civilian Coordination with the Palestinian Steering Committee. Presentation to James Wolfensohn. May 3, 2005.

The Palestine Delegation. Statement to the Middle East Peace Multilateral Negotiations: Working Group on Development of the Palestinian Economy, and Regional Economic Cooperation. Brussels: May 11, 1992.

Palestinian Draft for the ECF. Framework for the Conclusion of a Final Status Agreement Between Israel and the Palestine Liberation Organization. July 4, 1995.

Penn + Schoen Associates. American Jewish Attitudes Toward U.S. Role in Mideast Peace Process. Survey commissioned by Israel Policy Forum. February 7, 1997.

Perlman, Lee, and Raviv Schwartz. A Preliminary Stocktaking of Israeli Organizations Engaged in Palestinian-Israeli People-to-People Activity. Presented November 27 1999. Workshop on Evaluating Israeli-Palestinian Civil Society Cooperative Activities, Helsinki, November 27–28 1999.

Pgisha im Nasr Yussuf, yom shishi [Meeting with Nasr Yussuf, Friday]. September 9, 2005.

Pinhas Yechezikieli. Mitve letichun astrategi b'nose' maarekhet ha lo-formaliim im ha palestiniayim [Guidelines for strategic planning of cooperation with the Palestinians on the informal level]. June 26, 2000.

Powell, Jonathan. Talking to Terrorists: How to End Armed Conflicts. Unpublished manuscript, 209, 213.

PLO View: Prospects of a Palestinian Israeli Settlement. Palestinian Dossier, Arab Summit Conference. June 1988.

PM Rabin's Opposition to a Palestinian State. October 27, 1995.

PMO and Israeli National Security Council. Ptichat tium kalkali/ezrachi im hapalestinim swiw tochnit hahitnatkut: B'rashut hamshneh leroshhamemshala [The beginning of economic/civilian coordination with the Palestinians on the basis of the Disengagement Plan: Led by the Vice Prime Minister]. February 23, 2005.

Political Programme adopted by the Fifth General Congress of the Palestinian National Liberation movement (Fatah). Unofficial translation. August 8, 1989.

Pre-EPS Model. February 1, 1998.

Preparing for Negotiations with Shlomo's Boss. December 8, 1995.

Presentation of Cooperation North to European Partners during a tour in Europe. March 14–20, 1999.

The Principles of an Israeli-Palestinian Negotiating Plan, version 4. February 12, 1993.

The Principles of an Israeli-Palestinian Understanding. Sarpsborg III, Version 3. March 21, 1993.

Project Gildor, Comprehensive National Strategy and Action Plan for the Government of Israel. January 1, 2004.

Proposed Final Status Agreement. August 28, 1995.

Proposed Follow Up. January 16, 1996.

Proposed Israeli-Palestinian Strategy for Long-Term Cooperation.

Protocol: Meeting of February 15. 1989, 20.00 to 22.15, Notre Dame (Jerusalem). February 15, 1989.

Protocol: Meeting with Nabil Shaath at Gaza-Erez. September 6, 2001.

Protocol: Meeting in Nijmegen. April 18, 1990.

Protocol of ILP Secretariat Meeting. July 10, 1989.

Protocol of Meeting between Yossi Beilin and Mahmoud Abbas. April 30, 2001. Ramallah.

Protocol of Peres and Rashad Shawwa meeting. November 21, 1982.

Protocol of Phone Conversation between Yossi Beilin and Yair Hirschfeld. June 10, 2000.

Protocol of meeting of the Steering Committee of Cooperation North. Presentation to European partners. October 4, 1999.

Protocol on Security Implementation Procedures. November 24, 2005. Quartet Statement. Talking Points attached to the Text. May 4, 2004. New York.

Pundak, Ron. Dan Abram's Group with Shimon Peres. June 25, 1995.

———. Meeting between Larsen and Beilin. April 11, 1993.

Reform Agenda of the Palestinian Government. July 9, 2002.

Remarks by Hussein Agha and Ahmed Khalidi in Stockholm. June 24, 1999.

Report from the Office of the Special Envoy for Disengagement (James Wolfensohn). October 17, 2005.

Report of meeting with Ahmed Khalidi and Hanan Ashrawi in London and Follow-Up. January 29–30, 2002.

Report of Meeting with Dan Kurtzer, Yair Hirschfeld and Gidi Grinstein to Yossi Beilin, Nimrod Novik, Ron Pundak, Boaz Karni, and Daniel Levy [in Hebrew]. April 18, 1999.

Report of Meeting with ECF and van Mirlo [Dutch Minister of Foreign Affairs]. 10:00–10:45, September 13, 1994.

Report of Meeting with Faisal Husseini, Yair Hirschfeld, and Ron Pundak. November 7, 1995.

Report of Meeting with German Foreign Minister Fischer. October 26, 2001. Tel Aviv.

Report of Meeting with Israel Harel. November 9, 1995.

Report of Meeting of the Jerusalem Working Group. August 1–20, 1995. The Hague.

Report of Meeting between Yossi Beilin and Saeb Erekat. October 26, 2001. Jericho.

Report of meetings in Oslo. April 30 and May 1, 1993.

Report Re: Paris Seminar on Jerusalem (13–14 May 1995). May 17, 1995.

Report of the Sharm el-Sheikh Fact-Finding Committee. April 30, 2001.

The Road Ahead: Palestinian Policy in the Wake of US Terror Attacks. Anonymous Palestinian paper. September 16, 2001.

Road Map to Camp David II. October 12, 1997.

Roling, Sharon. Summary of the Joint Israeli-Palestinian Seminar on People-to-People Activities, Gaza, December 17–18, 1997, and December 20, 1997.

Sedaka, Dov, and Celine Touboul. Implications of the Disengagement from the Northern West Bank: Civilian Issues. October 16, 2005.

Seventh Joint Meeting of Palestinian & Israeli Team for History/Civics Project with Palestinian Center for Peace & Rothschild Foundation. May 22, 2000.

Sheelot politiot merkasiot hakshurot lapituah hakalkali bshtaschim [Paper prepared for a meeting of the Blumenthal group]. February 16, 1984.

Sicha im Karim Khalaf [Discussions with Karim Khalaf]. December 30, 1983.

Side Agreement on the Permanent Resolution of Palestinian Refugeeism. Draft number 1. September 13, 1999.

Sikum bikur bwashington [Summary of meeting in Washington]. October 10, 1999.

The Stockholm Group. First Progress Report. November 1994.

———. Guiding Principles for Reaching an Israeli-Palestinian Agreement on Final Status Issues. Session 1, Document 2. Stockholm. Final Agreed Draft. September 4, 1994.

———. Israeli-Palestinian Understanding Regarding Guidelines for Permanent Status Negotiations. Draft only. January 7, 1998.

———. Israeli-Palestinian Understanding Regarding Guidelines for Permanent Status Negotiations. In The Logic of Peace. April 21, 1999.

———. The Logic of Peace. April 23, 1998.

———. Phase II. February 1, 1997.

———. Preparing a Working Agenda for the Stockholm Group Phase 2. Draft. April 24, 1997.

———. Second Progress Report. May 1995.

———. Steps Towards a Future Middle East. Session 1, Document 4. Stockholm. Final Agreed Draft. September 4, 1994.

———. Working on the Logic of Peace: A Proposal for Action. Draft only. December 9, 1998.

———. Working Principles for the Stockholm Brainstorming Group for a Solution of the Palestinian Refugee Problem Within the Context of an Israeli-Palestinian Permanent Status Peace Agreement. Draft, non-paper. February 1997.

Summarized Report of the 3rd Sarpsborg Meeting. March 20–22, 1993.

Summary of Cross Border Cooperation Round Table. November 4, 1998. Jenin Governorate.

Summary of Meeting between Yossi B[eilin] and Faisal H[usseini]. (Based on report of Y.B. to Y.H. thereafter). Clingendael, July 13, 1995.

Summary Report on Meeting with Faisal Husseini and Hanan Ashrawi. 8:00–10:00 with Ashrawi, 12:30–12:50 with Husseini. February 27, 1989.

Tagar, Zecharya. The Disengagement Plan: Implications and Opportunities in the West Bank, Water, Wastewater, and Solid Waste. July 2005.

Talking Points for Maher. February 19, 1997.

Tochnit hapeula bshtachim 1 mea hayamim harishonim [Action program in the territories for the first hundred days]. Approximately February 1984.

Tochnit Hitnatkut bshlavim: Haekronot hamerkazim [Appendix A: A Phased Disengagement Program – Main Principles]. May 28, 2004.

Tochnit medinit-bitchonit lememshelet awoda [A policy and security program for a Labor government]. December 23, 2002.

Transfer of Assets and Infrastructure. September 2004.

Trust Fund Agreement between the Government of Israel and UNDP [United Nations Development Program] Regarding the Management of the Funds for the Deconstruction and Removal of Rubble of the Houses Demolished by Israel and the Evacuated Areas in the Gaza Strip. n.d.

Unofficial Draft, The Final Palestinian Proposal. August 7, 1993.

The William and Mary Declaration. Draft. November 21, 1996.

World Bank. *Two Years of Intifada, Closures, and Palestinian Economic Crisis: An Assessment.* March 2003.

Yeshayahu Folman Sipura shel Geder Hafrada [The story of the Security Fence Carmel]. 2003. Jerusalem.

100 Days: Negotiating an Economic Package for Gaza. December 15, 1995.

Israeli Labor Party Archives, Beit Berl College, Israel

Sartawi to Kreisky, Hotel Imperial Wien, Vienna. Circular B 14/77 attached as Annex I to the Report of a SI Fact Finding Mission to the Middle East. January 27, 1977.

Socialist International Fact-Finding Mission to the Middle East. SI Circular No. B32/74. March 8, 1974.

Mapai Archives, Beit Berl College, Israel

B/52. Correspondence with the Socialist International.

Tel Aviv University Archives, Israel

Litvak, Meir. "Imagining a National Past: The Palestinian Case." Submitted to the Rethinking Nationalism seminar, 1992–93. Department of Middle Eastern History and African Studies.

Tel Aviv University/Research Project on Peace, Promoting Academic Regional Cooperation. December 1979.

Interviews by the Author

Samih el-Abed. October 11, 2013.
Sufayn Abu Saideh. February 24, 2013.
Shaul Arieli. August 8, 2012.
Yossi Beilin. December 22, 2011; February 27, February 29, and June 4, 2012.
David Brodet. August 28, 2012.
Shlomo Brom. January 5 and January 24, 2012.
Ehud Dekel. March 14 and June 24, 2012.
Yuval Diskin. October 6, 2013.
Edward Djerejian. January 15, January 22, and December 10, 2012; November 18, 2013.
Aviad Friedman. April 19, 2012.
Eival Gilady. June 17 and August 2, 2012.
Dore Gold. January 22, January 23, and August 23, 2012.
Micha Goldmann. September 4, 2013.
Gidi Grinstein. August 21, 2012.
Eitan Haber. August 27 and August 28, 2012.
Avivit Hai. October 3, 2013.
Shalom Harari. March 29, June 13, June 21, and June 22, 2012; January 18 and September 11, 2013.
Tamar Hermann. September 28, 2013.
Boaz Karni. August 7 and August 21, 2012.
Motti Kristal. August 7, 2012.
Dan Kurtzer. May 11, August 2 and August 7, 2012; September 10, 2013.
Efraim Lavie. March 14, 2012.
Yitzhak Meir. July 22, 2013.
Dan Meridor. January 13, 2013.
Amnon Neubach. March 15 and April 19, 2012.
Nimrod Novik. January 12, January 13, January 15, January 25, June 24, August 7, and August 16, 2012; August 12, October 4, and October 10, 2013.
Danny Rothschild. January 4, 2012.
Dov Sedaka. June 14 and August 20, 2012; October 11, 2013.
Oren Shachor. August 21, 2012.
Ron Schatzberg. August 7 and September 6, 2012.
Othniel Schneller. March 4, April 3, and April 19, 2012; September 28, October 19, and December 12, 2013.
Rabbi Yuval Sherlov. June 2011.
Baruch Spiegel. March 5, August 17, and August 20, 2012; June 9, 2013.
Itamar Yaar. June 7, 2007; March 12, 2012.
Khalid Yazdji. June 8, 2006.

Personal Correspondence

Zuhair al-Manasreh to Dani Atar. June 20, 2000.

Minister Al Masri, Meridor and Nashashibi to Timothy J. Sullivan and the Honorable Charles S. Robb, January 1997. Draft Letter.

Yossi Beilin to Mahmoud Abbas [Abu Mazen]. Private and personal. September 20, 2000.

Economic Cooperation Foundation to Ehud Barak. Suggested Guidelines for the Meeting between Ehud Barak and Yasser Arafat. September 24, 2000.

Economic Cooperation Foundation to Partners and Friends of Cooperation North. Re: Minutes of the 7th Steering Committee Meeting (Dorot Center for Senior Citizens, Gilboa Regional Council). September 27, 2000.

Maher El-Kurd to Timothy J. Sullivan. Sub: The William and Mary Conference on "Investing in Peace." January 30, 1997.

Maher El-Kurd to Yair Hirschfeld and Ron Pundak. Israeli-Palestinian Relations: An Appraisal and Background for a Position Paper. April 19, 2001.

Gidi Grinstein to Dr. Eberhard Rhein. Sub: Summary Notes of Dr. Rhein's Visit to Israel, January 5–12, 1997. January 10, 1997.

Yair Hirschfeld to Shimon Peres. January 31, 1982.

Yair Hirschfeld to Yossi Beilin. March 19, 1982.

Yair Hirschfeld for Max van der Stoel. July 13, 1989.

Yair Hirschfeld to Molly Williamson. October 18, 1989.

Yair Hirschfeld and Ron Pundak to Shimon Peres, via Yossi Beilin. January 14, 1993.

Yair Hirschfeld and Ron Pundak to Yossi Beilin. *Pgisha im mishlachat ashaf* [Report of meeting with a PLO delegation]. January 24, 1993.

Yair Hirschfeld to Dan Kurtzer. January 26, 1993.

Yair Hirschfeld and Ron Pundak to Yossi Beilin. Report on the Meetings with a PLO Delegation. Ramat Yishai, February 13, 1993.

Yair Hirschfeld to Yossi Beilin. In continuation of report of February 13, 1993. February 18, 1993.

Yair Hirschfeld to Yossi Beilin. Evaluation of the Sarpsborg Proposals. February 18, 1993.

Yair Hirschfeld to Yossi Beilin. April 6, 1993.

Yair Hirschfeld and Ron Pundak to Yossi Beilin. April 13, 1993.

Yair Hirschfeld and Ron Pundak to Shimon Peres. Proposed Backchannel Negotiations Strategy. April 22, 1993.

Yair Hirschfeld and Ron Pundak to Shimon Peres, Yossi Beilin and Uri Savir. *Doch alimfgash bnorwegiya* [Report of meeting in Norway]. July 13, 1993.

Yair Hirschfeld to Yossi Beilin. Preparing for Israeli-Palestinian Final Status Negotiations. April 18, 1994.

Yair Hirschfeld to Yossi Beilin. Economic Issues (with political repercussions). July 17, 1994.

Yair Hirschfeld to Shimon Peres via Yossi Beilin. Very confidential. Report on Meeting with the Dutch Ambassador. November 18, 1994.

Yair Hirschfeld and Ron Pundak to Ahmad Khalidi, Hussein Agha. February 16, 1995.

Yair Hirschfeld and Ron Pundak to Yossi Beilin. Report on Analytical Statements made by Ahmed Khalidi and Hussein Agha. March 18, 1995.

Yair Hirschfeld to Yossi Beilin and Ron Pundak. April 7, 1995.

Yair Hirschfeld and Ron Pundak to Yossi Beilin. Talking Points for Meeting with Crown Prince Hassan. April 22, 1995.

Yair Hirschfeld to Ambassador C. Kroner. May 1, 1995.

Yair Hirschfeld to Yossi Beilin. June 20, 1995.

Yair Hirschfeld to Karl Schramek and Leo Radauer. June 23, 1995.

Yair Hirschfeld to Yossi Beilin. Proposed Coalition Moves – 100 Days. November 8, 1995.

Yair Hirschfeld to Yossi Beilin. Guidelines for a One-Year Programme for a Labour Government headed by Shimon Peres. November 9, 1995.

Yair Hirschfeld to Yossi Beilin. Summary of meetings on January 3 and January 7, 1996.

Yair Hirschfeld to Yossi Beilin, Nimrod Novik and Ron Pundak. Meeting with Maher el-Kurd, Paris. January 8, 1996.

Yair Hirschfeld to Aaron Miller. Re: Clinton-Netanyahu-Arafat Summit. October 1, 1996.

Yair Hirschfeld to Dan Kurtzer. Re: Clinton-Netanyahu-Arafat Summit. October 1, 1996.

Yair Hirschfeld and Ron Pundak to Sten Andersen. Three Weeks Later. December 24, 1998.

Yair Hirschfeld and Hussein Agha. January 22, 2000. Phone call.

Yair Hirschfeld to Gilead Sher. June 6, 2000.

Yair Hirschfeld to Rob Malley. July 7, 2000.

Yair Hirschfeld to Dan Kurtzer. April 11, 2002.

Yair Hirschfeld to Karim Nashashibi. December 21, 2007.

Yair Hirschfeld to Dan Kurtzer. Undated.

Faisal Husseini to Hans van Mierlo. July 6, 1995.

General Jones to Yair Hirschfeld. April 11, 2008.

Muhammad Masrouji (Secretary-General) to Dr. Otto Gatscha. Prime Minister's Office, Vienna, Jerusalem. August 3, 1980.

Memorandum of Understanding. December 16-17, 1997.

Nimrod Novik to Ambassador Bassiouni. October 4, 1989, 12:30 p.m. Phone call.

Nimrod Novik to M.K. Benjamin Fuad ben Eliezer, Deputy Chairman of the Knesset Committee for Foreign Affairs and Security. February 26, 1990.

Nimrod Novik to M.K. Micha Harish. Yosmat Baker (The Baker Initiative). October 18, 1989.

Nimrod Novik to Michael T. Clark. Re: Draft Memo to Minister Meridor. November 6, 1996.

Nimrod Novik to Danny Naveh. January 17, 1997.

Dr. Nimrod Novik to Dr. Osama al-Baz. Private & Personal, Urgent, Re: Mubarak Initiative. May 18, 1997.

Nimrod Novik to Ehud Barak and Yossi Beilin. January 7, 1998.

Nimrod Novik to Yuval Rotem-Frankl. Hahachanot Hapalestiniot [The Palestinian preparations]. January 18, 1998.

Nimrod Novik to Ehud Barak and Yossi Beilin. Emdot roshhamemschala lemachar [The positions of the Prime Minister for tomorrow]. January 19, 1998.

Nimrod Novik to Ehud Barak and Yossi Beilin. Ikareh hasicha Albright-Mel Salberg of January 16 [The main points of the meeting with Albright-Mel Salberg of January 16]. January 19, 1998.

Nimrod Novik to Ehud Barak and Yossi Beilin. Pgisha im Osama [Meeting with Osama]. January 25, 1998.

Nimrod Novik to Ehud Barak and Yossi Beilin. Hamitveh ha amerikai idkun [The American approach–update]. February 3, 1998.

Nimrod Novik to Ron Pundak and Daniel Levy. Update from Washington. February 15, 1998.

Nimrod Novik to Yair Hirschfeld. The Involvement of the European Union. February 15, 1998.

Nimrod Novik to Yossi Beilin. The Return of the Host (Bassiouni). February 23, 1998.

Nimrod Novik to Ehud Barak and Yossi Beilin (and Yair Hirschfeld and Ron Pundak). Update: the Committees for the Interim Agreement and Permanent Status. February 25, 1998.

Nimrod Novik to Ehud Barak and Yossi Beilin. Update. March 16, 1998.

Nimrod Novik to Ehud Barak. Update from Washington. April 15, 1998.

Nimrod Novik to Ehud Barak. Meetings in Cairo. April 29, 1998.

Nimrod Novik to Ehud Barak. The Dennis (Ross) Arafat Meeting, (April 26) with Martin Indyk, Abu Mazen, and Saeb Erekat present. April 29, 1998.

Nimrod Novik to Yossi Beilin. Update from London (on the Albright-Arafat meeting). May 5, 1998.

Nimrod Novik to Yair Hirschfeld. Bibi-Lingo. May 6, 1998.

Nimrod Novik to all. Additional information from London. May 8, 1998.

Nimrod Novik to Yair Hirschfeld and Ron Pundak. Update of the Process. June 25, 1998.

Nimrod Novik to Ehud Barak and Yossi Beilin. Albright fights back. June 28, 1998.

Nimrod Novik to Prime Minister Ehud Barak. April 25, 2000.

Nimrod Novik to Prime Minister Ehud Barak. Haaruz hapalestini [The Palestinian track]. March 6, 2000.

Nimrod Novik to Yossi Beilin, Yair Hirschfeld, Ron Pundak, and Boaz Karni. May 16, 2000.

Nimrod Novik to Yair Hirschfeld, Ron Pundak, and Boaz Karni. May 19, 2000.

Nimrod Novik to Rob Malley. July 10, 2000.

Nimrod Novik to Prime Minister Ehud Barak. Lepgishatcha im hamelech Abdallah [On your meeting with King Abdallah]. August 21, 2000.

Nimrod Novik to Prime Minister Ehud Barak. August 14, 2000.

Nimrod Novik et al. to Rob Malley. Enclosure. September 20, 2000.

Nimrod Novik to Yair Hirschfeld, Ron Pundak, and Boaz Karni. Cover note to Enclosure. September 20, 2000.

Nimrod Novik to Prime Minister Ehud Barak. Markiwej Iska [The components of the deal]. December 31, 2000.

Nimrod Novik to Yossi Beilin, Yair Hirschfeld, Ron Pundak, Boaz Karni, Daniel Levy, Avrum Burg, and Yuval Rotem. Tikvot Israel: Hityachsut rishonit [Israeli hopes: A first comment]. February 20, 2001.

Nimrod Novik to Eylon Javetz (ECF). July 25, 2001.

Shimon Peres to Faisal Husseini. January 10, 1993.

Dr. Margit Scherb to Dr. Daniel Levy and Rami Nassrallah, February 13 1997. Nord Sud Institute. Fax message.

Robert Serry to Yair Hirschfeld. October 16, 2000.

Max van der Stoel to Yair Hirschfeld. July 19, 1989. Fax sent to Boaz Karni.

Max van der Stoel to Yair Hirschfeld. September 4, 1989, 7:45 p.m. Phone call.

Published Documents and Reference Resources

Governments and International Organizations

EGYPT

Sadat, Anwar. Statement before the Egyptian People's Assembly. November 26, 1977.

EUROPEAN UNION

Civil Society – Israeli-Palestinian Dialogue and Cooperation. June 1998.

FRIEDRICH-EBERT FOUNDATION (GERMANY)

"Israeli-Palestinian Cooperation at Municipal Level." EU Workshop with the support of the European Commission. Brussels: December 10–14, 1997.
"The Water Economics in the Middle East – Main Problems and Possible Solutions." Tel Aviv: November 1996.

ISRAEL AND PALESTINE

Abdul Hadi, Mahdi F., ed. *Documents on Palestine – From the Negotiations in Madrid to the Post-Hebron Agreement Period.* Vol. 2. Jerusalem: PASSIA, 1997.
Benvenisti, Meron, and the West Bank Data Project. *1987 Report: Demographic, Economic, Legal, Social and Political Developments in the West Bank.* Jerusalem: West Bank Data Project, 1987.
Central Bureau of Statistics. *Year Book for 1990.* Tel Aviv: Israel Central Bureau of Statistics, 1990.
Feitelson, Eran, and Marwan Haddad. *Joint Management of Shared Aquifers: Final Report.* The Palestine Consultancy Group (PCG) and the Harry S. Truman Institute for the Advancement of Peace, Hebrew University of Jerusalem, December 1995.
Foreign Office. "Background Briefing No. 1, Wye River Memorandum: Status of Implementation as of January 1, 1999."
Gvirtzman, Haim. *Maps of Israeli Interests in Judea and Samaria: Determining the Extent of the Additional Withdrawal.* The Begin-Sadat Center for Strategic Studies, Bar Ilan University. *Security and Policy Studies* No. 34, December 1997.
Hachlata 563 shel hamemshala myom 19.6.67 [Israeli Government Decision Number 563. June 19. 1967].
Israeli Government Decree 145. November 11, 1979.
Israeli-Jordanian Treaty of Peace. October 26, 1994.
Mabat [Israeli newscast]. Excerpts from an interview with vice premier and foreign minister Shimon Peres on Israel TV's "Mabat" Newscast. By Yoram Ronen and Yigal Goren. May 13, 1987.
Medzini, Meron, ed. *Israel's Foreign Relations: Selected Documents, 1947–1974.* Vol. 1. Jerusalem: Ministry of Foreign Affairs, 1976.

Ministry of Foreign Affairs. Annex VI. September 28, 1995.

———. "Israeli-Palestinian Interim Agreement of the West Bank and the Gaza Strip." Washington, DC, September 28, 1995.

Netanyahu, Benjamin. Address to the Knesset. October 7, 1996.

Rabin, Yitzhak. Speech to the Knesset. October 5, 1995.

Sagie, Uri, and Gilead Sher. *Niyar Emda Medini* [A political position paper]. Jerusalem: Van Leer Institute, 2002.

Segal, Jerome. "Roundtable Discussion of an Interim Proposal: A Palestinian State with Sovereignty over Gaza/Jericho and Administrative Authority over the West Bank." May 1995.

JORDAN

King Hussein, *To the Arab Nation*, Centennial Speech. Amman Domestic Service in Arabic. July 31, 1988. 1701 GMT.

PALESTINE LIBERATION ORGANIZATION

Legal Unit of the Palestine Liberation Organization Negotiation Affairs Department. *Concept Paper: Framework Agreement*. Report to the Ad Hoc Liaison Committee. November 18, 1999. New York: September 25, 2013.

Official translation of the final statement of the 19th Session of the Palestine National Council held in Algiers, November 12–14, 1988, trans. Edward Said.

Organisation de Liberation de la Palestine, Conseil National Palestinien, 188ieme Session EXTRAORDINAIRE, Session de l'INTIFADA. [Declaration of Independence]. Algiers, November 12–15, 1988.

PLO Negotiations Affairs Department. *The Road Map Obligations: Road Map Status Report, Phase 1.* May 5, 2003. http://www.nad-plo.org.

UNITED NATIONS

UN Office for the Special Coordinator for the Middle East Peace Process. *Closing the Gap: Palestinian State-Building and Resumed Negotiations.* New York: September 25, 2013

———. *Economic and Social Conditions in the West Bank and Gaza Strip, Quarterly Report, Autumn 1996.* Gaza: October 29, 1996.

———. *Report on Economic and Social Conditions in the West Bank and Gaza Strip – Spring 1999.* Gaza: April 30, 1999.

UNITED STATES

Department of State. "Policy Paper Prepared in the Department of State, March 15, 1949." In *Foreign Relations of the United States, 1949,* Vol. VI. *The Near East, South Asia, and Africa,* 827–42. Washington, DC: US Government Printing Office, 1977.

Shultz, George P. Address to the Council of Jewish Federations and Welfare Funds, Atlanta. November 21, 1983.

———. Speech and Q&A Session before Washington Institute for Near East Policy. Wye Plantation, Maryland. September 16, 1988.

Text of the US-Russian announcement. March 10, 1993.

Newspapers

Abbas, Mahmoud. "Interview." *Al-Ayyam*. May 7, 2002.

"Advertisement: Palestinians Under Occupation Present Steps Toward Peace." *Washington Post; New York Times; Christian Science Monitor*, March 15, 1988.

Bitterlemons. "Fayyad's State-Building Plan." March 15, 2010.

Blitzer, Wolf, "Murphy's Assessment." *Jerusalem Post*, April 5, 1985.

Bruck, Connie. "A Reporter at Large: The Wounds of Peace." *The New Yorker*, October 14, 1996.

Diehl, Jackson. "Israelis Ease Opposition to Cairo Plan." *Washington Post*, October 3, 1989.

Fishman, Alex. "Bzel ha intifada nimshach ha mum bein Israel lepalastinaim gam b'idan Sharon [In the shadow of the intifada, Israeli-Palestinian negotiations continue]." *Yedioth Ahronoth*, March 16, 2001.

Freij, Elias. "A Palestinian Initiative for Peace." *Washington Post*, February 14, 1982.

Friedman, Thomas L. "For Orthodox Jews, the Choice Was Netanyahu or Pizza Hut." *International Herald Tribune*, September 23, 1996.

Globes. "Minister of Tourism Rehavam Zeevi Assassinated at Point-Blank Range in Jerusalem Hyatt." October 17, 2001.

Goren, Shlomo. "The Holy Land and the Value of Life." *Jerusalem Post*, October 6, 1989.

Greenberg, Joel. "Rabbi Eliezer Schach, 103, Leader of Orthodox in Israel." *New York Times*, November 3, 2001.

Gutman, Matthew, and David Rudge. "Groundbreaking Begins for West Bank Fence." *Jerusalem Post*, June 11, 2002.

Haaretz. "Bpitaron hogen jesh lehakzot, 94–96% m'shetach hagada lamedina hapalestinait [For a decent solution, 94–96% of the West Bank territory must be given to the Palestinian State]." December 31, 2000.

———. "Full Text of Netanyahu's Foreign Policy Speech at Bar Ilan." June 14, 2009.

———. "Hamagama blikud: lalechet lebchirot [The tendency in the Likud: to go to elections]." September 18, 1989.

———. "Moezet ashaf niftacha b Baghdad bsiman hilukiej de'ot charifim [The PLO Council opened in Baghdad under heavy differences of opinion]." October 15, 1989.

———. "Neum sar habitachon bfnej merkaz mifleget ha'awoad b 21.9.1989 [The speech of the Minister of Defense before the Central Committee of the ILP, 21.9.1989]." September 24, 1989.

———. "Rabin yoze haboker lepgischa im Mubarak [This morning Rabin is going to Cairo to meet Mubarak]." September 28, 1989.

———. "Shamir: Efarek et hamemshala im Rabin ve Peres vitmechu byosmato shel Mubarak" [Shamir: I will break up the government if Rabin and Peres will support Mubarak's initiative]." September 24, 1989.

Haaretz Editorial. "Foundations for Final Status." *Haaretz*, February 23, 1996.

Hanieh, Akram. "The Camp David Papers [English version]." *Al-Ayyam*, July 31, 2000.

Herman, Peter. "Siege in the Eighth Day as Zinni, Arafat Meet at Complex." *Baltimore Sun*, April 6, 2002.

Hubermann, Haggai. "Beilin et Eitan yechalku et Yerushalayim [Beilin and Eitan will divide Jerusalem)]." *HaZofe*, January 31, 1997.

Jerusalem Post. "Arafat Statements." December 14/16, 1988.

————. "Interview: The Americans Are the Critical Link." September 15, 1989.

Katz, Yaakov. "Analysis: Jewish Terrorism Gaining Steam." *Jerusalem Post*, October 4, 2011.

Keinon, Herb. "Jordan Valley Settlers Fume over Labor-Likud Position Paper." *Jerusalem Post*, January 10, 1996.

Litani, Yehuda. "Signed Bank Pact May Presage Israel-Jordanian Condominium, Hussein's W. Bank Push." *Jerusalem Post*, October 3, 1986.

Lustig, Robin. "After the Carrot, Jordan Tries the West Bank Stick." *Observer*, June 29, 1986.

Maariv. "Beilin, Novik and Sneh met Faisal el Husseini. February 16, 1989.

Makovsky, David. "Beilin Seeking Economic Deal for Peace with Syria." *Jerusalem Post*, June 21, 1995.

Matthews, Mark. "US, Soviets Agree to Pact on Arms Cuts." *Baltimore Sun*, October 4, 1990.

Miller, Judith. "Hussein Lauds 'Spirit' of Peres Peace Plan." *International Herald Tribune*, October 24, 1985.

Murphy, Richard, and John Marks. "Then, After the Gulf Is Settled..." *Los Angeles Times*, November 28, 1990.

Myre, Greg, and Steven Erlanger. "Clashes Spread to Lebanon as Hezbollah Raids Israel." *New York Times*, July 13, 2006.

Petreanu, Dan, David Makovsky, and Wolf Blitzer. "Shamir Seen Ready to Accept Baker Plan – but Likud Hardliners Balk." *Jerusalem Post*, November 3, 1989.

Radio Monte Carlo in Arabic. "Daily Report." July 30, 1988.

Rubin, Trudi. "Israel Tries to Outflank West Bank Leadership." *Christian Science Monitor*, August 28, 1981.

Samaha, Joseph. "The Rocky Road from Mitchell to Tenet to Zinni." *Daily Star*, April 6, 2002.

Schiff, Ze'ev. "A Very Careful Speech." *Haaretz*, December 6, 1998.

Schneller, Othniel. "Shkenut weshituf peula b'header shalom: Tfisat hahafrada a terro-demografit hahadzdadit kmanof legibush heskem kewa b'atid [Neighborhood and cooperation under no peace conditions: the concept of territorial-demographic separation as a lever for a Permanent Status Agreement]." *Yedioth Ahronoth*, June 2001.

Sciolino, Elaine. "PLO Aide's Plan has US Intrigued." *The New York Times*, June 28, 1988.

Shanks, Hershel. "Netanyahu's Tunnel Vision." *Washington Post*, September 27, 1996.

Wall Street Journal. "Hussein's Decision: Fears for His Kingdom, Sense of History Drove Monarch to Seek Talks." April 15, 1983.

Wilkinson, Tracy. "Bomb Kills Palestinian Military Chief." *Los Angeles Times*. January 15, 2002.

YNet News. "Leil hamikro fonim harishon: kach ze haya [The first microphone night: this is how it went]." November 30, 2004.

Yosef, Ovadia. "Nothing Must Stand in the Way of Saving a Life." *Jerusalem Post*, October 6, 1989.

Memoirs and Secondary Sources

Abbas, Mahmoud (Abu Mazen). *Through Secret Channels: The Road to Oslo – Senior PLO Leader Abu Mazen's Revealing Story of the Negotiations with Israel.* London: Ithaca Press 1995.

Abrams, Elliott. *Tested by Zion: The Bush Administration and the Israeli-Palestinian Conflict.* New York: Cambridge University Press, 2013.

Abu Maneh, Butrus. "The Husaynis: The Rise of a Notable Family in 18th Century Palestine." In *Palestine in the Late Ottoman Period: Political, Social and Economic Transformation,* edited by David Kushner, 93–108. Jerusalem: Yad Yizchak Ben Zvi, 1986.

Abu Odeh, Adnan. *Jordanians, Palestinians, and the Hashemite Kingdom in the Middle East Peace Process.* Washington, DC: United States Institute of Peace Press, 1999.

Abu Sitta, Salman. "The Right of Return: Sacred, Legal and Possible." In *Palestinian Refugees: The Right of Return,* edited by Naseer Aruri, 195–207. London: Pluto Press, 2001.

Al-Rachid, Loulouwa. *Summary Report: Arab States and Islamism: Strategies of Re-legitimization.* Paris: Institut Français des Relations Internationales, 1996.

Arafat, Yasser. "Address to the Swedish Parliament, Stockholm, 5 December 1998 (excerpts)," *Journal of Palestine Studies* 28, no. 3 (April 1999): 143.

Armstrong, Karen. *A History of Jerusalem: One City, Three Faiths.* London: Harper Perennial, 1996.

Aruri, Naseer Hasan. *Jordan: A Study in Political Development, 1921–1965.* Ann Arbor, MI: University Microforms, 1970.

Avnery, Uri. *My Friend, the Enemy.* London: Zed Books, 1986.

Bailey, Clinton. *Jordan's Palestinian Challenge, 1948–1983: A Political History.* Boulder, CO: Westview Press, 1984.

Baker, Alan. "Israel's Rights Regarding Territories and the Settlements in the Eyes of the International Community." In *Israel's Right as a Nation-State in International Diplomacy,* edited by Alan Baker, 65–74. Jerusalem: Jerusalem Center for Public Affairs – World Jewish Congress, 2011.

Baker, James A. III. *The Politics of Diplomacy: Revolution, War and Peace, 1989–1992.* New York: G. P. Putnam's Sons, 1995.

Ben Ami, Shlomo. *Scars of War, Wounds of Peace: The Israeli-Arab Tragedy.* New York: Oxford University Press, 2006.

Benvenisti, Meron. *Sacred Landscape: The Buried History of the Holy Land Since 1948.* Berkley: University of California Press: 2000.

Bialer, Uri. "Facts and Pacts: Ben Gurion and Israel's International Orientation." In *David Ben Gurion: Politics and Leadership in Israel,* edited by Ronald W. Zweig, 216–35. London: Frank Cass, 1991.

Castelli, Christopher J. "Jones: New Team Must Build on Israeli-Palestinian Progress in Jenin," interview. *Inside the Pentagon.* October 30, 2008.

Clinton, Bill. *My Life.* New York: Random House, 2005.

Cohen, Avraham. *Kalkalata shel hagada hamaaravit verezuat 'aza, 1922–1980* [The economy of the West Bank and Gaza Strip, 1922–1980]. Givat Haviva: Institute of Arabic Studies, 1986.

Davidson, William, and Joseph Montville. "Foreign Policy According to Freud." *Foreign Policy* 45 (Winter, 1981–82): 145–57.

Diker, Dan, ed. *Israel's Critical Security Needs for a Viable Peace*. Jerusalem: Jerusalem Center for Public Affairs, 2010.

Eisenberg, Laura Zitrain, and Neil Caplan. *Negotiating Arab-Israeli Peace: Patterns, Problems, Possibilities*. 2nd ed. Bloomington: Indiana University Press, 2010.

Feldman, Shai. *Nuclear Weapons and Arms Control in the Middle East*. Cambridge, MA: MIT Press, 1997.

Fischbach, Michael R. *Records of Dispossession: Palestinian Refugee Property and the Arab-Israeli Conflict*. New York: Columbia University Press, 2003.

Fitzduff, Mari. *Beyond Violence: Conflict Resolution Process in Northern Ireland*. Tokyo: United Nations University Press, 2002.

Gazit, Shlomo. *Hamakel ve Ha Gezer: Haminhal haisraeli b'yehuda yeshomron* [The stick and the carrot: The Israeli administration in Judea and Samaria]. Tel Aviv: Zmora Bitan, 1985.

Gelber, Yoav. *Palestine 1948: War, Escape and the Emergence of the Palestinian Refugee Problem*. Eastbourne, UK: Sussex Academic Press, 2001.

Gellner, Ernest, and John Waterbury, eds. *Patrons and Clients in Mediterranean Societies*. London: Duckworth, in association with the Center for Mediterranean Studies of the American Universities Field Staff, 1977.

Gilbert, Martin. *Israel: A History*. London: Black Swan, 1998.

Gold, Dore. *The Fight for Jerusalem*. Washington, DC: Regnery Publishing, 2007.

———. *Hatred's Kingdom: How Saudi Arabia Supports the New Global Terrorism*. Washington, DC: Regnery, 2003.

Grinberg, Lev. *Shalom medumyan, siach milchama: keshel hamanhigut, hapolitka yehademokratiya byisrael, 1922–2006* [Imagined peace, discourse of war: The failure of leadership, politics and democracy in Israel, 1992–2006]. Tel Aviv: Resling Publishing, 2007.

Halabi, Usama, Aron Turner, and Meron Benvenisti. *Land Alienation in the West Bank: A Legal and Spatial Analysis*. Jerusalem: West Bank Data Project. April 1985.

Hamann, Brigitte. *Hitler's Vienna: A Dictator's Apprenticeship*. Oxford: Oxford University Press, 1999.

Harkabi, Yehoshafat. *Milchama ve-strategia* [War and strategy], 593–605. Tel Aviv: Tsahal-Hotsaat Maarakhot/Misrad ha-bitahon, 1992.

Harnoi, M. "Trends of settlement of Judea, Samaria and Gaza regions" [in Hebrew]. *Judea and Samaria Research Studies – Proceedings of the Second Annual Meeting 1992*, edited by Zeev H. Erlich and Yaakov Eshel, 369–75. Kedumim: The College of Judea and Samaria, 1992.

Heller, Yosef. "Emdotejhem shel Ben Gurion, Weitzmann veJabotinski b'sheela haaravit: mechkar hashvaati" [The positions of Ben Gurion, Weitzmann, and Jabotinsky in regard to the Arab question: A comparative research]. In *Eidan Hazionut* [The era of Zionism], edited by Anita Shapra, Yehuda Reinharz, and Yaakov Haaris, 203–40. Jerusalem: Zalman Shazar Center, 2000.

Hirschfeld, Yair. "Jordanian-Israeli Peace Negotiations after the Six Day War, 1967–1969: The View from Jerusalem." In *Jordan in the Middle East, 1948–1988*, edited by Joseph Nevo and Ilan Pappe, 229–53. Newbury, UK: Frank Cass, 1994.

Hirschfeld, Yair. *Oslo Nushat Shalom* [Oslo: A formula for peace]. Tel Aviv: Am Oved, 1999.

Hooman, Majd. *The Ayatollah Begs to Differ: The Paradox of Modern Iran.* New York: Anchor Books, 2008.

Hurwitz, Harry, and Yisrael Medad, eds. *Peace in the Making: The Menachem Begin-Anwar el-Sadat Personal Correspondence.* Jerusalem: Gefen Publishing House, 2011.

Indyk, Martin. *Innocent Abroad: An Intimate Account of American Peace Diplomacy in the Middle East.* New York: Simon & Schuster, 2009.

Jafarzadeh, Alireza. *The Iran Threat: President Ahmadinejad and the Coming Nuclear Crisis.* New York: Palgrave Macmillan, 2007.

Katz, Samuel. *The Hunt for the Engineer.* Guilford, CT: Lyons Press, 2002.

Khalidi, Rashid. *Palestinian Identity: The Construction of a Modern National Consciousness.* New York: Columbia University Press, 1997.

Kissinger, Henry. *Years of Upheaval.* Boston: Little, Brown, 1982.

Klieman, Aharon. *Comprising Palestine: A Guide to Final Status Negotiations.* New York and Tel Aviv: Columbia University Press and Jaffe Center for Strategic Studies, 2000.

Kurtzer, Daniel C., Scott B. Lasensky, William B. Quandt, Steven L. Spiegel, and Shibley Z. Telhami. *The Peace Puzzle: America's Quest for Arab-Israeli Peace; 1989–2011.* Ithaca, NY, and Washington, DC: Cornell University Press and US Institute for Peace Press, 2013.

Lapidoth, Ruth, and Moshe Hirsch, eds. *The Arab-Israel Conflict and its Resolution: Selected Documents.* Boston: Martinus Nijhoff, 1992.

Lavie, Efraim. "Hapalestinim b gada ha maaravit: tfussei hitargenut politit tachat kibosh veshilton asmi" [The Palestinians in the West Bank: Patterns of political organisations under occupation and self-rule]. Unpublished doctoral thesis, Tel Aviv University, March 2009.

Lederach, John Paul. *Building Peace: Sustainable Reconciliation in Divided Societies.* Washington, DC: US Institute for Peace Press, 1997.

Liddle-Hart, B. H. *Strategy.* New York: Penguin, 1991.

Litvak, Meir. *The Islamization of Palestinian Identity: The Case of Hamas.* Tel Aviv: The Dayan Center, Tel Aviv University, September 1995.

Mayer, Tamar, and Suleiman Moura, eds. *Jerusalem: Idea and Reality.* London: Routledge, 2008.

Miller, Aaron David. *The Much Too Promised Land: America's Elusive Search for Arab-Israeli Peace.* New York: Bantam Books, 2008.

Muasher, Marwan. *The Arab Center: The Promise of Moderation.* New Haven, CT: Yale University Press, 2008.

Neeman, Uri. *Hachra'ot gvuliot* [Borderline choices]. Tel Aviv: Yedioth Ahronot, 2011.

Nusseibeh, Sari, with Anthony David. *Once Upon a Country: A Palestinian Life.* London: Halban, 2009.

Paffenholz, Thania. "Exploring Opportunities and Obstacles for a Constructive Role of Social Capital in Peace-Building: A Framework for Analysis." In *Social Capital and Peace Building: Creating and Resolving Conflict with Trust and Social Network,* edited by Michaelene Cox. New York: Routledge, 2009.

Peres, Shimon. *Battling for Peace: A Memoir,* ed. David Landau. London: Weidenfeld & Nicolson, 1995.

Peters, Joel. *Pathways to Peace: The Multilateral Arab-Israeli Peace Talks*. London: Royal Institute of International Affairs, 1996.

Porath, Yehoshua. *The Emergence of the Palestinian National Movement, 1918–1929*. London: Frank Cass, 1974.

———. *The Palestinian Arab National Movement, 1929–1939: From Riots to Rebellion*. London: Frank Cass, 1977.

Powell, Jonathan. *Great Hatred, Little Room: Making Peace in Northern Ireland*. London: Vintage Books, 2009.

Quandt, William B. *Peace Process: American Diplomacy and the Arab-Israeli Conflict since 1967*. Berkeley and Washington, DC: University of California Press and Brookings Institution, 1993.

Qurrie, Ahmed (Abu Ala'). *From Oslo to Jerusalem: The Palestinian Story of the Secret Negotiations*. London: I. B. Tauris, 2006.

Rabin, Yitzhak. *Rodef shalom: Neumej hashalom shel rosh hamemshela* [Pursuing peace: The peace speeches of Prime Minister Yitzhak Rabin]. Tel Aviv: Zmora Beitan, 1995.

Reich, Bernard, ed. *Arab-Israeli Conflict and Conciliation: A Documentary History*. Westport, CT: Praeger, 1995.

Rice, Condoleezza. *No Higher Honor: A Memoir of My Years in Washington*. New York: Random House, 2011.

Rosenne, Meir. "The Legal Perspective: Understanding UN Security Council Resolution 242 of November 22, 1967 on the Middle East." In *Defensible Borders for a Lasting Peace*, edited by Yuval Stienitz. Jerusalem: Jerusalem Center for Public Affairs, 2008.

Ross, Dennis. *The Missing Peace: The Inside Story of the Fight for Middle East Peace*. New York: Macmillan, 2005.

Sadat, Anwar. *In Search of Identity: An Autobiography*. New York: Harper & Row, 1978.

Sagie, Uri. *Ha Yad she Kafa* [The frozen hand]. Tel Aviv: Yedioth Ahronot, 2011.

Schiff, Zeev. *Israeli Preconditions for Palestinian Statehood, Policy Focus – Special Studies on Palestinian Politics and the Peace Process*. Research Memorandum Number 39. The Washington Institute for Near East Policy. May 1999.

Shlaim, Avi. *Lion of Jordan: The Life of King Hussein in War and Peace*. New York: Allen Lane, 2007.

Sicherman, Harvey. *Palestinian Self Government (Autonomy): Its Past and its Future*. Washington: Washington Institute for Near East Policy, 1991.

Smith, Rupert. *The Utility of Force: The Art of War in the Modern World*. London: Penguin Books, 2006.

Spiegel, Steven. *The Other Arab-Israeli Conflict: Making America's Middle East Policy, from Truman to Reagan*. Chicago: University of Chicago Press, 1985.

Sprinzak, Ehud. *Brother Against Brother: Violence and Extremism in Israeli Politics from Altalena to the Rabin Assassination*. New York: Simon & Schuster, 1999.

Susser, Asher. *Israel, Jordan, and Palestine: The Two-State Imperative*. Lebanon, NH: University Press of New England, 2012.

———. "Jordan, the PLO and the Palestine Question." In *Jordan in the Middle East, 1948–1988*, edited by Joseph Nevo and Ilan Pappe, 211–28. Newbury, UK: Frank Cass, 1994.

Takkenberg, Lex. *The Status of Palestinian Refugees in International Law*. Oxford: Clarendon Press, 1998.

Thompson, Leigh. *The Mind and Heart of the Negotiator.* Upper Saddle River, NJ: Prentice Hall, 1998.

Vilnay, Zev. *Legends of Jerusalem.* Philadelphia: Jewish Publication Society of America, 1973.

Wehrey, Frederic, David E. Thaler, Nora Bensahel, Kim Cragin, Jerrold D. Green, Dalia Dassia Kayer, Nadia Oweidat, and Jennifer Li. *Dangerous but Not Omnipotent: Exploring the Reach and Limitations of Iranian Power in the Middle East.* Washington, DC: RAND Corporation, 2009.

Weissglas, Dov. *Arik Sharon: Rosh Hamemshala—Mabit Ishi* [Arik Sharon: A prime minister]. Tel Aviv: Yedioth Ahronot, 2012.

Ya'alon, Moshe. *Derekg aruka kzara* [The longer shorter way]. Tel Aviv: Yedioth Ahronot, 2008.

Yatom', Dan. *'Shutaf Sod: msayeret Matkal vead hamossad* [The confidant: From Sayyeret Matkal to the Mossad]. Tel Aviv: Yedioth Ahronot, 2009.

Zertal, Idith, and Akiva Eldar. *Lords of the Land: The War Over Israel's Settlements in the Occupied Territories, 1967–2007.* New York: Nation Books, 2009.

Zwim, Michael. "Promise and Failure: Environmental NGOs and Palestinian-Israeli Cooperation." *Middle East Review of International Affairs (MERIA),* Vol. 5, No 4. (December 2001): 116–26.

Electronic Sources

Adwan, Sami, Dan Bar-On, Fida Obeidi, and Julia Chaitin. "A Study of Palestinian & Israeli Environmental Non-Governmental Organizations," April 2000–August 2001. http://vispo.com/PRIME/palisenvngos.htm.

Ashrawi, Hanan. "Unilateral Peace?" The Palestinian Initiative for the Promotion of GlobalDialogue&Democracy.October30,1999.http://www.miftah.org/Display.cfm?DocId=112&CategoryId=1.

Azam, Azam. "Azam Azam speaks out on his captivity in Egypt." YouTube video, 2:20, posted by "infolivetvenglish," January 30, 2010. https://www.youtube.com/watch?v=SKBqFsq6kCk.

"Carl in Jerusalem." "The truth about the 1948 battle for Jerusalem." *Israel Matzav.* June 2, 2008. http://israelmatzav.blogspot.ca/2008/06/truth-about-1948-battle-for-jerusalem.html.

"The Geneva Accord: A Model Israeli-Palestinian Peace Agreement." Palestinian Peace Coalition/Yes to an Agreement: The Geneva Initiative. n.d. http://www.geneva-accord.org/mainmenu/english.

Government of Israel. "Fifteenth Knesset: Government 28." 2014. http://www.knesset.gov.il/govt/eng/GovtByNumber_eng.asp?govt=28.

———. "IDF to leave Gaza by Monday morning." reliefweb.int. September 11, 2005. http://reliefweb.int/report/occupied-palestinian-territory/idf-leave-gaza-monday-morning.

———. "Israel's Response to the Road Map, May 25, 2003." 2003. http://www.knesset.gov.il/process/docs/roadmap_response_eng.htm.

———. "The Sharm el Sheikh Memorandum on Implementation Timeline of Outstanding Commitments of Agreements Signed and the Resumption of Permanent Status Negotiations." http://www.knesset.gov.il/process/docs/sharm_eng.htm.

"Hamas Covenant 1988: The Covenant of the Islamic Resistance Movement, 18 August 1988." The Avalon Project: Documents in Law, History and Diplomacy, Yale Law School. 2008. http://avalon.law.yale.edu/20th_century/hamas.asp.

Inbari, Pinhas, and Dan Diker. "The Murder of Mussa Arafat and the Battle for the Spoils of Gaza," *Jerusalem Issue Brief*, Vol. 5, No. 6 (October 10, 2005). Institute for Contemporary Affairs, founded jointly with the Wechsler Family Foundation, Jerusalem Center for Public Affairs. http://www.jcpa.org/brief /brief005-6.htm.

"Israel Health & Medicine: Israeli-Palestinian Health Cooperation, 1994–1998." Jewish Virtual Library. Accessed March 10, 2014. https://www.jewishvirtuallibrary .org/jsource/Health/pacoop.html.

Israel Ministry of Foreign Affairs, "Address by PM Ariel Sharon at the Fourth Herzliya Conference – December 18, 2003." Accessed March 10, 2014. http:// mfa.gov.il/MFA/PressRoom/2003/Pages/Adress%20by%20PM%20Ariel%20 Sharon%20at%20the%20Fourth%20Herliya.aspx.

———. "Guide to the Mideast Peace Process." Accessed March 10, 2014. http://www .mfa.gov.il/MFA/ForeignPolicy/Peace/Guide/Pages/GUIDE%20TO%20THE%20 MIDEAST%20PEACE%20PROCESS.aspx.

———. "Knesset Election Results: January 28, 2003." Accessed March 10, 2014. http:// mfa.gov.il/MFA/AboutIsrael/History/Pages/Knesset%20Election%20Results.aspx.

———. "PM Rabin in Knesset – Ratification of Interim Agreement." October 5, 1995. http://www.mfa.gov.il/mfa/mfa-archive/1995/pages/pm%20rabin%20in%20 knesset-%20ratification%20of%20interim%20agree.aspx.

———. "Terrorism deaths in Israel - 1920–1999." January 1, 2000. http://www.mfa .gov.il/mfa/foreignpolicy/terrorism/palestinian/pages/terrorism%20deaths%20 in%20israel%20-%201920-1999.aspx.

———. "The Western Wall Tunnel – Update." September 29, 1996. http://www.mfa .gov.il/MFA/MFA-Archive/1998/Pages/The%20Western%20Wall%20Tunnel%20 -%20Update.aspx.

Israel Security Agency. "Terrorist Attack against the Park Hotel in Netanya (2002)." 2010. Accessed March 10, 2014. http://www.shabak.gov.il/English/History/Affairs /Pages/theParkHotelinNetanya.aspx.

"Israeli Settlements and International Law." LA Jews for Peace. September 10, 2009. http://www.lajewsforpeace.org/SettlementsinPalestine.html.

Isseroff, Ami, and Zionism and Israel Information Center. "Israel Labor Party: Definition." The Encyclopedia and Dictionary of Zionism and Israel. May 1997. http://www.zionism-israel.com/dic/Labor_Party.htm.

"Kotel Tunnel Incident, 1996." PalestineFacts.org. 2013. Accessed March 10, 2014. http://www.palestinefacts.org/pf_1991to_now_kotel_tunnel_1996.php.

Palestinian Center for Policy and Research. "PSR Poll No. 48 – Joint Palestinian-Israeli Press Release." July 2, 2013, http://www.pcpsr.org/survey/polls/2013/p48ejoint .html.

"A Performance-Based Roadmap to a Permanent Two-State Solution to the Israeli-Palestinian Conflict" (press statement). US Department of State Archive. April 30, 2003. http://2001-2009.state.gov/r/pa/prs/ps/2003/20062.htm.

Petraeus, David. "Gen. Petraeus' Testimony to the Senate Armed Services Comm." April 8, 2008. *Real Clear Politics*. http://www.realclearpolitics.com/articles /2008/04/gen_petraeus_testimony_to_the.html.

"President Sadat Speech to the People's Assembly, November 26, 1977." Anwar Sadat Archives, Anwar Sadat Chair for Peace and Development, University of Maryland, College Park, MD. Accessed March 10, 2014. http://sadat.umd.edu/archives/speeches/AADK%20Sadat%20Speech%20after%20Jersusalem%2011.26.77.pdf.

"Second Lebanon War: Background and Overview," Jewish Virtual Library. Accessed March 10, 2014. http://www.jewishvirtuallibrary.org/jsource/History/lebanon2.html.

"Transcript of Ariel Sharon's speech at Egypt summit." February 8, 2005. Posted: 6:07 p.m. EST. CNN.com. www.cnn.com/2005/WORLD/meast/02/08/transcript.sharon/.

"Transcript of Mahmoud Abbas' speech at Egypt summit," February 8, 2005. Posted: 6:07 p.m. EST. CNN.com. www.cnn.com/2005/WORLD/meast/02/08/transcript.abbas/.

"UN Security Council Resolution 1397." MidEastWeb.org. March 12, 2002. http://www.mideastweb.org/1397.htm.

White, Steven, and P. J. Dermer. "How Obama Missed an Opportunity for Middle East Peace: Why did the president ignore the only part of the "peace process" that was working?" *Foreign Policy*, May 18, 2012. http://www.foreignpolicy.com/articles/2012/05/18/how_obama_missed_an_opportunity_for_middle_east_peace.

White House Office of the Press Secretary. "President Bush Calls for New Palestinian Leadership." June 24, 2002. http://georgewbush-whitehouse.archives.gov/news/releases/2002/06/20020624-3.html

White House Office of the Press Secretary. "Remarks by President Barack Obama to the People of Israel." March 21, 2013. http://www.whitehouse.gov/the-press-office/2013/03/21/remarks-president-barack-obama-people-Israel.

"Zinni's ceasefire plan." Al-bab.com. March 26, 2002. http://www.al-bab.com/arab/docs/pal/zinni2002a.htm.

Documentary Films

A Million Bullets in October. Directed by Moish Goldberg for Israeli television *Arutz 8.* 2007.

Dancing in Jaffa. Directed by Hilla Medalia. 2013.

The Gatekeepers. Directed by Dror Moreh. 2012.

Index

Abbas, Mahmoud (Abu Mazen): and Arafat, 391*n*10; and back-channel negotiations (1991–93), 129; and Camp David Summit (2000), 242; and deniability, 125; and Kerry Peace Initiative, 338, 341, 344; and multitrack diplomacy (1989–91), 69; and multitrack diplomacy (1996–99), 188–89, 199, 200, 201, 202; and Permanent Status negotiations (1993–96), 161, 162, 170, 173, 176–77, 183–84; and Permanent Status negotiations (1999–2001), 228, 236, 237, 243, 245, 250, 255, 322–23; and Permanent Status negotiations (2006–9), 311, 312, 313, 314, 345–46; and reform in Fatah movement, 281; resignation of, 293; and roadmap, 292–93; and state building, 345–46; and strategic reorientation, 262, 265, 388*n*88; and unilateral disengagement, 289, 301, 305, 324. *See also* Beilin–Abu Mazen Understanding

Abbington, Ed, 187, 206

Abdel-Meguid, Ahmed Asmet, 77, 80, 81, 82, 362*n*59

Abdel-Razzeq, Yehia, 161

Abdullah (King of Jordan), 14, 244

Abdullah II (King of Jordan), 282

Abram, Daniel, 374*n*92

Abramovitch, Ahron, 310

Abrams, Elliott, 309, 392*n*20, 397*n*7

Abu Ala': and back-channel negotiations (1991–93), 108, 109, 111, 117–23, 126–30, 366*n*61; and multitrack diplomacy (1996–99), 201, 379*n*58; and Permanent Status negotiations (1999–2001), 229, 236, 244, 250, 255; and Permanent Status negotiations (2006–9), 314; and strategic reorientation, 262, 270

Abu Dis, 171, 175, 179, 229–30, 236

Abu Jihad (Khalil al-Wazir), 44

Abu Mazen. *See* Abbas, Mahmoud

Abu Sharif, Bassam, 57, 62, 66, 90

access and movement, 299, 321–22. *See also* travel restrictions

Access and Movement Agreement (2005), 299

Achille Lauro hijacking (1985), 46

"adult supervision" of process, 331–32

Afghanistan, 275, 290